Communications
in Computer and Information Science 289

Maotai Zhao   Junpin Sha (Eds.)

Communications and Information Processing

International Conference, ICCIP 2012
Aveiro, Portugal, March 7-11, 2012
Revised Selected Papers, Part II

 Springer

Volume Editors

Maotai Zhao
Xueyuan Road 3, Taiyuan, Shanxi, China 030051
E-mail: zmaotai@163.com

Junpin Sha
Jinhua Road 4, Xi'an, Shanxi, China 710032
E-mail: deepakawal@gmail.com

ISSN 1865-0929   e-ISSN 1865-0937
ISBN 978-3-642-31967-9   e-ISBN 978-3-642-31968-6
DOI 10.1007/978-3-642-31968-6
Springer Heidelberg Dordrecht London New York

Library of Congress Control Number: 2012942224

CR Subject Classification (1998): I.2, C.2, H.4, H.3, I.4-5, D.2

Typesetting: Camera-ready by author, data conversion by Scientific Publishing Services, Chennai, India

Printed on acid-free paper

Springer is part of Springer Science+Business Media (www.springer.com)

Preface

It is our pleasure to welcome you to the proceedings of the 2012 International Conference on Communications and Information Processing (ICCIP 2012) held in Aveiro, Portugal. ICCIP 2012 was the first conference dedicated to issues related to communications and information processing. A major goal and feature of ICCIP 2012 was to bring academic scientists, engineers, and industry researchers together to exchange and share their experiences and research results about most aspects of communications and information processing, and discuss the practical challenges encountered and the solutions adopted.

The conference was both stimulating and informative with a wonderful array of keynote and invited speakers from all over the world. Delegates had a wide range of sessions to choose from and many had a difficult time deciding which sessions to attend.

The program consisted of invited sessions, technical workshops, and discussions with eminent speakers covering a wide range of topics in communications and information processing. This rich program provided all attendees with opportunities to meet and interact with one another.

We would like to thank the organization staff, the members of the Program Committees, and the reviewers. They worked very hard in reviewing papers and making valuable suggestions for the authors to improve their work. We also would like to express our gratitude to the external reviewers, for providing extra help in the review process, and the authors for contributing their research result to the conference. Special thanks go to Springer.

We look forward to seeing all of you next year at the ICCIP 2013. With your support and participation, ICCIP will continue its success for a long time.

Zhenli Lu

Organization

General Chair

Lu Zhenli   IEETA, University of Aveiro, Portugal

Program Committee

Lorenzo Bruzzone   University of Trento, Italy
Hans du Buf   University of the Algarve, Portugal
Tiberio Caetano   NICTA and Australian National University,
                                         Australia
Javier Calpe   Universitat de València, Spain
Rui Camacho   Universidade do Porto, Portugal
Gustavo Camps-Valls   University of València, Spain
Ramon A. Mollineda Cardenas   Universitat Jaume I, Spain
Xavier Carreras   UPC, Spain
Marco La Cascia   Università degli Studi di Palermo, Italy
Rui M. Castro   Eindhoven University of Technology,
                                         The Netherlands
Zehra Cataltepe   Istanbul Technical University, Turkey
Javier Ortega Garcia   Universidad Autnoma de Madrid, Spain
Marco Parvis   Politecnico di Torino, Italy
Kostas Plataniotis   University of Toronto, Canada
Fabio Roli   Università degli Studi di Cagliari, Italy
Arun Ross   West Virginia University, USA
Bulent Sankur   Bogazici University, Turkey
Gabriella Sanniti di Baja   CNR, Italy
Carlo Sansone   University of Naples Federico II, Italy
Bhavesh Patel   Shah & Anchor Kutchhi Polytechnic, India
Xu Ning   Wuhan University of Technology, China
Cao Jian   Shanghai Jiao Tong University, China
He Jin   Peking University, China
Sun Pengtao   University of Nevada, USA
Wong Pak Kin   University of Macau, Macau

Table of Contents – Part II

Table of Contents – Part I

Design of Adaptive Signal Separator
Based on Particle Swarm Optimization

Jie Zhang and Shiqi Jiang

Department of Control Engineering,
Chengdu University of Information Technology,
Sichuan Chengdu of China
zj@cuit.edu.cn

Abstract. Particle swarm optimization (PSO) is a new algorithm based on swarm intelligence heuristic search, which is easy to understand, easy to implement, it has global search capability and gets more attention in the field of science and engineering; it becomes one of the fastest growing intelligent optimization algorithms. Adaptive filter has received extensive attention and research because of its excellent performance in recent years, the adaptive algorithm is the core of the adaptive filter, the different performance of the algorithm has different influence on the filter. In the paper, PSO algorithm is proposed to design adaptive signal separator based on adaptive filter, which can separate the broad-band and narrow-band signal. The simulation and the results show that the particle swarm optimization has the better convergent performance and the better separate capability, the algorithm is proved the validity and practicability in signal separator.

Keywords: Adaptive Notch Filter, LMS algorithm, Particle Swarm Optimization (PSO), Quantum Particle Swarm Optimization (QPSO).

1   Introduction

The Particle Swarm Optimization (PSO) is a stochastic optimization approach simulating birds to prey for food. Assuming a scene like this: a group of birds are searching food randomly, only a piece of food in this district, and all birds do not know where the food is, but they know the distance from their position to the food [1]. What is the optimal strategy to find the food? Most simple and effective way is to search the surrounding district in where a bird which is closest to the food. In recently years, the PSO is applied in many fields based on the guidance thinking, the habitat of the birds in the swarm athletics models have an analogy to the solution of the optimal problem in the algorithm, the swarm move to the direction of the solution by the information transfer, in this process, the better solution is found. The bird in the swarm is abstracted the "particle" without any quality and volume, the particle are cooperate with the other particle and their information should be shared, the current position, direction and velocity of the particle are affected by the better position of the particle itself and the swarm in the history, on the other hand, it must deal with the relation between the

M. Zhao and J. Sha (Eds.): ICCIP 2012, Part II, CCIS 289, pp. 1–8, 2012.
© Springer-Verlag Berlin Heidelberg 2012

particle and the swarm so that they found the best solution in the complex solution space [2].

In Adaptive signal process, the main research object is the system that the structure can be changed or adjusted, the performance of the signal process can be improved by contacting with the outside environment. Compared with the normal digital filter, the adaptive filter's frequency is changed with the input signal automatically, so it has more application in many filed than the normal digital filter[5,6].

In this paper, PSO algorithm is proposed to design the adaptive signal separator based on the adaptive filter structure, because the structure adopt the swarm intelligence search algorithm replace the LMS algorithm, it has many advantages, the step-size can't affect the simulation results, and it can separate the board-band signal and the narrow-band signal very well.

2   Principle of Adaptive Signal Separator

Adaptive noise cancellation (ANC) system is always used in pick-up the useful signal, but the system ask the reference input signal is relevant with the noise, and it must irrelevant with the useful signal. In fact, the ANC is difficult to work because that the reference signal isn't easy to find. We can design an adaptive signal separator to pick-up the board-band signal and the narrow-band signal as Fig. 2.

In the Fig. 2, the structure of adaptive filter in the experiment is the FIR adaptive filter structure, which is shown in Fig.1, and the adaptive algorithm is PSO.

Input signal x(n) is mix-signal, which is consists of the cycle signal s(n) and the noise v(n), it can be made up of the board-band signal and the narrow-band signal too,

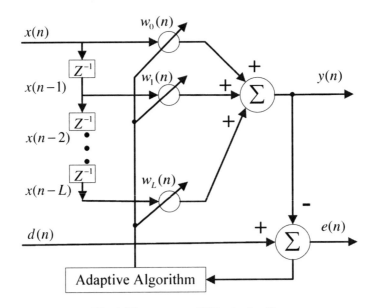

Fig. 1. The structure of FIR adaptive filter

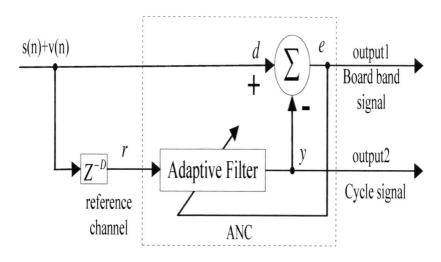

Fig. 2. Adaptive signal separator

s(n) and v(n) are irrelevant, but after x(n) is delayed D-step, it as the input port signal of adaptive filter:

$$x(n-D)=s(n-D)+v(n-D) \tag{1}$$

Because D is big enough that the x(n-D) and the x(n) are irrelevant, the output of adaptive filter is estimate value of cycle signal, y(n)≈s(n), after D-step delay, y(n) is relevant of s(n), but y(n) is irrelevant with v(n).

$$e(n)=x(n)-y(n)=s(n)+v(n)-y(n) \tag{2}$$

$$e(n)-v(n)=s(n)-y(n) \tag{3}$$

$$E\{[e(n)-v(n)]\}_{min}=E\{[s(n)-y(n)]\}_{min} \tag{4}$$

$$y(n)=s(n),e(n)=v(n) \tag{5}$$

From formula (5), output of the system y(n) is cycle signal s(n), on the other hand, y(n) is output of adaptive filter, which weight-value is adjusted by x(n-D), so, e(n) is the noise signal v(n), we separate the cycle signal and the noise signal through the system.

3   ASS Based on PSO Algorithm

Normal adaptive algorithm is LMS, but LMS have many problems, such as: results depend on step, and the maladjustment is influenced by the step, at the same time, the convergence velocity is very slowly.

The PSO is a stochastic optimization approach simulating birds to prey for food. In PSO, the solution of the optimal problem is a bird in search space, and we can name it "particle". All particles have fitness values which are evaluated by the fitness function to be optimized, and have velocities which direct the flying of the particles. Each particle being attracted towards the best solution found by the particle's neighborhood and the best solution found by the particle [4].

In this paper, PSO algorithm replaced the LMS algorithm. Adaptive FIR filter is expressed by difference equation:

$$y(n) = \sum_{m=0}^{M} b_m x(n-m) \tag{6}$$

Program Flow Chart of PSO is described in Fig.3.

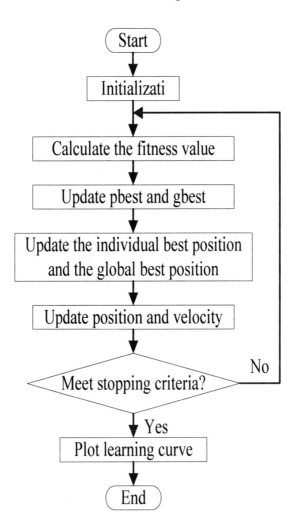

Fig. 3. PSO Program Flow Chart

The system is initialized with a group of random particles (solutions), and then the optimal solution is found by updating generations. During iteration, each particle is updated by tracking two "best" values. The first one is the optimal solution that the particle has achieved so far. This value is called individual extremum. Another "best" value is the optimal solution tracked by the particle swarm optimizer, and the solution is called the global extremum obtained so far by any particle in the population. After finding the extremum, particles update their velocity and position as follows:

$$V_{id}^{k+1} = w * V_{id}^{k} + c1 * rand() * (P_{best}^{k} - X_{id}^{k})$$
$$+ c2 * rand() * (G_{best}^{k} - X_{id}^{k})$$

(7)

$$X_{id}^{k+1} = X_{id}^{k} + V_{id}^{k+1}$$

(8)

Where Vid is the velocity of the current particle; Xid is the position of the current particle; Pbest is the position at which the particle has achieved its best fitness so far, and Gbest is the position at which the best global fitness has been achieved so far; w is called inertia weight which controls the momentum of the particle by weighing the contribution of the previous velocity-basically controlling how much memory of the previous flight direction will influence the new velocity;c1 and c2 are two study factors, and usually c1 and c2 are all equal to 2; rand() is a random numbers, uniformly distributed in [0, 1];k is the number of iteration. The particles find the optimal solution by cooperation and competition among the particles [3].

4   Simulation Result

Fig.4 shows the simulation results, in the Fig. 4(a) is the expected signal s(n), it is cycle signal, which is the useful signal. Fig. 4(b) is the input signal x(n), which is made up of s(n) and v(n).

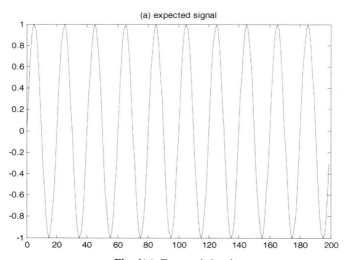

Fig. 4(a). Expected signal

ASS system model shows in Fig.2, board-band signal v(n) is Guess-white noise, cycle signal is: $s(n) = \sin(0.2\pi t)$

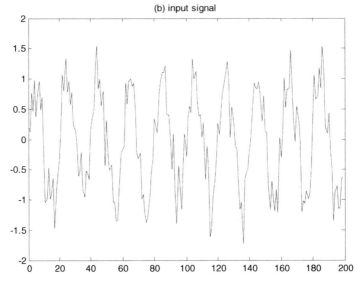

Fig. 4(b). Input signal s(n)+v(n)

Fig. 4(c) is the signal of output2 port, which is the cycle signal after the adaptive signal separator, Fig. 4 (d) is the signal of output1 port, which is the board-band noise signal after the adaptive signal separator. From the Fig. 4, we find it has separate the narrow-band signal and board-band signal based on the PSO algorithms, and it have fast convergence speed.

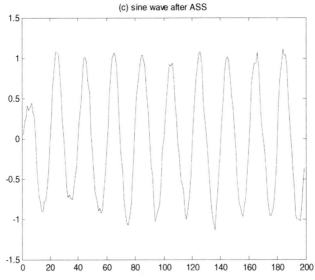

Fig. 4(c). Sinusoid wave after ASS

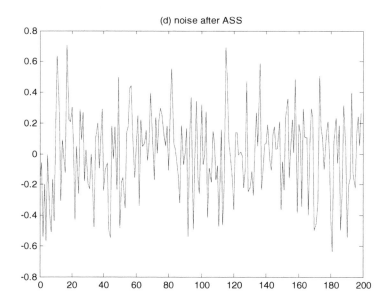

Fig. 4(d). Board-band noise signal after ASS

After many experiments, it proved that the adaptive signal separator based on PSO can separate the board-band signal and the narrow-band signal successfully.

5   Conclusions

Particle swarm optimization (PSO) is a kind of evolutionary computation technology which simulates the behavior of biological species. It is one of the most powerful methods for solving unconstrained and constrained global optimization problems. This method is an evolutionary computation. Evolutionary computation is a random optimization search technology which based on simulation of the biology evolutionary process. It is the research hotspot of intelligence computation field. In this paper, the idea is proposed that PSO algorithm replace the LMS algorithm to design the adaptive signal separator, after many experiments, the simulation shows the excellent separate effect. It can satisfied with the engineering require signal. A new method is provided in signal separate technology about the board-band signal and the narrow-band signal because that PSO algorithm was combined with the adaptive signal separator, it has provided some research foundation for engineering application.

Acknowledgement. This work was financially supported by aviation science Foundation (20101024005).

References

1. Zeng, J.C., Jie, Q., Cui, Z.H.: Particle swarm optimization algorithm. Science Press, Beijing (2004)
2. Clerc, M.: Particle swarm optimization. ISTE Publishing Company, London (2006)
3. Kennedy, J., Eberhart, R.: Particle swarm optimization. In: IEEE Int'l Conf. on Neural Networks, pp. 1942–1948 (1995)
4. Shen, F.: Adaptive signal processing. Xidian University Press, Xian (2003) (in Chinese)
5. Widow, B., Stearns, S.D.: Adaptive signal processing. Prenice-Hall, Inc., US (1985)
6. Luo, X.: A new variable step size LMS adaptive filtering algorithm. Acta Electronica Sinica 34(6), 1123–1126 (2006)
7. Shi, Y., Eberhart, R.: Empirical study of particle swarm optimization. In: International Conference on Evolutionary Computation, Washington, pp. 1945–1950 (1999)
8. Xu, X.: Improved particle swarm optimization based on Brownian motion. Application Research of Computers 28(7) (July 2011)
9. Wei, C.: Quantum-behaved particle swarm optimization dynamic clustering algorithm. Application Research of Computers 28(7) (July 2011)

A Fast Subdividing Research
for Grating Signal Based on CPLD

Nuan Song[1], Changhong Ding[1,2], Chunhui Liu[2,3], and Wei Quan[1,4]

[1] Air Force Aviation University, Chang Chun, JiLin, China
[2] Baicheng Ordance Test Center of China, Baicheng, JiLin, China
{bluebirdsong,dingchanghong777,quanweiron}@163.com,
502723842@qq.com

Abstract. With the development of science and technology, the precision of various precise detection technology has put forward more advanced requirement. Moiré fringe based on the optical grating of optical grating measuring system have some merit, such as high degree of accuracy, high resolution, wide range, better anti-interference and higher speed of measurement. Because of so many good characteristics, it has been applied in the region of precise detection widely. This paper presents a new dividing method based on electronics, we apply new-style CPLD of logic devices to implement four dividing and sensing of moiré fringe signal, Twenty dividing fraction will realize by amplitude of grating signal and looking up table of software.

Keywords: grating, moiréfringe, subdividing technology, CPLD.

1   Introduction

Along with the development of science and technology, all kinds of precision detection techniques of precision also put forward higher request. Grating as a precision measuring tools, has been widely used in precision instrument, coordinate measuring, accurate orientation, high precision processing, etc. Measuring grating is mainly composed of scale grating and instructions grating, measuring principle is formed on the basis of the moire fringe grating, the traditional method of improving precision can improve by the linear density to achieve, but this will cause scribed line difficulties, the cost is high, therefore, a fast subdividing circuit design for moire frenge grating is very necessary.

This system avoid the disadvantages which the traditional monostabtle pulse count when the system is instability in higher frequency, it adopt the method of the resistance dephasing and state comparison to make the grating sensor output signal 20 subdivision, the system stability and anti-jamming has greatly improved.

M. Zhao and J. Sha (Eds.): ICCIP 2012, Part II, CCIS 289, pp. 9–16, 2012.
© Springer-Verlag Berlin Heidelberg 2012

2   The Working Principle

The system is composed of grating optical system signal acquisition circuit and signal processing circuit two parts, the total diagram shown in fig.1. Grating optical system signal acquisition circuit mainly refers to the grating sensor and signal processing circuit include a fast subdividing circuit and the identifying direction circuit two parts, the identifying direction circuit is composed of plastic circuit and CPLD counts circuit; Subdivision circuit [1] is composed of difference amplifier circuit, triangle wave building circuit, A/D converter circuit and single-chip microcomputer.

The systemic principle diagram shown in figure 1. The light from the light source after grating modulation, will convert the mechanical displacement to the light information, will be changed into the alternating electric signals along with the light modulation by the photoelectric receiving converter, through a variety of signal processing and the transformation, it can achieve various corresponding mechanical geometric displacement quantity. Grating sensor [2] output four road each phase difference 90 °AC signals, then after deal with the two road differential amplifiers, eliminate the circuit zero drift, get two road phase differ 90 ° and the AC signal U_5 and U_6.

$$U_5 = U_m \sin \theta(x) \quad ; \quad U_6 = U_m \cos \theta(x)$$

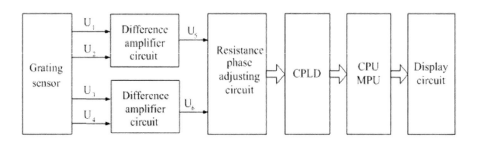

Fig. 1. The operation principle diagram

Among them: $\theta(x) = \dfrac{x}{d} 2\pi$, d is the grating sensor mechanical angular displacement, x is the relative displacement quantity between scale grating and instructions grating, U_m is the signal amplitude.

Due to a linear relationship between the mechanical angular displacement $\theta(x)$ and displacement x , so to any displacement quantity is transformed into the measurement of the phase angle $\theta(x)$, as long as $\theta(x)$ phase shifting segmentation, then in digital circuit judge $\theta(x)$ the phase condition, can be used for the displacement of the subdivision of the x .

3   The System Hardware Design

The traditional subdivision circuit inverse each square wave respectively, get the original square wave signal and the reverse square wave signal, then use differential type monostable trigger to generate pulse in every rising edge moment of square wave signal, and then stack up the pulse, but the width of pulse signal which monostable trigger produced depends on parameters of the external resistance and capacitance. We require 500 kHz grating signal output highest, the pulse should be subdivided to 10 MHz, so we must choose very small RC time constant, to produce a very narrow pulses, the edge and amplitude of the pulse signal which circuit generated is difficult to meet all the requirements of the counter stability[3].

The phase shifting circuit of this system design is composed of 10 group phase shifting resistances, the phase shifting principle of the phase shifting resistances shown in fig 2. the sine signal phase can be shifted via choose the appropriate value of R_{1n} and R_{2n} [4].

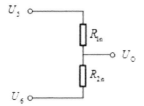

Fig. 2. The phase shifting resistances chain

Set the input signal for: $U_5 = U_m \sin \theta(x)$,

$U_6 = U_m \cos \theta(x)$; The output signal is : $U = \beta U_m \sin \theta(x + \varphi)$ among them,

$$\beta = \frac{\sqrt{R_{1n}^2 + R_{2n}^2}}{R_{1n}^2 + R_{2n}^2} , \quad \varphi = \arctan \frac{R_{1n}}{R_{2n}} , \varphi \text{ is to move Angle.}$$

Select the appropriate resistance R_{1n} and R_{2n} make each group of resistance from phase shifting for 18 °, and then after zero comparator comparison, got 10 phase difference in turn 18 ° of square wave[5]. Detection total design of the moire fringe grating signal.

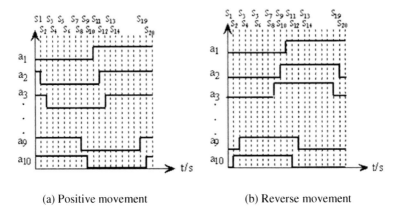

(a) Positive movement   (b) Reverse movement

Fig. 3. The waveform of the Positive or Reverse movement state

Since in a grating cycle, from the phase shifting circuit can output 10 road different phase signals, as shown in fig. 3 shows, analysis this 10 signals relationship of the level state, 10 signals at the same time can make 20 state, as shown in figure 3(a) shows, from state $S_1 - S_{20}$, there a_n phase is ahead of a_{n+1} 18 °in phase. Figure 3(a) is for grating sensor positive motion of a state chart, and figure 3(b) similarly in figure 3(a), to reverse motion of sensor state chart. So according to the 20 state put a grating cycle divided into 20 copies, can get 20 subdivision.

After signal subdivision, sensor is very sensitive to the displacement, if sensor appears a slight shaking return phenomena will cause error counter, and identify the movement direction is necessary[6]. When sensor positive motion counter add 1, when the reverse move just the opposite order, sensor reverse move counter minus 1, as shown in figure. 4 shows:

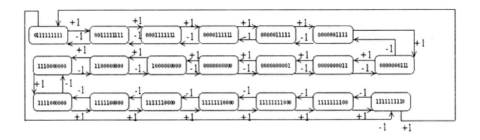

Fig. 4. Signals state change direction and operation

According to the above analysis, we compared the state before with the current state of the 10 signals, the change accords with one of them in figure 4, the counter does corresponding operation add1 or minus 1, this system with CPLD realize this function to avoid tedious design to the relationship of checking, comparison, trigger. The circuit by using the programmable device CPLD to realize subdivision and identifying direction technology, the system time delay is small, the system measurement precision has been improved, dismissed the intrinsic defects of traditional circuit, use convenient and flexible, circuit modulation simple. Using the external clock to make count operation synchronization, and greatly improve the system of anti-interference ability.

4   The Synthesis of Triangle Wave

In order to obtain precise displacement value, it must be to displacement subdivided. In a cycle, the sine function is with phase or space displacement is one-to-one, as long as it can measure the size or the positive and negative of the sine function, it can measure the grating amplitude of the relative displacement quantity. But because of sinusosineprotractor of the grating signal [7] in a different part of the cycle, slope is very different (in $90°$ and $270°$ nearby linear is very bad), and the alternate use sine and cosine signal with noise because of the actual will signal can cause join error, so use two orthogonal the moire fringe grating signal through the simulation way circuit synthesis approximate triangular wave, again by single chip subdivision. On the one hand because of the slope of the synthetic signal is approximately equal, the whole cycle has the same sensitivity; On the other hand, the frequency of the signal is original synthesis is (cosine) signal frequency double. Therefore, with the grating signal amplitude synthesis can improve fine scores, and at the same time, improve measurement accuracy.

Specific triangle wave functions such as type shows:

$$U = |u \sin a| - |u \cos a|$$

This design adopt precise full-wave detection principle to realize the absolute value circuit of the sine and cosine signal. Analog the whole synthesis triangle wave circuit, is to be the cosine signal after absolute value circuit [8] into $|\sin \theta|$ and $-|\cos \theta|$ respectively, and by the LM324 gain for 1 adder circuit, namely get design grating signal amplitude synthesis requirements. Through the experiment of the triangle wave to obtain synthetic for an isosceles triangle wave standard, the circuit diagram as shown in figure 5 shows:

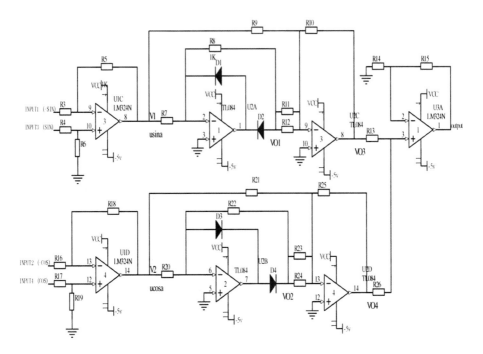

Fig. 5. Total circuit diagram of the triangle wave amplitude combining

5   The Software Design

Before you begin to format your paper, first write and save the content as a separate text file. Keep your text and graphic files separate until after the text has been formatted and styled. Do not use hard tabs, and limit use of hard returns to only one return at the end of a paragraph. Do not add any kind of pagination anywhere in the paper. Do not number text heads-the template will do that for you.

Finally, complete content and organizational editing before formatting. Please take note of the following items when proofreading spelling and grammar[9].

According to the above analysis, we compared the state before with the current state of the 10 signals, the counter does corresponding operation add1 or minus 1, this system with CPLD :realize this function to avoid tedious design to the relationship of checking, comparison, trigger, the main program flow chart is as follows

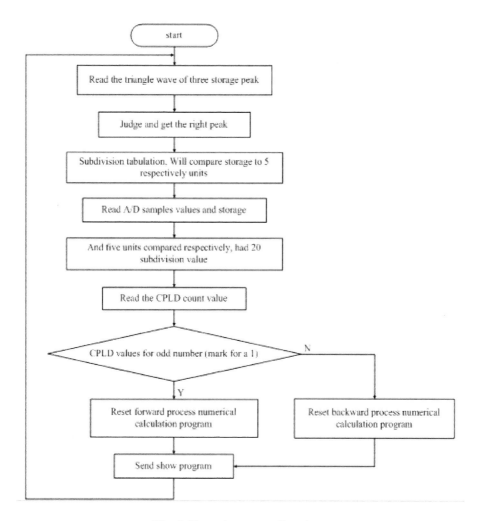

Fig. 6. The main program flow chart

The circuit by using the programmable device CPLD to realize subdivision and identifying direction technology, the system time delay is small, the system measurement precision has been improved, dismissed the intrinsic defects of traditional circuit, use convenient and flexible, circuit modulation simple. Using the external clock to make count operation synchronization, and greatly improve the system of anti-interference ability[10].

The equations are an exception to the prescribed specifications of this template. You will need to determine.

6   Conclusion

The system uses the CPLD to grating moire fringe fast subdivision, sich orientieren and count, this circuit saves traditional monostable trigger devices such as resistors, capacitors, and overcomes the unstable shortcomings which the monostable trigger working. Circuit introduction of external synchronous clock, enhance the anti-interference ability of the system. In the design of sensor is less than 500 kHz output signal completed 20 subdivision, counting frequency can be as high as 10 MHz. Experiment results show that the measurement system have strong commonality and stability.

References

1. Liu, W., Dug, E., Li, S., et al.: Design and Realization of Uniform Fiber Bragg Gating Used in Dense Wavelength Division Multiplexing Systems. Semiconductor Photonics and Technology 08(02), 96–102 (2002)
2. Jeong, M.-S., Kim, S.-W.: Color grating projection moire with time-integral fringe capturing for high-speed 3-D image. Opt. Eng. 41(8), 1912–1917 (2002)
3. Liao, Y.: Fiber Optics, pp. 28–36. Tsinghua University Publishing House, Beijing (2000)
4. Yang, J.M.: BP neural network algorithm is discussed in this paper. The Development and Economic and Technology Information (3), 241–242 (2006)
5. Beaver, Wang, W., Zhang, W.: Equality Based on the maximum likelihood intelligent mines passive sound array to direction. The PLA University of Science and Technology Journal (Natural Science Edition) 4, 74–76 (2003)
6. Ming, Y., Hua, J.Z., Feng, T.W., Chaoyi, C.: Signal-Obtaining System of Miniature ESG. Journal of Chinese Inertial Technology 10(4), 39–43 (2002)
7. Federico, P., Augusto, S., Stefano, T.: Improving the performance of edge localization technigues through error compensation. Signal Processing: Image Communication 12, 33–47 (1998)
8. Risk, W.P., Lenth, W.: Room temperature CW 946nm Nd: YA G laser pumped by laser-diode-array and intra-cavity frequency doubling to 473nm. Opt. Lett. 12(12), 993–995 (1987)
9. Zhang, R.Z., Wang, J.Z., Xue, A.K.: Passive sound detection nets data simulation system design and implementation. Hangzhou University of Electronic Science and Technology Journal 25(2), 33–36 (2005)
10. Gao, L., Tan, H.: Compact and Efficient 600 mW Blue Laser with a Composite Nd:YAG. Acta Photonica Sinica 33(1), 8–10 (2004)

The Design of the Underlying
Network Communication Module Based on IOCP

Wei-guo Zhang[1], Dong-hui Shi[1], and Li-feng Li[2]

[1] College of Computer Science and Technology,
Xi'an University of Science and Technology, Xi'an China
[2] Department of Satcom Products,
Xi'an Space Stellar Space Technology Application Co., Ltd
zhangwg@xust.edu.cn, 81855071@qq.com

Abstract. The I/O completion port(IOCP) mechanism is adopted in the design, on the basis of it, many optimization technology of the system performance are integrated, such as multithreaded, object pool and the ring buffer zone and memory management etc. The underlying network communication module is designed in this paper to focus on solving some issues, such as the huge amount of client connections, a malicious client to connect and the frequent sending and receiving of small amounts of data packets etc. And it also improves the efficiency of customers' connectivity and sending and receiving messages and reduces the system overhead. Through strict test of pressure and performance, the design has made the good performance in actual application of network game projects.

Keywords: IOCP, network communication, Object pool, Ring buffer zone.

1   The Mechanism of IOCP

The key development part of the network game is how to design an effective game serve, which can't only provide services for more customers as possible as it can, but also is of the biggest scalability and high stability. The so-called scalability is that the serve can always meet customers' demands whether few or more customers. The so-called stability is that the serve can support long time stable services for network customers without errors. These are depended on the performance of network communications layer in large measure. The Socket I/O model is programming in the development of TCP/IP protocol network services, such as WSAAsyneSelect I/O model, WSAEventSelect I/O model, and Overlapped I/O model. When these models encounter massive connections, the systems need to start a large number of threads to serve. However, many threads which are performed together simultaneously would immediately drop the system performance a lot, because the operating system needs to be constantly context switch and switch between the many threads have wasted a lot of time of CPU, seriously affecting the efficiency of the system. In addition, the thread is a system resource, which is limited. In order to solve the questions, developing the port model [1] on a Win32 platform can be adopted. That is the best choice of designing

M. Zhao and J. Sha (Eds.): ICCIP 2012, Part II, CCIS 289, pp. 17–24, 2012.

servers of high performance and scalable, and also is the best processing scheme to a large number of concurrent connections [2].

IOCP (I/O Completion Port), that is an I/O model with the best performance, is a handling mechanism that the applications call few threads for asynchronous I / O requests. The overlapped I/O must be required when we use I/O completion port. Meanwhile, completion port is an efficient way to handle the overlapped I/O. It could deal with requests of the overlapped I/O by a number of working threads to provide service for the request of completion ports. Compared with other I/O models, it can manage any number of socket handles and be consists of the queue of waiting threads and I/O completion queue. A completion port object can be associated with multiple socket handles. For example, the system wouldn't add an I/O complete package until the asynchronous I/O operations initiated by a socket handle are complete.

The completion port is served by working threads to deal with completion notifications that reached the completion port. That means: when an I/O operation is completed, an overlapping I/O completion event notification will be put into this port's completion queue. And then a single working thread will be woken up, which would call GetQueuedCompletionStatus. If there are finished packages in the queue, the current call would obtain data for subsequent processing and then return.

Compared with other I/O models, the biggest advantage of IOCP is its high efficiency for mass connections. It makes full use of system resources to serve a large number of customers only by few threads. Constantly other socket I/O models, such as WSAAsyneSelect I/O model, WSAEventSelect I/O model, overlapped I/O model [3], need that the system starts a lot of threads to serve. However, a large number of thread's scheduling must waste a lot of resources and time in CPU if multiple threads executed concurrently. Therefore the design of completion port is the basis of applications that are of high-performance and massive scalability.

2   Based on the General Design of the Completion Port

2.1   Architecture Design

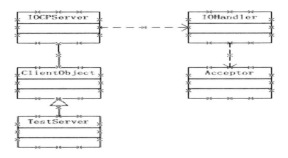

Fig. 1. Modular design architecture

Figure 1 shows the model design. Here is the analysis of functions of main classes in Figure 1.

2.1.1   IOCPServer Class

It is the server basic communication classes, using the IOCP mechanism of Windows workbench. the main functions are :

- Initial server basic configuration and the IOHandler class.
- Open listening.
- Close Server.
- Open work thread for client to sends data and so on.

2.1.2   IOHandler Class

It is created by IOCPServer class, the main functions are:

- The new client connection processing
- Management client connection list
- Create receiving thread.
- Create connection thread.
- The client disconnected or connection error processing.
- Management pending accept request list.

2.1.3   Acceptor Class

It is created by IOHandler class; its main function is to process client new connection.

2.1.4   ClientObject Class

It combines the low level of network with the practical project development, its main functions are:

- Sending data interface to the client.
- Processing interface after receiving data from the client.

2.1.5   TestServer Class

It is a test class, which is mainly used for demonstrating how to derive a real application server on the basis of ClientObject and to introduce that it needs to overload and implement virtual functions of ClientObject.

2.2   System Communication Part of the Module Function Design and Multi-threading Design

Multi-threaded [4] is a very good technology to improve the performance of the server program. The thread pools used for network server program under Win32 workbench can be divided into two classes: One is work thread pool which is maintained by completion port object, and it is mainly responsible for the network layer correlation processing (such as delivery asynchronous read or write operation, etc; Another kind of thread pool is responsible for the logical processing, and it is specifically for application layer to use: The communication module in this paper are shown in figure 2. All kinds of the communication module and the function of the thread are as follows:

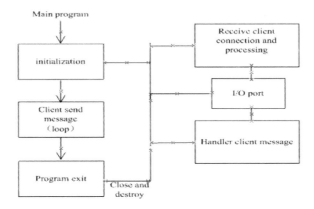

Fig. 2. Program execution flow

2.2.1   Main Thread: It Completes Communication Module Initialization, Sends the Client News and Links to Error of Treatment, etc

- **Communication Initialization Module**

When starting server, it conducts initialization work of communication system in the main thread.

The following are implemented: Create completion port, create work threads related to completion port, create accept client connection thread, create list of connection client, etc. Meanwhile, it needs to create the server listening socket Listensocket, to associate with the completion port, and begin to monitor. Create and initialization m ready and client connection socket Clientsocket and ClientSession class object (customer information).(Here with the memory pool, connection pool to carry efficiency, which will be introduced in detail in the subsequent performance optimization) Use the socket created to delivery m AcceptEx requests, and begin to wait for customers of connection

- **Send Data**

Connection list of circulation client remove data from each ClientSession Object's receiving queue buffer and call send interface to send messages to client.

- **Client Message Processing**

Connection list of circulation client remove data from each ClientSession Object's outgoing queue buffer and call application program logic processing interface to process messages.

- **Regularly Check Each Customer Connections from the Connection List**

Process "empty connection" and "death connect", and process client that be long time to connect to the server but don't make any operation request to reduce server load.

2.2.2   Receive Client Connection Thread

It mainly execute to receive connection processing modules, which is a cyclical process, used when the connection requests from our customers, therefore the customer allocate a ClientSession class (customer information) object and assign it, and then this object will be added to the client connection list.

2.2.3   Receive Client Message Thread

The module is used to serve clients that connect to the server: when receiving messages from clients, the messages would be write into the ring buffer of the client's information object to prepare the application programs' subsequent processing.

2.2.4   System Exit Processing Module

In the main thread, when a system exits, it must do some work such as close and cleanup. It mainly close the completion port that have been created and destroy memory pool, connection pool, and close threads that were created in initialization.

3   Performance Optimization

3.1   Object Pool, the Comprehensive Use of the Location of Customer Information

In the Windows platform, Socket actually is taken as a kernel object handle. Many Windows API which support traditional HANDLE parameters also support Socket. For example, CreateIoCompletionPort support to introduce and call Socket handles instead of HANDLE parameters. So, we create and destroy a Socket handle, which actually create a kernel object in the internal system. For Windows, creating and destroying a Socket kernel object cost is pretty high actually. Especially for some connection-oriented Socket application, the server tend to manage lots of representatives client communication Socket objects, and because of the customer variability, it mainly faces a lot of operations in addition to the general sending and receiving data, and the rest are constantly creating and destroying Socket handle. For frequent access and broken server applications, creating and destroying Socket performance price will come out immediately now. In this case we usually like to not a simply "destroyed" for broken Socket object, but expect to reuse this Socket object. Facing the above problems, we can create a group of Socket object in advance to compose a "pool", in time of needing you can "reuse" the Socket object, or throw Socket object into the pool.

Object pool [5,6] is the memory management way, which is designed for a particular application, and it will promote memory allocation and release performance in some cases. The default memory management function (new/delete or malloc/free) has its shortcomings, if the application frequently distribute and free memory in pile, then it will not only lead to loss of performance, but also make the system appear large amounts of memory pieces, which will reduce the utilization rate of memory.

The so-called object pool is that application can call for the one-time size of the appropriate advance memory block through the system memory allocation, and then divide this piece of memory into a size of the same object, according to the size of a specific object. If the object pool has no free object, you can apply the same size of the system memory block for system again. If the object after using is directly put into the pool, the memory management strategy can effectively improve program performance.

The application of object pool and client message location in the system will be introduced. In IOCP model in order to determine the client object represented by currently return Socket according to the function of GetQueuedCompletionStatus, module needs to rewrite the OVERLAPPED structure for delivering so as to add object point in the client information class:

```
struct OVERLAPPEDEX : public OVERLAPPED
{
……
    ClientSession* ClientSession;
};
```

During initialization, n objects of ClientSession (customer information class) are created and be initialized at first. Their information includes IP address corresponding to client, port number, Socket variable information and so forth. Of course, the number of objects of ClientSession should be based on actual projects, and the ClientSession objects created would be in a unified management. When using LPFN_ACCEPTEX delivery AcceptEx request, a object would be fetched and its object address would be assigned to ClientSession .When a client connection comes, LPFN_GETACCEPTEXSOCKADDRS would get the client's necessary information and SOCKADDR_IN variable of the client information class would be assigned.

Calling for CreateIoCompletionPort, the Socket handles and Socket address of client information object will be associated with completion port and WSARecv will be delivered. IOCP will response this I/O when receiving data from client. At this moment, the value of CompletionKey [7] from GetQueuedCompletionStatus is the point of the current client information class. When the client disconnected, the client's information will be initialized again and delivered again by AcceptEx, which do not destroy objects so as to improve the performance of server program.

3.2   Malicious Client Connection Problems

How to provide AcceptEx function for receiving buffer, overlap operations of AcceptEx delivery don't return until accepted to link and receive the data. But some malicious customers constantly call only connection function to connect to the server. That is to say, not send data and also don't close the connection, which will cause a lot of overlap AcceptEx delivery operation can't return. In order to satisfy the needs of customers, the server have to deliver more accept I/O, taking up a lot of system resources. To avoid this incident, server records all client connection and set DWORD m_lastTime parameters for each connection customers. Every time it receives client news, it will update m_lastTim data, and traverse them in threads in time to check how long receive no messages, if time is too long, its connection will be closed.

3.3   Packet Double-Ranked Problem

For the same asynchronous IO equipment, first submitted asynchronous IO requests always are executed first. That means first submitted, first finished. However, because the thread of asynchronous IO request and the thread of processing asynchronous IO may not be the same one, and thread scheduling order is unsteady, that is to say, first completed asynchronous IO may not be firstly processed.

If IOCP only has one thread to each connection and work the same time only executes a asynchronous IO request, there will be no message order disorder. But this will violate the goal of developing network service program by IOCP which is used to improve the performance and simultaneity. And more work threads will be needed. Meanwhile, multiple asynchronous IO requests would be executed at the same time. It means that reordering data packages is inevitable. The process of reordering packages is: define two mutexes variables in each Socket to indicate the current order of reading or writing and put them in the client information class. Then define other two variables to indicate the order of asynchronous IO request and put them in the derived class of OVERLAPPED. When the receiver has one finished asynchronous IO request, it will extract the order of current need data module and compare its order with the order of current asynchronous IO. If the two numbers are the same, then the data can be further processed. If the two numbers are different, the data packet will be cached and it will be processed until previous data packets are processed. For writing operations we use the same method. The only difference is when a writing operation is completed; another wiring operation can be applied. When work threads get a writing request, it can directly get order from client information class which is taken as the current order of asynchronous IO request to obtain the right data to write.

3.4   Ring Buffer Zone

Server application programs based on TCP protocol, it is necessary to spell a packet processing process. Because the logical data packets should be decomposed from the receiving buffer, so generally memory copy will be involved. But too much memory copy will reduce system performance. And using ring buffer can avoid this kind of circumstance and improve the system performance.

This paper tells the specific application of the ring buffer: Every customer news class maintains a receiving ring buffer and a sending ring buffer. When delivering WSARecv, it will firstly call receiving ring buffer to get their unused space first address and length to assign variable WSABUF, which would make the newly received data packets directly copy into the end of data in receiving ring buffer and directly do the next logical analysis to avoid the frequently calling the memory copy function. Send ring buffer also uses the same methods of operation. In the IOCP processing, even in other processing needing high efficiency processing data transceiver network model of the receiving, it should be a widely used optimized scheme.

4   Last Words

Completion port has a huge advantage and application in the management of mass concurrent users' connection request. It is a good solution to use completion port to develop network servers that support lots of clients. The design uses many kinds of optimization technology such as object pool, message orientation, and ring buffer and so on, which were tested carefully and made good performance in practical projects.

References

1. Jones, A., Ohlund, J.: Network Programming For Microsoft Windows, 2nd edn. (2002)
2. Ma, J.-X., Yuan, D.: Research and Implementation of High Concurrent Server Based on IOCP. J. Communications Technology (July 2009)
3. Gong-Yi, Dong, D.-F., Wang, J.: Computer network high-level software programming technology (2008)
4. Yue, Q.-B., Ma, Y., Lei, W.-M.: One kind thread pool design with realizes in high concurrent request. In: Ninth Session of Computer Science and Technical Graduate Student Symposium Collection, Beijing (2006)
5. Jin, M., Li, W.-Y.: IOCP mechanism application on the network communication system in the P2P model. Microcomputer Information (24) (2007)
6. Hou, J., Chun-Qiu, Chi-Nei: Memory Pool's design philosophy painless application. J. Programmer 9, 94–97 (2002)
7. Jones, A.: Amol Deshpande: Windows Sockets2.0: writescalable winsock apps using completion ports [DB/OL] (2000), http://msdn.microsoft.com/zh-cn/magazine/cc302334(enus).aspx

Study and Implementation on Stereoscopic Display in Virtual Reality

Yuding Zang, Dehui Kong, and Yong Zhang

College of Computer Science and Technology, Beijing University of Technology,
Beijing Municipal Key Laboratory of Multimedia and Intelligent Software Technology,
Pingleyuan. 100, 100124 Beijing, China
yudingzang@163.com

Abstract. Stereoscopic display is a key technology of virtual reality system, and it can enhance the characteristic of immersion. However, in most method the depth of scene is got incorrectly because of inaccurate parallax. This paper focuses on the stereoscopic display technology and proposes a stereoscopic display method based on binocular parallax. In the method, eye separation is determined by focal length and vertical parallax is eliminated. Experimental results show that stereoscopic effect can be obtained well in our method.

Keywords: stereoscopic display, binocular parallax, focal length, vertical parallax.

1 Introduction

Computer vision is that use computer to achieve human visual function such as perception, recognition, understanding and so on that human can get from three-dimensional scene of the objective world [1]. As an important branch of computer vision, computer stereo vision simulates directly the way in which human vision process scenes. Since the objective world is three-dimensional in space, so that stereo vision has become one of the hot keys about computer vision. It can bring depth sense and make people have an immersive feeling. Stereo vision is applied in many areas such as virtual reality, multimedia teaching, robot vision, industrial product design, art sculpture, architecture.

In the stereoscopic display method based on binocular parallax, the important factor is how to obtain stereo pairs correctly. So far there are two ways to obtain stereo pairs: stereo camera recording, computer drawing. Eagles ham B. S. and other people who work in the Cornell University of America adapt the method of CLSM (Confocal Laser Scanning Microscope) to obtain stereo pairs, so as to observe bacteria conveniently. However, such approach requires at least two or more cameras which are calibrated strictly in optical, mechanical, electrical and other properties. This increases the difficulty of capturing stereo pairs. Drawing stereo pairs with computer has attracted widespread interest in domestic and foreign scholars. Austrians called Habbware developed a component to generate stereo images or video by three-dimensional model. But this method needs users to adjust the parameters themselves and users don't know what parameters make the best stereoscopic display.

M. Zhao and J. Sha (Eds.): ICCIP 2012, Part II, CCIS 289, pp. 25–36, 2012.

Inspired by the method of computer rendering, a new binocular parallax method is designed in this paper, and this method combines the relationship between eye separation and focal length and the technology of eliminating vertical parallax, realize stereoscopic display for three-dimensional scenes.

2   Background

2.1   Stereoscopic Principles

So far there are many technologies about computer stereo vision, and binocular parallax is a research hot. When people watch some objects with both eyes, the two pieces of visual image received by left and right eye is different because of the distance between two eyes. Physical depth cues will be generated through the brain fusion of the two views. This is the basic principle of binocular stereo vision [2, 3]. We can obtain binocular stereoscopic views by taking advantage of binocular stereo vision technology [4]. In brief, binocular stereo view is a process that acquits, generates, and transmits a space scene. And at the end of the process a stereoscopic view will be put forward.

In addition, there are other stereoscopic technologies not based on the principle of binocular parallax, Such as dimensional holographic, volume display and so on [10, 11]. Holographic technology is that we record the special wavelengths of light given by the object in the form of interference fringes based on the theory of interferometry, to form a piece of hologram. Because holographic is a kind of real 3D display technology, people will receive the same feeling as viewing real objects in daily life. Although the technology has some significant advantages in stereoscopic feeling and visual fatigue, their products are not yet mature, and also need for future research.

The stereoscopic function of eye can help people sense the distance between near and far objects in the eye area [12]. Usually the two different views obtained by left and right eyes are called left view and right view. In the display, if we use certain devices to make left and right eye only see the correspond view that displayed simultaneously on the screen, we will obtain stereoscopic view through the fusion of brain [7]. In the figure 1, A_1 is the left view point of A and A_2 is the right view point of A; B_1 is the left view point of B and B_2 is the right view point of B. If A_1 and B_1 are only seen by left eye

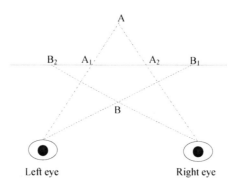

Fig. 1. Principle of binocular

and A_2 and B_2 are only seen by right eye, then the depths of A and B will be reflected in human brain. The projection of point A locates behind the screen and the projection of point B locates in front of the screen.

At first let's define some variables: X is the separation between left eye and right eye, L is the distance between the eye and the screen, S_A is the distance between A_1 and A_2, and S_B is the distance between B_1 and B_2. Then the depth of A is:

$$D_A = \frac{S_A}{x-S_A} L \tag{1}$$

Similarly the depth of B is:

$$D_B = \frac{S_B}{x-S_B} L \tag{2}$$

2.2   Stereoscopic Display

Because of the limitations of two-dimensional display device, the real three-dimensional scene just show two-dimensional features when displayed in the flat display equinment. We only see the plane image, and can't feel the stereoscopic sense. It's a issue how to display stereoscopic view on the two-dimensional screen, attracts many researchers' attention who wok in the virtual reality area. For this, a variety of solutions have been proposed, such as   head-monitor, 3D glasses and so on. Recnetly, some countries have developed stereoscopic monitor.

Stereoscopic display with glasses is divided into three categories according to working principle. The first method bases on the wavelength, sunch as red-blue glasses. It is praised for maturity and low cost, but can not display color images. The second method bases on alternating time. Syschronous signal control liquid crystal shutter glasses in order to alternate left and right view. The third method bases on polarized light [5]. The fourth method bases on spectral. Display the left and right views with different RGB color scheme and left and right eyes can see different scenes. Then people can feel the depth of scene.

In the method of head-mounted, two monitors are placed before left and right eye, so left eye and right eye only see the scene displayed on each monitor [6]. Then the parallax images bring people a feeling of immersion. This approach also has some drawbacks such as only for one user, low resolution, heavity of monitor and so on.

Grating stereoscopic monitor is the widespread type in stereoscopic display[9]. This kind of monitor is formed by a combination of flat screens and gratings. Left and right parallax views are displayed on the flat screen according to certain rules, and with the spectroscopic function of gratings, the rays of left and right views can be propagated in different directions. In that case, when the viewer stand at the absolute position the left and right eyes can observe respectively at left and right scenes. Then people can feel the depth with brain fusion.

3   Design of Stereoscopic Display

The scheme designed and implemented in this paper aims for active stereoscopic projection display based on binocular parallax. In active display, left and right parallax views are projected alternately onto the screen in accordance with time, and then human eyes receive left and right parallax projections according to time series by wearing special glasses. In this scheme, the most important aspect is to obtain correct parallax image pairs in order to have a good fusion effect. To achieve this goal, this paper takes two methods: first, focal length determines the eye-separation; second, elimination of vertical parallax. Figure 2 shows the stereoscopic display model designed in this paper. In the model, the relative positions of left and right view-point are determined according to the selected focal length. We adopt parallel projection for view frustum in order to eliminate vertical parallax. After that the binocular pairs can be projected in the style of active stereoscopic display.

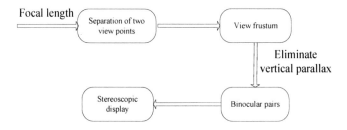

Fig. 2. Architecture of stereoscopic projection

3.1   Separation of Left and Right View Point

The degree of the stereo effect depends on both the distance of the view point to the projection plane and the separation of the left and right view point [8]. Too large a separation can be hard to resolve and is known as hyper stereo. Experiments show that a good ballpark separation of the left and right view point is 1/20 of the distance to the projection plane; this is generally the maximum separation for comfortable viewing. When the separation of two points is between 1/30 and 1/20 of the distance of the view point to the projection plane, the stereo effect is relatively good. Another constraint in general practice is to ensure the negative parallax does not exceed the eye separation. As figure 3 shows, appropriate range of eye separation is from Focal Length*1/30 to Focal Length*1/20.

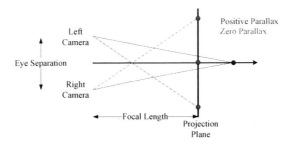

Fig. 3. Binocular disparity

The stereo effect can be measured by a variable which is named parallax angle. The definition of parallax angle id described by equation 3 where DX is the horizontal separation of a projected point between the two eyes and d is the distance of the eye form the projection plane. For easy fusing by the majority of people, the absolute value of theta should not exceed 1.5 degree for all points in the scene.

$$thea=2arctan(DX/2d) \tag{3}$$

3.2   Circumvention of Vertical Parallax

For stereoscopic display, the important factors are stereo pairs which make people feel the depth of scene. How to calculate stereo pairs is an important issue. There are a couple of methods of setting up a virtual camera and rendering two stereo pairs, many methods are strictly incorrect since they introduce vertical parallax. An example of this is called the "Toe-in" method; while incorrect it is still often used because the correct "off-axis" method requires features not always supported by rendering packages. Toe-in is usually identical to methods that involve a rotation of the scene. The toe-in method is still popular for the lower cost filming because offset cameras are uncommon and it is easier than using parallel cameras which requires a subsequent trimming of the stereo pairs. The following describes the details of these two typical methods.

Toe-in. In this projection, as figure 4 shows the camera has a fixed and symmetric frustum; each camera is pointed at a single focal point. And left and right horizontal angle is equal in value.

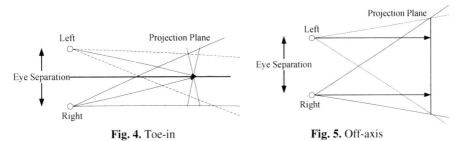

Fig. 4. Toe-in   **Fig. 5.** Off-axis

In figure 4, view frustum drawn by imaginary lines expresses what left eye see and view frustum drawn by solid lines expresses what right eye see. The two frustums 'central axes point to the same focus point. It just needs a simple rotation to produce stereo pairs. But the vertical parallax it introduces will cause increased discomfort levels.

Off-axis. Shown as figure 5, this is the correct way to create stereo pairs. It introduces no vertical parallax and is therefore creates the less stressful stereo pairs. The view frustum is non-symmetric. In this projection method, FOV vectors of the two viewpoints keep parallel and the projection planes of the two view frustums overlap each other. So this eliminates the vertical parallax and brings a more comfortable viewing experience.

4   Implementation of Stereoscopic Display

The stereoscopic display technology mentioned in this paper is realized by cylindrical projection shown as figure 6. We use the technology of double channel to achieve large resolution of cylindrical screen with a horizontal FOV of 100°and a vertical FOV of 33.461°. The cylindrical screen is formed by two channels with a fusion area of 20% and the channel's horizontal FOV is 55.556°. The radius, chord length, arc length and height of this cylindrical are 4700mm, 7200mm, 8203mm and 2500mm respectively. The double channels of the projection system are realized based on the hardware and we should provide view pairs with certain aspect ratio to the projection system.

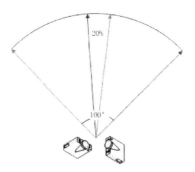

Fig. 6. Projection of double channels

4.1   Hardware Platform of Projection System

Experiments mentioned in this paper are done with projectors produced by Barco Company. There are many drawbacks in traditional active stereoscopic display, such as great luminance decay, bulky glasses, dizziness and nausea and so on. Barco adopts INFITEC skill to overcome the drawbacks occur in traditional active and passive stereoscopic skills. This skill has a better performance in practical terms and display effects, and don't require that the screen should have feature of polarization. INFITEC is now recognized as a good skill about stereoscopic display. It uses high-quality light filter to separate spectrum for each eye of people and generates stereoscopic views without ghosting. Compared with the traditional active stereo, it doesn't bring flicker and is equipped with appropriate glasses. Besides, compared with other passive stereo, it is characterized with good consistence for no dependence on screen.

4.2   Definition of Symmetrical Frustum

Shown as figure 7, left and right frustum is obtained through rotation of the frustum got upon single viewport, so we must determine the symmetrical frustum in single viewport at first.

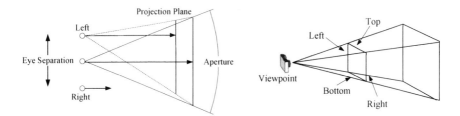

Fig. 7. Left and right frustum   **Fig. 8.** Definition of frustum

The definition of frustum is shown as figure 8, referring to several parameters. Besides, the values of parameters must keep consistent with particular hardware of display device.

The values of left, right, top, bottom, near and far are selected upon the devices we used in lab. These parameters should fulfill constraints described by formula 4 and formula 5. The two formulas ensure frustum adapt horizontal and vertical FOV of cylindrical screen.

$$\arctan(\frac{right-left}{2*near}) = \frac{5\pi}{18} \tag{4}$$

$$\arctan(\frac{top-bottom}{2*near}) = \frac{33.461\,\pi}{180} \tag{5}$$

4.3   Calculation of Eye Separation

As mentioned in chapter 3.2, eye separation is usually set between 1/30 and 1/20 of focal length, so we just to determine the focal length of virtual camera at first. Focal length is the distance of the view point from the projection plane. Usually when we conduct projection calculation, we make the y of projected point between -1 and 1. In this situation, focal length can be determined as long as the vertical FOV of frustum is known.

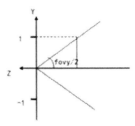

Fig. 9. Focal length

According to fovy (vertical FOV) shown in figure 9, we can calculate the value of focal length by formula 6, and also determine the range of eye separation.

$$\text{FocalLength} = 1 * \text{arccot}(\frac{\text{fovy}}{2})$$

(6)

4.4   Calculation of View Pairs

During the calculation of view pairs, an important point is to avoid the generation of vertical parallax. In chapter 3.2, we discuss two methods for this problem, and off-axis can deal with vertical parallax well, obtain good visual effect and comfortable feeling. View pairs are obtained through translation of frustum and non-symmetric projection. The following gives a description about process details.

Parameter Description

Table 1. Matrix and parameters

Heading level	Single viewport	Left frustum	Right frustum
View matrix	**MVIEW**	**MLVIEW**	**MRVIEW**
Projection matrix	**MPROJ**	**MLPROJ**	**MRPROJ**
Translation matrix	**MTRANSF**	**MLTRANSF**	**MRTRANSF**
The coordinates of left vertex on x-axis of frustum	**l**	**lL**	**lR**
The coordinates of right vertex on x-axis of frustum	**r**	**rL**	**rR**

In addition, d is half of the eye separation; t, b, f_{Near} and f_{Far} correspond to top, bottom, near and far in figure 8 respectively. According to the positions of left and right viewpoint, we can know that t, b, f_{Near} and f_{Far} in left frustum are equal to that of right frustum.

Calculate View Pairs with Off-axis. In this situation, the view matrix has no rotation around Z-axis and the projection frustum is non-symmetric. During rendering, we make a translation for view matrix of single viewport to obtain view matrixes of left and right viewpoint. According to the perspective projection matrix, we do a certain transformation to obtain non-symmetric projection matrixes of left and right viewpoint. Finally, we do a multiplication operation on view matrix and perspective projection matrix for left and right viewpoint respectively, and then we make normalization on the results to convert to screen coordinates. Now the view pairs are calculated completely, and we just output them to the devices with stereoscopic function in order to have a stereoscopic display of virtual scenes.

$$M_{LVIEW} = M_{VIEW} \bullet M_{LTRANSF}$$
$$M_{RVIEW} = M_{VIEW} \bullet M_{RTRANSF}$$

$$M_{LTRANSF} = \begin{bmatrix} 1 & 0 & 0 & -d \\ 0 & 1 & 0 & 0 \\ 0 & 0 & 1 & f_{Far} \\ 0 & 0 & 0 & 1 \end{bmatrix} \tag{7}$$

$$M_{RTRANSF} = \begin{bmatrix} 1 & 0 & 0 & d \\ 0 & 1 & 0 & 0 \\ 0 & 0 & 1 & f_{Far} \\ 0 & 0 & 0 & 1 \end{bmatrix} \tag{8}$$

$$M_{PROJ} = \begin{bmatrix} \dfrac{2 \bullet f_{Near}}{r - l} & 0 & \dfrac{r+l}{r-l} & 0 \\[2ex] 0 & \dfrac{2 \bullet f_{Near}}{t-b} & \dfrac{t+b}{t-b} & 0 \\[2ex] 0 & 0 & -\dfrac{f_{Near}+f_{Far}}{f_{Far}-f_{Near}} & -\dfrac{2 \bullet f_{Near}}{f_{Far}-f_{Near}} \\[2ex] t & 0 & -1 & 0 \end{bmatrix} \tag{9}$$

$$M_{LPROJ} = \begin{bmatrix} \dfrac{2 \bullet f_{Near}}{r_L - l_L} & 0 & \dfrac{r_L+l_L}{r_L-l_L} & 0 \\[2ex] 0 & \dfrac{2 \bullet f_{Near}}{t-b} & \dfrac{t+b}{t-b} & 0 \\[2ex] 0 & 0 & \dfrac{f_{Near}+f_{Far}}{f_{Near}-f_{Far}} & \dfrac{2 \bullet f_{Near}}{f_{Near}-f_{Far}} \\[2ex] t & 0 & -1 & 0 \end{bmatrix} \tag{10}$$

$$
M_{RPROJ} = \begin{bmatrix} \dfrac{2 \cdot f_{Near}}{r_R - l_R} & 0 & \dfrac{r_R + l_R}{r_R - l_R} & 0 \\[2ex] 0 & \dfrac{2 \cdot f_{Near}}{t-b} & \dfrac{t+b}{t-b} & 0 \\[2ex] 0 & 0 & \dfrac{f_{Near} + f_{Far}}{f_{Near} - f_{Far}} & \dfrac{2 \cdot f_{Near}}{f_{Near} - f_{Far}} \\[2ex] t & 0 & -1 & 0 \end{bmatrix} \qquad (11)
$$

5   Experimental Results

We have tested the proposed method on a binocular active projection system. We applied this method to a railway simulation system. Results are shown in figure 10 and 11. Scenes without stereoscopic function are described in figure 10, and we can see that elements in the scene are displayed clearly and observers can't feel the depth difference between elements. We also find that edges of elements are fuzzy in figure 11. This is the result of separation of left and right view. When we watch the two views corresponding to the left and right eye our brain will fuse the separate views and extract the depth information as it does in normal watching. In the experiments of simulation system, we can obviously feel the distance while the train is moving along railway.

Fig. 10. Scene without stereoscopic function

Fig. 11. Scene with stereoscopic function

Our method has a great effect at the aspect of calculating stereo pairs. Appropriate eye separation and avoidance of vertical parallax play a very important role in improving stereoscopic effects. If stereo pairs are created with a conflict of depth cues then one of a number of things may occur: one cue may become dominant and it may not be the correct/intend one, the depth perception will be exaggerated or reduced, the image will be uncomfortable to watch, the stereo pairs may not fuse at all and the viewer will see two separate images. Too large or too small a separation and vertical parallax all reduces the performance in stereoscopic display. Too large a separation can be hard to resolve and too small a separation cannot produce depth perception. Figure 12 shows the performance of our method and our brain can easily fuse the stereo pairs for its appropriate eye separation. Figure 13 shows the performance of incorrect pairs and we cannot get the perception of depth for the hard fusion. The incorrect stereo pairs are caused by the horizontal parallax that cannot math focal length. In addition, vertical parallax also influences the formation of correct pairs.

Fig. 12. Correct stereo pairs

Fig. 13. Incorrect stereo pairs

6   Conclusion

This paper presents a method for stereoscopic display based on binocular parallax.   In particular, it describes the process of calculating eye separation and how to eliminate vertical parallax. Our method can determine appropriate eye separation more suitable for focal length and further obtain correct view pairs. In addition, circumvention of vertical parallax also helps us have a comfortable visualization.

Besides, there are still some shortcomings in our method. In the process of calculating view pairs, we put the whole scene as a single object to deal with, ignoring the differences between the various elements.

In most scenes, there are interesting areas that attract observers' attention. For the hot area, we may have a good stereoscopic sense by enlarging the eye separation corresponding to this area. In general, people are likely to focus on the mass objects located in the central area. Following this rules, we can adjust eye separation for every local area in the whole scene so as to enhance stereoscopic effects of significant areas.

Acknowledgments. This paper is supported by the National Natural Science Foundation of China (Nos. U0935004, 60825203), National Key Technology R&D Program (No. 2007BAH13B01) and Beijing Natural Science Foundation (No. 4102009).

References

1. Zhang, Y.: Image understanding and computer vision. Tsinghua University Press, Beijing (2000)
2. Hou, C., Yu, S.: A novel method of picture conversion from 2D to 3D. Acta Electronica Sinica 30(12), 1861–1864 (2002)
3. Zhou, L.: Study on stereoscopic technique for virtual reality. Computer Applications 19(4), 24–26 (1999)
4. Zhu, Q., Liu, R., Xu, X.: Properties of a binocular stereo vision model, pp. 831–834. World Scientific Press (2005)
5. Jung, S.M., Park, J.U., Lee, S.C.: A novel polarizer glasses type 3D displays with an active retarder. SID Symposium Digest of Technical Papers J. 40(1), 348–351 (2009)
6. Kellerk, Statea, Fuchsh: Head mounted displays for medical use. Journal of Display Technology 4(4), 468–472 (2008)
7. Mao, C.D., Wang, Y.Q.: Multiview auto-stereoscopic projection system. Opto-Electronic Eng. 33(4), 59–62 (2006)
8. Tanaka, K., Hayashi, J., Inami, M., et al.: TWISTER: An immersive autostereoscopic display. In: Proceeding of VR 2004, pp. 59–66. IEEE Computer Society, Chicago (2004)
9. Perlin, K., Paxia, S., Kollin, J.S.: An autostereoscopic display. In: Proceedings of SPIE, San Jose, CA, USA, pp. 64900M-1–64900M-12 (2007)
10. Lipton, L., Feldman, M.: A new autostereoscopic display technology. The Synth Gram TM. In: Proceeding of SPIE, San Jose, CA, USA, pp. 229–235 (2002)
11. Dodgson, N.A., Moore, J.R., et al.: A time sequential multi-projector autostereoscopic diplay. Journal of the Society for Information Display 8(2), 1–12 (2000)
12. Schwerdtner, A.: Autostereoscopic 3D display. In: Proceedings of SPIE, San Jose, CA, USA, vol. 6055, pp. 1–10 (2006)

Application Layer DDoS Detection Model Based on Data Flow Aggregation and Evaluation

Mi Zhang, Wei Zhang, and Kuan Fan

College of Computer,
Nanjing University of Posts and Telecommunications,
Nanjing, China
zhangmi222@gmail.com, 1999zhangwei@163.com,
xiaokuan_ff@yahoo.com.cn

Abstract. Distributed Denial of Service (DDoS) attacks have been one of the most effective attacks to the Internet. With the rapid development of Web applications, the application layer DDoS attacks gradually become the main attacks which can make the server deny legitimate users' requests by exhausting the bandwidth of the target network and the resources of the server hosts. An application layer DDoS detection model is proposed based on data flow aggregation and evaluation in this paper. In the model users' data first is aggregated to data flows according to the surface characteristics, average scan time and sequence of page requests. Second, it extracts the deep features of data flows, hot-spot access and resource consumption. Then the model utilizes D-S evidential theory to evaluate the data flows so that it can identify and isolate the attack flows. The experimental results show that this model can thwart typical application layer DDoS attacks effectively.

Keywords: application layer, DDoS, data flows, D-S evidential theory.

1 Introduction

With the rapid development of the Internet, various network attacks emerge, in which Distributed Denial of Service (DDoS) attacks are the primary security threats. Traditional DDoS attacks usually occur in the network layer, such as SYN Flood, ICMP Flood, etc. Currently, many research achievements have made it possible to detect and prevent DDoS attacks in the network layer[1]. As the web applications develop rapidly and become more and more complex, the application layer DDoS attacks gradually become the main attacks which mainly take advantage of the defects of the high layer service. Attackers send packets to the target server through victims or proxy servers in order to exhaust the bandwidth of the target network or CPU resources to make the server deny legitimate users' requests. The attackers establish legal connections and send the normal packets so it can easily pass the low-level detection system to the application layer. However, it is more complex to deal with the data of application layer than that of lower layer. The application layer attack is a

M. Zhao and J. Sha (Eds.): ICCIP 2012, Part II, CCIS 289, pp. 37–45, 2012.

kind of asymmetric attack, by which only a few bandwidth or host resource of the attacker can cause a tremendous exhaust of the server's resources. It makes the attacks more destructive, and the attacks can be implemented more easily since it works in the application layer[2].

At present, the famous application layer attacks include HTTP flood attack, CC(Challenge Collapsar) attack, spam mail attack, SQL worm king attack and so on. Owing to the diversity and difference of the application protocols, we propose a detection model based on the aggregation and evaluation of data flows for popular HTTP. In the model, first we aggregate users' traffic to data flows according to the surface characteristics, average scan time and sequence of page requests. Second, it extracts the deep features of data flows, hot-spot access and resource consumption, then utilizes D-S evidential theory[4-6] to evaluate the data flows so that it can identify and isolate the attack flows.

2   Related Work

Currently most application layer attacks can be classified into two categories: the bandwidth exhausting and the host resource exhausting. The former occupies the bandwidth of the target network by a large number of forged HTTP requests, so that normal users cannot access the Web, such as HTTP flood attacks. The characteristic of this attack is that the server receives many HTTP packets which have the same IP in a short term, and the requests have the same URL, or repeat a few different URLs. The latter uses a small amount of HTTP requests to ask the server to return large files, such as images, video files, etc. The latter can also ask the server to run some complex scripts, such as complex data processing, calculation and verification of password, etc. Its purpose is to exhaust the resources of the target host, such as CPU, memory, Socket, etc. This approach can quickly exhaust the resources of the host without a high attack rate, and it can also be hidden easily, such as CC attacks.

Currently, the study of the application-layer DDoS attacks detection aboard is to distinguish between normal traffic and attack traffic. The methods proposed in [7-9] identify attack traffic based on user access behavior. Xie, Y. et al [7] propose a detection method based on semi-hidden Markov model, which describes users' access behavior with HsMM. It uses the deviation of most normal users' access features as a measurement of the flow's abnormal degree, which can effectively detect application-layer DDoS attacks, however, the computation is complex. Yatahai, T. et al [8] detect HTTP-Get flood attacks by using two algorithms that whether the same IP user is browsing the page in the same order and comparing the relationship between browsing time and the size of the page information. However, the implicit prerequisite of the algorithm is that the attacks adopt the same sequence of the requests, and some normal users may also access web sites with the same sequence in reality, causing a high rate of false positive in the method. Park, K. et al [9] propose a model adopting the Turing test, which sends the behavior detection program to the client, then analyzes whether there are normal user behaviors, such as mouse movements, and analyzes whether the user's access request is consistent with normal browsing behaviors to determine a normal user or a robot. Walfish, M. et al [10] propose a method of speak-up to protect against application layer DDoS. Contrary to the traditional filtering methods of slowing or weakening the attacker, speak-up approach asks all clients increase the sending rate, but the attacker in order to achieve better effects of attacks usually takes to the maximum attack ability principle. The attacker uses maximum transmission rate in the beginning, so the users who increase the sending rate are legitimate users, which can identify legitimate traffic. However, this method will undoubtedly increase the burden on the server and may crash the system, especially when the server is busy.

3   Application Layer DDoS Detection Model Based on Data Flow Aggregation and Evaluation

3.1   Overview of the Detection Model

To detect and isolate the attack traffic real-timely, we intercept the traffic before they reach the server. And we extract the average scan time and the sequence of page request's characteristics from the traffic of each IP address. Generally, for a DDoS attack, the attack software running on the victims send the same attack packets, so we can aggregate the attack traffic to one flow according to the similarity of the surface characteristics. Moreover, due to the difficulty of code implementation, the attack software cannot completely mimic the normal users' sequence of requests. It can only repeat one or several requests. Since few normal users will have the same sequence of requests, few of normal users will be aggregated to the attack flow incorrectly.

We assume each flow as the input focal elements of the evidential theory. As to the application layer, DDoS attacks especially to the low-speed attacks, the attack software usually requests the pages that will need server hosts to perform complex operations. We extract two deep features of data flows as two mass functions, m_1, m_2, hot-spot access and resource consumption. According to the combined value of $m_{1,2}$, we assign a priority label to each flow and put the data flows into the user queue. The overall framework of the model is as Fig. 1.

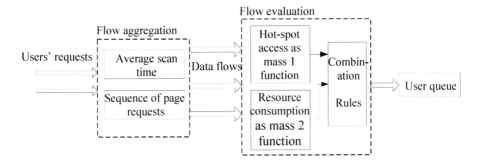

Fig. 1. Framework of the model

3.2   Data Flow Aggregation

To reduce the number of input focal elements of the evidential theory, we aggregate users' traffic with similar surface characteristics to the same flow. If each single user is dealt as a focal element, it will result in a reduction in the probability assigned to every focal element, then we cannot distinguish the normal traffic and the attack traffic effectively.

The process of aggregation can be divided into two parts, extraction of surface characteristics and aggregation of the data flows.

3.2.1   Extraction of Surface Characteristics

(a)   Average Scan Time
Every time when normal users click on a link in a web page, there will be a request. We denote the time between two requests as Scan Time (ST) and calculate the Average Scan Time (AST) of each IP user[11]. The formula is as follows:

$$AST[i+1] = AST[i] \cdot (1 - W_{ST}) + ST[i] \cdot W_{ST} \quad . \tag{1}$$

In (1) variable i indicates the request index, $AST[i+1]$ indicates the average scan time after receiving the No.i+1 request, and $ST[i]$ indicates the time between No.i request and No.i+1 request. W_{ST} is a constant weight smaller than 1.

(b)   Sequence of Page Requests
We number the pages on a web server side to represent every user's sequence of requests. And use an access vector to represent the sequence of requests: $\mathbf{V} = (v_1, v_2, v_3, ..., v_n)$. The vector length n indicates the total number of the web pages and v_i indicates the accessed times of the page i.

The difference of the sequence of page requests can be represented by the Euclidean distance between two vectors as follows:

$$\Delta(\mathbf{V_p}, \mathbf{V_q}) = \sqrt{(v_p^1 - v_q^1)^2 + (v_p^2 - v_q^2)^2 + ... + (v_p^n - v_q^n)^2} \quad . \tag{2}$$

3.2.2   Data Flow Aggregation

We aggregate the IP users' data with similar average scan time and sequence of page requests to one flow. The pseudo-code is as follows:

```
If |AST_p − AST_q| ≤ TH_t
    If (V_p − V_q) ≤ TH_v
        Then p and q belong to the same flow
```

In the pseudo-code TH_t and TH_v indicate the threshold of average scan time and access vector.

3.3   Data Flow Evaluation

Through data flow aggregation, we get one sequence of data flows denoted as $S = (S_1, S_2, S_3, ..., S_m)$. Each data flow owns some properties, which can be denoted as $P = (p_1, p_2, p_3, ..., p_n)$. Taking account into the universality of detection method, we choose two features, hot-spot access and resource consumption as mass functions m_1, m_2 of D-S theory. Then we combine m_1 and m_2 to get $m_{1.2}$. The value of the function represents the probability of the data flow to be an attack flow. We set a threshold of mass function and determine a flow is an attack flow or not with the threshold. Finally, we put the traffic of the flow into the priority queue to send to the server according to its probability.

3.3.1   D-S Evidential Theory

D-S evidential theory which is proposed by A.P. Dempster first and then developed by G. Shafer is a theory of dealing with uncertainty problems. D-S theory use a prior probability to get a posterior range of evidence, which quantifies the credibility of a proposition. It can assign evidence to assumptions or propositions.

There is an environment represented by θ which is a set with mutually exclusive and exhaustive elements in D-S theory. Basic probability assignment (BPA) function is a function m called mass function where $2^\theta \rightarrow [0,1]$. And it meets $m(\varnothing) = 0$ and

$$\sum_{A \in \theta} m(A) = 1.$$ We call the A a focal element if $m(A) > 0$.

To $\forall A \in \theta$, the combination rule of two mass functions m_1 and m_2 in θ is as follows:

$$m_1 \oplus m_2(A) = \frac{1}{K} \sum_{B \cap C = A} m_1(B) m_2(C) \ . \tag{3}$$

$$K = \sum_{B \cap C \neq \varnothing} m_1(B) m_2(C) = 1 - \sum_{B \cap C = \varnothing} m_1(B) m_2(C) \ .$$

Because evidential theory is an axiom system weaker than probability theory and it has the ability to express "unknowing" and "uncertain", we choose evidential theory to evaluate the data flows to distinguish the normal flows and attack flows.

3.3.2   Mass Functions

(a)   Hot-Spot Access
We use data flows' hot-spot access feature as mass function m_1. The value of m_1 represents the probability of the flow to be an attack flow.

Keep an access vector on the server side to add up all the users' sequence of page requests in normal state and then calculate each page's access frequency to generate a normalized frequency vector $\mathbf{F} = (f_1, f_2, f_3, ..., f_n)$ while $\sum_{i=1}^{n} f_i = 1$. The access vector of data flow S_k is denoted as $\mathbf{V_k}$. Define a vector $\mathbf{I} = (1, 1, ..., 1)$, then

$$m_1(S_k) = \frac{(\mathbf{I}-\mathbf{F}) \times \mathbf{V}_k^T}{\sum_{i=1}^{m}(\mathbf{I}-\mathbf{F}) \times \mathbf{V}_i^T} \quad . \tag{4}$$

(b) Resource Consumption

The application layer DDoS attacks especially the low-speed attacks is purposed to exhaust target server's host resources, such as CPU, memory, sockets, etc. When we analyze the features of attack flows we can discover that the requested URLs are almost the pages that will need server hosts to perform complex operations. So we use the ratio of accessing for the pages that need complex operations as mass function m_2.

Keep a table to record the pages that need complex operations. To each data flow S_k's access vector $\mathbf{V}_k$, we count the pages that need complex operations by looking up the table to get a number denoted as P_k. So

$$m_2(S_k) = \frac{P_k}{\sum_{i=1}^{n}P_i} \quad . \tag{5}$$

3.3.3   Combination of Evidence

While the data flow is aggregated from different users' traffic, so there will be no intersection among focal elements. To one data flow, its mass function of hot-spot access will not be zero. But the mass function of resource consumption can be zero. So we set a threshold denoted as TH_{m_1} to the mass function of hot-spot access. If the value of m_1 is larger than the threshold, we don't need to combine m_1 with m_2. Instead, we determine the flow to be an attack flow directly.

Combine the two mass functions m_1 and m_2 according to (3). To data flow S_k

$$m_{1,2}(S_k) = m_1 \oplus m_2(S_k) = \frac{1}{K} \sum_{B \cap C = S_k} m_1(B)m_2(C) \quad . \tag{6}$$

$$K = \sum_{B \cap C \neq \varnothing} m_1(B)m_2(C) = 1 - \sum_{B \cap C = \varnothing} m_1(B)m_2(C) \quad .$$

$m_{1,2}(S_k), (k = 1, 2, ..., m)$ represents the probability of the data flow S_k to be an attack flow.

3.4   Discussion

An important part of this model is the determination of the constants and thresholds. We should consider the number of focal elements in D-S theory and the similarity of users' traffic in a data flow. The constant used in calculating the AST generally is set at 0.1[11]. And the threshold of AST can be (maximum of AST — minimum of AST)/n, where n represents a division number of the AST. Generally, we set n at 5. The threshold of the hot-spot access is based on the number of web pages and the distance of each access vector. We don't need to consider the vector which is deviated from the general vector seriously. To determine the flow to be an attack flow, we set the threshold of the two mass functions at 0.5.

4   Experimental Results and Analysis

We set up a web server deployed with 10 web pages in our campus network. The home page is numbered 1. Other pages can be clicked in from home page and are numbered from 2 to 10. There are two pages numbered 9 and 10 needing querying the database. Server cost about 0.01s to get the response of no.9 page or no.10 page while the other common pages only need a few milliseconds. The access frequency vector as the web has counted in a normal state is $F = (0.20, 0.15, 0.09, 0.06, 0.06, 0.06, 0.11, 0.06, 0.15, 0.06)$. We visit the web server through 10 PCs simultaneously. Six of them simulate normal users, and the other four simulate attackers with the attack software running on it.

Our detection module intercepts and analyzes the traffic before they reach the server host. The surface characteristics we extract at one time is as Table 1, where C2,C5 are HTTP Flood attackers and C6,C10 are CC attackers. We aggregate users' traffic to data flows and set the threshold of average scan time at 0.5 while the threshold of access vector at 3. The aggregated flows are shown as Table 2.

We set the threshold of mass function m_1 at 0.5 and the threshold of $m_{1,2}$ at 0.3. Due to flow S2's m_1 function value is larger than 0.5, we determine flow S2 to be an attack flow directly. Among the remaining four flows as S4's $m_{1,2}$ function value is 0.8714 larger than 0.3, we determine S4 to be an attack flow and drop it.

Table 1. Surface characteristics of users

Client	AST	V
C1	25	(1,1,1,0,0,1,1,0,2,0)
C2	1	(179,0,0,0,0,0,0,0,0,0)
C3	18	(1,0,1,1,0,0,1,0,1,0)
C4	21	(1,1,0,0,0,0,1,0,0,1)
C5	1	(181,0,0,0,0,0,0,0,0,0)
C6	15	(0,0,0,0,0,0,0,0,10,0)
C7	17	(1,2,0,0,0,1,0,1,1,1)
C8	16	(2,0,1,1,0,0,1,0,0,0)
C9	18	(1,1,0,0,2,0,0,1,1,0)
C10	14	(0,0,0,0,0,0,0,0,13,0)

Table 2. Data flows' combination of mass functions

Stream	m1	m2	m1,2
S1(C1,C4)	0.0285	0.1	0.0555
S2(C2,C5)	0.8983	0	0
S3(C3,C8)	0.0260	0.033	0.0167
S4(C6,C10)	0.0583	0.767	0.8714
S5(C7,C9)	0.0289	0.1	0.0563

The experimental results show that the model can aggregate and filter attack flows. The false positive rate of this model is 4.5%, and the false negative rate is 5.7% through a test of large amounts of data.

This method is able to thwart typical HTTP Flood attacks and CC attacks while the model in [8] can only defend HTTP Flood attacks and is hard to detect the low-speed attacks of application layer. The calculation of the method in [7] is complex while the complexity of our model is far less than traditional algorithms.

5   Conclusion

We propose a detection model based on the aggregation and evaluation of data flows against application layer DDoS attacks in this paper. In the model, first we aggregate users' traffic to data flows according to the surface characteristics, average scan time and sequence of page requests. Then it extracts the deep features of data flows, hot-spot access and resource consumption. We use D-S evidential theory to evaluate the flows, and get the probability whether it is an attack flow. Finally, we put the data flows into the priority queue according to the probability. Due to using the statistical flow information, the proposed method can detect various application layer DDoS attacks.

Acknowledgments. We would like to thank Nanjing University of Posts and Telecommunications for the support of Students Technological Innovation Training Program (STITP2011).

References

1. Douligeris, C., Mitrokotsa, A.: DDoS attacks and defense mechanisms: classification and state-of-the-art. Computer Networks 44, 643–666 (2004)
2. My Doom virus, http://www.us-cert.gov/cas/techalerts/ta04-028a.html
3. Chen, Z.H., Zhang, L.Y., Wang, X.M.: CC attack detection method. Telecommunications Science 5, 62–65 (2009)
4. Xu, C.F., Geng, W.D.: Evidence reasoning theory and application review. Pattern Recognition and Artificial Intelligence 12, 424–430 (1999)

5. Xu, L.Y., Zhang, B.F., Xu, W.M.: Evidence loss analysis and improvement methods of D-S theory. Journal of Software 15, 69–75 (2004)
6. Yang, J.B., Xu, D.L.: On the evidential reasoning algorithm for multiple attribute decision analysis under uncertainty. IEEE Transaction on Systems Man and Cybernetics 32, 289–304 (2002)
7. Xie, Y., Yu, S.Z.: A large-scale hidden Semi-Markov model for anomay detection on user browsing behaviours. IEEE/ACM Transactions on Networking 17, 54–65 (2009)
8. Yatahai, T., Isohara, T., Sasase, I.: Detection of HTTP-GET flood attack based on analysis of page access behaviour. In: IEEE Pacific Rim Conference on Communications, Computers and Signal Processing (Pacrim), pp. 232–235. IEEE Press, Victoria (2007)
9. Park, K., Pai, V., Lee, K., Calo, S.: Securing Web service by automatic robot detection. In: Annual Conference on USENIX 2006 Annual Technical Conference, Boston, pp. 23–28 (2006)
10. Walfish, M., Vutukuru, M., Balakrishnan, H., Karger, D., Shenker, S.: DDoS defense by offense. In: Conference on Applications, Technologies, Architectures, and Protocols for Computer Communications, Pisa, Italy, pp. 303–314 (2006)
11. Doron, E., Wool, A.: WDA: A Web farm Distributed Denial Of Service attack attenuator. Computer Networks 55, 1037–1051 (2011)

CPN-Based Composition in Modeling Command and Control of Surface Air Defense

Xiaoyu Kang[1,2], Guishi Deng[2], Shiliao Zhang[1], and Bo Wang[2]

[1] School of Management Dalian University of Technology,
116000 Dalian, China
[2] Dept. of Sciences Research Dalian Naval Academy,
116018 Dalian, China
{kxyzykn,zsjz_1516}@163.com, denggs@dlut.edu.cn,
sonzywb@hotmail.com

Abstract. In order to model command and control procedure of surface air defense by reusing existent simulation models, a composition model based on hierarchy color Petri net(HCPN) is advanced. The model can describe the composition process of simulation models with strict formalization and also can support the validation analysis of accuracy of composition flow. For illustration, a procedure of modeling surface fleet air defense command and control process supported by an early-warning aircraft is presented. With the CPN Tools, the model is used to calculate dynamic response time and throughput of surface fleet air defense command and control (C2) system. Empirical results show the validity and practicability of the composition description model.

Keywords: HCPN, Surface Air Defense, C2, Modeling and Simulation.

1   Introduction

Surface fleet air defense combat involves many complex command and control (C2) features, and modeling and simulating its process is an important content in researching and designing surface command systems. Under the condition of diversifications of aerial threat and changing of combat modality, composing the existing simulation models flexibly to form new simulation applications is required urgently, so it can meet changing requirements of fleet air defense.

Facing to the requirements of composition of simulation applications, the U.S. Department of Defense Modeling and Simulation Office proposed a combined mission space, as early as 2002, to comprehensively improve the reusability and the interoperability of models and simulation, and to implement combination of model and simulation agilely and rapidly. Simulation systems developed by the U.S. military then, have raised the requirements of model composition. In JWARS (Joint Combat System), models are described by Battle Space Entity which supports composition in modeling weapon, C2, communication, detection, etc in level of entity. OneSAF takes

M. Zhao and J. Sha (Eds.): ICCIP 2012, Part II, CCIS 289, pp. 46–53, 2012.
© Springer-Verlag Berlin Heidelberg 2012

modularization and composition as a fundamental principle for system designing [1]. FLAMES (Flexible Analysis Modeling and Exercise System) defines a common model set, and determines interfaces of models, which give a limit of model compositions [2].

In theoretic research, Petty, Eric, etc worked with the theory of simulation model composition systematically, which established a lexicon of model composition, defining a hierarchy of composition, analyzed the computational complexity of selection of composition and researched the relations between the semantic compositions and DEVS [3-5]. Mathias proposed composition structures and interface descriptions for discrete event models. Claudia advanced a hierarchical component modeling framework, defined a model composition process by EBNF syntax-based grammar composition rules which provided methods for composition validation [6-7].

Petri net is an effective tool in describing and analyzing synchronization, contacting and resource-allocation in concurrent processes and widely used in describing and analyzing and simulating discrete event system. However, there are two basic disadvantages of Petri net:

(1) No data concepts. Data is described by a network structure (place or transition).

(2) No level concepts. It can not build a large complex model with a series of sub-models with favorable interfaces.

Colored Petri Net (CPN) solves these two problems effectively. CPN bands both advantages of PN and programming language together to provide synchronization primitive graphs to describe concurrent process, and to increase basic units to define data types and operations of data value. Meanwhile, CPN also provides means of hierarchical description, which can be used to construct a large system model by combining small CPNs.

According to the description of CPN simulation model, the paper defines a hierarchy CPN (HCPN) to describe the simulation model composition (SMC), with which a C2 modeling process supported by an early warning aircraft (EWA) is established, and the real-time ability of the C2 model of surface fleet air defense is simulated and analyzed.

2   Model of SMC_HCPN

Here, we have the definition of SMC_HCPN [8][9]:

$$SMC\_HCPN = (HCPN, T_s, ST, PA) \tag{1}$$

1) $HCPN(\Sigma, P, T, A, C, G, E, I)$ is a non-hierarchy CPN:

a) Σ is a set of data types involved in simulation models.

b) P is a nonempty finite set of data token which buffers parameters of simulation.

c) $T = T_c \cup T_0 \cup T_s$ a non-empty finite transition set, where Tc is a common transition set and collects simulation models, T_0 is a zero transition set for auxiliary expression, and Ts is a replacement transition set, a collection of simulation sub-models, and each corresponds to a SMC_HCPN.

d) $A \subseteq P \times T \cup T \times P$ is a finite set of data arcs, and

$$P \cap T = P \cap A = T \cap A = \Phi \tag{2}$$

e) C is a data type function, defined as $C : P \to \Sigma$, and the data type of place $p \in P$ is $C(p)$.

f) G is a guard function, defined as $G : T \to G(t)$ satisfying

$$\forall t \in T : Type(G(t)) = B \wedge Type(Var(G(t))) \subseteq \Sigma \tag{3}$$

which designates the fulfilled preconditions of triggering transition.

g) E is a function on the arc A, and defined as $E : A \to E(a)$ and satisfies

$$\forall a \in A : Type(E(a)) = C(p)_{MS} \wedge Type(Var(E(a))) \subseteq \Sigma \tag{4}$$

Here, p is the place of $A(a)$; $C(p)_{MS}$ is a multi-set on sets of data types of p, and E is input and output data of the simulation model.

h) I is an initialization function, defined as a closed expression from p to $I(p)$, satisfying $\forall p \in P : Type(I(p)) = C(p)_{MS}$.

2) Ts is the replacement transition set, $\forall t \in T_s : t = (SMC\_ECPN, P_p, PT)$.

The network including t is called an ultra-page and the network corresponding t is called a sub-pages:

a) Ts is a set of sub-model, and if $T_s = \phi$, the SMC_HCPN degrades to non-hierarchical.

b) P_p is a set of port places, and also dual places of sub-pages and ultra-pages.

c) PT is a type function of port place, defined as $P_p \to \{in, out, io\}$, where in is an input place, out is an output place, io is an input and output place.

3) ST is a type function of socket places, which map the socket place and the replacement transition to $\{in, out, io\}$. To $\forall t \in T_s$, there is

$$ST(p,t) = \begin{cases} in & p \in (*t - t*) \\ out & p \in (t* - *t) \\ io & p \in (*t \cap t*) \end{cases} \tag{5}$$

4) PA is a port distribution function associating a socket place of ultra-page with a port place of sub-page, defined as a binary relation from Ts to:

a)

$$\forall t \in T_s : PA(t) \subseteq (*t \cup t*) \times t.P_p \tag{6}$$

$t.Pp$ expresses a set of port places of replacement transition t.

b)

$$\forall t \in T_s \forall (p_1, p_2) \in PA(t) : ST(p_1, t) = t.PT(p_2) \tag{7}$$

$t.PT(p)$ is a type function of port place for replacement transition t.

c)

$$\forall t \in T_s \forall (p_1, p_2) \in PA(t) : C(p_1) = C(p_2) \wedge I(p_1) <>= I(p_2) <> \tag{8}$$

Composing simulation models with sub-models starts from basic structures which include selection, sequence, parallel, loop, which can be easily expressed by above composition structures.

3   Composition in Modeling C2 of Surface Air Defense

3.1   C2 Process of Surface Air Defense Analysis

Entities in C2 process of surface fleet air defense with EWA are shown in Fig.1, including air target, EWA, shipborne anti-air fire-control units (SAFU) and command posts (CP). The fleet CP entity is further divided into fleet CP (including fleet combat command systems), fleet air defense CP and member-surface CP (including member-surface C2 systems).

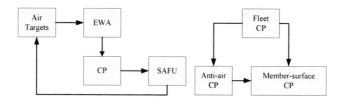

Fig. 1. Entities in C2 of Surface air defense

Based on above analysis, fleet air defense C2 process can be divided into 5 steps:

1) *Early warning and detection.* The process is to obtain target information, which will be throughout the whole process of combat. The fleet CP organizes EWA, radars and electronic surveillance equipments in member-surface for air-searching, EWA and surfaces transmit the information of found targets to the fleet CP.

2) *Threat evaluation.* The fleet CP determines the threat levels by target's tracks and its tactical actions. It is popularly divided into 3 levels: high, middle and low.

3) *Command assignment.* Fleet CP assigns tasks to air defense CP by threat levels of targets, and targets distribution orders commands of air defense CP to member-surface CPs. The CPs in member-surfaces order commands of target designation.

4) *Missile recovery.* When targets enter the recovery area of anti-air missile, anti-air missile will be launched against the targets.

5) *Terminal defense.* When the anti-surface missiles approaching the fleet, electronic combat equipments, short-range weapon systems and other soft and hard weapons on each member-surface will be counterattack at the same time.

3.2   Modeling C2 Process of Surface Air Defense Compositively

The processes in 3.1 can be modelled based on SMC_HCPN. There are 6 sub-models and 1 top model, namely, *the air target model, the EWA models, the fleet CP model, the air defense CP model* and *the CP model in other member-surfaces.* Here, we mainly explain the CP models and the top model.

1) *Fleet CP model*

The model includes model of fleet CP (BZ) and model of fleet combat command system (C3I_BZ), shown in Fig. 2. Both the BZ and the C3I_BZ model contain 4 transitions and 5 places. P1 is an input port, which means target information from the EWA. P6 is an output port, which means the command from fleet CP to air defense CP.

The meanings of transitions are following:

a) *SA*: An evaluated situation after integrating the input data.

b)*IF*: An integrated situation evaluation after information fusion.

c)*CI*: Command interpreter, which means strategies and principles from the system after command interpreting the situation evaluation.

d)*RS*: Decision-making according to certain strategies and principles.

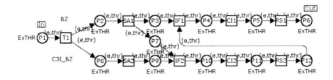

Fig. 2. Fleet CP Model

2) *Fleet Air Defense CP Model*

The model contains 6 transitions and 10 places, shown in Fig. 3. P1, P10 as an input ports, respectively descript the target information from the EWA and the anti-air commands from fleet air defense CP. P6 as an output port, denotes air defense fire allocation command from the air defense CP to member-surfaces. The meanings of *SA, IF, CI, RS* are the same as fleet CP. *RE* means preparation for operation after receiving information of long-range early warning from the fleet combat control system. The guard function [*thr = midnear*] denotes that transitions only respond under the condition of targets closing to the fire range.

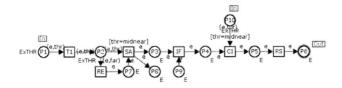

Fig. 3. Fleet Air Defense CP Model

3) *Member-surface CP model*

The model is shown in Fig. 4, including member-surface command model (WARSURFACE), member-surface C2 system (C3I_WARSURFACE) model and the member-surface air defense combat post model. The member-surface command model consists 4 transitions and 4 places, and the member-surface C2 system model consists 5 transitions and 6 places, and the member-surface air defense combat post model contains 2 transitions and 2 places. P1, P17 and P18 as input port, respectively denote target information from the EWA, situation information from the fleet CP and fire allocation commands from fleet air defense CP. P16 as output port is the target detonation information from shipborne air defense fire units. The meaning of *SA, IF, CI, RS* are the same as fleet CP. *RE1* and *RE2* respectively mean preparation for operation after receiving the formation of long-range early warning from the fleet combat control system. The guard function [*thr = midnear*] denotes that transitions only respond under the condition of targets closing to the fire range.

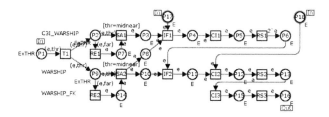

Fig. 4. Member-surface CP Model

4) *Top Model*

The top model of fleet air defense C2 is built base on SMC_HCPN, after the 6 sub-models have been completed, shown in Fig. 5, which includes 6 transitions (including 4 replacement transitions) and 6 places. The 4 replacement transitions represent the 4 sub-pages.

Transitions between the various replacement places are interfaces between the sub-pages. The arc pointing to a replacement place is input information from interfaces to sub-pages and the arc deviating from a replacement place is output information from sub-pages to ports.

The replacement transition *early_warning_plane* expresses the sub-model of the EWA, the replacement transition *command_control* is the CP model, the replacement transition *anti_air_weapen* is the sub-model of shipborne air defense fire unit, and the replacement transition *target* is the sub-model of the air target.

Transitions *T1* is an attacking probability of replacement transition *anti_air_weapon* and *T2* is a zero transition.

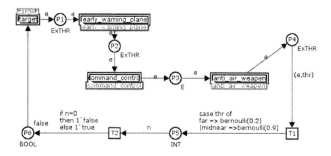

Fig. 5. Fleet Air Defense C2 Top Model

4   Simulation and Analysis

The real-time ability of C2 system is normally described by its *response time* and *throughput*. The response time measures a delay time from receiving information to sending response messages. The throughput is a completed workload by system per unit time. To C2 system we have the following assumptions: the system start time is 0, and the transition trigger time is μ_i which is processing time that the transition needs to complete the task.

(1) System Response Time
Suppose the system dynamic response time is RT and the response time for system to complete N inputs is $RT_N = \dfrac{T_m^N}{N}$. Here, T_m^N is time of output transition T_m to complete N inputs.

In fleet air defense operation, response time is a very important indicator for C2 system, which can express target processing capabilities in different situations at different levels of C2 structure of CP.

(2) Throughput
Assuming that the system is stable-running processing K inputs per unit time, throughput is defined as $\varphi = \dfrac{K}{\pi}$

Throughput describes C2 system to handle number of aerial threat targets per unit time. If the input rate of aerial threat target information exceeds this, the excess target information will not be treated timely; thereby it will reduce the combat effectiveness of the fleet.

Assuming aerial threat target number is 10 batches, the following 4 cases should be considered.

a) *Case 1*: Each CP dealing with an aerial threat target each time, and the processing time of each transition is 1 time unit.

b) *Case 2*: Each CP dealing with 2 aerial threat targets each time, and the processing time of each transition is 1 time unit.

c) *Case 3*: The target processing ability is same as Case 2, but the transition processing time is different. The processing time of each transition in EWA is 2 time unit but is 1 in other CPs.

d) *Case 4*: Each CP ability of dealing with target is 3, the replacement processing time of CP SA is 2 time unit, IF is 3, CI is 4 and RS is 1.

The real-time ability of fleet air defense C2 system is simulated and calculated with CPN Tools. The results were shown in Table 1.

Table 1. Simulation Results

	Case 1	Case 2	Case 3	Case 4
Period (π)	32	24	32	81
Target Numbers (K)	1	2	2	3
Throughput (φ)	0.125	0.333	0.25	0.143
Dynamic Response Time (RT_{10})	32	12.8	16.8	33.6

5   Conclusion

Modeling and simulating fleet air defense C2 system is an effective way to study its ability and efficiency. The SMC_HCPN model based on CPN presented in this paper can accurately describe the process of combining simulation models and it is independent from the specific programming languages which can be converted into a description of a specific programming language and implement conveniently.

The fleet air defense C2 system models based on SMC_HCPN can not only realistically simulate the air defense C2 process with fewer transitions and places but can easily be extended to facilitate the research on the problems of fleet air defense decision-making, the maximum information processing capacity and processing bottlenecks from different point of view. It also provides a new way to combining models in molding and simulation.

References

1. Parsons, D., Surdu, L.J., Jordan, B.: OneSAF: A Next Generation Simulation Modeling the Contemporary Operating Environment. In: Euro-Simulation Interoperability Workshop, 05E- SIW-19. IEEE Press, Toulouse (2005)
2. Ternion Corporation FLAMES, http://www.ternion.com/
3. Petty, M.D., Weisel, E.W.: A Formal Basis for a Theory of Semantic Composability. In: SISO Spring Simulation Interoperability Workshop, 03S-SIW-056. IEEE Press, Florida (2003)
4. Petty, M.D., Weisel, E.W., Mielke, R.R.: Computational Complexity of Selecting Components for Composition. In: Proceedings of the 37th Winter Simulation Conference, pp. 2472–2481. IEEE Press, Florida (2003)
5. Weisel, E.W.: Validity of Models and Classes of Models in Semantic Composability. In: SISO Spring Simulation Interoperability Workshop, 03S-SIW-076. IEEE Press, Florida (2003)
6. Szabo, C., Teo, Y.M.: On Syntactic Composability and Model Reuse. In: First Asia International Conference on Modeling & Simulation, pp. 230–237. IEEE Computer Society Press, Phuket (2007)
7. Szabo, C., Teo, Y.M.: An Approach for Validation of Semantic Composability in Simulation Models. In: Proceedings of the 2009 ACM/IEEE/SCS 23rd Workshop on Principles of Advanced and Distributed Simulation, pp. 3–10. IEEE Press, New York (2009)
8. Yuan, C.Y.: Principle and Application of Petri Net. Publishing House of Electronics Industry, Beijing (2005)
9. Li, J.X., Cheng, J.J.: Hierarchical Colored Petri Net Description Model for Web Service Composition. Computer Engineering 35, 39–44 (2009)

Design of Industrial PLC Based on ZigBee Protocol

Meihua Xu, Peng Xu, and Jingji Xu

School of Mechatronics Engineering and Automation,
Shanghai University,
Shanghai, 200072, China
mhxu@shu.edu.cn

Abstract. According to the view of Intelligent Industry, this paper proposes a real-time system which can monitor the Programmable Logical Controller (PLC) working parameters like the relay states and response to abnormal ones. This system includes the ARM micro-processor, wireless RF transceiver modules and PLC. The wireless RF transceiver module owns a micro-controller to collect PLC parameters. Then the obtained parameters will be sent to ARM microprocessor by a RF transceiver using ZigBee protocol. The microprocessor stores the collected parameters and analyses received data, if parameters do not accord with a standard one, the microprocessor will inform the user by sounding the beeper. Even the microprocessor can directly stop PLC, if necessary.

Keywords: ZigBee, ARM, PLC, Intelligent Industry.

1 Introduction

With the rapid development of national economy, science and technology has developed and improved a lot. PLC has been used widely in various industries at home and abroad. In the Stiernberg Consulting (serving Electronic Systems Industry) whitepaper, it points out that lots of applications and technology require close and detailed monitoring; some need only a watchful eye to changes. Caught early enough, shifting working patterns can save unnecessary cost [1] .So it is very promising to monitor PLC working condition, which now has been used widely in industry.

From the current industrial applications of PLC, some are not necessary to control PLC, but environment may be terrible in industry so some need industrial PC auxiliary. In such harsh situation, it is rather tough for operators' participation. Therefore transmitting PLC's output to a remote terminal for operators' monitoring has great practical significance. It can not only reduce the negative effects of the environment, but also view the output of PLC real-time data, which is convenient to check whether output is in accordance with the requirements and do changes to adjust to parameters. This system reflects people-oriented, which not only meets the needs of the development of the intelligent industry, but also can greatly reduce unnecessary spending [2].

M. Zhao and J. Sha (Eds.): ICCIP 2012, Part II, CCIS 289, pp. 54–61, 2012.
© Springer-Verlag Berlin Heidelberg 2012

2   Hardware Design of the System

2.1   Overall Design of the System

This paper aims to monitor the relay states and controls PLC remotely. Fig.1 shows the overall frame of the monitoring system. This system links ARM and the microcontroller with the ZigBee module, respectively. The microcontroller collects data, and this data will be received by ARM. Through the MCU with ARM data exchanging, we can implement a real-time remote monitoring. Also we have developed an application to display the PLC's working parameters and save data in time. Meanwhile ARM analyses and processes saved data. The user will be alerted immediately when data is abnormal.

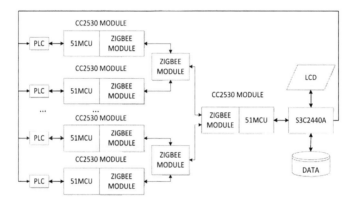

Fig. 1. Overall Frame of the System

2.2   Related Controllers

In this system, we mainly use three controllers. One is the PLC. PLC is mainly used in industry. In this system, PLC sends data out. The other is the CC2530. It is a wireless microcontroller integrating a ZigBee module inside, which is used for receiving data from PLC and transmitting data in this system. Another is S3C2440A, which is ARM 920T based micro-processor.

2.2.1   PLC

PLC is a computer used in industrial controlling essentially. It also has its own CPU, memory, and input and output devices, but the difference is that PLC can be used in place of terrible environment and work stably. Early PLC is mainly used to replace the relay logic control. Until now, PLC still mainly controls relays to achieve its control function. Currently, PLC is an indispensable industrial control part. In this system, PLC sends out the relay parameters to the UART and these parameters will be received by a CC2530 controller.

2.2.2   CC2530

CC2530 is a true system on chip (SoC) CMOS solutions. This solution can improve performance and meet the ZigBee-based applications and low power requirements. The CC2530 combines the excellent performance of a leading RF transceiver with an industry-standard enhanced 8051 MCU [3]. Its internal structure can be roughly shown in Figure 2. Here we choose 2.405GHz as the communication channel of this system. If the UART received data, the controller will transmit it to its neighboring ZigBee node unless it is related with an ARM microprocessor.

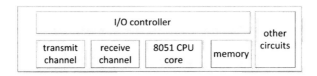

Fig. 2. Rough Internal Structure of CC2530

2.2.3   S3C2440A

S3C2440A is designed to provide hand-held devices and general applications with low-power, and high-performance microcontroller solution in small die size. And it provides a low cost, low power, high performance solution for small micro-controller for handheld devices and general types of applications [4]. Thence it is easy to show received data far away from harsh environment in our hands.

2.3   System Components

This monitoring system can be divided into three modules; the collection module, the transition module and the terminal module.

2.3.1   Collection Module

Fig. 3 shows the hardware structure of the collection module. PLC converts the analog signal of the relay states into digital signals, and transmits these signals to the CC2530 module. After receiving data, CC2530 will display them by LCD, and transmit data to transition module through the ZigBee wireless transmission module.

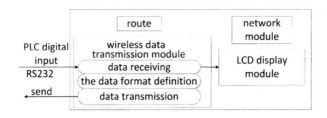

Fig. 3. Hardware Structure of the Collection Module

2.3.2   Transition Module

Fig. 4 shows the hardware structure of transition module. In this system, the transition module receives data from collection module. It can be seen as a transfer station. On the one hand, the transition module shows the received data by LCD. On the other hand, it also transfers the data to the terminal module.

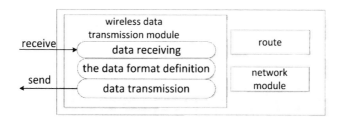

Fig. 4. Hardware Structure of the Transition Module

2.3.3   Terminal Module

Fig. 5 shows the hardware structure of the terminal module. In this system, the terminal module consists of the ZigBee module and the microprocessor. The ZigBee module receives data from the transition module and passes it to the microprocessor through the serial port. And then ARM will display data by LCD and store the data in memory.

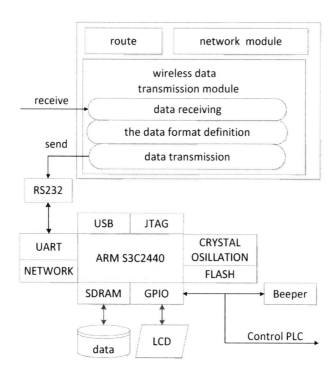

Fig. 5. Hardware Structure of the Terminal Module

3   Software Design of the System

In this paper, ZigBee transmission of data is completed as the main software design. It is mainly about achieving the data exchange among ZigBee modules. Also we implement the serial communication and application development.

3.1   Data Transmission

In order to ensure the feasibility of practical application, the system uses a ZigBee network. At first, the transition module sets up a network, and waits for other modules to add into this network. Its flow diagram can be seen in the Fig.6. Then other modules begin to transfer data to the terminal module. At last, the terminal module displays the data. The structure of the software flow diagram is shown in Fig.7. In this part, the most important is primitive communication [5].

The ZigBee protocol consists of four layers. The IEEE 802.15.4 implements the PHY layer and MAC layer. Based on that, ZigBee implements network layer and application layer [6]. For ZigBee protocol, the most important layer is the network layer. Implemented at the network layer is mainly about the node joins the network, the node leaves the network, data transmission and other functions. Each layer provides certain services to its upper layer. Usually data service entity provides data transmission services; management entity provides all of other management services. Each services entity provides an interface for its upper layer through Service Access Point (SAP), each SAP perform the corresponding functions through the primitives [7].

In ZigBee protocol, there are four kinds of primitive, namely request, confirm, response and indication. For example, when node A wants to join a network, at a higher layers will send request primitive to the lower layer, at last this request primary will be sent to PHY layer. Then the PHY layer transmits it through ZigBee protocol to PHY layer of the coordinator B. Then the PHY layer of B will send indication primary to inform upper layer node A wants to join. No matter whether B allows A to join, the higher layer of B will send a response primary to the lower layer with joining status of A. Then these data transmit to the PHY layer of A. After receiving data from B, the PHY layer of A will send a confirm primary to higher layer regardless of receiving data. While the NWK layer received this data, it will decide whether B allows it to associate. If node A joins the network successfully, the route table will be update [8][9].

We implement these primitives by calling functions or processing it indirectly. By using this mechanism, we can communicate between layers and implement the whole wireless network.

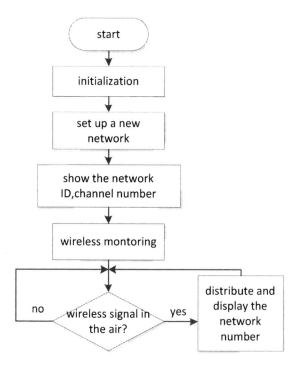

Fig. 6. Flow Chat of the Transition Module

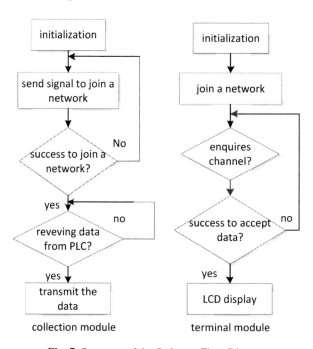

Fig. 7. Structure of the Software Flow Diagram

3.2   Serial Communication

Serial port can save the cost of hardware and keep the steady of the data transition. As a serial communication interface, serial ports are widely used in industrial equipment. There are many different serial standards, such as RS-232 standard, RS-449 standard. In this system, we implement serial communication functions by using RS-232C standard.

When this system starts to work, the collection module receives data from the serial port of PLC, and then sends the data out by wireless signals. When the terminal module gets data, it will pass data to S3C2440A microprocessor by the serial port.

Serial devices can be seen as a stream interface device. Therefore, the serial port can be opened, closed, perform serial port operations, sending and receiving data, connection management functions [9]. At first, we open serial port, and then we read data from serial port. When this system stops, we need to close serial port.

3.3   Embedded Application Development

In order to implement the real-time monitoring, we need to show received data into LCD to display. So we write an application based on S3C2440A. Qt is used widely for its good portability in the embedded system. We also use Qt in this system. We designed a graphics user interface (GUI).We success to add some modification into this GUI to make it friendly. Then we begin to read data from serial port. After getting data, S3C2440A transmits it to GUI to display and analyzes data quickly. If data is abnormal, the S3C2440A will alert the user immediately by sounding the beeper, or stop the PLC if necessary.

4   Conclusion

This paper is applying to the traditional PLC, and on the basis of that, we introduce the real-time monitoring in PLC, and put forward a new real-time monitoring system based on the ZigBee protocol. Through designing a reliable wireless communication module, it provides a good detection mechanism for the running state of the PLC and explores a new way and certain significance for the future development of the intelligent industry.

Acknowledgments. The authors would like to acknowledge the financial support by National College Students' Innovation Fund No.CXSJ-11-048 and the Shanghai Absorption of Imported Technology and Innovation Annual Projects No.11XI-15.

References

1. Stiernberg_Q209_whitepaper, http://www.stiernberg.com
2. Zhang, X.M., Chen, G.H., Chen, Q.G.: Human-Oriented Safety Management in Modern Industry. Electrical and Mechanical Safety, 9–12 (2004)

3. CC2530 Datasheet, http://www.ti.com
4. S3C2440A Datasheet, http://www.armkits.com
5. Gao, S.W., Wu, C.Y.: ZigBee Technology Hands-on Tutorials. Beijing Aerospace University Press, Beijing (2009)
6. Ji, W.Z., Duan, C.Y.: ZigBee Introduction and Practice of Wireless Network Technology. Beijing Aerospace University Press, Beijing (2007)
7. Fred, F.: Hands-On ZigBee Implementing 802.15.4 with Microcontrollers. Newnes, Burlington (2007)
8. Farahani, S.: ZigBee Wireless Networks and Transceivers. Newnes, Burlington (2008)
9. ZigBee specification (2005), http://www.ZigBee.org
10. Wang, J.Q., Gong, B.Y., Fang, Z.P.: Research on Implementing Information Terminal Communication Based on PDA. Computer Engineering and Applications, 201–203 (2005)

Modeling the Ship Degaussing Coil's Effect Based on Magnetization Method

Cunlong Xiao[1], Changhan Xiao[1], and Guanglei Li[2]

[1] College of Electrical and Information Engineering,
Naval Univ. of Engineering,
Wuhan, China
[2] Office of Navy Representative in Jiujiang,
Jiujiang, China
xiaocunlong@yahoo.com.cn

Abstract. Before the warship building, it needs to calculation the degaussing coil's effect to design the degaussing coil arrangement. The paper proposed the method of modeling ship degaussing coil's effect based on magnetization. The new method calculation the ship degaussing coil's effect split less element than presently method, calculation fast but still with high accuracy. The result of calculation on the simple mathematic model shows that the method is reliable and feasible.

Keywords: degaussing coil, magnetization method, finite element method, magnetic protection.

1 Introduction

The warship assembly degaussing coil that in order to compensating the induced magnetic field of ship; reducing the magnetic signal characteristics; improving the ship's magnetic defense capability. Before the ship construction, according the degaussing coil's effect and the ship induced magnetic characteristics to design the degaussing coil arrangement. The good design will use less energy and greatly enhance the ship's magnetic protection ability, otherwise, get half the result with double the effect. The magnetic protection ability of ship influenced by the accuracy of the ship's induced magnetic and degaussing coil's effect, but presently there is a lot of research on the ship's induced magnetic and less on the degaussing coil's effect [1-4], at home and abroad. In the domestic, there is two main method to get the effect of degaussing coil[5], the one is layout the degaussing coil in the proportion of ship, through repeated measurements to determine a winding optimal layout position, this method with high accuracy, but quite laborious. The other is calculation the hollow coil's effect, and then according to the experience of multiplying a proportional coefficient, gets the degaussing coil's effect, this method is more convenient, but lack of rigorous in theory and the accuracy is bad. In foreign , using finite element analysis method to calculation the degaussing coil's effect[6-8], and has made great

M. Zhao and J. Sha (Eds.): ICCIP 2012, Part II, CCIS 289, pp. 62–69, 2012.

development , some companies have developed a number of commercial software, such as FLUX 3D[9], the British thorn company developed TOSCA software package. However, the finite element method in structural boundary conditions, must be on a ship, include large area space division, usually following the division of the elements will reach a million, so the storage space and the solution of linear equations algorithm raised very tall requirement.

In this paper, introduce a new method based on the magnetization calculation the degaussing coil's effect. First , derived hollow polygon coil's induced magnetic three dimensional analytical expressions, then based on magnetization built mathematical model to calculate the effect of iron shell adds to hollow polygon coil's induced magnetic field, at last under the magnetic field can be superposition principle, get the degaussing coil's effect. The new method only needs to split the ship shell, and the split element much less than finite element method, conducive to the calculation. The results of calculation on the simple mathematic model show that the method has high accuracy through with less split element.

2   3D Induce Magnetic Field of Hollow Polygonal

According to the magnetic field can be superposition principle, arbitrary polygon coil's induce magnetic field is equivalent to the straight wire generates induce magnetic field vector addition, which composition of the polygon coil. As follow, we derivate the analysis express of electric straight wire.

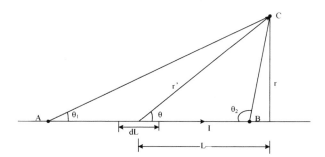

Fig. 1. The position relation of electric straight wire and the field point

By the Biot-Savart theorem [6], we know that the induce magnetic field in point C create by current element IdL in the conductor AB as follow:

$$dH = \frac{1}{4\pi} \frac{IdL \times e_{r'}}{r'^2} \tag{1}$$

According to the right-hand screw rule, the magnetic field H in the direction of vector n must be perpendicular to the plane ABC , so

$$n = \overrightarrow{AC} \times \overrightarrow{BC} = \begin{vmatrix} i & j & k \\ x_0 - x_1 & y_0 - y_1 & z_0 - z_1 \\ x_0 - x_2 & y_0 - y_2 & z_0 - z_2 \end{vmatrix} \tag{2}$$

Simplification formula (1)

$$dH = \frac{1}{4\pi} \frac{IdL\sin\theta}{r'^2} \cdot n \tag{3}$$

By figure 1, $r' = r/\sin\theta$, $L = r\cot\theta$, $dL = -rd\theta/\sin^2\theta$, so

$$H = -\int_{180^\circ - \theta_2}^{\theta_1} \frac{I}{4\pi r}\sin\theta d\theta = \frac{I}{4\pi r}(\cos\theta_1 + \cos\theta_2) \cdot n \tag{4}$$

$r = |AC||\sin\theta_1|$, by trigonometric cosine theorem

$$\cos\theta_1 = \frac{|AC|^2 + |AB|^2 - |BC|^2}{2|AC||AB|} \tag{5}$$

$$\cos\theta_2 = \frac{|BC|^2 + |AB|^2 - |AC|^2}{2|BC||AB|} \tag{6}$$

Simplification formula (4)

$$H_x = \frac{Im(a+b)(c+a+b)(c-a-b)}{4\pi\sqrt{(2a^2b^2 + 2a^2c^2 + 2b^2c^2 - a^4 - b^4 - c^4)}ab\sqrt{(m^2 + n^2 + p^2)}} \tag{7}$$

$$H_y = \frac{In(a+b)(c+a+b)(c-a-b)}{4\pi\sqrt{(2a^2b^2 + 2a^2c^2 + 2b^2c^2 - a^4 - b^4 - c^4)}ab\sqrt{(m^2 + n^2 + p^2)}} \tag{8}$$

$$H_z = \frac{Ip(a+b)(c+a+b)(c-a-b)}{4\pi\sqrt{(2a^2b^2 + 2a^2c^2 + 2b^2c^2 - a^4 - b^4 - c^4)}ab\sqrt{(m^2 + n^2 + p^2)}} \tag{9}$$

Unit is A/m , and

$$m = z_0 y_2 - z_0 y_1 + z_1 y_0 - z_1 y_2 + z_2 y_1 - z_2 y_0 \tag{10}$$

$$n = x_0 z_2 - x_0 z_1 + x_1 z_0 - x_1 z_2 + x_2 z_1 - x_2 z_0 \tag{11}$$

$$p = y_0 x_2 - y_0 x_1 + y_1 x_0 - y_1 x_2 + y_2 x_1 - y_2 x_0 \tag{12}$$

We calculate the induce magnetic field of electric straight wire in an arbitrary point. The induce magnetic field of N edge coil is $H_{Np} = \sum_{i=1}^{N} H_i$, H_i is the magnetic field straight wire which compose of N edge coil.

3   Ferromagnetic Object Internal Magnetization

Ferromagnetic material in the presence of free charge in the case, from the view of magnetic charge, magnetic scalar potential Poisson integral equation solution can be expressed as:

$$H_m(r_p) = -\frac{1}{4\pi} \nabla_p \int_V M(r_Q) . \nabla_Q (\frac{1}{|r_{pQ}|}) dv_Q \tag{13}$$

In the formula, V is ferromagnetic object volume, $M(r_Q)$ is the additional magnetization of the electric wire in ferromagnetic object internally, r_p is field vector, r_Q source vector, $r_{pQ} = r_p - r_Q$, $H_m(r_p)$ is the three component magnetic field column vector of the point r_p , ∇_Q is the source point gradient calculation, ∇_p is the field point gradient calculation.

The ferromagnetic material is split into many discrete, magnetization and magnetic parameters can treated as a constant equivalent uniformly magnetized body, each of the split unit inside have $\nabla_Q \cdot M_Q = 0$, and by the vector identity and Gauss theorem, the formula (13) simplification as

$$H_m(r_p) = -\frac{1}{4\pi} \nabla_p \int_S (\frac{M(r_Q) \cdot n}{|r_{pQ}|}) ds_Q \tag{14}$$

According to the magnetic field principle of superposition, the whole ferromagnetic object's magnetic field equal to all split element's magnetic field superposition.

$$H_m(r_p) = \frac{1}{4\pi} \sum_{i=1}^{N} \int_{S_i} \frac{M(r_{Qi}) \cdot n_i}{|r_{pQ}|} r_{pQ} dS_Q \tag{15}$$

In the formula, N is ferromagnetic object split element number, $M(r_{Qi})$ is the magnetization of split element i . In the uniform magnetized body there is $M_i = \chi_i H_i$, so formula (15) can express as:

$$H_m(r_p) = \frac{1}{4\pi} \sum_{i=1}^{N} S_{PQi} \chi_i H(r_{Qi}) \tag{16}$$

$$S_{pQi} = \begin{pmatrix} S_{p_x Q_{ix}} & S_{p_x Q_{iy}} & S_{p_x Q_{iz}} \\ S_{p_y Q_{ix}} & S_{p_y Q_{iy}} & S_{p_y Q_{iz}} \\ S_{p_z Q_{ix}} & S_{p_z Q_{iy}} & S_{p_z Q_{iz}} \end{pmatrix} \tag{17}$$

S_{pQi} is area element coupling coefficient matrix, physical meaning is the contribution coefficient matrix of a split element's magnetic field in field point P. when solution the source area magnetic field equation, need to put the point P in the split element center, in the area element coupling coefficient matrix , because of r_{Qi} on the split element surface, while r_p in the split element center, the integrand function does not exist integral singular, does not need to deal with it as volume coupling coefficient matrix.

After using hexahedral element discrete ferromagnetic objects, can get each hexahedron element node data information. Based on this information, the key to solution formula (16) is three types of surface integral [1], as follow

$$\begin{cases} S_{lx} = \int_{Sl} \frac{x_p - x_{Ql}}{|r_p - r_Q|^3} dS_Q \\[2mm] S_{ly} = \int_{Sl} \frac{y_p - y_{Ql}}{|r_p - r_Q|^3} dS_Q \\[2mm] S_{lz} = \int_{Sl} \frac{z_p - z_{Ql}}{|r_p - r_Q|^3} dS_Q \end{cases} \tag{18}$$

First in the hexahedron element built local coordinate system of each surface respectively, then get S_{lx} , S_{ly} , S_{lz} analytical expression, as follow

$$S_{lx} = -I_1(c_{11}, L_{11}, L_{12}, x_1, y_1, z_1) + I_1(c_{21}, L_{11}, L_{12}, x_2, y_1, z_1) - \\ I_1(c_{31}, L_{21}, L_{22}, x_1, y_1, z_1) + I_1(c_{41}, L_{21}, L_{22}, x_2, y_1, z_1) \tag{19}$$

And

$$I_1(c_1, L_1, L_2, x, y, z) = \left[\frac{1}{\sqrt{1+c_1^2}} \ln(y_Q - c_2 + \sqrt{(y_Q - c_2)^2 + c_3 - c_2^2}) \right]_{L_1}^{L_2} ;$$

$c2=(y+c1x)/(1+ c12)$, $c3=(x2+y2+z2)/(1+c12)$; each parameter is $c11=dx/dy$, $L11=0$, $L12=dy$, $x1=xp, y1=yp$, $z1=zp$; $c21=0$; $c31=dy/(dx-cx)$, $L21=dx$, $L22=cx$, $y2=yp+c31cx$; $c41=by/bx$, $L31=0$, $L32=bx$; $c51=by/(bx-cx)$, $L41=bx$, $L42=cx$, $y3=yp+c51cx$. S_{ly}, S_{lz} analytical expressions also can be getting the same as S_{lx}.

Paper [1] provides a detailed narrative; here no longer give unnecessary details.

In order to obtain every split element's magnetic field, usually put field point P in each split element center, using the formula as follow; get the N demission equation groups.

$$H(r_p) = \frac{1}{4\pi} \sum_{i=1}^{N} Sp_{Qi} \chi_i H(r_{Qi}) + H_S(r_{pj}) \tag{20}$$

In the formula, $j=1, 2\cdots N$, χ_i is susceptibility of each split element. The iron shell magnetization belongs to the category of weak magnetic field, so each split element's susceptibility set as the initial susceptibility of ferromagnetic material, $H_S(r_{pj})$ is the magnetic field of straight wire in each split element center, it can be get formula (7)-(9). After get the magnetization in the split element center, according to formula (16) can calculation the addition magnetic field which the ferromagnetic materiel influence on electric coil.

4 Degaussing Coil's Effect

Degaussing coil's effect is defined as: the magnetic field of signal coil with 1A current, it is composed of two parts, the one is the magnetic field H_s of hollow polygonal, the other is the addition magnetic field H_m of ferromagnetic material[10].

$$H = H_s + H_m \tag{21}$$

Degaussing coil is equivalent to signal wire stack [9], so get the signal coil's effect, then superimposed can get the corresponding degaussing coil's effect.

5 Example Analysis

As shown in figure 2, the plate with a length 1000 cm, width 20 cm, high 0.6 cm, initial magnetization rate is about 140, placed in the east-west direction. Two 30 cm apart energized conductor placed on the plate, (considering the background magnetic field is large, in order to reduce the measurement errors caused by instrument, each wire is connected to the current 10A)measuring plate longitudinal center line below 21cm a   total of 21 points to the magnetic field , each measuring point spacing 5cm. The results show in figure 3.

Fig. 2. Experimentation model

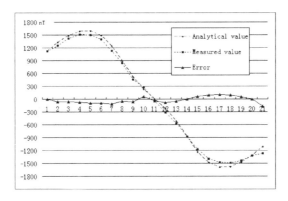

Fig. 3. Analyze the result of induced magnetic Z component

Through the above figure, the difference between measured magnetic value and simulated is very little, the error is less than 150nT, and the relative error is less than10%. Analysis of the experiment the error sources are mainly as follow:

(1) Error from the simulation model split. Integral equation method obtain solutions of ferromagnetic material is actually numerical solution, exit error between the theoretical. In theory, only if the split element is small enough it can be consider as uniformly magnetized body. But if split element is small, the split element number will much more, the computation time will increase substantially. How to find a new method with high accuracy and less computation time will be the next research work.

(2) It can be seen from the figure, the fixed magnetic field is large, it must make influence to the plate internal magnetic susceptibility, but in simulation model we think the magnetization is uniform.

(3) Magnetic field measurement error. Measurement apparatus have inherent error, artificial measurement errors and errors caused by magnetic environment etc.

6   Conclusion

The paper propose a new method of calculation ship degaussing coil's effect based on magnetization, and validation of the method with a simple mathematical model, the result show that the method with less calculation amount, high accuracy, obvious physical meaning, can be applied to calculation the shell body ship degaussing coil's effect, and with high engineering application value.

Acknowledgment. Changhan XIAO(1949—), male, professor, main research is electromagnetic environment and defendable technology.

References

1. Zhou, G., Xiao, C., Liu, S., Gao, J.: 3D Magnetostatic Field Computation With Hexahedral Surface Integral Equation Method. Transactions of China Electrotechnical Society 24(3), 1–7 (2009)
2. Guo, C., He, M., Zhou, Y.: Calculation of induced magnetic fields of ships by integral equation method. Journal of Naval University of Engineering 13(6), 71–74 (2001)
3. Froidurot, B., Rouve, L.L., Foggia, A., et al.: Calculation of electrical machine magnetic stray fields. IEE Proc. Sci. Meas. Technol. 149(5), 190–193 (2002)
4. Hafla, W., Buchau, A., Groh, F., et al.: Efficient integral equation method for the solution of 3Dmagnetostatic problems. IEEE Transactions on Magnetic 41(5), 1408–1411 (2005)
5. Zhang, G.: Warship degaussing system. Naval University of Engineering Press, Wuhan (1994)
6. Le Dorze, F., Bongiraud, J.P., Coulomb, J.L., Labie, P., Brunotte, X.: Modeling of Degaussing Coils Effects in Ships by the Method of Reduced Scalar Potential Jump. Transactions on Magnetic 34(5), 2477–2480 (1998)
7. Aird, G.J.C.: Moldelling the Induced Magnetic Signature of Naval Vessels. Department of Physics and Astronomy University of Glasgow (2000)
8. Chadebec, O., Coulomb, J.L., Bongiraud, J.P., et al.: Recent improvements for solving inverse magnetostatic problem applied to thin shells. Transactions on Magnetic 38(2), 1005–1008 (2002)
9. Xiao, C., Xiao, C., Li, G.: Fast calibration of distributed degaussing system coils' compensatory current. Journal of Naval University of Engineering 23(4), 100–103 (2011)
10. Flux3D CAE software for ship magnetization (2005), http://flux-ship-magnetisation.pdf
11. Fan, M., Yan, W.: Electromagnetic Field Integral Equation Method. China Machine Press, Beijing (1991)

More Efficient Sparse Multi-kernel
Based Least Square Support Vector Machine

Xiankai Chen, Ning Guo, Yingdong Ma, and George Chen

Center of Digital Media Computing, Shenzhen Institutes of Advanced Technology,
Shenzhen 518055, P.R. China
xk.chen@siat.ac.cn

Abstract. Multiple Kernel Learning (*MKL*) has been one of the most important methods for learning kernels. Multi-kernel based east square support vector machine (*LSSVM-MK*) can be handled by semi-definite programming (*SDP*) and quadratically constrained quadratic program (*QCQP*). Unfortunately *SDP* and *QCQP* can only handle the problem with small scale sample and kernels size. In this paper we introduce a more effective algorithm to solve the *LSSVM-MK* with larger kernel size and sample size. The experimental results show that the proposed algorithm is more effective than *SDP* and *QCQP* in terms of the number of kernel matrixes and samples.

Keywords: Least Square Support Vector Machine, Learning Kernels, *SILP*, Sparsity.

1   Introduction

Multiple kernel learning (*MKL*) aims at learning appropriate kernels for kernel-based methods. *MKL* also can be used to combine multiple sources, where different sources correspond to different kind of kernels. *MKL* has been one of the most import methods to learn kernels [1-5] . *MKL* has the practical values, for instance, instead of using the cross-validation method to choose the best kernel for learning, and *MKL* can learn a series of kernels thorough linear combination of kernel matrix, so we just need to choose probable kernel parameters to construct kernel matrixes. In practice, data can be obtained from multiple sources, such as vector, tree, string and graphics and *MKL* offers the advantage of integrating these kinds of data. *MKL* has been successfully applied in feature selection and heterogeneous data combination [1, 6-9].

   MKL is firstly proposed in [1], where *QCQP* and *SDP* are used to handle *MKL* problem to obtain better accuracy than traditional support vector machine (*SVM*). Unfortunately *QCQP* and *SDP* are suitable for problems with small scale sample size and a few kernels. In [2], semi-infinite linear programming (*SILP*) is employed to learn kernels, which makes it possible to handle problems with large scale sample size and kernel size. Another advantage of *SILP* is that it learns the kernel weights and the Lagrange multipliers of *SVM* in a wrap-based way. The primal problem is designed to a continue formulation in [13], which can be effectively solved by the reduced-gradient

M. Zhao and J. Sha (Eds.): ICCIP 2012, Part II, CCIS 289, pp. 70–78, 2012.
© Springer-Verlag Berlin Heidelberg 2012

method (*RG*). Note that linear constrain for kernels leads to the sparse solution, but it may discard some useful information for learning model. In [10], the kernels are combined with a nonlinear constrain which is solved by semi-infinite programming (*SIP*). KLOFT et al. employed the Mirror Descend (*MD*) method for non-spares multiple kernel learning [4].

Least square support vector machines (*LSSVM*) is a popular kernel method since it can be formulized as linear systems[11]. To improve the generalization ability of *LSSVM*, some researchers implement model selection using analytical methods and achieve better performance [12, 13]. Jian et al. designed a multiple kernel learning method for *LSSVM* by employing *SDP* and *QCQP* method [14]. Unfortunately the algorithm proposed in [14] is only feasible for small problems with limited sample size and a few kernel matrixes. In this paper, we propose a novel algorithm, called *SILP*, to solve multi-kernel based *LSSVM*. We design a new formulation which leads to convexity and Lipchitz continuously differentiability. The problem is then solved by using the *SILP* method.

The rest of this paper is organized as follows. Section 2 presents the proposed algorithm. Section 3 introduces the optimization, while section 4 reports the experimental results on both real world and synthetic dataset. Finally, Section 5 is the conclusion.

2   Multi-kernel Based LSSVM

Consider the supervised learning problem, given a sample set $\mathcal{D} = \{(\mathbf{x}_1, y_1), (\mathbf{x}_2, y_2), ..., (\mathbf{x}_l, y_l)\}$, with $\mathcal{X} \subseteq \mathcal{R}^n$ input feature space and $\mathcal{Y} \subseteq \mathcal{R}^n$ label space. The object of *LSSVM-MK* is to learn an appropriate hypothesis that works well on new samples. Considering that M kernel matrixes are combined, $\mathcal{H}_m$ corresponds to the m_{th} Reproduce Kernel Hilbert Space with the kernel $K_m = K_m(\mathbf{x}, \mathbf{z})$. The formulization of multi-kernel based *LSSVM* was proposed in [5] according to [1]. The *MKL* problem is solved by the formulation *SDP* where contains the linear matrixes constraint. However, as we known, the *SDP* is time-consuming. [14] also introduced *QCQP* to handle the *LSSVM-MK* problem, which is more effective than *SDP*. But *QCQP* is still computational intensive since the object function and constraints are quadratic and the number of quadratic constraints is increased when the algorithm is going on. Therefore *SDP* can handle small scale problems and *QCQP* is feasible for middle scale problems. Inspired by [2, 3, 10], we propose to address the problem by solving the following convex problem and we refer to this as the primal *LSSVM-MK* problem:

$$\min_{\{f_m\}, \mathbf{d}, \xi, b} \frac{1}{2} \sum_{m=1}^{M} \frac{1}{d_m} \|f_m\|^2_{\mathcal{H}_m} + \frac{C}{2} \sum_{i=1}^{l} \xi_i^2$$

$$s.t. \quad y_i = \sum_{m=1}^{M} f_m(x_i) + b - \xi_i \quad \forall i = 1, ..., l \tag{1}$$

$$\sum_{m=1}^{M} d_m = 1, d_m \geq 0 \quad \forall m = 1, ..., M$$

where kernel weight d_m control the l_2 -norm of f_m in the objective function. ξ_m is the relaxation factor of sample x_i. We use the wrapped-based strategy to solve this problem. Firstly, find the optimal solution $\{f_m^*\}_{m=1}^M$ and b^* by fixing $\mathbf{d}$. Secondly, find the optimal solution $\mathbf{d}^*$ by fixing $\{f_m^*\}_{m=1}^M$ and b. Then the primal problem (1) can be rewritten as follows:

$$\min_{\mathbf{d}} Q\left(\mathbf{d},\{f_m^*\}_{m=1}^M,b^*\right), s.t. \sum_{m=1}^M d_m =1, d_m \geq 0 \quad \forall m=1,...,M \tag{2}$$

where

$$Q\left(\mathbf{d},\{f_m^*\}_{m=1}^M,b^*\right)=$$

$$\begin{cases} \min_{\{f_m\},b} -\dfrac{1}{2}\sum_{m=1}^M \dfrac{1}{d_m}\|f_m\|_{H_m}^2 +\dfrac{C}{2}\sum_{i=1}^l \xi_i^2 \\ s.t. \quad y_i = \sum_{m=1}^M f_m(x_i)+b-\xi_i \quad \forall i=1,...,l \end{cases} \tag{3}$$

The problem of (3) is a traditional *LSSVM*, and it can be solved by its dual formulation. By introducing the Lagrange technology, The dual problem of (3) can be formulated as follows:

$$P(\mathbf{d},\mathbf{\alpha}^*)=$$

$$\begin{cases} \max_{\alpha} \sum_{i=1}^l y_i\alpha_i -\dfrac{1}{2}\sum_{i,j=1}^l \alpha_i\alpha_j \sum_{m=1}^M d_m K_m(x_i,x_j)-\dfrac{1}{2C}\sum_{i=1}^l \alpha_i\alpha_i \\ s.t. \quad \sum_{i=1}^l \alpha_i =0 \quad \forall i=1,...,l \end{cases} \tag{4}$$

It can be solved by a positive definite system as follows [15]:

$$\begin{bmatrix} \mathbf{H} & 0 \\ 0 & \mathbf{1}_n^T \mathbf{H}^{-1}\mathbf{1}_n \end{bmatrix}\begin{bmatrix} \mathbf{\alpha}+\mathbf{H}^{-1}\mathbf{1}_n b \\ b \end{bmatrix}=\begin{bmatrix} \mathbf{y} \\ \mathbf{1}_n^T \mathbf{H}^{-1}\mathbf{y} \end{bmatrix} \tag{5}$$

where $\mathbf{H}=\sum_{m=1}^M d_m \mathbf{K}_m +\dfrac{1}{C}\mathbf{I}$, $\mathbf{K}_{m_{ij}} = K_m(x_i,x_j)$, $\mathbf{I}$ indicates a unit matrix, $\mathbf{1}_n$ denotes a n-dimensional vector of all ones, and $\mathbf{y}=(y_1,y_2,...,y_l)$, then the optimal solution of Lagrange dual variables $\mathbf{\alpha}$ and bias term b are obtained solely by:

$$\begin{cases} b^* = \mathbf{1}_n^T \mathbf{H}^{-1}\mathbf{y}\left(\mathbf{1}_n^T \mathbf{H}^{-1}\mathbf{1}_n\right)^{-1} \\ \mathbf{\alpha}^* = \mathbf{H}^{-1}\left(\mathbf{y}-b^*\mathbf{1}_n\right) \end{cases} \tag{6}$$

According to (4), (2) can be rewritten as:

$$\min_{\mathbf{d}} P(\mathbf{d},\mathbf{\alpha}^*), s.t. \sum_{m=1}^M d_m =1, d_m \geq 0 \quad \forall m=1,...,M \tag{7}$$

where the optimal solution $\alpha*$ is calculated by the first equation of (6).

Suppose we have obtained the optimal solution of $\alpha*, b^*$ and $\mathbf{d}^*$. Given a new sample x without label, we can classify it by computing the following decision function:

$$f(x)=\sum_{i=1}^l \alpha_i^* \sum_{m=1}^M d_m^* K_m(\mathbf{x}_i,\mathbf{x})+b^* \tag{8}$$

In the next section, we introduced a novel algorithm to solve problem (7).

3   Optimization

SILP has been successfully used in *MKL* problem[2]. In this section we employ *SILP* to handle the situation of *LSSVM* with multiple kernels. We rewrite formulations of (2) and (4) as follow:

$$\min_{\mathbf{d},\eta} \eta$$
$$s.t. \ \|\mathbf{d}\|_1 = 1, \mathbf{d} \geq 0$$
$$P(\mathbf{d},\boldsymbol{\alpha}) \leq \eta \quad for \ all \ \boldsymbol{\alpha} \in R^N \tag{9}$$
$$with \ the \ constrain \ \|\boldsymbol{\alpha}\|_1 = 0$$

Problem (9) can be resolved in an iterative algorithm[10]. Algorithm 1 describes the detail procedures of our proposed method. Line 1 initializes algorithm parameters, such as penalty C, kernel weight and the epsilon of algorithm; Line 3 calculates the Lagrange multipliers $\boldsymbol{\alpha}^t$ by formulation (6) with the single kernel; Line 4 calculates the value of objective function; Line 6 updates the $\mathbf{d}^{t+1}, \eta^{t+1}$ by solving a linear programming problem. Please note that the number of constraints would increase when iteration is going on. Line 5 is used to determine whether the algorithm achieves the optimal condition. Note that *SILP* algorithm for *LSSVM* with multiple kernels can handle the problem of large scale sample and kernel matrixes size. Because *SILP* $\boldsymbol{\alpha}^t$ is updated by *LSSVM* with single kernel matrix and it can be easily calculated by two equations in formulation (6). Our experimental results will support our claim in next section.

Algorithm 1. *SILP* algorithm for *LSSVM*-MK.

1	Initialize: $S^0 = 1, \eta = -\infty, d_m^1 = \frac{1}{M}, \varepsilon = 10e-2$, set C as some positive real number.
2	For t = 1,2,...
3	Compute $\boldsymbol{\alpha}^t$ by (6) where $\mathbf{H} = \sum_{m=1}^{M} d_m^t \mathbf{K}_m + \frac{1}{C} \mathbf{I}$
4	Compute $P^t = P(\mathbf{d}^t, \boldsymbol{\alpha}^t)$ by (4);
5	If $\left\|1 - \frac{P^t}{\eta^t}\right\| \leq \varepsilon$,then return
6	update $(\mathbf{d}^{t+1}, \eta^{t+1}) = \arg\min_{\mathbf{d},\eta} \eta$ $s.t. \ \|\mathbf{d}\|_1 = 1, \mathbf{d} \geq 0$ $P(\mathbf{d},\boldsymbol{\alpha}^i) \leq \eta \ \forall i = 1,...,t$
7	End for

4   Experiments

In this section we design the experiments on real world datasets and toy dataset to support our claims. We compare *SILP* with relevant algorithms, including *SDP* and *QCQP*. We use *MOSEK* to solve *SDP* and *QCQP*. The problem at Line 6 in Algorithm 1 is a linear program, which can be effectively solved by *MOSEK*[16]. The first experiment focuses on the performance, including training time, the number of selected kernels and accuracy. The second experiment explores the scalability, including kernel size and sample size. Note that all kernel matrixes are pre-computed. All experiments are implemented in a personal computer with 2.99GHz *CPU* and 2GB *RAM*.

Table 1. Font sizes of headings. Table captions should always be positioned *above* the tables. Average performance for *SDP*, *QCQP* and *SILP*. l denotes the sample size, M is the kernel size. #Kernels indicate the number of kernels, #Time indicates the training time (second), and #Accuracy indicates the performance of precision. Method denotes the used algorithm.

Dataset	Method	#Accuracy	#Time	#Kernels
Liver	*SDP*	0.65±0.04	85.45±8.92	86.9±1.51
(l=173,	*QCQP*	0.67±0.04	4.81±0.16	3.10±1.30
M=91)	*SILP*	0.65±0.04	4.73±1.74	3.60±1.36
Pima	*SDP*	—	—	—
(l=384,	*QCQP*	—	—	—
M=117)	*SILP*	0.77±0.01	17.79±2.40	6.60±0.80
Sonar	*SDP*	—	—	—
(l=104,	*QCQP*	0.80±0.02	73.36±0.87	14.90±1.70
M=793)	*SILP*	0.80±0.03	394.72±298.17	15.50±2.66
Wpbc	*SDP*	0.76±0.04	155.30±41.32	437.70±22.51
(l=99,	*QCQP*	0.76±0.03	22.06±0.46	8.20±1.25
M=442)	*SILP*	0.77±0.04	11.10±1.51	7.00±1.10
Ionosphere	*SDP*	—	—	—
(l=176,	*QCQP*	0.94±0.02	71.56±2.62	12.70±1.19
M=442)	*SILP*	0.94±0.02	99.00±17.38	14.6±1.69

4.1   Performance on Real World Dataset

We compare the performance of our approach with that of *SDP* and *QCQP* on five real world datasets which come from *UCI*, namely Liver, Pima, Ionosphere, Wpbc and Sonar. We generate kernel matrixes as [17]. We do cross-validate on penalty parameter C and then use the best C to run 20 times on training set and testing set where the sampling rate is 50%. All the experimental results contain two parts, namely mean and variance. We use 3 measures, including training time, selected kernels and accuracy, to evaluate algorithms.

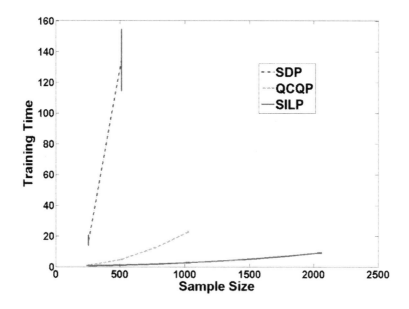

Fig. 1. Training time with varying number of samples for algorithms

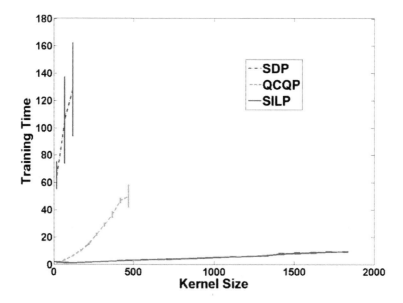

Fig. 2. Training time with varying number of kernels for algorithms

Table 1 reports the performance of five real world datasets. For the accuracy, we find that three algorithms achieve similar generalization ability.

For the selected kernels, *QCQP* and *SILP* algorithms also keep almost the same number of kernels. *SDP* loses the sparsity for kernels because of the constraint of kernel weight. For example, *SDP* choose all kernels for building model on dataset Liver and Wpbc.

For the training time, *SILP* can handle all dataset but *QCQP* cannot tackle the Pima and *SDP* cannot process the Pima, Sonar, and Ionosphere, which indicates that our algorithm can handle problems with various kernel sizes. *SDP* spends more time than other algorithms and *SILP* is faster than *QCQP* on Liver and Wpbc. In particular, *SILP* is 2 times faster than *QCQP* on Wpbc dataset. Note that *SILP* is slower than *QCQP* on Sonar and Ionosphere. But *SILP* is feasible for problems with larger scale kernel size and sample size. It can be proofed in the next section.

4.2   Scalability

In this section we compare *SILP* with *SDP* and *QCQP* on training time. We show different aspects of our approach including the scalability of kernel size and sample size. The dataset is generated by a typically function, called Sinc, and 5% noises are added.

For the scalability of sample size, we generate 100 kernel matrixes with Gaussian kernel which are obtained by evenly sampling the interval $[2^{-20}, 2^6]$ on a logarithmic scale. We generate the data from Sinc function in the interval $[-1, 1]$. We generate data points with 256, 512, 768, 1024..., For each fixed sample size, we obtain training time by running 20 times. Figure 1 shows the training time with varying number of samples for *SDP*, *QCQP* and *SILP*. For the max sample size, *SDP* only achieves 512, *QCQP* achieves 1024, and our approach achieves 2048, 2 times more than *QCQP* and 4 times more than *SDP*. For the training time, our approach cost the least time, 3 times faster than *QCQP* and almost 10 times faster than *SDP*. In fact, our algorithm can handle various scale problems. We find that the termination of *SILP* is due to the problem of out of memory in Matlab and the termination of *QCQP* and *SDP* are due to the same problem in *MOSEK*. Thus we believe that *SILP* can handle large scale sample size under other more effective environment, such as *C/C++*.

For the scalability of kernel size, we generate 512 data points which are evenly split in training set and testing set with 5% noise added. The kernel size is obtained by evenly sampling the interval $[2^{-20}, 2^6]$ on a logarithmic scale. Here we set the penalty C as 550. The training time is obtained by running 20 times for each fixed kernel size. Figure 2 shows the training time with varying number of kernels for *SDP*, *QCQP* and *SILP* algorithms. For the max kernel number, *SDP* can only handle about 120 kernels, *QCQP* can tackle about 470 kernels and our approach can deal with about 1820 kernels. Note that the termination of our algorithm is due to the problem of out of Memory in Matlab. In fact our approach can handle more kernels, for example 100,000 levels, when it is implemented in *C* or *C++* environment. For the training time, *SDP* is almost 2-3 times slower than *QCQP* and almost 10 times slower than *SILP*. We find that the training time of *SILP* increases rarely when kernel size increases.

In summary, our proposed algorithm is more efficient than *SDP* and *QCQP*. Moreover, it can handle problems with large scale kernel and sample size.

5   Conclusion

SDP and *QCQP* algorithms for *LSSVM* with multiple kernels optimize the kernel weight and Lagrange multipliers at the same time. Both of them are time-consuming methods. In order to address this problem, we propose a more effective algorithm, called *SILP*, for the issue of *LSSVM* with multi-kernels in this paper. The proposed algorithm optimizes the kernel weights and Lagrange multipliers in a wrapped-based way. The experimental results show that our algorithm is not only feasible for problems with large scale kernels and sample size but also keeps the same accuracy and selects similar number of kernels for various scale problems. Our algorithm can be directly implemented without more effect. From the practical point of view, *LSSVM-MK* can be easily applied in lots of applications, such as pattern recognition, time serial prediction and bioinformatics.

For the future work, Firstly, we will explore how to learn the kernel matrixes and penalty *C* parameter at the same time. Secondly, we will extend constrain of kernel form 1-norm to *p*-norm ($p \geq 2$). Thirdly, we explore more efficient algorithm to tackle problems with larger scale kernel and sample size, such as level method and stochastic gradient method.

Acknowledgments. This work was sponsored by National Nature Science Foundation of China (#61070147). The first two authors have the same contribution.

References

1. Lanckriet, G.R.G., Cristianini, N., Bartlett, P., El Ghaoui, L., Jordan, M.I.: Learning the kernel matrix with semidefinite programming. Journal of Machine Learning Research 5, 27–72 (2004)
2. Sonnenburg, S., Ratsch, G., Schafer, C., Scholkopf, B.: Large scale multiple kernel learning. Journal of Machine Learning Research 7, 1531–1565 (2006)
3. Rakotomamonjy, A., Bach, F.R., Canu, S., Grandvalet, Y.: SimpleMKL. Journal of Machine Learning Research 9, 2491–2521 (2008)
4. Kloft, M., Brefeld, U., Sonnenburg, S., Zien, A.: l(p)-Norm Multiple Kernel Learning. Journal of Machine Learning Research 12, 953–997 (2011)
5. Aflalo, J., Ben-Tal, A., Bhattacharyya, C., Nath, J.S., Raman, S.: Variable Sparsity Kernel Learning. Journal of Machine Learning Research 12, 565–592 (2011)
6. Qiu, S., Lane, T.: Multiple Kernel Support Vector Regression for siRNA Efficacy Prediction. In: Măndoiu, I., Wang, S.-L., Zelikovsky, A. (eds.) ISBRA 2008. LNCS (LNBI), vol. 4983, pp. 367–378. Springer, Heidelberg (2008)
7. Yan, F., Mikolajczyk, K., Kittler, J., Tahir, M.: A Comparison of l(1) Norm and l(2) Norm Multiple Kernel SVMs in Image and Video Classification. IEEE, New York (2009)

8. Yeh, C.Y., Huang, C.W., Lee, S.J.: A multiple-kernel support vector regression approach for stock market price forecasting. Expert Syst. Appl. 38, 2177–2186 (2011)
9. Longworth, C., Gales, M.J.F.: Multiple Kernel Learning for speaker verification. In: 33rd IEEE International Conference on Acoustics, Speech and Signal Processing, pp. 1581–1584
10. Kloft, M., Brefeld, U., Laskov, P.: Non-sparse multiple kernel learning. In: NIPS workshop on Kernel Learning: Automatic Selection of Optimal Kernels (2008)
11. Suykens, J.A.K., Gestel, T.V., Brabanter, J.D., Moor, B.D., Vandewalle, J.: Least Squares Support Vector Machines. World Scientific, Singapore (2002)
12. Cawley, G.C., Talbot, N.L.C.: Preventing over-fitting during model selection via Bayesian regularisation of the hyper-parameters. Journal of Machine Learning Research 8, 841–861 (2007)
13. Adankon, M.M., Cheriet, M.: Model selection for the LS-SVM. Application to handwriting recognition. Pattern Recognition 42, 3264–3270 (2009)
14. Jian, L., Xia, Z.G., Liang, X.J., Gao, C.H.: Design of a multiple kernel learning algorithm for LS-SVM by convex programming. Neural Networks 24, 476–483 (2011)
15. Ojeda, F., Suykens, J.A.K., De Moor, B.: Low rank updated LS-SVM classifiers for fast variable selection. Neural Networks 21, 437–449 (2008)
16. http://www.mosek.com/index.php?id=22
17. Haiqin, Y., Zenglin, X., Jieping, Y., King, I., Lyu, M.R.: Efficient Sparse Generalized Multiple Kernel Learning. IEEE Transactions on Neural Networks 22, 433–446 (2011)

Design Optimization of Ultrasonic Transducer for Medical Application Based on an Integrating Method

Ying Chen, Bingdong Liu, and Rui Kang

School of Reliability and System Engineering,
Beihang University Beijing, China
{Ying Chen,Bingdong Liu,Rui Kang,cheny}@buaa.edu.cn

Abstract. Ultrasonic Transducer are widely used in manufacture and medical surgery. A new method to optimize ultrasonic transducer for medical application is introduced, which is characterized by integrating Analytical Method, Finite Element Method and Constrained Variable Method. In our optimization process, the optimization aim is output power of the transducer, which is the most important parameter to value the performance of a transducer and could be achieved by the product of impact force at the tip of the ultrasonic transducer and vibration velocity amplitudes. Design variables are dimensions of certain part of the transducer, constrain functions are stresses of the stress-concentration zone. Optimization results showed that compared with the given initial parameters, the velocity of the optimum parameters was dramatically increased. Experiments were also performed and the results were in great agreement with the theoretical one.

Keywords: Ultrasonic Transducer, Design Optimization, FEA, Analytical Method, Constrained Variable Method.

1 Introduction

The main difficulties to design piezoelectric transducers with wide bandwidth and high output power come from variation loads during operation and the surgeon's demand for lightweight tools [5-6]. At the same time the stress of the vibrating transducer should not concentrated, which would result in break when vibrating. Thus the optimization of ultrasonic bone cutter is a problem with multi-object and multi constraint.

Previous studies of ultrasonic transducers optimization were mostly based on electrical equivalent circuit or based on experience of the designers [1-4]. Here we present a new method to optimize ultrasonic transducers. The method is characterized by integrating Finite Element method, Analytical Method and Constrained Variable Method, and employ output power of the transducer as optimization aim, which is the most important parameter to value performance of an ultrasonic transducer.

Constrained Variable Method is an excellent non-linear constrained optimization algorithm, which was firstly introduced by Wilson in 1963 and consummated by Han

M. Zhao and J. Sha (Eds.): ICCIP 2012, Part II, CCIS 289, pp. 79–88, 2012.
© Springer-Verlag Berlin Heidelberg 2012

in 1977[7] and Powell in 1978[8]. Thus this optimization algorithm is also called WHP method.

Theories for these three methods are introduced and optimization is carried out and the optimum transducer is designed. Results are tested by measuring the velocity amplitude at the tip of ultrasonic transducers.

2   Theory of Analytical Method

Typical structure of a piezoelectric ultrasonic transducer is shown in Fig. 1.

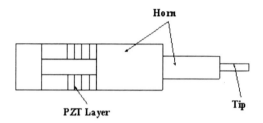

Fig. 1. Simplified structure of ultrasonic transducer

Ultrasonic transducer mainly includes three parts: PZT parts, horn and tip, which transform electric energy into mechanical vibration. The function of horn is to magnify vibration signal. The tip vibrates longitudinally to cut, emulsify, and dissect tissues. Key technology to design high performance transducers is to couple the three parts to vibrate at resonance frequency during surgical operation. There are many methods to design and analyze the scalpel.

One-dimensional analytical method to design ultrasonic transducer is based on the hypothesis that each part of an ultrasonic transducer can be treated as thin rod shown in Fig. 2.

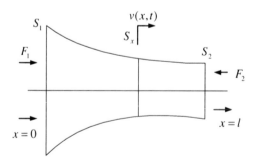

Fig. 2. Model of one dimensional thin rod vibrate longitudinally

The vibration velocity equation is,

$$\frac{\partial^2 v}{\partial x^2} + \frac{1}{s}\frac{\partial S}{\partial x}\frac{\partial v}{\partial x} + k^2 v = 0 \tag{1}$$

Where: v ——Vibration velocity
$\quad\ S$ ——Cross-section area
$\quad\ k$ ——Wave number, $k = \omega / c$
$\quad\ \omega$ ——Circular frequency
$\quad\ c$ ——Velocity of longitudinal wave

Stress distribution $\sigma(x)$ is,

$$\sigma(x) = \frac{E}{j\omega}\frac{\partial v}{\partial x} \tag{2}$$

The harmonic solution of (1) is,

$$v(x) = \frac{1}{\sqrt{S}}(A\sin k_1 x + B\cos k_1 x) \tag{3}$$

A and B can solve with the vibration boundary condition. ($v\big|_{x=0} = v_1 \quad v\big|_{x=L} = v_2$)
and force balance boundary condition ($F\big|_{x=0} = -F_1 \quad F\big|_{x=L} = -F_2$), Then,

$$F_1 = \frac{\rho c}{j2k}\frac{\partial S_1}{\partial x}v_1 + \frac{\rho ck_1 S_1}{jktgk_1 L}v_1 - \frac{\rho ck_1\sqrt{S_1 S_2}}{jk\sin k_1 L}v_2 \tag{4}$$

$$F_2 = \frac{\rho ck_1\sqrt{S_1 S_2}}{jk\sin k_1 L}v_1 - \frac{\rho ck_1 S_2}{jktgk_1 L}v_2 + \frac{\rho c}{j2k}\frac{\partial S_2}{\partial x}v_2 \tag{5}$$

Analyze each part individually and combines them in series, we can obtain the vibration velocity and stress distribution of the whole system.

Though simple in theory, Analytical Method will be very complex when design different ultrasonic transducer. In addition, if transverse size of an ultrasonic transducers is large, the thin rod hypothesis is no longer reasonable, and the error of Analytical Method will be intolerable.

3   Finite Element Analysis

The piezoelectric finite element in commercial FEA software ANSYS enables convenient access to perform both model and harmonic analyses for a given systems. In this paper, model and harmonic response of the aspirator transducer are performed using ANSYS to analyze system mode, resonant frequency and tip displacement.

Properties of steel, titanium, and PZT8 ceramic are listed in Table I). Piezoelectric rings are modeled using 3-D Coupled-Field Solid Elements SOLID5.

Table 1. Material Properties

Materials	Young's Modulus (N/m)	Density(Kg/m3)	Poisson's ratio
Steel	2.1×1011	7896	0.29
Titanium	1.05×1011	4450	0.33
PZT8	N/A	7500	N/A

Modal analysis is performed using the Lancoze method. Then harmonic analysis is performed using Sparse Matrix Solver. The input voltage varied sinusoidally between +/-1000. Output of harmonic analysis includes displacement, velocity amplitudes and maximum equivalent stress etc..

4   Theory of Optimization Algorithm

The online version of the volume will be available in LNCS Online. Members of institutes subscribing to the Lecture Notes in Computer Science series have access to all the pdfs of all the online publications. Non-subscribers can only read as far as the abstracts. If they try to go beyond this point, they are automatically asked, whether they would like to order the pdf, and are given instructions as to how to do so.

Please note that, if your email address is given in your paper, it will also be included in the meta data of the online version.

WHP optimization algorithm is composed of four parts, quadratic programming, imprecise 1-Dimension search, revision of matrix B based on BFGS method and sensitivity analysis and convergence rules, which will be introduced below in detail.

4.1   Quadratic Programming

The optimization problem can be described as

$$x = \left[x_1, x_2, \ldots, x_n \right]^T \tag{6}$$

$$\min \quad f(x)$$
$$\text{s.t.} \quad g_j(x) \geq 0 \quad j = 1,2\ldots,m$$
$$\underline{x}_i \leq x_i \leq \overline{x}_i \quad i = 1,2,\ldots,n$$

In which, x is design variable vector, g (x) is constrain function and f(x) is object function. $\underline{x}_i$, $\overline{x}_i$ are the minimal and maximum limit of design variable.

The corresponding quadratic programming problem is

$$d = [d_1, d_2, \ldots\ldots, d_n]^T$$

$$\min \quad \frac{1}{2} d^T B^k d + \nabla f(x^k)^T d \tag{7}$$

$$\text{s.t} \quad g_j(x^k) + \nabla g_j(x^k)^T d \geq 0 \quad j = 1, 2, \ldots\ldots, m$$

$$\underline{x}_i \leq x_i^k + d \leq \overline{x}_i \qquad i = 1, 2, \ldots\ldots, n$$

In which d is search direction, which could be obtained by repeatedly solve (7), and iterate based on Newton method. The solution of the original problem could be gained. B is revision matrix.

4.2   Imprecise 1-Dimension Search

The first thing to do when solve (6) by Newton Method is to find search direction and then 1-dimensional method would be used to gain search step. To increase convergence speed, imprecise search is usually adopted.

To search with imprecise 1-Dimension method, certain 1-Dimensional rule should be satisfied. The rule we adopt is

$$\Phi(\alpha_k) \leq \Phi(0) + 0.1\alpha_k \Phi'(0) \tag{8}$$

In which, α is search step and $\Phi(\alpha)$ is a segment function, and can be described as follows.

$$\Phi'(0) = \nabla f(x^k)^T d^k + \sum_{i \in I_1} \mu_i d_i^k + \tag{9}$$

$$+ \sum_{i \in I_2} \mu_i(-d_i^k) + \sum_{j \in J} \lambda_j(-\nabla g_j(x^k))^T d^k$$

Where

$$I_1 = \left\{ i \,\middle|\, x_i^k - \overline{x}_i > 0 \right\} \cup \left\{ i \,\middle|\, x_i^k = \overline{x}_i \cup d_i^k > 0 \right\} \tag{10}$$

$$I_2 = \left\{ i \,\middle|\, \underline{x}_i - x_i^k > 0 \right\} \cup \left\{ i \,\middle|\, \underline{x}_i = x_i^k \cup d_i^k < 0 \right\} \tag{11}$$

$$J = \left\{ j \,\middle|\, g_j(x^k) < 0 \right\} \tag{12}$$

Firstly let $\alpha = 1$, then calculate (8), if (8) is not correct, then let $\alpha = 0.1, 0.01...$ until (8) is correct.

4.3   Revision of Matrix B Based on BFGS Method

BFGS formula was used to revise B^k here. Let $L(x, u, \lambda)$ as the Lagrange function of problem (6), where u^k and λ^k are the factors to be solved through quadratic programming.

$$s = x^{k+1} - x^k \tag{13}$$

$$y = \nabla_x L(x^{k+1}, \mu^k, \lambda^k) - \nabla_x L(x^k, \mu^k, \lambda^k) \tag{14}$$

$$z = \theta y + (1 - \theta) B^k s \tag{15}$$

In which,

$$\theta = \begin{cases} 1 & y^T s \geq 0.2 s^T B^k s \\ \dfrac{0.8 s^T B^k s}{s^T B^k s - y^T s} & y^T s \leq 0.2 s^T B^k s \end{cases} \tag{16}$$

Then the revision formula of B_k is,

$$B^{k+1} = B^k - \frac{B^k s s^T B^k}{s^T B^k s} + \frac{z z^T}{z^T s} \tag{17}$$

It can be proved that B^k is positive definite, so does B^{k+1}.

4.4   Sensitivity Analysis and Convergence Rule

The sensitivity analysis formula of Finite Difference Method is given as

$$\frac{\partial u_i}{\partial x_j} = \frac{u_i(x + \Delta x_j) - u_i(x)}{\Delta x_j}, \quad j = 1, 2, ..., n \tag{18}$$

In which Δx_j is step size, and can be selected according to experience and condition. If the given value is too large or too small, precision and convergence velocity will be affected. u is objective function or constraint function.

Here we adopt dual convergence rule, one is according to design variable and the other is according to objective function.

(1) When the distance between the same design variable of two iterations is small enough,

$$\left\| x^{k+1} - x^k \right\| \leq \varepsilon_1 \tag{19}$$

(2) When difference between two iteration objective function values is small enough,

$$\frac{\left| f(x^{k+1}) - f(x^k) \right|}{\left| f(x^k) \right|} \leq \varepsilon_2 \tag{20}$$

ε_1 and ε_2 are given based on experience.

The flow chart of this program is shown in Fig. 3.

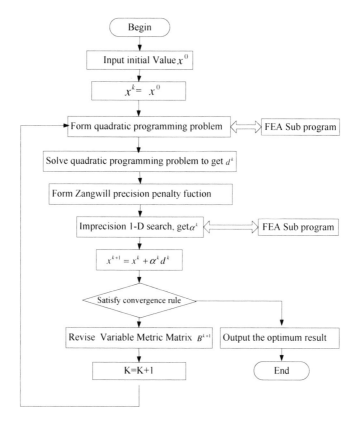

Fig. 3. Flow chart of the optimization program

The procedure of the optimization method can be briefly described as, firstly analytical method is used to create initial design variables then these parameters will be sent to FEA software. Output parameters are the calculated constrain functions and object function. Input these parameters into optimization program based on Constrained Variable Method, and then a new group of design variables is yield and ready for new optimization cycle.

5   Case Study

Structure of the ultrasonic transducer in the case is shown in Fig.4.

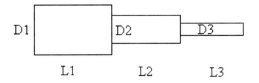

Fig. 4. Optimization model

Mathematics model of the transducer optimization problem is given as

$$\{x^*\} = \{L1^*, L2^*, D2^*\}^{lT}$$

min $f(x)$
Constrained by,

$$g(x) = 1 - \frac{\sigma}{[\sigma]} \geq 0$$

In which: $f(x)$ is output power, which could be achieved by the product of impact force at the tip of the ultrasonic tool and vibration velocity amplitudes. $g(x)$ is constrain function to prevent fatigue break. Here we select two dangerous stress concentration zone, and accordingly two constrain functions were given. σ is the maximum equivalent stress and $[\sigma]$ is allowable stress.

In addition, L3 can be calculated by the optimization program considering that the length of the tool is multiple of half wavelength. D1 and D3 are predetermined by analytical method, which has been introduced in [9]. The initial input parameters are shown in Table 2, and optimum value is achieved after 5 times iteration and 31 times FEA calculation.

Table 2. Optimization results

Length(m)	L1	L2	D2
Initial	0.030	0.0405	0.012
Optimum	0.05805	0.0257	0.01

Two ultrasonic Transducers, which have the dimension of the initial input parameters and optimization parameters, were machined and assembled. The resonance of the two tools measured by dynamic signal analyzer is 29.46KHz and 29.73KHz, which are very closely to the design value 30KHz.

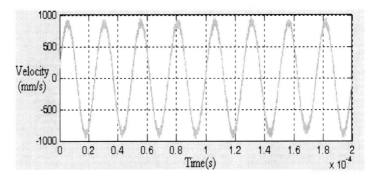

a) Ultrasonic transducer with initial design parameters

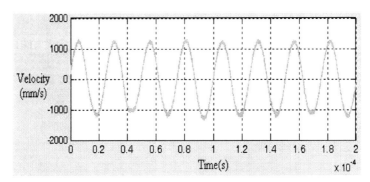

b) Ultrasonic transducer that has been optimized

Fig. 5. Vibration velocity of the two ultrasonic transducers

Animal experiments were done to test the performance of the two transducers. Fig. 5 shows the vibration velocity of the two ultrasonic transducers when cutting the same spongy bone. It can be seen from Fig.3 that the transducer after optimization has larger vibration velocity when cutting bones.

6   Conclusion

Here we present a new method for the optimization of ultrasonic transducers, which integrate FEA, Analytical Method and Constrained Variable Method. From this method, the given dimension parameters calculated by analytical method could be optimized to achieve high performance, such as larger vibration velocity and improved cutting ability. At the same time, the optimal ultrasonic transducer has less possibility to break due to fatigue. Experiments results were in great agreement with the optimization results.

References

1. Sergio, S.: Design of an optimized high-power ultrasonic transducer. In: Muhlen Ultrasonics Symposium, pp. 1631–1633 (1990)
2. Eisner, E., Seager, J.S.: A longitudinally resonant stub for vibrations of large amplitude. Ultrasonics, 88–98 (April-June 1965)
3. Pascal, C.: Optimizing Ultrasonic Transducers Based on Piezoelectric Composites Using a Finite-Element Method. IEEE Transactions on Ultrasonics, Ferroelectrics and Frequency Control 37(2), 135–140 (1990)
4. Lockwood, G.R., Stuart Foster, F.: Modeling and optimization of high-frequency ultrasound transducers. IEEE Transactions on Ultrasonics. Ferroelectrics and Frequency Control 41(2), 225–230 (1994)
5. Sun, D., Zhou, Z., Liu, Y.H., Shen, Z.: Development and application of ultrasonic surgical instruments. IEEE Trans. on Biomedical Engg. 44(6), 462–467 (1997)
6. Gu, Y.J., Zhou, Z., Yao, J.: Ultrasonic vibration system Four Terminal Network Method and its application. Jixie Gongcheng Xuebao/Chinese Journal of Mechanical Engineering 33(3), 94–101 (1997)
7. Han, S.P.: A Globally Convergent Method for Nonlinear Programming. JOTA 22(3), 7–31 (1977)
8. Powell, M.J.D.: Algorithms for Nolinear Constraints that Use Lagrangian Function. Math. Prog. 14, 224–248 (1980)
9. Chen, Y., Zhou, Z., Cao, Q., Luo, X.: Design and Analysis of Ultrasonic Scalpel. In: Proceedings of the International Symposium on Test and Measurement, vol. 1, pp. 241–244 (2003)

A Unified Design and Implementation for Creating, Reading, Updating and Deleting Operations Based on ADO.NET Entity Framework

Xiang Yang and Hongjun Shen

School of Physics & Electrical Information Engineering, Ningxia University,
Yinchuan, 750021, China
yangxiang.cn@gmail.com, shenhongj2004@126.com

Abstract. The code for creating, reading, updating and deleting (CRUD) operations based on ADO.Net Entity Framework (EF) was similar, mixed with business logic (BL) and distracted developers' concentration from BL. This paper proposed a unified design and implementation (UDI) for CRUD based on EF to avoid above problems. Through Generics, Reflection and Lambda expression tree, the repetitive code was reduced. It was found that internal CRUD procedure was definite and external entity's BL was changeable. So Inversion of Control (IoC) pattern which enabled the BL separating with persisting code was applied. The paper took the MVCMusicStore as an example to apply UDI. The modified example ran as well as the original one. Then the applying results were discussed. Finally, it was concluded that UDI for CRUD based on EF was useful to avoid repetitive code, reduce the mixture of BL code with CRUD and help the developers concentrate on BL.

Keywords: ADO.NET Entity Framework, CRUD, unified design and implementation.

1   Introduction

Creating, reading, updating and deleting (CRUD) operations are principal functions for data-oriented application. ADO.NET Entity Framework (EF) provides a set of model-driven tool to create Entity Data Model (EDM), and maps automatically from the conceptual model to relational storage schema in runtime [1]. Obviously, object-oriented CRUD based on EF is easier than before.

However, with EF's facility, there were also obviously similar CRUD codes found inside a project and among projects. The only differences were the name of entity, entity's property, entity set and entity container. In addition, business logic (BL) code mixed with persisting code was hard to concentrate on BL, comprehend and maintain code. These cases had been noticed by a few developers. Reference [2] described a unified searching model to look up entities. It received parameters with predefined syntax, and used dynamic Lambda expression tree to unify searching implementation. Maybe the model was designed for web-based application, its parameters' syntax was

M. Zhao and J. Sha (Eds.): ICCIP 2012, Part II, CCIS 289, pp. 89–98, 2012.

restrictedly designed so that it could not accept composite conditions composed by "logic and" and "logic or".

This paper proposed a unified design and implementation (UDI) for CRUD operations based the EF to avoid repetitive CRUD code, reduce the mixture of BL code with CRUD and help designers pay more concentration on BL. Contents were arranged as follow:

1. General thinking, some presetting and terms in this paper were given.
2. Since searching operation was independent with CRUD, its UDI was described ahead of the others. How to design infix or postfix query expression (I/PQE) was shown.
3. UDI for creating was shown. By analysis of creating procedure, Inversion of Control (IoC) was used to design the procedure framework.
4. UDI for updating was similar with creating, so only the key different point was given.
5. UDI for reading and deleting was easier than creating and updating, so they were omitted.
6. IoC required the entity to provide some new methods for BL. The implementing way of the new methods was chosen.
7. UDI was applied to "MVCMusicStore [3]" example.
8. The result of UDI applied to MVCMusicStore was listed.
9. The result was discussed.
10. The conclusion was drawn.

2   Methods

2.1   General Thinking

In general, the thinking of UDI for CRUD was based on Generics, Reflection, Lambda expression tree, IoC.

Generics were an idea to avoid writing repetitive code with the same structure. Entity container (EC) was changed with different EDMs. Many Entities was in an EDM. But the operations on EC and entity were completely same. It was appropriate to use generics type to replace concrete EC and entity classes [4]. The UDI class for CRUD was designed as follow:

```
public class YXUnifiedCRUD<TEC, TEO>
   where TEC : ObjectContext, new()
   where TEO : YXEntityObject, new()
```

Reflection was a mechanics to access class, property, method at run time [5].

Lambda expression was an abbreviate code style for method. Reflection and Lambda expression tree were together used to setup dynamic queries conditions for reading operation [6].

IoC was an idea that converted flow control right from caller to callee. The callee controlled the entire procedure, and the caller provided the BL. IoC was proper for those internal changeless procedure and external variable BL [7]. After carefully analyzing CRUD procedure, it was found that the procedure was definite, while the BL was changeable with concrete entity. So the CRUD operations became a procedure framework, and the developer only wrote the entity's BL instead of writing CRUD procedure mixed with BL.

2.2 Presetting and Terms in this Paper

1. Environment was .Net Framework 4.0, Visual Studio.Net 2010, C#. It didn¡⁻t mean that the thinking of the UDI was not applied other version, while the code may be modified slightly.
2. In order to use C# generics, made the entity name the same with entity set name.
3. "Pks" presented primary keys. "NonIdPks" meant that Pks properties values were not auto incremented or from Global Unique Identifier (GUID). "NonPkUps" meant that properties refused repetition and did not belong to PKs. If Pks/NonPkUps had more than one property, they would be dynamically connected by "logic and" lambda expression tree.
4. If the parameter type of the method was "NameValueCollection", it meant the name was entity's property name and value was entity's property value. And also it was the parent class of "FormCollection" which was used in web application and directly converted. If the parameter was "String ids", it meant that Pks of an entity were split with "," and the same order with Entity.EntityKey.
5. "TEC" meant a generics type for entity container. TEO meant entity generics type.
6. The basic CRUD methods were named like this:

```
public ReturnType CRUDTEO(Parameters)
```

"ReturnType" would be replaced with "void", "int", and so on. "CRUDTEO" would be replaced with CreateTEO, ReadTEO, and etc. "Parameters" would be replaced with concrete parameter decided by the method.

2.3 UDI for Searching Using I/PQE as Query Conditions

The "ReturnType" was replaced by IQueryable<TEO> that present an entity result set. The "Parameters" were 2 parameters: NameValueCollection nvc, ref int total.

The first parameter nvc including the property name and value pairs, such as page number, page count, sorting name, sorting order and I/PQE. The I/PQE was shown in table 1.

The reason for splitting each element instead of a whole expression was as much as possible to avoid query operators conflicting with property name or property value, especially in web application. The operators and their priorities were shown in table 2.

Table 1. The content of I/PQE

Name	Meaning
fix	Alternative value: in, post.
qecount	Elements count of the fix
1,2,...,qecount	Every element (property name, property value, operators) ordered by the fix

Table 2. The I/PQE operators and their priorities

Priority	Operators	Meaning
5(highest)	(,)	Only with infix expression.
4	!	Logic not
3	^	String starts with
	$	String ends with
	%	String likes
	==, !=, <, <=, >, >=	Relation operators
2	&&	Logic and (must escape sequence in web)
1(lowest)	‖	Logic or

The infix was converted to postfix firstly. And then Lambda query expression tree was dynamically constructed, executed, and result entity set was returned [2, 6].

2.4 UDI for Creating Used IoC

Taken the creating procedure as an example, IoC was used to design the procedure framework. The "ReturnType" was replaced by NameValueCollection that present an entity Pks. The "Parameters" had 2 overloads. The unified creating procedure could be divided into 4 steps:

1. Creating entity by inputted parameters

How to instantiate entity from inputted parameters was fully known by itself. The static method called "CreateEntity" automatically generated by EF did not check the constraints for inputted parameters, so it was discarded. New creating methods were designed for entity to accept property name and value pairs as follow:

```
public virtual bool Create(NameValueCollection nvc)
```

This style of inputted parameter often came from html form or Ajax post. It returned false if nvc was not satisfied constraints.

2. Checked extra constraints of the entity set

When adding an entity to entity set, it must be checked whether new entity violated unique constraints. E.g., in many systems, User entity had auto incremented Pks "ID" and NonPkUps "Name". It was not allowed to add a new User the same name with existing User. So the User entity refused repeated name. But in an online shopping system [8], LineItem entity had NonIdPks "Order id, Product id" and no NonPkUps. It accepted a LineItem with same NonIdPks that just added the LineItem.quantity with 1. It was inferred from the above 2 examples that the entity itself knew whether to accept the new entity with same NonIdPks/NonPkUps, i.e., how to dispose entity with same NonIdPks/NonPkUps was entity's BL.

The two entity methods were defined for getting the NonIdPks/NonPkUps as follow:

```
public NameValueCollection GetNonIdPksAndValues()
public NameValueCollection GetNonPkUpsAndValues()
```

If the entity had one or both of them and the same NonIdPks/NonPkUps entity had existed, there would be three corresponding methods for entity to decide whether to continue creation:

```
public bool ContCreateByNonIdPks(YXEntityObject newTEO)
public bool ContCreateByNonPkUps(YXEntityObject newTEO)
public bool ContCreateByBoth(YXEntityObject newNonPks)
```

If any one of them refused to add the same entity, returned false and CreateTEO threw an exception; otherwise did something with new entity information, and then returned true.

3. Added/updated to entity set

If the same entity did not exist in step 2, TEC.Add was used to add new entity to entity set. If the same entity was accepted in step 2, TEC.ApplyCurrentValues was used to accept value to the existed entity.

4. Saved changes to storage

Finally, TEC.SaveChanges was called to save the changes to storage. Try-catch structure should be used to capture the known/unkonwn exceptions in order to show friendly error information.

2.5 UDI for Updating Similar with Creating

The unified updating was similar with creating except one key point: if the properties to be updated were NonIdPks/NonPkUps, it was equivalent with creating a new entity. Unique constraints were still checked whether entity with updated properties had existed. If existed, and also three continuing methods like creating were designed for existed entity disposing its updating BL. And then if updating NonIdPks/ NonPkUps were accepted, it still deleted the entity by original NonIdPks/NonPkUps.

2.6 Unified Reading and Deleting an Entity

Unified reading and deleting an entity was without anything newer not mentioned above.

The whole design for YXUnifiedCRUD was shown in Fig. 1.

Fig. 1. Class diagram of YXUnifiedCRUD implementing UDI

2.7   Implementing New Entity BL Requried by IoC

During the process of the UDI for CRUD, some of new methods for entity were defined. They provided BL outside the CRUD procedure. There were three mechanics to design and implement those entity methods:

1. New entity methods could be packaged in interface mode implemented by TEO. In most condition, entity with NonIdPks/NonPkUps refused to duplicate, so the default implementation of the new methods should be given to avoid wasting time. The interface mode was aborted.
2. New entity methods could be implemented in extension mode. The extension method did not support virtual method, and only used in concrete entity class. So it was also aborted.
3. The last was abstract class. It inherited EntityObject and derived concrete entity class. Not only it supported virtual method, but also allowed default methods implementation. So the abstract class YXEntityObject was designed shown in figure 2.

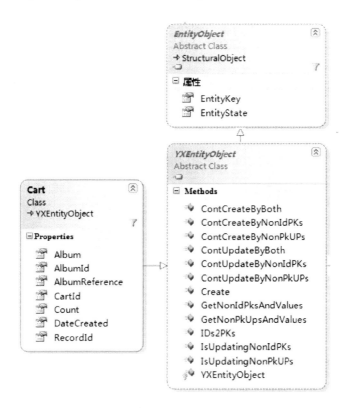

Fig. 2. Abstract class YXEntityObject and its inheritance relation. Child class Cart was only an entity example depicted in section 2.8.

The entities in EDM are automatically generated by T4. It was in vain to modify directly *.Designer.cs by replacing EntityObject with YXEntityObject. EDM generating template could be customized [9]. Followed its step, then replaced <#=BaseTypeName(entity, code)#> with YXEntityObject in the template file with extension "tt".

2.8   Applied UDI to MVCMusicStore

"MVC Music Store v1.0" [3], is a frequently mentioned example based on ASP.Net MVC 2 and EF 4.0. The BL was mainly implemented by ShoppingCart class. The Cart entity had identity Pks "RecordId", NonPkUps "CartId" and "AlbumId". It was found inside ShoppingCart.AddToCart method that Cart entity accepted new entity with the same NonPkUps. The original code was as follow:

```
public void AddToCart(Album album)
{
  var cartItem = storeDB.Carts.SingleOrDefault(
    c => c.CartId == shoppingCartId &&
```

```
      c.AlbumId == album.AlbumId);
  if (cartItem == null)
  {
    // Create a new cart item
    cartItem = new Cart
    {
      AlbumId = album.AlbumId,
      CartId = shoppingCartId,
      Count = 1,
      DateCreated = DateTime.Now
    };
    storeDB.AddToCarts(cartItem);
  }
  else
  {
    // Add one to the quantity
    cartItem.Count++;
  }
  // Save it
  storeDB.SaveChanges();
}
```

So it was proper to take the ShoppingCart.AddToCart as a UDI applying example.

1. Compile the UDI code as the class library named YXEntityPersistence.dll. It defined a namespace YXEntityPersistence that included classes such as YXUnifiedCRUD, YXEntityObject etc.
2. Added a reference to YXEntityPersistence.dll in MVCMusicStore project.
3. According [9], replaced <#=BaseTypeName(entity, code)#> with YXEntity Persistence.YXEntityObject. Then the class diagram of Cart entity was shown in figure 2.
4. Added partial Cart class, imported YXEntityPersistence namespace, and overrode the virtual methods inherited form YXEntityObject.

```
public partial class Cart
{
  public override bool Create(NameValueCollection nvc)
  {
    Count = 1;
    DateCreated = DateTime.Now;
    return base.Create(nvc);
  }
  public override bool ContCreateByNonPkUPs
    (YXEntityObject newTEO)
  {
    Count++;
    return true;
```

```
  }
  public override NameValueCollection
    GetNonPkUpsAndValues()
  {
    NameValueCollection nvcUps = new
      NameValueCollection();
    nvcUps.Add("CartId", CartId);
    nvcUps.Add("AlbumId", Convert.ToString(AlbumId));
    return base.GetNonPkUpsAndValues();
  }
}
```

5. Rewrote the ShoppingCart.AddToCart.

```
public void AddToCart(Album album)
{
  YXUnifiedCRUD<MusicStoreEntities, Cart> ucrud =
    new YXUnifiedCRUD<MusicStoreEntities, Cart>();
  NameValueCollection nvc = new NameValueCollection(2);
  nvc.Add("CartId", shoppingCartId);
  nvc.Add("AlbumId", Convert.ToString(album.AlbumId));
  ucrud.CreateTEO(nvc);
}
```

3   Results

After debugging and running, the result of applying UDI to MVCMusicStore was listed as follow:

- Modified MVCMusicStore ran the same as original one. Every function of UDI worked.
- The code about creating and updating was reduced and clear.
- The code quantities and readability compared original one with ReadTEO were the same.
- The developer only programmed entity BL.

4   Discussion

The code of reading and deleting operations in original MVCMusicStore was short and readable, so it was hard for UDI to promote the two operations.

In MVCMusicStore example, UDI was more properly applied to improve creating and updating procedure. Based on IoC, the developer spent more concentration on entity BL.

It seemed that the code about NameValueCollection were superfluous. The reason was that the original MVCMusicStore used the Strong-typed View. If it submited data with property name and value pair, the data would be directly converted from FormCollection to NameValueCollection.

5   Conclusion

The UDI for CRUD operations based on ADO.NET EF was done by Generics, Reflection, Lambda expression tree and IoC. It was concluded that it was useful to avoid repetitive CRUD code, reduce the mixture of BL code with CRUD and help designers pay more concentration on BL. The UDI was still a little, so there are many further jobs as follow:

- Applying it to more system, improving design and implementation, and becoming a mature framework.
- Providing more automatic UDI code generation through T4.
- Updating code for .Net Framework 4.1 to support simple class creation through code-first paradigm.

Acknowledgments. This research was supported by the Natural Science Foundation of Ningxia Hui Autonomous Region, China (Grant No. NZ1139), all support is gratefully acknowledged.

References

1. Blakeley, J.A., Campbell, D., Muralidhar, S., Nori, A.: The ADO.NET Entity Framework: Making the Conceptual Level Real. SIGMOD Record 35(4), 31–38 (2006)
2. Chsword: EfSearchModel Demo (2011), http://searchmodel.codeplex.com/
3. Galloway, J.: ASP.NET MVC Music Store Tutorial, Version 1.0 (2010), http://mvcmusicstore.codeplex.com/releases/view/53639
4. Microsoft: Introduction to Generics (C# Programming Guide), http://social.msdn.microsoft.com/search/en-us?query=Generics
5. Microsoft: Reflection   Overview,   http://msdn.microsoft.com/en-us/library/f7ykdhsy(v=vs.80).aspx
6. Microsoft: Use Expression Trees to Build Dynamic Queries, http://msdn.microsoft.com/en-us/library/bb882637.aspx
7. Wikipedia: Inversion of control, http://en.wikipedia.org/wiki/Inversion_of_control
8. Fakhroutdinov, K.: Online Shopping UML Examples, http://www.uml-diagrams.org/examples/online-shopping-example.html
9. Efdesign: Customizing Entity Classes in VS 2010 (2009), http://blogs.msdn.com/b/efdesign/archive/2009/01/22/customizing-entity-classes-with-t4.aspx

Task Scheduling in AD Hoc Network Positioning System Using Ant Colony Optimization

Jun Mao[1] and Hui Li[2]

[1] College of Computer Science and Technology Henan Polytechnic University,
JiaoZuo 454000, China
[2] School of Foreign Studies Henan Polytechnic University,
JiaoZuo 454000, China
morejune@gmail.com, Lihui@hpu.edu.cn

Abstract. Efficient scheduling of nodes for an application is critical for achieving high performance in AD hoc network positioning System. The node scheduling has been shown to be NP complete in general case and also in several restricted cases. The paper introduces a novel framework for node scheduling problem based on Ant colony optimization (ACO). The performance of the algorithm is demonstrated by a Matlab program for producing effective schedules for random node sets.

Keywords: Ant Colony Optimization, AD hoc network positioning System.

1   Introduction

AD hoc network positioning System, which is an international and archival journal providing a publication vehicle for complete coverage of all topics of interest to those involved in ad hoc and sensor networking areas. The Ad Hoc Networks considers original, high quality and unpublished contributions addressing all aspects of ad hoc and sensor networks, is a collection of separate co-operating and communicating modules called routers and nodes. Nodes can be executed in sequence or at the same time on two or more routers. An efficient node scheduling avoids the situation that some routers are idle while others have multiple jobs queued up. The node scheduling activity determines the execution order. To meet the computational requirements of a larger number of current and emerging applications, a satisfactory algorithm for node matching and scheduling is able to enhanced the parallelization functions.

One of the key challenges of such heterogeneous systems is the scheduling strategy. Given an application modeled by a dependence graph, the scheduling problem deals with mapping each node of the application onto the available routers in order to minimize make span. The node scheduling problem has been solved for years and is known to be NP complete [1]. Several heuristic algorithms are proposed in literature to solve this problem. These heuristics are classified into different categories such as list scheduling algorithms, clustering algorithms, but there have been being limitations. For example, the solution quality is not guaranteed for large sized problems.

M. Zhao and J. Sha (Eds.): ICCIP 2012, Part II, CCIS 289, pp. 99–106, 2012.

Reliability of the heterogeneous systems has a vital role in scheduling the application on to the routers. As heterogeneous systems become larger and larger, the issue of reliability of such systems needs to be addressed. This problem can be prevented by a constructive algorithm based approach, called Ant colony Optimization (ACO).

2   Methodology

Parallel programming systems is based on scheduling the nodes to be executed. Suppose that n nodes from m nodes terminals are submitted to work center. A parallel programming systems has a number s of router terminals to execute the nodes. Our node is to place each node to a right router terminal in order to maximize the outcome for the parallel programming system. The different priority level will also be given to node terminals refering to their past contribution to the system. In this research we do not focus on how the methods of measuring the contribution of a node terminal. Instead we suppose the priority level is given.

The main difficulty is how to build up the path and the route when one applies ACO to solve a certain problem. To express our approach we use the following variables to express the methodology in this research.

Sets of nodes   from node   terminals: $\{o_1,\ldots,o_m\}$

Prices for different router terminals: $\{t_1,\ldots,t_s\}$, per second (depends on performance ,customers' satisfactions ,response speed etc. of each router terminals)

Maximum available time for each router   terminal: $\{u_1,\ldots,u_s\}$

Nodes index by different node   terminals: $\{c_{11},\ldots,c_{1n_1};\ldots;c_{m1},\ldots c_{mn_m}\}$,

$n_1+\cdots+n_m=n$.

Priority level of node   terminals: $\{e_1,\ldots,e_m\}$

Timetable of routering   in time (sec.):

an $s\times m$ matrix (b_{ij}), $i\in\{1,\ldots,s\},j\in\{1,\ldots,m\}$.

The revenue of a timetable is calculated by

$$f=\sum_i t_i(\sum_j b_{ij}w_{ij}),\qquad\qquad(1)$$

where, w_{ij} is a $0-1$ binary matrix. The elements of matrix (w_{ij}) are divided to n groups, each group corresponds to a router terminal. All w_{ij} in the k-th group take value 1 if all nodes c_{ki_k} of router terminal o_k are routersd. Otherwise, All w_{ij} in the k-th group take value 0.

Now we apply ACO to find a global optimal timetable. We start with allocating an ant to an node c_{ki_k} based on the credit information on the advertiser by a probability

$$p_{c_i} = \frac{c_i}{\sum_{i \in N} c_i} \tag{2}$$

A high priority level is given a higher priority to have its node to router. After a node determined according to the priority level information (2), a break is determined to router the node according to rules of (1) and (2). Then the above router is repeated until a timetable completed. The objective value f is obtained according to (1). This value is used to give pheromone η_{kj} on the path from k to j.

The reason for applying the ACO algorithm in this research is to exploit its excellent searching ability to maximize the objective f over all feasible timetables. The complete algorithm is listed below:

Algorithm AcoMaxOutput

Step 1 form an initial pheromone by set $\eta_{ij} = e_i + t_j$ for c_{in_i} going to time slot j.

And $\tau_{ij} = 1$. Set all parameters .

Step 2   choose an node c_{kn_k} according to (2).

Uniformly generate an random value p.

If $p \geq p_0$, compute probabilities according to (2) and local update according to (2.3) to determine a break subject to u_i.

If $p < p_0$, compute (1) to find a time j to air c_{kn_k}.

Step 3 If a timetable is not completed, go to Step 2.

Step 4 compute f according to (1).

If f is currently best, set $V = f$. Global update according to (2) on the path of current best timetable.

If f is less that current best, set $V = 1$. Global update according to (2) on the rest of the path of current best timetable.

Step 5 go to Step 2 and repeat several times.

We will see that the initial values $\eta_{ij} = e_i + t_j$ contribute to obtain a better f within initial iterations. At Step 2 c_{kn_k} is chosen by credit information of advertiser. This setting is very important to control no-show risk.

3   Numerical Experiments and Discussions

To investigate the performance of AcoMaxOutput, we conducted numerical experiment using a dataset of node times (in second) and price for different router terminals. Dataset node times (in second) are showed in table2 according to second. We have 207 nodes in total. Price for different router terminal is listed below in detail:

Table 1. Price value for different router terminal

60 40 40 40 40 40 60 60 60 60 60 80 80 60 60 60 100 80 100 100 100 100 80 60

The nodes come from twelve different nodes terminals. The detailed times are listed as follows:

Table 2. Node time in second

Nodesterminal O_1 : 12,13,15,14,15,14,14,14,15,14,15,15,15,15,15,13

Nodesterminal O_2 : 15,16,15,15,15,15,14,14,16,14,17,14,15,16,14,14

Nodes terminal O_3 15,14,13,15,14,14,14,14,16,16,16,15,16,17,16,15,17

Nodesterminal O_4 : 17,15,15,14,16,15,15,15,14,15,15,17,15,14,15,15,15,16

Nodesterminal O_5 : 15,14,16,15,14,14,16,16,14,14,15,16,16,15,14,17,15,16,15,

Nodesterminal O_6 : 15,16,15,13,15,14,13,14,15,14,15,15,16,15,15,16,12,16,15,

Nodesterminal O_7 : 14,13,15,16,15,16,15,14,16,13,14,15,15,15,13,16,16,14,16

Nodesterminal O_8 : 16,16,17,15,14,17,14,15,15,14,14,15,15,15,16,16,16,14,15,

Nodesterminal O_9 : 15,16,14,18,15,15,16,14,14,15,15,15,16,15,15,16,16,16,15,

Nodesterminal O_{10} : 15,15,14,15,19,15,14,16,13,15,15,15,14,15,15,14

Nodesterminal O_{11} : 15,15,15,14,15,13,14,14,17,15,14,15,13,14,15,17

Nodesterminal O_{12} : 15,18,16,16,14,15,16,16,14,15

12 nodes terminals provide 219 nodes. The value of t_i in the algorithm is replaced by the data in this table.

We suppose that priority level of 12 nodes terminals as follows.

Table 3. Priority level of 12 nodes terminals

450	300	200	450	400	280	400	450	200	400	450	200
1300	1450	200	400	450	200	400	450	260	400	50	50

Credit information is measured by many methods. Variety of this dataset influences the revenue for the broadcasting station.

ACO algorithm works with many parameters, some of them are very sensitive to its convergence. Therefore, setting better parameters can be a key to make ACO algorithm work efficiently. After running AcoMaxOutput using the trail parameters with small-scale data, we eventually set the important parameters and other two initial data as follows:

Table 4. Initial data setting

α	β	ρ	ρ_g
2	1	0.2	0.2
Maximum time limitation for each_break		total_number_ of_iterations	
50		500 and 100	

A wrong initial dataset may make the algorithm not to be convergent. Search ability and convergence are two main criteria. We found that our algorithm provides quite good results with the dataset in this table under the above two criteria.

A program based on AcoMaxOutput was coded using Matlab. The program was executed 10 times with the credit information described in Table 3. We obtained two sets of 10 better output in the following Table 5. The results in 2nd &5throw and 3rd &6throw correspond to the 2nd dataset and 3rd dataset in Table 3, respectively.

Table 5. 10-run results

# of run	1	2	3	4	5
Best Revenue 1	80410	80400	80280	80040	80120
Best Revenue 2	80080	80200	80180	80060	80020
# of run	6	7	8	9	10
Best Revenue 1	80060	80210	80260	80160	80400
Best Revenue 2	80160	80200	80060	80260	80030

The bset output we obtained each time is relatively stable.

One of the 10 runs are depicted in below Figure 1. We see that the algorithms starts with a very good Output value. We believe that this good result is benefited from the setting $\eta_{ij} = e_i + t_j$ in Step 1 of AcoMaxOutput. Actually.

The numerical experiments show that the optimal output is influenced by the priority level of nodes terminals, we found that the first Output value can be declined to less than 3000 while we set $\eta_{ij} = 1$ as the initial data.

When the credit information is changed slightly (see dataset in 3rd row in Table 3), we see that the best revenues in 3rd row (Best Output2) of the 10 runs in Table 5 were changed slightly as well. Figure 2 portrays the f value in each iteration of one of the 10 runs. We see the stability and higher search ability of AcoMaxOutput.

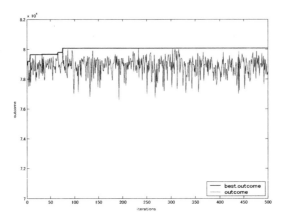

Fig. 1. Output and iterations

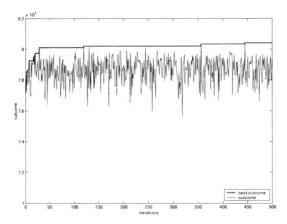

Fig. 2. Output using a different dataset of priority level

The numerical experiments show that the optimal output is influenced by the priority level of nodes terminals.

4   Conclusion and Future Research

We have studied how to apply the ACO algorithm to maximize the outcome for parallel program system. Different with TSP, there do not exist explicit paths and routes, which are needed to put the pheromone on and make ACO work well. The main contributions of this research are

(1) proposed a method to build a route in order to store the pheromone to maximize the output.
(2) based on above ideas, we proposed algorithm AcoMaxOutput to solve this revenue problem using credit information of advertiser.
(3) found a good initial data $\eta_{ij} = e_i + t_j$ in Step 1 of AcoMaxOutput, while the most other ACO-based algorithms use $\eta_{ij} = 1$ or a constant number suggested by, such   as, Karpenko, Shi and Dai (2005).

The results show that AcoMaxOutput works efficiently and credit information can influence the optimal revenue. We know that substantial experiments should be conducted in this research field. There many topics we are interested in area such as how does the Priority level influent the Output and how deep it could be. We consider doing this research in near future.

Acknowledgments. The paper was completed by author when he was Supported by the Opening Project of Key Laboratory of Mine Information, Henan Polytechnic University .The authors appreciates Professor Wentao Zhao and the fellows in the Laboratory for providing advices and helps in this research.

References

1. Smith, T.F., Waterman, M.S.: Identification of Common Molecular Subsequences. J. Mol. Biol. 147, 195–197 (1981); Freund, R.F., Siegel, H.J.: Heterogeneous routing. IEEE Comput. 26 (6), 13–17 (1993)
2. Della Croce, F., Oliveri, D.: Scheduling the Italian Football League: an ILP-based approach. Computers & Operations Research 33, 1963–1974 (2006)
3. Solimanpur, M., Vrat, P., Shankar, R.: Ant colony optimization algorithm to the inter-cell layout problem in cellular manufacturing. European Journal of Operational Research 157, 592–606 (2004)
4. Dorgio, M., Maniezzo, V., Colorni, A.: Ant System Optimization by a colony of Co operating agents. IEEE Trans. Syst. Man Cybern. B 26(91), 29–41 (1996)
5. Dorigo, M., Shützle, T.: Ant Colony Optimization. MIT Press, Cambridge (2004)
6. Tsang, C.H., Kwong, S.: Multi-Agent Intrusion Detection System in Industrial Network using Ant Colony Clustering Approach and Unsupervised Feature Extraction. Proceedings of the IEEE, 51–56 (2005)

 7. Chiang, C.W., Lee, Y.C., Lee, C.N., Chou, T.Y.: Ant colony optimization for node matching and scheduling. IEE Proc.-Comput. Digit. Tech. 153(6) (November 2006)
 8. Shen, J.Q., Zheng, X.F., Tu, X.Y.: Humanoid Grid Management Model and its Implementation Frame. In: 2006 International Symposium on Distributed Computing and Applications to Business, Engineering and Science (2006)
 9. Dorigo, M., Gambardella, L.M.: Ant colonies for the travelling salesman problem. Biosystems 43, 73–81 (1997)
10. Karpenko, O., Shi, J., Dai, Y.: Prediction of MHC class II binders using the ant colony search strategy. Artificial Intelligence in Medicine 35, 147–156 (2005)

HSRP Protocol Based on High Reliable Redundant Campus Network Design

Fenge-Wang[1] and Chang-xing-Zhu[2]

[1] College of Computer Science Technology Henan Polytechnic University,
Jiaozuo, China
[2] School of Civil Engineering Henan Polytechnic University, Jiaozuo, China
zcx7685@yahoo.com.cn

Abstract. Network core layer has come true by high-speed data transmitted of three layer switches between the router of VLAN in big network. Routers and three layer switches are key equipments in the network. When network plan is designed, redundancy backup of these key equipments must be accomplished to improve network reliability and stability. How to realize network routing redundancy and load balancing by the HSRP technique is particularly described in this article.

Keywords: VLAN, HSRP protocol, virtual router, backup group, router redundancy, load balancing.

1   Introduction

With the rapid development of Internet, network application has rapidly increased in college, and higher stability requirements have been put forward. In order to ensure mutual connections between terminal device of internal network and external network based on TCP/ IP protocol in campus network, and default route must be configured in these devices (setting static default gateway). If the default gateway router down, redundant communication has not defined by Ethernet and TCP / IP protocol. If default gateway appears problem, but the host is unable to automatically switch gateway which results in mutual disconnect between the internal network and external network terminal device. Even if redundant router in the network can serve as the default gateway of network segments, any dynamic method can't make the equipment get new default gateway address, and HSRP does not cause confusion in IP flow failure transfer and allow the host use a single router, also router in the actual first hop failure conditions can maintain the connectivity between routers. When host router is down, standby route equipment timely accept transmitting work. It solves the problem of the router switch and improves the reliability of computer network.

M. Zhao and J. Sha (Eds.): ICCIP 2012, Part II, CCIS 289, pp. 107–114, 2012.
© Springer-Verlag Berlin Heidelberg 2012

2   Introduce of the HSRP Protocol

2.1   Overview of HSRP Protocol

HSRP is a router protocol of hot backup. In order to achieve redundancy of gateway and automatic switches, Cisco has developed redundancy protocol based on HSRP, which can provide a redundancy of gateway. When the network edge device or access link occurs error, the protocol ensures that the user can quickly and transparently restore communications and provide redundancy and fault tolerance, and enhance routing function for IP network. Condition of HSRP is that system has at least two routers, which forms a group, and main members of the group are as followed: active router, standby route and virtual router. At any given moment, a group has only one active router that transmits data packets. If the active router fails, it will choose a backup router to replace active router. Virtual router has its own IP address and MAC address, and this network within the host remains link, which is not affected by fault effects. So the problem of the router switch has been solved.

2.2   Working Principle of HSRP Protocol

Firstly, HSRP protocol has used a priority scheme to decide which configuration of the HSRP protocol router becomes the default active router. If priority setting of a router is higher than other routers, the router becomes the active router and fault priority is 100. If the router with the priority is sameness, higher IP address of the router becomes the active router.

HSRP priority has broadcast among its protocol router setting, and its protocol chosen the active router. If the predetermined period time(Hold Time defaults) is 10 seconds ,active router can't send hello message, or information of active router can't be detected by HSRP. It will think that active router has fault, then the HSRP will choose the highest priority standby router change active router, at the same time, HSRP priority in the configuration of the HSRP router chooses a router as a new standby router.

HSRP protocol has been configured in a set of routers, and there are a virtual router for the host computer in the LAN, Default gateway of network workstations will point to the virtual address, and active router elected is responsible for transmitting the virtual address in the packet of the workstation.

The working principle of HSRP protocol and VRRP protocol are similar, but VRRP includes a protective mechanism of VRRP packet which is not append by another remote network. Setting TTL = 255 and checking it stops much defect, and the TTL value is 1 by application of HSRP.

2.3   Router Status and Status Transition in the HSRP

Each router runs a simple state machine in a hot standby group, which converts into a different state through the current state and event trigger. It includes the following state:

1) Initial state. When state of HSRP turns on, HSRP is not running. Generally changing the configuration or just starting port comes into state.

2) Learning state. The virtual IP address not decided by router, also the certification and activate routers from HELLO message of router in this state. The router is still waiting for the HELLO message of activate router.

3) Monitor router. The router has been a virtual IP address. It is not active router and waiting router. It has been monitored from the HELLO message of active router and waiting router .

4) Speaking status. The router periodically sends a HELLO message, and actively participates in campaign of the activities or waiting router in the state.

5) Waiting state. The router is the next candidate active router in the state, and regularly sends HELLO message.

6) Active state. The active router assumes the task of transmitting packets. These packets are sent to the virtual MAC address. It sends out a HELLO message.

In addition, each router has three calculagraphes, namely, the activating, waiting and calling calculagraph. Event arouses state changes t, and different events on different status in will generate different actions, such as starting a calculagraph and a paper, etc..

2.4   Link Polymeric Technology

Link polymeric technology has been named Trunking or Bonding, which can overlap multiple port bandwidth and form a greater bandwidth logical port, namely. Two devices of several physical link are dummied into a logic data path which is called a aggregation link. As shown in Figure 1.Tthe physical link, Link 1, Link2 and L ink3 constitute a polymeric link circuit. On the one hand it can expand the bandwidth of the network to solve the network bottleneck problem, on the other hand, it can provide automatic network redundancy.

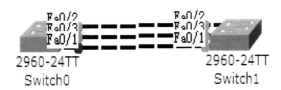

Fig. 1. Link aggregation technology

3   High Reliable Redundant Design Scheme of Campus Network Based on HSRP Protocol

3.1   Redundancy Design of Campus Network

Investment of network equipment accounts for a large proportion during the course of campus network construction, but reliable degree of device ensures the reliability of the network, and the price of grade and reliability network equipment are high. But link redundancy and equipment redundancy are essential in the design of network. Many colleges may not be equipped with special high-grade equipment redundancy due to funds limited during the construction of the campus network. The router is core and hear of the whole network. If a router appears fatal failure, it will result in paralysis of the local network. If the router is a backbone router, it will affect the broad range, and the loss is difficult to estimate. But the price of routers and three layer switches is very high. Therefore, the router or three layer switch using a HSRP is an inevitable choice to improve network reliability. If a router can't work, all functions of the system will be completely took over by another standby router until the emergence of router can work.

Cisco company has put forward three layer network design model. The structure of model can simplify the structure of network and load balancing, and each layer has a specific function. When problems of network arises, people are easier to debug. Two routers or three layer switch form the core layer, and connect by polymerization link, which not only improves the bandwidth of network, but also provides automatic link redundancy. In order to enhance the reliability of the network, the router or three layer switch complete the routing switch by HSRP technology, and provide redundant gateway within the campus network users.

Switches of distribution layer (Network Center, administration building, the library, institutes) and each routers of core layers or three layer switch have connected, also router of core layer and the switches of distribution layer use HSRP technology, which can provide redundant network for distribution layer switches. Lower user connect more access layer switch (such as students, teachers, families of Residence building ,computer experimental center, etc.). It can ensure that the terminal user visit speed and provide an automatic network redundancy by connecting the polymerization link and the distribution layer switches. At the same time, in order to ensure the reliability of the campus network server (double CPU, double power providing equipment redundancy),it can be connected between the dual card switch and the core. As shown in figure 2:

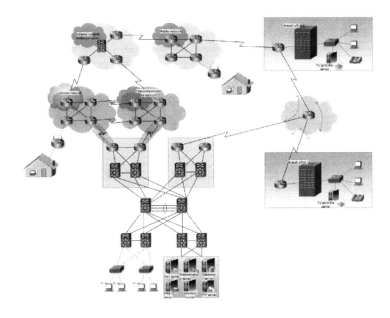

Fig. 2. Campus network topology

3.2   Design and Implementation

Single standby group applies in HSRP, and a router is online as the Master. The other routers only act as a backup which does involve transfer, and idle equipment, and link are not used (as shown in Fig.3).

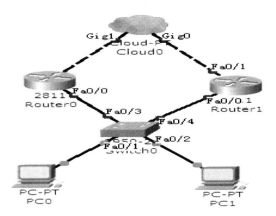

Fig. 3. HSRP single backup group topology

If three layer switch of two sets belong to the same class, and configure HSRP double standby group. So, the two devices involve in data transmission, and achieve double effect of redundancy and load balancing. Configuration three layer switch of two sets belongs to the mutual standby for two HSRP active group. Configuration schemes are as shown (Figure 4).

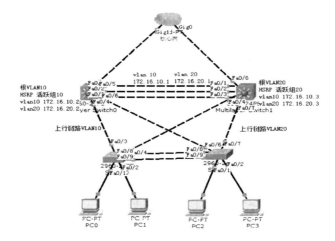

Fig. 4. Double standby group configuration of HSRP

Switch0 act as the main control equipment in the active group 10, also Switch1 act as the main control equipment active in group 20. Default gateway of other part of the host is set active group of 10 virtual IP address, namely, 172.16.10.2, and default gateway of another part of host is set as active group of 20 virtual IP address, namely, 172.16.20.3. If Switch0 fails, Switch1 is main router of two HSRP active group, all host connect between Switch1 and the Internet. Correspondingly, if Switch1 fails, Switch0 will become two alternate groups of master control switch. It not only has realized the load balancing function, but also improved the reliability of the network and effectively made use of equipment resources.

A. Configuration steps

a. A HSRP of configuration router interface

Before equipping router of hot backup, hot backup group of router and virtual router of the group are defined. The format of its command is as follows:

Router (config-it) # standby [group-number] ip [ipaddress],

Group-number is number In the command, and   ip-address is the address of virtual router.

b. configure router priority

After equipping the virtual router, configuration of two router should set priority. Specific command format is as follows:

Router (config-it) # standby [group-number] priority priority-number

The priority-number is set priority in the command.

c. preemption right of configuration HSRP

Robbing the active potency commands of the Standbv mode router equipment rob is as follows:

Router (config-if standby preempt) # [group-number]

d. Port track of configuration HSRP

Configuration command of port track is as follows:

Router (config-if) # standby [group-number] track interface-type interface-number [priority-number]

The priority-number should be deleted In the command.

B.   According to the configuration of Switch0, its code of implementation is :

```
switch(config)#spanning-tree vlan 10 root primary
switch(config)#spanning-tree vlan 20 root secondary
switch(config)#interface vlan 10
switch(config-if)#ip address 172.16.10.2 255.255.255.0
switch(config-if)#standby 10 ip 172.16.10.1
switch(config-if)#standby 10 priority 110
switch(config-if)#standby 10 preempt
switch(config-if)#standby 10 track 50
switch(config)#interface vlan 20
switch(config-if)#ip address 172.16.20.2 255.255.255.0
switch(config-if)#standby 20 ip 172.16.20.1
switch(config-if)#standby 20 priority 90
switch(config-if)#standby 20 preempt
```

The code implementation of switch1 configuration is similar to the Switch0.

4   Summary

The design of HSRP protocol is very simple, which has boost the reliable network in college network. Load balancing is effectively achieved. HSRP makes use of three layer switches of multiple Ethernet to plot the function of many business segments. Only multiple Ethernet routers or three layer switches in the application of HSRP can realize share of two routers, and it is no failure of single point, but implementation and normal operation can adapt complex network environment as a system. they are still many aspects to be improved in the future. The biggest problem hasn't provided security protection for the HSRP protocol. When VRRP protocol is used, the network can be further improved.

References

1. Kenyon, T.: High-Performance Network Design: Design Techniques and Tools (2001)
2. Cisco System. Hot Standby Router Protocol Features and Functionality [EB//OL] (May 25, 2006), http://www.cisco.com/en/US/tech/tk648/tk362/technologies_tech_note09186a0080094a91.shtml/

3. Cisco System.Load Sharing with HSRP [EB/OL] (August 10, 2005),
   `http://www.cisco.com/en/US/tech/tk648/tk362/technologies_`
   `configuration_example09186a0080094e90.shtml/`
4. Cisco System.How to Use the standby preempt and standbytrack Commands [EB/OL]
   (August 10, 2005), `http://www.cisco.com/en/US/tech/tk648/tk362/`
   `technologies_tech_note09186a0080094e8c.shtml/`
5. Shinn, S.K.: Fault Tolerance Virtual Router for Linux Virtual Server, pp. 273–275. IEEE
   Computer Society (2009)
6. Kenyon, T.: Designing Reliable Network. Data Networks, 391–470 (2002)
7. Lin, J.-W.: Fault -tolerant design for wide -area Mobile IPv6 Networks. Journal of Systems
   and Software 82(9), 1434–1446 (2009)
8. Long, J.: Network Devices. Penetration Tester's Open Source Toolkit, 317– 357 (2005)
9. Van Den Heuvel: Protocol -transparent resource sharing in hierarchically scheduled real -
   time systems. In: Proceedings of the 15th IEEE International Conference on Emerging
   Technologies and Factory Automation, ETFA 2010 (2010)
10. Behnam, M.: Overrun and skipping in hierarchically scheduled real -time systems. In:
    Proceedings- 15th IEEE International Conference on Embedded and Real-Time
    Computing Systems and Applications, RTCSA 2009, pp. 519–526 (2009)
11. Song, S.: Scalable fault - tolerant network design for ethernet - based wide area process
    control network systems. In: IEEE Symposium on Emerging Technologies and Factory
    Automation, ETFA 2001, pp. 315–323 (2001)
12. Khosravi, H., et al.: Requirements for Separation of IP Control and Forwarding, RFC 3654
    (2003)
13. Yang, L., et al.: Forwarding and Control Element Separation (ForCES) Framework, RFC
    3746 (2004)
14. Moy, J., et al.: OSPF Version 2, RFC2328 (1998)
15. Li, T., et al.: Cisco Hot Standby Router Protocol, RFC2281 (1998)
16. Knight, S., et al.: Virtual Router Redundancy Protocol, RFC2338 (1998)
17. Moy, J., et al.: Graceful OSPF Restart, RFC 3623 (2003)
18. Linux-HA (heartbeat), `http://www.linux-ha.org`

Stability Classification of Surrounding Rock Based on Support Vector Machine Classification Theory

Chang-xing-Zhu[1] and Fenge-Wang[2]

[1] School of Civil Engineering Henan Polytechnic University, Jiaozuo, China
[2] College of Computer Science Technology Henan Polytechnic University, Jiaozuo, China
zcx7685@yahoo.com.cn

Abstract. The classification of rock surrounding has an important significance for guiding design and construction of underground engineering. Past classification systems have not successfully been used because of complex classification index and much unascertained information. In order to better define stability classification of surrounding rock, support vector machine classification(SVM) theory is used. SVM is a good diagnosis method for small sample stability classification of surrounding rock system, which overcomes some deficiencies of traditional methods. Surrounding rock classification data collected are defined as training and forecasting samples, which can classify stability type surrounding rock. Therefore, the results show that the SVM model can be used to predict the classification of underground engineering surrounding rock, and the prediction accuracy is reliable and feasible.. It is a new way to be used for predicting the classification of surrounding rock of underground engineering.

Keywords: Stability classification of surrounding rock, support vector machine, training and forecasting samples, assessment system.

1 Introduction

Since the nineties of the 20th century, more and more irrigation works, transportation, energy and defense projects. have started in some areas at home, for example, JINPING's diversion tunnel, SANXIA's hydroelectric station, South-to-North water, etc.. Rock classification is the fundamental of underground engineering design and construction. It is also all important basis of evaluation and analysis of rock stability, shape design, construction methods and lining. Surrounding rock classification is considered an important problem of foundation research of underground engineering which can guide design and construction of underground engineering .Whether evaluating result of surrounding rock stability is right or wrong, it immediately affects construction of underground engineering. In order to better define stability classification of surrounding rock, now, many estimate methods of surrounding rock stability is used for example, RQD classification, Q system classification, RMR

M. Zhao and J. Sha (Eds.): ICCIP 2012, Part II, CCIS 289, pp. 115–122, 2012.
© Springer-Verlag Berlin Heidelberg 2012

classification, etc.. In recent years, many people are manage in classification of surrounding rock who made use of some nonlinear theory, such as the artificial neural network theory ,fuzzy theory and so on. these theories have very good modeling capability, can carry on nonlinear operation, and has a strong self-learning ability and adaptive ability. Therefore, they are some good solution to nonlinear problems. Since the 1990s, Vapnik, etc. have developed one kind of new general machine learning method – Support Vector Machine (SVM), which displays many advantages by solving small sample, nonlinear and high dimensional model identification, and extensively applied some domains of the function fitting, pattern recognition, the recognition of personal face and the text retrieval and so on. Compared with the traditional artificial neural networks, not only the structure of SVM is simple, but also each kind of technical performance, especially generalization ability is enhanced distinctly, which has been massively confirmed. Some scholars adopt new theories and methods to study the classification of surrounding rock, but SVM theory is rarely applied surrounding rock classification. How to utilize information known to classification. From classified standpoint, this article tentatively applies SVM to solve stability classification of surrounding rock according to some samples known. The results validates that the classification method is reliable.

2   Theory of Support Vector Machine

SVM is a classification algorithm based on statistical learning theory. With the SVM, multiple indicators can be easily handled with a feature vector and no thresholds need to be empirically determined for each indicator. Furthermore, it has been proved that SVM can handle the classification problem successfully in small sample. It has been successfully used to tackle several biological problems, such as functional prediction, membrane gene classification and structural classification. In SVM model there exists an optimal class hyper plane, which can not only separate different classes correctly, but maximize the margin. Training sample points lying nearest to the class hyperplane is named support vector, as shown in fig.1.

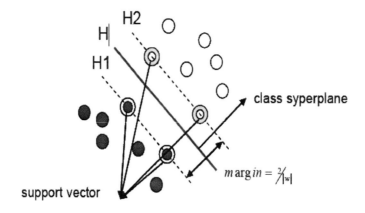

Fig. 1. The optimal class hyperplane

SVM develops from optimal hyperplane under the condition of linear bipartition, so, the linear separable sample set

$$y_i\left((\omega \cdot x_i)+b\right) \geq 1 \qquad i = 1, 2, \cdots, l \tag{1}$$

where y_i is the class index, the value is $+1$ for all WO pairs, and -1 for all TUB pairs; ω is the weight vector; b is the offset value. $\vec{x}_i = \left(x_{i1}, x_{i2}, \cdots, x_{in}\right)^T$.

With respect to the task of classification, genes pairs fall into two classes: WO pairs that are treated as positive data and TUB pairs that are treated as negative data. The margin, denoting the distance of the hyperplane to the nearest of the WO and TUB pairs, $2/\|\omega\|$ is and evaluates the classification ability of SVM. For optimal resolution of the data, the SVM analysis should arrive at an optimized hyper plane with a maximal margin. Given all that, the optimized hyperplane is constructed under the condition of linear bipartition that can be expressed as the following quadratic programming problem:

$$\begin{cases} \min & \varphi(\omega) = \dfrac{1}{2}(\omega \cdot \omega) \\[2mm] s.t. & y_i\left((\omega \cdot x_i)+b\right) \geq 1 \qquad i = 1, 2, \cdots, l \end{cases} \tag{2}$$

The theory of SVM had been widely described in the literature, thus only a simplified introduction into the basic ideas behind SVM for the two class classification problems is given here. By introducing Lagrange multipliers αi, the optimal hyperplane problem constructed converts into a simpler dual form that is a quadratic programming problem,:

$$\begin{cases} \max & W(a) = \displaystyle\sum_{i=1}^{l} a_i - \dfrac{1}{2}\sum_{i.j} a_i a_j y_i y_j\left(x_i \cdot x_j\right) \\[3mm] s.t. & \displaystyle\sum_{i=1}^{l} a_i y_i = 0, \qquad a_i \geq 0, i = 1, 2, \cdots, l \end{cases} \tag{3}$$

Where W(a) is maximize function , and ai is the Lagrange coefficient corresponding to formula 3. ai is a restriction condition ,and meets to $a_i \geq 0, i = 1, 2, \cdots, l$.

By resolution, the optimal class function is

$$f(x) = \mathrm{sgn}\{(\omega x)+b\} = \mathrm{sgn}\left\{\sum_{i=1}^{l} a_i y_i\left(x_i \bullet x\right)+b\right\} \tag{4}$$

SVM can not only solute linear separable question, but linear inseparable.

In linearly separable case, to find the separable hyperplane in practical applications, a margin slack variable ξ_i is added the terms, equation (1) becomes (5)

$$y_i\left((\omega \cdot x_i)+b\right) \geq 1 - \xi_i \qquad \xi_i \geq 0, i = 1, 2, \cdots, l \tag{5}$$

The object function is modified as

$$\varphi(\omega, \xi) = \frac{1}{2}(\omega \cdot \omega) + C \sum_{i=1}^{l} \xi_i \qquad (6)$$

In non-linearly separable cases, the SVM technology introduces the slack variable to the definition of hyperplane

$$y_i\left((\omega \cdot x_i) + b\right) \geq 1 - \xi_i \qquad \xi_i \geq 0, i = 1, 2, \cdots, l \qquad (7)$$

and the problem can be converted into a quadratic programming problem

$$\begin{cases} \max W(a) = \sum_{i=1}^{l} a_i - \frac{1}{2} \sum_{i=1}^{l} \sum_{j=1}^{l} a_i a_j y_i y_j x_i^T x_j \\ s.t. \sum_{i=1}^{l} a_i y_i = 0 \\ 0 \leq a_i \leq C \qquad i = 1, 2, \cdots, l \end{cases} \qquad (8)$$

where C>0 is a pre-specified value that defines regularization. It is a QP problem with linear inequality constraints(described as equation 1). SVM maps the input variable into a high dimensional feature space with a kernel function $K(x_i, x_j)$. We derive its dual by introducing the Lagrange coefficients α_i as follows:

$$\begin{cases} \max W(a) = \sum_{i=1}^{l} a_i - \frac{1}{2} \sum_{i=1}^{l} \sum_{j=1}^{l} a_i a_j y_i y_j K\left(x_i, x_j\right) \\ s.t. \sum_{i=1}^{l} a_i y_i = 0 \\ 0 \leq a_i \leq C \qquad i = 1, 2, \cdots, l \end{cases} \qquad (9)$$

There are two typical kernel functions: linear kernel and RBF kernel:

$$K(x, x_i) = \begin{cases} x^T x_i \\ \exp\left(-\gamma |x - x_i|^2\right) \end{cases} \qquad (10)$$

After solving it, we can obtain the following separating hyperplane in the feature space

$$f(x) = \mathrm{sgn}\left(\sum_{i=1}^{l} y_i a_i K(x, x_i) + b\right) \qquad (11)$$

For a given problem, once the kernel function and the regularity parameter C are selected, the constructed SVM system can be used to solve related problems. The article has tested two kernel functions, namely, linear kernel and RBF kernel.

3   Stability Classification of Surrounding Rock Based on SVM Theory

Now, classification methods usually divided into two kinds: single factor index and multi-factor indexes, single factor is simple, but not accurate, for example uniaxial compressive strength or protodyaknove's number(f), RQD classification; multi-factor indexes are usually complex, such as Q system classification, RMR classification, etc..but not convenient to use. The author use multi-factors to evaluate and analyze the stability of surrounding rock in underground engineering. Whether evaluating result of surrounding rock stability is right or wrong affects cost and quality of support. Surrounding rock stability of the roadway in mine is ensured by many factors which intercross between each other. Now, it is not possible and necessary for people to consider all factors based on SVM theory, but in order to better define stability classification of surrounding rock and validate the SVM method , therefore, the other author's data are used, some parameters are as followed:

①Rock quality designation(RQD,%);
②Rock uniaxial saturated compressive strength(Rw, MPa);
③Rock integrity coefficient(Kv);
④ Structure plane strength(Kf);
⑤The amount of underwater seepage(Qw,L-min).
Specific classification indexes shown table 1.

Table 1. The classification indexes of surrounding rock stability

number	RQD(%)	R_w (MPa)	K_v	K_f	$Q_w / \left[L \cdot (min \cdot m)^{-1} \right]$	surrounding rock sort
1	>90	>120	>0.75	>0.80	<5	I
2	90~75	120~60	0.75~0.45	0.80~0.6	5~10	II
3	75~50	60~30	0.45~0.30	0.6~0.4	10~25	III
4	50~25	30~15	0.30~0.20	0.4~0.2	25~125	IV
5	<25	<15	<0.20	<0.2	>125	V

According to "Specification for design of hydraulic tunnel" and the domestic and international experience of surrounding rock stability classification, surrounding rock stability is divided into 5 levels. In order to prove the method used that is right ,30 samples data collected from literature and are defined as training and predicting samples (as shown in tab.2).

The former 24 samples are trained, furthermore, the later 6 are predicted. Research result shows that method adopted is rational (as shown in tab.3). Table 2,3 show the result are consistent with actually ones from the classification according to the code of hydraulic tunnel design, and Network methods used.

Table 2. On-site test parameters of surrounding rock

No	RQD (%)	R_w (MPa)	K_v	K_f	Q_w L.$(min.m)^{-1}$	Surrounding rock stability
1	52	25	0.22	0.52	12	**IV orIII**
2	41.5	25	0.22	0.35	12.5	**IV**
3	50	40.5	0.38	0.55	10.5	**III**
4	28	26	0.32	0.3	18	**IV**
5	51	45	0.35	0.5	5	**III**
6	93	156.5	0.78	0.82	3.2	**I**
7	50	35	0.32	0.35	10	**III**
8	76	63.9	0.65	0.62	10	**II**
9	23.5	13.4	0.15	0.16	120	**V**
10	78	58.6	0.57	0.55	10.5	**I**
11	81	65.2	0.56	0.65	6	**I**
12	24.2	12.5	0.13	0.18	125	**V**
13	92	125	0.82	0.83	3.5	**I**
14	80	100	0.65	0.7	8	**II**
15	82	110	0.6	0.65	9	**II**
16	72	50	0.35	0.55	20	**II**
17	70.5	40	0.4	0.57	18	**IV**
18	40	25	0.28	0.35	35	
19	40.5	20	0.25	0.3	30	**IV**
20	20	10	0.18	0.19	130	**V**
21	176	40.5	0.43	0.55	15.5	**I**
22	70.5	40.5	0.43	0.55	15.5	**III**
23	80	100	0.58	0.7	8	**II**
24	21.5	13.5	0.1	0.15	135	**V**
25	46	38	0.28	0.32	6	**IV**
26	65	54	0.23	0.52	13	**IV**
27	26	48	0.57	0.55	15	**V**
28	91	48	0.57	0.55	5	**III**
29	23	25	0.28	0.17	14	**V**
30	87	42	0.58	0.66	12	**III**

Table 3. Predicting sort of surrounding rock stability between ANNs and SVM

No	RQD ($\%$)	R_w (MPa)	K_v	K_f	Q_w $L.(min.m)^{-1}$	Stability of ANNs method	Stability of SVM method
25	46	38	0.28	0.32	6	**IV**	**IV**
26	65	54	0.23	0.52	13	**IV**	**IV**
27	26	48	0.57	0.55	15	**V**	**V**
28	91	48	0.57	0.55	5	**III**	**III**
29	23	25	0.28	0.17	14	**V**	**V**
30	87	42	0.58	0.66	12	**III**	**III**

The results show the method is rational and prediction result is very right. Compared with some nonlinear methods, the computation process of the SVM measure is more simple. It is a new way to be used for predicting the classification of rocks surrounding about underground engineering.

4   Summary

In order to better control displacement of surrounding rock, it is necessary for scientific personal to classify types of surrounding rock stability classification. The author use six factors indexes evaluate and analyze the stability of surrounding   rock. Classification data of surrounding rock collected which were defined as evaluation index are relativity small. So, non-linear relationship between surrounding rock stability and factors influenced based on SVM, which can better classify stability type of   surrounding rock. The results show the method is rational and   prediction result is very right. Compared with some nonlinear methods, the computation process of the SVM measure is more simple, other advantages are as follows: 1) SVM is a good diagnosis method for small sample. 2) Some deficiencies of conventional methods which measure is not accurate and criterion is not uniform are avoided. 3) The classification of surrounding rock based on SVM is usually classification, especially for parameters of multi-dimension. Its classification methods have some advantages to compare with other methods. So, it is a new way to be used for predicting the classification of rocks surrounding about underground engineering, furthermore.

References

1. Melville, P., Mooney, R.J.: Creating diversity in ensembles using artificial data. Information Fusion 6(1) (2005)
2. Zhu, K.J., Su, S.H., Li, J.L.: Optimal number of clusters and the best partition in fuzzy C-mean. Systems Engineering-Theory & Practice 25(3), 52–61 (2005)

3. Liu, Y.T.: A genetic clustering algorithm for data with non-spherical shape cluster. Pattern Recognition Letter 33(1), 1251–1259 (2000)
4. Pham, D.L.: Fuzzy clustering with spatial constraints. In: Proceedings of the IEEE International Conference on Image Processing, vol. 2, pp. 65–68. IEEE Computer Society, New York (2002)
5. Zhang, S.H., Sun, J.X., Zhu, K.: Sampling fuzzy C means clustering algorithm based on genetic optimization. Systems Engineering-Theory & Practice 24(5), 121–125 (2004)
6. Chen, S.-C., Zhang, D.-Q.: Robust image segmentation using FCM with spatial constraints based on new kernel-induced distance measure. IEEE Transactions on Systems, Man, and Cybernetics 34(4), 1907–1916 (2004)
7. Zhang, X.-G.: Introduction to statistical learning theory and support vector machines. Acta Automatica Sinica 26(1), 32–42 (2006) (in Chinese)
8. Cervantes, J., Li, X., Yu, W.: SVM classification for large data sets by considering models of classes distribution. In: 6th Mexican International Conference on Artificial Intelligence, Special Session, pp. 51–60 (2008)
9. Kuncheva, L.I., Whitaker, C.J.: Measures of diversity in classifier ensembles and their relationship with the ensembleaccuracy. Machine Learning 21(2), 181–207 (2003)
10. Windeatt, T.: Diversity measures for multiple classifier system analysis and design. Information Fusion 6, 21–36 (2005)
11. Shin, H.W., Sohn, S.Y.: Selected tree classifier combination based on both accuracy and error diversity. Pattern Recognition 38(2), 191–197 (2005)
12. Valentini, G., Dietterich, T.G.: Bias-variance analysis of sup-port vector machines for the development of SVM based ensemble methods. Journal of Machine Learning Research 5, 725–775 (2004)
13. Wang, S., Mathew, A., Chen, Y., et al.: Empirical analysis of support vector machine ensemble classifiers. Expert Systems with Applications:an International Journal 36(3), 6466–6476 (2009)
14. Liew, A.W., Yan, H., Law, N.F.: Image segmentation based on adaptive cluster prototype estimation. IEEE Transactions on Fuzzy Systems 13(4), 444–449 (2005)
15. Dong, L., Hu, D., Bai, Y., Liu, Y.: Unascertained Average Grade Model for Surrounding Rock Classification on Hydraulic Tunnels. In: The 2008 International Symposium on Safety Science and Technology, vol. 1, pp. 2227–2231 (2008) (in chinese)
16. Jiang, H., Meng, C., Yang, S., Luo, J.: The SVM Information Model Based on AI-ESTATE. In: 8th International Symposium on Test and Measurement, vol. 1, pp. 323–326 (2009) (in chinese)
17. Wang, G.: The unascertqined Measurementtailled Elvation on a city Evaluation on a City's Environmental Quality. Systems Engineering Theory & Practice 23(4), 52–58 (1990) (in Chinese)
18. Wei, L.: Study on fuzzy theory applied in surrounding rock classification of highway tunnel. Journal of Highway and Transportation Research and Developmem 21(11), 63–65 (2004) (in Chinese)
19. Huang, X., She, C.: Research on methods of surrounding rockmasses stability classification based on extension theory. Rock and Soil Mechanics 27(10), 1800–1814 (2006) (in Chinese)
20. Zhou, C., Zhang, L., Huang, X.: Classification of rock surroundings tunnel based on improved BP network algorithm. Earth Science Journal of China University of Geosciences 30(4), 480–486 (2005) (in Chinese)
21. Dong, L., Wang, F.: Comprehensive evaluation∞seismic stability of slopes based on unascermined measurcmem. The Chinese Journal of Geological Hazard and Control 18(4), 74–78 (2007) (in Chinese)

Three IP Soft-Core Designs
of ADC and FPGA Verification

JiangFeng Sun and Feng Chen

School of Computer Science and Technology, Henan Polytechnic University,
Jiaozuo, 454000, china
sjffly@hpu.edu.cn

Abstract. Analog to Digital Converters (ADC) are important components of the
Input /Output system in a Large-Scale Integrated Circuit, And the applied value
is very high. Such as wireless communications, medical imaging, portable test
equipment, video equipment, radar and guide, portable instrumentation, etc. in
this paper, by researching and exploring the multiplexing design
methodology, the paper achieves three quasi-digital IP soft cores of 8-bit, 10bit
and 16bit. The AD Converters are comprehensive certificated, and meet the
requirements, they can be directly applied to the SoC and the front parts of
ASIC.

Keywords: Field Programmable Gate Array, Intellectual Property core, Analog
to Digital Converter, Random Logic, Quartus II.

1   Introduction

IP Core in the semiconductor industry can be applied in chips based on ASIC, SoC
and PLD etc. It is an electric circuit module which is designed in advance, and has the
intellectual property rights. At present, there are many kinds of ADC chips in the
domestic and foreign production, but these chips are analog or analog - digital mixed
type. In recent years, with the development of digital technology researches on all-
digital ADC are ongoing[1,2,3], The literature[4] gives an ideas about DAC based on
random logic theory that has attempted on the 8 bit DAC principle confirmation. In
this foundation this paper attempts to develop the design ideas into three complete IP
Cores. Through the design and verification of the ADC this paper explores the
feasibility of the ADC which can be used in practical as a commercial soft-core which
is designed for PLD Applications and ASIC designs as a functional module.

2   Principle of ADC

2.1   Principle of DAC Based on Random Logic Theory

Ortega presents a DAC design based on random logic theory as shown in Figure 1 in
1995 [5]. As the figure1 shown, a_n is the sequence that will be converted to digital

M. Zhao and J. Sha (Eds.): ICCIP 2012, Part II, CCIS 289, pp. 123–130, 2012.

signals, b_n is the sequence of random sequences generated by LFSR. Firstly, a_n is stored in the digital register. Then the digital signal a_n compares with the random signal b_n which is the output of pseudo-random generator (LFSR) .From the output of the comparator a digital pulse sequence proportional to the digital signal a_n can be acquired, the sequence contains the information of a_n . Finally, this sequence is sent to RC low-pass filter, after filtering out high frequency digital to analog conversion can be achieved.

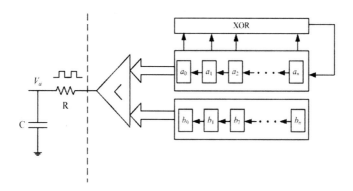

Fig. 1. DAC's structure based on random logic

2.2   Principle of ADC Based on Random Logic Theory

As the design of the DAC based on random logic circuits has been acquired [6], on this basis by the method of mixed circuit, the circuit structure of ADC based on random logic can be achieved as shown in Figure 2. Relative to the DAC, which adds an analog comparator and a successive approximations register (SAR).

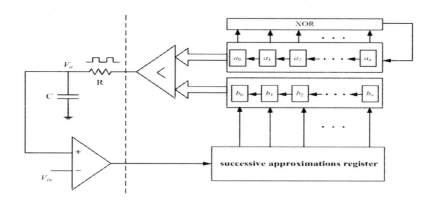

Fig. 2. ADC's structure based on random logic

The ADC Works as follows: V_{in} is the analog voltage waiting for conversion after control system sampling, it is sent to inverting input of the analog comparator. V_a is the feedback voltage that is obtained after the random logical sequence pass the low-pass filter, it is sent to the positive input of the analog comparator. In the system initialization, the highest bit of SAR is set to '1'. Then the digital signal is read into data register M of DAC. After the completion of a DAC conversion, V_a is acquired ,it is the analog voltage corresponding to the digital signal in data register M. V_a is sent to analog comparator Compared with the input sample voltage V_a, from the comparator output there is a signal to control Changes of the corresponding bit in SAR. When $V_a \geq V_{in}$, the number in M is too big, and the analog comparator output is high voltage, the SAR's highest bit is set to '0'. The second highest bit is set to '1'. When $V_a \leq V_{in}$, the number in M is too small, and the analog comparator output is low voltage, the SAR's highest bit is unchanged, and the second highest bit is set to '1'. By comparison of each bit form high to low, a digital signal corresponding d analog voltage V_{in} in SAR is eventually obtained.

Figure 2 shows that the function of SAR is to produce the final digital signal through the successive displacement. Besides, the SAR is connected to a DAC and an analog comparator, DAC is responsible for producing pseudo-random sequence and restoring the analog values by Successive approximation. Analog comparators are analog part which is responsible for comparing between analog values restored and analog values to be converted.

3   The Design of ADC's Digital Circuit

3.1   The Design and Simulation of ADC8 Circuit Module

Figure 2 shows that in addition to a RC filter circuit and an analog comparator, other parts of the ADC are digital circuits. Digital circuits can be described in VHDL language. Figure 3 is 8-bit ADC's top-level circuit module realized through Quartus II 6.0.

It can be concluded from Figure 3 that Top-level module consists of a successive gradual shift register (sar8), an 8-bit successive gradual shift register clock module (SAR_CLK) and a digital comparator (comp8). There are three input signals in which c is the analog comparator output signal, start is enable when the falling edge of Voltage is coming, clk is the system clock signal. There are four output signals of the top-level module in which random_array8 is the digital pulse sequence which contains information on input signal, CLK_SAR is an output clock as the clock signals of sar8. d[7 .. 0] is the final digital signal converted from the input analog signal. At the end of conversion, Eoc will send the signal of the end of a conversion to the module SAR_CLK. the timing simulation waveforms of 8-bit ADC shown in Figure 4.

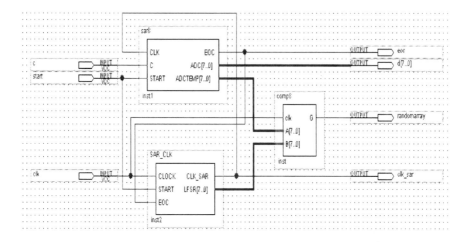

Fig. 3. The top-level circuit module of ADC8

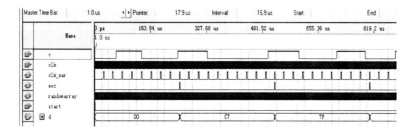

Fig. 4. Timing simulation waveforms of ADC8

It is can be seen from Figure 4: clk_sar is the clock signal of SAR8. At the eighth rising edge of clk_sar, the lowest bit conversion is completed. At the increased rising edge of the 9th clock (only one CLK clock cycle), the digital date is locked in digital register of the ADC. The locked date is outputted through date line of d[7..0] such as 00、C7、7F which are the final digital signal converted from the input analog signal. When the start is equal to 1 or Eoc equal to 1 the ADC will start next conversion.

3.2   The Design and Simulation of ADC10 and ADC16

Compared with ADC8, the important design is the gradual shift register clock module which needs to redesign of feedback bits, the output sequences must be maximum period of 10-bit and 16-bit random sequences. In addition, the count value also needs to redesign so that the appropriate is moderate. The calculation of Conversion time is shown in formula (1).

$$T = T_{clk} \times n \times count \times 2^n \qquad (1)$$

In formula (1), n is the resolution, T_{clk} is the ADC's input clock, *count* is the successive gradual shift register clock module's count value.

Timing simulation waveforms of ADC10 and ADC16 are shown in Figure 5 and Figure 6.

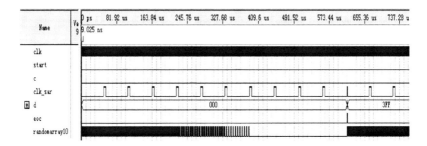

Fig. 5. Timing simulation waveforms of ADC10

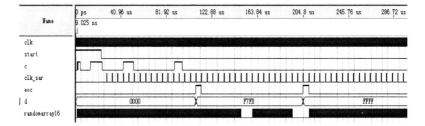

Fig. 6. Timing simulation waveforms of ADC16

3.3   Factors that Affect the Conversion Time of Digital Circuits

Factors that affect the conversion time of Digital circuits are clock frequency and resolution, when the clock frequency is constant, the higher the resolution, the longer the conversion time, conversion time increased exponentially with the resolution. When the resolution is fixed, the conversion time is inversely proportional with the clock frequency.

When the clock frequency is set to 50MHz and *count* is set to 10, the conversion time is ADC8's Digital is 0.410ms, the conversion time is ADC10's Digital is 2.05 ms, the conversion time is ADC16's Digital is 210ms.

4   The Design and Verification of Hardware Circuit of ADC

4.1   The Design of Hardware Circuit of ADC

The design of hardware circuit of ADC is that the digital part of ADC is downloaded to the main chip EP1C3T144C8 of EDA Experiment Box developed by Hang Zhou KonXin SOC Co, .Ltd, The Experiment Box Model is GW48-CK+, so a lot of modules such as the clock circuit module, the signal generator module, power supply circuit module, display module can be used directly. Analog part is composed of a RC filter circuit and an analog comparator.

4.2   The Verification of Hardware Circuit of ADC

The PLD chip chose is EP1C3T144C8, its parameters and the hardware test results are shown in Figure 7, Figure8 and Figure 9.

Conversion time	Clock frequency	Conversion voltage	Resistance value	Capacitance value	LE Number	Resources occupied(%)
2.311ms	10MHz	0-5.5V	2.6K	0.1uF	81	3
0.152ms	50MHz	0-5.5V	5.2K	0.01uF	81	3
0.232ms	100MHz	0-5.5V	2.6K	0.01uF	81	3

Fig. 7. Test results parameters and the test results of ADC8

Conversion time	Clock frequency	Conversion voltage	Resistance value	Capacitance value	LE Number	Resources occupied(%)
18.41ms	10MHz	0-5.5V	8.3K	1uF	84	3
3.794ms	50MHz	0-5.5V	1.7K	1uF	84	3
1.818ms	100MHz	0-5.5V	8.3K	0. 1uF	84	3

Fig. 8. Test results parameters and the test results of ADC10

Conversion time	Clock frequency	Conversion voltage	Resistance value	Capacitance value	LE Number	Resources occupied(%)
18.16s	10MHz	0-5.5V	1.7K	1uF	119	4
3.631ms	50MHz	0-5.5V	3.6K	1uF	119	4
1.843ms	100MHz	0-5.5V	1.7K	0. 1uF	119	4

Fig. 9. Test results parameters and the test results of ADC16

As can be seen from the figure 7. When n is equal to eight there are two factors affecting conversion time. One factor is the target chip's clock speed, another factor is the time of RC filter and time of analog comparator. The clock frequency is on a leading role in improving conversion time. When the clock frequency Increases from 10MHz to 100MHz conversion time is approximately one-tenth of the original time. Resources occupied by the LE take up 3% of the total, resources occupied by the I/O take up 13% of the total.

After verification, the function of three ADCs are correct, timing meet logic, as the resolution is set to 8 or 10, the clock frequency is set to 50MHz, the conversion time of is less than 3ms, However, when the resolution is set to16 the conversion time is longer to 3.6s or so, It can not be applied to the actual.

5   The Usability Evaluation of ADC's IP Core

As a reusable IP soft core it must have the following characteristics: The design of the header files about project is standard; Codes written are standard and can be integrated; Validation strategies, verification platform and validation test set are complete; Guidance document is detailed and easy to understand. In this thesis, the ADC's IP soft-cores are to meet the above requirements.

6   Summary

Reuse Technology of IP core in SoC's design is one of the key technologies. Based on the traditional ADC, as well as all digital ADC around the world, combined with the current situation of the rapid development of digital circuits. This paper has designed successfully three "quasi-digital" IP soft-cores of 8-bit, 10bit and 16bit. After verification, the ADC's function is correct, timing is also logical. As 50MHz clock frequency chosen the conversion rate is higher, the conversion time is of less than 3ms. Compared with the ADC of the traditional successive approximation, the 8-bit and 10-bit "quasi-digital" ADCs' conversion time are similar. It can be applied to medium-speed or low speed, medium-precision data acquisition and intelligent devices, such as measurement and control instrumentation, the ADC's IP soft-cores possess certain reference value and practical value.

References

1. Ascota, A.J., Rueda, A., Huertas, J.L.: A VHDL-based Methodology for the Design and Verification of Pipeline A/D Converters. In: Proceedings of Design, Automation and Test in Europe Conference and Exhibition, pp. 534–538 (March 2000)
2. Buenzli, C., Owen, L., Rose, F.: Hardware/Software Codesign of a Scalable Embedded Radar Signal Processor. In: VHDL International Users' Forum, pp. 200–208 (October 1997)
3. Chen, C.-C., Chen, P., Hwang, C.-S., Chang, W.: A Precise Cyclic CMOS Time-to-Digital Converter With Low Thermal Sensitivity. IEEE Transactions on Nuclear Science 52(4), 834–838 (2005)

4. Marin, S.L.T., Reboul, J.M.Q., Franquelo, L.G.: Digital Stochastic Realization of Complex Analog Controllers. IEEE Transactions on Industrial Electronics 49(5) (October 2002)
5. Ortega, Janer, C.L., Quero, J.M., Franquelo, L.G., Pinilla, J., Serrano, J.: Analog to Digital and Digital to Analog Conversion Based on Stochastic Logic. In: IEEE Intl. Conf. on Ind. Electr., IECON 1995, Orlando (November 1995)
6. Toral, S.L., Quero, J.M., Franquelo, L.G.: Stochastic Pulse Coded Arithmetic. In: IEEE International Symposium on Circuits and Systems, Geneva, Switzerland, May 28-31 (2000)

A Novel Dual Fuzzy Neural Network to Civil Aviation Aircraft Disturbance Landing Control

Kaijun Xu

Department of Air Navigation, School of Flight Technology, Civil Aviation Flight University
of China Guanghan, Sichuan, 618307, P.R. China
K_j_xu@163.com

Abstract. A novel dual fuzzy neural network to civil aviation aircraft disturbance landing control is presented in this paper. Conventional automatic landing system (ALS) can provide a smooth landing, which is essential to the comfort of passengers. However, these systems work only within a specified operational safety envelope. When the conditions are beyond the envelope, such as turbulence or wind shear, they often cannot be used. The objective of this paper is to investigate the use of dual fuzzy neural network in ALS and to make that system more intelligent. Firstly the dual fuzzy neural network is trained from available flight data and then that trained neural network controls the landing, roll, pitch and altitude hold of the airplane. Current flight control law is adopted in the intelligent controller design. Tracking performance and robustness are demonstrated through software simulations. The neural network control has been implemented in MATLAB and the data for training have been taken from Flight Gear Simulator. Simulated results show that control for different flight phases is successful and the dual fuzzy neural network controllers provide the robustness to system parameter variation.

Keywords: Dual Fuzzy Neural Network, Disturbance Landing Control, Flight Gear Simulator, MATLAB.

1 Introduction

Civil aviation aircrafts in the initial stages compulsorily needed continuous attention of a pilot for smooth flight and effective control. Early development of aircraft had created a very high demand on aircraft crew concentration and thus rendered pilot's job extremely tedious and challenging. The auto landing system (ALS) in modem aircraft are designed to give a satisfactory performance under nominal operating conditions and are generally unable to cope with failures such as control surfaces being stuck at certain deflections.

Most conventional control laws generated by the ALS are based on the gain scheduling method [1]. Control parameters are preset for different flight conditions within a specified safety envelope, which is relatively defined by Federal Aviation Administration (FAA) regulations. According to FAA regulations, environmental conditions considered in the determination of dispersion limits are: headwinds up to

M. Zhao and J. Sha (Eds.): ICCIP 2012, Part II, CCIS 289, pp. 131–139, 2012.

25 knots; tailwinds up to 10 knots; crosswinds up to 15 knots; moderate turbulence, wind shear of 8 knots per 100 ft from 200 ft to touchdown [2]. If the flight conditions are beyond the preset envelope, the ALS is disabled and the pilot takes over. An inexperienced pilot may not be able to guide the aircraft to a safe landing.

Between 2000 and 2010, 22.6% of the flight safety events are due to weather factors. Among them, 62% are attributed to wind disturbances. It is therefore desirable to develop an intelligent ALS that expands the operational envelope to include more safe responses under a wider range of conditions. This paper has demonstrated that the proposed a novel dual fuzzy neural network controller can automatically guide the aircraft to a safe landing in different wind disturbance environments.

Most of the improvements in the ALS have been on the guidance instruments, such as the Global Navigation Satellite Systems Integrity Beacons, Global Positioning System, Microwave Landing System, and Auto-land Position Sensor [3]. By using improvement calculation methods and high-accuracy instruments, these systems provide more accurate flight data to the ALS to make the landing smoother. However, these researches did not include weather factors such as wind disturbances. There have also not been many researches on the problem of intelligent landing control [4]–[6].

An early use of neural networks in auto-landing is given in [7] where the neural network was trained off-line to generate the desired trajectories for landing under wind disturbances and worked in conjunction with a conventional PID landing controller. A feed-forward network neural network, trained off-line is used as an auto-landing controller in [8]. Here, the neural network replaced the original PID controller and similar performance has been observed.

In some of the above work [9], a feed-forward neural network with back propagation learning algorithm has been used. The main drawback of such a scheme is that the neural network requires a priori training on normal and faulty operating data. Also, the size of the neural network needs to be fixed beforehand. An alternate neural network is the Radial Basis Function Network (RBFN) with Gaussian functions, which have good local interpolation and global generalization ability [10]-[11].

The controller proposed in this paper is comprised of a fuzzy logic controller (FLC) in the feedback configuration and two dynamic neural networks in the forward path [12]-[13]. A novel dual fuzzy neural network controller is used to control the intelligent landing system, and being employed to learn the weighting factor of the fuzzy logic. It is envisaged that the integration of fuzzy logic and neural network based-controller will encompass the merits of both technologies. The fuzzy logic controller, based on fuzzy set theory, provides a means for converting a linguistic control strategy into control action and offering a high level of computation. On the other hand, the ability of a dynamic recurrent network structure to model an arbitrary dynamic nonlinear system is incorporated to approximate the unknown nonlinear input −output relationship using a dynamic back propagation learning algorithm.

The paper is structured as follows: Section 2 deals with the description of civil aviation aircraft auto landing system. Then we will discuss the dual fuzzy neural network controller in Section 3. In Section 4, our concept of the dynamic learning process will be presented. We mainly focus on the learning model and the adaptive control in the dual fuzzy neural network control system. Finally, we conclude with a discussion and an outlook in Section 5.

2   System Description

The overall block diagram of the civil aviation aircraft auto landing system controller is shown in the Figure 1. ALS controller is used for taking and sending data from aircraft using data sensor. First the data is taken from civil aviation aircraft for different flights environment that is used for training the neural network as shown in Figure1.

The training of neural network has been done by using back propagation algorithm. When training phase is completed, the trained neural network is attached to ALS controller to control the flight. The objective of trained network is to send corrective output signal to flight gear simulator to get desired results as shown in Figure 2. Any changes in the pitch or roll are detected by a vertical gyroscope. The altitude is detected by a barometric sensor in real aircraft but here inputs for neural networks are directly taken from flight gear. The altitude, roll (bank) and the pitch are the signals available in the model for the feedback, whereas the elevator, aileron and throttle are the control outputs for all three controllers.

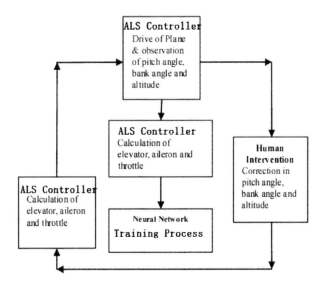

Fig. 1. Neural Network Training

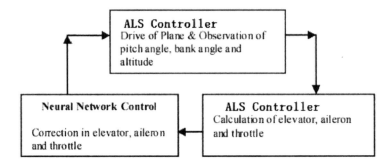

Fig. 2. Execution Under Neural Network Control

3   Dual Fuzzy Neural Network Control System

The disturbance parameters of environments have to be known in order to control the ALS with conventional control techniques since the disturbance affects the whole system.

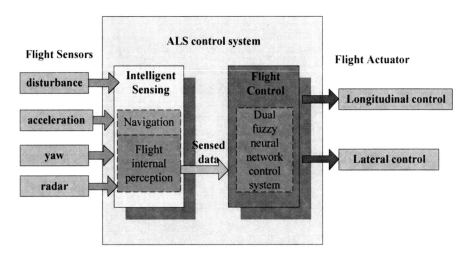

Fig. 3. Block-diagram of the disturbance ALS control system

Research on civil aviation aircraft disturbance landing control mainly focused on control laws and the learning process that enhanced comfort and lowered fuel consumption by moderating the aircraft's accelerations. In the flight control part, we designed the dual fuzzy neural network control system which used the sensed data to control the aircraft.

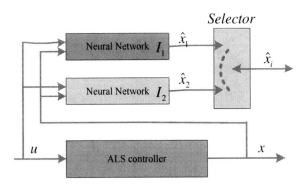

Fig. 4. The structure of dual fuzzy neural network controller

The flight controller is comprised of the system identifier and two recurrent neural networks. The system identifier inspect the control strategy which is not satisfied the real system after a while, it changes two dynamic neural networks function. The learning neural network which has suitable strategy became to control the adaptive cruise control system. The former control network became to learning the new strategy. The identifier combines two parts: performance index and selector.

Consider an nth-order nonlinear control system governed by the following differential equation:

$$x^{(n)}(t) = f(X;t) + G(X;t)U(t) + d(X;t)$$

$$y(t) = x(t)$$

$$(1)$$

$X = (x, x', ... x^{(n-1)})$ $y(t)$ $d(X;t)$ are unknown nonlinear and bounded continuous function; is control input, is a disturbance term, is the output of the control system; State vector is observable. Define the tracking error vector as following:

$$E = (e, e', ... e^{(n-1)})$$

$$e(t) = x_d(t) - x(t),$$

......

$$e^{(n-1)}(t) = x^{(n-1)}{}_d(t) - x^{(n-1)}(t)$$

$$(2)$$

Where, $x_d(t)$ is the desired output, and $x_d(t) \ldots x^{(n-1)}{}_d(t)$ can be obtained. The perfect control law that is designed in the sense of feedback linearization can be defined as following:

$$U^*(t) = G(X;t)^{-1}(x_d^{(n)} - f(X;t) - d(X;t) + K^T E)$$

$$(3)$$

Where, $K = (k_n, k_{n-1}, ..., k_1)^T, k_i (i = 1, 2, ..., n)$ are positive constants and such that:

$$e^{(n)} + k_1 e^{(n-1)} + ... + k_n e = 0$$

$$(4)$$

Where K is positive constants and If K is properly chosen such that the roots of the characteristic polynomial of Eq. (4) lie strictly in the open left half of the complex plane, then we get $\lim_{t \to \infty} e(t) = 0$. In this study, the force control command $U^*(t)$ is the output of the proposed dual fuzzy neural network.

4   Disturbance Learning Process

The design of the civil aviation aircraft ALS controller proposed in this paper consists of a fuzzy logic controller (FLC) in the feedback configuration and two dynamic neural networks, i.e. a disturbance control network (DCN) and a disturbance learning network (DLN). The FLC computes the excursion for the adaptive cruise control system. The DCN computes the output of the adaptive cruise control system and the result is input to the disturbance learning network (DLN). The DLN is employed to learn the disturbance weighting factor of the FLC. Both networks are trained on-line.

The network structure is made up of three layers with the hidden layer neurons have a dynamic self-recurrent connection relationship. The mapping relationship of this kind of network can be described as follows.

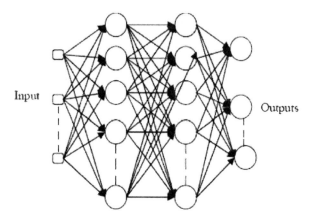

Fig. 5. Graphical Presentation of Neural Networks

Input layer: $I_i(k) = x_i(k)(i = 1, 2, 3)$ (5)

Hidden layer: $O_j^2(k) = f(net_j(k))(j = 1, 2, ..., m)$

$$net_j(k) = w_j^{(2)} O_j^{(2)}(k-1) + \sum_{i=1}^{3} w_{ij}^{(1)} x_i(k)$$ (6)

Output layer: $O^{(3)}(k) = \sum_{k=1}^{m} w_k^{(3)} O_k^{(2)}(k)$ (7)

The error function is defined as: $E_I = \frac{1}{2}(y(k) - y_d(k))^2$ (8)

The DLN is used to learn the weighting factor a of the FLC. It is a three layer dynamic neural network structure, not unlike the DCN, but the output of the DLN is nonlinear. The weighting factor ranges from zero to 1, so the nonlinear activation function is taken as $f(x) = \dfrac{1}{1 + e^{-x}}$. The mapping relationship between the inputs and output of the DLN is defined as:

Input layer: $I_i^1(k) = x_i(k)(i = 1, 2, 3)$ $\qquad\qquad\qquad\qquad\qquad\qquad\qquad$ (9)

Hidden layer: $O_j^2(k) = f(I_j^{(2)}(k))(j = 1, 2, ..., m)$

$$I_j^{(2)}(k) = v_j^{(2)}O_j^{(2)}(k-1) + \sum_{i=1}^{3} v_{ij}^{(1)}x_i(k) \qquad\qquad (10)$$

Output layer: $I^{(3)}(k) = \sum_{k=1}^{m} v_k^{(3)}O_k^{(2)}(k)$

$$O^{(3)}(k) = f(I)^{(3)}(k) = a \qquad\qquad\qquad (11)$$

The error function is defined as: $E_L = \dfrac{1}{2}(r(k) - y(k))^2$ $\qquad\qquad$ (12)

where $r(k)$ is the input to the manipulator system and $y(k)$ is the actual output of the manipulator system.

The weights of DLN can be updated by applying the following expression:

$$v(k+1) = v(k) + \alpha(-\frac{\partial E_L}{\partial v}) + \sigma(v(k) - v(k-1)) \qquad (13)$$

where v are the weights $v_{ij}^{(1)}$, $v_j^{(2)}$, $v_k^{(3)}$ of the DLN; α is adaptive learning rate, and σ is moment factor.

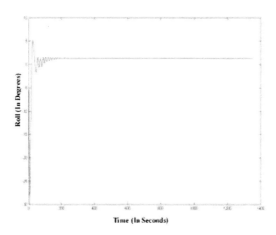

Fig. 6. Roll Control Near to Zero Degree

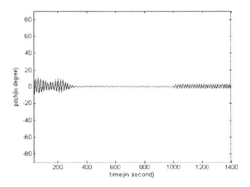

Fig. 7. Pitch Control for Altitude Hold

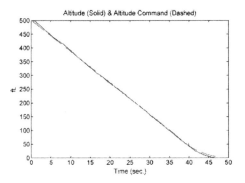

Fig. 8. Aircraft altitude and command

5   Conclusion and Future Work

The ALS of an airplane is enabled only under limited conditions. If severe wind disturbances are encountered, the pilot must handle the aircraft due to the limits of the ALS. The purpose of this paper is to investigate the use of dual fuzzy neural networks in ALS and to make these systems more intelligent. A modified learning through time process is adopted in the intelligent controller design. Tracking performance and robustness are demonstrated through software simulations. MATLAB tools were utilized to the simulations.

For the safe landing of an aircraft using a conventional controller with fixed gains, the wind speed turbulence limit is 30 ft/s. controllers can successfully guide the aircraft flying through wind speeds of 20 to 65 ft/s. A well-trained dual fuzzy neural network controller can overcome turbulence up to 65 ft/s without using the gain scheduling technique. From these simulations, proper type of neural network controller can be used to successfully replace the conventional autolander. The intelligent controller can act as an experienced pilot and guide the aircraft to a safe landing in severe wind disturbance environments.

Considering the great potential on safety issues we received from the dual fuzzy neural network model and its ability to be easily expandable, our future works should consider the extension of this model. However, we should also continue the improvement of our identifier algorithm, which could help improving the overall results of our model. We should finally investigate the possibility of extending the dual fuzzy neural network model with intelligent sensor and reinforcement learning applied to the real civil aviation aircraft disturbance landing control system.

Acknowledgement. This work is supported by the Open Foundation of Civil Aviation Flight University of China (Grant No.F2011KF04). Also be supported by Research Foundation of Civil Aviation Flight University of China (Grant No. J2011-04).

References

1. Buschek, H., Calise, A.J.: Uncertainty modeling and fixed-order controller design for a hypersonic vehicle model. J. Guid. Control Dyn. 20(1), 42–48 (1997)
2. Federal Aviation Administration, Automatic Landing Systems. AC 20-57A (January 1971)
3. Cohen, C.E., et al.: Automatic landing of a 737 using GNSS integrity beacons. In: Proc. ISPA, pp. 247–252 (1995)
4. Advanced Auto Landing System from Swiss Federal Aircraft Factory, Real-Time Journal, Sprint (1995)
5. Cooper, M.G.: Genetic design of rule-based fuzzy controllers, Ph.D.dissertation, Univ. California, Los Angeles (1995)
6. Jorgensen, C.C., Schley, C.: A neural network baseline problem for control of aircraft flare and touchdown. In: Neural Networks for Control, pp. 403–425. MIT Press, Cambridge (1991)
7. Iiguni, Y., Akiyoshi, H., Adachi, N.: An intelligent landing system based on human skill model. IEEE Trans. Aerosp. Electron. Syst. 34(3), 877–882 (1998)
8. Jorgensen, C.C., Scheley, C.: Neural network baseline problem for control of aircraft flare and touchdown. In: Neural Networks for Control, pp. 402–425. MIT Press, Cambridge (1990)
9. Iiguni, Y., Akiyoshi, H., Adachi, N.: An intelligent landing system based on a human skill model. IEEE Trans. Aerospace Electron. Syst. 34(3), 877–882 (1998)
10. Li, Y., Sundararajan, N., Saratchandran, P.: Analysis of minimal radial basis function network algorithm for real-time identification of nonlinear dynamic systems. IEE Proc. Control Theory Appl. 147(4), 476–484 (2000)
11. Sundararajan, N., Saratchandran, P., Li, Y.: Fully Tuned Radial Basis Function Neural Networks for Flight Control. Kluwer Academic, Boston (2001)
12. Xu, K.J., Zou, L., Lai, J.J., Xu, Y.: An application of Dual-Fuzzy Neural-Networks to Design of Adaptive Fuzzy Controllers. In: The 3rd International Conference on Natural Computation (ICNC 2007) (2007)
13. Xu, K.J., Lai, J.J., Li, X.B., Pan, X.D., Xu, Y.: Adjustment strategy for a dual-fuzzy-neuro controller using genetic algorithms -application to gas-fired water heater. In: 8th International FLINS Conference On Computational Intelligence in Decision and Control (2008)

The Transaction Processing of Heterogeneous Databases Application in Web Service

Wentao Zhao[1,2] and Xiaohong Zhang[2]

[1] Provincial Open Laboratory for Mine Information Key Disciplines,
[2] School of Computer Science and Technology,
Henan Polytechnic University, Jiaozuo, China
{zwt,xh.zhang}@hpu.edu.cn

Abstract. In this paper, we analyze the mechanism of the traditional database transaction, and the characters of web services. The transaction is one of the import techniques ensuring data consistency. However, web service can't support transactions. To provide transactions in web service, we propose a AOP mode. AOP simulates the mechanism of traditional transactions. We can develop business applications and transaction management systems based on AOP. The codes of the applications and the systems can be reusable easily.

Keywords: Heterogeneous database, Web service, Transaction processing, Data interface, AOP mode.

1 Transaction Problems in Web Service

A large number of heterogeneous databases in existence, making the information resources can not co-ordinate a unified platform for the effective integration of heterogeneous database is very much needed. Transaction is one of the critical techniques to build reliable distributed applications. It uses a collection of atomic operations to acheive data consistency in application. Web service can't provide consistency and reliability without transaction management. Web service provide different services cross platform and programming languages with the help of XML, and it can be applied in can be used in Many applications provides the integration of heterogeneous database based on Web Service. However, web service is stateless, and it cannot support transactions. Web Services only provides provide data communication standards among applications, and provide coarse-grained service.

2 The Operating Principle of Tradition Database Transaction Processing

Transactions have ACID properties:

1) Atomicity: all operations in transaction are indivisible in the database.
2) Consistency: The results of several transactions which execute parallelly must be consistent to the results according to the serial exection of these transactions.

M. Zhao and J. Sha (Eds.): ICCIP 2012, Part II, CCIS 289, pp. 140–147, 2012.

3) Isolation: The execution of a transaction cannot disturb the execution of other transactions. the have The intermediate results of a transaction   must be transparent for other transactions.

4)   Durability: For submitted transactions, systems must make sure that the changes made by the transactions must be written to database, even if the database is broken down.

A transaction can be partitioned into two stages. In the first stage, the transaction manager executes a persist processing for each participant in the transaction. Each participant must capture the change of the status in the transaction, and send the change to the transaction manager. The manager makes a desion on wheter to roll back or commit the transaction according to the executing results of the transaction. If each participant doesn't throw SQL Exceptions to transaction manager in the first stage, and the transaction will be committed in the second stage, and the durable information will be written to database simultaneously.

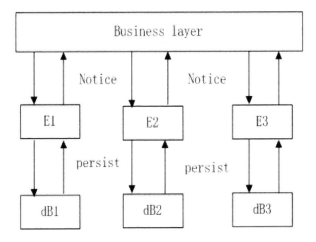

Fig. 1. The preparation phase of the transaction mechanism

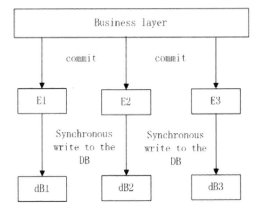

Fig. 2. The Transaction commit phase of the transaction mechanism

To keep data consistency, the participant which responded commit requests must be in the state of synchronization after responded in the first stage before the participant receives the message from partners. Meanwhile, the other participants cannot use the resource occupied by the participant. Otherwise, the ACID behavior will occur. If the partners failed before transmitting the message, the participant keeps in "synchronization" before the partner recovers.

3   Heterogeneous Database Integration

Integration of heterogeneous database systems need to be addressed shield platforms and environments, heterogeneous data model conversion, mode conversion and integration, distributed transaction management.

3.1   Heterogeneous Database Integration Issues to Be Addressed

Determine the characteristics of heterogeneous databases need to be addressed in the integration of heterogeneous database. the autonomy of the subsystem is a naturally occurring, and will not change because of the integration of various databases. The focus needs to be considered is the distribution and heterogeneity. Distribution and heterogeneity features make access transparent and heterogeneous data needs to be an effective solution.

1) Heterogeneity problem: Heterogeneous database integration technologies focused on how to solve the database heterogeneity. Business units by a number of relatively independent departments, each department has a different database systems from relatively independent. This fact makes a huge enterprise information classification, and repeatedly distributed in multiple heterogeneous database systems. Enterprises in the sharing of resources between the various departments of the subsystem, accurate and rapid transmission of information, efficient global search, you at least need to address three aspects of heterogeneity:

Host heterogeneity: each subsystem resides in a different hardware platform, using a different operating system. Communication protocols between the different host naturally not uniform.

Heterogeneous database systems: The various departments of the subsystem can be the same as the third generation of relational database systems, can also be a different data model database systems coexist, coexistence, such as relational, hierarchical, network and database system composed of a heterogeneous database system.

Semantic heterogeneity: semantic heterogeneity by the developers of the differences arising from the same data in different sub-database system name meaning, describe scope. Due to the different departments of the database system independent design and development of the different development teams, to participate in the overall database integration between the other sub-databases may produce a variety of semantic conflicts, including the table structure conflicts and data conflicts.

2) Transparency: Heterogeneous database systems, distributed and heterogeneous co-produced the opaque data access. Transparency of the heterogeneous database

integration need to address the key issues. Transparency with higher scores indicating higher integration, the function of the system the more perfect and more convenient to use. Transparency, including a platform of transparency, the system transparency, transparency of data sources and semantic transparency.

Platform transparent: from the physical host and the logical host distribution and heterogeneous platform opaque, heterogeneous database integration, you need to encapsulate the underlying implementation, hidden hardware, operating systems and communication protocols, such differences. For the user requesting the service, users do not need to care about the ins and outs of the data, the underlying implementation details, as long as the requests get feedback, get satisfactory service can be no difference in the use of ordinary single-database system.

System transparent: Heterogeneous database system, the system opaque. Heterogeneous database integration needs to be differences of the members of the DBMS of the database, data model and SQL commands, etc. to hide, for users who request service, each member of the database use the same data model, with a DBMS, and the same SQL commands to operate, manage and maintain.

Data source transparency: Traditional database integration hides the details and descriptions of distributed heterogeneous data sources, determine the data source of the data stored by the system automatically searches for dynamic data set translation formatting, visible to the user a logical data source. Heterogeneous databases in a unified platform for this study design in the traditional database integration technology based on the increase for customers of the actual data source is visible and the right to a separate operating functions.

Semantic transparency: Through the design of local wrapper translation, transformation, data and format, hide in terms of meaning, description, and the scope of the same or related data name. For users, the integrated system has a consistent table structure and a unified data structure.

3.2   Heterogeneous Database Integration Strategy

Heterogeneous database integration, mainly through conversion and standardization to achieve the strategy adopted by the following:

Common Programming Interface is widely used of heterogeneous database access interface. Heterogeneous database data exchange must provide a separate database management system, a unified programming interface and a common database, SQL-based access methods. Enterprise-class J2EE and JDBC, JTA, and other technology just is able to achieve a better solution for this requirement.

The public database gateway is connected to its own database products through third-party development tools, users do not need to waste existing applications can use the gateway to connect them with the new database technology, thereby protecting existing investments.

Public agreement is to standardize the format and protocol of communication between the client and server, and database languages. The method to manipulate the database efficiency is relatively high, but the amount of programming, the application does not generally.

3.3   Heterogeneous Database Integration Approach

Heterogeneous database integration has gone through decades of development, a variety of excellent and effective integration into a virtual view methods and the data warehouse to achieve.

Virtual view methods is a kind of integration in the view layer, upon request by the user to integrated systems, integrated systems analysis request and the role of the corresponding child data source. Virtual view methods as the theoretical basis, in the integrated structure, there are two integrated system of Federated Database System (FDBS) and Mediated System. Child data source in FDBS belongs database system independent of each other and with each other. Have autonomy to each sub-data source, can be used independently, but the composition FDBS increased after the mutual constraints, constraints to achieve is to provide access to interface between the child data source.Mediated System through an intermediary in the view layer reunification process the request and results.Mediated System data source is not limited to traditional databases, storage management data software system can become a data source, including network, text, etc. In this way shielding the user, heterogeneous data sources in the user opinion is just an ordinary database systems.

The data warehouse method need to create a warehouse used to store data, the data warehouse to be stored on a regular basis by the ETL (Extract, the Transform and load) tool from the data source to filter data for user queries. Corresponding to the virtual view wears, we call this method for the Eager method.

More practical solutions to data integration using the integrated virtual view. In this method defines one or more of the Mediated Schema mode usually refers to the global mode. They are just used to query data without data storage, data is still stored in the local data source. When users apply to the integrated system for a query, the query will be translated into a set of queries for each data source, then will the results returned to the user. Use this solution to make the query results to the latest data, and because of the emergence of XML standardized description of various data information possible to make the system easier access between the different data sources.

Heterogeneous database integration can be divided into two phases. The main research directions of the first phase of a multi-database system. The second stage is the generic Heterogeneous Data Integration. Data integration system is not limited to the database, and also non-database data, such as XML data, multimedia data. Database integration system has strong expansion, at any time to add new data sources, and have the ability to hot deploy.

4   The Solution of JTA

The participants in a transaction act as the data access objects (DAO) to the same database. They also play the roles of DAO of distributed heterogeneous databases. Java provides the local transaction management of Java DataBase Connection (JDBC) and the global transaction management of distributed JTA, respectively. In the paper, we only focus on the transactions in distributed heterogeneous database, and only pay attention to the solutions of global transaction in web service.

The applications based on JTA commits transactions through two phases. two-phase commit transactions. JTA is a well-defined transaction services, it provides a kind of services which can be used directly by J2EE application developers. In real applications, most enterprise-class J2EE WEB containers are integrated with JTA transaction manager which insteads of the developer to manage the transactions, which is convenient for developers to construct business logic. Considering the excellent performance in a distributed transaction management, we adopt JTA in heterogeneous database integration solutions that based on web service. web service as a middleware, providing unified transmission and data access interface for the applications, it also cuts off the communication between transaction participants and transaction manager. In essence, Web service can't run on the transaction context which run before web service calls, and it also can not send a transaction context to another component.

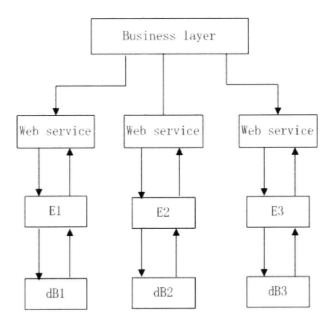

Fig. 3. Participant status change message is shielded by web service

5   The Simulative Realization of Distributed Transaction Management Framework with Aspect Oriented Programming

Aspect Oriented Programming（AOP）is a programming concept which is a an supplement of OOP. AOP separates cross businesses, and takes them as independent units called Aspects. Aspects are the modular realizations of cross businesses. They encapsulate the behaviors which have effects on all classes. Aspects ban be reused by different business.

Transaction simulation module and business logic module discussed in the paper are two kinds of disparate businesses. They are tight-knit cross businesses. So weaving these two modules by AOP is an excellent designing pattern.

For example, figure 4 shows with reference to the working mechanism of the traditional transaction, web service in the upper deck of the business logic should have similar Traditional transactions have some excellent characters, i.e. capturing the SQL Exceptions thrown by the participants, rolling back or committing transactions according to the results of the transactions. AOP adopts these excellent characters, and providing commands to implement these characters.

According to the designing concept of AOP, when clients calls business logic methods, the modules of transaction management should be woven, which is implemented by JAVA Dynamic Proxy mode. Java Dynamic Proxy Mode encapsulates transaction processing codes into a class called Advicer, and generates the proxy of business logics dynamically. Then it weaves Advice into business logic, and hence the business logic can provide transactions.

Advicer simulates transactions. It handles the basic operations of database, i.e. selecting operations, inserting operations, updating operations and deleting operations.

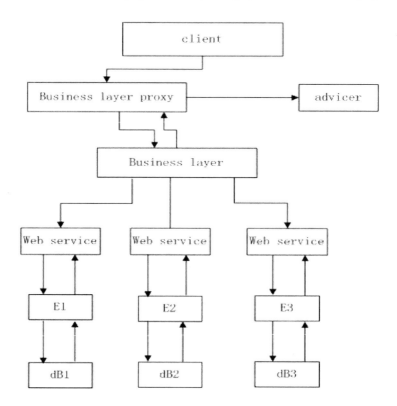

Fig. 4. Integrate transactions into the business logic via AOP

The following problem is how the Adviser to simulate the transaction. With the four database operations, namely insert, delete, update and query, we will make   specific analysis in the following:

1) select: selecting operations are read-only operations. The security of these operations can be guaranteed without transactions. So we need not implement transaction processing logics for these operations.

2) Insert: inserting operations add new data to into database. They are writing operations. Advicer saves the ORM (Object Relational Mapping) before executing the business logic, and calls the deleting data method of the web service to remove the ORM from the database after the business logic captures SQL exceptions.

3) update: updating data into the database is a writing operation. It needs transaction management to provide security and data consistency. Advicer stores the data returned by the reading data method of web service before executing the business logic, and select the data which should bee updated into databases. Then it calls the updating data method of web service to store the selected data after the business logic captures SQL exceptions.

4) Delete: deleting the data from databases is a write operation, and it also need transaction management to provide security and consistency. Advicer stores the data of the reading data method of web service before executing the business logic, and Reads the data which should be updated into Advicer. Then it calls the update data method of the web service to store the data after the business logic captures SQL exceptions.

The operations of above have realized the consistency and durability of the transaction characteristics, also achieved the atomicity on macroscopically.

6   Conclusions

In this paper, we propose a solution to provide transactions in Web service. The solution performs very well on the simulation of transaction processing, and it is not realize the perfect goal to manage the business. However, it could be used as a glancing reference for the other researchers.

References

1. Web Service Workgroup [S/OL], http://www.w3.org/2002/ws/
2. Web Services Transaction (WS - Transaction) Specification [S/OL], http://www.ibm.com/developerworks/library/ws-transpec
3. Gan, Z.B., Li, Z.X., Peng, B.: Research on Multi-heterogeneous Integrated Model. Application Research of Computers 20(10), 16–18 (2003)
4. Chai, X.L., Y.: Web Services technology, framework and Application. Publishing House of Electronics Industry (2003)
5. Li, Z.Y.: The new progresses of database technologies. Tsinghua University Press
6. Shi, S.: Application Integration of Distributed Heterogeneous System Based on Web Services. Microcomputer Information, 7–3 (2005)

The Aircraft Sonic Feature Extraction Based on the Daubechies(dbN)

Nuan Song, Xingwen Dong, Jihang Cheng, and Yang Jiao

Air Force Aviation University, Chang Chun, JiLin, China
{Bluebirdsong,dongxingwen,jiaoyang}@163.com,
cjhahang@yahoo.com.cn

Abstract. This paper mainly based on Daubechies(dbN)the wavelet analysis of aircraft audio feature extraction. The aircraft passive sonic detects and identification technology as a traditional means of reconnaissance is an important component of airborne early-warning system. Based on the two kinds of battlefields targets about the audio spectrum characteristics , using the characteristic pick-up arithmetic of the wavelet decomposition measure detail signal domain energy which is based on wavelet theory, and using this algorithm obtains lower-dimensional feature vector.

Keywords: Aircraft, Audio Signal, Features Extraction, Wavelet Analysis, Pattern Recognition.

1 Introduction

The aircraft sonic feature target recognition belongs to the category of pattern recognition, as shown in Fig. 1 shows, pattern recognition system mainly divided into data acquisition, pretreatment, feature extraction and selection, classification and decision-making four parts.

Fig. 1. Diagram Aircraft Sonic Feature Target Identification System

In the aircraft passive sonic feature recognition system, target recognition is key to the feature extraction and classifier design. Among them, the feature extraction was more key, it had decided the classifier classification effect quality. The more information contained in the category from the eigenvector from feature extraction, the less information will be interfered, the effect of classification will be better.

M. Zhao and J. Sha (Eds.): ICCIP 2012, Part II, CCIS 289, pp. 148–155, 2012.
© Springer-Verlag Berlin Heidelberg 2012

2   Aircraft Audio Characteristic Analysis

2.1   The Armed Helicopter Target Audio Characteristic Analysis

The causes of the armed helicopter noise is very complicated. The noise characteristics of the armed helicopter mainly consists of three parts, namely the rotor noise, tail rotor noise and engine noise. Among them, the engine noise is a broadband high-frequency noise[1], it is different from the main rotor and the tail rotor noise, it must be treated separately. Because of its energy partial collection in high frequencies, in the far field air attenuated fast, this paper does not consider the impact. So the rotor noise (including tail rotor) became the main noise source of detection system. The tail rotor noise generating mechanism and estimation methods is the basic same as the main rotor. From the analysis of the results look: the noise spectrum of the helicopter from discrete spectrum and broadband spectrum composition, it is a typical noise spectrum which on the basis of the broadband spectrum superimposed a series of discrete spectrum.

The rotor noise includes spin noise and broadband noise. The rotor spin noise is caused by the load periodic disturbance and blades thickness. When role in the lift of the blades and resistance with blades in different position and cyclical change, the surrounding air force with blades rotate together and presents to periodic disturbance. Thickness noise is caused by the thickness of the blades. Through the blades rotate, the thickness of the blades forced displacement periodic filling the volume of a gas around, from this the noise produced. The rotor broadband noise is the main role in the blades pulse power on random and cause.

Predictably, the typical helicopters noise spectrum is based in broadband noise superimposed on a series of discrete linear spectrum, the Frequency of the linear spectrum were respectively leaf through the frequency BPF (Blade Passing Frequency) and its every harmonic frequency. The main energy of the helicopter noise is generally concentration in the 1000 Hz less than. At low frequency (10-100 Hz), Lord propeller noise is dominant, noise occurs in the BPF and every harmonic; At the medium frequency band (100-500 Hz) the main contribution of noise is from the tail rotor, noise occurs in the tail rotor BPF and every harmonic; At the higher frequency band, noise present broadband characteristics[2]. The helicopter flying state of the audio signal waveform time domain is shown in Fig. 2.

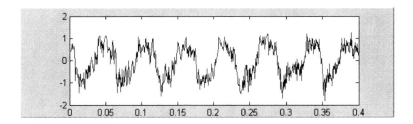

Fig. 2. The helicopter flight state audio signal waveform time domain

2.2   Fighter Planes Target Audio Characteristic Analysis

The aircraft noise is all kinds of the acoustic radiation comprehensive when the aircraft flight. The aircraft noise is basically divided into two kinds, namely the propulsion system noise and air dynamic noise. The propulsion system noise is including the propeller noise, jet noise, fan/compressor noise, turbine noise and combustion noise, etc[3]. Air power noise is caused by blowing air flow through the air pressure produced disturbance, also called the noise. For different types of aircraft, the noise source in the plane of the proportion of the total noise is not the same. In the case of fighter, the noise is mainly from the aircraft noise, fan/compressor noise and jet noise etc.

The noise mainly contains: the wing and the rear wing noise, landing device noise, rear edge flap noise and front wing noise seam. In normal flight condition, the main noise is from the wing broadband noise. The grooves and the discrete points in the smooth surface produce the low frequency pure tone. About the Large High-Bypass Ratio Turbofan Aeroengine for contemporary, fan/compressor noise has a prominent place. For high speed rotating fan/compressor, discrete noise is dominant. The interference in the leaf between the rotor and the stator interaction produce cyclical change unsteady aerodynamic is fan/compressor discrete noise generation principal principle. The jet noise generation is when the rest of the jet flows into or slower airflow velocity, the jets around the rest of the media and relatively sharp mixed, thus make the jet boundary layer formed in the strongly turbulent pulse. Gas of the need to change the momentum by force to balance and in no solid boundary of pure air flow, the forces of change is caused by the pressure change, flow pressure in the area and cause density ups and downs, it spread to the flow of the regions outside the media, they form a jet mixture noise[4].

Fighters noise signal is from a low frequency to high frequency broadband signal, the main energy concentrated in the low frequency (500 Hz below), for medium, low continuous spectrum, within 800 Hz the low frequency is obviously characteristic peak. The medium frequency noise is by higher harmonic caused by extension. The time domain noise signal waveform of fighter planes flying noise is shown in Fig. 3.

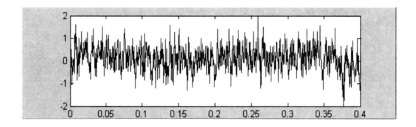

Fig. 3. The fighter flight state audio signal waveform time domain

This paper focused on two kinds of aircraft, attacking helicopters and a certain type of fighters, using the wavelet analysis method. First, the multi-resolution analysis nature by using wavelet transform, After 10 a layer of decomposition from the passive audio signal of the aircraft, extract the wavelet coefficients from every layer. Finally, calculate the energy of each layer, then take the power for normalization. get the vector after the three steps as the characteristics vector of aircraft target[5].

3   Based on Daubechies (dbN) Thewavelet Analysis

Fighter planes, helicopters audio signal is a kind of non-stationary process. Therefore, the audio signal analysis needs to be a suitable tools for non-stationary process signal processing. The characteristics of the wavelet transform has decided, it is very suitable for analysis of passive audio signal of the Fighter planes and helicopter fighters. The wavelet analysis method is a window size (namely the window size) fixed but its shape can change, time window and frequency window are may change the time-frequency localization analysis method. That is in the low frequency part provided with high frequency resolution and low time resolution, in the high frequency part has high time resolution and low frequency resolution, so is known as math microscope. Because of this characteristics ,the wavelet transform has the adaptability to signal. The time-frequency window shape after the wavelet transform has for the two rectangular $[b-a\Delta\Psi,b+a\Delta\Psi]\times$ $\left[(\pm\omega_0-\Delta\hat{\Psi})/a,(\pm\omega_0+\Delta\hat{\Psi})/a\right]$, window center for $(b,\pm\omega_0/a)$, window and frequency window wide is respectively for $a\Delta\Psi$ and $\Delta\hat{\Psi}/a$. Which b only affect the time axis position of window in phase plane, which a not only influence in a window on the shaft frequency position, also influence the shape of the window. So the wavelet transform to different frequency of sampling in time domain is the step length of regulatory, namely in low frequency wavelet transform time resolution is poorer, and high frequency resolution; When in the high frequency of wavelet transform time resolution is higher, and low frequency resolution, that is in the low frequency signal changes slowly and the characteristics of the high frequency signal change quickly.

This paper is mainly adopt with the Daubechies wavelet function to the passive audio signals flying to make the wavelet analysis. Daubechies function is the world famous by wavelet analysis scholars Inrid Daubechies constructed wavelet function, besides db1 (i.e. haar wavelet) outside, other wavelet no clear expression, but the conversion function of square mould h was very clear. Hypothesis:

$$P(y) = \sum_{k=0}^{N-1} C_k^{N-1+K} y^k$$

Among them, C_k^{N-1+K} is for the coefficient of binomial, then:

$$\left|m_0(\omega)^2\right| = (\cos^2 \frac{\omega}{2})^N P(\sin^2 \frac{\omega}{2}) \tag{3.1}$$

Among them,

$$m_0(\omega) = \frac{1}{\sqrt{2}} \sum_{k=0}^{2N-1} h_k e^{-kw} \tag{3.2}$$

The effectively support of the length wavelet function ψ and the scale functions of Φ is 2N-1, the order of wavelet vanishing moment of the wavelet function ψ is N. dbN mostly don't have symmetry[6]; For some wavelet function, asymmetry is obvious. Regular characteristic with serial number N increased. At the same time, the function is orthogonal. Daubechies wavelet function offers more effective analysis and comprehensive than Haar function. Daubechies department of wavelet base notes for dbN, N is for serial number, and N = 1, 2, ..., 10.

4   The Aircraft Audio Signal Feature Extraction

The wavelet transform can be described as a function $f(t) \in L^2(R)$ through the bandpass filter output response. Therefore, the wavelet transform will change a signal into a logarithmic coordinates with the same size of multimodal band set. The resolution cells with scale factor d change and change, when a more hours, the frequency domain distinguish performance is poorer, time domain distinguish performance is better; When a increases, the frequency domain distinguish performance increases[7], and the time domain resolution is reduced. The wavelet transform due to its good time scale positioning properties, make it not only can well reflect the characteristics of the signal frequency domain, but also can be well gived its time domain of the description, therefore, by using wavelet transform extracted features has stability.

The wavelet transform is the essence of the original signal filtration process, the wavelet function selection is different, the decomposition results are different. But no matter how to select the wavelet function, each decomposition scale of filter center frequency and bandwidth used a fixed proportion, it will have the so-called "constant Q" characteristics. So the space of the smooth signal and detail signal can provide the original signal frequency when local information, especially it can provide different frequency band on the structure of the information signal. If the different scale of signal decomposition for energy out, then can according to scale these to an order form feature vector for identify with. This is the basic principle which based on wavelet transform to extract the multi-scale space energy characteristics. For microphones, the battlefield target radiation noise contains the distribution of the energy spectrum and the size the of goal, shape and type closely related. Therefore, after the wavelet decomposition of the scale space can be thought of as the energy distribution is the essential characteristics of target, used for recognition.

In theory, can use any form of the wavelet function to decomposition the target signal. In order to calculate and reduce the characteristic dimension, here using the binary wavelet transform to extract the energy on the scale space distribution. Among them, the binary wavelet decomposition process can use Mallat fast algorithm to realize. Specific multi-scale space energy distribution characteristics and the extraction of target recognition process flow is shown in Fig. 4. Among them, the time-frequency pretreatment process is to the aircraft audio signal energy normalization. If the last identification results insufficient ideal, can go to the mutual close process, then the energy of the normalized. Selected parts of scale space of energy characteristic vector, is mainly refers to choose those relatively concentrated energy of the scale of the space. This can make full use of aircraft audio signals prior information, make the main energy target signal characteristics can strengthen, and can reduce the characteristic dimension, speed up the classification speed. But if a priori information is not clear or for reducing the characteristic dimension classification has ability to reduce[8], so it should still composition of the final characteristic vector with all scale space energy.

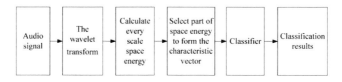

Fig. 4. Based on the wavelet transform multi-scale space energy feature extraction

In this paper using the wavelet Daubechies respectively, the two types of aircraft target level 10 data the scale of wavelet decomposition is calculated, and all of the scale space normalization energy. Set e_j to the first level of detail space scale j energy, the scales of energy level 10 characteristic vector can be expressed as:

$$F = (e_1, e_2, e_3, e_4, e_5, e_6, e_7, e_8, e_9, e_{10})\qquad(4.1)$$

Signal subspace of energy in each can be expressed as:

$$E_j = \sum_{k=0}^{n_j} (d_{j,k})^2 \qquad(4.2)$$

In the expression, n_j is the coefficients for j layer wavelet. Then, using $e_j = E_j / E_{max}$, make the subspace energy normalization[9], among them $E_{max} = \max(E_j)$.

Table 1. Helicopter and fighter characteristic vector extraction one of the results

Each scale detail signal energy normalization value				
Helicopter **1**	**2**	**3**	**4**	**5**
0.1004	0.0850	0.0810	0.1204	0.2788
6	**7**	**8**	**9**	**10**
1.0000	0.2000	0.1977	0.2385	0.2225
Fighter **1**	**2**	**3**	**4**	**5**
1.0000	0.1636	0.2827	0.1004	0.0535
6	**7**	**8**	**9**	**10**
0.0182	0.0555	0.1102	0.1518	0.1189

Table 1 data isn't intuitive enough, and make this data direct, helicopters and fighter jets were made the scale of energy distribution histogram respectively, shown in Fig. 5. We can see, the scale energy distribution of helicopters and fighter is different obvious, audio signal wavelet decomposition scale details signal energy distribution can be used to characterize the characteristics of target indeed. Therefore, the energy from the scale as a aircraft audio features is feasible.

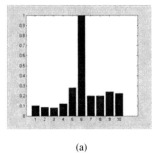   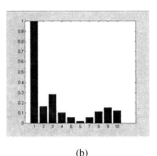

(a)   (b)
(a) The helicopter each scale energy distribution   (b) The energy distribution scale fighter

Fig. 5. Two kinds of aircraft each scale energy distribution

5 Conclusion

This paper mainly studied the aircraft audio feature extraction based on the wavelet analysis. The feature extraction using db2 wavelet, the signal is 10 layer decomposition, extract the every layer of the scale of coefficient, and calculated the different scale of energy decomposition signal, then normalized. Make a group of the normalized data after a histogram, the difference is obvious that using wavelet analysis can be used to extract the characteristics of aircraft audio signal recognition. Finally, make these power forming feature vector according to the scale order for the following classifier design and recognition.

References

1. Jain, A.K., Duin, R.P.W.: Statistical Pattern Recognition:A Review. IEEE Transactions on Pattern Analysis and Machine Intelligence 22(1), 4–37 (2000)
2. Al-Taani, A.T.: An Efficient Feature Extraction Algorithm for the Recognition of Handwritten Arabic Digits
3. Blumenstein, M., Verma, B., Basli, H.: A Novel Feature Extraction Technique for the Recognition of Segmented Handwritten Characters. In: Proceedings of the Seventh International Conference on Document Analysis and Recognition, ICDAR 2003 (2003)
4. Shmulevich, I., Yli-Harja, O., Coyle, E.: Perceptual Issues in Music Pattern Recognition:Complexity of Rhythm and Key Finding. Computers and the Humanities 35, 23–35 (2001)

5. Spannnenburg, L., Slump, C.: Preparing for Knowledge Extraction in Modular Neural Networks. In: Proc.3rd IEEE Benelux Signal Processing Symposium (SPS 2002), Leuven, Belgium (2002)
6. Guan, S.-U., Li, S., Tan, S.K.: Neural Network Task Decomposition Based on Output Partitioning. Journal of The Institution of Engineers 44(3) (2004)
7. Zheng, Z.R., Zhong, W.J., AnKe, X.: Passive sound detection nets data simulation system design and implementation. Hangzhou University of Electronic Science and Technology Journal 25(2), 33–36 (2005)
8. Moreaut, F., Gibertt, D.: Wavelet analysis of potential fields. Inverse Problems 13, 165–178 (1997)
9. Smith, T.F., Waterman, M.S.: Identification of Common Molecular Subsequences. J. Mol. Biol. 147, 195–197 (1981)

Multi-parameter Multi-objective Algorithm to Solve VRP

Jianhua Zhang[1] and Zhe Zhang[2]

[1] General Education Center
Beijing Normal University Zhuhai Campus, P.R. China
zhuhaijianhua@yahoo.com.cn
[2] Technical Logistics, University Duisburg-Essen,
Duisburg, Germany
engel_2002@msn.com

Abstract. First of all, the paper simply describes the VRP (Vehicle Routing Problem), and systematically describes the classification of the "ant colony algorithm and logistics solutions". Finally, this article details the multi-parameter multi-objective algorithm and program design.

Keywords: Ant Colony Algorithms, TSP, VRP, Logistics management.

1   Introduction

Traveling Salesman Problem, TSP, the first description is to study the knight tour problem in 1759 for Euler (Swiss mathematician and physicist).

Vehicle routing problem (VRP) was first proposed by Dantzig and Ramser in 1959, it refers to a certain number of customers, each with a different number of goods demand, distribution centers to provide customers with the goods, by a team responsible for distribution of goods, organization of appropriate traffic routes, the goal is to make the customer's needs are met, and under certain constraints, to achieve the shortest distance, minimum cost, least time-consuming and so on purpose.

The TSP is a special case of VRP, due to Gaery has proved the TSP problem is NP-hard, therefore, the VRP is one of NP. Since 1959,the vehicle routing problem be proposed, it has been one of the most fundamental problems in the network optimization problem, due to its wide application and significant economic value, it has been subject to extensive attention from scholars.

About TSP and VRP, the two issues seem to have similarities, but after careful analysis, we will find is very different between the two. The latter is be solved, but must be have subject to many conditions, the algorithm of which belongs to solve the problem of multiple parameters, that is a much more complex problem.

In reality, transportation logistics companies plan a programs of the actual logistics and distribution, will be affected by a variety of constraints, such as: certain goods in transit are not allowed to mix load, there are transit time limits for certain goods, LTL cargo to used transit mode, the optimal path selection, the design of multi-start node and multi-objective node and so on. With the expansion of scale of operations, the

M. Zhao and J. Sha (Eds.): ICCIP 2012, Part II, CCIS 289, pp. 156–162, 2012.
© Springer-Verlag Berlin Heidelberg 2012

algorithm will be more complex, the program design will be had more difficulty. The reality of Transportation and distribution programs is belong of the multi-parameters multi-objective algorithm to solve VRP.

The use of ant colony algorithm to solve the VRP, is only in recent years has proposed research topic. The difficulty does not lie in the difficulty of ant colony algorithm, but in logistics management, the transport and distribution plan are face the more conditions and requirements is too complicated. In fact, using different search options, there will be some differences in the results obtained. Also, the algorithm optimization and efficiency is very different too.

Based of our recent research work on this, we propose, this solution can be called the ACALDS(Ant Colony Algorithms and Logistics Distribution Solutions).

2   Transport Distribution of the Basic Plan and Program

In order to facilitate depth to study algorithm and program design, by means of the related concepts of mathematics, we divided them as the following three types: "Single-parameter single-target algorithm"; "Multi-parameter single-objective algorithm"; Multi-parameter multi-objective algorithm".

3   Multi-parameter Multi-objective Algorithm and Program Design Features

We introduced four questions.

3.1   The Choice of Starting Point

Since we have the goods transported to other nodes in the node called "starting node", then when a transport and distribution orders have more than one "starting node" in the case, how should we arrange transport tool? Of course the transport and distribution work is the sequential arrangement according some principles. The principles are as follows.

To better illustrate the specific algorithms and programming, we call the node is the "first node" that will be arranged transportation task at first. The node with the basic conditions is: first, there are more goods or goods to be transported to other receiving point (the node is often the largest cargo assembled and forward node). Second, that is the "Bus Terminal" node, that is, in order to complete transport task, all transport vehicles are starting from this node to other node. After completed their task, all vehicles must return to this node and wait for the next batch of orders arrangement.

3.2   Priority Arrange the Orders That Had Special Required

In a transport distribution orders, may be some task request transport goods are not allowed to mix, or have time constraints and so on. According to different levels, we will write it into the "Priority Task List". All of the statistics completed, according the priority right of each task to arrange the transportation task. Task completed, all of the empty trucks don't need return to the start node, to stop and waiting for the other transport tasks on this node.

3.3   Accordance with the Full Load Mode to Arrangement All Other Nodes Transport Task

At First, accordance with the full load mode to arrangement the "first node" transport task, to send goods from the first node to other nodes. Arrange principles are: according of the size of the vehicle fully loaded descending order to arrange and processing, until the goods to send is zero, or the surplus goods is LTL. LTL transportation will be processed using another ways. After completed their task, all vehicles must return to this node and wait for the next batch of orders arrangement.

The next step should plan all of the other nodes using the full load transport task.

The Planning all of the Another Nodes Using the Full Load Transport Task
Every other node, there may be two cases, the first possibility this node is no goods to send to other nodes. The second possibility this node had received another nodes goods. We will deal the transport task of each node, following one by one. Specific operations are: the current node are known as the "current starting node", the current starting node if there are transport vehicles ("first node" node cargo had been sent to this node, the vehicle has not been returned), we can arrange these vehicles join to the current starting node vehicle transport task. If this is a not transport task node or the vehicles is too little to not meet by the current starting node full load goods, then must using vehicles of another node. The selected node should have the following conditions: The first condition is the node is from the "current starting node" more close proximity, the second condition is there are empty transport vehicles in this node, and the vehicle model is exactly suitable for use. The third condition is that if this node having goods will be transported to the "current starting node", that of course is the best. In addition to these three conditions, if the node is selected from the "current starting point" relatively close to (but not recently), but it is the node suitable the conditions 1, 2 and 3, it can also be selected. Of course, the "relatively close" standard, we can set a default value in the program.

According to the above two steps, we can complete all the nodes of the vehicle fully loaded transport tasks.

3.4   LTL Freight

When the full load vehicle transport is completed, each node has three characteristics: One is: this node there is no transport task to another node, or only a little LTL awaiting delivery to the other nodes. The second is the weight of LTL is less than the cargo volume of minimum truck. Third, this node is another node's transport target, at least there are empty trucks can transport goods to another nodes, or this node is not the end of the transport of goods, then the node does not have any empty truck, then this transport task need to use the neighboring nodes truck. Based on three characteristics above, take the following search methods are more.

First, the searching method still based on multi-parameter single-task algorithm.

Second, from the "first node" start node, according of the "loading merged" method handles LTL business.

Third, we processed LTL transport task of all of other node subsequently, excepting the "first node".

Fourth, each node LTL transport work is completed, the entire batch transport arrangements in place. Finally, each node empty truck will be return to "the first starting point", and calculated all the no-load transportation costs.

After calculating the total no-load transportation cost, can then in accordance with certain principles, sharing to every the transport customer.

4   Practical Issues Affecting Transportation Costs

The following conditions need to pay attention.

4.1   Trucks Cargo Capacity

Logistics companies should configure what kind of cargo capacity truck will save transportation costs? This seems to be a "Does not matter" thing, but it is not true.

We first analyze the things around us. The current market circulation in China, there is 13 kinds of par the "yuan". Cardinality of the various denominations is 1, 2, 5, people clearly understand that no 3, 4, 6, 7, 8, 9 number of nominal value. Why is this?

It turned out that in the 1 - 10 of these 10 natural numbers, people divide them into two categories, that is "important number" and "non-important number" two. 1, 2, 5, 10 is the "important number". The "important number" characteristics is that will be able to least the addition and subtraction combinations, composed other number. Such as 1 +2 = 3, 2 +2 = 4, 1 +5 = 6, 2 +5 = 7, 10-2 = 8, 10-1 = 9. If you use any of a "non-important numbers" instead of the four "important number", it will need more than two the addition and subtraction combinations, composed other number. That is tedious operations. A greater negative impact is, in order to keeping the normal circulation of RMB in the market, you need to produce more number of RMB. The increased number of results will lead to the issuance of RMB costs of natural increase in ancillary costs (storage, transport related labor management costs, equipment and energy consumption, etc.) Naturally increases.

Similarly, the value of amount of lorry laden is different to "important number" and "non-important number" two, only different is, in the 10 natural numbers, the important number is 1, 2, 5, 8. This is ideal solution. At most configure up to 2 kinds of models to transport, can guarantee and meet a 1-10 (integer) tonnage cargo transport. At most, configure up to 4 kinds models to transport, can guarantee and meet the 1-100(integer) tonnage cargo transport. Because the goods at full load transportation, transportation costs is the least. So the most ideal truck cargo capacity is the 0.1,0.2,0.5,0.8,1,2,5,8,10,20,50,80 ton.

Please note that the mathematical relationship:

$$N = 2 \times f \tag{1}$$

Which, N is the needing of largest number of transport vehicles; f is the right value of the Decimal number.

4.2   The Sum of Costs Should Include the Cost of No-Load Transport

It goes without saying that the no-load transportation costs that must be considered. Of course, different types of vehicles, their no-load transportation costs are different. Depending on the circumstances, it is converted into correlation coefficients or right weights, reflected in the above transportation and distribution solution.

4.3   The Complexity of the Transport Situation Will Affect the Cost of Transportation

Road grades and road conditions, locations, altitudes and even the status of the weather, all of them will affect the transportation cost. Depending on the circumstances, it be converted into correlation coefficients (right weights), or as the third parameter reflected in the transportation and distribution solution. Of course, if as the third parameter to deal with, the overall algorithm and program design will be more complex.

5   Preliminary Analysis the Complexity of the Algorithm

First, we can assume that all transportation tasks as a node N are the order of the queue, with that the "Nn". Suppose there are 10 nodes:

$$Nn \mid n = 1; 2; 3; \dots 10; \tag{2}$$

M stands the number of the type of the variety of trucks, stands the number of the load of the variety trucks.

Suppose there are four types of trucks, there are:

$$G_M = 1; 2; 3; 4 \tag{3}$$

If we can freely use various types of vehicles laden with a cargo mode, so, loading methods are

$$F_M = 4 \ ! \tag{4}$$

Because there are a variety of loading methods, the cost of the transport vehicle is a different value.

After the fully loaded transport, the remaining LTL goods may be different, even, have all been transported to be completed. Of course, this is the best idea. It allows we get maximum transport efficiency.

Second, we analyze the vehicle fully loaded or similarly to fully loaded situation.

W_n stands a certain node LTL weight, n still assume that the number of nodes, and set initial value is 10, there are the LTL cargo weight to each node:

$$W_n \mid n=1; \ 2; \ 3; \ \cdots 10 \tag{5}$$

According to general conditions:

$$W_n < G_M \tag{6}$$

And

$$\sum_{n}^{m} W_n \le G_M \tag{7}$$

Then according to the mathematical permutations and combinations formula,

$$C_n^m = \frac{n!}{m!(n-m)!} \tag{8}$$

Can have a variety of loading combinations of:

$$1 \le C_n^m \le \frac{n!}{m!(n-m)!} \tag{9}$$

Third, in order to obtain the best efficiency, to get the actual distance between two points is different. In accordance with the formula of permutations and combinations can have a variety of paths as follows?

$$p = \frac{n!}{(n-m)!} \tag{10}$$

Fourth, more complex, in the actual transport, often in the outside the initial starting point, there are goods prepared want to transport to other node. Namely, to use the Loading merge method, the tonnage of actual task is different in each path, because there are amount of different loading and unloading to other node. Thus, there are more kinds of transportation options.

Each node can have up to $\frac{n!}{m!(n-m)!}$ kinds Loading merge method of transport, we said it using M_N then there are different options, we said it using N:

$$N= M_1 \times M_2 \times ... \times M_N \tag{11}$$

This is more complex option, will bring out the greater difficulty in programming and design in order to solve the VRP.

6   Conclusions

Described above, the work in the search process, all of data are interrelated, and, the data is always changing. Through programming, control this task processes, and ultimately we can get the satisfaction results. Of course, the program design is essential. And it is a very important aspect.

References

1. Haibin, D.: Ant Colony Algorithm and its Applications. Sciences Press, China (2005); ISBN 978-7-03-016204-5
2. Cao, C., Wang, N.: Intelligent Computing. Tsinghua University Press, China (2004); ISBN7-302-09412-8/TP.6570
3. Yun, G.S., Ling, Q.W.: Discrete Mathematics. Higher Education Press, China (2004)
4. Yuan, P., Xu, B.: 2011 6th IEEE Joint International Information Technology and Artificial Intelligence Conference, vol. 2, pp. 424–426 (2011)
5. Toth, P., Vigo, D.: The Vehicle Routing Problem. Society for Industrial and Applied Mathematics, Philadephia (2002)
6. Fisher, M.L.: Vehicle Routing. Handbooks in Operations Research & Management Science 8, 1–33 (1995)
7. Clarke, G., Wright, J.: Scheduling of vehicles from central depot to a number of delivery points. Operations Research 12, 568–581 (1964)
8. Osman, I.H.: Meta-strategy simulated annealing an Tabu search algorithms for the vehicle routin problem. Annu. Oper. Res. 41, 77–86 (1993)
9. Ombuki, B.M., Nakamura, M., Osamu, M.: Ahybri search based on genetic algorithm s and tabu search for vehicle routing. Brock University T echnica Report:#CS-02-07 5, 1–7 (2002)
10. Bent, R., Van Hentenryck, P.: A two-stage hybri local search for the vehicle routing problem with tim windows.Technical Report, CS-01-06, Brown University 9, 1–30 (2001)

Forest Topology Generation Algorithm Based a Metric in Wireless Mesh Networks

Zimian Hao

Hubei Urban Construction Vocational and Technical College,
Hubei, 430075, China
haozimian@yahoo.com.cn

Abstract. This paper proposed a network topology generation strategy based on a metric which consider hops of the node and the expectations transmission times in the topology generation. Based on the metric proposed a algorithm (BMFSP) with low routing cost and congestion control. Especially suit the uniform network environment.

Keywords: Forest topology, wireless mesh networks, load balancing, algorithm.

1 Introduction

To construct a wireless mesh network topology which is of high connectivity and is helpful for channel assignment and routing algorithm is a problem deserving of study. As the actual wireless mesh networks often have multiple gateway nodes through which the nodes complete external network access, a tree topology is formed with each gateway node as the root. The key issue to be discussed in this part is how to effectively select the gateway node to join. When establishing a forest topology, such factors as reliability rate, link quality, delay and interference should be considered, thus a criterion is required to ensure the acceptance and rejection of relevant links.

Aiming at the above-mentioned problems and the bottleneck to network throughput performance in the gateway caused by most of the flows of wireless mesh network going to the internet just through a small amount of gateways after gathering at the backbone routers, the concept of link reuse degree is introduced to reduce routing overhead and attain efficient traffic aggregation. Based on the method of the shortest path tree (SPT), BMFSP algorithm is proposed to realize the congestion control of multi-gateways nodes in wireless mesh networks.

2 Problems Definition and Description

2.1 Network Model

In the network model, Let graph G = (V, E) denotes a backbone network of wireless mesh network. V denotes the set of wireless routers, E denotes the set of wireless

M. Zhao and J. Sha (Eds.): ICCIP 2012, Part II, CCIS 289, pp. 163–170, 2012.
© Springer-Verlag Berlin Heidelberg 2012

links between the nodes, g∈V denotes gateway node, r∈V denotes a node which is not gateway nodes, e∈E denotes a link in the set E, the number of already deployed gateway nodes is M.

2.2   Problem Definition and Description

With a given network graph and the gateway number of network, to solve the forest topology generation method is the aim of this paper.

Literatures [1~3] describes the methods of tree generation for wireless mesh networks, here no longer narrative, but mostly description is based on node degree and the hop from gateway node as topology generation criterion, or simple considering the homogeneous rate of a node, not a very good use of the advantage of multi gateways to come to load balance, resulting in throughput drops, and most general algorithms design for single tree, not fully considering the coordination between the trees. In order to facilitate formal analysis, a series of definitions are given as follows:

Define 1 layer of the node: in a given propagation tree $Tree_i$ (V_i, Ei), the layer of node $r_i \in V_i$ can be expressed as

$$L(r_i) = | L(r_j) + 1 |, r_i, r_j \in V_i \tag{1}$$

r_j is the upper node of r_i, the root node set the layer number is 0.

In general, the distance from a node to gateway is the closer and the delay between the two nodes is the smaller. From gateway node to the following nodes, the breadth first search (BFS) can realize the recent hop, the same hop count nodes is on the same layer.

The quality of a link in Wireless network may measure with expectations transmission times (ETX), the smaller of the ETX then the higher of the link quality, the link which is nearer to the root node will have a greater traffic load, that is, with the BFS method, there is more traffic load between the nodes in the lower layer number and their children, so criterion of the node join a tree can be defined as follows:

Define 2 criterion of the node join a tree: node r_i join the current tree that must meet the following conditions:

$$Min\ \lambda_{ij} = \alpha T_{ij} + (1 - \alpha)L_{ij}, v_i \in V, v_j \in r \tag{2}$$

λ_{ij} denotes the criterion of the node join a tree, the first part in the above formula T_{ij} is ETX of a link $(V_i, V_j) \in E$, to be fair here T can take its average of the history window.

α denotes the weight factor and its value must be picked between 0 and 1. In general it is equal or greater than 0.5, this means that the link quality between nodes is more important in this criterion. So consider reason is that T influences the packet retransmission times, retransmission times are more, and the performance of the system is lower.

3   Forest Topology Formulation

Forest topology generation can be described as a integer programming problem, given M a gateway node, with each gateway node is the root according to certain strategy can generate M tree, resulting in a forest topology. Three optimization targets must achieve: minimize node to gateway's hop and minimize criterion of the node join a tree, through define in the second section it is minimized λ_{ij}. Table 1 shows multi channel assignment model symbols.

Table 1. Related symbol

symbol	signification
λ_{mj}	*criterion of the node join a tree*
L_{mj}	**The layer numbers** *from Node* $v_j \in r$ **to** *gateway node* $g_n \in g$
x_v	*Boolean variable,* x_v **=1** **express the node is gateway, else** x_v **=0**
A_{mj}	*Boolean variable,* A_{mj} **=1** **express the root of node** v_j *is* *gateway* $g_m,$ *else* A_{mj} **=0**
L	*A constant to limit the value of* L_{mj}
M	*The number of gateway nodes*
α	*A constant* **the** *adjustment factor for the weight*

This paper only considers the problem of network topology generation without involving the questions of network nodes deployed , experiment can assume already using literature [5~7] mentioned methods joints, such initial deployment topology generation algorithm can achieve better results.

Then the problem of forest topology generation can describe become integer linear programming optimization problems:

Target function:

$$Min \sum_{g_m \in g, v_j \in r} \lambda_{mj} \tag{3}$$

Constraint condition:

$$\sum_{v \in g} X_v = M \tag{4}$$

$$\sum_{g_m \in g} L_{mj} = 1, \forall v_j \in r \tag{5}$$

$$\sum_{g_m \in g} \sum_{v_j \in r} A_{mj} L_{mj} \leq L \tag{6}$$

$$L_{mi} A_{mi} A_{mj} = \sum L_{mj} A_{mi} A_{mj} + 1, \forall v_j, v_i \in r, (v_i, v_j) \in E, g_m \in g \tag{7}$$

$$T_{ij} \leq \beta \tag{8}$$

$$\lambda_{mj} \geq A_{mj} \sum \alpha T_{mj} + (1 - \alpha) L_{mj}, \forall g_m \in g, v_j \in r \tag{9}$$

$$A_{mj}, X_v \in \{0,1\}, \forall g_m \in g, v_j \in r \tag{10}$$

Constraint (4) ensure the number of trees in forest topology is equal to the number of gateway nodes, constraint (5) there is only one gateway node for any nodes which are not gateway nodes and must have one connection gateway node, this is a necessary condition, constraint (6) is the value limit of node layer, constraint (7) ensure a node and its parent must connect to a same gateway node and the layer value is less than its parent's, this is an other necessary condition for tree topology, constraint(8) is a threshold of the expectations transmission times which ensure the performance of the topology generation, constraint (9) is the criterion of the node join a tree.

A matter worthy of note, the meaning of above constraints (7) is the same as the symbol   in table I, it is used for judging that if have different non-gateway nodes connect with the same gateway node, it is for avoiding quadratic of condition which can lead to nonlinear programming.

4   Forest Topology Algorithm

4.1   BMFSP Algorithm

In a given network, the nodes send a message "Hello" in a public control channel When the system is idle, the node which received the message will regard send-node as their neighbors and save its relevant information, and at the same time reply a Response message back to its neighbor node, so that every node will get their neighbors related topology information in the wireless mesh network. Also every node will send their neighbors topology information through the public channel to each gateway node in a unit time interval, each gateway node combines to obtain the whole wireless mesh network topology information.

In the process of forest and tree network topology construction, one of the most important problems is the standard to choose parent node for a child node, namely the criterion of the node join a tree. Wireless mesh network's main business is between the gateway node and child nodes,, the algorithm based on the definition 2 which is a comprehensive weights about the parameters hop of node to gateway node, link quality and delay. According to the design idea, the process is a top-down method.

For a given wireless mesh network graph G (V, E), algorithm for all nodes will figure G generating an $M \times N$ adjacency matrix, M denotes the number of gateway nodes, N denotes the node which are not gateway nodes. the number in the matrix denotes the L_{mj} ,when there is not path or the path-hop is greater than the constant L, $L_{mj} = \infty$. L value selected should o ensure each node at least have a non infinite weights in the matrix, namely each column of the matrix must exist an effective weights, to ensure all nodes can be added into forest structure. The forest topology algorithms can be simply described as follow:

//Algorithm Forest_BMFSP()

```
Input:G=(V,E), L
Output:BMFSP_Forest
Gnum=n;
Mrnum=m;
Treegi=Null;
BMFSP_Forest=Null;
Xrij=0;
 For i=1 to n Do
For j=1 to m Do
  rij=GetNeighbor(G,i);
   ij=GetMetric(G,L);
  If MinMetric( ij) and Xrij=0 Then
    Treegi=AddTree(gi,rj);
        Xrij=1;
     EndIf
   EndFor
   BMFSP_Forest=BMFSP_Forest•Treegi;
EndFor
```

Function *GetMetric()* is used to calculate and statistics the criterion set of the current node to all of the neighbor node, when there is not exist one direct path or the node layer outnumber limit value, ,function *GetNeighbor()* is used to select neighbor node, function *MinMetric()* is used to judge that if the vule of is the minimum, function *AddTree()* is used to add the current node into a tree.

4.2   Algorithm Time Complexity

BMFSP algorithm time complexity is mainly depended on the number of the nodes in the network, let G denotes the number of gateway nodes, $|V|$ denotes the number of the other nodes in the network, because the runtime of functions *GetNeighbor()* and *MinMetric()* in the algorithm is affected by the neighbors node number $|V|$, so each node has done the above function, the time is O $|V|$), and time complexity of the whole network nodes related with the number of gateways G and the number of nodes $|V|$, so the entire time complexity of the algorithm required for $O(G*|V|^2)$.Because G denotes the number of gateway node generally not great, so this time complexity of the algorithm is mainly depends on the number of the nodes in the network.

Through the comparison with other algorithms, when gateway nodes are far less than the number of the other nodes in the network, the time complexities of algorithms are nearly.

5   Simulation and Comparison

5.1   Simulation Environment

To evaluate the effectiveness of BMFSP algorithm from different aspects, we perform a simulation in the NS2, and compare with BLBFSP and SPT algorithms. Simulation environment is as follows:

In the simulation environment, 100 nodes are randomly and independently distributed in rectangular network domain of 1000×1000 square meters, each node fitted with 2 wireless interface and communications scope is as the same value, By the cbrgen tools randomly generated the stochastic network flow each of node size and carries on normalization processing, L values is equal to 3 in the simulation. In order to verify the algorithm better, algorithm will be in uniform network and non-uniform network two different scenarios to make the comparison. In uniform network, gateway nodes and other nodes are random distributed in the area. And in non-uniform network, 70% gateway nodes and 30% other nodes are disturbed in the left domain. This is to compare the adaptability of different algorithms for different environment. When a given network nodes and gateway nodes number, Simulation randomly generated 20 topology. The final data is data on average of 20 different topology produced.

Here compared BMFSP algorithm performance with BLBFSP and SPT algorithms, increase gateway node number in turn from 2 to 8. When a given network node and gateway node number, simulation randomly generated 20 types of topologies, the average of the data is used.

5.2   Simulation Results Analysis

In the simulation environment described above, by changing the number of gateway nodes to observe the algorithm performance of the BMFSP algorithm, SPT algorithm and BLBFSP algorithm.

Figure 1 shows throughput of network by varying number of gateways in the uniform network environment. No matter which kind of algorithms the network throughput are increasing as the gateways number increasing, this can be as simple proof that the correctness of algorithm. And overall performance varies slightly. This is mainly because three algorithms in different extent consider the basic factors hop-count. While in the uniform network environment, the performance BMFSP algorithm is the best among the other two algorithms, this is mainly because BMFSP algorithm considers not only the hop-count element but also expectations transmission times. When gateway Numbers are from one increased to three, the network throughtput most obviously increases, when gateway node over five, network throughput increasing is slowdown, it is mainly caused by the gateway numbers is to a certain degree, the nodes in network in satisfactory way connected to the gateway node, when gateway node increase to eight, the network throughput reach saturation shows that this network all gathered flow can be successful transmission.

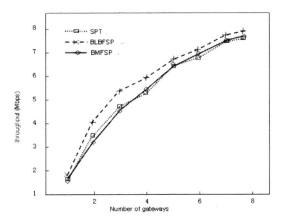

Fig. 1. Throughput by varying number of gateways

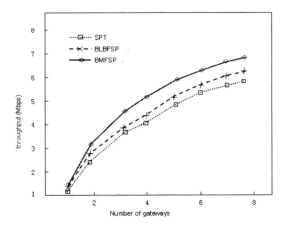

Fig. 2. Throughput by varying number of gateways

Compared with Figure 1 in the uniform network environment, in non-uniform network environment figure 2, compared with figure 1, performance of three methods overall declined, the main reason is nodes distribution uneven and cause of forest structure produced to be a serious imbalance. Leading the domain of gateway to hot spots for data transmission, and the other nodes are too free. Through the observation can see, in non-uniform distribution network environment the performance of BMFSP algorithm than other two algorithms has obvious advantages, the main reason is SPT and BLBFSP algorithms mainly are based on network node to gateway hop count as the main judgment standard node for topology generation, but the BLBFSP algorithm maintain certain stability.

6   Conclusion and Future Work

This paper researches the forest topology generation problem, based on the expectations transmission times and the node layer, proposed a metric for a node join to a tree, and by the metric proposed the forest topology generation scheme. BMFSP algorithm in addition to consider distance from gateway node hops factors, but also selects the parent node to link with the metric. Experimental results show that the proposed algorithm can effectively deal with different network environment, especially in the uniform network environment improves the network performance. The next work is going to combine channel allocation strategies with topology, further improve the performance of wireless mesh network.

References

1. Park, J.C., Kasera, S.K.: Expected data rate: an accurate high-throughput path metric for multi-hop wireless routing. In: IEEE Communications Society Conference on Sensor and Ad Hoc Communications and Networks (SECON 2005), pp. 218–228. IEEE Press, Santa Clara (2005)
2. KyaSanur, P., Vaidya, N.H.: Routing and Interface Assignment in Multi-Channel Multi-Interface Wireless Networks. In: Proceedings of IEEE WCNC 2005, pp. 205–2056. IEEE Press, New Orleans (2005)
3. Malekesmaeili, M., Shiva, M., Soltan, M.: Topology optimization for backbone wireless mesh networks. In: Communication Networks and Services Research Conference (CNSR), pp. 221–230 (May 2007)
4. Gupta, P., Kumar, P.R.: The Capacity of Wireless Networks. IEEE Transactions on Information Theory 46(2), 388–404 (2000)
5. Aoun, B., Boutaba, R., Iraqi, Y., Kenward, G.: Gateway placement optimization in wireless mesh networks with QoS Constraints. IEEE Journal on Selected Areas in Communications 24(11), 2127–2136 (2006)
6. Li, F., Wang, Y., Li, X.-Y.: Gateway Placement for throughput optimization in wireless mesh networks. In: IEEE International Conference on Communications (ICC), Scotland, pp. 24–28 (June 2007)
7. Papadaki, K., Friderikos, V.: Gateway selection and routing in wireless mesh networks. Computer Networks, 319–329 (2010)

The High-Speed Data Acquisition System Based on LabVIEW and PCI

Yinhan Gao[1,2], Junjie Gu[2], Kaiyu Yang[1,2], Rongjiang Tang[2], Litong Zhang[2], Tianhao Wang[2], RuiminZhou[2], and Bing Song[2]

[1] State Key Laboratory of Automobile Simulation and Control, Jilin University, Changchun 130026, China
[2] College of Instrumentation & Electrical Engineering, Jilin University, Changchun 130026, China
yinhan@jlu.edu.cn, gujunjiesimon@126.com

Abstract. In order to meet the requirements of acquiring transient signal, a high-speed data acquisition system which is based on virtual instrument platform LabVIEW and PCI data acquisition card has been developed. The system achieves the functions of synchronous data acquisition, signal noise reduction, data storage and real-time display for multi-channel analog voltage signal and digital signal. In the application of balloon burst test results show that: the system can effectively complete the task of data acquisition, data processing, data storage and display for transient signal in a synchronized and high-speed way with convenient operation, stable and reliable performance, high accuracy and strong practical applicability in engineering application.

Keywords: LabVIEW, transient signal, high-speed, data acquisition, synchronous.

1 Introduction

In modern industrial control and monitoring, the data acquisition system plays a significant role. It is the link between the external physical world and computer. In practice, different test occasions have different requirements to the data acquisition system. For example, the object being measured has short duration (ms level) and the cost of testing is high in the tests of airbag explosion, explosive, missile-launching and so on, which requires the data acquisition system could collect the most effective data in a very short period of time, but the traditional instruments could not meet this requirement. This article describes a high-speed data acquisition system with the function of synchronized acquisition which is designed by NI Company's PCI data acquisition card and LabVIEW software platform. The system is based on 32-bit PCI bus architecture, the maximum sampling rate could reach to $2\,MS/S$, and it can acquire 8-channel channel differential analog input signal and 2-channel counter input signal simultaneously.

M. Zhao and J. Sha (Eds.): ICCIP 2012, Part II, CCIS 289, pp. 171–178, 2012.

2   The Design of Hardware

According to the characteristics of the signal being measured and combining the advantages of LabVIEW, the system chooses NI PCI-6133 card as the core of collection which is responsible for data acquisition and sending the data to the computer and the computer which is installed Windows XP as the control center, responsible for receiving data and data processing, storage, waveform display and printing. The PCI-6133 card is superior in quality and the operation is simple. Its main performances are: $3\ MS/S$; 14-bit; 16 single-ended/8 differential analog inputs; synchronous sampling; two 24-bit counters; digital trigger. It can be used in the occasions of realizing synchronized stimulus and response measurement between high-speed continuous data acquisition, analog I/O, digital I/O and counter/timer operations. Hardware structure is shown in Figure 1.

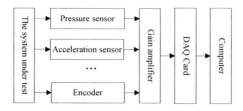

Fig. 1. Hardware structure

3   The Realizing of System Synchronous Acquisition Function

The synchronous data acquisition function is achieved by the acquisition technology and test system of data acquisition card and starting mode of the system being measured.

3.1   The Process of Achieving Multi-channel Synchronous Acquisition

Due to the conversion tasks of multi-channel analog signal are all focused on one piece of A/D chip, the acquisition speed of typical multi-way acquisition and single channel A/D converter data acquisition technology is limited; Secondly, the time of sample holding is so long that the voltage in holding capacitor drops and the error occurs; Furthermore, when using a piece of A/D realizes the multiple signals acquisition, there exists phase difference among each signal and which is not conducive to the instantaneous comparison and analysis of the signals in each channel.

In order to solve these technical deficiencies in the high-speed data acquisition applications, a multi-channel data acquisition technology (Multi-channel Synchronous Data-Acquisition Technique) is proposed [1]. PCI-6133 is built on this technology, the different A/D converters driven by a same sampling clock signal, it can achieve the synchronous data acquisition by setting up multiple data acquisition channels in parallel, this approach is not only conducive to high-speed data acquisition, but also good for the instantaneous signal analysis among different channels. The operating principle of multi-channel simultaneous data acquisition system is shown in Figure 2.

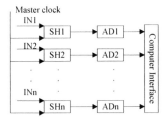

Fig. 2. The operating principle of multi-channel simultaneous data acquisition system

3.2   The Process of Achieving Synchronization between the Test System and the System under Test

In order to ensure not missing any important signals, the typical data acquisition system acquires signal by the way of continuous sampling. This will not only increase the software overhead, but take up computer resources. The concept of Trigger is introduced in order to make data acquisition system can acquire genuine useful signals accurately.

The users need to set specific conditions for starting data collection when collecting data. Only meet the conditions, data acquisition cards begin to collect data. That is the principle of Trigger [2]. The types of Trigger are Post-Trigger, Pre-Trigger, Delay-Trigger and so on. The system chooses Post-Trigger trigger mode, the data card under this mode works as follows: the users issue orders to start collecting, collecting cards waiting for a trigger event, when the TTL signal which has meet the conditions of trigger enters into the data acquisition card, it will drive A/D circuit sampling immediately until the end of the sampling procedure. Post-Trigger trigger mode data acquisition is shown in Figure 3.

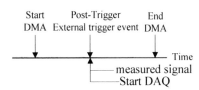

Fig. 3. Data acquisition with Post-Trigger trigger mode

In practice, the trigger (TTL-level output standard) output end is connecting with the trigger end of both data acquisition card and the system being measured, which enables data acquisition and system being tested start simultaneously.

4   The Design of Software

A typical data acquisition system is including data acquisition, analysis and preservation three parts. If these three parts are achieved, the design of system software is done. The followings are take data acquisition and analysis as important points to introduce the design and implementation of software system.

4.1   The Design and Implementation of Data Acquisition Module

Using LabVIEW to realize data acquisition is to control PCI-6133 completing a specific function under the support of DAQ mx driver. DAQ mx driver function is given in the form of sub-VI; through this sub-VI, it can access to the underlying registers easily, and conduct I/O operations to acquisition card directly. The software flow chart of data acquisition system is shown in Figure 4.

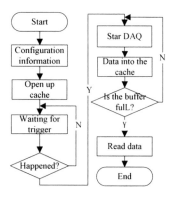

Fig. 4. Data acquisition flow chart

Master some important functions before writing acquisition procedure:

DAQ mx Create Task function: to create a single or multiple virtual channels, and add it to the task, DAQ support multi-channel setup tasks and multiple channels can set up a task. The polymorphism inputs are available to VI, such as analog input/output, counter input / output and so on.

DAQ mx Read function: read user-specified task or virtual channel data, the polymorphic VI can return to the different sample formats.

DAQ mx Timing function: configurate the samples which are going to be obtained or generated, and create the required buffer. Rate port appoints per channel a specified sampling rate f; samples per channel port setting up the number of samples N for each channel. These two parameters determine the time span of DAQ card sampling, the sampling time $t = N * 1 / f$.

DAQ mx Trigger function: a variety of triggers and trigger types of configuration tasks.

LabVIEW data acquisition has limited sampling and cycle sampling two sampling methods; the limited sample used for high-speed data acquisition applications, and the cycle sampling used for the occasions of slow signal conversion and low sampling rate. Combining the features of system, the limited sampling approach is applied.

System is only related to A/D converter for the collection of analog voltage and the measurement methods are continuous acquisition and limited collection. While the acquisition of speed is the acquisition of pulse value, the pulse value is the square wave which is made of high level and low level exported by encoder. There are a variety of measurement methods, but the high frequency (with 2 Counters) and low frequency (with 1 counter) methods are often being used in test actually. However, the measurement of pulse is not support triggering and also the displayed set clock. In order to solve this problem, the sequence structure function was added, just like Figure 5. Only when the trigger event occurs, the procedure can implement the next frame of sequence structure. Mandatory pulse and analog quantity start to collect synchronously making use of sequence structure. And counting and analog inputs share an analog clock, which would address the problem of pulse value does not support the trigger and achieve the collection of analog quantity and pulse value synchronously in software [3].

When write data acquisition program, the main function of analog quantity acquisition is configured to: DAQ mx Create Task function is analog voltage input; DAQ mx Timing function is the limited sampling, the front panel sets the sampling rate and number of samples per channel; DAQ mx Trigger function is the digital edge trigger and the falling edge is effective; DAQ mx read function is analog 1D wave function > N-channel> N samples. The main function of digital pulse acquisition is configured to: DAQ mx create task function is the CI edge count; the sampling rate f and the sampling points N of DAQ mx Timing function are the same with analog quantity and share a sampling clock with analog sampling. Combining analog sampling and digital pulse sampling, the preparation of the sampling procedure is shown in Figure 5.

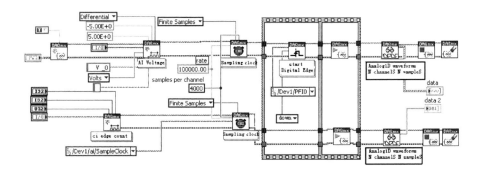

Fig. 5. Data acquisition block diagram

4.2   The Design and Implementation of Data Analysis Module

The Application of Queuing Technology. During the process of high-speed acquisition, we hope that both data acquisition and data analysis can work synchronously and keep relative independent at the same time. To be specific, that is to use multiple concurrent circulation processing different tasks; each cycle has independent thread and they do not interfere with each other. In the high-speed data acquisition, the data collection period is often less than the analysis data cycle. If using a local or global variable reads the variant content of data analysis circulation, the unprocessed data would be covered. In order to solve this problem, the queuing technology was introduced.

Queuing is a FIFO structure which can ensure the ordered data transmission and avoid competition or conflict. Its working principle is like that: the acquisition procedures transmit the collected data to the queue space, analysis program read and analyze the data from queue space, and the data which were not analyzed will be cached in the queue. As long as the queue is not full, it won't lose data. When all data analysis is completed, the program is over [4]. Thus the improved production\consumer model was constituted between collection and analysis procedures, and realizes the ordered transmission of data during the process of high-speed data acquisition. The application of queue was shown in Figure 6.

Signal Noise Reduction. A variety of noises will be inevitably introduced in signal acquisition and transmission process. In order to reduce the effect of noises to experimental results effectively, after the data enter into analysis program, some measures must be taken to reduce noise. Wavelet analysis provides a kind of adaptive analysis method in which the time domain and frequency domain can be localized at the same time and it can automatically adjust the window of time domain no matter analyzing the low frequency local signal or high frequency local signal. An important application of the wavelet analysis is used to signal noise reduction and the noise reduction processing method is:

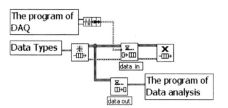

Fig. 6. The application of queuing technology

The first thing is to wavelet decompose the signal, using threshold value and many other forms decompose the wavelet coefficient, its purpose is to reduce or even eliminate the coefficient completely produced by noise and reserve the coefficient of true signals furthest at the same time; then reconstruct the original signal through the processed wavelet coefficient and get a optimal estimation of the real signal, and then achieve the purpose of noise reduction [5]. The definition of wavelet transform is:

$$W_f(a,b) = |a|^{-1/2} \int_R f(t)\psi((t-b)/a)dt \tag{1}$$

In this formula, $f(t)$ is energy limited signal, $a > 0$; $\psi(t)$ is called wavelet generating function, its energy concentrate on the domain which treat t as the center; a is scale parameter and b is displacement parameter. When generating function meet the following enabled condition:

$$C_\Psi = \int_R (|\Psi(w)|^2 / w)dw < +\infty \tag{2}$$

The inverse transformation of wavelet transform exists:

$$f(t) = C_\Psi^{-1} \int_R \int_R W_f(a,b)\psi_{a,b}(t)a^{-2}dadb \tag{3}$$

Among, $Y_{a,b}(t) = a^{-1/2}Y((t-b)/a)$,it can recon figurate the primary signal accurately according to the wavelet coefficient. In the practical application, a and b can only take discrete value, let a=2^j , $b = 2^j k$, binary system wavelet $\psi_{j,k} = 2^{j/2}\psi(2^{-j}t-k), j,k \in Z$, if

$$\int\psi_{j,k}(t)\psi_{m,n}(t) = \begin{cases} 1 & j=m, k=n \\ 0 & other \end{cases} \tag{4}$$

$\psi_{j,k}(t)$ is binary orthogonal wavelet. When in actual noise reduction, the wavelet basis function chooses db04 wavelet, and disassembles scale sets to 5, threshold value sets to 0.10000. This kind of filtering type can filter the tiny burrs doping in the whole waveform commendably and the waveform mutation part becomes clearer; this can increase the SNR substantially and gain a good noise reduction effect [6]. The signal before and after noise reduction by making use of binary orthogonal wavelet are shown in figure 7, a is the signal before noise reduction, b is the signal after noise reduction.

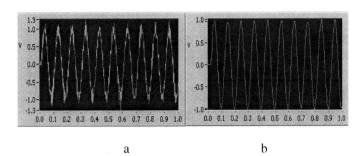

a   b

Fig. 7. The voltage signal before and after noise reduction

The Design of Data Storage and Display Module. The main program passes the analyzed data to Report subVI, and the subVI is responsible for generating excel form of the managed data by certain order. The excel form can save and print the testing form and curve in the form of excel conveniently. Meanwhile, the data curve is shown in front panel.

This system treats cars airbags blasting as the tested object and collects the pressure signals of 4 channels, the acceleration signal of one channel and the pulse signal of one channel, the sampling frequency is 100 *kHz* and the sample number per channel is 1600. 4 pressure curves and resultant curve, angular speed curve, acceleration curve are shown in figure 8. The system achieves the synchronous and high speed data collection and treatment of transient signals efficiently and gains excellent test result.

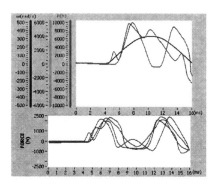

Fig. 8. Experimental curves show

5   Conclusion

The high speed data acquisition system based on Lab VIEW and PCI data acquisition card design achieves the functions of synchronous acquisition, signal noise reduction, data storage and display of transient signal with strict and synchronous collection per channel, obvious noise reduction effect and high accuracy, which has achieved the expected design aim and demand. This design scheme has largely shortened the development time, lessened the development cost, increased the reliability of test system and has strong practicability in practical application compared with the traditional data acquisition device which is slow in sampling speed, low in measurement accuracy, large number in test instrument and long in construction cycle.

References

1. Lin, J., Ren, R., Liu, F.: Multi-channel parallel data collection technology. Changchun Geological College Journal 26, 93–98 (1996)
2. Chen, X., Zhang, Y.: LabVIEW8.20 program design from introduction to proficient, pp. 5–90. Tsinghua University Press, Beijing (2007)
3. Lin, J., Lin, Z., Zheng, F.: LabVIEW virtual instrument program design from introduction to proficient, pp. 313–343. Beijing people's post and press (2010)
4. Ye, F., Zhou, X., Bai, X., Guo, Z., Yuan, C.: The data acquisition system design based on LabVIEW queuing state machine. Virtual Instrument and Application
5. Wan, W., Luo, H.: The filtering method based on the wavelet transforms. Mine Warfare and Ship Self Defense 15, 12–15 (2007)
6. Bi, S., Lan, H., Liu, L.: MIG welding arc acoustic signal acquisition and analysis system design. Harbin University of Science and Technology Journal 18, 52–56 (2010)

Fault Diagnosis of Sucker-Rod Pumping System Using Support Vector Machine

Jilin Feng[1], Maofa Wang[1,*], Yiheng Yang[2], Fangping Gao[1], Zhian Pan[1], Weifeng Shan[1], Qingjie Liu[1], Qiuge Yang[1], and Jing Yuan[1]

[1] Department of Information Technology, Institute of Disaster Prevention, Beijing 101601, P.R. China
[2] College of Applied Science, Beijing Information Science and Technology University, Beijing 100101, P.R. China
wangmaofa2008@126.com, fengjilin@cidp.edu.cn

Abstract. It is interesting thing to diagnose the faults of Sucker-rod Pumping System by analyzing dynamometer cards, which is inexpensive and easy to obtain. But conventional statistical methods are often ineffective to diagnose the faults of Sucker-rod Pumping System. One reason is that there are more parameters or smaller sample sizes than a simple model in analyzing dynamometer cards, so that their degree of freedom is reduced. Another reason is that the accurate structure of the conventional statistical model diagnosing the faults of Sucker-rod Pumping System is hard to make certain, because of that statistical criteria are crucially dependent on such assumptions as normality, homogeneity, independence. In the paper, we present a SVM-based approach for fault diagnosis of Sucker-rod Pumping System by analyzing dynamometer cards. With the method, we can get the working status of the Sucker-rod Pumping System.

Keywords: Support Vector Machine, Classifier, Pattern Recognition, Dynamometer card, Cross-validation, Oil well rod pump.

1 Introduction

Sucker-rod pumping is the most widely used means of artificial lift. It is reported in [1] about 85% to 90% of all producing wells in the USA use rod-pumped system. Thus, a reliable method of analyzing these pumping systems is a necessity. For many years, a down-hole dynamometer has been used to analyze sucker-rod systems.

Recently, a variety of useful statistical methods have been raised in analyzing down-hole dynamometer cards of sucker-rod pumping system. With these study methods, people wish to get more work status information of sucker-rod pumping system and clearly know which type of fault is occurring, so that we can take a well-timed intervention when some fault is occurring. For example, artificial neural network have been proposed to establish pattern classes of down-hole dynamometer cards in oil well rod pump systems such as shown in [2, 3, 4] and so on.

---

* Corresponding author.

M. Zhao and J. Sha (Eds.): ICCIP 2012, Part II, CCIS 289, pp. 179–189, 2012.
© Springer-Verlag Berlin Heidelberg 2012

Traditionally, neural networks were proved to be a powerful method on intelligent fault diagnosis. Reliable training methods have been developed mainly thanks to interdisciplinary studies and insights from several fields including statistics, systems and control theory, signal processing, information theory and so forth. Despite many of these advances, there still remains a number of weak points such as, difficulty in choosing the number of hidden units, over-fitting problem, existence of many local minimal solutions, and usually needing an abundant training samples. In order to overcome those tough problems, major breakthroughs have been made at this point with a new class of neural net-works called support vector machines (SVM), which developed in the area of statistical learning theory and structural risk minimization. SVM has many advantages, such as automatic selection of model complexity, few local minimal solutions, no loss of dimensionality, good generalization performance. SVM has been recently introduced for solving pattern recognition and function estimation problems. In this paper we will discuss the faults classification of Sucker-rod Pumping System by analyzing down-hole dynamometer cards with SVM.

Throughout the whole processing course, there are mainly the following approaches: preparing down-hole dynamometer cards data sets which is a set of vector points whose two corresponding weights are load and displacement, extracting characteristic values from input dynamometer cards data, transforming the characteristic values to the format of an SVM method, conducting simple scaling on the data, considering to use the RBF kernel X, using cross-validation to find the best parameter C and γ, using the best parameter C and γ to train the whole training set, giving the faults classification labels of testing data set.

2   SVM Classification Algorithm

A lot of studies about SVM Classification algorithm have been proposed in [5, 6, 7, 8], and the summary of the SVM Classification algorithm is described as the following:

Suppose we have N given Observations. Each observation object consists of a pair of data: a vector F and a class label $y_i \in \{+1, -1\}$ for each vector x_i. We say x_i belongs to class I if $y_i = +1$, and x_i belongs to class II if $y_i = -1$. These data pairs build the training data sets. For linearly separable data, we can determine a hyper-plane $f(x)$ that separates the data sets. For a separating hyper-plane $f(x) \geq 0$ if the input x belongs to the positive class, and $f(x) < 0$ if x belongs to the negative class.

$$f(x) = w \cdot x + b = \sum_{j=1}^{m} w_j x_j + b \qquad (1)$$

$$y_i f(x_i) = y_i (w \cdot x_i + b) \geq 0, \quad i = 1, \cdots, N \qquad (2)$$

where w is an m-dimensional vector and b is a scalar. $w \cdot x$ is the inner production of w and x. If we additionally require that w and b is such that the points closest to the hyper-plane has a distance of $1/|w|$, the equation (2) should be written as

$$y_i(w \cdot x_i + b) \geq 1, \quad i = 1, \cdots, N \tag{3}$$

The separating hyper-plane has the maximum distance between the hyper-plane and the nearest data, i.e. the maximum margin, is called the optimal separating hyper-plane. The classification ability is maximized with the optimal hyper-plane. A sketch of an optimal separating hyper-plane of two data sets is shown in Fig. 1, where H is the optimal separating hyper-plane. The optimal hyper-plane can be obtained by solving the following convex quadratic optimization problem:

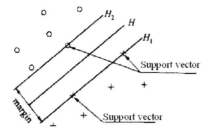

Fig. 1. A sketch of an optimal separating hyper-plane

$$\text{minimize} \quad 1/2 \|w\|^2 \tag{4}$$

$$\text{subject to } y_i(w \cdot x_i + b) \geq 1, \ i = 1, \cdots, N \tag{5}$$

This problem can be transformed into the equivalent Lagrange dual problem as:

$$Q(a) = \sum_{i=1}^{N} \alpha_i - 1/2 \sum_{i,k=1}^{N} \alpha_i \, \alpha_k \, y_i y_k x_i \cdot x_k \tag{6}$$

$$\text{subject to } \sum_{i=1}^{N} y_i \alpha_i = 0 \ , \ \alpha_i \geq 0, \ i = 1, \ \cdots, \ N \tag{7}$$

where $\alpha = (\alpha_1, \alpha_2, \cdots, \alpha_i)$ is the Lagrange factor. Each sample has corresponding α_i, $i = 1, \cdots, N$. Those samples for whose $\alpha_i > 0$ are called support vectors, and are ones where the equality condition holds in equation (5). All other training samples having $\alpha_i = 0$ can be removed from the training set without affecting the optimal hyper-plane.

Let us assume that optimal solution of α for the dual problem is α^*, the solution of w and b are w^* and b^* which can be given by:

$$w^* = \sum_{i=1}^{N} \alpha_k^* y_i \cdot x_i = \sum_{sup\,port\,vectors} \alpha_i^* y_i \cdot x_i \tag{8}$$

$$b^* = 1 - w^* \cdot x_i \qquad for \ x_i \ with \quad y_i = 1 \tag{9}$$

After training, the classifier can be used to classify a new sample x by the decision functions:

$$f(x) = sign(\sum_{j=1}^{N} \alpha_j^* y_j x_j \cdot x + b^*)$$ (10)

$$x \in \begin{cases} class\ I, & if\ f(x)=+1 \\ class\ II, & if\ f(x)=-1 \end{cases}$$ (11)

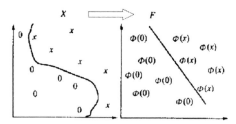

Fig. 2. A sketch of mapping from the original data space X to the feature space F

   The SVM classifier is based on a non-linear kernel function, which maps the original data space X where the samples may be non-linear classified to a data space F where the samples can be linearly classified. The new data space F is called the feature space of X. This is depicted in Fig. 2. Now, using the non-linear vector function $\Phi(x) = (\Phi_1(x), \cdots, \Phi_l(x))$, which maps the d-dimensional input vector x into the l-dimensional feature space, the linear decision function in dual form is given by:

$$f(x) = sign(\sum_{i=1}^{N} \alpha_i y_i \Phi(x_i) \cdot \Phi(x) + b^*)$$ (12)

Noticing that in Equation (12) as well as in the optimization problem Equation (6), we only concern the inner productions of samples. So, in the higher dimensional space (feature space), we only deal with the data in the form of the inner product $\Phi(x) \cdot \Phi(z)$. If the dimension of F is very large, then it will be difficult or very expensive computationally. However if it is possible to find a kind of function to calculate inner products of feature space in the original data space, this function is called a kernel function, $k(x,z) = \Phi(x) \cdot \Phi(z)$. Then we use this kernel function in place of $k(x) = \Phi(x) \cdot \Phi(z)$ everywhere in the optimization problem and never need to know explicitly what Φ is. Using a kernel function, the decision function will be:

$$f(x) = sign\left[\sum_{sup\ port\ vectors} \alpha_i^* y_i(x_i, x) + b^* \right]$$ (13)

$$x \in \begin{cases} class\ I, & if\ f(x)=+1 \\ class\ II, & if\ f(x)=-1 \end{cases}$$ (14)

However, all kernels do not correspond to inner products in some feature space F. With a so-called Mercer theorem it is possible to find out if a kernel K depicts an inner product in that space where Φ is mapped. Some typical kernel functions are:

$$\text{Polynomial Function}: K(x, y) = (x \cdot y + 1)^d, \, d = 1, \, 2, \cdots \quad (15)$$

$$\text{Radial Basis Function}: K(x, y) = \exp(-\|x - y\|^2 / 2\sigma^2) \quad (16)$$

$$\text{Sigmoid Function}: K(x, y) = \tanh\left[b(x \cdot y) - c\right] \quad (17)$$

In our research, Radial Basis Function is adopted.

3   Preparing Down-Hole Dynamometer Cards Data Sets

For many years, the surface dynamometer has been used to analyze sucker-rod systems. Interpretation of actual pump conditions from surface dynamometer cards is often difficult, even not impossible. Results obtained from surface cards are strictly qualitative and are dependent on the analyzer's expertise. The ideal analysis procedure would be to measure the actual pump conditions with a down-hole dynamometer. However, this situation is not economically feasible. Therefore, an accurate method of transforming down-hole pump cards from measured surface cards is needed. Several transforming methods have been widely studied [9, 1, 10-11]. In our research, we can calculate down-hole pump cards using a quick recursion arithmetic which is depicted by Peng et al. [12].

There occurs about 200-300 vector points in each one down-hole pump card, where these vector points indicate the displacement and the tension values of the sucker rod in time sequence in one stoke course. Then we give out the class label of every one down-hole pump card in an empirical manner. In experimental stage, a part of dynamometer cards need to be divided into three classes: the first fault class is normal operation, the second is no enough fluid supplying, and all other types of faults are regarded as the third fault which includes leaking standing valve, worn out pump, stuck piston, gas interference and so on. Those divided dynamometer cards data will be used to train the classification model. In the following application, the training dynamometer cards could be divided into more classes.

The detail information extracting from a training dynamometer cards finally is saved as a text table, whose structure is shown as table 1. From which, we can gain the main dynamometer card parameters including fault class-label, minimal and maximal tension of sucked-rod and, minimal and maximal displacement of sucked-rod, and 200-300 common vector points of displacement and tension. A true value of class-label can be only one of 1, 2 and 3, which are respectively corresponding to 3 types of work operations: normal, no enough fluid supplying, and other types of fault. For a given well, all the card parameters have the same values in minimal and maximal tension, minimal and maximal displacement.

If training data size is too small, the representative of samples will be dubious, and if training data size is too large, a heavy workload will be need to empirically and manually divide the samples to different classes. So that for each type of fault, preparing 50-100 training data tables of dynamometer cards is feasible.

Table 1. The detail information extracting of a training dynamometer

Class-label	Min-displacement	Min-tension	Max-displacement	Max-tension	Displacement	Tension
2	2.649e-001	-1.970e+001	2.380e+000	7.99e+000	2.649e-001	1.970e+001
					2.380e+000	7.990e+000
					2.814e-001	1.578e+001
					2.701e-001	1.488e+001
					2.649e-001	1.398e+001
					2.650e-001	1.315e+001
					2.685e-001	1.243e+001
					2.732e-001	1.181e+001
					2.776e-001	1.123e+001
					2.807e-001	1.059e+001
					2.826e-001	9.781e+000
					2.841e-001	8.684e+000
					2.864e-001	7.231e+000

......

4   Extracting Characteristic Values from Per Input Dynamometer Card

Because of that there are 200-300 vector points of displacement and tension in per down-hole dynamometer card, so the whole calculation quantities will be very large if we use directly these vector points' data as parameters to train and get classification model. Therefore, we need extracting relatively few and effective feature parameters from vector points of down-hole dynamometer cards as input parameters of classification function, which is important for the accuracy of the final fault diagnosis.

According to analysis to abundant typical down-hole dynamometer cards, we will extract 13 dimension feature parameters from a dynamometer card in total. The detailed extraction arithmetic of the 13 dimension feature parameters is depicted as the following:

4.1   Normalizing Dynamometer Card

To enhance the robustness of parameters and get right classification model which can use dynamometer cards from different wells, we firstly need normalize all the dynamometer cards from different wells. Eq. (18) and Eq. (19) shows the normalization processing.

$$dis = (dis - min\text{Dis})/(max\text{Dis} - min\text{Dis}) \qquad (18)$$

$$ten = (ten - min\text{Ten})/(max\text{Ten} - min\text{Ten}) \qquad (19)$$

where dis is the displacement of one point in a dynamometer card, ten is the tension, $min\text{Dis}$, $max\text{Dis}$, $min\text{Ten}$ and $max\text{Ten}$ respectively corresponds to minimal displacement, maximal displacement, minimal tension and maximal tension of a well.

4.2 Calculating the 5 Points Having Maximal Curvature Values of Every One Training Down-Hole Dynamometer Card

Suppose there are three adjacent points: $A(x_1, y_1)$, $B(x_0, y_0)$, $C(x_2, y_2)$ in a dynamometer card where x and y represents displacement and tension respectively. And point A is the prior point of point B, C is the backward point of B, and the curvature of point B can be calculated such as Eq. (20-24)):

$$area = 1/2 \begin{vmatrix} 1 & 1 \\ x_1 - x_0 & y_1 - y_0 \\ x_2 - x_0 & y_2 - y_0 \end{vmatrix} \qquad (20)$$

$$\alpha = \sqrt{(x_1 - x_0)^2 + (y_1 - y_0)^2} \qquad (21)$$

$$\beta = \sqrt{(x_2 - x_0)^2 + (y_2 - y_0)^2} \qquad (22)$$

$$\delta = \sqrt{(x_2 - x_1)^2 + (y_2 - y_1)^2} \qquad (23)$$

$$cur = 2.0 * area / (\alpha * \beta * \delta) \qquad (24)$$

where $area$ is the area of the triangle ABC, α is the length of line segment AB, β is the length of line segment BC, δ is the length of line segment AC, and cur is the final curvature result of point B.

After calculating curvature values of each one point in a down-hole dynamometer card, we choose the 5 feature points: P_1, P_2, P_3, P_4, P_5, whose curvature values are larger than all other points. Physically, the five points corresponds to the shut and open positions of standing valve and traveling valve respectively.

4.3 Calculating 13 Dimension Feature Parameters for Every Training Dynamometer Card Using the 5 Feature Points

Firstly, the displace values of the 5 feature points are used as the first 5 dimension feature training parameters. After that, we calculate the 5 slope values between every two adjacent points in the 5 feature points, and the 5 slope values are used as the second five dimension feature parameters. Eq. (25) gives the slope formula.

$$slope_i = (y_{i+1} - y_i) / (x_{i+1} - x_i), \quad i = 1, 2, 3, 4, 5 \qquad (25)$$

where if $i = 5$, we give the formula $i+1$ the value of 1.

Further, we need to calculate the means of tension in the up and down stroke respectively. And the two means are used as other two dimension training feature parameters.

Finally, the area of pentagon $P_1 P_2 P_3 P_4 P_5$ is calculated as the 13th dimension feature parameter by the Eq. (26) and Eq. (27).

$$area_{i-1} = 1/2 \begin{vmatrix} 1 & 1 \\ x_i - x_1 & y_{i-}y_1 \\ x_{i+1} - x_1 & y_{i+1-}y_1 \end{vmatrix} \quad i = 2,3,4,5 \tag{26}$$

$$area = \sum_{i=1}^{4} area_i \tag{27}$$

where $area_{i-1}$ is the area of the triangle $P_1 P_i P_{i+1}$, $i = 2,3,4,5$, and $area$ is the area of pentagon $P_1 P_2 P_3 P_4 P_5$.

The feature extraction transforms an observation space of dimension m', which is the down-hole dynamometer cards data, into the characteristic space of dimension q', where q<m, in order to simple the classification task. The structure of input data of classification function is shown as table.

Table 2. The training class-label and 13 dimension feature parameter of a well

Class-label	13 dimension feature parameter
3	1:0.658324 2:0.870865 3:0.785629 4:0.187915 5:0.037599 6:-0.538457 7:8.932224 8:-0.202505 9:-1.395537 10:0.877966 11:0.445880 12:0.830548 13:0.296384
1	1:0.174935 2:0.755881 3:0.667865 4:0.160072 5:0.011953 6:-0.108655 7:5.409379 8:0.402619 9:-1.583537 10:3.123769 11:0.385190 12:0.750632 13:0.187650
2	1:0.101126 2:0.277251 3:0.803453 4:0.336088 5:0.072731 6:-1.545776 7:0.135796 8:0.928083 9:0.123108 10:23.488199 11:0.208683 12:0.879103 13:0.244993
2	1:0.086994 2:0.449671 3:0.308260 4:0.070871 5:1.000000 6:-0.134627 7:1.688092 8:1.976799 9:-2.394027 10:0.000000 11:0.158584 12:0.554462 13:0.183187

······

5   Training and Testing

In our research, we have developed our own software written with C++ language to diagnose faults of sucker-rod pumping system, where the open-source code *libsvm* written by Chang and Lin [13] has been modified and integrated into our software system, and the chosen type of the SVM Classification is C-SVC, and Radial Basis kernel function is adopted.

5.1   Rescaling Feature Extraction Data Set

The structure of original training and testing data are shown as table 2, and the test data allows of no class-label weight. And these data may be too huge or small in range, thus we can rescale them to the proper range so that training and predicting.

The scale function is described by Lin (2009), and the upper limit of scaling is 1, and the lower limit is -1. Table 3 is the scale date set of a training feature extraction data set, where range of every dimension parameter is between -1 and 1.

Table 3. The scale date set of a feature extraction data

Class-label	13 dimension feature parameter
3	1:0.423166 2:0.739168 3:0.421755 4:-0.639625 5:-0.595141 6:0.259807 7:-0.66034 8:0.0250785 9:-0.68137 10:-0.515415 11:0.112075 12:0.698365 13:-0.365323
1	1:-0.621825 2:0.506918 3:0.10347 4:-0.695841 5:-0.637648 6:0.261752 7:-0.683111 8:0.0632464 9:-0.682275 10:-0.503679 11:-0.0604729 12:0.495139 13:-0.647683
2	1:-0.781386 2:-0.459839 3:0.469929 4:-0.340459 5:-0.536911 6:0.255249 7:-0.7172 8:0.0963898 9:-0.674066 10:-0.39726 11:-0.562301 12:0.82184 13:-0.498775
2	1:-0.811936 2:-0.111578 3:-0.868447 4:-0.875941 5:1 6:0.261634 7:-0.707166 8:0.162537 9:-0.686173 10:-0.520003 11:-0.704738 12:-0.0037204 13:-0.659272
	......

5.2 Cross Validating to Get Optimized SVM Training Parameters

The two most critical parameters for SVM training model are cost and gamma. After getting nice parameters: cost and gamma, we will use them to train the training data to get the best training mode and use the mode for final prediction on test data with unknown class-label. The whole process to get nice parameter cost and gamma is called cross validation. In our research, the cross validation can be formalized to the following six-step procedure:

$a)$ Split the training data to 3 sets of pre-classified data randomly.
$b)$ Obtain a pair of cost and gamma by the following:

$for \quad i = 1, 2, 3 \cdots, 20 \quad do$

$for \quad j = 1, 2, 3 \cdots, 10 \quad do$

$c = 0.01 + 0.5 * i$, $g = 0.01 + 0.5 * j$

$c)$ Train two sets of pre-classified data with parameters c and g obtained by Eq. (27), and predict third set of data to calculate the accuracy.

$d)$ Choose another two sets of pre-classified as training data, the other data as predict set, repeat step 3. So that we will get the average accuracy with this set of parameter: cost and gamma.

$e)$ Repeating *Step 2*, *Step 3*, and *Step 4*, we can obtain the maximum of accuracy with a given set of parameter: cost and gamma, which is the best training parameters.

$f)$ Train all the training data with above calculated parameter: cost and gamma to obtain the training model. The structure of the training model file is described as in Chang and Lin. (2001).

5.3   Predict the Testing Data

The testing data might have no class-labels. In the last step, we predict their labels using the obtained training model. The average accuracy rate of training is higher than 87%, which are calculated by the consistent percent of original label to predict label. The structure of predict result file is shown as Table 4.

Table 4. The predict result of a well

Accuracy class-label	Original class-label	Predict
91%	3	3
	1	1
	2	2
	3	3
	1	1
	2	2
	1	1
	2	2
	....	

6   Conclusion and Prospect

The present study have get good classification effects even with a few training sample, and more hopeful to analyze the faults of sucker-rod pump in slope well later.

We also write the correlative software with c++ codes, which applies the above processing algorithms. Using the software, we can easily and automatically give out the class-label of the faults, which could actually occurs in hundreds of meters deep underground.

If more detailed fault classification is required such as no less than 3 fault classes, giving out the fault class-label of training data in an empirical manner will become difficult even if the training data size is no so large. So the study about how to automatically label the faults of trainning data is going on now in our team.

Acknowledgment. Two of Authors (Jilin Feng, Maofa Wang) thank the financial support from funding program of scientific researching for teachers of China seismology bureau (20100105).

References

1. Everitt, T.A., Jennings, J.W.: An Improved Finite-Difference Calculation of Downhole Dynamometer Cards for Sucker-Rod Pumps. SPE Production Engineering 7, 121–127 (1992)
2. Abello, J., Houang, A., Russell, J.: A Hierarchy of Pattern Recognition Algorithms for the Diagnosis of Sucker Rod Pumped Wells. In: Conference on Computing and Information-ICCI, pp. 359–364 (1993)
3. Bezerra, M.A.D., Schnitman, L., Barreto Filho, M.D.A., Felippe De Souza, J.A.M.: Pattern Recognition for Downhole Dynamometer Card in Oil Rod Pump System using Artificial Neural Networks. In: International Conference on Enterprise Information Systems- ICEIS, pp. 351–355 (2009)

4. Felippe de Souza, A.M., Bezerra, M.A.D., Barreto Filho, M., de, A., Schnitman, L.: Using artificial neural networks for pattern recognition of downhole dynamometer card in oil rod pump system. In: AIKED 2009: Proceedings of the 8th WSEAS International Conference on Artificial Intelligence, Knowledge Engineering and Data Bases, pp. 231–235 (2009)
5. Vapnik, V.N.: Nature of Statistical Learning Theory, pp. 100–300. Springer Press, New York (2001)
6. Burges, J.C.: A Tutorial on Support Vector Machines for Pattern Recognition. Data Mining and Knowledge Discovery 2(2), 121–167 (1997)
7. Mulier, F.: Vapnik-Chervonenkis(VC) Learning Theory and Its Applications. IEEE Trans. on Neural Networks 10(5), 985–987 (1999)
8. Li, L.J., Zhang, Z.S., He, Z.J.: Mechanical Fault Diagnosis Using Support Vector Machine. International Journal of Plant Engineering and Management 8(3), 180–183 (2003)
9. Chen, J.L.: A method A Fast Algorithm of calculating down-hole dynamometer cards of Sucker-rod Pumping System. Acta Petrolei Sinaca 9(3), 105–113 (1998)
10. Gibbs, S.G.: Predicting the Behavior of Sucker-Rod Pumping Systems. Journal of Petroleum Technology 15, 769–778 (1963)
11. Gibbs, S.G., Neely, A.B.: Computer Diagnosis of Down-Hole Conditions in Sucker Rod Pumping Wells. Journal of Petroleum Technology 1, 91–98 (1996)
12. Peng, Y., Yan, W.H., Wang, S.H.: A quick recursion arithmetic of calculating pump dynamo-graph of the sucker-rod pumping system. Drilling & Production Technology 24(6), 45–47 (2004)
13. Chang, C.C., Lin, C.J.: LIBSVM: A library for support vector machines. University of Taiwan, http://www.csie.ntu.edu.tw/~cjlin/papers/libsvm.pdf (accessed August 23, 2011)

Evolutionary Design of Image Filter Using PicoBlaze Embedded Processor

Kai-feng Zhang, Hua-min Tao, and Shan-zhu Xiao

National Key Laboratory of Automatic Target Recognition (ATR),
National University of Defense Technology,
Changsha, Hunan, P.R. China
zkf0100007@163.com

Abstract. This paper proposed an evolutionary design method of image filter based on PicoBlaze embedded processor. Experiment was conducted to test the validity of the evolvable system, experimental results and analyses demonstrate that the optimal evolved filter outperforms traditional filters both on performance and implementation costs. In comparison with evolutionary methods of image filter existing, evolutionary method based on PicoBlaze not only improves the speed of evolution, but also brings more flexibility and little logic resource utilization.

Keywords: evolvable hardware, image filter, PicoBlaze, evolutionary algorithm.

1 Introduction

Image is inevitably contaminated during acquisition, compression and transmission. In order to improve the image quality, image filter has to be incorporated before post-processing. In case of traditional image operator design, the designer has to (1) analyze an input image, (2) design an algorithm (an operator), which will perform a required operation, and (3) prepare a circuit implementation (e.g. a configuration of an FPGA). The design process is mostly based on experimental work with the images and it leads to a very time consuming job [1].

Evolvable hardware (EHW) refers to hardware that can change its architecture and behavior dynamically and autonomously by interacting with its environment [2]. EHW usually use evolutionary algorithm (EA) as their main adaptive mechanism. EHW was introduced to the design of image filter, due to the limitations of traditional image filter design methods. A number of works have been done on this issue. Sekanina introduced a concept of complete hardware evolution (CHE), which means that evolving filter as well as the EA is implemented on a single chip [3]. A PowerPC based hardware evolution method was proposed by Sekanina latterly [4], due to lack of flexibility of CHE. PowerPC is a hard core only embedded in high-end FPGA of Xilinx. According to the limitation, an evolutionary method based on PicoBlaze embedded processor was proposed. PicoBlaze is a soft core can be widely used in most all of the FPGA, even some CPLD can also support it.

M. Zhao and J. Sha (Eds.): ICCIP 2012, Part II, CCIS 289, pp. 190–197, 2012.

The rest of the paper is organized as follows. Section 2 gives a brief introduction to PicoBlaze and JTAG_loader. Section 3 describes in detail the design methodology and the hardware implementation details of evolvable system based on PicoBlaze embedded processor. Section 4 reports the simulations and experiments conducted to verify the validity of the evolvable system and demonstrate its effectiveness. Section 5 concludes with a brief summary of the features and advantages of the proposed evolutionary design methodology and discussed future directions.

2   PicoBlaze Embedded Processor and Design Tools

2.1   PicoBlaze

The PicoBlaze microcontroller is a compact, capable, and cost-effective fully embedded 8-bit RISC microcontroller core optimized for the Spartan and Virtex FPGA families. The PicoBlaze microcontroller provides cost-efficient micro controller-based control and simple data processing [5]. (see block diagram of PicoBlaze in Fig. 1).

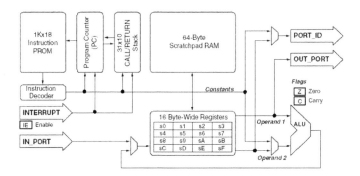

Fig. 1. Block diagram of PicoBlaze

The structure and features of PicoBlaze could be summarized as follows:

- 16 byte-wide general-purpose data registers.
- 1K instructions of programmable on-chip program store, automatically loaded during FPGA configuration.
- Byte-wide Arithmetic Logic Unit (ALU) with CARRY and ZERO indicator flags.
- 64-byte internal scratchpad RAM.
- 256 input and 256 output ports for easy expansion and enhancement.
- Automatic 31-location CALL/RETURN stack.
- Predictable performance, always two clock cycles per instruction, up to 200 MHz or 100 MIPS in a Virtex-II Pro FPGA.
- Fast interrupt response; worst-case 5 clock cycles.
- Assembler, instruction-set simulator support.

2.2   pBlazIDE

The Mediatronix pBlazIDE software is a free, graphical, integrated development environment for Windows-based computers [5]. Its features are as follows:

- Syntax color highlighting
- Instruction set simulator (ISS)
- Breakpoints
- Register display
- Memory display
- Source code formatter
- KCPSM3-to-pBlazIDE import function/syntax conversion
- HTML output, including color highlighting

With the help of pBlazIDE, software of PicoBlaze could be simulated before implementation on FPGA, which could help for error debugging in early process.

2.3   JTAG_loader

JTAG_loader is a small tool used for modifying the content of BRAM online. Program stored in BRAM could be reloaded by JTAG_loader easily, eliminating the process of re-synthesis, implementation and generation of new bit stream. According to this feature, software development process could be accelerated substantially.

3   Evolvable System Design and Implementation

3.1   Evolvable System Overview

Evolvable system consists of a PicoBlaze embedded processor, a UART macro, two SRAM, a fitness unit (FU), a programmable function element array(PFEA), a configuration RAM (CFG RAM) and a population RAM.

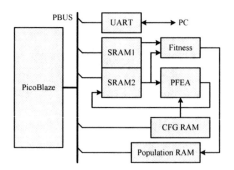

Fig. 2. Block diagram of evolvable system

As seen from Fig. 2, PicoBlaze embedded processor is the core of the whole system, all operations are controlled by it, which communicates with other components using PBUS.UART is a macro provided by Xilinx, by which the original image data is received from PC. Two SRAM is used for storing original image data, corrupted image data and data output filtered by the PFEA. The fitness unit calculates individual fitness by comparing the outputs of PFEA with original image data. Population information stores in population RAM, which is also responsible for configuring PFEA. PFEA is a reconfigurable unit, whose function and interconnection is depended on the data storing in population RAM. Once the system evolution is finished, the results could be transmitted to the PC by UART interface.

3.2   Programmable Function Element Array

PFEA is a two dimensional arrays, which consists of PFE and MUX (see schematic of PFE array in Fig. 3).

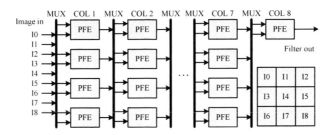

Fig. 3. Schematic of PFE array

It consists of 29 PFEs allocated in a grid of 8 columns and 4 rows. The last column includes only one PFE, and the output of which is the filtered pixel output of PFEA. The first column receives the image data to be filtered, including I4 and its 8-neighbor pixels. The MUX controls the interconnections of PFEs. In this paper, we chose L=1, which means that the input of PFE in column l can only connect to the output of PFE in column l-1.

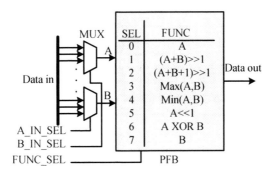

Fig. 4. Schematic of PFE

Fig. 4 shows the schematic of PFE. A PFE consists of two MUX and a programmable function block (PFB). A_IN_SEL and B_IN_SEL stands for the input selection bit-string, the input A and B is controlled by them. FUNC_SEL determines the function of PFB. We use 3 bits for FUNC_SEL here, as a result that PFB can operation in 8 different modes.

3.3   Chromosome Coding

Genotype-phenotype mapping plays an important role in hardware evolution. In this paper, the encoding of a digital circuit into a genotype is based on the methods of Wang et al. [6]. The genotype is a fixed-length binary bit string, which defines the interconnections of PFEs and functions performed by PFEs. The structure of chromosome encoding is shown in Fig. 5.

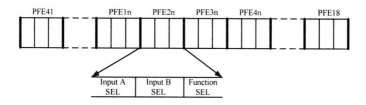

Fig. 5. Structure of chromosome encoding

PFEs in column 1 have 9 inputs, which needs 4 bit for input selection. PFEs in other columns have only 4 inputs, which needs only 2 bit for input selection. So the total length of the chromosome is (4+4+3)*4+(2+2+3)*4*6+(2+2+3) =219bit.

3.4   Evolutionary Algorithm

In this paper, the EA is a simple form based on the 1+λ evolution strategy (ES) [7], where λ=4. According to the results of earlier researchers, crossover operators have little contributions on improvement of the quality of evolutionary search [8]. As a result, we use mutation operators only during the evolution. The evolution flow of the employed algorithm is as follows:

1)   Initial population of λ individuals is randomly generated.
2)   Configure PFEA by writing phenotype information to CFG RAM.
3)   Evaluate all individuals. The corrupted image is filtered by PFEA, and calculates the fitness of each individual. If expected circuit is evolved or predefined EA maximum generation number is exhausted, then go to step 5.
4)   Create next generation using evolutionary operators, and then go to step 2.
5)   Evolution terminated.

For evolutionary design of image filter, usually two fitness functions are used, of which one is PSNR (Picture Signal Noise Ratio) and the other is MDPP (Mean Difference Per Pixel). In this paper, MDPP is used for fitness evaluation.

$$d = \sum_{i=1}^{R-2} \sum_{j=1}^{C-2} |v(i,j) - w(i,j)|$$

$$MDPP = \frac{d}{(R-2) \cdot (C-2)} \tag{1}$$

$$fitness = 255(R-2) \cdot (C-2) - d$$

The definition of MDPP and fitness function are shown above, where $v(i,j)$ and $w(i,j)$ stand for pixel of filtered image and original image; and R and C are the height and width of the image.

We employed all the evolutionary operations implemented in the PicoBlaze embedded processor, but only the MDPP fitness function was carried out in hardware calculation, as it is computationally easier for hardware calculation, but time consuming for software.

It is worth mentioning that the random number used in this paper is true random number, in contrast to pseudo random number in other cases [3][4][6]. True random number generator is based on the earlier model of Wold [9], which could be easily implemented on Xilinx FPGA.

4   Experimental Results

We designed the experiments to verify the validity of proposed evolvable system. The evolved image filter was tested on processing Salt & Pepper noise (the image contains 5% corrupted pixels with white or block shots) which was independent of the image itself. In our experiment, Baboon image was used as training input, which was a grey scale (8 bit each pixel) image of 256*256 pixels.

Evolution strategy was used here, where λ=4, mutation=5%, and no crossover operation employed. The termination condition of ES is defined as: (1) MDPP less than 5; or (2) maximum generation 20000 reached. We perform 100 independent runs, and 91 runs find the expected circuit, the other 9 runs failed to achieve the goals during 20000 generations.

Median filter usually used for Salt & Pepper noise corrupted image filtering, Table 1 shows the performance comparison of evolved filters and median filter.(see filtering results in Fig. 6)

As showed in Figure 6, although median filter eliminated most noise, also lead to image detail loss significantly. On the contrary, although the image filtered by evolved filter (EF) still leave some noisy point, the detail retained better. The data in Table 1 also proved the fact.

To verify the generality of evolved filter, Cameraman image and Baboon image corrupted by Salt & Pepper noise with the same parameters are also used for filtering. The filtering results also show that evolved filter could have better performance than median filter, although the evolved filter was trained by Lena image. So we can draw a conclusion that the evolved filter has good generality characteristic.

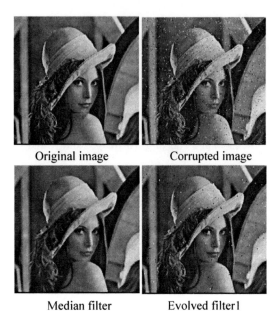

| Original image | Corrupted image |
| Median filter | Evolved filter1 |

Fig. 6. Filtering results of Lena

The performance comparison of evolved filter and conventional filter such as median filter is shown in Table 1.

Table 1. Performance comparison of filters

Filters	Item to be compared(using Lena image)		
	MDPP	*logic resource utilization (Slice)*	*Convergence generation*
Median filter	3.496	256	—
EF1	2.350	71	17273
EF2	3.391	89	11208
EF3	4.273	295	7581

As can be seen from Table 1, optimal evolved filter evolved filter outperforms traditional filters both on performance and implementation costs. The evolvable system was implemented on Xilinx Spartan-3 Starter Kit, where PicoBlaze runs at 50MHz. Each fitness evaluation could be done within about 2.8ms. On the other hand, each fitness evaluation spent 8.3ms using MATLAB (R2007b) on a PC which equipped with Intel 2.4GHz Dual Core E6600 processor, 2GB DDR II SDRAM and Windows XP SP2 OS. However, although the clock frequency of the PC is 48 times greater than on the FPGA, the evaluation speed is around 3 times slower conversely.

In comparison with evolvable system using 32bit embedded processor such as PowerPC or MicroBlaze, our evolvable system has little improvement in speed of evolution, but little logic resource utilization needed.

5   Conclusions

The paper has presented a novel approach to evolutionary design of image filter based on PicoBlaze embedded processor. Experiment was conducted to verify the validity of our proposed method, and the result demonstrated that evolutionary method based on PicoBlaze not only improve the speed of evolution, but also bring more flexibility and little logic resource utilization for the evolvable system design.

Most evolutionary algorithm was implemented in software, which became the speed bottleneck of the evolvable system due to the frequently function calls. Some method could be employed to accelerate the evolution speed, such as user-customizable instruction which supported by PicoBlaze and its design tool chains.

References

1. Sekanina, L., Drabek, V.: Automatic Design of Image Operator Using Evolvable Hardware. In: 5th IEEE Design and Diagnostics of Electronic Circuits and Systems Workshop, pp. 132–139. IEEE Press, Brno (2002)
2. Yao, X., Higuchi, T.: Promises and Challenges of Evolvable Hardware. IEEE Trans. on Systems, Man, and Cybernetics 29, 87–97 (1999)
3. Martínek, T., Sekanina, L.: An Evolvable Image Filter: Experimental Evaluation of a Complete Hardware Implementation in FPGA. In: Moreno, J.M., Madrenas, J., Cosp, J. (eds.) ICES 2005. LNCS, vol. 3637, pp. 76–85. Springer, Heidelberg (2005)
4. Vasicek, Z., Sekanina, L.: An Evolvable Hardware System in Xilinx Virtex II Pro FPGA. International Journal of Innovative Computing and Applications 1, 63–73 (2007)
5. Ug129, http://www.xilinx.com/support/documentation/ip_documen tation/ug129.pdf
6. Wang, J., Piao, C.H., Lee, C.H.: FPGA Implementation of Evolvable Characters Recognizer with Self-adaptive Mutation Rates. In: Beliczynski, B., Dzielinski, A., Iwanowski, M., Ribeiro, B. (eds.) ICANNGA 2007. LNCS, vol. 4431, pp. 286–295. Springer, Heidelberg (2007)
7. Job, D., Vassilev, V.K.: Principles in The Evolutionary Design of Digital Circuits. Genet. Program. Evol. 1, 8–35 (2000)
8. Miller, J.F., Thomson, P.: Cartesian Genetic Programming. In: Poli, R., Banzhaf, W., Langdon, W.B., Miller, J., Nordin, P., Fogarty, T.C. (eds.) EuroGP 2000. LNCS, vol. 1802, pp. 121–132. Springer, Heidelberg (2000)
9. Wold, K., Tan, C.H.: Analysis and Enhancement of Random Number Generator in FPGA Based on Oscillator Rings. International Journal of Reconfigurable Computing 2009, 1–8 (2009)

Study and Application of Risk Evaluation
on Network Security Based on AHP

Chun Yan and Bo Qiao

Computer Science and Technology School,
Wuhan University of Technology,
Wuhan, China
Yanchun@whut.edu.cn, qiaoboxy@163.com

Abstract. Based on risk evaluation techniques for network security, this paper establishes evaluation criteria system of risk evaluation on network security by Delphi method, and constructs an analytical hierarchy process (AHP) model for risk evaluation on network security. Based on this evaluation model, a software of comprehensive evaluation system is developed. Using this software the risk of a university network security is evaluated. The investigation results show that this model can be used to a comprehensive evaluation of network security risk levels effectively.

Keywords: risk evaluation, evaluation criteria, analytical hierarchy process.

1 Introduction

With the computer networks continuous development and widely application, network security issues become increasingly prominent. Strictly speaking, in the real applications, almost all network systems exist security risk. The so-called network security risk is that due to the existence of the vulnerability of the system, man-made or natural threats lead to the probability of security incidents and the impact they caused. Risk evaluation on network security is a basic work to be carried out to establish network protection systems and implement risk management procedures. Through risk evaluation, it can identify the size of risk, and thus make the network security policy. It takes appropriately control objectives and control methods to control the risk. The risk is avoided, transferred or reduced to an acceptable level. Therefore, the network security risk assessment study has important practical significance. The paper uses typical integrated risk assessment methods – AHP. It establishes a network security risk assessment model, and for the practical application doing the specific analysis.

2 Construct Network Security Risk AHP Evaluation Model

The thought of AHP (Analytic Hierarchy Process, AHP) is that according to the nature of the problem need to be analyzed and the overall goal achieved, the problem is

M. Zhao and J. Sha (Eds.): ICCIP 2012, Part II, CCIS 289, pp. 198–205, 2012.
© Springer-Verlag Berlin Heidelberg 2012

broken down into different elements, and in accordance with elements of the inter-related, impact and affiliation, the elements will be aggregated combinations by different levels to form a hierarchical analysis structure model. Finally, the systems analysis will come down to the decision of relative importance weight of the lowest level relative to the highest level or the sorting problem of the order of the relative merits. The core of this approach is to give decision-makers to quantify the experience to judge, so as to provide decision makers with quantitative basis for decision making [1]. Using the AHP method to assess the risk of network security, the basic steps [2] are as follows:

2.1 Determine Evaluation Criteria System of Risk on Network Security

The method of determining the criteria system is: the factors included in the research questions are divided into different levels, such as the target layer, rule layer, criteria layer, etc. It builds hierarchical hierarchy model, and uses different forms of diagram to indicate the affiliation between the hierarchical structure of the layers and factors.

In this paper, when it determines evaluation criteria system of risk evaluation on network security, it uses Delphi method [3] which is the most widely used currently. Firstly, through the systems analysis, it initially protocols the evaluation criteria [4] [5]; then, it composites experience and subjective judgments of some experts to evaluate the indicator of the degree of importance; finally, it uses feedback and information control to make the dispersion evaluation suggests successively converge to a coordinated, thereby screening out 22 evaluation criteria of risk on network security. The evaluation criteria system of risk on network security consists of the 22 indicators shown in Figure. 1. And top to bottom is the target layer, rule layer and target layer.

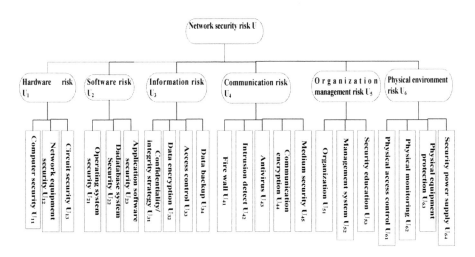

Fig. 1. Evaluation criteria system of risk on network security

2.2   Construct the Judgment Matrix of the Risk on Network Security

The method of constructing the judgment matrix is: using knowledge and experience of policy makers, as shown in Table 1 indicator scale method. It compares the importance of the factors of the same layer to the upper layer in the hierarchical structure model to generate judgment matrix:

$$A = \begin{bmatrix} a_{11} & a_{12} & \cdots & a_{1n} \\ a_{21} & a_{22} & \cdots & a_{2n} \\ \cdots & \cdots & \cdots & \cdots \\ a_{n1} & a_{n2} & \cdots & a_{nn} \end{bmatrix},$$

where, a_{ij} represents the value of the relative importance of the i-th factor and the j-th factor in the same layer, on the term of factor of the upper layer.

In this paper, on the base of evaluation criteria system of risk evaluation on network security, according to expert opinions, it compares the importance of various factors and constructs network security risk judgment matrix as shown in Table 3.

Table 1. Indicator Scale Method

a_{ij}	Two objectives compare
1	The i-th factor is the same important as the j-th factor.
3	The i-th factor is slightly important than the j-th factor.
5	The i-th factor is obvious important than the j-th factor.
7	The i-th factor is more important than the j-th factor.
9	The i-th factor is extreme important than the j-th factor.
2 4 6 8	Between the two cases above the adjacent two objectives
Reciprocal	in turn.

Table 2. The judgment matrix of the network security risk of the objective layer

U	U_1	U_2	U_3	U_4	U_5	U_6
U_1	1	1/2	1/4	1/3	5	3
U_2	2	1	1/3	1	5	4
U_3	4	3	1	3	7	6
U_4	3	1	1/3	1	7	3
U_5	1/5	1/5	1/7	1/7	1	1/2
U_6	1/3	1/4	1/6	1/3	2	1

Table 3. All kinds of risk judgment matrix in criterion layer

Hardware risk judgment matrix				
U1	*U11*	*U12*	*U13*	
U11	1	1	3	
U12	1	1	3	
U13	1/3	1/3	1	

Software risk judgment matrix				
U2	*U21*	*U22*	*U23*	
U21	1	1	1	
U22	1	1	1	
U23	1	1	1	

Information risk judgment matrix				
U3	*U31*	*U32*	*U33*	*U34*
U31	1	1/3	1/5	1/4
U32	3	1	1/3	1/2
U33	5	3	1	2
U34	4	2	1/2	1

Communication risk judgment matrix					
U4	*U41*	*U42*	*U43*	*U44*	*U45*
U_{41}	1	5	2	3	7
U_{42}	1/5	1	1/4	1/3	3
U_{43}	1/2	4	1	2	6
U_{44}	1/3	3	1/2	1	5
U_{45}	1/7	1/3	1/6	1/5	1

Organization and management risk judgment matrix			
U_5	U_{51}	U_{52}	U_{53}
U_{51}	1	1/5	1/3
U_{52}	5	1	3
U_{53}	3	1/3	1

Physical environment risk judgment matrix				
U6	*U61*	*U62*	*U63*	*U64*
U61	1	1/6	1/3	1/5
U62	6	1	4	2
U63	3	1/4	1	1/3
U64	5	1/2	3	1

2.3   Compute the Single Weight of the Criteria of Network Security Risk

The method to calculate the single weight of the criteria is: solving the maximum eigenvalue of the judgment matrix and the corresponding eigenvectors. The eigenvectors are normalized to get the relative weight vector $W = [w_1, w_2, \cdots, w_n]^T$. The weight vector represents for an element of the upper layer. The n elements associated with the relative weights in the layer. In practice, it uses root method to approximately calculate eigenvectors. That is:

$$\overline{w_i} = \sqrt[n]{\prod_{j=1}^{n} a_{ij}} \quad (i = 1, 2, \cdots, n)$$

the $\overline{w_i}$ is normalized and gets the weights:

$$w_i = \frac{\overline{w_i}}{\sum_{j=1}^{n} \overline{w_j}} \quad (i = 1, 2, \cdots, n)$$

After obtaining the relative weight vector, the judgment matrix also need the consistency test, in order to ensure the conclusion from the application of AHP to be reasonable. Consistency test is conducted through the consistency indicator CI and test coefficient CR,

$$CI = \frac{\lambda_{max} - n}{n - 1}, \quad CR = \frac{CI}{RI}$$

Where, RI is the average consistency indicator. It can be found in Table 4. In general, when CR <0.1, the judgment matrix can be considered to be conformance with satisfaction, or need to re-adjust the judgment matrix.

Table 4. Consistency test cross-references

Degree	1	2	3	4	5	6
RI	0.00	0.00	0.58	0.90	1.12	1.24
Degree	7	8	9	10	11	12
RI	1.32	1.41	1.45	1.49	1.52	1.54

According to the constructed network security risk judgment matrix, it can get the weight vector of the criterion layer in the risk of network security evaluation criteria system for objective layer. And the weight vector is: $W_U^{(1)} = [0.112, 0.187, 0.411, 0.201, 0.033, 0.056]^T$. From consistency test we can obtain that: $\lambda_{max} = 6.2325$, $CI = 0.0465$, $RI = 1.24$, $CR = 0.0375 < 0.1$. It can be seen that the judgment matrix has satisfaction consistency.

As the same way, the weight vector of indicator layer on criterion layer are:

$$W_{U_1}^{(2)} = [0.4285, 0.4285, 0.143]^T \qquad W_{U_2}^{(2)} = [0.334, 0.333, 0.333]^T$$

$$W_{U_3}^{(2)} = [0.072, 0.17, 0.473, 0.285]^T$$

$$W_{U_4}^{(2)} = [0.427, 0.08, 0.277, 0.176, 0.04]^T \quad W_{U_5}^{(2)} = [0.105, 0.637, 0.258]^T$$

$$W_{U_6}^{(2)} = [0.061, 0.495, 0.133, 0.311]^T$$. It can obtain the CR are 0, 0, 0.0189, 0.0303, 0.0332, 0.0292, through respectively consistency test. They are all less than 0.1, and it can be seen that each judgment matrix has satisfaction consistency.

2.4 Compute the Indicator Comprehensive Weight of the Risk of the Network Security

The method of calculating the indicator comprehensive weight is: given the weight vector of the criterion layer on the objective layer W(1) and the weight vector of indicator layer on the criterion layer W(2), then the indicator comprehensive weight vector is W = W(1)×W(2). It represents the weight of all the elements in the indicator layer on objective layer, the weight of each component represents its corresponding indicator accounts the share or proportion of the objective. The indicator comprehensive weight also must be taken consistency test, test formula is:

$$CI = \sum_{i=1}^{n} w_i CI_i \qquad RI = \sum_{i=1}^{n} w_i RI_i$$

.Where, CIi and RIi represent the consistency indicator and test coefficient of the corresponding judgment matrix of the ith criterion in the criterion layer. If it meets CR < 0. 1 (CR = CI/R I), then we think that the calculation results of indicator comprehensive weight has satisfied consistency.

According to the weight vector of the criterion layer on the objective layer W(1)and the weight vector of indicator layer on the criterion layer W(2), we can obtain the comprehensive weight vector of the indicator layer on the objective layer:

$$W = W^{(1)} \times W^{(2)} = [0.048, 0.048, 0.016,$$
$$0.062, 0.062, 0.062, 0.03, 0.07, 0.194, 0.117,$$
$$0.086, 0.016, 0.056, 0.035, 0.008, 0.003,$$
$$0.021, 0.009, 0.003, 0.028, 0.007, 0.017]^T$$

From the consistency test, we can obtain that: $CI = 0.016$, $RI = 0.838$, $CR = 0.0191 < 0.1$. It can be seen that the results of the comprehensive weight have satisfied consistency.

3 Application Analysis

The use of integrated weight of risk indicators on network security, can evaluate the risk on practical network security. Generally, the results of risk evaluation on network security will be divided into five levels, such as high-risk, higher risk, medium risk, lower risk, and low risk. The total points of the model is set to be 100 points, scores of corresponding to the level of risk are shown in Table 5.

Table 5. The levels of the risk on network security and scores

levels	high-risk	higher risk	medium risk	lower risk	low risk
score	80-100	60-80	40-60	20-40	0-20

First, ask the experts on network security risks of the individual indicators to assess the risk level by one and give a specific score, then according to the formula $V = S \cdot W$ (V is a comprehensive assessment score, S is the individual indicators to evaluate the vector, W is comprehensive weight vector). It makes weighted sum of the evaluation results of the individual indicators, to get the comprehensive assessment results of the network security risk from the experts, and finally the comprehensive assessment results are averaged, the final results of the assessment will be obtained.

This paper has invited five experts, for a university campus network to conduct a comprehensive security risk assessment, the experts on the evaluation of the individual indicators shown in Table 6. Through calculating, we can obtain the result from comprehensive assessment of the network security risk is 30 points, belonging to a lower level of risk..

Table 6. Experts evaluation results

	U11	U12	U13	U21	U22	U23
Expert1	20	23	30	24	26	32
Expert2	25	15	35	20	25	27
Expert3	22	20	28	25	28	22
Expert4	20	22	25	22	28	30
Expert5	18	18	30	27	20	25
	U31	U32	U33	U34	U41	U_{42}
Expert1	40	24	45	22	28	40
Expert2	35	28	52	25	25	35
Expert3	45	20	47	20	26	38
Expert4	44	25	40	18	32	45
Expert5	48	22	50	20	30	42
	U_{43}	U_{44}	U_{45}	U_{51}	U_{52}	U_{53}
Expert1	30	27	18	24	26	25
Expert2	36	23	20	25	28	28

Table 6. (*continued*)

Expert3	39	21	20	20	24	26
Expert4	34	25	25	19	25	27
Expert5	32	20	22	23	30	30
	U_{61}	U_{62}	U_{63}	U_{64}		
Expert1	40	30	15	22		
Expert2	36	36	20	25		
Expert3	38	34	17	20		
Expert4	44	29	15	18		
Expert5	45	28	18	22		

4   Conclusion

In this paper, trough study of the risk evaluation techniques for network security, it determines the reasonable evaluation criteria system of risk on network security, builds a scientific AHP-based network security risk assessment model and develops practical software about risk assessment system of network security. From using the system it can effectively assess the risks of network security, and then it enables timely to make control strategies of risks on network security, and thus improves network security and survivability.

References

[1]   Feng, D., Zhang, Y., Zhang, Y.: Information security risk assessment and reviewed in this paper. Journal on Communications 25(7) (2004)
[2]   Xu, S.: Principle of analytic hierarchy process. Tianjin University Press, Tianjing (1988)
[3]   Hou, D., Wang, Z.: Nonlinear assessment theory exploration and application. China Science and Technology University Press, Hefei (2001)
[4]   Chen, J.: Information security risk management, evaluation and control study. Jilin University, Jilin (2008)
[5]   Xu, F.Y., Shen, J., Li, J.Y.: Network security comprehensive evaluation method of research and application. Computer Engineering and Design 27(8) (2006)

Virtual Reality and Its Application in the Coal Mine

Zhijie Hao[1], Wei Hao[2], and Guoxia Yang[3]

[1] Department of Information Engineering, Cangzhou Technology Institute,
065201 Cangzhou Hebei, China
haozhijie@126.com
[2] Department of Information Technology, Institute of Disaster Prevention,
101601 Beijing, China
conniehao@126.com
[3] College of Information Science and Engineering, Hebei University of Science and
Technology, 050018 Shijiahuang Hebei, China
yangguoxia@126.com

Abstract. The technology of three-dimensional visualization can well describe the object, and it is a research hotspot in spatial information visualization. On the base of research actuality about virtual reality technology, application of it in the Geosciences and the coalmine is expounded. Now, virtual reality is used in mine system, virtual workface, virtual laneway and simulation laneway, mine accident and training, etc, and its wide application prospect in coalmine is shown.

Keywords: virtual reality, visualization, geosciences, mine.

1 Introduction

At the era of the information exploding, the VR comes into being accompanied with the implementation of the "Digital Earth". And with the development of VR, new issue emerges. The knowledge structure of VR has been the subject of numerous researching areas in recent years, and the knowledge acquisition and knowledge representation are the bottleneck problem. The former one is about the acquisition of special information in one domain, confirming the information model. It is the key to determine the practicality degree of the system. The latter is the main segment of KBS of VR. Built on a complex model to research the expression and usage of knowledge is the basis of building a high-powered repository.

The government of America, Britain, Japan, and many big companies pay special attention to the research of virtual reality technology, invest a large amount of funds in its exploitation and have acquired some fruits. Now its application has involved scientific research engineering, architecture, medicine, trade, movie and TV, art, amusement, education and training, military affairs etc.[1] The 21st century will be an era of the virtual reality technology.

M. Zhao and J. Sha (Eds.): ICCIP 2012, Part II, CCIS 289, pp. 206–213, 2012.

2   Virtual Reality Technology

2.1   Virtual Reality

Virtual reality technology is a sort of computer interface technology. In nature, virtual reality technology is a sort of computer user's interface. It facilitates consumer's operation to the largest extent by providing simultaneously all kinds of intuitional, natural, Real-time, perceptive and alternative measures, such as seeing, hearing and feeling etc., thereby lightens consumer's burden, heightens the whole system's working efficiency.

Virtual reality technology originated from 1960s. But due to its broad and embedded technical base-area, especially the restriction of the real-time and three-dimensional computer graph, it didn't attract worldwide attention, except for being applied in war industry and national defense. It was not until late 1980s that active researches were carried out and rapid growth was achieved in virtual reality technology, with the development of LED and CRE display technology, high-speed graphics technology, multimedia technology and tracer technology.

Virtual reality technology has four main features [2]:

- Multi-perception: ideal virtual reality technology should have those perceptive functions that a natural person bears, such as, multi-perceptive channels which include the senses of seeing, hearing, feeling, smelling as well as tasting. At present, virtual reality technology has not reached such a high level, only limiting to the senses of seeing, hearing, movement, feeling and etc.
- Presence: namely being on the scene, it indicates the sense of reality that a consumer feels when existing in stimulant environment as a leading actor. Ideal stimulant environment should achieve such an effect that it is difficult for users to differentiate the true from the false.
- Alternation: it refers to the operability of the objects in the stimulant environment and the naturalness (including the degree of being Real-time) of the feedback which is gained from the environment. For example, the user can grasp the object that is in the stimulant environment directly, and then he can feel like holding something in his hand and have an idea of the object's weight. The object that is grasped will also move with the moving of his hand in sigh.
- Self-determination: it refers to the object's accordance to the physics law when moving in the stimulant environment. For instance, the object will move, turn over or slide from the table to the ground in the direction of power when it is pushed.

2.2   VR Limitations and Solutions

One of the challenges presented to the user of a VR application is the need to become accustomed to rather cumbersome interface hardware devices such as head-mounted displays, trackers, or haptic devices. The first display and tracking devices were developed with the earliest VR system created by Ivan Sutherland [3~4]. However, with the use of these tools, it is still difficult to achieve the level of performance required for many tasks. Lack of haptic feedback is the main hardware problem. There has been some research done and some commercial products have been created in order to improve haptic feedback devices, but most of them still restrict the mobility of the user. Hardware devices currently represent serious limitations for VR, but these limitations will be somewhat overcome with advances in technology. This issue will not be considered in this dissertation.

Many of the benefits of virtual reality are dependent upon the sense of immersion or presence, which the user experiences. However, many applications fail to provide an effective sense of immersion because of an ineffective use of the capabilities of the three-dimensional interface or because of poor operating performance. In order to overcome these deficiencies, improved VR design will be advanced to make VR applications more successful. VR interface and performance are the two major elements to be considered in order to improve VR design. Much research has been done to improve VR visualization and interaction techniques.

Fine-grained interaction with virtual objects is particularly hard to achieve because of inaccurate tracking devices, lack of haptic and acoustic feedback, and limited input information. A dominant paradigm of interaction using windows and motif widgets has existed on conventional desktop computers for some time. However, in the VR environment, there is not yet a unified interface. Conventional graphics provide unambiguous input actions and do not restrict the required performance, but they are not always the most reliable within the context of the three-dimensional environment of virtual reality applications. Thus, a systematic investigation of fine-grain and 3D interactions with three- dimensional geoscience's data has been a major focus of this research.

3   The Present Condition of Virtual Reality Technology

Although virtual reality technology can be applied in any field, in a certain degree its actual engineering application is restricted by software and hardware environment, funds shortage. For the moment, its application in the field of aviation and spaceflight develops the most quickly. That design of Boeing 777 transporters without using papers, the astronaut's training before the repair of the Harbo outer space telescope and the success of stimulant flight proved the potentiality of the virtual reality technology [5].

At abroad, the United States is the cradle of virtual reality. The United States' level of research in virtual reality technology represents basically that of the world. The basic researches of America in this field mainly focus on four aspects: perception, consumer interface, backstage software and hardware. Ames laboratory of the space navigation bureau of the United States has perfected HMD and applied VLP's data gloves to engineering. Now, it is dedicated to a trial plan named Virtual Planet Exploration. This project can make "Virtual Explorer" use virtual environment to investigate the faraway planet. North Carolina University began to be engaged in the research of virtual reality technology in the 70s of this century and established virtual reality laboratory. MIT built medium laboratory in 1985 and started the formal research of virtual environment. In addition, it carried out the "path study" and "movement study". At the same time, SRI research center, Washington technical center of Washington University, advanced robot research LTD. In England, about 50 graduate schools in Germany were in the process of virtual reality technology study and acquired marvelous fruits.

In China, governmental departments and scientists have begun to pay attention to the research, exploitation and application of virtual reality technology. The computer department of Peking aviation and Spaceflight University is one of the earliest units that carry out the study of virtual reality. For example, the Virtual Palace Museum system exploited by virtual reality technology is established according to the true size of the Palace Museum by using Real-time software to build a three-dimensional model, running stimulant procedure and riding bicycle in the Virtual Palace Museum with crash helmet display. This kind of system is still a pioneer at local. The exploitation of the Virtual Palace Museum greatly promotes the development of the local virtual reality technology.

4   Application of the Virtual Reality in Coal Mine

4.1   Requirements for Geosciences Visualization in VR

A review of the VR applications in scientific visualization clearly indicates that VR provides intuitive manipulation, better 3D imaging, and more useful information than conventional data displays are able to provide. So, new visualization technologies enable technicians to interpret 3D data more completely, handle more data at one time, and communicate results more accurately than they can with conventional media.

Due to the current limitations of the hardware used in VR, these five phases of data interpretation may sometimes only be applied successfully to a sub volume of the data set if the performance requirements of VR are to be satisfied. Hardware limitations may become a concern if there are over1, 000,000 polygons in a single virtual scene or if the size of the texture used is greater than the size of the texture memory.

Dr.Loftin initially formulated the functional requirements for this VR application in geoscience visualization in collaboration with geoscientists and software developers at Broken Hill Proprietary Company Limited. The functional requirements for this VR environment are listed below:

Overall Interaction

- Translate and rotate the whole model
- Zoom in and zoom out
- Navigate to an area of interest
- Provide an arbitrary cutting plane for the entire data world
- Import surfaces and volumes from one of the vendor interpretation packages

Geological Surfaces

- Surface selection
- Extract surface out of the data world to view it independently

- Change color mapping of surface
- Move the surfaces
- Edit the surfaces

Seismic Data

- Preview seismic data
- Show selected inline, cross, or time slices
- Move inline, cross line, or time slices of seismic data
- Change color mapping of data
- Create geological surfaces
- Enable an arbitrary cutting plane for seismic data only
- Display annotation associated with cursor position
- Support for 3D volume rendering and interpretation techniques
- Color editor

4.2   Application of the Virtual Reality in Coal Mine

The mostly characteristics of coal mining are the working under the ground, the stagger tunnel and the complicated working procedure. So there are lots of uncertain factors. At the same time, the coal mine is an industry, which is the enormous investment, is the long production cycle, is the excessive danger and the accident frequently occurs. Along with the virtual reality proposed as well as in each profession application, also the certain researches in the mining industry have been started. For instance, the work system of truck in the strip mine of the AIMS, the simulate system of the room and pillar mining, the assessment system of risk in virtual reality, the accident reappearance and so on.

Virtual Mine System. The virtual mine system is an important aspect in the application of the virtual reality in coal mine. At present, the engineer carry on the mine design under the two-dimensional coordinate system, like the ichnography of mining, the project ichnography and the well compare drawing, etc. In fact, these project drawings describe the spatial structure of mine, which completely rely on the designer or others imagines. This virtual mine system can translate the ideals of designer into visualization. It can provide three-dimensional model to exhibit deportation, transportation, ventilation that is designed based on the virtual reality. These models may realize interacting with the designers, willfully choosing roams the way and exhibiting design achievement. Designed virtual mine, each three-dimensional entity of mine may be saved in the model storehouse. When designed, the entity models which needs to synthesize the virtual mine can be chosen from the model storehouse, which calls the constructional virtual mine [6-8].

Virtual Workface. The virtual workface included the mining coal workface and tunneling workface. The workface is one of the important cores in the entire mine system. The status of running directly affects the production efficiency of the coal mine. The machines are large and various, the accident formation rate are high and the system structure complex, which is in the workface. The mining coal workface and the tunneling workface are independent. One is called the virtual reality system of mining coal workface; the other is called the virtual reality system of tunneling workface. There not only include the static virtual environment (for example tunnel, roof, floor and so on) but also include the dynamically interactive virtual entity.

The virtual reality system on synthesis workface of Taiyuan University of Technology is the system on simulated mining coal. This system not only may automatically demonstrate the entire process about mining coal, but also may carry on the simple man-machine interaction, which is rising, falling, moving and so on by the mouse or keyboard.

Virtual Laneway and Simulation Laneway. The laneway is the key position of join the mine production system. Its primary function is the transport coal, ventilation, draining water, walling and so on. If function of the laneway is different, its form of section, support form and supplementary equipment are also along with them respectively different.

At present, there are many the virtual laneway models in our country. Like the virtual mine in Shanxi coal museum. It contains the track laneway, the leather belt laneway, the workface as well as the partial machine. The virtual laneway of the Heilongjiang Jixi Mining Company of the East Sea coal mine has the lifter, the leather belt, the support equipment and the supplementary equipment to drill the workface and so on. All these equipments may revolve and exhibit the work scene on virtual reality in the certain degree, so they can provide direct viewing understanding to the visitor. But they are expensive. The former is more than one million Yuan, the latter is also more than 200,000 Yuan. The equipments all are racing, the unconventional froth or the cement manufactures the laneways. So it cannot actually serve for the working and the training. But the virtual laneway of the texture mapping or the triangle geometry surface may play an important role. And these mechanical devices also may carry on the man-machine interactive [8-10].

Application of the Virtual Reality in Mine Accident. The each kind of accident occurs can be fast effectively reappeared by a series of three-dimensional pictures on the computer screen. So the accident causes can be discovered, including system design and scene personnel's behavior. Meanwhile the parameter or the condition in this VR model may be changed through the interaction, thus others and the correlative hazard can be prevented.

The mine fires and firedamp explosion are the main disaster, which the mine staffs face. The solution that is the complex ventilation of the disaster on the network has been into possibly. When the mine fires occur, the ventilation can be correctly controlled which can guarantee the mine staff safely to withdraw, can prevent the fire and the noxious gas, the mist and dust from spreading. In recent years, hydrodynamics has widely used in the industry fire, the detonation and the coalmine fire. CFD can nearly accurate forecast the temperature of the fire area, the pressure of the fire wind and the real-time distributed condition of the combustion product by calculating the mathematical model of the fire and the explosive material.

At present the AIMS researchers are devoting to the mine fire VR system development. This system may really demonstrate the fire or the dynamic process of the detonation occurs through the really simulated work environment of the mine, the network analysis and the simulated result of the CFD. This system not only can simulate the condition on the fire smoke but also can show the human factor by man-machine interaction. This kind of system may be widely used in the mine fire preventing, disaster relief, training and so on [11-13].

Application of the Virtual Reality in Training. In the mining industry, all kinds of complex work environment can be simulated on the VR system. This can provide the training for the mining engineering student, which is both, may reduce the practice expense and may reduce the teaching time. So more people can accept the higher education, meanwhile mineshaft can be carried on the beforehand operation and safe education training. The kind of the dangerous situation can be simulated. The trainer can learn that how to process the kind of the dangerous situation, so the personnel quality can be improved, the accident hidden danger can be eliminated [14-16].

5   Conclusion

Along with information time arrival, the people will contact the massive information. The traditional information processing way was difficult to adapt this kind of magnanimous information analysis and processing. This question is especially prominently for the complex and huge spatial information. The people are urgent to have the new method to analyze and to process this magnanimous spatial information. The spatial information visible is precisely this kind of technology. The space information can be expressed by the graph or the picture. So people can better understand space information by people's visual sensation. In recent years, along with the function of computer enhancement, all kinds of display device as well as the visible software development, the technology on the spatial information visualization can be able to implement in the ordinary computer. Now it already has become a kind of data processing plan that the people popularly accepted.

A number of VR applications have been developed for scientific visualization. Data visualization also has important uses in the geosciences, especially in coalmine.

References

1. Jia, C.-H., Xiao, W.-G.: Discussion on virtual reality technique and simulation application, vol. 18, pp. 27–31. Xi'an Institute of Technology (1998)
2. Ma, L.-M.: Virtual Reality and its Application. Computer Era, 1–2 (February 2005)
3. Sutherland, I.: The Ultimate Display. In: Proc. IFIP Congress, pp. 506–508 (1965)
4. Sutherland, I.: A Head-Mounted Three-Dimensional Display. In: Proc. The Fall Joint Conference on Computers, pp. 757–764 (1968)
5. Zheng, Y.-P., Yan, P., Jun, H.: Applied condition of Virtual reality and its application. Information Technology, 94–95 (December 2005)
6. Li, C.-C., Wang, B.-S., Wei, Z.-Y.: Design of Mine Virtual Reality System Based on OpenGL and Its Implementation. Industry and Automation, 103–105 (April 2008)

7. Ye, B., Bao, N., Bai, Z.: The Study on Building of Virtual Reality System in Large Surface Coal Mine. In: Li, D., Liu, Y., Chen, Y. (eds.) CCTA 2010, Part III. IFIP AICT, vol. 346, pp. 173–178. Springer, Heidelberg (2011)

8. Chen, S.-H.: Realization of 3D Coal Mine Virtual Realistic System. Jilin University (2008)

9. Li, Y.-L., Bi, X.-S., Zhang, J.-W.: Application of Virtual Reality Technology in Coal Mine. Coal Technology 25, 111–113 (2006)

10. Meng, Q.-W., Ming, F., Shen, W.-L.: The Development of Coal Mine Virtual Reality System Based on Maya and Virtools. Shanxi Coking Coal Science & Technology 56, 43–45 (2011)

11. Jiang, X.-T., Lin, B.-Q., Wang, C.: The Research of the 3D Reconstruction of the Colliery Outburst Accident Based on Virtual Reality Technology. Journal of Electrical & Electronic Engineering Education 30, 38–39 (2008)

12. Wang, C.-C., Zhang, C.-H., Chen, Y.: Simulation and Analysis of Mine Accident Base on Virtual Reality. Jilin Normal University Journal:Natural Science Edition 30, 58–61, 64 (2009)

13. Kuang, Y.-H., Wang, C., Jiang, X.-T.: Representation of Colliery Outburst Based on Virtual Reality Technology. Computer Measurement & Control 18, 2885–2887 (2010)

14. Wang, B.-J., Zhang, Y.-.W., Yang, Z.-W.: Application of virtual reality technology in coal mine safety training. Journal of Henan Polytechnic University (Natural Science) 28, 561–565 (2009)

15. Wang, B.-J., Zhang, S., Zhang, Y.-W.: Application of Virtual Reality Technology in Coal Mine Safety Training. Coal Science and Technology 37, 65–67 (2009)

16. Yang, J.-Y.: Frame Design of Virtual Training System for Coal Mine Safely. Mining Saftey & Environmental Protection 38, 34–37 (2011)

Research on TD-LTE Interference
with WCDMA in Adjacent Frequency Band

Changpeng Ji[1] and Yun-fei Huang[2]

[1] School of Electronic and Information Engineering,
Liaoning Technical University,
No.188, Longwan South St., Huludao, Liaoning Province, 125105 P.R. China
ccp@lntu.edu.cn
[2] Institute of Graduate,
Liaoning Technical University
Hyunfei1987@163.Com

Abstract. TD-LTE, as the evolution of TD-SCDMA, and WCDMA systems may coexist in one area. It will result in the coexistent interference between these two systems. The inter-system interference may cause the performance loss. We analyze the performance loss of TD-LTE interference with WCDMA in adjacent frequency band. The system simulation model was modeled based on Monte Carlo, and the simulation results of the three scenarios were presented. ACIR model and interference model are improved to accommodate to the coexistence of TD-LTE and WCDMA. Then capacity loss is discussed in detail with different carrier frequencies, geographic location offsets, bandwidths, and power control parameters. What's more, ACIR values are provided about system coexistence. It provides valuable reference for the research of hybrid network planning and optimizing.

Keywords: TD-LTE, WCDMA, interference, coexistence, ACIR.

1 Introduction

TD-LTE, as the evolution of TD-SCDMA, has been set up trial network construction on a certain scale which is proprietary intellectual property rights of China. Due to the shortage of frequency resource, these two systems inevitably are coexistence in the same geographical area with adjacent frequency band. Therefore, the coexistence of TD-LTE and WCDMA is the issue that the mobile communication systems must be tackled to reduce inter-system interference and improve system performance.

Relative research for the interference of TD-LTE and WCDMA was proposed and made some achievements. For example, MCL method is adopted and project solutions are proposed, which is simple to use and gives a worst case of link budget, as in [1, 2]. The mutual interference between TD-LTE and WCDMA systems is investigated using Monte Carlo method, and analyzes different carrier frequencies and offsets influence on the interference between the systems, as in [3, 4]. We analyze data service

M. Zhao and J. Sha (Eds.): ICCIP 2012, Part II, CCIS 289, pp. 214–223, 2012.
© Springer-Verlag Berlin Heidelberg 2012

for TD-LTE interference with 12.2kbit/s speech service for WCDMA, with round-robin scheduling. For TD-LTE downlink, each user occupies one Resource Block (RB). RB is minimum resource allocation unit of TD-LTE system, which is defined as 12 consecutive sub-carriers in frequency domain and one slot in time domain. For uplink, each e-Node B will serve 5 users at the same time, as in [5, 6]. By using Monte Carlo simulation method, we research the performance loss of TD-LTE and WCDMA when they are deployed in adjacent channel. Adjacent channel interference ratio (ACIR) model and interference model are adopted into simulations, which are modified to accommodate to the coexistence of TD-LTE and WCDMA systems. Then we get the required ACIR of two coexistent systems, as in [7].

2   System Model

2.1   Network Topological Structure and Path Loss Model

This paper mainly researches the coexistence of TD-LTE and WCDMA systems in a macro scenario. 19 Hexagon macro cellular deployments with 3 sectors per site are adopted. Wrap Around technology is used to eliminate boundary effect in simulation. In order to research the influence of geographical position of BS, the position of interferer system BS is shifted. Suppose inter-site-distance is D, so the offset distance d are $0, D/\sqrt{3}, D/2\sqrt{3}$, which denotes respectively that the two systems are co-site, interferer site is located at the edge of victim system cell and the middle of two positions above.

The path loss model of BS to UE and BS to BS is used car propagation model in UMTS 30.03 and double slope model respectively, as in [8].

2.2   ACIR Model

In the uplink, ACIR depends on the UE adjacent channel leakage ratio (ACLR), ACLR model is depicted in Table 1. X serves as step (dB), $X=$ …, -10, -5, 0, 5, 10 …

Table 1. ACLR model of TD-LTE interference with WCDMA

TD-LTE	ACLR (dB)	
	Adjacent to edge of victim RBs	Non Adjacent to edge of victim RBs
5MHz	30+X (less than5RBs)	43+X (more than 5RBs)
10MHz	30+X (less than 7RB)	43+X (less than 7RBs)

For downlink, all frequency resource blocks calculate inter-system interference with the same ACIR. In order to get different performance losses, we adopt ACIR changed from 20dB to 55dB with step size 5dB, as in [9].

2.3   Interference Model

For WCDMA system, signal to noise ratio (SINR) for UE n is calculated by

$$SINR_n = \frac{P_{rx,n}}{I_{intra,n} + I_{inter,n} + N_0} \ . \tag{1}$$

Where N_0 is thermal noise; $P_{rx,n}$ is received power of use n, which is defined as

$$P_{rx,n} = P_{tx,n} G_n / L_n \ . \tag{2}$$

Where $P_{tx,n}$ denotes transmitting power of user n in uplink, or in downlink transmitting power of BS to user m; G_n is the antenna gain; L_n presents path loss between user n and BS which is serviced by it.

In WCDMA system, $I_{intra,n}$ denotes the intra-system interference to user n, $I_{inter,n}$ is the inter-system interference from TD-LTE. They are calculated by

$$\begin{cases} I_{intra,n} = (1-\alpha) \sum_{\substack{k \in cell\ m \\ k \notin n}} P_{tr,k} \cdot G_k / L_{k,m} \\ \qquad + \sum_{\substack{j \in all\ cell \\ j \notin cell\ m}} P_{tr,j} \cdot G_j / L_{j,m} \ . \\ I_{inter,n} = \sum_k \frac{P_{tr,k} \cdot G_k}{ACIR_k \cdot L_{k,m}} \end{cases} \tag{3}$$

Where α is joint detection factor, $L_{k,m}$ and $L_{j,m}$ are the path losses between interference user k, j and BS m of victim user n. $ACIR_k$ is the ACIR linear value, which is user k of TD-LTE system to user n of WCDMA system.

For TD-LTE system, we can obtain SINR through

$$SINR_n = \frac{P_{rx,n}}{I_{intra,n} + I_{inter,n} + N_0} \ . \tag{4}$$

Where the calculation of $P_{rx,n}$ is similar with WCDMA system as in (2); $I_{intra,n}$ is the intra-system interference user n, which is obtained from (5). Due to the sub-carriers orthogonality, the interference from UEs occupy the same RB position with user n. $I_{inter,n}$ denotes the interference from WCDMA to TD-LTE, which is calculated by

$$\begin{cases} I_{intra,n} = \sum_{UEs\ on\ same\ RB} P_{tr,k} G_k / L_{k,m} \\ I_{inter,n} = \sum_k \frac{P_{tr,k} \cdot G_k}{ACIR_n \cdot L_{k,m}} \end{cases} \ . \tag{5}$$

2.4   Power Control

For TD-LTE system, power control in uplink is showed in (6).

$$P_t = P_{max} \times min\left\{1, max\left[R_{min}, \left(\frac{L}{L_{x-ile}}\right)^{\gamma}\right]\right\} .$$ (6)

Where P_{max} is the maximum transmitting power; R_{min} is the ratio of the minimum power to the maximum, which is used to prevent users of good transmission channel with a low rate. L is the path loss of user, L_{x-ile} is per-set path loss value (including shadow fading), which denotes the $x\%$ of users that have the highest path loss will transmit at the maximum transmitting power. γ is the balance factor for users with good transmission channel and that with the poor channel, $0<\gamma\leq1$. In simulation, when the bandwidth of TD-LTE system is 10MHz, two sets of power control parameters are adopted: set1: $\gamma=1$, $L_{x-ile}=112$; set2: $\gamma=0.8$, $L_{x-ile}=129$.

For TD-LTE downlink, no power control is used, suppose each frequency RB has the same power and divides the total power.

In WCDMA system, closed-loop power control is adopted. For uplink, we can use (7) to determine the transmitting power of UEs in order to make the signal from UE to BS with the same E_b/N_0 value.

$$P_{tx} = max\left(P_{min}, min\left(P_{max}, P_{old} + E_b/N_{0(target)} - E_b/N_{0(measured)}\right)\right) .$$ (7)

Where P_{tx} is transmitting power of UE after power control, P_{old} is transmitting power of UE before power control, P_{max} and P_{min} denote the maximum and minimum transmitting power of UE respectively, $E_b/N_{0(target)}$ is UE received target E_b/N_0 value at BSs, $E_b/N_{0(measured)}$ is UE received E_b/N_0 value before power control.

For downlink, in order to make transmitted signal from all the BSs to UEs with the same E_b/N_0, we still can use (7) to calculate transmitting power from BS to UE. At this time, P_{tx} is transmitting power of BS to UE after power control, P_{old} is transmitting power of BS before power control, P_{max} and P_{min} denote the maximum and minimum transmitting power of BS respectively, $E_b/N_{0(target)}$ is UE received target E_b/N_0 value, $E_b/N_{0(measured)}$ is UE received E_b/N_0 value before power control.

3   Experiment Simulations

3.1   Simulation Scheme

Monte Carlo simulation method suggested is used to research the interference between TD-LTE and WCDMA systems. Then build system model according to system characteristics, topology structure, simulation scenario, propagation model and so on. Due to every sampling obeys uniform distribution, so we can simulate various positions of users in the actual system as long as simulation times are enough. In simulation, the data collected by snapshots are analyzed by statistics. Each snapshot contains the following steps, and take TD-LTE UEs interference with WCDMA BSs for example, simulation flow is showed in Fig. 1.

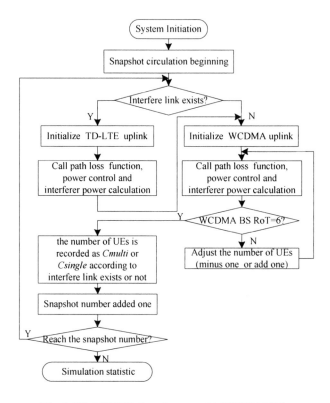

Fig. 1. TD-LTE UEs interference with WCDMA BSs

1) Initialize WCDMA system. The topology structure of 19 cells cellular is generated, initialize parameters and N users of WCDMA is distributed randomly;

2) Calculate link gain from each UE to BS, and then store them into link gain matrix G of internal system. Call soft handover function, interference model, and power control. What's more, the whole power control iterates 150 times, and power control step is 1dB;

3) Data statistics. For WCDMA uplink, the number of users through power control loop makes the raise of thermal noise reach 6dB. So we get single system uplink limit capacity;

4) Choose an *ACIR* value, the *ACIR* value is selected with steps of 5dB. TD-LTE and WCDMA are regarded as interference system and victim system respectively;

5) Initialize TD-LTE system and calculate link gain. Generate the topology structure and initialize parameters, 5 users are distributed randomly into each section. Then calculate link gain in internal system;

6) Call power control function of TD-LTE uplink. Two sets of parameters, set1 and set2, are simulated respectively, and then record the transmitting power of UEs;

7) Calculate the link gain matrix from TD-LTE UEs to WCDMA BS;

8) Simulate double systems after introducing TD-LTE. Then repeat steps 1~3 for WCDMA. What we get through the third step is the limit capacity of WCDMA uplink.

By simulation we can obtain the average relative capacity loss for the system after analyzing the data, which is collected by snapshots of the two systems, as in [10].

3.2   Simulation Parameters

The key simulation parameters are showed in Table 2.

Table 2. Simulation parameters for TD-LTE and WCDMA systems

Parameters	TD-LTE	WCDMA
Carrier frequency (GHz)	2.6	
Inter-site-distance (m)	1000	
MCL (dB)	BS-UE: 70; BS-BS: 50	
Antenna gain of BS (dBi)	15	14
Maximum transmission power of BS (dBm)	43/46	43
Target RoT value of BS (dB)	-	6
Maximum transmission power of UE (dBm)	24	21
Minmum transmission power of UE (dBm)	-30	-50
Target E_b/N_0 value of BS (dB)	-	6.1
Target E_b/N_0 value of UE (dB)	-	7.9
Active set size	1	2

3.3   Capacity Criteria

For uplink, WCDMA system is adopted 6dB noise rising standards (corresponding to the load of 75%). And for downlink, satisfaction rate for users' criteria is 95%. When dropping rate is 5%, the numbers of users are downlink capacity. The capacity loss is calculated by

$$Capacity loss = 1 - C_{multi} / C_{single} .$$ (8)

Where C_{single} is the numbers of average users in stable single system, C_{multi} is the capacity for the two coexistent systems.

4   Simulation Analyses

4.1   TD-LTE BSs Interference with WCDMA BSs

The simulation platform is established about TD-LTE downlink of 5MHz interference with WCDMA uplink. What Fig. 2 depicts is that offset value and different carrier frequencies influence on average relative capacity loss of WCDMA uplink.

By Fig. 2, when carrier frequency f=2.6GHz, for the same *ACIR* value, the greater relative offset d is, the smaller the average relative capacity loss of WCDMA is, the smaller interference system suffer. This is because path loss rises with the increasing of the two systems inter-site-distance accordingly, and interference power to the receiver also decreases. When offset d is 577, 288.5 and 0m, the required *ACIR* value should be at least 110.2, 94.5 and 93.8dB respectively to ensure that WCDMA system uplink capacity loss is less than 5%.

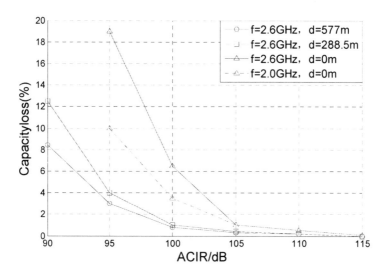

Fig. 2. TD-LTE BSs interfere with WCDMA BSs

When the two systems are co-site, which is the worst scenario of coexistence, d=0, reduce carrier frequency from 2.6GHz to 2.0GHz. At this time, in order to ensure WCDMA uplink capacity loss less than 5%, the required ACIR at 2.0GHz is lower 3.5dB than that at 2.6GHz.

4.2   TD-LTE BSs Interference with WCDMA UEs

The simulation result of TD-LTE BSs interference with WCDMA UEs is showed in Fig. 3. B is the bandwidth of TD-LTE system. We can get the following conclusions through the simulation analysis:

1) WCDMA downlink capacity loss rises with the increase of *ACIR* value;

2) TD-LTE of wider bandwidth interferes with WCDMA UEs more serious;

3) TD-LTE BSs of 10MHz is regarded as interfere source, when offset distance is 577, 288.5 and 0m, the required *ACIR* value should be at least 25, 32 and 33dB respectively to ensure that capacity loss is less than 5%. In additional, the required *ACIR* is increased by 3dB when TD-LTE BSs of 5MHz is regarded as interfere source.

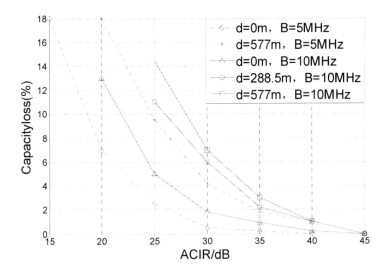

Fig. 3. TD-LTE BSs interfere with WCDMA UEs

4.3   TD-LTE UEs Interference with WCDMA BSs

What Fig. 4 depicts is the average capacity loss of TD-LTE UEs interference with WCDMA BSs, where *B* is bandwidth of TD-LTE system. We can obtain the following conclusions through the simulation analysis:

1) TD-LTE of smaller bandwidth generates less interference to WCDMA BSs.

2) When 5MHz TD-LTE interferes with WCDMA system, the required *ACIR* is less 3~4.5dB than that 10MHz TD-LTE;

3) As power control parameters set1 is adopted, the users of higher transmitting power increase. It could improve TD-LTE system performance, but it causes more interference with WCDMA than using power control parameters set2. So using set2 is more advantageous to the two systems coexistence.

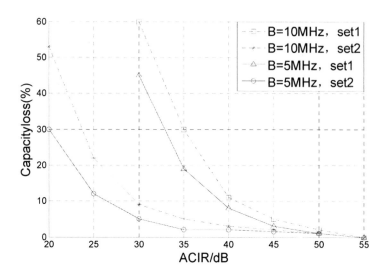

Fig. 4. TD-LTE UEs interfere with WCDMA BSs

5   Conclusion

By classical Monte Carlo method, the coexistence interference of TD-LTE and WCDMA systems was researched only in a macro-to-macro cells scenario. We analyzed that the offset, carrier frequency, bandwidth and power control parameters influence on coexistence system capacity. The simulation analysis shows that interference from TD-LTE BSs to WCDMA UEs decreases with the small bandwidth of TD-LTE. The worst case occurs when TD-LTE BSs interfere with WCDMA BSs, the stricter *ACIR* values are needed to solve system coexistence. In order to ensure high performance of systems, we must make two BS antennae have enough isolation, so that the interference could be avoided or minimized. When TD-LTE UEs interferes with WCDMA BSs, using power control parameters set2 is more advantageous to the systems coexistence. So we should take into account various factors for reasonable planning. Simulation platform proposed by this paper can be modified slightly to research the coexistence of other wireless systems, it has strong expansibility.

References

1. Iskra, S., Thomas, B.W., Mckenzie, R., Rowley, J.: Potential GPRS 900/180-MHz and WCDMA 1900-MHz Interference to Medical Devices. IEEE Transactions on Biomedical Engineering 47, 1858–1866 (2007)
2. Ratasuk, R., Ghosh, A., Xiao, W., Love, R., Nory, R., Classon, B.: TDD Design for UMTS Long-Term Evolution. In: 19th IEEE International Symposium on Personal, Indoor and Mobile Radio Communications, pp. 1–5. IEEE Press, Cannes (2008)

3. JingXin, C., Grace, D., Mitchell, P.: Capacity Analysis of Coexisting TD-SCDMA/WCDMA Systems. In: 18th IEEE International Symposium on Personal, Indoor and Mobile Radio Communications, pp. 1–5. IEEE Press, Athens (2007)
4. Meng, Z., Guofang, T., Shuangchun, L.: Interference Analysis between Macro WCDMA and Macro WIMAX Coexisted in Adjacent Frequency Band. In: International Conference on Wireless Communications, Networking and Mobile Computing, pp. 910–913. IEEE Press, Shanghai (2007)
5. Stefania, S., Toufik, I., Baker, M.: LTE–The UMTS Long Term Evolution from Theory to Practice, Chichester, United Kingdom (2009)
6. Tarokh, V.: New Directions in Wireless Communications Research, New York (2009)
7. Mugen, P., Wenbo, W.: Technologies and Standards for TD-SCDMA Evolution to IMT-Advanced. Communications Magazine 47, 50–58 (2009)
8. 3GPP TR 25.942 v10.0.0: Radio Frequency (RF) System Scenarios, Release 10 (2011)
9. 3GPP TR 36.942 v9.0.1: E-UTRA Radio Frequency (RF) Systems Scenarios (Release 9) (2010)
10. Larsson, E.G.: Model-Averaged Interference Rejection Combining. IEEE Transactions Communications 55, 271–274 (2007)

Research on 3-D Image Reconstruction Concerning Radices Dentis Based on VTK

Changpeng Ji and Dian Liu

School of Electronic and Information Engineering,
Liaoning Technical University,
No.188, Longwan South St., Huludao, Liaoning Province, 125105 P.R. China
ccp@lntu.edu.cn

Abstract. In modern dental operations, dentists need to fix the position of radices dentis accurately in the process in order to relieve suffering of patients. Three-dimensional image reconstruction concerning radices dentis can help dentists achieve this aim and improve the vivacity and interaction of diagnosis greatly. In this research we adopt visualization tool kit with strong function based on VC6.0, acquire several CT images of a healthy person in DICOM format as the research objects, use the VTKfilter and Laplacian sharpening template for preprocessing of the images, and then adopt the Ray-Casting Algorithm which is developed for volume rendering to construct a three-dimensional visualization model, at last we complete three-dimensional image reconstruction successfully.

Keywords: Three-dimensional image reconstruction, DICOM, VTK, volume rendering, Ray-Casting Algorithm.

1   Introduction

In recent years, as the fast development of computer three-dimensional graphic image processing technique as well as the lossless and high spatial resolution CT technology has been widely used in the medical field, adopting two-dimensional medical image sequence to reconstruct the three-dimensional model and then offering comprehensive, intuitive and accurate information of lesions or normal tissues to doctors has become the research focus in the medical field. Three-dimensional image reconstruction is one of the significant research directions of computer visualization [1], foreign scholars have achieved some results in the field, for example, Lorensen came up with the MC(marching cube) Algorithm. In China, VTK has been widely used for CT three-dimensional reconstruction and surgical simulation but it still needs to be improved.

2   Brief Introduction of VTK

VTK(Visualization Tool Kit) is developed by the United States Kitware Inc. It is based on OpenGL library, open source and used in three-dimensional graphics, image

M. Zhao and J. Sha (Eds.): ICCIP 2012, Part II, CCIS 289, pp. 224–231, 2012.

processing and visualization, the newest version now is 5.8.0 [2]. VTK adopts the object-oriented technology which is popular recently, the code can be written in C++, Tcl, Java or Python, it is implemented in open cross platform development environments and can be installed and operated in the environment of Windows, Unix and so on [3], but its kernel is independent of operating system. In fact, VTK is an open source class library rather than a single system, it encapsulates numerous and frequently-used graphical operation and image processing algorithms in different classes, these classes are easy to be understood and called. The object libraries can be embedded into applications; we can also develop the library functions of ourselves on the base of VTK's basic functions. At the same time VTK has excellent streaming and cach, processing three-dimensional data produces a high memory demanding, once the program fails to request memory to the operating system, the program will make mistakes, sometimes the failure even leads to program crash, the efficient streaming and cach can solve the problem better, in addition, VTK also supports multithreading processing and has high execution efficiency. Compared with MATLAB and OpenGL library, VTK has the advantages of flexible application, better reconstruction quality and higher reconstruction speed; it can also accomplish manipulation such as image shrinking, rotating, shifting and feature extraction. The initial aim of developing VTK is the application in the medical field, VTK contains many advanced modelings and a series of visualization algorithms such as the MC Algorithm, The Ray-Casting Algorithm and so on. Since the appearance, VTK has been widely valued, used and improved continually, now it has become the most famous software development kit in the image visualization field.

VTK consists of two subsystems, one is the C++ Class Library written in C++, the other one is the interpretive layer and the layer is constructed according to certain rules, it supports script languages. The structure not only can generate effective algorithms with C++ but also keeps the characteristic of script languages at the same time, which means the users can choose their familiar languages and these languages all have their own GUI development support.

VTK adopts the pipeline architecture and sets two types of rendering processes (surface rendering and volume rendering) in the architecture of the data pipeline; the two processes adopt different visualization algorithms. The most salient characteristic of VTK programs is the pipeline, it means that a VTK program is a complete render pipeline, the forepart of the pipeline is the Visualization Model Pipeline which consists of data source, reader, filter and so on, it is used for obtaining image and preprocessing (image segmentation, smoothing and sharpening) source data information and then transforming the information into graphic data. The posterior part is the Graphic Model Pipeline, which consists of actor, camera, ray, property, mapper, renderer, render window and so on; it is used for transforming the graphic data into image. In other words, the visualization process establishes the geometric expression and then the graphic process processes it. The render pipeline can accomplish three-dimensional reconstruction of point, line and surface [4].

As VTK is an open source and free software with powerful 3D graphics processing function, an excellent architecture, high flexibility, outstanding portability and expandability, recently it is widely used in image processing, computer graphics and visualization in scientific computing; meanwhile, it has become a good choice for development of medical image visualization.

3   3-D Image Reconstruction Concerning Radices Dentis

3.1   The Ray-Casting Algorithm

The research of volumn rendering began in the 1980s. Volumn rendering is frequently used in the field of medical visualization [5].Compared with surface rendering based on the Marching Cubes Algorithm which can only display the outline of the tissues and organs, volumn rendering directly researches the relationship among the voxels which rays pass through in the volumn data field, there is no need to construct surface model, volumn rendering can display the internal and external structure of the organs we want to observe more clearly, and it offers more three-dimensional information, including properties, attributes, shape features and spatial relations among different organs, these detail information can contribute to medical diagnosis and research, however, volumn rendering has the disadvantages of high algorithmic complexity, huge amount of data and low arithmetic speed, this is a challenge in the field of medical image visualization all the time and VTK can solve these problems perfectly.

The Ray-Casting Algorithm is one of the main methods of volumn rendering based on VTK, it is a typical volumn rendering algorithm based on the object spatial scanning technology and can generate images of high quality. Its basic principle is that ray casting are stared out at every pixel on screen along the viewpoint direction and pass through the three-dimensional data field [6], we select several equidistant sampling points along the lines. Then we figure out the color value and opacity value of a certain sampling point on a line with the Tri-linear Interpolation Algorithm, the data we use for calculating are the color values and opacity values of the eight voxels closest to this sampling point. After acquiring the color values and opacity values of all the sampling points on the line, we combine the color value and opacity value of every sampling point by method of front to back or back to front, thereby figure out the color value of the pixel which gives off the ray on the screen, then write it into frame buffer, at last we can get the image wanted.

VTK offers the users three kinds of Ray-Casting Algorithm transfer functions [7]:The Iso Surface Rendering Function; The Maximum Density Projection Function; The Synthesized Volumn Rendering Function.

In this research we adopt the Synthesized Volumn Rendering Function, it is frequently used in the medical field, its principle is that taking the weighted sum of the density values of all the pixels on every ray as the final density value of the pixels on the projective plane of image, more specifically, we can transform the volumn data to optical properties such as color value and opacity value with the transfer function, then combine the properties to the pixels on the screen and finally acquire the 3D image. The algorithm is relatively simple.

3.2   Acquisition, Importing and Format Conversion of CT Images

In this research we use several CT images in DICOM format of healthy people's head, they are provided by the traditional Chinese medicine hospital in Fuxin, Liaoning Province, China, the size is 512×512×234, and interval between layers is 0.2mm.

First, we adopt the vtkVolume16Reader class or the vtkDICOMImageReader class to read CT image data, as VTK can't recognize CT image data in DICOM format, we have to use the vtkImageShiftScale class or the vtkImageCast class to convert the data type of short(DICOM format) to that of unsigned short or unsigned char(BMP format) which can be processed by VTK [8]. The partial code is shown as follows:

```
vtkDICOMImageReader *reader = vtkDICOMImageReader::New();
reader->SetDataByteOrderToLittleEndian();
reader->SetDirectoryName("E:/vtksrc/ct/radices dentis/");
reader->SetDataSpacing(3.2, 3.2, 1.5);
reader->SetDataOrigin(0.0, 0.0, 0.0);
vtkImageCast *readerImageCast = vtkImageCast::New();
readerImageCast->SetInputConnection(reader-> GetOutputPort());
readerImageCast->SetOutputScalarTypeToUnsignedShort();
//SetOutputScalarTypeToUnsignedChar();
//readerImageCast->SetOutputScalarTypeToFloat();
//readerImageCast->SetOutputScalarTypeToShort();
readerImageCast->ClampOverflowOn();
reader->Delete();
```

3.3   Data Preprocessing

After acquisition and format conversion, there exists a large amount of noise and impurity in the images. In order to extract and analyse the object's characters later, we must acquire the high-definition images so volumn data preprocessing is necessary. The data preprocessing module adopts the median filtering method to accomplish image smoothing and filtering, the median filtering method is a kind of local average smoothing technology, when the pray values in an image differ little, the method can effectively restrain various kinds of noise interference in the generation and transmission process and improve image quality, at the same time it can also restrain the fuzzy phenomenon on the edge of image caused by filtering. Its principle is that sorting the scalar value of one point and those around it and then we take the intermediate value as the scalar value of this point. In the research we choose a kind of mixed median filtering method, it can solve the problems of producing fillet and getting rid of thin line efficiently. The basic code is shown as follows:

```
vtkImageHybridMedian2D *hybird = vtkImageHybridMedian2D::New();
hybird->SetInputConnection(read->GetOutputPort());
```

In addition, after filtering, in order to outstand the information in the images we are interested in, meanwhile, decay the unimportant information, we need to sharpen the images, here we adopt the Laplace sharpening algorithms in space domain to achieve this aim. The Laplace sharpening algorithms need to call the SetNumberOfInteractions class in VTK. Through repeated tests we acquire the appropriate sharpening times for better effect of treatment.

The main purpose of data preprocessing is to furthest keep the integrality of image information, restrain interference caused by noise and impurity and make the images' visual effect better [9].

3.4   Three-Dimensional Image Preconstruction and Mapping

After data preprocessing we can acquire the relatively complete and clear volume data, then we use the volumn data to reconstruct the three-dimension images. The outstanding point and crux of the Synthesized Volumn Rendering is setting different opacity values for voxels which have different gray values, the opacity values determine the final display effect. The general aim of volumn rendering is to display several organs in an image at the same time and we can observe the spatial relations among them clearly. In the research we set the opacity values of outer organs(for example, skin) bigger so that ray can reach inner organs(for example, skeleton) through the outer organs, for this reason we should know the extent of outer organ's gray value. As the difference between gray values of two positions or layers of skin, we have to test repeatedly to acquire an appropriate extent and manage to do this. VTK offers the vtkFixedPointVolumeRayCast class as the encapsulation of the Ray-Casting Algorithm.

The partial code is shown as follows, thereinto, we use the vtkPiecewiseFunction class for setting opacity value, the vtkColorTransferFunction class for setting color value [10], the vtkVolumeProperty class for setting various kinds of properties of the volumn data and at last we adopt the vtkVolume class, the vtkVolumeRayCastCompositeFunction class and the vtkVolumeRayCastMapper class to accomplish sampling, composition, mapping and then the final three-dimensional image construction.

Opacity value setting

```
vtkPiecewiseFunction *opacityTransferFunction = vtkPiecewiseFunction::New();
opacityTransferFunction->AddPoint(10, 0.0);
//Gray value and opacity value
opacityTransferFunction->AddPoint(50, 0.1);
opacityTransferFunction->AddPoint(200, 0.1);
opacityTransferFunction->AddPoint(2900, 0.1);
opacityTransferFunction->AddPoint(2950, 0.8);
opacityTransferFunction->AddPoint(3050, 1);
//Opacity is set to 1, it means completely opaque.
opacityTransferFunction->ClampingOff();
```

Color value setting

```
vtkColorTransferFunction *colorTransferFunction =
vtkColorTransferFunction::New();
colorTransferFunction->AddRGBPoint(0.0,0.91,0.65,0.66); //Gray value and RGB
color value.
colorTransferFunction->AddRGBPoint(30.0,0.91,0.65,0.66);
colorTransferFunction->AddRGBPoint(128.0,0.91,0.65,0.66);
colorTransferFunction->AddRGBPoint(1200.0,0.43,0.43,0.43);
```

```
colorTransferFunction->AddRGBPoint(1800.0,0.43,0.43,0.43);
colorTransferFunction->AddRGBPoint(2950.0,0.9,0.0,0.0);
colorTransferFunction->AddRGBPoint(3050.0,0.9,0.0,0.0);
colorTransferFunction->ClampingOff();
```

Volumn data properties setting

```
vtkVolumeProperty *volumeProperty = vtkVolumeProperty::New();
volumeProperty->SetColor(colorTransferFunction); //Loading the color value
mapping function.
volumeProperty->SetScalarOpacity(opacityTransferFunction);
//Loading opacity mapping.
volumeProperty->SetGradientOpacity(gradient);
//Loading gradient mapping.
volumeProperty->ShadeOn();
volumeProperty->SetInterpolationTypeToLinear(); //Adopting linear interpolation.
```

Volumn rendering function and mapping

```
vtkVolumeRayCastCompositeFunction *compositeFunction =
vtkVolumeRayCastCompositeFunction::New();
vtkVolumeRayCastMapper *volumeMapper =
vtkVolumeRayCastMapper::New();
volumeMapper-> SetVolumeRayCastFunction(compositeFunction);
//Loading the volumn rendering algorithm.
volumeMapper->SetInput(append->GetOutput());
//Loading image data.
volumeMapper->SetSampleDistance(0.5);
vtkVolume *volume = vtkVolume::New();
volume->SetMapper(volumeMapper); //setting mapping.
volume->SetProperty(volumeProperty); //setting property.
```

3.5   Drawing and Display

After the process above we have reconstructed the fairly complete three-dimensional images and they need to be displayed in the VTK render window [11]. First, we create the vtkRenderer object and the vlkRenderWindow object, add the vtkActor object to the vtkRenderer, and then add the vtkRenderer object to the vtkRenderWindow, for accomplishing interactive image manipulation, we create the vtkRenderWindowInteractor object, and at last we set the vtkRenderWindow object as the interactive render window.

```
vtkRenderer *aRenderer = vtkRenderer::New();
//Creating renderer.
vtkRenderWindow *renWin =
vtkRenderWindow::New(); //Creating render window.
renWin->AddRenderer(aRenderer);
//Add renderer torender window.
```

```
vtkActor *skin = vtkActor::New(); //Creating actor.
Skin->SetMapper(skinMapper);
vtkRenderWindowInteractor *iren =
vtkRenderWindowInteractor::New(); //Creating objects for interactive
manipulation, such as mouse, keyboard and so on.
iren->SetRenderWindow(renWin);
vtkPolyDataMapper *skinMapper =
vtkPolyDataMapper::New(); //Creating mapping object.
skinMapper->SetInputConnection(skinNormals->
GetOutputPort());
skinMapper->ScalarVisibilityOff();
```

We can acquire the effect drawings as shown in Fig. 1.

In the drawings we can see the three-dimensional configuration of radices dentis, the configuration is relatively clear and complete. The final three-dimensional images contain abundant detail information. In general, the rendering effect is rather good.

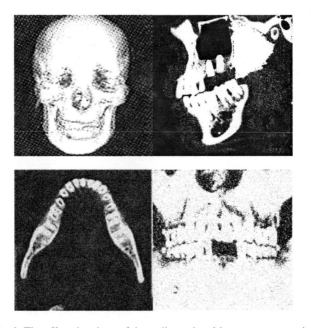

Fig. 1. The effect drawings of three-dimensional image reconstruction

4   Conclusion

This research has the aid of powerful Visualization Tool Kit to establish the visualization development environment on Visual Studio 6.0. First, we import the two-dimensional CT image data, then through image smoothing and sharpening we can ensure the completeness and sharpness of images' details, at last, we manage to reconstruct the highly precision 3D model of radices dentis with the Ray-Casting Algorithm and display the result in the visualization render window. We can observe the configuration of radices dentis clearly in the effect drawings and manipulate the images reconstructed interactively such as enlargement, shrinking and rotating [12].In general, the research achieves the expected result and lays a good foundation for the further research later.

References

1. Liu, Z., Zheng, Y.: The Three-dimensional Medical Image Reconstruction Based On VTK. Information Technology and Informatization 33, 59–61 (2009)
2. Lorensen, W.E., Cline, H.E.: Marching Cubes: A Light Resolution 3D Surface Construction Algorithms. J. Computer Graphics 21, 163–169 (1987)
3. Pang, K.C.H., Miller, J.P., Fortress, A., et al.: Age-related Disruptions of Circadian Rhythm and Memory in the Senescence Accelerated Mouse(SAMP8). J. Age 28, 283–296 (2006)
4. Schroeder, W., Avilal, M., et al.: The VTK User's Guide. Kitware Inc., New York (2000)
5. Chen, J., Bao, S.: The Applied Research of Abdomen Medical Image Volume Rendering Based on VTK. Computer Engineering and Science 32, 83–84 (2010)
6. Han, Q.: 3D Visualization Technology of Medical Images and Its Applications. J. Changchun Science and Technology University Journal 34, 56–58 (2006)
7. Yuan, G., Xie, M.: Medical Image Processing and Comprehensive Strategies of 3D Reconstruction (in press)
8. Wang, X., Li, Y., Zhang, H.: 3D Reconstruction of CT Images of Liver Based on VTK. International Journal of Biomedical Engineering 33, 28–29 (2010)
9. Gonzales.: Digital Image Processing. Beijing Electronics Industry Publishing House, Beijing (2003)
10. Hong, T., Pan, Z.: The Application and Implementation of 3D Reconstruction of Medical Images. Computer Systems and Applications 20, 127–128 (2011)
11. Leng, D., Zhou, T.: 3D Reconstruction of Permanent Teeth. Wuhan University Journal 32, 920–921 (2010)
12. Zhu, L., Xu, H.: 3D Visualization Volumn Rendering of Liver Based on VTK. Computer and Digital Engineering 22, 121–122 (2010)

An Intelligent Fire Alarm System Based on GSM Network

Yue-jiao Wang[1] and Xiao-kui Ren[2]

[1] Institute of Graduate,
Liaoning Technical University,
No.188, Longwan South St., Huludao, Liaoning Province, 125105 P.R. China
[2] School of Electronic and Information Engineering,
Liaoning Technical University
wyj0905@163.com

Abstract. Aiming at the shortcomings of the fire alarm system, a kind of intelligent fire alarm system based on GSM network is proposed. The system uses AT89S52 microcontroller as the core of the control system to implement the collection of temperature and smoke information and the fire automatic alarm processing. Communication with the users is fulfilled through the GSM global mobile communication in this system. Its short message transmission mode has broken the geographical constraints. It can achieve that the fire information is sent to the mobile phone of the relevant personnel accurately and timely when a fire occurs. It brings the convenience of taking the fire-protection measures in time. Experimental result is the effect. It can meet the design challenge.

Keywords: GSM, temperature sensor, smoke sensor, alarm system.

1 Introduction

In many disasters, fires have become recurrent, destructive and most influential disasters. With the rapid development of urban construction, the occurrence probability of the great fire and other special disasters also increased year by year [1]. Fires in the early detection and early warning are an important way to extinguish the fires promptly and avoid great casualties and property loss. Therefore, in some key fire prevention places are required to install intelligent fire alarm system [2].

The communication method of the traditional fire alarm system mostly adopts the radio or radio trucking communication. Their data transmission distance is short, transmission reliability is low, system maintenance is difficult and the cost is high. Compared with the traditional communication method, the communication method of GSM short message makes full use of public mobile network resources; it can achieve the remote fire alarm using the GSM communication module to send and receive text messages. It can save construction investment greatly and reduce maintenance cost. At present, this communication method has been widely used in timing remote monitoring, remote alarm system, location services, office automation and other aspects.

M. Zhao and J. Sha (Eds.): ICCIP 2012, Part II, CCIS 289, pp. 232–240, 2012.

Therefore, this paper designs an intelligent fire alarm system based on GSM network, it can realize intelligent fire detection, the signal transmission network and automatic alarm control, and it has a very good application prospect.

2   System Function

Fire alarm system mainly consists of information processing module, single chip microcomputer control module and alarm module. When a fire occurs in the environment, there will be change of the temperature and smoke concentration. Sensors are very sensitive to these changes. At this time, they will change the usual normal state and generate an analog signal. This signal will be sent into the single-chip microcomputer after a series of processing. Through analyzing and processing of the single-chip microcomputer, if it found abnormal, the system sends AT commands to operate the global mobile communication module through the serial port. The fire information is sent to the mobile phone of the relevant personnel in short message form to realize the function of the fire short message alarm. Block diagram of the system shown in Fig. 1.

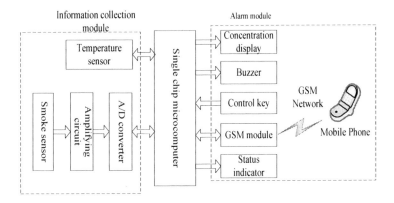

Fig. 1. Block diagram of system

3   Hardware Design

3.1   Control Chip

The core of the main control computer is AT89S52. It is a low-power, high-performance CMOS 8-bit microcontroller. With 8k bytes Flash, it can provide a large enough storage space for the design of the system; RAM of 256 bytes, 32 bit I/O port lines, three 16-bit timer/counter, A six-vector two-level interruption structure, a full duplex series interface, chip internal crystal oscillator and clock circuit. In addition, AT89S52 in the power failure protection mode, the content of RAM to be saved, and the crystal oscillator is frozen, single chip microcomputer all work stopped until the next interrupt or hardware reset.

The AT89S52 in this system is responsible for receiving corresponding analog signal of temperature and smoke that sent by the sensor on one hand, on the other hand, analyzing and processing the two signals and sending the action control command to the follow-up circuit. When the collected information value is sent into reality software, it usually requires the single chip microcomputer has faster operation speed. Most importantly, it can save the data in RAM in power-down mode. Compared with other chips, it has stronger maneuverability, low cost and good reliability.

3.2   Design of Information Collection Module

Selection of Temperature Sensor. The temperature sensor used in this design is DS18B20 temperature sensor. The sensor is a digital sensor, with high precision, good stability, simple circuit, convenient control, temperature range is wide, a huge expansion space and anti-interference ability. Signal from DS18B20 acquired will be input to the single chip microcomputer eventually. Because it is a digital chip, it can be connected to the single chip microcomputer directly. DS18B20 has two power supply mode, one is the power supply mode, and the other one is the parasitic power supply mode. But the adaptation ability of the second mode is poor and easy to be damaged [3], so here using the first mode. Its output port is connected with the P3.0 pin of single chip microcomputer.

Selection of Smoke Sensor. MQ-2-type smoke sensor is tin dioxide semiconductor gas-sensing material. It has good sensitivity for combustible gas, especially for propane, methane, liquefied petroleum gas, hydrogen, etc. Its long life, low cost, good stability and drive circuit is simple [4]. In addition, it also has good repeatability and anti-interference performance and can accurately rule out the interference information of irritating non-combustible smoke. When the environment generates smoke, smoke sensor can not be normal to collect the information immediately; it must take some time to preheat. After preheating, with the increase of concentration of the smoke in the environment, the conductivity of sensor will increase constantly. We can use this fact to obtain the information of the existence of smoke. Comprehensive comparison, this design chose this smoke sensor.

Implementation of Information Collection Circuit. The analog signal output by the sensor, is usually very weak. So generally it must be amplified by operational amplifier, so that it can meet the requirement of A/D converter for the input analog amplitude and polarity, and then meet the requirement of single chip microcomputer for input signal. However, the temperature sensor used in this design is a digital sensor, so it can be connected with the single chip microcomputer directly. But MQ-2 type smoke sensor is semiconductor resistive sensor; the weak voltage signal which collected from the sensor is amplified by the amplifier firstly. Then, after converted to digital signal through the A/D converter, it can be sent to the single chip microcomputer.

The amplifier used in information collection circuit is LM324. The amplifier is inexpensive, simple to use, it is more prominent compared with other amplifiers. In addition, LM324 is a monolithic high gain four operational amplifier. It can work in single or dual supply of a wide voltage range. Its supply current is small and the supply voltage is independent. The four operational amplifiers have good consistency, the input bias resistance is temperature-compensated, so it don't need external frequency compensation and can make the output level compatible with digital circuitry. It also adds a reference voltage and introduces zero adjustment function in the amplifier circuit. It is more convenient to solve the problem of zero change caused by the different sensors. The circuit uses slide rheostat to generate a reference voltage V_{ref}, and then the voltage is inputted to the voltage reference point of the operational amplifier circuit through the voltage follower. At this time, the reference voltage of amplifier circuit can be changed directly by adjusting the slide rheostat. Amplifier circuit structure is shown as Fig. 2.

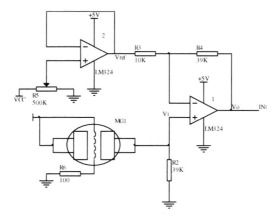

Fig. 2. Diagram of amplifier circuit structure

In Fig. 2, the role of the voltage follower is used to match the impedance to prevent the impact of R3 and R4 for the slide rheostat output voltage. When sampling, the analog signal of sensor output is sent to LM324 amplifier from V_i terminal for amplifying, and then it is sent to A/D converter circuit after output from the V_o terminal.

A/D converter is used to convert the analog signal into digital signal and then the signal will be input to the single chip microcomputer. The system uses 8-bit 8-channel modulus conversion chip ADC0809, the output terminal of smoke sensor is connected with ADC0809's IN0 pin. The channel selection address of ADC0809 is provided by the output of the address latches 74LS373, while the input of 74LS373 is provided by P0.0~0.2 of AT89S52. When P2.7=0, it controls the strobe of ADC0809 with the write signal WR. The ALE pin is connected with START pin, writes the address signal in the leading edge of the WR signal and starts the conversion in the trailing edge. The EOC of ADC0809 is connected with the INT1 pin of AT89S52. When the A/D conversion is completed, the EOC pin will become a high level. This indicates the end of conversion and generates an interrupt. In the terminal services program, the converted data will be sent to the designated storage unit. Because there is no clock within the ADC0809, an external crystal oscillator is needed in the CLOCK pins of ADC0809 to get clock.

3.3   Design of Alarm Module

Analysis of GSM Module and the Program Design. The GSM short message module used in this design is TC35; it is a new generation of wireless communications GSM module which is launched by Siemens Company. As a terminal product, it embeds TC35 wireless module and integrates standard RS232 interface and SIM card, the SIM card contains all the information of the users [5]. TC35 supports the standard AT commands; it can connect with microprocessor serial directly and send AT commands to operate by the serial. The GSM module realizes the control for short message through the asynchronous communication interface. The short message mode has two modes: Based on the AT command text (TEXT) model and based on the AT command protocol data unit (PDU) model [6]. The structure of receiving and sending short message shows in Fig. 3.

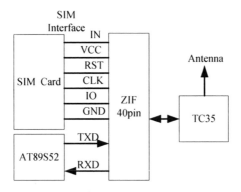

Fig. 3. The structure of receiving and sending short message

As shown in Fig 3, microprocessor serial can be connected with the GSM module directly, microprocessor uses the AT command to operate GSM module after power system start, initializes the GSM and sending and receiving short massage. The operation process is as follows:

(a) Set port parameter: The baud rate of TC35 ranges from 300bps to 115000bps. The baud rate is settled as 9600bps. In addition, it still needs to set the data bit, stop bit, parity bit and other parameter.

(b) Set ATE: set ATE as ATE0, it means the information does not display back.

(c) Set the receiving mode: when receiving the short message, it will be written into SIM card for store firstly, and read through AT+CMGR=X.

(d) Set the form of short message: TC35 supports two message forms, PDU and TEXT. The design uses PDU form, that is to set AT+CMGF=0<CF (Enter)>.

(e) Send short message: when the above process are completed, it sends AT+CMGS="target mobile phone number" <CR> to the module firstly. After the module responds, it sends the content of the message and presses "Enter", then begin to send the message.

(f) Short message receiving: After the GSM module receives a short message, the information will be sent to the serial of the data and equipment. Its receiving form is: header of message + additional message + valid message + the end of message marker [7].

Design of Sound Alarm Circuit. The circuit uses active buzzer to alarm and output, adopting DC power supply. When the concentration of the combustible gas or temperature exceeds a preset standard value, the P2.0 pin of the single chip microcomputer will be set to low level, at this time the triode turns on, the speaker beeps and alarms.

Select of Display Module. The system uses LCD1620 liquid crystal display. It has high display quality, digital interface, small volume, light weight and low power consumption. It can display 32 characters, LCD1620 liquid crystal module internal character generation memory has stored 160 different lattice character graphics. These characters can be Arabic numerals, capital and small English letters, conventional symbol and Japanese Kana, etc. Therefore, it uses more quickly and conveniently.

The D0~D7 pins of LCD1620 are connected with the P0.0~P0.7 of single chip microcomputer respectively. RS, RW and E are connected with the P3.1, P3.4 and P3.5 of single chip microcomputer respectively. BLK is connected with the ground, BLA connects to the supply after connecting a series resistance, and VL is connected with a sliding rheostat and then connected with a power supply.

Design of Status Indicators and Key Circuit. Status indicators are used to detect whether there is a fire danger in the environment. Green light indicates a normal status; there isn't a fire hazard in the environment. The yellow light indicates the heating wire of sensor is disconnected or bad contact. Red light indicates the concentration of smoke and temperature in the environment exceed the preset standard value, it is used to alert users to take appropriate security measures as soon as possible. The status indicators are controlled by P2.2, P2.3 and P2.4 of the single chip microcomputer.

Control key circuit adopts the independent button design. When the concentration of the smoke and temperature exceed the preset standard value, alarm will beep, the user arrived at the scene, press the button to stop the alarm beeps. If the concentration of the smoke and temperature in environment exceed the standard value once again, the alarm will beep again to remind the user. The four keys of the control key are connected to P1.0, P1.1, P1.2 and RST of the single chip microcomputer respectively.

4   Design of Software

When the temperature or smoke concentration detected by sensors exceeds the preset standard value, alarm system will send AT commands and the content of alarm message to GSM by the controller module. At the same time, the system will alert. The flow chart of short message alarm system is shown in Fig. 4.

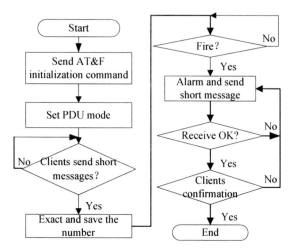

Fig. 4. Flow chart of short message alarm system

The software part of the short message alarm is implemented in C Programming Language. The core of the entire system software is to send alarm messages, including port initialization, TC35 module initialization, setting the number of SIM card short message service center and etc.

A part of C program of short message sending shown as follows:

```
//Set PDU mode.
void GSM_SetPDUmode(void)
{uchar atcmd[]={"AT+CMGF=0/r/n"};
 U1_TxOpen(0);
 U1_SendStr(atcmd);}
// Judge whether return to 'OK'.
uchar GSM_IsOK(void)
{uchar i=0;
  while(U1_Buf[i])
  {if(U1_Buf[i]=='O'&&U1_Buf[i+1]=='K')
  {cldata(U1_Buf,sizeof(U1_Buf));
  return OK;
  }
  i++;
  if(i>sizeof(U1_Buf))
    break;
 }
 return ERROR;
}
//Send messages.
void GSM_SendMess(uchar *phone,uchar *mess)
{uchar strl;
```

```
uchar atcmd[]={"AT+CMGS="};
uchar mspre[]={"000800"};
uchar *str="AT+CMGS=24";
GSM_PackPhone(phone);
strl=(strlen(gsm.set)+strlen_f(Gsm_Mspre)+strlen(mess)-
2);
//strl=(strlen(gsm.set)+strlen_f(Gsm_Mspre)+strlen_f(mess
)-2);//The hexadecimal number of the message length
except for the short message center.
strl/=2;
strl=tobcd(strl);//Be converted into BCD decimal.
gsm.messlen[0]=pgm_read_byte(ASC_NUM+(strl>>4));
gsm.messlen[1]=pgm_read_byte(ASC_NUM+(strl&0x0F));
U1_TxOpen(0);
U1_SendStr(atcmd);//Send CMGS command.
U1_SendData_C(gsm.messlen,sizeof(gsm.messlen));//Send
the length of the message.
U1_SendByte('/r');//Send '0x0D'.
U1_SendStr(gsm.set);//Send the phone number of message
center and the target.
U1_SendStr(mspre);//Send the message prefix.
U1_SendStr(mess);//Send message content.
U1_SendByte(0x1A);//Send 'Ctrl+Z'.
GsmState.GSM_SED=1;//Message has been sent.
```

5   Conclusion

In this paper, the intelligent fire alarm system based on GSM network was introduced. Information collection and short message alarm modules were designed respectively in detail. Combining AT89S52 with GSM module, it improved the reliability of intelligent fire alarm system by sending short message in GSM network. The design solved the problem that the transmission distance of traditional fire alarm system is too short and the coverage area is too small. In addition, since GSM network has the advantage of excellent compatibility, real-time, high performance-price ratio, and easy to realize, it is a better selection of the intelligent fire alarm system.

References

1. Holborn, P.G., Nolan, P.F., Golt, J.: An analysis of fatal unintentional dwelling fires investigated by London Fire Brigade between 1996 and 2000. Fire Safety Journal, 1–42 (2003)
2. Yan, Z.: Design of remote fire alarm system based on GSM /GPRS network. Journal of Zheng Zhou University, 123–125 (2006) (in Chinese)
3. Xue, H., Guoping, J.: Application of digital temperature sensor DS18B20 in greenhouse environment monitoring. Instrument Technology and Sensor, 29–31 (2002) (in Chinese)

4. Changgeng, L., Yuxin, Z.: Design of multi-senser data acquisition systerm based on wirless RF. Microcomputer Information, 151–153 (2008) (in Chinese)
5. Yutian, W., Ruiguang, W., Xifeng, Z.: GSM module TC35 and its application. Computer Measurement and Control, 557–560 (2002) (in Chinese)
6. Ke, M., Heping, C.: Design and implementation of fire short message alarm system. Computer engineering and Design Journal, 2387–2389 (2008) (in Chinese)
7. Xiongwei, L., Panqing, W.: Design of GSM short message module interface basedon the characteristic string. Computer Measurement and Control, 1407–1408 (2010) (in Chinese)

Based on Cloud-Computing's Web Data Mining

Shen Ruan

Department of Mathematics and Computer Science,
Liuzhou Teachers College,
Liuzhou, Guangxi 545004, China
Playboy0217@163.com

Abstract. On the Internet, huge amounts of data generated is distributed, heterogeneous, dynamic, more complex, if the use of the existing centralized data mining methods can not meet the application requirements. To solve these problems, proposed a cloud computing- based Web data mining method, the massive data and mining tasks will be decomposed on multiple computers parallely processed. We use open platform--Hadoop to establish a parallel association rules mining algorithm based on Apriori, and it tests and veriftes the efficiency of system. This paper proposed a design thinking that migrate the calculation to the store, the calculation will be implemented on the locals to rage nodes, thus it can avoid the large amount of data transmission on the network, and will no take a lot of band width.

Keywords: Cloud computing, data mining, parallel association rules.

1   Introduction

Found in the data collection data mining useful information is a hot research. Web data mining is based on the amount of data analysis on the Web Shanghai based on the use of data mining algorithms to effectively collect, select and store the information of interest and an increasing number of information in the discovery of new concepts and the relationships between them, to achieve automation of information processing. This is outside the enterprise to obtain useful and reliable information on the course of commercial operations to collect, analyze data to make the right decision has great significance.

Currently, Web log mining to be studied there are two main problems: First, how to deal with distributed integration and Web log; second is how to develop high-performance, scalable distributed parallel mining algorithms, to ensure the efficiency of mining. Research in recent years [1, 2] focus on platform based GlobusToolkit parallel data mining algorithms to achieve with the improvements. However, the lack of commercial grid computing to achieve, and GlobusToolkit is based on middleware technology, need to be programmed or set to build the underlying infrastructure installed, increasing the difficulty of system implementation [3].

Web data mining is a massive data processing, and the exponential growth, while the design to the mining algorithm is quite complex, and some algorithms need to scan the database many times, when the increased amount of data will increase the

M. Zhao and J. Sha (Eds.): ICCIP 2012, Part II, CCIS 289, pp. 241–248, 2012.

cost of scanning; some algorithms need to store the sequence of the relevant information, when a large amount of information, there will be storage problems[5,6]. Therefore, cloud computing will be integrated into Web data mining has a very important practical significance, can solve the mass distribution on the Internet wide area data mining problem.

2   MAP / Reduce Programming Model

Map / Reduce is a large amount of data used for the calculation of the programming model, but also an efficient task scheduling model, it will be a lot more fine-grained tasks into subtasks, these subtasks can be in the idle processing nodes between the dispatching, faster processing speed makes more nodes handling the task, thus avoiding the slow processing speed of the nodes to extend the task completion time. Express it as a large-scale distributed computing on the data key / value pairs for serialization of distributed operations, including Map (mapping) and Reduce (Simplify) in two stages. Map is a sub-process, is used to split the input data with a large number of data segments, and each piece of data assigned to a computer processing, to the effect of distributed computing, and Reduce put together to separate the data together the final results will be aggregated output. Map / Reduce implementation by the two different types of nodes responsible for, Master and Worker. Worker is responsible for data processing, Master is responsible for task scheduling and data sharing between different nodes. Implementation of a Map / Reduce operation requires five steps: the input file, the file split and assigned to the parallel execution of multiple worker, a local writing intermediate file, merge the intermediate files and output the final result[7].

2.1   Outline

Cloud-based Web data mining system on the Internet is vast amounts of data and wide-area distributed computing resources of the environment found in the data model and access to new knowledge and the law. Cloud-based Web data mining with traditional Web data mining the same basic process is divided into data preprocessing, data mining, pattern evaluation of three stages, only in the data processing means are different, the difference is the use of the Hadoop MapReduce ideas: 1) the collection of data, a change in the tradition of all data, files stored in the data warehouse unified approach to wide-area distributed on the Web through the vast amounts of data filtering, cleaning, transformation and consolidation, and into semi-structured XML file, save to the distributed file system. Copy the same file will be copied and stored in different storage nodes, so that not only can solve the prevalent traditional Web data mining and storage capacity expansion I / O operations issues, but also can effectively avoid because of mechanical failures caused by data loss problems. 2) in the implementation of a specific mining task, the task master node (Master) is responsible for the control of the entire work, create a child node of the subordinate tasks, and then by the idle computing resources on the Web (ServiceNode) to deal with, Service-Node will status and completion information to report to the Master. Finally, the results from the Master is responsible for all merger.

2.2   Integration of Computing and Storage

In the Internet, network bandwidth is relatively scarce resources. Map / Reduce the Map in the operation of each node, processing the data transmission does not work normally, but in the process need to Master Reduce transmission results for Web data mining this data-intensive computing tasks, this method saves a lot of data transfer time. As network transmission speeds far less than the CPU calculation speed, and it was proposed to calculate the exchange for communication of program strategies. Let the input data can be stored in the machine's local disk form clusters on the way to reduce the network bandwidth overhead. We can be the size of the data file into blocks of 64M, stored on a different machine copy of the block. By the Master to save the block location information, and in the appropriate input data block stored on the device perform Map task. This approach makes the most of the input data are read in the local machine does not take up network bandwidth.

2.3   Data File Backup

Cloud computing in the design of the system, not only to consider the integration of computing and storage must also be taken into account in the calculation of node failure and storage migration. General cloud computing (Hadoop) for storage migration, but migration of computing and storage simultaneously is done well, the migration of computing is based on the data block must copy strategy, so that migration can be re-calculated to find the data to be processed. General point of view of information through the network is relatively slow migration, the migration can be calculated by the system be completed soon, in a copy of the policy system, only need to find a copy of the location, the calculation of migration in the past to complete the migration of storage and computing work, so the efficiency is very high.

2.4   System Architecture

In this paper the design of Web-based cloud computing data mining system (see Figure 1), the node is divided into three categories. One is the master node (Master), in the cloud, Master only one responsible for scheduling and coordinating work between the process of computing nodes; a class of algorithm storage node is the node responsible for storing the necessary data mining algorithms; there is a category node is a service node (ServiceNode), good for storage sub-block XML file and perform the tasks assigned by the Master, and the results returned to the Master. Accordingly, cloud-based Web data mining system is divided into three layers: the data storage layer, business process mining algorithms layer and layer.

Data storage layer

This layer should have the following functions:① able to collect documents on the Web, such as Web log files automatically parse the XML file into a semi-structured, and into distributed storage system;② can automatically copy the XML file, copy the XML file is stored in a DataNode at random on a DataNode prevent data loss caused by paralysis of the problem;③ long-term memory contains user information, the user basic information file;④ large distributed data sets provide access to the interface; ⑤ distributed file system, a new DataNode DataNode add or delete the old, can automatically update.

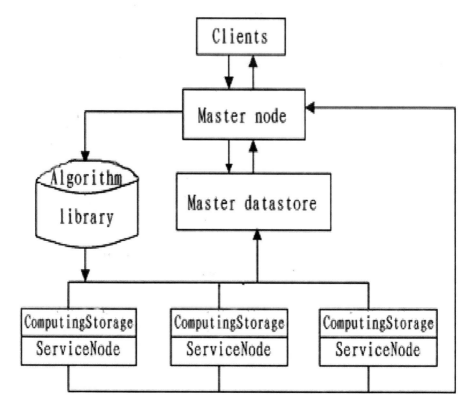

Fig. 1. Cloud-based data mining system architecture of the Web

Distributed file system is responsible for storing and reading the XML file, which consists of a master node (NameNode) and a number of child nodes (DataNode) composition. In practice, a single storage node failure is often present in the system design must be shielded trusted node failure within the system, so the file system copy of the copy storage file systems strategy to achieve high reliability. A paper copy of each XML, are stored in two DataNode on.

Shown in Figure 2, NameNode each XML file stores the metadata, these metadata include the IP address of the XML file, through which the node can be stored in the system of distributed file system access and processing XML files. NameNode also responsible for managing file storage services, but the actual data is not stored in the NameNode on. DataNode for actual data storage, access to data on the DataNode is not passed on NameNode, but to establish data communication with the user directly. DataNode from time to time to the Name-Node sends a signal to show that the DataNode is working correctly, there is no failure. If NameNode did not receive the signal, then DataNode fails, NameNode will save a copy on the other node to another DataNode, always keep the system in each XML document has two, so as to ensure the system's high reliability.

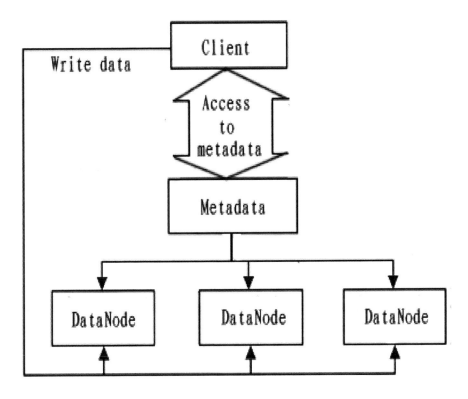

Fig. 2. File storage system architecture

The operation of the user to save the XML file as follows: First, to save NameNode submit a request, NameNode the XML file into multiple sub-file of size 64M, and query the metadata tables to find free DataNode, and then store the data DataNode IP address returned to the user, and notify the other to receive a copy of the DataNode, while the file's metadata (sub-divided into several files, each file is stored in which DataNode sub on) to write the metadata table. User based on the results directly with the corresponding DataNode connection, DataNode in the sub-file is written.

elmining algorithm

The layer (algorithm library) for storing various data mining algorithms are based on the traditional mining algorithms improved cloud computing platform for parallel data mining algorithms. The actual call, the first node from the Master to get metadata (which is called algorithm, the implementation of the algorithm the location of the node), then transferred to the corresponding algorithm on the node where the original data. This parallel implementation is based on association rule mining algorithm Apriori algorithm improvement.

Business process layer

Distributed data mining subsystem design is the task scheduling, all unified by the Master Miner is responsible for scheduling, the implementation process is as follows: ServiceNode time to time send a signal to the Master, to prove that the ServiceNode working properly. Master the ServiceNode into the free node list. M aster to receive the user's business applications, access to the data blocks required to store the information and call mining algorithms, and then to apply for the mining algorithm storage node mining algorithm is the node directly to the algorithm where the data is sent to the original ServiceNode nodes, computing tasks in the file storage server place immediately start calculations, completed only relevant results to the Master sent, not sent to the Master file data blocks, Master summary generated after the final result to the user. This process is not a file transfer and restructuring process, a computing and storage nodes in the above, save the data transfer time.

2.5   Cloud-Based Web Data Mining Algorithms

For a wide range of data mining algorithms, such as association rules, clustering, classification, association rule mining in which the Web log analysis, personalized information recommendations, and many play an important role, widely used in the field of Web data mining. Mining association rules in two steps, first step is to find all frequent itemsets; second step is the basis of the frequent itemsets to generate association rules. In order to find all frequent itemsets are commonly used iterative methods, namely: First, identify the frequent 1 - itemsets L 1, then find the set of frequent 2-L 2, has been to a k such that L k is empty, the end of the final algorithm. When seeking L k, the first through the L k-1 of the candidate itemsets generated from connection Ck, Ck then check each element to meet the user-defined minimum support threshold element is L k elements. Obviously, this wide-area data sources on the Web to validate the elements Ck is a bottleneck in the algorithm will produce a large number of candidate sets and repeat the scan database. In this paper, cloud-based platform for more than two Apriori algorithm will assign work to multiple computing nodes ServiceNode cloud parallel processing, that each compute node ServiceNode were obtained each local frequent itemsets, then the statistics by the Master of the frequent items set the total number of global support, and ultimately determine the global frequent itemsets, which can greatly improve the efficiency of mining Apriori algorithm.

This parallel implementation of Web data mining algorithms is to improve on the traditional Apriori algorithm, the mining process is as follows:① user through a Web browser made the request data mining services, association rules specified minimum support and minimum confidence.② M aster after receiving a request to dig, to NameNo de apply for the XML data files, and access a list of free nodes, the ServiceNode the metadata (machine name, IP address is free) to return to the M aster. Master will be sent to the algorithm stored in the metadata node, storage node algorithm algorithms Aprior i will send to the original data where the nodes.③ The ServiceNode first scan the local database, statistical database transaction number, the number of occurrences of each item, and then the mining process and the Apriori algorithm to get the local candidate 1 - itemset, then statistics and local candidates

1 - Item set is sent to the Master calculated the overall 1 - itemsets, and then global frequent 1 - itemsets sent to all ServiceNode generate more accurate local frequent 1 - itemsets, and then by the local 1 - draw local candidate itemsets 2-- itemsets, scan the local database transactions, statistics, number of occurrences of each item, the new local candidate 2-- itemsets and results sent to the Master repeat until the generation in line with user-defined to meet the minimum support frequent item sets, and finally generated according to rules threshold confidence level.④ Master of association rules will be returned to the user.

2.6   Algorithm Results

The system consists of multiple servers (both Linux and Hadoop installation cloud computing), of which 1 unit as a client and the master node, 1 storage node as an algorithm, five as a service node ServiceNode. In parallel execution, the time consumed mainly in the connection between each node and data transmission. First, all data on the primary node directly call Aprior algorithm to calculate the execution time; then the data set is divided into 5 sub-files are stored in five ServiceNode on the Aprior algorithm from the algorithm in parallel on the storage node spread 1,3,5 ServiceNode run, calculate the time; finally Aprior algorithms are copied to the 5 ServiceNode on the data files to run on 1,3,5 a ServiceNode to calculate the time. Through three experiments comparing the efficiency can be found with increasing amount of data significantly improved. Meanwhile, with the increase in the amount of data to the storage node transmission time of the algorithm is also significantly less than the nodes transmit data to the algorithm. This cloud-based platform to improve the Aproior algorithm, each node because of its frequent item sets are in the global side filtering, so that neither the loss of valid association rules, it does not produce valid association rules [7] .

3   Conclusion

Traditional data mining systems that run on UNIX minicomputer centralized platform, which in large amounts of data and Web mining applications in increasingly complex subject to many restrictions. Compared with traditional Web data mining, cloud-based Web data mining system resources to complete more than one cloud in the original excavation undertaken by a working node, so that resources are fully utilized to improve the efficiency of the process of data mining. Cloud-based data mining is of great significance, not only can improve the mining efficiency, but also to overcome the shortcomings of the grid environment can be for business applications, more valuable.

References

1. Li, J., Xu, C., Tan, S.-B.: A Web data mining system design and research. Computer Technology and Development 19(2), 55–58 (2009)
2. Tao, Z.: Web Data Mining Analysis. Friends of Science 6(17), 68–73 (2009)

3. Branch, C.K., Dashun, Y.: Web data integration in data mining research. Computer Engineering and Design 8(27), 271–350 (2006)
4. Jun, J.: A cloud-based data mining platform architecture design and implementation. Qingdao University, Qingdao (2009)
5. Zheng, J.: Grid-based parallel implementation of data mining algorithms. Fujian University of Technology 2(8), 20–24 (2010)
6. Ye, Y.-B., Chiang, C.C.: A Parallel Apriori Algorithm f or Frequent Item set s Mining. In: Proceedings of the Fourth International Conference on Software Engineering Research Management and Applications (SERA 2006), pp. 7–94 (2006)
7. Zheng, J.: Grid-based parallel implementation of data mining algorithms. Fujian University of Technology 2(8), 57–64 (2010)

Soft Sensor of Biomass in Nosiheptide Fermentation Process Based on Secondary Variable Weighted Modeling Method

Qiangda Yang[1] and Fusheng Yan[2]

[1] School of Materials & Metallurgy, Northeastern University, P.B. Box 345,
110819 Shenyang, China
[2] Research Institute, Northeastern University, P.B. Box 318,
110819 Shenyang, China
daqiang9666@163.com

Abstract. Biomass is hard to be measured on line in Nosiheptide fermentation process, which brings difficulties to control and optimization of this process. To solve this problem, soft sensor technique is applied to implement the on-line estimation of biomass, and a secondary variable weighted modeling method is proposed. Based on the unstructured model for Nosiheptide fermentation process, the secondary variables are selected according to the implicit function existence theorem. Then, each secondary variable is self-adaptively weighted according to its different effect on biomass, and a soft sensor model of biomass is developed by using the secondary variable weighted modeling method. The testing results show the effectiveness of the proposed method.

Keywords: Nosiheptide fermentation, soft sensor, secondary variable, weighted, modeling.

1   Introduction

Fermentation is a common mode of production in modern process industry, which has been widely used in the production of medicine, food, chemical products, and so on. Biomass is an important indicator that can reflect the course of fermentation process, and its real-time acquisition is of great significance for process optimization and control. However, until now there are no practical on-line sensors that can be used to measure biomass directly. In the industrial production, biomass is mostly measured through off-line analysis [1]. Off-line analysis has large time-delay, which brings many difficulties for the real-time monitoring and direct quality control of this process. Therefore, for fermentation process, one of the key problems to be solved is how to fulfill the on-line measurement of biomass under existing technical conditions.

Soft sensor is a technique that can estimate hard-to-measure primary variables using easily available secondary variables, which provides an effective way for solving the above problem. Many soft sensor modeling methods have been proposed over the last 30 years for fermentation process, and one of the typical modeling methods is developing soft sensor models for fermentation process using artificial

M. Zhao and J. Sha (Eds.): ICCIP 2012, Part II, CCIS 289, pp. 249–256, 2012.

neural network [2-4]. In the course of modeling, the above methods regard the position of each secondary variable as equal. However, the effect of each secondary variable on primary variables is different in fermentation process, so in order to improve the accuracy of soft sensor, it needs to give each secondary variable different degrees of consideration. In addition, the above modeling methods still have a shortage that the selection of secondary variables is not strict in theory.

Based on the above, a secondary variable weighted soft sensor modeling method is proposed for the estimation of biomass in Nosiheptide fermentation process. Based on the unstructured model for Nosiheptide fermentation process, the secondary variables are selected properly according to the implicit function existence theorem. Then, each secondary variable is self-adaptively weighted according to its different effect on biomass, and a secondary variable weighted soft sensor model of biomass is developed. Lastly, experiment is performed based on the production data from Nosiheptide fermentation process, and the results show the effectiveness of the proposed method.

2   Selection of Secondary Variables

In this paper, the secondary variables are selected based on the unstructured model for Nosiheptide fermentation process and the implicit function existence theorem, which makes the selection be strict in theory. The selection process is as follows.

According to the actual conditions of Nosiheptide fermentation process and the research results of [5-9], the unstructured model for Nosiheptied fermentation process can be written as

$$\begin{cases} \dfrac{dX}{dt} = \mu X = \dfrac{\mu_{max} S}{K_s X + S} \cdot \Omega(C_O) \cdot \Gamma(T) \cdot \Pi(pH) X \\[2mm] \dfrac{dS}{dt} = -(m_s + \dfrac{\mu}{Y_{X/S}} + \dfrac{\beta}{Y_{P/S}}) X \\[2mm] \dfrac{dP}{dt} = \beta X - \lambda P \\[2mm] \dfrac{dC_O}{dt} = g(N,Q) \cdot (C_O^* - C_O) - (m_O + \dfrac{\mu}{Y_{X/O}} + \dfrac{\beta}{Y_{P/O}}) X \\[2mm] CER = (m_{CO_2} + \dfrac{\mu}{Y_{X/CO_2}}) X \end{cases} \tag{1}$$

Where X is biomass, μ is the special growth rate, μ_{max} is the maximum special growth rate, S is the substrate concentration, K_S is the saturation constant, C_O is the dissolved oxygen concentration, T is the temperature of fermentation broth, pH is the pH value of fermentation broth, m_S, m_O and m_{CO2} are the maintenance factors, $Y_{X/S}$, $Y_{X/O}$ and $Y_{X/CO2}$ are the growth yield coefficients, β is the special product rate, $Y_{P/S}$ and $Y_{P/O}$ are the product yield coefficients, P is the product concentration, λ is the product degradation coefficient, N is the agitation speed of electromotor, Q is the air flow rate,

C_O^* is the saturation concentration of dissolved oxygen, CER is the evolution rate of carbon dioxide, $\Omega(C_O)$ is a continuous function with respect to C_O, which is subject to $0<\Omega(C_O)\leq1$, $\Gamma(T)$ is a continuous function with respect to T, which is subject to $0<\Gamma(T)\leq1$, $\Pi(pH)$ is a continuous function with respect to pH, which is subject to $0<\Pi(pH)\leq1$, and $g(N,Q)$ is a continuous function with respect to N and Q, which is subject to $0<g(N,Q)\leq1$.

Based on the fourth and fifth equations in (1), construct a subsystem described as

$$\begin{cases} f_4(\dot{C}_O, C_O, CER, pH, T, N, Q, X, S) \\ = g(N,Q) \cdot (C_O^* - C_O) - \left(m_O + \dfrac{\mu}{Y_{X/O}} + \dfrac{\beta}{Y_{P/O}} \right) X - \dot{C}_O = 0 \\ f_5(\dot{C}_O, C_O, CER, pH, T, N, Q, X, S) \\ = \left(m_{CO_2} + \dfrac{\mu}{Y_{X/CO_2}} \right) X - CER = 0 \end{cases} \tag{2}$$

For the subsystem satisfying (2), it can be proved that the corresponding determinant of its Jacobian matrix denoted as J ($J = \partial[f_4\ f_5]/\partial[X\ S]$) is not zero. Then according to the implicit function existence theorem [10], (2) can determine a functional relation described as

$$X = \Phi(\dot{C}_O, C_O, CER, pH, T, N, Q) . \tag{3}$$

From (3), it can be seen that the secondary variables which should be selected are $\dot{C}_O$, C_O, CER, pH, T, N and Q.

There are unknown functional expressions in the unstructured model for Nosiheptied fermentation process, so it is very difficult to describe the relationship between secondary variables and biomass by analytical expression. In this paper, artificial neural network is used to approximate the functional relation given by (3).

3   Soft Sensor of Biomass Based on Secondary Variable Weighted Modeling Method

With the development of research, we find that the interaction between each process variable and biomass is different in Nosiheptied fermentation process. On the one hand, the effect of each control variable such as the temperature and pH value of fermentation broth on biomass is different; on another hand, the effect of biomass on each display variable such as the content of carbon dioxide in end gas is also different. Secondary variables are coming from process variables, so the effect of each secondary variable on biomass is also different.

Based on the above knowledge, a secondary variable weighted soft sensor modeling method is proposed with reference to the feature weighted conception in categorization field. The method takes a secondary variable weighted measure to reflect the different effect of each secondary variable on biomass, and then improves the accuracy of soft sensor of biomass.

3.1   Determination of Weights

For the secondary variable weighted soft sensor modeling method, the reasonable selection of weights is the key. Generally, weights are determined by people according to experience. For this determination method, there is inevitably some subjectivity. Therefore, a novel determination method of weights is proposed in this paper. It is thought that all the above seven secondary variables fluctuate in a certain range, but the fluctuations are all in the allowed range. Thus, it can be thought that the effects of secondary variables with large fluctuations on biomass are relatively low, so the weights of them are also relatively small. The concrete steps of the determination of weights are as follows.

① Let P denote the matrix consisting of secondary variables, then it can be written as

$$\mathbf{P} = \begin{bmatrix} p_{11} & p_{21} & p_{31} & p_{41} & p_{51} & p_{61} & p_{71} \\ p_{12} & p_{22} & p_{32} & p_{42} & p_{52} & p_{62} & p_{72} \\ \vdots & \vdots & \vdots & \vdots & \vdots & \vdots & \vdots \\ p_{1L} & p_{2L} & p_{3L} & p_{4L} & p_{5L} & p_{6L} & p_{7L} \end{bmatrix}. \tag{4}$$

Where p_1, p_2, p_3, p_4, p_5 and p_6 are $\dot{C}_O$, C_O, CER, pH, T, N and Q, respectively. L is the total number of modeling data.

② Calculate the mean value of each secondary variable by

$$\mu_i = \frac{1}{L} \sum_{l=1}^{L} p_{il}. \tag{5}$$

Where $\mu_i(i=1,2,\cdots,7)$ is the mean value of each secondary variable.

③ Calculate the standard deviation of each secondary variable by

$$\sigma_i = \sqrt{\frac{1}{L-1} \sum_{l=1}^{L} [p_{il} - \mu_i]^2}. \tag{6}$$

Where $\sigma_i(i=1,2,\cdots,7)$ is the standard deviation of each secondary variable.

④ Measure the fluctuation degree of each secondary variable by

$$\gamma_i = \frac{\mu_i}{\sigma_i}. \tag{7}$$

From (7), it can be seen that the smaller the fluctuation degree of p_i is, the greater is the value of its corresponding γ_i.

⑤ Calculate the weight of each secondary variable by

$$\beta_i = \frac{\gamma_i}{\sum_{n=1}^{7} \gamma_n}. \tag{8}$$

Where $\beta_i(i=1,2,\cdots,7)$ is the weight of each secondary variable.

3.2   Implementation Steps of Soft Sensor of Biomass

The concrete steps of the implementation of soft sensor of biomass in Nosiheptied fermentation process by using the secondary variable weighted modeling method are as follows.

① Distribution of weights of secondary variables

Eliminate outliers in modeling data and determine the weight of each secondary variable by the method stated in Section 3.1. Then, normalize the secondary variables to eliminate the negative effect of the difference of variable dimensions, and distribute corresponding weights to the normalized secondary variables.

② Development of soft sensor model of biomass

As one kind of artificial neural network, RBF neural network has the universal approximation nature and the best approximation performance [11], so RBF neural network is used in this paper to develop the soft sensor model of biomass in Nosiheptied fermentation process with its inputs and output being the normalize weighted secondary variables and biomass respectively. The number of the hidden layer node is determined by the mean square error between estimation values and actual values of biomass and the complexity of soft sensor model. The center of each hidden layer node is determined by k-means clustering algorithm. The spread of each hidden layer node is determined by neighbor rules [11]. The link weights from hidden layer to output layer are determined by the least-square algorithm.

③ On-line estimation of biomass

When estimating biomass on line by using the developed soft sensor model, firstly, the on-line measurement values of secondary variables are normalized and weighted, and then they are inputted into the developed soft sensor model, and the on-line estimation values of biomass are obtained by calculation.

4   Experimental Research

4.1   Acquisition of Experimental Data

The experimental data are collected from Nosiheptide fermentation process in a "211 Projects" fermentation laboratory of Northeastern University, and the main body of fermentation equipment system of this laboratory is shown in Fig. 1. The production cycle of Nosiheptide fermentation process is about 96 hours. In this paper, experimental data from 5 batches of normal fermentation processes are used as soft sensor modeling data, and experimental data from 1 batch of normal fermentation process are used as testing data. Among the above 6 batches of data, biomass is obtained by manual sampling and off-line analysis with the sampling cycle being about 3 hours, and the secondary variables are obtained by DCS system with the sampling cycle being 5 minutes.

Fig. 1. Main body of fermentation equipment system

4.2   Performance Analysis of Soft Sensor Model

Based on the above data, a soft sensor model of biomass in Nosiheptide fermentation process is developed by the method stated in Section 3.2, and it is denoted as $Model_1$. After $Model_1$ is developed, the normalized weighted secondary variables of testing data are inputted into this model, and then the soft sensor result of biomass is obtained, as shown in Fig. 2 (*solid line*).

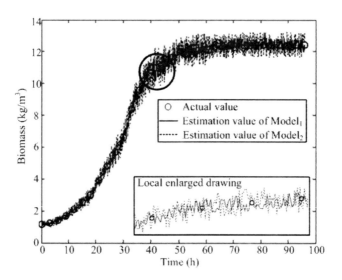

Fig. 2. Estimation results of biomass

From the curves of actual values of biomass and estimation values of $Model_1$ as shown in Fig. 2, it can be seen that $Model_1$ can estimate biomass in Nosiheptide fermentation process with high accuracy.

In addition, to reflect the advantage of the secondary variable weighted soft sensor modeling method, based on the same training method, the same modeling data and the same testing data, a soft sensor model of biomass in Nosiheptide fermentation process is developed by the traditional soft sensor modeling method (the secondary variables are not weighted in the course of modeling) in this paper, and it is denoted as $Model_2$. The inputs of $Model_2$ are $\dot{C}_O$, C_O, CER, pH, T, N and Q, and the output of $Model_2$ is biomass.

The estimation result based on $Model_2$ is shown in Fig. 2 (*dotted line*). The estimation errors of the two soft sensor models are shown in Table 1.

Table 1. Error comparison using two soft sensor models

Error Model	$Model_1$	$Model_2$
Average relative error	3.57%	6.13%
Maximum relative error	6.11%	9.55%

From Fig. 2, the outputs of the two soft sensor models can all reflect objectively the trend of biomass in Nosiheptide fermentation process. From Table 1, the estimation errors of biomass of the soft sensor model based on the proposed secondary variable weighted soft sensor modeling method is less than the soft sensor model based on the traditional soft sensor modeling method, which clearly demonstrates that the proposed soft sensor modeling method is superior to the traditional soft sensor modeling method.

5   Conclusion

Aiming at the problem that biomass is hard to be measured on line in Nosiheptide fermentation process, a secondary variable weighted soft sensor modeling method is proposed in this paper. Based on the unstructured model for Nosiheptide fermentation process, the secondary variables are selected according to the implicit function existence theorem, which makes the selection be strict in theory. Then, each secondary variable is self-adaptively weighted according to its different effect on biomass, and a secondary variable weighted soft sensor model of biomass is developed by using RBF neural network. The testing results show that the estimation performance of the soft sensor model based on secondary variable weighted soft sensor modeling method is good, and compared with the soft sensor model based on traditional modeling method, the estimation accuracy of the secondary variable weighted soft sensor model is improved obviously and the secondary variable weighted soft sensor model accords closer with the practice condition that the effect of each secondary variable on biomass is different in Nosiheptide fermentation process.

Acknowledgments. This work was financially supported by the Fundamental Research Funds for the Central Universities (N090302006).

References

1. Schügerl, K.: Progress in monitoring, modeling and control of bioprocesses during the last 20 years. Journal of Biotechnology 85, 149–173 (2001)
2. Shene, C., Diez, C., Bravo, S.: Neural networks for the prediction of the state of Zymomonas mobilis CP4 batch fermentations. Computers and Chemical Engineering 23, 1097–1108 (1999)
3. Rosales-Colunga, L.M., García, R.G., De León Rodríguez, A.: Estimation of hydrogen production in genetically modified E. coli fermentations using an artificial neural network. International Journal of Hydrogen Energy 35, 13186–13192 (2010)
4. Adilson, J., Rubens, M.: Soft sensors development for on-line bioreactor state estimation. Computers and Chemical Engineering 24, 1099–1103 (2000)
5. Beluhan, D., Beluhan, S.: Hybrid modeling approach to on-line estimation of yeast biomass concentration in industrial bioreactor. Biotechnology Letters 22, 631–635 (2000)
6. Koutinas, A.A., Wang, R., Kookos, I.K., Webb, C.: Kinetic parameters of Aspergillus awamori in submerged cultivations on whole wheat flour under oxygen limiting conditions. Biochemical Engineering Journal 16, 23–34 (2003)
7. Noor, S.K., Indra, M.M., Singh, R.P.: Modeling the growth of Corynebacterium glutamicum under product inhibition in L-glutamic acid fermentation. Biochemical Engineering Journal 25, 173–178 (2005)
8. Ruchi, S., Subhash, C., Ashok, K.S.: Batch kinetics and modeling of gibberellic acid production by Gibberella fujikuroi. Enzyme and Microbial Technology 36, 492–497 (2005)
9. Birol, G., Undey, C., Cinar, A.: A modular simulation package for fed-batch fermentation: penicillin production. Computers and Chemical Engineering 26, 1553–1565 (2002)
10. Wu, M.D., Li, Z.X., Song, S.H.: Mathematical analysis. National Defense University Press, Changsha (2003)
11. Li, C.F., Wang, G.Z., Ye, H.: Operating regime based soft sensing of polypropylene melt flow rate. Journal of Chemical Industry and Engineering 56, 1916–1921 (2005)

The Neural Network Analysis Method Applied in Prediction of Coal-Bed Methane Content

Xing-peng Jing

Shaanxi Xi'an 710054, China
Xi'an Research Institute of China Coal Technology & Engineering Group Corp
jingxingpeng@163.com

Abstract. The article applied neural net-work analysis method in prediction of coal-bed methane content. And use this method to analysis the main prediction factors of coal-bed methane content. And then the paper based on the neural network built the mathematics prediction models and system structure of coal-bed methane content. At last we applied this model in prediction of coal-bed methane content in Qinshui coal mine. Projections show that use neural network to predict the methane content of coal-bed is feasible.

Keywords: Coal-bed methane content, neural network, mathematical prediction, network structure.

1 Introduction

The reservoir parameters tested about China's coal bed methane (also known as coal gas) mainly include reservoir pressure, methane content of coal seam permeability, the survey radius, skin factor and in-situ stress, etc. There are two most important indicators to evaluate the exploitation of CBM are coal seam gas content and permeability. CBM content is the gas contented in per unit coal mass (mainly composed of methane, CH_4).So the gas content of coal-bed is the basic indicator to evaluate CBM exploration, appraisal and development. And also it is the key data of measuring coal mine's gas. Therefore, it is the main work to have a accurate test and prediction of CBM content of development and utilization of CBM. In the process of coal-bed methane content prediction, often choose geology, characteristics of coal itself, coal coring process and technical of testing as well as other factors to analyze the character of coal-bed gas. The number of indicators are even or more than ten. So it is difficult for choosing main factors to get better prediction. Therefore, in this paper used neural net-work system to analyze and predict the coal-bed methane content could greatly reduce the prediction error [1-3].

2 Main Factors of Methane Content

There are many factors include geology, coal, technology of coal coring, temperature pressure, operating processing and other factors etc. These factors not only affect the

M. Zhao and J. Sha (Eds.): ICCIP 2012, Part II, CCIS 289, pp. 257–264, 2012.

occurrence characteristics of coal-bed methane also affect the accuracy of test results about the gas content.

(1) Geology factor mainly includes geological conditions and geological structure. And the geological conditions mainly include coal seam depth, closed characteristic of roof and floor rock, nature of fracture and underground hydrogeology conditions. Geological structure can cause the coal rock's stress uneven distribution, and also has a significant impact on coal-bed methane content. Therefore, geological factors have dual nature such as water heating, tectonic stress, water dynamics in different times and parts. Eventually, leading to the large number of coal-bed methane escaped so as to affecting the content of coal-bed methane.

(2) Seam factor. It mainly includes the coal seam thickness, seam inclination, the metamorphic grade of seam, coal structure and thickness of soft coal seam layer etc. And they have a different impact on coal-bed methane gas content. Through the analysis and comparison about the test results of different coal mines in china, which the results show that it has a large deviation on the content of gas even in the same coal seam.

(3) Temperature and pressure factor, temperature and pressure have a great effect on the gas content. A certain amount of coal, with the increase of pressure, the gas content would increase, but if the temperature increasing, the gas content would reducing. Therefore, it has a direct relationship between temperature and pressure and the gas content [4].

(4) Technology of coal coring. Generally, it requires to using rope to drill coal core when test the gas content. This method use core-drilling tools take the coal core to drilling well, then load the coal core into coal core test container quickly, and start to simulate the coal seam state begin to desorbed gas. The time must within 2 minutes in 100m from coal seam to drilling well. So in the process of coring, the coring technology has a direct influence on gas content[5].

(5) Process of gas content testing, if the testers not check the test equipment carefully, the operation is not standardized, inaccurate reading, not timely recording and some man-made operational errors which have a significant influence on gas content test results.

3   Neural Networks

A neural network is a system that takes numeric inputs, performs computations on these inputs, and outputs one or more numeric values. When a neural net is designed and trained for a specific application, it outputs approximately correct values for given inputs. Similar to the brain, artificial neural nets consist of elements, each of which receive a number of inputs, and generate a single output, where the output is a relatively simple function of the inputs.

Neural nets have large degrees of freedom. Thus they are capable of modeling extremely complex functions by capturing the non-linearity of the process studied providing an efficient alternative to the more traditional statistical methods. Nowadays, there exists a range of sophisticated algorithms for neural net training differing in structure, kinds of computations performed, and training algorithms. One type of neural network is the Multi-Layer Feed Forward Network (MLF). With MLF nets, we specify if there should be one or two layers of hidden elements or neurons, and how many neurons the hidden layers should contain. The other types of neural network are the Generalized Regression Neural Nets (GRN) and Probabilistic Neural Nets (PN) (Specht, 1990, 1991). These are closely related, with GRN used for numeric prediction and the PN for category prediction/classification. With GRN/PN nets, there is no need for the user to make decisions about the structure of a net. These nets always have two hidden layers of neurons, with one neuron per training case in the first hidden layer, and the size of the second layer is determined by some facts about training data. Training a GRN net consists of optimizing smoothing factors to minimize the error, and the conjugate gradient descent optimization method is used to accomplish that. Mean square error is used during training to evaluate different sets of smoothing factors. When computing the mean square error for a training case, that case is temporarily excluded from the Pattern Layer because the excluded neuron would compute a zero distance, making other neurons insignificant in the computation and prediction (Palaside Corporation manual, 2005). Therefore, the neural network method is to find the minimum error function of the number of samples and through repeated learning to get weights of the connection layers and bias values of neurons in each layer, and be saved in order to predict the samples values which are not learned, and finally calculated the predicted results [6-8].

4   Research of Gas Prediction by Neural Networks

Neural network is a non-linear and complex network system that constitute of a large number of interconnected processing units who are similar to neurons. It could simulate human brain's neurons to complete processing, memory, identification and other information processing functions, and also it is a manifestation of the artificial intelligence. Neural network model usually simulate a given mapping by learning a algorithm. In the process of learning, the first step is to provide a set of samples which are consist of input samples and output samples. If the provided samples were much enough, and also have a strong representation, the networks would identify the host factors and the non-linear relationship between the evaluation indexes by self-organizing and adaptive ability. The samples are divided into learning sets and testing sets, the learning sets are for learning and training. The networks accord to the learning algorithm to adjust the functions and parameters until meet the requirements of predicted values. The learning sets are used to evaluate the learned network's performance whether it is a non-linear function, and in the end get a satisfactory predicted value and predicted model.

4.1   The Design of Gas Prediction System Based on Neural Network

(1) The selection of learning and training samples. Learning and training samples usually selected from the history gas data which must represent the test samples. The input parameters are determined based on the gas factors. Because there are many factors, so according these factors, we selected effectively buried depth of coal seam, reservoir temperature, coal structure and reflectance 4 factors as the main controlling factors to be the basic factors to predict the gas content.

(2) Numerical processing of learning samples. Learning samples should have a numerical processing. Some conceptual description must be transformed into numerical value in order to be identified and dealt by the neural network. So before input the samples into the neural network, the input and output samples must have a numerical processing.

(3) Determine the network structure. Based on the gas factors we determined a 4 input layers. For the hidden neural network layer, only some empirical formula could be adopted to determine its' number. According the studies when input layer has N nodes the hidden layer should has 2N+1 nodes, only in this way the gotten prediction result could reflect the real condition and ensure the accuracy of neural network computing. In fact, the hidden layer's node is not fixed but adjusted through learning. Based on the above analysis, the gas prediction model adopts 4 input layers, so there are 9 hidden layers. Finally, we determined a 4-9-1neural network, and the specific network was shown in fig.1.

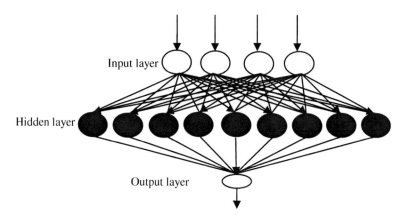

Fig. 1. The coal-bed methane content of neural net-work structure

(4) Determine the weights and thresholds of neural network. In the neural network of gas prediction system, there are 4 input parameters which are effectively buried depth of coal seam, reservoir temperature, coal structure and reflectance, that is input parameters vector of $X = (X_1, X_2, \cdots, X_n)^T$, in the vector of X, there are 3 input nodes, and in the output parameters vector of $Y = (Y_1, Y_2, \cdots, Y_m)^T$, there is only 1 output node. Therefore, the data need have a normalized processing in order to improve the accuracy of neural network's prediction. Use the following formula normalized the learning samples so as to get the output value of each node is in 0-1.

$$X i = \frac{X_i' - X_{min}}{X_{max} - X_{min}}$$

Here, X_i' ——the actual measured value; X_{min} ——the minimum value of original samples; X_{max} ——the maximum value of original samples. Before learning, for the numerical samples and the output data through the above formula can be normalize, so get the output value is in 0-1. After an iteration processing the neural network that would get convergence in the end. Finally used the gradient descent algorithm calculates the weights of input layers and out put layers and the threshold of nodes in order to get the prediction result of neural network system.

4.2   The Learning Processing of Gas Prediction Based on Neural Network

Applied neural network to the predicting processing of the gas content: ①Give the network initial weights and threshold in random. For the network, if the initial weights are equal to each other, the network can not have a normal learning and training ②Calculate the networks' actual output of each hidden layer and output layer forwardly. ③Calculate the error of each node of networks' output layers. ④Calculate the error signal of each node of networks backward. ⑤ Correct the networks' connection weights and node thresholds. ⑥ Judging the results whether it meets the network connection weights conditions, if meets, go on performing, or go back to ②. ⑦Judging the results whether it meets the nodes' thresholds' conditions, if meets, stop and save the got weights and threshold of networks, or go back to①.

4.3   Analysis the Neural Network Gas Prediction Result

Working the gas samples as the known samples to learn and train. The learning and training samples of gas content are shown in Table 1, where effectively buried depth of coal seam, reservoir temperature, coal structure and reflectance as 4 the mainly controlling factors, and the output factor is the prediction result of gas content. And with 40 prediction results and actual test values' comparison in order to learn and train samples, among the results there are 34 dates as learning and training, 6 dates as the test samples.

Table 1. The statistics of neural network prediction learning samples and prediction results

Sample number	Effective buried depth of coal seam /m	Coal structure	Reflectance /%	Reservoir temperature /°C	G_{yc}	G_{sc}	$G_{yc}-G_{sc}$	Accuracy /%
1	416. 95	columnar	4. 30	19. 35	11. 89	11. 72	0. 17	98. 55
2	514. 83	columnar	4. 27	21. 15	29. 91	31. 03	−1. 12	96. 39
3	377. 87	massive	4. 24	19. 25	9. 89	9. 26	0. 63	93. 20
4	460. 90	columnar	4. 02	20. 15	19. 10	18. 30	0. 80	95. 63
5	464. 30	columnar	4. 27	20. 05	18. 56	17. 79	0. 77	95. 67
6	530. 15	columnar	4. 25	22. 00	22. 93	22. 81	0. 12	99. 47

Table 1. (*continued*)

Sample number	Effective buried depth of coal seam /m	Coal structure	Reflectance /%	Reservoir temperature /°C	G_{yc}	G_{sc}	$G_{yc}-G_{sc}$	Accuracy /%
7	448.06	short column	4.28	19.20	17.52	17.63	−0.11	99.38
8	546.20	massive	4.11	21.20	30.24	29.09	1.15	96.05
9	367.69	columnar	4.28	17.30	12.04	11.99	0.05	99.58
10	499.70	columnar	4.31	20.15	22.89	22.78	0.11	99.52
11☆	591.68	massive	4.27	23.20	29.93	27.19	2.74	89.92
12☆	645.55	columnar	4.17	21.20	27.52	27.66	−0.14	99.49
13	648.95	columnar	4.31	21.20	28.83	28.75	0.08	99.72
14	743.48	columnar	4.36	25.50	45.89	45.70	0.19	99.58
15	642.80	columnar	4.26	22.20	24.35	24.13	0.22	99.09
16	636.79	long column	4.26	22.00	25.51	24.26	1.25	94.85
17	653.81	columnar	4.33	23.10	29.72	29.86	−0.14	99.53
18	655.31	columnar	4.28	23.10	28.73	28.61	0.12	99.58
19☆	658.78	columnar	4.33	22.20	26.62	26.48	0.14	99.47
20☆	481.10	massive	4.25	22.00	19.24	18.99	0.25	98.68
21	655.20	columnar	4.36	23.60	30.13	31.82	−1.69	94.69
22	471.10	columnar	4.31	21.60	22.92	22.83	0.09	99.61
23	368.16	columnar	4.19	18.00	17.65	17.23	0.42	97.56
24	460.86	columnar	4.20	20.00	28.12	27.79	0.33	98.81
25	454.63	columnar	4.19	20.00	20.81	20.97	−0.16	99.23
26	549.01	columnar	4.20	22.00	33.56	33.23	0.33	99.01
27	321.85	massive	4.22	18.00	18.82	20.04	−1.22	93.91
28	416.51	massive	4.23	20.00	35.98	32.53	3.45	89.39
29	418.16	massive	4.22	20.00	32.15	31.22	0.93	97.02
30	400.25	columnar	4.23	20.00	26.78	26.87	−0.09	99.67

Table 1. (*continued*)

Sample number	Effective buried depth of coal seam /m	Coal structure	Reflectance /%	Reservoir temperature /°C	G_{yc}	G_{sc}	$G_{yc}-G_{sc}$	Accuracy /%
31	416. 30	fragment	4. 14	22. 00	25. 14	24. 95	0. 19	99. 24
32	348. 81	columnar	4. 22	20. 00	24. 06	23. 93	0. 13	99. 46
33☆	352. 30	columnar	4. 26	20. 00	22. 95	22. 75	0. 20	99. 12
34☆	497. 50	columnar	4. 19	22. 00	28. 56	29. 96	−1. 40	95. 33
35	348. 04	columnar	4. 24	19. 00	12. 76	12. 20	0. 56	95. 41
36	460. 15	columnar	4. 26	20. 70	34. 56	31. 00	3. 56	88. 52
37	454. 60	massive	4. 21	20. 60	27. 48	27. 35	0. 13	99. 52
38	288. 41	columnar	4. 20	16. 00	26. 76	26. 47	0. 29	98. 90
39	374. 45	Broken kernel	4. 31	20. 20	22. 14	22. 32	−0. 18	99. 19
40	443. 70	columnar	4. 23	18. 70	18. 52	18. 44	0. 08	99. 57

In the table, Gyc—the prediction of gas content/$cm^3 \cdot g^{-1}$, Gsc—actual tested value/$cm^3 \cdot g^{-1}$; accuracy=$[1-(G_{yr}-G_{sc})/G_{sc}]100\%$, ☆—test samples.

From the 40 comparison results show that the accuracy of gas content by neural network is very high. The error between the prediction and actual test is very small. The accuracy is as high as 90%. According to the learning and training samples of gas content and the 6 known samples (11,12,19,20,33,and 33) as the test samples which based on the neural network, at the certain learning conditions the error of prediction results and actual test results is very small. The actual tested gas results which are worked as the learning and training samples. And the accuracy of the gas prediction based on the neural network model is generally greater than 90% (the error is ±10%). Therefore, we can get the conclusion that the prediction result based on neural network is steady and reliable.

5   Conclusions

(1) Although there are so many factors of gas content, we can accord to the characters of coal seam itself and through the comprehensive analysis of the factors in order to get the main controlling gas content factor, they are effectively buried depth of coal seam, reservoir temperature, coal structure and reflectance.

(2) Because there is a comprehensive non-linear relationship between the gas content factors, even some of them are random, vague and in short term, so it is hard to process the date by traditional mathematical method theory.

(3) The gas content neural model is a network structure which is based on the 4 factors that are effectively buried depth of coal seam, reservoir temperature, coal structure and reflectance and 1 output parameter: 4-9-1model. The error of used neural network to predict the gas content is small, usually the accuracy is greater than 90%.Theregfore, the neural network can be promoted in predicting the gas content's usage.

Acknowledgments. The author acknowledges the experiment support of this work by Xi'an Research Institute of China Coal Technology & Engineering Group Corp.

References

1. Jing, X.: Researching of gas pressure distribution law in south coal-bed of Qin Shui, p. 16. Xi'an University of Science and Technology, Xi'an (2010) (in Chinese)
2. Pang, X., Jing, X., Wang, W.: Coal-Bed Gas Content Experiment Research Based on Desorption by Raising Temperature. Safety in Coal Mines 41(11), 1–3 (2010) (in Chinese)
3. Yu, B.: Manuals of coal mine gas disaster prevention and the gas use technical, pp. 1–38. Coal Industry Press, Beijing (2005) (in Chinese)
4. Qian, K., Zhao, Q., Wang, Z.: The theoretical and experimental testing technology of coal bed methane's exploration and development, pp. 1–15. Petroleum Industry Press, Beijing (1997) (in Chinese)
5. GB/T19559-2008: The testing methods of coal gas. Standards Press of China, Beijing (2008) (in Chinese)
6. Zhou, Z., Cao, C.: The application of neural network, pp. 1–56. Tsinghua University Press, Beijing (2000) (in Chinese)
7. Hao, J., Yuan, C.: The application of the fuzzy network techniques in prediction of coal and gas outburst. Journal of China Coal Society 24(6), 624–627 (1999) (in Chinese)
8. Shi, H.: The application of neural network, pp. 1–79. Xi'an Jiaotong University Press, Xi'an (1987) (in Chinese)

A Delegation Model
Based on Directed Acyclic Graph

Xiujuan Zhang[1], Dianming Zhang[2], Yuanke Zhang[1], and Junhua Wu[1]

[1] School of Computer Science, Qufu Normal University, Rizhao, China
[2] Department of Information Engineering, Shandong Water Polytechnic, Rizhao, China
{zhangxiujuan1207,zdm1111,yuankezhang,shdwjh}@163.com

Abstract. Delegation in access control is used to deal with exceptional circumstances, in case of a regular user is unable to perform their normal job and delegates all or part of it to others. Delegation can be identified by a directed acyclic graph, called the Delegation Graph, with a rigorous formal modeling. In this study, we first proposed the definition and the storage structure of the Delegation Graph and then discussed the properties of the Delegation Graph. At last, we presented the algorithms about how to implement delegation, how to judge a directed acyclic graph and how to revoke delegation.

Keywords: information security, access control, delegation algorithm, directed acyclic graph.

1   Introduction

Delegation is an important aspect of access control, which is usually treated as a special case in security tasks. Many situations require the temporary transfer or granting of access rights belonging to a user/role to another user/role in order to accomplish a task. For example, a department chair may delegate his privilege to the assistant chair while he is traveling. The entity that transfers or grants his privileges temporarily to an-other entity is referred to as the delegator and the entity who receives the privilege is known as the delegatee. Delegation has been considered as a critical requirement in various domains [1-4].

In 2000, Barka and Sandhu[5] first proposed the delegation in role-based access control (RBAC). In their studies, various properties of delegation are discussed, such as permanent/temporary, monotonic/non-monotonic, and total/partial, self I acted/agent-acted and single-step/multi-step. RBDM0[6] was then proposed, which was a total delegation model since all the permissions of the delegator were delegated to the delegatee. RBDM1[7] furthermore added role hierarchies and source dependent cascading revocation. And then, the permission-based delegation model, called PBDM[4], was proposed with fully supports partial and multi-step delegation. In the following years, delegation theory has been further developed in various aspects[9-12].

The most common types of delegation include user-to-machine, user-to-user, and machine-to-machine delegation [5]. Although the entities involved in these delegation

M. Zhao and J. Sha (Eds.): ICCIP 2012, Part II, CCIS 289, pp. 265–272, 2012.

types are different, they have the same consequence—the propagation of permissions. In the study, we discussed only the user-to-user delegation. In this case, one employee, i.e. the delegator, can delegate their job to another employee, i.e. the delegatee; then the delegatee can be on behalf of the delegator and finish the task.

Delegation has many properties. Temporary delegation means that the term of delegation is short. After the term ends, delegated authority is revoked or expired. There are three types of situations where delegation takes place [8]: backup of role, decentralization of authority, collaboration of work. The first and third cases need temporary delegation of permissions. Total and partial delegation means that the delegator can delegate totally or partially the job to the delegatee. Multi-step delegation is permitted, but is not unlimited. When the delegator delegates its permissions to the delegatee, there are two cases: the delegator loses its permissions (monotonic delegation) or the delegator does not lose its permissions (nonmonotonic delegation).

Nyanchama et al.[13] propose a graph-based reference model for role-based access control and discuss how separation of duties can be represented in this model. Chen and Crampton [14] develop the representation based on graph for the spatio-temporal RBAC. Vertices represent the RBAC entities while their relationships are represented by the edges of a directed graph. But not much work appears in the context of verifying delegation using graph-theoretic notation. Our work is commited to this. Delegation can be formally modeled by directed graph with label. Directed graph has mature algorithms to help us discuss delegation's properties. Our discussion is based on RBAC model.

The following parts of this paper are organized as follows. In section 2, we gave the definition of the Delegation Graph and other basic elements definition. The algorithms of how to implement delegation and how to revoke delegation are presented in section 3 and section 5. In section 4, Delegation Graph's properties are discussed. Finally, section 6 concluded this paper.

2   Assumptions and Basic Elements

RBAC96[15] presents the basic components of the RBAC model: users (U), roles (R), permissions (P), sessions (S), administrative users (AU), administrative roles (AR) and administrative permissions (AP). A user is a human being or an independent entity that has rights to access data. A role is a position in an organization that has authority and responsibility to do a job. Permission is the right to access an object in the system. A session represents a user logged on to a system. $AU \cap U = \varphi$, $AR \cap R = \varphi$ and $AP \cap P = \varphi$. In our paper, UAU= AU∪U, and PAP= AP∪P.

The employee $u1 \in UAU$, i.e. the delegator can delegate their job $p \in P$ or their permission's set to another employee $u2 \in UAU$, i.e. the delegatee, which is called the delegation. In the access control system, all delegation at a time is called Delegation Status.

The following is the definition of the Delegation Graph. The Delegation Graph G (V, E) can present delegation Status. G (V, E) is a directed graph, where V is the vertex set and E is the labeled directed edge set. $\forall v \in V$, $\exists u \in UAU$, injective function $\lambda(v)=u$ is satisfied. $\forall v1, v2 \in V$, if $\lambda(v1)$ monotonically delegates the permission to $\lambda(v2)$, a directed edge from v1 to v2 is established whose label is σ; if λ(v1) non-monotonically delegates the permission to λ(v1), a directed edge from v1 to v2 is also established whose label is σ and differently the staring of this edge is a small black spot.

In the Delegation Graph G (V, E), let the in-degree of a vertex v be the number of edges directed into v. That is, the in-degree of v1 is the cardinality of the set {(v2, v1)|(v2, v1)∈E}. If injective function λ(v1)=u1 is satisfied, the in-degree of v1 represents the total number of user u1 delegate permissions. Similarly, the out-degree of v1 is the number of edges directed out of v1, that is, the cardinality of the set {(v1, v2)| (v1, v2)|∈E}. In the Delegation Graph G (V, E), an in-neighbor is a vertex v1 that has a directed edge (v2, v1) to v1, and an out-neighbor is a vertex v1 such that v1 has a directed edge (v1, v2) to v2.

Each directed edge label could be a four-tuple (σ, t, yndelegate, c). σ, t and c, respectively, represent delegation label, delegation time, delegation constraint. If yndelegate is 1, the user who gains the delegation can delegate it to other user; if yndelegate is 0, the user can't.

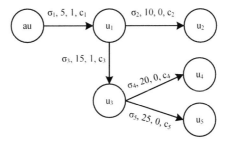

Fig. 1. An Example of the Delegation Graph

Figure 1 shows a simple example of the Delegation Graph. Root vertex represents a system administrative user au, au∈AU. The permission delegated from the vertex is user's basic permission or role. There may be more than one root vertex because system may have more than one administrative user.

The definition and the algorithm in this paper also apply for the role delegation, but the role delegation is more difficult due to role hierarchy.

3   Storage Structure

When the Delegation Graph represents Delegation Status, delegation process changes into increasing vertices and edges in the Delegation Graph. Revocation of delegation turns into deleting vertices and edges. In order to discuss the algorithms to insert, delete, query in the Delegation Graph, we customize chain storage structure of the Delegation Graph. We use the storage structure adopting adjacency list. An adjacency-list representation of a graph gives a list of out-neighbors of for each vertex. Proved by graph theory, it saves more storage space with adjacency list than with adjacency matrix when the edges are sparse and associate with much information.

VertexID	InDegree	OutDegree	FirstArc

Fig. 2. Storage Structure of the Vertex

Located on the Delegation Graph with n user vertices, each vertex creates a linked list. Figure 2 shows storage structure of the vertex. VertexID is the only identifier of the delegation. One vertex maps to one user, so it can also be used DelegatorID to identify. InDegree is the in-degree of the vertex, which indicates the delegation number that the vertex user acts as delegatee. OutDegree is out-degree of the vertex, which denotes the delegation number that the user vertex acts as delegator. FirstArc is the pointer linking to the first node, which grants the vertex user as the delegator.

DelegateID	DelegateeID	DelegateTime	YNDelegate	NextArc

Fig. 3. Storage Structure of the Directed Edge

Figure 3 shows storage structure of directed edge. One directed edge presents one delegation. DelegateID is the only identifier of this delegation. DelegateeID comes from the VertexID set, which denotes the delegatee of this delegation. DelegateTime is the time of this delegation. YNDelegate is a logical value in which 1 means that the delegatee can pass gained permission to another user, and 0 means that the delegatee can not. NextArc is the pointer linked to the next edge node. According to the specific system, vertex node and edge node may be store more information, such as delegation constraint.

Using adjacency list is a good idea. User vertices use array to store. Therefore, the user's search is random. Once the user is found, this user's number who acts as delegator and as delegatee is found. There should be extra data structure to map the number of vertices n and the number of edges k. The user number |UAU|=m, n<=m is supposed. The runtime is O(n) to find the user and the number of delegation through adjacency list.

However, to determine whether there is a delegation relationship between any two users, we need to search both users' delegation chain list. It is not as easy to use adjacency list as to use adjacency matrix. Figure 4 shows the storage structure of the above Delegation Graph example.

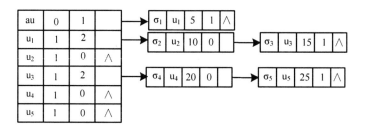

Fig. 4. Storage Structure of the Delegation Graph Example

4   Delegation Algorithm

We adopt delegation algorithm to delegate in the Delegation Graph as shown in Algorithm 1.

Algorithm 1. delegate(G (V,E), req(σ), u_2, u_3)

Input: G (V,E), current Delegation Graph G(V,E); req(σ), delegation requisition; u2, delegator; u3, delegatee

Output: G (V', E'), new Delegation Graph

Begin

if JudgeValid (req(σ)) ==0 //JudgeValid (req(σ)) is a algorithm to judge the validity of delegation requisition.

    return G(V,E)

else

    if exist vi, vj, and vi≠vj, λ(vi)=u2, λ(vj)=u3,

    then create a directed edge (vi ,σ ,vj) that is from vi to vj.

    if not exist vj, and vi≠vj, λ(vj)=u3,   // if req(σ)is valid requisition, then vi should exist.

    then create vertex vj and create a directed edge (vi ,σ ,vj) that is from vi to vj.

    return G(V', E')

End

Given an adjacency-list representation of the delegation graph G (V, E), it is easy to find a vertex' information, to insert a vertex's information and to insert a edge in linear time.

5   Delegation Graph Properties

The delegation relationship of users is anti-reflexive, anti-symmetric, and transitive. If user u_1 delegates the permission p to user u_2 and user u_2 delegates the same permission p to user u_3, we say that u1 indirectly delegate the permission p to user u_3. Thus, the Delegation Graph should be anti-reflexive, anti-symmetric, and transitive. Users grant permissions to themselves is seen meaningless and should be banned. Therefore, delegation cycle is granted as insecure policy and is forbidden in any access control system. To ensure there is no loop between users, the Delegation Graph should not have circle .So the Delegation Graph is directed acyclic graph (DAG).

A predecessor of vertex v is any vertex w such that there is a directed path from w to v. Similarly, a successor of v is any vertex u such that there is a directed path from v to u. A vertex is a source in a DAG if its in-degree is zero and a sink if its out-degree is 0. A path tree rooted at vertex v is a subset of the edges that form a tree rooted at v, oriented away from v, and reaching every successor of v. The above definitions will help us to implement algorithms of the Delegation Graph.

At any time, the Delegation Graph G (V, E) should not have a delegation loop. G is called controllable.

The following is the algorithm to judge whether a Delegation Graph have circle. Firstly, find out a vertex whose in-degree is zero, then output. Secondly, delete this vertex and the directed edges, which begin with the deleted vertex. Finally, we process the rest of the Delegation Graph with the same approach until all vertices have been output or no vertex's in-degree is zero in the directed graph. In the latter case there is a loop in the graph.

Algorithm 2. Status YNCircle(G (V, E))

begin

CountInDegree (G, indegree); //calculate the in-degree of each vertex and save in indegree[0..n-1],

InitStack(S);

for (i=0; i<n; ++i)   //n is the number of the vertices

if (!indegree[i]) Push(S, i); //push the vertex with zero indegree into the stack

count=0;   // count the output vertices

while (!EmptyStack(S)) {

Pop(S, j);   //pop the vertex with zero indegree from the stack to process

++count;

for (p=G.vertices[j].FirstArc; p;   p=p->NextArc){

- -indegree[j];

if (!indegree[j])   Push(S, j);   // push the new vertex with zero indegree

into the stack

}

}

if (count<n)   return ERROR;

else return OK;

end

If the graph is the Delegation Graph, executing the algorithm as shown in Algorithm 2 always returns OK. Based on this algorithm, we can find a depth-first search forest since source vertex is likely to more than one.

More, there is no isolated vertex in the Delegation Graph G (V, E); G is called reachable. The Delegation Graph also must ensure that. An isolated vertex is defined as one that is unreachable and therefore cannot be used. The isolated vertex can be determined by considering the in-degree and out-degree of each vertex. The isolated vertex's in-degree and out-degree equal to zero.

The above algorithm needs the in-degree and out-degree of each vertex. To get the in-degree and out-degree, we have to count the number of edges connected to each vertex. Given $n=|V|$ and $m=|E|$, the process of detecting isolated vertex can be done in $O(m*n)$ time. However, we can improve it by recording the in-degree and out-degree of each vertex. Each time the vertex or the edge is added to or removed from the graph, we update the in-degree and out-degree of the related vertices. So this update process can be done in $O(m)$. Once such values is recorded for every vertex, the detection can be done in $O(n)$.

6   Revocation in Delegation Graph

Revocation of delegation is very important. It expresses various revocation dimensions suggested in the literature [6, 16] such as propagation, dominance, grant dependency, automatic revocation. We focus our work on two aspects of revocation. The first aspect is how to perform the revocation and the effect of the revocation on other delegations (e.g. cascade revocation). The second issue is how to manage the right of revocation, i.e. who is permitted to revoke delegations.

Time-out revocation is enforced by the system. The system will check the expiration time in the label of the edge. If it has expired, the delegation is revoked and the delegation edge is deleted from the system. Depending on the system setting, if the system is ensured to use cascading revocation, then all delegations on the delegation path are revoked at the same time. If the system is not using cascading revocation, then only the expired delegations are revoked. Similar to time-out revocation, the constraint violation revocation is also configured by the system. If a constraint in C is violated, then the delegation is revoked. This revocation also can lead to a cascading revocation.

Algorithm 3. cascadingRevocation(G, s, u)

Input: G(V,E), current Delegation Graph; s, delegation that requires to revoke; u, the user who revoke the delegation;
Output: G(V', E'), new Delegation Graph
Begin
    if not exist s or no user u, return G(V,E)
    else
        get the starting vertex vi , the end vertex vj and yndelegate according to s
        delete delegation edge s
        if vi becomes an isolated vertex, then delete vi
        while yndelegate ==1
            vi=vj
            get s' from vertex vi
            get the end vertex vj and yndelegate according to s'
            delete delegation edge s'
            if vi becomes an isolated vertex, then delete vi
        return G(V', E')
End

Naive cascading revocation algorithm is presented in Algorithm 3. In fact, it is very complex because cascade revocation involves the revocation of all the permissions belonging to the delegatee. The revocation should not affect the permissions belonging to other delegator. The reason is that if the delgatee has received all the permissions not from one delegator, then if one of these delegations is revoked, the delegatee still has the right to have the permissions belonging to other delegator. It need further support from the graph theory. Of course, a strong cascade revocation will affect the other delegation associated with the same delegatee.

7   Conclusions

This paper contains a thorough discussion of delegation presented by a directed acyclic graph, i.e. the Delegation Graph. We have analyzed various prosperities of the Delegation Graph, such as anti-reflexivity, anti-symmetry, transitivity, controllability, reach ability. We have given algorithms of how to implement delegation, how to judge a directed acyclic graph and how to revoke delegation. Thus, we find graph theory helpful to the principal problems of delegation.

In our future work, the combination of delegation and graph theory needs to be further to solve various delegation problems.

Acknowledgment. This work was supported in part by Award Foundation Project of Excellent Young scientists in Shandong Province(BS2009DX024, BS2010DX013), Science and Technology Plan Project of colleges and universities in Shandong Province (J09LG34), Soft science research projects in Shandong Province (2008RKB399), Youth fund project of Qufu Normal university (XJZ200814). The authors would like to thank the anonymous reviewers for providing valuable comments and suggestions that were used in this paper.

References

1. Wainer, J., Kumar, A., Barthelmess, P.: DW-RBAC: A formal security model of delegation and revocation in workflow systems. Information Systems 32(3), 365–384 (2007)
2. Crampton, J., Khambhammettu, H.: Delegation in role-based access control. International Journal of Information Security 7(2), 123–136 (2008)
3. Hasebe, K., Mabuchi, M., Matsushita, A.: Capability-based delegation model in RBAC. In: Proceeding of the 15th ACM Symposium on Access Control Models and Technologies (2010)
4. Alam, M., Zhang, X., Khan, K., Ali, G.: xDAuth: A Scalable and Lightweight Framework for Cross Domain Access Control and Delegation. In: Proceedings of the 16th ACM Symposium on Access Control Models and Technologies, Innsbruck, Austria (2011)
5. Barka, E., Sandhu, R.: Framework for role-based delegation models. In: Proceedings of 16th Annual Computer Security Applications Conference, pp. 168–176 (2000)
6. Barka, E., Sandhu, R.: A role-based delegation model and some extensions. In: 23rd National Information Systems Security Conference, pp. 396–404 (2000)
7. Barka, E., Sandhu, R.: Role-based delegation model/hierarchical roles (RBDM1). In: 20th Annual Computer Security Applications Conference, Tucson, AZ, USA, pp. 396–404 (2004)
8. Zhang, X., Oh, S., Sandhu, R.: PBDM: a flexible delegation model in RBAC. In: Proceedings of 8th ACM SACMAT, pp. 149–157. ACM Press (2003)
9. Zhang, L.H., Ahn, G.-J., Chu, B.-T.: A rule-based framework for role-based delegation. In: Proceedings of the 6th ACM Symposium on Access Control Models and Technologies, New York, pp. 153–162 (2001)
10. Tolone, W., Ahn, G.-J., Pai, T., Hong, S.-P.: Access control in collaborative systems. ACM Computing Surveys 37(1), 29–41 (2005)
11. Hasebe, K., Mabuchi, M., Matsushita, A.: Capability-based delegation model in RBAC. In: Proceeding of the 15th ACM Symposium on Access Control Models and Technologies (2010)
12. Schiman, J., Zhang, X., Gibbs, S.: DAuth: Fine-grained Authorization Delegation for Distributed Web Application Consumers. In: Proceeding of IEEE Symposium on Policies for Distributed Systems and Networks (2010)
13. Nyanchama, M., Osborn, S.: The role graph model and conflict of interest. ACM Transactions on Information and System Security 2(1), 3–33 (1999)
14. Chen, L., Crampton, J.: On Spatio-Temporal Constraints and Inheritance in Role-Based Access Control. In: Proceedings of the 2008 ACM Symposium on Information, Computer and Communications Security, Tokyo, Japan, pp. 205–216 (2008)
15. Sandhu, R., Coyne, E.J., Feinstein, H.L., Youman, C.E.: Role-based access control models. J. IEEE Computer 29(2), 38–47 (1996)
16. Hagström, Å., Jajodia, S., Parisi-Presicce, F., Duminda, W.: Revocations-a classification. In: Proceedings of the 14th IEEE Computer Security Foundations Workshop, Nova Scotia, Canada, pp. 44–58 (2001)

Soft Sensor of Biomass in Fermentation Process Based on Robust Neural Network

Qiangda Yang[1] and Fusheng Yan[2]

[1] School of Materials & Metallurgy, Northeastern University,
P.B. Box 345, 110819 Shenyang, China
[2] Research Institute, Northeastern University,
P.B. Box 318, 110819 Shenyang, China
daqiang9666@163.com

Abstract. In the course of soft sensor modeling of biomass in fermentation process using neural network, it will usually make the modeling accuracy and estimation performance of soft sensor model worsened when there are outliers in modeling data. To solve this problem, a soft sensor modeling method based on robust neural network is proposed in this paper. Firstly, the anomaly degree of each modeling data pairs is calculated using k-nearest neighbor algorithm, and the weight of each modeling data pairs is determined according to the calculated anomaly degrees. Then, the soft sensor model of biomass based on robust neural network is developed. Simulation is performed using the production data from Nosiheptide fermentation process, and the simulation results show the effectiveness of the proposed method.

Keywords: robust neural network, fermentation, biomass, soft sensor, k-nearest neighbor.

1   Introduction

Fermentation process is a kind of complicated dynamic process with high nonlinearity. Biomass is an important indicator that can reflect the course of fermentation process, and its real-time acquisition is of great significance for process optimization and control. However, until now there are no practical on-line sensors that can be used to measure biomass directly. In the industrial production, biomass is mostly measured through off-line analysis [1]. Off-line analysis has large time-delay, which brings many difficulties for the real-time monitoring and direct quality control of this process. Therefore, the implementation of the on-line estimation of biomass using soft sensor technique has important actual significance.

Until now, there have been many soft sensor modeling methods for fermentation process, and one of the typical modeling methods is developing soft sensor models using artificial neural network [2-8]. The above methods need to use the historical data of secondary variables and primary variables to complete the development of soft sensor model, so the accuracy of the developed soft sensor model is dependent on the accuracy and validity of the obtained modeling data to a great extent. However, due to

M. Zhao and J. Sha (Eds.): ICCIP 2012, Part II, CCIS 289, pp. 273–280, 2012.

the complexity of field environment, sensor failures and other factors, there are inevitably some outliers in the historical data, which will directly affect the modeling accuracy and estimation performance of soft sensor model.

Therefore, a soft sensor modeling method based on robust neural network is proposed to develop the soft sensor model of biomass in fermentation process. Firstly, the anomaly degree of each modeling data pairs is calculated using k-nearest neighbor algorithm, and the weight of each modeling data pairs is determined according to the calculated anomaly degrees and 3σ rule. Then, a soft sensor model of biomass in fermentation process based on robust neural network is developed. Lastly, simulation research on performance of the proposed method is performed using the production data from Nosiheptide fermentation process.

2   Soft Sensor of Biomass in Fermentation Process Based on Robust Neural Network

In the introduction, it is mentioned that there are inevitably some outliers in the soft sensor modeling data from fermentation production field, and outliers can badly affect the modeling accuracy and estimation performance of soft sensor model. Therefore, a soft sensor modeling method of biomass in fermentation process based on robust neural network is proposed to diminish the effects of outliers on the developed soft sensor model. In this method, it is thought that the important degree of each modeling data pairs is different and a corresponding weight should be distributed to each modeling data pairs according to its anomaly degree when developing the soft sensor model of biomass in fermentation process. A training error weighted method is adopted to reflect the important degree of each modeling data pairs, and its detailed description is as follows.

When developing the soft sensor model of biomass in fermentation process using traditional neural network, the error function is

$$e=\sum_{i=1}^{n_p}(y_i-\hat{y}_i)^2 \quad . \tag{1}$$

Namely, the course of developing the soft sensor model of biomass in fermentation process using traditional neural network is the course of solving the problem described as

$$\min_{\theta} J(\theta)=\sum_{i=1}^{n_p}(y_i-\hat{y}_i)^2 \quad . \tag{2}$$

In (1) and (2), θ is the parameters of neural network, y_i is the actual value of biomass, $\hat{y}_i$ is the estimation value of biomass, and n_p is the total number of modeling data pairs.

The optimization problem shown in (2) does not take into account the effects of outliers on the developed soft sensor model. To diminish the effects of outliers on the developed soft sensor model, the error function shown in (1) is modified into

$$e=\sum_{i=1}^{n_p} h_i(y_i - \hat{y}_i)^2 \quad . \tag{3}$$

Meanwhile, the optimization problem shown in (2) is modified into

$$\min_{\theta} J(\theta)=\sum_{i=1}^{n_p} h_i(y_i - \hat{y}_i)^2 \quad . \tag{4}$$

In (3) and (4), h_i is the weight of the i-th modeling data pairs, and the meanings indicated by other symbols are the same as in (2). From (4), in the course of modeling, the smaller the value of h_i is, the weaker is the effect of the training error of the i-th modeling data pairs ($e_i = (y_i - \hat{y}_i)^2$) on the estimation of the parameters of soft sensor model (θ). Therefore, to diminish the effects of outliers on the developed soft sensor model, it needs to distribute relatively small weights to the modeling data pairs with relatively large anomaly degrees and distribute relatively large weights to the modeling data pairs with relatively small anomaly degrees. Thus, for the soft sensor modeling method of biomass in fermentation process based on robust neural network, the reasonable selection of weights is the key.

2.1   Determination of Weights

The k-nearest neighbor algorithm is originally proposed by Cover and Hart [9], and it is widely used in pattern recognition and content similarity based information retrieval [9, 10]. Firstly, the anomaly degree of each modeling data pairs is calculated using k-nearest neighbor algorithm with secondary variables and biomass selected as features and attribute of cases respectively. Then, the weight of each modeling data pairs is determined according to the calculated anomaly degrees and 3σ rule. The concrete steps are as follows.

① Normalize the secondary variables of modeling data $<x_i, y_i>(i=1,2,\cdots,n_p)$ (where x is the secondary variables, y is biomass, and n_p is the total number of modeling data pairs) to eliminate the negative effect of the difference of variable dimensions. The normalization formula used in this paper is

$$x_{ri}' = \frac{x_{ri} - x_{r\min}}{x_{r\max} - x_{r\min}} \quad (r = 1, 2, \cdots, n_d; i = 1, 2, \cdots, n_p) \quad . \tag{5}$$

Where x_{ri}' is the r-th secondary variable value of the i-th normalized modeling data pairs, $x_{r\max}$ and $x_{r\min}$ $(r = 1, 2, \cdots, n_d)$ are the maximum value and minimum value of the r-th secondary variable respectively.

② Deposit the normalized modeling data pairs $<x_i', y_i>$ $(i=1,2,\cdots,n_p)$ to database D, and meanwhile establish database D_{Temp}.

③ Choose randomly a modeling data pairs $<x_i', y_i>$ from D, and meanwhile deposit this data pairs from D to D_{Temp}. Then find out the k-nearest subset of this data pairs from D and D_{Temp} (the value of k generally takes 5-10% of n_p), and denote them as $S_i = \{<x^{'1}, y^1>, <x^{'2}, y^2>, \cdots, <x^{'k}, y^k>\}$.

④ Calculate the anomaly degree of $<x_i', y_i>$ by

$$\delta_i = \left| (\sum_{n=1}^{k} y^n /n) - y_i \right| .\tag{6}$$

Where, δ_i is the anomaly degree of the i-th modeling data pairs, and $y^n(n=1,2,\cdots,k)$ is the value of biomass of the n-th modeling data pairs belonging to the k-nearest subset of $<x_i', y_i>$. From (6), the larger the value of δ_i is, the greater is the difference between the value of biomass of $<x_i', y_i>$ and the modeling data pairs in its k-nearest subset, that is to say $<x_i', y_i>$ is more likely to be an outlier. So we use (6) to measure the anomaly degrees of modeling data pairs in this paper.

⑤ Repeat Step ③ and ④ till no modeling data pairs in database D.

⑥ Denote the mean value and the standard error of δ_i ($i=1, 2, \cdots, n_p$) as μ and σ. Then, they can be written as

$$\mu = \sum_{i=1}^{n_p} \delta_i / n_p ,\tag{7}$$

$$\sigma = \sqrt{\frac{1}{n_p-1} \sum_{i=1}^{n_p} [\delta_i - \mu]^2} .\tag{8}$$

According to 3σ rule and the characteristic that the smaller the value of δ_i is, the bigger is the possibility that the corresponding modeling data pairs being a normal data pairs, it can be thought that the i-th modeling data pairs is normal when $\delta_i - \mu \leq 3\sigma$; on the contrary, they are abnormal when $\delta_i - \mu > 3\sigma$. Based on the above, the formula adopted in this paper to determine the weight of each data pairs is

$$h_i = \begin{cases} 1, \delta_i - \mu \leq 3\sigma \\ (\dfrac{3\sigma}{\delta_i - \mu})^\alpha, \delta_i - \mu > 3\sigma \end{cases} .\tag{9}$$

Where, α is a positive constant, and in this paper it is chosen to be equal to 1. From (9), when a modeling data pairs is an outlier, the larger the value of δ_i is, the smaller is the weight of this modeling data pairs.

2.2   Implementation Steps of Soft Sensor of Biomass

The concrete steps of the implementation of soft sensor of biomass in fermentation process using the soft sensor modeling method based on robust neural network are as follows.

① Determine the corresponding weight of each modeling data pairs by the method stated in Section 2.1.

② Develop the soft sensor model of biomass. As one kind of artificial neural network, BP neural network has the characteristics of simple structure and easy implementation, so robust BP neural network that combines BP neural network and the above robust modeling method is used in this paper to develop the soft sensor model of biomass in fermentation process with its inputs and output being the normalized secondary variables and biomass respectively. The structure of neural network is determined by the mean square error between estimation values and actual values of biomass and the complexity of soft sensor model. The parameters of neural network are determined by the solution of the optimization problem shown in (4) using gradient descent method.

③ Estimate biomass on line. When estimating biomass on line using the developed soft sensor model, firstly, the on-line measurement values of secondary variables are normalized; then, they are inputted into the developed soft sensor model and the on-line estimation values of biomass are obtained by calculation.

3   Simulation Research

3.1   Simulation Data and Selection of Secondary Variables

The simulation data are collected from Nosiheptide fermentation process in a "211 Projects" fermentation laboratory of Northeastern University, and the main body of fermentation equipment system of this laboratory is shown in Fig. 1. The production cycle of Nosiheptide fermentation process is about 96 hours. In this paper, experimental data from 5 batches of normal fermentation processes are used as soft sensor modeling data, and experimental data from 1 batch of normal fermentation

Fig. 1. Main body of fermentation equipment system

process are used as testing data. Among the above 6 batches of data, biomass is obtained by manual sampling and off-line analysis with the sampling cycle being about 3 hours, and the secondary variables are obtained by DCS system with the sampling cycle being 5 minutes.

Based on deep analysis of the mechanism of Nosiheptide fermentation process, dissolved oxygen concentration (*DO*), one ordered derivative of dissolved oxygen concentration ($\dot{DO}$), evolution rate of carbon dioxide (*CER*), pH value of fermentation broth (*pH*), temperature of fermentation broth (*T*), agitation speed of electromotor (*N*) and air flow rate (*Q*) are selected as the secondary variables in this paper.

3.2   Performance Analysis of Soft Sensor Model

Based on the above data, a soft sensor model of biomass in Nosiheptide fermentation process is developed by the method stated in Section 2.2, and it is denoted as $Model_1$. After $Model_1$ is developed, the normalized secondary variables of testing data are inputted into this model, and then the soft sensor result of biomass is obtained, as shown in Fig. 2 (*solid line*).

From the curves of actual values of biomass and estimation values of $Model_1$ as shown in Fig. 2, it can be seen that $Model_1$ can estimate biomass in Nosiheptide fermentation process with high accuracy.

In addition, to reflect the advantage of the soft sensor modeling method based on robust neural network, estimation results are compared between the soft sensor model based on robust BP neural network and the soft sensor model based on BP neural network in this paper. A soft sensor model of biomass in Nosiheptide fermentation process is developed by the soft sensor modeling method based on BP neural network, and it is denoted as $Model_2$. The estimation result based on $Model_2$ is shown in Fig. 2 (*dotted line*). The estimation errors of the two soft sensor models are shown in Table 1.

From Fig. 2, the outputs of the two soft sensor models can all reflect objectively the trend of biomass in Nosiheptide fermentation process. From Table 1, the biomass estimation errors of the soft sensor model based on robust BP neural network are less than those of the soft sensor model based on BP neural network, which clearly demonstrates that the proposed soft sensor modeling method in this paper is superior to the soft sensor modeling method based on traditional neural network. By the analysis of experimenters in the fermentation laboratory, it can be found that the value of *pH* of the 23rd modeling data pairs is abnormal, the values of *CER* of the 30th and 146th modeling data pairs are abnormal, the value of *T* of the 40th modeling data pairs is abnormal, the values of *DO* and $\dot{DO}$ of the 76th modeling data pairs are abnormal, the value of *Q* of the 123rd modeling data pairs is abnormal, while the rest 159 modeling data pairs have no obvious abnormalities. The reason why the estimation accuracy of the soft sensor model based on BP neural network is lower than that of the soft sensor model based on robust BP neural network is that the above 6 outliers cannot truly reflect the mapping relation between secondary variables and biomass, and the soft sensor modeling method based on BP neural network cannot overcome the effects of outliers on the soft sensor model developed by it.

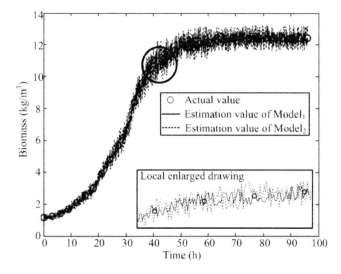

Fig. 2. Estimation results of biomass

Table 1. Error comparison using two soft sensor models

Error Model	Model$_1$	Model$_2$
Average relative error	5.34%	7.91%
Maximum relative error	9.57%	11.29%

4   Conclusion

In this paper, a soft sensor modeling method of biomass in fermentation process based on robust neural network is proposed to diminish the effects of outliers on the developed soft sensor model. Firstly, the anomaly degree of each modeling data pairs is calculated using k-nearest neighbor algorithm, and the weight of each modeling data pairs is determined according to the calculated anomaly degrees and 3σ rule. Then, a soft sensor model of biomass is developed by training error weighted neural network. The simulation results based on the production data from Nosiheptide fermentation process show that the estimation performance of soft sensor model based on robust neural network is good, and compared with soft sensor model based on traditional neural network, the robustness of soft sensor model based on robust neural network is improved obviously and soft sensor model based on robust neural network is more suitable for the soft sensor modeling problem in actual fermentation process.

Acknowledgments. This work was financially supported by the Fundamental Research Funds for the Central Universities (N090302006).

References

1. Schügerl, K.: Progress in monitoring, modeling and control of bioprocesses during the last 20 years. Journal of Biotechnology 85, 149–173 (2001)
2. Riverol, C., Cooney, J.: Estimation of the ester formation during beer fermentation using neural networks. Journal of Food Engineering 82, 585–588 (2007)
3. Nagy, Z.K.: Model based control of a yeast fermentation bioreactor using optimally designed artificial neural networks. Chemical Engineering Journal 127, 95–109 (2007)
4. Shene, C., Diez, C., Bravo, S.: Neural networks for the prediction of the state of Zymomonas mobilis CP4 batch fermentations. Computers and Chemical Engineering 23, 1097–1108 (1999)
5. Rosales-Colunga, L.M., García, R.G., De León Rodríguez, A.: Estimation of hydrogen production in genetically modified E. coli fermentations using an artificial neural network. International Journal of Hydrogen Energy 35, 13186–13192 (2010)
6. Adilson, J., Rubens, M.: Soft sensors development for on-line bioreactor state estimation. Computers and Chemical Engineering 24, 1099–1103 (2000)
7. Beluhan, D., Beluhan, S.: Hybrid modeling approach to on-line estimation of yeast biomass concentration in industrial bioreactor. Biotechnology Letters 22, 631–635 (2000)
8. Craninx, M., Fievez, V., Vlaeminck, B., De Baets, B.: Artificial neural network models of the rumen fermentation pattern in dairy cattle. Computers and Electronics in Agriculture 60, 226–238 (2008)
9. Cover, T.M., Hart, P.E.: Nearest neighbor pattern classification. IEEE Transactions on Information Theory 13, 21–27 (1967)
10. Aci, M., İnan, C., Avci, M.: A hybrid classification method of k nearest neighbor, Bayesian methods and genetic algorithm. Expert Systems with Applications 37, 5061–5067 (2010)

Accelerated Additive Operator Splitting Differential Algorithm for Qual Currency Exchange Option Pricing Model

Xiaozhong Yang[1], Gaoxin Zhou[1], and Guanghui Wang[2]

[1] Dept. Mathematics and Physics, North China Electric Power University,
102206, Beijing, China
[2] State Key Laboratory of Severe Weather (LaSW),
Chinese Academy of Meteorological Sciences, 100029, Beijing, China
yxiaozh@ncepu.edu.cn,
zhougaoxin0913@yeah.net, earth54@126.com

Abstract. Black-Scholes equation of dual currency exchange option pricing is a typical multi-asset option pricing model. It is important to research numerical solution of this equation. In this paper, accelerated additive operator splitting (AOS) differential algorithm is used to transform the multi-dimensional Black-Scholes equation into equivalent one-dimensional equations. Then 'explicit-implicit' and 'implicit-explicit' schemes will be constructed. These schemes proved to be stable and convergent unconditionally and they have second-order accuracy. Finally, the numerical example shows the effectiveness of the accelerated AOS difference algorithm. It illustrates that accelerated AOS algorithm effectively avoids the computational complexity of the high-dimensional Black-scholes equation, and dramatically improves the computational speed. Therefore, it is applicable for multi-asset option pricing.

Keywords: dual currency exchange option, accelerated AOS algorithm, 'explicit-implicit' scheme, 'implicit-explicit' scheme, error analysis, numerical example.

1 Introduction

In the financial market, option is a kind of important financial derivatives. Along with development of financial market, it is difficult to meet the needs of financial traders by only using European, American and other single asset options. Therefore, financial institution designs more complex multi-asset options. Exchange option is a typical multi-asset option. It is a contract, and the holder of which has the right but not the obligation to exchange one asset to another. Many domestic investors may purchase foreign exchange options, however they pay domestic currency, they will face two risk assets and the risk of exchange rate. Therefore it is important to research the pricing of dual currency exchange options.

Suppose that domestic price of exchange option is $V(S_1, S_2, F, t)$, the option pricing formula is[1,4]:

M. Zhao and J. Sha (Eds.): ICCIP 2012, Part II, CCIS 289, pp. 281–290, 2012.

$$\frac{\partial V}{\partial t} + G_1 + G_2 + H - r_d V = 0, \tag{1}$$

$$G_1 = \frac{\sigma_{S_1}^2}{2} S_1^2 \frac{\partial^2 V}{\partial S_1^2} + \rho_{S_1 S_2} \sigma_{S_1} \sigma_{S_2} S_1 S_2 \frac{\partial^2 V}{\partial S_1 \partial S_2} + \frac{\sigma_{S_2}^2}{2} S_2^2 \frac{\partial^2 V}{\partial S_2^2},$$

$$G_2 = \rho_{S_1 F} \sigma_{S_1} \sigma_F S_1 F \frac{\partial^2 V}{\partial S_1 \partial F} + \rho_{S_2 F} \sigma_{S_2} \sigma_F S_2 F \frac{\partial^2 V}{\partial S_2 \partial F} + \frac{\sigma_F^2}{2} F^2 \frac{\partial^2 V}{\partial F^2},$$

$$H = \sum_{i=1}^{2} (r_d - q_i) S_i \frac{\partial V}{\partial S_i} + (r_d - r_f) F \frac{\partial V}{\partial F}.$$

Here, S_1, S_2 is the foreign price of two overseas risk assets, F is the exchange rate, r_d, r_f is the risk of domestic and foreign interest rates, and q_1, q_2 is the interest rate of S_1, S_2. Equation (1) is the three-dimensional equation. Yaxiong Li and Lihong Huang (2011) firstly proposed the analytical solution of Black-Scholes equation of dual currency exchange options pricing[4], Xiaozhong Yang, Lifei Wu(2011) put forward the 'explicit-implicit' and 'implicit-explicit' difference schemes for the Black-Scholes equation of options payment[6], however it did not consider the multi-asset options; Joachim(1998) firstly used the additive operator splitting (AOS) method to solve the multi-dimensional partial differential equations[7]; Yi Zhang, Xiaozhong Yang(2010) proposed the accelerated AOS schemes for nonlinear diffusion filtering[8], this method reduce the computation time and storage space, but it used the Hopscotch method to deal with the one dimensional equation, which is only conditionally compatible; This paper discussed the dual currency exchange option pricing model under several different exchange rates. Firstly, the accelerated AOS algorithm is used to converse (1) into equivalent one dimensional equation set. Then it constructed the 'explicit-implicit' and 'implicit-explicit' schemes for the every one dimensional equation. Meanwhile this paper analyzed the compatibility, stability, convergence and accuracy of the scheme. Finally, some numerical examples verified the effectiveness of this scheme.

2   Accelerated AOS Differential Algorithm

2.1   Initial-Boundary Value Problem under Different Rate

In theory, the solving area of (1) is:

$$\{(S_1, S_2, t) \mid 0 < S_1 < \infty, 0 < S_2 < \infty, t = [0, T]\}$$

But in the actual transaction, the price of the underlying asset will not always appear to be zero or infinity. Therefore, the financial institution provides a small enough value $S_{\min} (S_{\min} > 0)$ as the lower bound and a large enough value $S_{\max} (S_{\max} < \infty)$ as the upper bound. Then the pricing problem can be solved in a bounded area:

$$\Omega = \{(S_1, S_2, t) \mid S_{1\min} < S_1 < S_{1\max}, \ S_{2\min} < S_2 < S_{2\max} , \ t \in [0, T]\}$$

To construct the difference scheme of dual currency exchange pricing equation, this paper gains the boundary condition of (1). For example, the foreign option is the call option. For the reason that option pricing is a backward problem, the initial condition is the value at the time: t=T.

However, because of difference of rate, profitable function of the due date will be difference as well:

i.   In the fixed exchange rate system, profitable function of dual currency exchange options at the due date is:

$$V(S_1, S_2, T) = F_0 \max(S_1(T) - S_2(T), \ 0).$$

Here F_0 is the fixed rate between the two countries.

ii.   In a floating exchange rate system, because of the difference rate, the profitable function of dual currency exchange options at the due date $t = T$ can be divided into three cases:

$$\begin{cases} V(S_1, S_2, F, T) = F(T) \max(S_1(T) - S_2(T), \ 0), & F(T) \text{ is the rate of due date} \\ V(S_1, S_2, F, T) = F_0 \max(S_1(T) - S_2(T), 0), & F_0 \text{ is a fixed rate} \\ V(S_1, S_2, F, T) = \max(F_0, F(T)) \max(S_1(T) - S_2(T), 0). \end{cases}$$

Boundary conditions are as follows:

$$V(S_{1\min}, S_2, t) = 0, \quad V(S_{1\max}, S_2, t) = 0,$$
$$V(S_1, S_{2\min}, t) = 0, \quad V(S_1, S_{2\max}, t) = 0.$$

In order to solve (1), we can substitute its variable as follows [5]:

$$x = \ln S_1, \ y = \ln S_2, \ z = \ln F, \ \tau = T - t.$$

Then this pricing model will be transformed into the initial-boundary value problem of partial differential equation with constant coefficients:

$$\frac{\partial V}{\partial \tau} - G_1 - G_2 - H + r_d V = 0,$$

$$G_1 = \frac{\sigma_{S_1}^2}{2} \frac{\partial^2 V}{\partial x^2} + \rho_{S_1 S_2} \sigma_{S_1} \sigma_{S_2} \frac{\partial^2 V}{\partial x \partial y} + \frac{\sigma_{S_2}^2}{2} \frac{\partial^2 V}{\partial y^2},$$

$$G_2 = \rho_{S_1 F} \sigma_{S_1} \sigma_F F \frac{\partial^2 V}{\partial x \partial z} + \rho_{S_2 F} \sigma_{S_2} \sigma_F \frac{\partial^2 V}{\partial y \partial z} + \frac{\sigma_F^2}{2} \frac{\partial^2 V}{\partial z^2},$$

$$H = (r_d - q_1) \frac{\partial V}{\partial x} + (r_d - q_2) \frac{\partial V}{\partial y} + (r_d - r_f) \frac{\partial V}{\partial z}. \tag{2}$$

Initial conditions are different under different exchange rate:

i.   In the fixed exchange rate system, the initial condition will be transformed into:

$$V(x, y, 0, F) = F_0 \max(e^x - e^y, 0) \tag{3}$$

ii.   In a floating exchange rate system, the initial conditions will be transformed into:

$$\begin{cases} V(x, y, F, 0) = F(0) \max(e^x - e^y, \ 0), & F(0) \text{ is the rate of due date} \\ V(x, y, F, 0) = F_0 \max(e^x - e^y, \ 0), & F_0 \text{ is a fixed rate} \\ V(x, y, F, 0) = \max(F_0, F(0)) \max(e^x - e^y, 0). \end{cases}$$

Boundary conditions will be transformed into:

$$V(x, \ln S_{1\min}, y, F, t) = 0, \quad V(x, \ln S_{1\max}, y, F, t) = 0,$$
$$V(x, \ln S_{2\min}, F, t) = 0, \quad V(x, \ln S_{2\max}, F, t) = 0. \tag{4}$$

2.2   Construction of Accelerated AOS Arithmetic

Firstly, transform the equation (2) into equivalent equation set along with the x, y and z axis:

$$
\begin{cases}
\dfrac{\partial V}{\partial \tau} - \dfrac{3}{2}\sigma_{S_1}^2 \dfrac{\partial^2 V}{\partial x^2} - 3\left(r_d - q_1 - \dfrac{\sigma_{S_1}^2}{2}\right)\dfrac{\partial V}{\partial x} - \dfrac{3}{2}\rho_{S_1 S_2}\sigma_{S_1}\sigma_{S_2}\dfrac{\partial^2 V}{\partial x \partial y} - \dfrac{3}{2}\rho_{S_1 F}\sigma_{S_1}\sigma_F \dfrac{\partial^2 V}{\partial x \partial z} + r_d V = 0 \\[3mm]
\dfrac{\partial V}{\partial \tau} - \dfrac{3}{2}\sigma_{S_2}^2 \dfrac{\partial^2 V}{\partial y^2} - 3\left(r_d - q_2 - \dfrac{\sigma_{S_2}^2}{2}\right)\dfrac{\partial V}{\partial y} - \dfrac{3}{2}\rho_{S_1 S_2}\sigma_{S_1}\sigma_{S_2}\dfrac{\partial^2 V}{\partial x \partial y} - \dfrac{3}{2}\rho_{S_2 F}\sigma_{S_2}\sigma_F \dfrac{\partial^2 V}{\partial y \partial z} + r_d V = 0 \\[3mm]
\dfrac{\partial V}{\partial \tau} - \dfrac{3}{2}\sigma_F^2 \dfrac{\partial^2 V}{\partial z^2} - 3\left(r_d - r_f - \dfrac{\sigma_F^2}{2}\right)\dfrac{\partial V}{\partial z} - \dfrac{3}{2}\rho_{S_1 F}\sigma_{S_1}\sigma_F \dfrac{\partial^2 V}{\partial x \partial z} - \dfrac{3}{2}\rho_{S_2 F}\sigma_{S_2}\sigma_F \dfrac{\partial^2 V}{\partial y \partial z} + r_d V = 0
\end{cases}
\tag{5}
$$

Then the pricing problem can be solved in a bounded area:

$$
\Omega = \left\{(x,y,z,t)\big| \ln S_{1min} < x < \ln S_{1max}, \ln S_{2min} < y < \ln S_{2max}, \ln F_{min} < z < \ln F_{max}, \tau \in [T,0] \right\}
$$

Make a mesh partition on the area Ω. Let h_1, h_2, h_3 as the space step and k as the time step:

Denote that $V_{i,j,k}^{n} = V\left(x_i, y_j, z_k, \tau_n\right)$, the initial conditions under difference rate will be transformed.

i.   In the fixed exchange rate system, the initial conditions will be transformed into:

$$
V_{i,j,k}^{0} = F_0 \max\left(e^{ih_1} - e^{ih_2}, 0\right)
\tag{6}
$$

ii.   In a floating exchange rate system, the initial conditions will be transformed into:

$$
\begin{cases}
V_{i,j,k}^{0} = e^{kh_3}(0)\max\left(e^{ih_1} - e^{jh_2}, 0\right), & F(0) \text{ is the rate of due date} \\[2mm]
V_{i,j,k}^{0} = e_0^{kh_3} \max\left(e^{ih_1} - e^{jh_2}, 0\right), & F_0 \text{ is a fixed rate} \\[2mm]
V_{i,j,k}^{0} = \max\left(e_0^{kh_3}, e^{kh_3}(0)\right)\max\left(e^{ih_1} - e^{jh_2}, 0\right)
\end{cases}
\tag{7}
$$

Boundary conditions will be transformed into:

$$
V_{0,j,k}^{n} = 0, \quad V_{M_1,j,k}^{n} = 0, \quad V_{i,0,k}^{n} = 0, \quad V_{0,M_2,k}^{n} = 0, \quad V_{i,j,0}^{n} = 0, \quad V_{i,j,M_3}^{n} = 0
\tag{8}
$$

Firstly, construct the 'explicit-implicit' scheme. We adopt the explicit scheme at the odd number floor, and implicit scheme at the even number floor.

In the x axis direction:

$$
\begin{cases}
\dfrac{V_{i,j,k}^{2n+1} - V_{i,j,k}^{2n}}{k} = \dfrac{3}{2}\sigma_{S_1}^2 \dfrac{V_{i+1,j,k}^{2n} - 2V_{i,j,k}^{2n} + V_{i-1,j,k}^{2n}}{h_1^2} + 3\left(r_d - q_1 - \dfrac{\sigma_{S_1}^2}{2}\right)\dfrac{V_{i+1,j,k}^{2n} - V_{i-1,j,k}^{2n}}{2h_1} + M_1 - r_d V_{i,j,k}^{2n} \\[3mm]
\dfrac{V_{i,j,k}^{2n+2} - V_{i,j,k}^{2n+1}}{k} = \dfrac{3}{2}\sigma_{S_1}^2 \dfrac{V_{i+1,j,k}^{2n+2} - 2V_{i,j,k}^{2n+2} + V_{i-1,j}^{2n+2}}{h_1^2} + 3\left(r_d - q_2 - \dfrac{\sigma_{S_1}^2}{2}\right)\dfrac{V_{i+1,j,k}^{2n+2} - V_{i-1,j,k}^{2n+2}}{2h_1} + M_2 - r_d V_{i,j,k}^{2n+2}
\end{cases}
\tag{9}
$$

$$
M_1 = \dfrac{3}{2}\rho_{S_1 S_2}\sigma_{S_1}\sigma_{S_2}\left(V_{xy}\right)_{i,j,k}^{2n} + \dfrac{3}{2}\rho_{S_1 F}\sigma_{S_1}\sigma_F \left(V_{xz}\right)_{i,j,k}^{2n}
$$

$$M_2 = \frac{3}{2}\rho_{S_1 S_2}\sigma_{S_1}\sigma_{S_2}\left(V_{xy}\right)^{2n+2}_{i,j,k} + \frac{3}{2}\rho_{S_1 F}\sigma_{S_1}\sigma_F\left(V_{xz}\right)^{2n+2}_{i,j,k}$$

$$\left(V_{xy}\right)_{i,j,k} = \frac{V_{i+1,j+1,k} - V_{i+1,j-1,k} - V_{i-1,j+1,k} + V_{i,j,k}}{4h_1 h_2}$$

$$\left(V_{xz}\right)_{i,j,k} = \frac{V_{i+1,j,k+1} - V_{i+1,j,k-1} - V_{i-1,j,k+1} + V_{i,j,k}}{4h_1 h_3}$$

In similar, we can get the same result in y, z axis direction.

If the computation is done in the x axis direction, the result $V_{i,j,k}$ of (9) is denoted as $\left(V_{i,j,k}\right)_x$, in the y, z axis the result is denoted as $\left(V_{i,j,k}\right)_y$, $\left(V_{i,j,k}\right)_z$ respectively. The arithmetic mean value of $\left(V_{i,j,k}\right)_x$, $\left(V_{i,j,k}\right)_y$ and $\left(V_{i,j,k}\right)_z$ is the final value:

$$V_{i,j,k} = \frac{\left(V_{i,j,k}\right)_x + \left(V_{i,j,k}\right)_y + \left(V_{i,j,k}\right)_z}{3} \tag{10}$$

Similarly, if we adopt the implicit scheme at the odd number floor, and explicit scheme at the even number floor, we can construct the 'implicit-explicit' scheme of accelerated additive operator splitting algorithm for qual currency exchange option pricing model.

3   Analysis of the Compatibility and Accuracy of 'explicit-implicit' Scheme

Add up the two equations of (9), we can eliminate $V^{2n+1}_{i,j,k}$:

$$\frac{V^{2n+2}_{i,j,k} - V^{2n}_{i,j,k}}{k} = \frac{3}{2}\sigma^2_{S_1}(G_1 + G_2) + M_1 + M_2 - 3r_d\left(V^{2n}_{i,j,k} + V^{2n+2}_{i,j,k}\right)\left(r_d - q_1 - \frac{\sigma^2_{S_1}}{2}\right)G_3$$

$$G_1 = \frac{V^{2n}_{i+1,j,k} - 2V^{2n}_{i,j,k} + V^{2n}_{i-1,j,k}}{h_1^2},$$

$$G_2 = \frac{V^{2n+2}_{i+1,j,k} - 2V^{2n+2}_{i,j,k} + V^{2n+2}_{i-1,j,k}}{h_1^2}$$

$$G_3 = \frac{V^{2n}_{i+1,j,k} - V^{2n}_{i-1,j,k}}{2h_1} + \frac{V^{2n+2}_{i+1,j,k} - V^{2n+2}_{i-1,j,k}}{2h_1} \tag{11}$$

Suppose $V(x,y,z)$ is the analytical solution of (5), and substitute $V(x_i,y_j,z_k,t_n)$ by $V^{2n}_{i,j,k}$ in the above equation. Then make difference between the two side of the equation, and we will get the truncation error:

$$\left(R^{2n}_{i,j,k}\right)_1 = \frac{V^{2n+2}_{i,j,k} - V^{2n}_{i,j,k}}{k} - \frac{3}{2}\sigma^2_{S_1}\left(\frac{V^{2n}_{i+1,j,k} - 2V^{2n}_{i,j,k} + V^{2n}_{i-1,j,k}}{h_1^2} + \frac{V^{2n+2}_{i+1,j,k} - 2V^{2n+2}_{i,j,k} + V^{2n+2}_{i-1,j}}{h_1^2}\right) -$$

$$3\left(r_d - q_1 - \frac{\sigma^2_{S_1}}{2}\right)\left(\frac{V^{2n}_{i+1,j,k} - V^{2n}_{i-1,j,k}}{2h_1} + \frac{V^{2n+2}_{i+1,j,k} - V^{2n+2}_{i-1,j,k}}{2h_1}\right) - M_1 - M_2 + r_d\left(V^{2n}_{i,j,k} + V^{2n+2}_{i,j,k}\right)$$

Then expand $\left(R_{i,j,k}^{2n}\right)_x$ as the Taylor Series at the point $\left(x_i, y_j, z_k, \tau_{2n}\right)$, and simplify it to get [2, 8]:

$$\left(R_{i,j,k}^{2n}\right)_x = O\!\left(h_1^2 + k^2\right) \tag{12}$$

Similarly, in the y and z axis direction:

$$\left(R_{i,j,k}^{2n}\right)_y = O\!\left(h_2^2 + k^2\right),$$
$$\left(R_{i,j,k}^{2n}\right)_z = O\!\left(h_3^2 + k^2\right). \tag{13}$$

Finally, take the arithmetic mean value of (11), (12) and (13):

$$R_{i,j,k}^{2n} = \frac{1}{3}\left[\left(R_{i,j,k}^{2n}\right)_x + \left(R_{i,j,k}^{2n}\right)_y + \left(R_{i,j,k}^{2n}\right)_z\right] = O\!\left(h_1^2 + h_2^2 + h_3^2 + k^2\right) \tag{14}$$

Therefore, we can get:

Theorem 1: The 'explicit-implicit' scheme (9) of accelerated AOS algorithm has second-order accuracy, and it is compatible with (5) unconditionally.

Apply the same method on the 'implicit-explicit' scheme, we will get similar theorem:

Theorem 2: The 'implicit-explicit' scheme of accelerated AOS algorithm has second-order accuracy, and it is compatible unconditionally.

4   Analysis of the Stability and Convergence of 'explicit-implicit' Scheme

As to the 'explicit-implicit' scheme, take the Fourier transformation on the two sides of the equation (11), and simplify it to get [6]:

$$\left(1 + r_d k - \frac{3}{2}\sigma_{S_1}^2 \frac{k}{h_1^2}\left(e^{i\xi} - 2 + e^{-i\xi}\right) - \frac{3}{2}\frac{k}{h_1}\left(r_d - q_1 - \frac{\sigma_{S_1}^2}{2}\right)\left(e^{i\xi} - e^{-i\xi}\right)\right)\tilde{V}^{2n+2}(\xi) = $$
$$\left(1 - r_d k + \frac{3}{2}\sigma_{S_1}^2 \frac{k}{h_1^2}\left(e^{i\xi} - 2 + e^{-i\xi}\right) + \frac{3}{2}\frac{k}{h_1}\left(r_d - q_1 - \frac{\sigma_{S_1}^2}{2}\right)\left(e^{i\xi} - e^{-i\xi}\right)\right)\tilde{V}^{2n}(\xi) \tag{15}$$

Therefore, the growth factor is:

$$G(\xi) = \frac{1 - r_d k - 6\sigma_{S_1}^2 \dfrac{k}{h_1^2}\sin^2\!\left(\dfrac{\xi}{2}\right) + 3\dfrac{k}{h_1}\left(r_d - q_1 - \dfrac{\sigma_{S_1}^2}{2}\right)\sin(\xi)i}{1 + r_d k + 6\sigma_{S_1}^2 \dfrac{k}{h_1^2}\sin^2\!\left(\dfrac{\xi}{2}\right) - 3\dfrac{k}{h_1}\left(r_d - q_1 - \dfrac{\sigma_{S_1}^2}{2}\right)\sin(\xi)i} \tag{16}$$

Denote that:

$$P = r_d k + 6\sigma_{S_1}^2 \sin^2\!\left(\frac{\xi}{2}\right)$$

$$Q = 3\frac{k}{h_1}\left(r_d - q_1 - \frac{\sigma_{S_1}^2}{2}\right)\sin(\xi)$$

Then the equation (16) can be transformed into:

$$G(\xi)=\frac{1-P+Qi}{1+P-Qi} \tag{17}$$

And we can get that:

$$|G(\xi)|^2 = \frac{(1-P)^2 + Q^2}{(1+P)^2 + Q^2} \leq 1 \tag{18}$$

By the Von Neumann Theorem, we can get that the AOS difference scheme (9) in the x axis direction is stable unconditionally. Similarly, we can get that the scheme in the y and z axis direction is also unconditionally stable.

Then we can get:

Theorem 3: The 'explicit-implicit' scheme (9) of accelerated AOS algorithm is unconditionally stable.

In addition, due to the Lax Theorem, we can get:

Corollary1: The 'explicit-implicit' scheme (9) of accelerated AOS algorithm is convergent.

Apply the same method on the 'implicit-explicit' scheme, we will get similar theorem:

Theorem 4: The 'implicit-explicit' scheme of accelerated AOS algorithm is unconditionally stable and convergent.

5   Numerical Example

Here, we consider an America investor have a Nikkei index option A. However, he forecast the profit of Nikkei index option B will be better than A, then he purchase a dual currency exchange option to gain more profit. Suppose that the price of A and B is 20000 yen, the dividend rate of the Nikkei is 0.03, the volatility is 0.2, the correlation coefficient between the Nikkei and the yen is 0.2, the risk-free interest rate of American is 0.08, the risk-free interest rate of Japan is 0.04, the Strike price of option is 30000 yen. When the deadline of the option is 3, 6, 9 and 12 months consider the price of this dual currency exchange option under following considers:

(1) The yen exchange rate is a fixed exchange one.
(2) The yen exchange rate is the exchange rate on the due day.

Take one dimensional equation for example, the main step of AOS Algorithm is:
Firstly, define the time and space step and a bounded area omega.

```
float dt, dx, xmax

MX=round(xmax/dx);

N=round(T/dt);

dx=xmax/M;

dt=T/N;
```

Secondly, simplify (9) and get the coefficient matrix V, then decompose U by LU method.

[L,U]=lu(2*eye(M-1)-U);

Finally, calculate the result.

VX=U/L/(M+g0)
%g0 is the initial condition.

We adopt the 'explicit-implicit' scheme to calculate this example under the Matlab environment, and the result is as follows.

Table 1. Comparison of Analytical and AOS Algorithm Under Fixed Exchange Rate

Time(m)	Analytical Solution[4]($)	AOS Algorithm($)	Relative Error
3	55.9434	54.6594	0.0229
6	58.5042	56.3906	0.0361
9	61.5346	58.2783	0.0539
12	64.9671	60.7630	0.0647

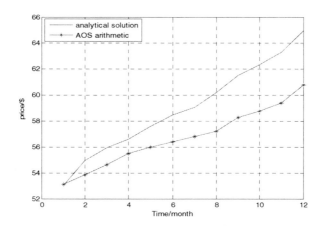

Fig. 1. Comparison of Analytical and AOS Algorithm under Fixed Rate

Table 2. Comparison of Analytical and AOS Algorithm under Rate of Due Date

Time(m)	Analytical Solution[4]($)	AOS Algorithm($)	Relative Error
3	67.1949	65.852	0.0199
6	70.6950	68.9076	0.0252
9	73.2849	70.5948	0.0367
12	76.1257	72.5439	0.0470

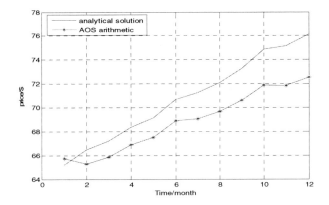

Fig. 2. Comparison of Analytical and AOS Algorithm under Rate of Due Date

From the above table and figure, we can see that the accelerated AOS differential algorithm has higher calculation accuracy.

6   Conclusion

In this paper we construct the accelerated additive operator splitting differential algorithm for qual currency exchange option pricing model. The main idea of the algorithm is to split the multi-dimensional Black-Scholes equation into equivalent one-dimensional equations, and then construct the 'explicit-implicit' and the 'implicit-explicit' scheme. This scheme is second-order accuracy, stable and convergent unconditionally, and the total computation of these schemes is only a quarter of the traditional AOS scheme.

The main advantages of accelerated AOS differential algorithm are as follows. Firstly, the AOS algorithm splits the high dimensional equation into low ones. This method can avoid the complexity of using difference method directly on high dimensional equation. AOS differential algorithm is very applicable to deal with the high dimensional equations. Secondly, the 'explicit-implicit' and 'implicit-explicit ' scheme also has prominent advantage. Classical implicit scheme hides the potential stability, which is no use in the calculation, but when it is applied in the alternate scheme, this potential stability just cover the stability shortage of explicit scheme. Finally, the implicit scheme calculates the approximate value of the analytical solution from above, and the explicit scheme calculates it from below. Every two steps produce errors with the opposite symbol, which can counteract with each other, and then obtain the more accurate result.

Acknowledgments. This work is supported by a grant from National Natural Sciences Foundation of China (No. 10771065, No. 40875066) and Invite Foreign Expert Key Project of the Ministry of Education (2010).

References

1. Wilmott, P., Howison, S., Dewynne, J.: The mathematics of financial derivative. Cambridge University Press, England (1996)
2. Jiang, L.: Mathematical Modeling and Methods of Option Pricing. Higher Education Press, Beijing (2008) (in Chinese)
3. Jiang, L., Xu, C., Ren, X.: Mathematical model and case analysis of the pricing of financial derivatives. Higher Education Press, Beijing (2008) (in Chinese)
4. Li, Y., Huang, L.: The Study of dual currency and delay option. Hunan University Press (2011) (in Chinese)
5. Per, L., Persson, J., von Sydow, L., Tysk, J.: Space-time adaptive finite difference method for European multi-asset options. Computers Mathematics with Applications 5(8), 1159–1180 (2007)
6. Yang, X., Wu, L.: A new kind of effective difference schemes for solving the payment of dividend Black-Scholes equation. In: Third International Conference on Computer and Network Technology, vol. 5, pp. 304–309 (2011)
7. Weickert, J., ter Haar Romeny, B.M., Viergever, M.A.: An efficient and reriable scheme for nonlinear diffusion filtering. Transaction on image Processing 7(3), 398–410 (1998)
8. Zhang, Y., Yang, X.: On the acceleration of AOS schemes for nonlinear diffusion filtering. Journal of Multimedia 5(6), 605–612 (2010)
9. Zhao, S.: Finance derivative tools pricing. China Financial and Economic. Publishing House, Beijing (2008) (in Chinese)
10. Zhang, S.: Finite difference numerical calculation for parabolic equation with boundary condition. Science Press, Beijing (2010) (in Chinese)
11. Yang, X., Liu, Y.: A Study on a New Kind of Universal Difference Schemes for Solving Black-Scholes Equation. International Journal of Information and Science System 3(2), 251–260 (2007)
12. Persson, J., von Sydow, L.: Pricing European Multi-asset Options Using a Space-time Adaptive FD-method, Technical report 2003-059, ISSN 1404-3203
13. Smereka, P.: Semi-Implicit Level Set Methods for Curvature and Surface Diffusion Motion. Journal of Scientific Computing 19(1-3) (2003)
14. Weickert, J.: Applications of nonlinear diffusion in image processing and computer vision. Acta Math, Univ. Comenianae LXX, 30–35 (2001)
15. Company, R., Gonzalez, A.L.: Numerical Solution of Modified Black-Scholes Equation Stock Options with Discrete Dividend. Mathematical and Computer Modeling 44(12), 1058–1068 (2006)
16. Elliott, R.J., Kopp, P.E.: Mathematics of Financial Markets. Springer, New York (1999)

Radial Basis Function Neural Networks Optimization Algorithm Based on SVM

Jifu Nong

College of Science, Guangxi University for Nationalities
Nanning, China

Abstract. Support vector machine (SVM) resembles RBF neural networks in structure. Considering their resemblance, a new optimization algorithm based on support vector machine and genetic algorithm for RBF neural network is presented, in which GA is used to choose the SVM model parameter and SVM is used to help constructing the RBF. The network based on this algorithm is applied on nonlinear system identification. Simulation results show that the network based on this algorithm has higher precision and better generalization ability.

Keywords: support vector machines, neural networks, genetic algorithm, system identification.

1 Introduction

Radial basis function (RBF) networks is one of new and effective feed-forward neural networks, which can approximate any continuous function with arbitrary precision. RBF networks are always with simple architecture, and trained fast. In RBF networks, the number and place of hidden center vector are key points concerned to the performance of the RBF networks. There exits obvious defectiveness to certain the parameters of RBF networks by the traditional ways.

Based on statistical learning theory, support vector machines (SVM) algorithm has a solid mathematical theoretical foundation and rigorous theoretical analysis, which has the advantage of theoretical completeness, global optimization, adaptability, and good generalization ability. It is largely solved the past problems of choosing machine learning model, over-fitting, non-linear, the curse of dimensionality, local minimum points and so on. It uses the structural risk minimization principle, which minimizes the empirical risk; at the same time effectively improve generalization ability of the algorithm.

SVM has the structure similarities with RBF network, in this paper, we study the intrinsic link between these two algorithms, and propose RBF optimization algorithm based on SVM and genetic algorithm, which use GA to choose the parameters for SVM, then to be used for structuring RBF networks. This algorithm effectively improves generalization and don't need a large number of experiments or empirical experiences to pre-specify network structure.

M. Zhao and J. Sha (Eds.): ICCIP 2012, Part II, CCIS 289, pp. 291–298, 2012.
© Springer-Verlag Berlin Heidelberg 2012

2   SVM Providing Theoretical Foundation for Structure and Parameters of RBF

Radial basis function (RBF) networks typically have three layers: an input layer, a hidden layer with a non-linear RBF activation function and a linear output layer. RBF network from input to output mapping is non-linear, but in terms of the weights of network output is linear. The kth hidden unit's output is

$$\phi_k(x) = \exp\left(-\frac{\|x-c_k\|^2}{2\sigma_k^2}\right) \tag{1}$$

where $\|\cdot\|$ is Euclidean norm, x_i is the ith input vector, c_k is the center vector of hidden units, σ_k is the width of hidden units. N denotes the number of the hidden units, w_k is the weights between the hidden units and the outputs, then the outputs of RBF networks is

$$f(x) = \sum_{k=1}^{N} w_k \phi_k(x)$$

$$= \sum_{k=1}^{N} w_k \times \exp\left(-\frac{\|x-c_k\|^2}{2\sigma_k^2}\right) \tag{2}$$

According to Mercer Conditions, SVM adopts kernel function to map a sample vector from the original space to feature space. Gaussian kernel function used here is

$$K(x, v_i) = \exp\left(-\frac{\|x-v_i\|^2}{2\sigma_i^2}\right) \tag{3}$$

SVM in regression form is the linear combination of the hidden units, then

$$f(x) = \sum_{i=1}^{g} w_i K(x, v_i) + b$$

$$= \sum_{i=1}^{g} w_i \times \exp\left(-\frac{\|x-v_i\|^2}{2\sigma_i^2}\right) + b \tag{4}$$

SVM network architecture can be indicated as shown in Figure1,which is similar to a RBF network.

SVM has a similarity in structure with the RBF network, so the number g of support vector which is gotten from the training of SVM can be the number of the hidden units in RBF networks, support vector can be the center vector of radius function, the width selected by SVM can be the width of RBF.

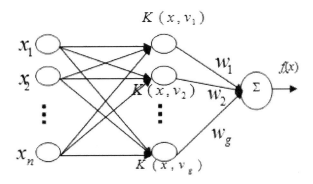

Fig. 1. The structure of SVM

3   GA Providing SVM Models Parameters

In designing SVM, the parameter σ, penalty factor C, insensitive loss function ε are the important factors to affect the performance of SVM, especially in small samples learning condition, so selecting proper σ、C and ε will be very important to the learning machine performances. We will use the most widely used genetic algorithm to select those three parameters.

The algorithm is to use genetic algorithm to optimize the SVM model parameters, the basic steps of it are as follows:

(1) Choose the initial population of individuals randomly;

(2) Evaluate the fitness of each individual in that population;

(3) Select a new generation of population from the previous generation by using selection operator;

(4) Take the crossover and mutation operation on the current population, then take the evaluation, selection, crossover and mutation operation on the new breed, and continue.

(5) If the fitness function value of optimal individual is large enough or the algorithm have run many generations, and the optimal fitness value of the individual can't be changed obviously, then we get the optimal value of kernel function parameter σ, penalty factor C, and insensitive loss function ε, and we can also get the optimal classifier by the training datum.

How to construct fitness function is the key point of genetic algorithm. We use the promotion theorem of SVM in high-dimensional space to construct fitness function. We set

$$fit = \frac{1}{T + 0.01} \qquad (5)$$

where $T = \dfrac{R^2}{l\gamma^2}$ is the testing error boundary, R is the radius of super-sphere which contain all the datum, $\gamma = \dfrac{1}{\|w\|}$ is the interval value, l is the number of the samples.

4   SVM Providing Networks Structure and Parameters for RBF

For support vector regression machine, its learning process can be concluded to be a quadratic programming problem under the linear constrains, then we can use the regression machine which have been trained well to certain the structure and parameters of RBF networks.

First considering the linear regression conditions, the sample are $(x_1, y_1),(x_2, y_2),...,(x_n, y_n) \in R^n \times R$, the linear function is set to be $f(x) = w \cdot x + b$, then the optimization problem will be a minimization problem.

$$R(w,\xi,\xi^*) = \frac{1}{2}w \cdot w + C\sum_{i=1}^{n}(\xi_i + \xi_i^*) \tag{6}$$

The conditions are

$$f(x_i) - y_i \le \xi_i^* + \varepsilon$$
$$y_i - f(x_i) \le \xi_i + \varepsilon \tag{7}$$
$$\xi_i, \xi_i^* \ge 0, i = 1,...,n$$

Introducing Lagrange function, we can get

$$L(w,b,\xi,\xi^*,\alpha,\alpha^*,\eta,\eta^*)$$
$$= \frac{1}{2}(w \cdot w) + C\sum_{i=1}^{n}(\xi_i + \xi_i^*) - \sum_{i=1}^{n}\alpha_i[\varepsilon + \xi_i + (w \cdot x_i) + b - y_i]$$
$$- \sum_{i=1}^{n}\alpha_i^*[\varepsilon + \xi_i^* - (w \cdot x_i) - b + y_i] - \sum_{i=1}^{n}(\eta_i\xi_i + \eta_i^*\xi_i^*) \tag{8}$$

where $\alpha_i, \alpha_i^* \ge 0, \eta_i, \eta_i^* \ge 0, i = 1,...,n$.

Solving this quadratic optimization problem, we can get α_i, α_i^* , then $w = \sum_{i=1}^{n}(\alpha_i^* - \alpha_i)x_i$,we can also get b by

$$\begin{cases} b = y_i - w \cdot x_i - \varepsilon \\ b = y_i - w \cdot x_i + \varepsilon \end{cases} \tag{9}$$

So the regression function is

$$f(x) = (w \cdot x) + b = \sum_{i=1}^{n}(\alpha_i^* - \alpha_i)(x_i \cdot x) + b \tag{10}$$

Non-linear regression use kernel function $K(x, y)$, if the kernel function is turned to be Gaussian function, then the regression function will be

$$f(x) = \sum_{i=1}^{n} (\alpha_i^* - \alpha_i) K(x, v_i) + b \tag{11}$$

When $\alpha_i^* - \alpha_i$ is not equal to zero, the according samples will be support vectors, we assume the number of the support vectors which are gotten after SVM training is $g \, (g \leq n)$, support vector are $v_i, i = 1, ..., g$, the weight factors are $w_i = \alpha_i^* - \alpha_i$, the bias is b, then we use these to construct RBF networks.

5   Application and Simulation Research

We use RBF networks optimized by SVM in system identification to test the learning performances and generalization abilities of this algorithm, we also compare it with generalized regression neural network.

Consuming the identification system denoted by the non-linear discrete function

$$y(k) = \frac{y(k-1)}{1 + y^2(k-1)} + u^2(k) \tag{12}$$

To this system, we use cascade- parallel models, the RBF network has two inputs and one output. The twenty samples $(u(1), u(2), ..., u(20))$ are selected from [0,2], started from zero, the interval value is 0.1, and the responding outputs are $(y(1), y(2), ..., y(20))$,when the identification is finished, we use the follow stimulus signal to test the generalization abilities of the networks.

$$u(k) = 0.15 \sin\left(\frac{2k\pi}{25}\right) + 0.22 \sin\left(\frac{2k\pi}{35}\right) + 0.2, k = 1, 2, ..., 100$$

(1) Generalized regression neural network select Gaussian function as the kernel function, the distribution density Spread is 0.7, the identification results is shown in figure2 , the mean squares error between identification results and output matrix is 0.0842.And the testing results is shown in figure 3, the mean squares error between testing results and expected output matrix is 0.0282.

(2) In optimizing neural networks by SVM, we set the maximum genetic generations is 20, we get the maximum value of fitness by genetic algorithm searching, so we get the model parameters x=[379.9678 1.0221 0.0426],that penalty factor C is 379.9678, the width of Gaussian function σ is 1.0221, the insensitive loss function ε is 0.0426, furthermore we get the number of support vectors is 4 by the learning of input and output datum, so we set the number of hidden units in RBF network is 4, the Gaussian function center vector are the support vectors, the width of Gaussian function is the same with the regression machine. According to $w_i = \alpha_i^* - \alpha_i$, we know the

responding network weights $w=[-1.7610\ \ 1.0219\ \ -1.0406\ \ 1.7797]$, the bias value is -0.0012, which are used to be the weights and bias value of RBF networks, then the RBF is constructed, just as shown in figure 4.According to identification results shown in figure 5, the mean squares error between identification results and output matrix is 0.0036.And the testing results is shown in figure 6, the mean squares error between testing results and expected output matrix is 0.0134.

In terms of identification accuracy and generalization abilities, the simulation results show that RBF networks optimized by SVM algorithm is superior to generalized regression neural network, also needn't pre-specify the structure by a lot of experiments.

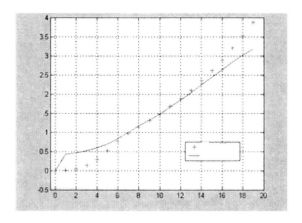

Fig. 2. The identification results of generalized regression neural network

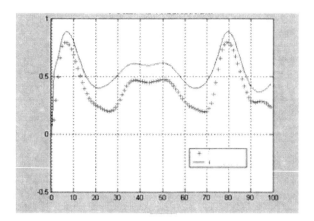

Fig. 3. The testing results of generalized regression neural network

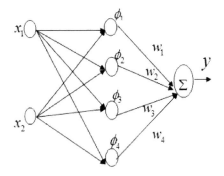

Fig. 4. RBF network structure based on SVM

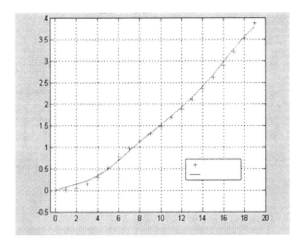

Fig. 5. The identification results of RBF optimized by SVM

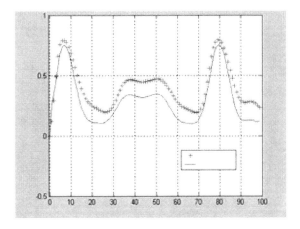

Fig. 6. The testing results of RBF optimized by SVM

6   Conclusion

The algorithm we proposed in this paper first use genetic algorithm to optimize SVM model parameters, then to make certain the structure and parameters of RBF networks by SVM, which is applied in system identification. The simulation results show this algorithm is more efficient in learning and training, with good identification accuracy and generalization capacity in term of system identification.

References

1. Peter, A.: The equivalence of support vector machine andregularization neural networks. Neural Processing Letters 15(2), 97–104 (2002)
2. Yuan, X.-F., Wang, Y.: A Hybrid Learning Algorithm for RBF Neural Network Based on Support Vector Machines and BP Algorithm. Journal of Hunan University 32(3), 88–92 (2002)
3. Zhang, G.-Y.: Support Vector Machine and its application Research. Hunan University, Hunan (2006)
4. Zhu, M.-X., Zhang, D.-L.: Study on the Algorithms of Selecting the Radial Basis Function Centre. Journal of Anhui University 24(1), 72–78 (2002)
5. Yang, X., Ji, Y.-B., Tian, X.: Parameters Selection of SVM Based on Genetic Algorithm. Journal of Liaoning University of Petroleum & Chemical Technology 24(1), 54–58 (2004)
6. Zheng, C.-H., Jiao, L.-C.: Automatic model selection for support vector machines using heuristic genetic algorithm. Control Theory & Applications 23(2), 187–192 (2006)
7. Chai, J., Jiang, Q.-Y., Cao, Z.-K.: Function Approximation Capability and Algorithms of RBF Neural Net Works. Pattern Recognition and Artificial Intelligence 15(3), 310–316 (2002)
8. Shan, X.-H.: RBF Neural Networks based on Genetic Algorithm and its Applications in System identification. Qingdao University, Shandong (2006)

Conditions for RBF Neural Networks to Universal Approximation and Numerical Experiments

Jifu Nong

College of Science, Guangxi University for Nationalities
Nanning, China

Abstract. In this paper, we investigate the universal approximation property of Radial Basis Function (RBF) networks. We show that RBFs are not required to be integrable for the REF networks to be universal approximators. Instead, RBF networks can uniformly approximate any continuous function on a compact set provided that the radial basis activation function is continuous almost everywhere, locally essentially bounded, and not a polynomial. The approximation is also discussed. Some experimental results are reported to illustrate our findings.

Keywords: universal approximation, radial basis function networks, numerical experiments.

1   Introduction

Universal approximation by feedforward neural networks has been studied by many authors. Under very mild assumptions on the activation functions used in the hidden layer, it has been shown that a three-layered feedforward neural network is capable of approximating a large class of functions including the continuous functions and integrable functions.

The known results in literature are mainly built upon the three-layered neural networks with one linear output node. In this paper, we adopt this standard setting. The class of functions realized by a three-layered feedforward neural network has the following form

$$\sum_{i=1}^{N} c_i g(x, \theta_i, b_i)$$

where N is the number of hidden nodes, $x \in R^n$ is a variable, $c_i \in R, \theta_i \in R^n, b_i \in R$ are parameters, and $g(x, \theta_i, b_i)$ is the activation function used in the hidden layer. Notice that most activation functions used in the hidden layer can be categorized into two classes: the ridge functions and radial basis functions. A ridge function has the following form

$$g(x, \theta, b) = \sigma(\theta^T x + b)$$

M. Zhao and J. Sha (Eds.): ICCIP 2012, Part II, CCIS 289, pp. 299–308, 2012.
© Springer-Verlag Berlin Heidelberg 2012

where σ is a mapping from R into R, $x \in R^n$ is a variable, $\theta \in R^n$ is a 'direction vector', and $b \in R$ is a 'threshold'. The commonly used sigmoid function $g(x) = 1/(1 + \exp(-(\theta^T x + b)))$ is an example. A radial basis function has the following form

$$g(x, \theta, b) = \phi\left(\frac{x - \theta}{b}\right)$$

The research on ridge activation functions is extensive (Cybenko, 1989; Hornik, 1990, 1993; Leshno et al., 1993). The work of Leshno et al. (1993) could be one of the most general results. They showed that if the ridge activation function used in the hidden layer is continuous almost everywhere, locally essentially bounded, and not a polynomial, then a three-layered neural network can approximate any continuous function with respect to the uniform norm.

In this paper, we extend Park and Sandberg's result by showing that the integrability assumption is not necessary for the radial-basis function networks to be universal approximators. Instead, the relaxed conditions are more like the results of Leshno. More specifically, we show that, if the radial-basis activation function used in the hidden layer is continuous almost everywhere, locally essentially bounded, and not a polynomial, then the three-layered radial-basis function network can approximate any continuous function with respect to the uniform norm. Moreover, Radial Basis Function (RBF) networks can approximate any function in $L^p(\mu)$ and μ is any finite measure, if the radial-basis activation function used in the hidden layer is essentially bounded and not a polynomial.

2   Basic Definitions and Notations

Throughout this paper, R^n denotes the n-dimensional Euclidean space, K is a compact set in R^n, $C(K)$ is the set of all continuous functions defined on K, with the uniform norm $\| f \|_{C(K)} = \max_{x \in K} | f(x) |$.

The essential supremum of a given function $f(x)$ is defined by

$$\operatorname*{ess\,sup}_{x \in R^n} f(x) = \inf\{\lambda \mid \mu\{x : | f(x) | \geq \lambda\} = 0\}$$

where μ is a measure. We also denote the essential supremum as

$$\| f \|_{L^\infty(R^n)} = \operatorname*{ess\,sup}_{x \in R^n} f(x)$$

Moreover, for a finite measure, μ and $1 \leq p < \infty$,

$$\| f \|_{L^p(\mu)} = \left(\int_{R^n} | f(x) |^p \, d\mu(x)\right)^{1/p}$$

We say a function is continuous almost everywhere (with respect to a measure), if the measure of the set of all discontinuous points of the function is zero. A set S of functions is said to be dense in $C(K)$, if for any $\varepsilon > 0$ and $f \in C(K)$, there is a function $g \in S$, such that $\| g - f \|_{L^{\infty}(K)} < \varepsilon$.

The convolution of two functions is defined as $f * g(x) = \int f(x-t)g(t)dt$.

The Fourier transform of a Fourier transformable function f is denoted as $\hat{f}$. The support of function f is denoted by supp f. An n-tuple $\alpha = (\alpha_1, \cdots, \alpha_n)$ of non-negative integers is called a multi-index. We define $|\alpha| = \alpha_1 + \cdots + \alpha_n$ and $\alpha! = \alpha_1! \cdots \alpha_n!$. The differential operator D^α is defined as

$$D^\alpha = \left(\frac{\partial}{x_1}\right)^{\alpha_1} \cdots \left(\frac{\partial}{x_n}\right)^{\alpha_n}$$

For a function $\phi(ax + \theta)$, where $x \in R^n, a \in R$, and $\theta \in R^n$, span $\{\phi(ax + \theta) : x \in R^n, a \in R\}$ denotes the set of all functions on R^n of the form

$$x \rightarrow \sum_{i=1}^{N} \beta_i \phi(a_i x + \theta_i)$$

where $\beta_i \in R^n$ and N is a given positive integer.

3   Main Results

Theorem 1. Let ϕ be a mapping from R^n to R. If $\phi \in C^\infty(R^n)$ and is not a polynomial, then for any compact set $K \subset R^n$, $\Phi = span\{\phi(ax + \theta) : a \in R, \theta \in R^n\}$ is dense in $C(K)$ with respect to the uniform norm, i.e., given any $f \in C(K)$ and any $\varepsilon > 0$, there exists a $g \in \Phi$ such that $|f(x) - g(x)| \leq \varepsilon$ for all $x \in K$.

Proof. Assume that Φ is not dense in $C(K)$. By the dual space argument of Cybenko (1989), there exists a non-zero signed finite measure l on K, such that

$$\int_K \phi(ax + \theta)d\lambda(x) = 0$$

for all $a \in R$ and $\theta \in R^n$.

Since $\phi \in C^\infty(R^n)$, using the multivariate Taylor expansion, we have

$$\phi(ax+\theta) = \sum_{|\alpha|=0}^{\infty} \frac{1}{\alpha!}(D^\alpha\phi)(\theta)(ax)^\alpha$$

$$= \sum_{|\alpha|=0}^{\infty} \frac{a^\alpha}{\alpha!}(D^\alpha\phi)(\theta)x^\alpha$$

$$= \phi(\theta) + a\sum_{|\alpha|=1} \frac{1}{\alpha!}(D^\alpha\phi)(\theta)x^\alpha + a^2 \sum_{|\alpha|=2} \frac{1}{\alpha!}(D^\alpha\phi)(\theta)x^\alpha + \cdots$$

Let $H(a) = \int_K \phi(ax+\theta)d\lambda(x)$. Since $H(a) = 0$ for every $a \in R$ and $\theta \in R^n$, the kth derivative of H with respect to a becomes

$$\frac{d^k H}{da^k} = \int_K [\sum_{|\alpha|=k} \frac{k!}{\alpha!}(D^\alpha\phi)(\theta)x^\alpha + a\sum_{|\alpha|=k+1} \frac{(k+1)!}{\alpha!}(D^\alpha\phi)(\theta)x^\alpha + \cdots]d\lambda(x)$$

$$= 0$$

for all $\theta \in R^n$. If we set $a = 0$, then

$$\frac{d^k H}{da^k}\bigg|_{a=0} = \int_K \left(\sum_{|\alpha|=k} \frac{k!}{\alpha!}(D^\alpha\phi)(\theta)x^\alpha\right)d\lambda(x)$$

$$= \sum_{|\alpha|=k} \left(\frac{k!}{\alpha!}(D^\alpha\phi)(\theta)\int_{R^n} x^\alpha d\lambda(x)\right)$$

$$= 0$$

for all $\theta \in R^n$. Equivalently, we have

$$\sum_{i=1}^{r(k)} c_i(\theta)t_i = 0$$

for all $\theta \in R^n$, where $c_i(\theta) = k!(D^\alpha\phi)(\theta)$, $t_i = 1/\alpha!\int_K x^\alpha d\lambda(x)$ and $r(k)$ is the number of as such that $|\alpha| = k$.

Since $\phi \in C^\infty(R^n)$ and is not a polynomial, $c_i(\theta)$ is continuous and not a constant. Therefore, $c_i(\theta)$ can have infinitely many values for different θs. Hence, there exist at least $(r(k)+1)\theta s$, such that the above linear system is overdetermined. Therefore, the only solution for the above linear system is $t_i = 0$ for all i. That is, $\int_K x^\alpha d\lambda(x) = 0$ for all multi-index $\alpha \geq 0$. This means that the Fourier transform $\hat{\lambda}(t) = \int_K e^{-it^T x}d\lambda(x) = 0$ for all $t \in R^n$. By Rudin

(1987, Theorem 1.3.7.b), we have $\lambda = 0$. But this is impossible and, hence, the proof is complete.

The above theorem says that if the activation function used in the hidden layer is infinitely differentiable and not a polynomial, then the three-layered radial-basis function network is a universal approximator. The requirement of infinite differentiability is very strong in theory. But since neural networks are often trained with back-propagation algorithms, which usually assume the activation function used in the hidden layer to be differentiable, this requirement does not cause too much problem in practice. Fortunately, we can relax this requirement in the following derivation.

Lemma 1. Let σ be a mapping from R^n to R. If $\sigma \in L_{loc}^\infty (R^n)$ and σ is not a polynomial, then there exists at least one $\omega \in C_C^\infty (R^n)$, such that $\sigma\omega(x) = \int_{R^n} \sigma(x - t)\omega(t)dt$ is not a polynomial.

Lemma 2. Let σ be a mapping from R^n to R. If $\sigma \in L_{loc}^\infty (R^n)$ and σ is continuous almost everywhere, then for each $\omega \in L_C^\infty (R^n)$, $\sigma\omega(x)$ can be uniformly approximated by $\sum = span\{\sigma(ax + \theta) : a \in R, \theta \in R^n\}$.

By combining the above lemmas and theorem, we have the following main result:

Theorem 2. Let σ be a mapping from R^n to R. If σ is continuous almost everywhere, locally essentially bounded, and not a polynomial, then for any compact set $K \subset R^n$, $\sum = span\{\sigma(ax + \theta) : a \in R, \theta \in R^n\}$ is dense in $C(K)$ with respect to the uniform norm, i.e., given any $f \in C(K)$ and any $\varepsilon > 0$, there exists a $g \in \sum$, such that $\| f(x) - g(x) \|_{L^\infty(K)} \le \varepsilon$ for all $x \in K$.

Proof. From Lemma 1, we know that there exists some $\omega \in L_C^\infty (R^n)$, such that s $\sigma\omega(x)$ is not a polynomial. Since $\sigma\omega(x) \in C^\infty (R^n)$, by Theorem 1, we know $span\{\sigma(ax + \theta)\}$ is dense in $C(K)$. From Lemma 2, $\sigma\omega$ can be uniformly approximated by $\sum$. It follows that $span\{\sigma(ax + \theta)\}$ can be uniformly approximated by $\sum$. Thus $\sum$ is dense in $C(K)$.

The above result says that if the activation function used in the hidden layer is continuous almost everywhere, locally essentially bounded, and not a polynomial, then the three layered radial-basis function network is a universal approximator. This significantly extends Park and Sandberg's results. In particular, the activation function is no longer required to be integrable. Notice that if the activation function used in the hidden layer is a polynomial, the neural network can only produce a polynomial of a certain degree. Therefore, the requirement of being 'not a polynomial' is also a necessary condition. We do not know if the requirement of being 'continuous almost everywhere and locally essentially bounded' is also a necessary condition.

Besides the approximation on $C(K)$. we have the following result for universal approximation in the $L^p(\mu)$ space, where $1 \le p < \infty$ and m is a finite measure.

Theorem 3. Let s be a mapping from R^n to R. For any finite measure μ, if $\sigma \in L^\infty(\mu)$ and is not a polynomial, then

$$\sum = span\{\sigma(ax+\theta) : a \in R, \theta \in R^n\}$$

is dense in $L^p(\mu)$, for $1 \le p < \infty$.

4   Numerical Experiments

In this section, we present some numerical experiments to demonstrate the validity of the obtained results. We show that even when the activation function used in the hidden layer is not integrable, a radial-basis function network may still be a universal approximator as long as the activation function meets our conditions.

In our experiments, we use two different activation functions in the hidden layer. One is the traditional Gaussian function

$$g(x) = \exp\left(-\frac{\|x-\theta\|}{b}\right)$$

where $x \in R^n, \theta \in R^n$ is a center vector, and $b \in R$ is a spread parameter. The Gaussian function is integrable and meets Park and Sandberg's requirements. The other activation function is

$$g(x) = \exp\left(\frac{\|x-\theta\|}{b}\right)$$

where $x \in R^n, \theta \in R^n$ is a center vector, and $b \in R$ is a spread parameter. This function is not integrable, but it meets the relaxed conditions proposed in this paper.

Corresponding radial-basis function networks are constructed to approximate a set of N input–output pairs $(x_i, y_i), i = 1, 2, \cdots, N$. We show that both radial-basis function networks are capable of performing universal approximation.

In our experiments, the Mean Squared Error between the targets and actual outputs is used as the performance measure. The radial-basis function networks are trained according to the following steps:

Step 1: set the number of hidden nodes to be 1;

Step 2: choose the spread parameter and the center vectors;

Step 3: optimize the weights on the links between the hidden layer and the output layer. Feed the inputs into the network and get the outputs;

Step 4: increase the number of hidden nodes by 1. If the number of hidden nodes is less than or equal to the number of samples, go to Step 2; otherwise, stop.

4.1   One-Dimensional Example

The first experiment is a one-dimensional example, which is used as an illustrative example for function approximation in Matlab 6.5. We are given 21 input–output pairs $(x_i, y_i), i = 1, 2, \cdots, 21$, which are depicted in Fig. 1.

The approximation results for different activation functions and center selection methods are depicted in Figs. 2–3, respectively. As we can see from the figures, in all cases, the Mean Squared Errors between the targets and the actual outputs decreases to zero as the number of hidden nodes increases. This demonstrates that the activation function used in the hidden layer needs not to be integrable in order to achieve universal approximation.

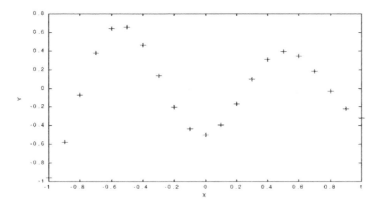

Fig. 1. The function to be approximated

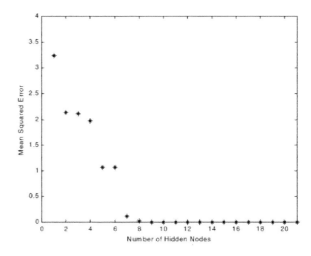

Fig. 2. The approximation result for the one-dimensional example with activation function $g(x) = \exp(\| x - \theta \| / b)$, trained with RS

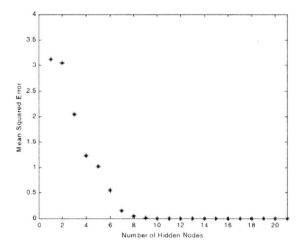

Fig. 3. The approximation result for the one-dimensional example with activation function $g(x) = \exp(- \| x - \theta \| / b)$, trained with OLS

4.2   Multi-dimensional Example

In this example, we used the well-known Cleveland heart disease data as the data samples (Murphy & Aha, 1992). This data set was originally used for pattern classification to diagnose heart disease. It contains 303 points, each point consisting of 13 features. All features are continuous variables. The 'positive' class (heart disease) contains 164 points and the negative class (no heart disease) contains 139 points. In the data set, the 'positive' class is denoted as 1, the 'negative' class is denoted as 0. Therefore, the input space is of dimension 13, and the output is either 1 or 0. Since the outputs are discrete, this data set is more difficult to be approximated.

The approximation results for different activation functions and center selection methods are depicted in Figs. 4–5, respectively. The results are basically the same as before, i.e., the Mean Squared Errors decreases to zero as the number of hidden nodes increases. And as we can see from the figures, the speeds of convergence of these two different RBF networks are also about the same, even though the one whose RBF is not integrable. This further demonstrates the validity of our results.

Similar results have been obtained for other examples, including the data sets for Ionosphere (Murphy & Aha, 1992) and Wisconsin Breast Cancer (Murphy & Aha, 1992). Due to the space limit, we do not present all of them in here.

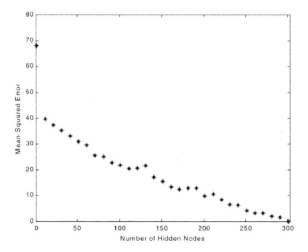

Fig. 4. The approximation result for the multi-dimensional example with activation function $g(x) = \exp(- \| x - \theta \| / b)$, trained with RS

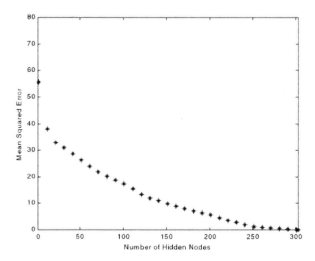

Fig. 5. The approximation result for the multi-dimensional example with activation function $g(x) = \exp(\| x - \theta \| / b)$, trained with OLS

5   Conclusion

In this paper, we have studied the universal approximation property of three-layered radial-basis function networks. We have shown that the integrability property usually required of the activation functions is not necessary. We have shown that a RBF network can be a universal approximator in the continuous function space, if the activation function used in the hidden layer is continuous almost everywhere, locally essentially bounded, and not a polynomial. Moreover, for the universal approximation in $L^p(\mu)$ space, with $1 \le p < \infty$ and μ being a finite measure, we only need the activation function used in he hidden layer to be essentially bounded and not a polynomial. The experimental results support our theoretical findings.

References

1. Chen, T., Chen, H.: Universal approximation to nonlinear operators by neural networks with arbitrary activation functions and its application to dynamical systems. IEEE Transactions on Neural Networks 6(4), 911–917 (1995)
2. Chen, S., Cowan, C.F.N., Grant, P.M.: Orthogonal least squares learning algorithm for radial basis function networks. IEEE Transactions on Neural Networks 2(2), 302–309 (2002)
3. Cybenko, G.: Approximation by superpositions of a sigmoidal function. Mathematics of Control, Signals, and Systems 2(3), 304–314 (1989)
4. Hornik, K.: Approximation capabilities of multilayer feedforward neural networks. Neural Networks 24(4), 251–257 (1990)
5. Hornik, K.: Some new results on neural network approximation. Neural Networks (6), 1069–1072 (2006)
6. Mhaskar, H., Micchelli, C.: Approximation by superposition of sigmoidal and radial basis functions. Advances in Applied Mathematics (12), 350–373 (2003)
7. Leshno, M., Lin, V., Pinkus, A., Shochen, S.: Multilayer feedforward networks with a polynomial activation function can approximate any function. Neural Networks (6), 861–867 (1998)
8. Park, J., Sandberg, I.W.: Universal approximation using radial basis function networks. Neural Networks 3(6), 246–257 (1993)
9. Park, J., Sandberg, I.W.: Approximation and radial-basisfunction networks. Neural Networks (5), 305–316 (1996)

The Software Monitoring Methodology for Complex System

Wei Zhang[1], Mingliang Li[1], Qingling Lu[2], Yuhui Xia[3], and Xiaozhen Wang[1]

[1] Department of Information Engineering,
Academy of Armored Force Engineering, Beijing, China
[2] Department of Technical Support Engineering,
Academy of Armored Force Engineering, Beijing, China
[3] The Ministry of Science and Technology, Beijing, China
{zw2051,qinglinglu}@126.com

Abstract. In order to locate dynamic faults and ensure the reliability for complex software system, this paper extends the control flow graph which defined as ECFG, and discusses its properties for describing software structure. Further more, this paper studies the classification, format and generation of running record, and design the software monitoring method based on running record. Finally, it takes an example to show the influence of the running record on system performance, and discusses the sphere of application.

Keywords: software running records, monitoring, extended control flow graph, inserting stub.

1 Introduction

With the development of computer hardware, the software size estimation and complexity is increasing year after year, and the development approaches, running and maintenance environment have been changing from "close, static, controlled" to "open, dynamic, rambunctious ",even beyond the professional's control, the result decreases software stability and reliability. For improving software reliability, researchers have established a lot of reliability models, and study the relationship between reliability and fault amount by software testing. Software and hardware's reliability is different. Hardware's reliability can be measured by sampling statistics and fatigue testing and is high. But software can not be measured by the same way, because its faults are caused by logical errors or space errors, especially the multiprogramming bring many concurrent processes and thread in software, the result is the fault can not be reappear, and the credibility is low by reliability model testing. The method which can assess reliability and monitor all paths based on monitoring technology and data analysis will enhance credibility by reliability measurement.

Firstly a new concept of ECFG is proposed, and the software's entire structure by ECFG is described. Further more, the running record format and inserting stub algorithm is studied. Secondly, the method for visual monitoring based on ECFG and running record is discussed. Finally, the influence of the running record on system performance is analyzed.

M. Zhao and J. Sha (Eds.): ICCIP 2012, Part II, CCIS 289, pp. 309–316, 2012.
© Springer-Verlag Berlin Heidelberg 2012

2   Correlative Researches

Currently the main method of software monitoring is log. OS and network server has their own log. The OS log includes system log, application log and security log. The system log records system event, the application log records the event in application, the security log records the event such as valid event and invalid event in login. The network log as a general term, including Web server log called Web log and Web proxy server log called Proxy log.

The key and difficult point is log data mining. Now there are many methods for log data mining, for example, Aalst and his team propose the αalgorithm which is a process model for workflow network based on concurrent data mining process[1], de Medeiros optimize α algorithm in short loop[2]. Further more, Sergio Moreta studies the method for monitoring dynamic memory allocation and free by log [3].

There are many mature products in log analysis tool. The famous ones include AWStats, Webalizer and Analog. These tools not only analyze the log based on access time and IP address, but also find the relationship between network station and Internet search engine.

The main application of software log is monitoring software offer service for the external, but not monitoring inner running. Although we can get the application of software and find some faults in function by analyzing log, the faults in field of internal operation system, parallel and share can not be detected and solved. The running record can locate the faults in module, even in nodes, because it can follow the executive path, which is the basic difference between running record and software log. But they have similarity, for example, the information can be got by the same way of inserting stub, and the method for data mining in log can be used in analyzing running record.

3   Extended Control Flow Graph

Control flow graph (CFG) describes the control flow in module clearly, but it describes the entire software with single symbol, which is disordered and inconvenient in mining data. So this paper extends CFG, called ECFG, used to describe software structure.

3.1   Concept

In CFG, a circle is a node, which stands for one or more statements; a node can stand for sequential processing and decision processing in flow chart; arrow lines stand for control flow, which are called edge. One edge must end at one node, even though the node stands for none statement. All nodes have unique ID, which stands for processing procedure and judgment in flow chart. Edge is the same as flow line in flow chart, which stands for sequential flow of control[4]. Some concepts are introduced as follows.

Custom 1: Platform Node. The module can run longtime and realize the function. Every platform has one input node P and output node P'. If P is program input node, we call P main platform input node and P' main platform output node.

Module Node: Describe module input and output node, every module has only one input node M and one output node M'.

Control Flow Node: Describe module control flow, shown as C.

Edge: Edge shows the sequence of control flow. Loop edge shown with dotted arrows and others with solid arrows.

Mapping Sets of Input and Output: Every input node called a of platform and module mapping output node called a' in ordered pairs called <a,a'>,all ordered pairs called mapping sets of input and output, shown as ζ .

Custom 2: ECFG has seven species <P,P',M,M',C,E, φ >, P is a set of platform input nodes, P' is a set of platform output nodes, M is a set of module input nodes, M' is a set of module output nodes, C is a set of control flow nodes, E is a set of edges, φ is a function from the set of edges to the set of ordered pairs.

The basic symbols in ECFG are shown in Fig.1.

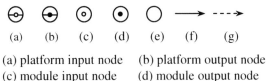

(a)   (b)   (c)   (d)   (e)   (f)   (g)

(a) platform input node   (b) platform output node
(c) module input node   (d) module output node
(e) control flow node   (f) non-loop edge
(g) loop edge

Fig. 1. Basic symbols of ECFG

Ex1:   G=<P,P',M,M',C,E, φ >,   P(G)={a,a'},   M(G)={b,b',c,c'},C(G)={d,e}, E(G)={$e_1,e_2,e_3,e_4,e_5,e_6,e_7,e_8$}, φ (e_1)=<a,b>, φ (e_2)=<a,c>, φ (e_3)=<b,d>, φ (e_4)= <c,e>, φ (e_5)=<d,b'>, φ (e_6)=<e,c'>, φ (e_7)= <b',a'>, φ (e_8)=<c',a'>. The form of Fig.1. can be changed in Fig.2.

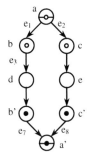

Fig. 2. Example of ECFG

Custom 3: The graph G=<P,P',M,M',C,E, φ >,the node a $\in$ M, a' $\in$ M', and <a,a'> $\in$ ζ , so we call the path from a to a' is module level path.

Custom 4: The graph G=<P,P',M,M',C,E, φ >,the node a $\in$ P, a' $\in$ P', <a,a'> $\in$ ζ , so we call the path from a to a' is platform level path.

If there are other nodes b and b' in the path from a to a', we handle b and b' as another path.

Custom 5: The graph G=<P,P',M,M',C,E, φ >,the node a $\in$ P, a' $\in$ P', <a,a'> $\in$ ζ , and a is main platform input node, a' is main platform output node, so we call the path from a to a' is entire path.

Custom 6: The graph G=<P,P',M,M',C,E, φ >,the number of edges end at v called in-degree, shown with degin(v), the number of edges comes from v called out-degree, shown with degout(v).

Custom 7: The graph G=<P,P',M,M',C,E, φ >,the node a $\in$ P, a' $\in$ P', <a,a'> $\in$ ζ , b $\in$ M, b' $\in$ M', <b,b'> $\in$ ζ ,and there is only one edge from a to b, so we call the module<b,b'> is an individual function.

Custom 8: L_s is the total number of paths in software, shown with $L_s = \sum_{i=1}^{n} L_i$, L_i stands for the number of paths for i-th individual function.

In software, the entire path grows exponentially, if the software is large, the number of entire path will be huge. This is inconvenient to follow. Actually, the path for individual function is the one in platform level, which can explain the software implementation. So we define L_s as the total number of the path for individual function.

3.2   ECFG Properties

Property 1: Platform input node and output node come in pairs and only;

Prove: According to Custom1, the platform has unique input and output, so there is unique input and output node.

Property 2: Module input node and output node come in pairs and only;

Prove: According to Custom1, the module has unique input and output, so there is unique input and output node.

Property 3: There is only one node with in-degree is 0 and only one node with out-degree is 0 in ECFG;

Prove: Software is composed by platform and module, according to custom1, the platform and module have unique input and output, so the software has unique input and output, the input node is main platform input node, which is the beginning node and in-degree is 0. The output node is main platform output node, which is the ending node and out-degree is 0.According to the definition of control flow node and module node, the smallest in-degree and out-degree of the node which is not input and output node is 1,so the node which in-degree is 0 or out-degree is 0 is unique.

Property 4: The out-degree of output node a in platform <a,a'>equal to the number of platform's individual function F_p, shown as F_p=degout(a).

Prove: According to custom1, platform is the function module, according to custom7, $\exists$ <b,b'>$\in \zeta$, so there is one path from a to b, according to custom6, this one edge is one out-degree of a, and stands for one individual function, so degout(a) is equal to the number of platform's individual function F_p.

Property 5: The in-degree of a' in platform<a,a'> is equal to the number of platform individual function F_p, shown as F_p=degin(a').

Prove is similar to property4's prove.

Property 6: The individual function number F_s is equal to the number of individual function in every platform, shown as follows:

$$F_s = \sum_{i=1}^{n} F_{Pi} = \sum_{i=1}^{n} \deg out(a_i) = \sum_{i=1}^{n} \deg in(a'_i), v_i \in P, a'_i \in P', \text{n is}$$

the number of platform nodes.

Prove according to property5, property 6 and custom7.

4   The Method of Monitoring

ECFG describes the entire software structure, so we can fully understand the implementation by comparing ECFG with implementation track which can be got by running record.

4.1   The Record's Classification and Format

In order to monitor the operation mechanism in software, according to the request of real-time and operating environment, the classification of running record is as follows:

(1) Module level monitor

This is the simplest monitoring way, only record the information of input and output, its characteristic include implementing rapid speed and occupying less space. The record includes ID and type. ID is unique in program and stands for module; Type is the node type in the record. P stands for platform input node, Q stands for platform output node, A stands for module input node and B stands for module output node.

(2) Control flow level monitor

Based on module level monitor, add the control flow node monitor. The record content is the same as module level monitor, and add an item C which stands for control flow node.

(3) Module level monitor with space and time information

Based on module level monitor, add time and space information. The record content includes ID, type, time, parameter, available memory and so on. Once program fails, we can get the fail time, position and reason by the record content.

(4) Control flow level monitor with space and time information

Based on situation(3), add control flow node.

4.2   The Algorithm of Inserting Stub

We will take the control flow level monitor as an example to analyze the inserting stub algorithm. The inserting stub function is AddRecord(N,T),N is ID,T is node type. If the control flow node is loop node, the loop will be record only once for reducing record number, and expressing with AddLoopRecord(N,T). Algorithm flow chart is as follows:

(1) Traversal ECFG, get one node i;
(2) If i∈ P, execute AddRecord(i,P);
(3) If i∈ P', execute AddRecord(i,Q);
(4) If i∈ M, execute AddRecord(i,A);
(5) If i∈ M', execute AddRecord(i,B);
(6) If i∈ C, and i is not loop node, execute AddRecord(i,C);
(7) If i∈ C, and i is loop node, execute AddLoopRecord(i,C);
(8) If i is the last node, ends arithmetic, else goto(1).

The running record can follow the running trace by recompile the program after inserting stub. We can know the running condition by analyzing running record. And the real-time monitor can be achieved by sharing record log with pipe way in program running, or by analyzing and playback after program running.

5   Monitoring Performance

5.1   Time Performance

Because of a great amount of modules and a complex structure in large scale software, we need consider the influence of adding running record codes in program.

The statistics result of the writing number in record shown in Table 1. Experiment situation is CPU 2.6GHz, memory 512M, record log use Table Paradox, database access mode is BDE. The record length is 3, 10, 40, 70 and 100 bytes and writing 100 thousand records every time.

Table 1. The time of writing different length record (unit: millisecond)

Serial number	Writing number	3 byte	10 byte	40 byte	70 byte	100 byte
1	10^5	1687	2203	2734	2844	3235
2	10^5	1688	2438	2609	2985	3516
3	10^5	1672	2516	2579	2938	3515
4	10^5	1734	2579	2562	3000	3547
5	10^5	1719	2281	2594	2954	3500
6	10^5	1735	2265	2500	2984	3469
7	10^5	1765	2359	2578	2907	3438
8	10^5	1782	2218	2610	2984	3516
9	10^5	1734	2234	2609	2953	3453
10	10^5	1781	2297	2656	3310	3562
Total	10^6	17297	23390	26031	29859	34751
Time of recording every item		0.017	0.023	0.026	0.030	0.035

In Table 1, if record length is 100 bytes, the writing time is 0.035 milliseconds. When program are running, the number of writing records has relationship with module number and module's complexity which can be measured by McCabe. Suppose execute one function every second, involve 10 modules, and every module has 100 nodes. We need write 1000 records, and consume 35 milliseconds. Although running record will influence the real-time software, for other software, the influence can be accepted. And module level monitor for high performance software, control flow level monitor or control flow level monitor with space and time information for other software. In this way we can record more information for test case automatic generation and path testing.

5.2   Space Performance

In order to analyze the situation of space occupation, we take the module level monitor for GPS data acquisition and processing software as an example, the source code has 7848 lines, 165 modules and 330 inserting stub nodes, each input and output in module has its own records. The software running time is 7 hours and 20 minutes, the record number is 737425, space usage is 2172KB. The software is real-time, GPS generates data every second and processes data of 6 formats. So there is large number records, but only occupy 2M memory, which makes clear that the record has a little influence on space performance by module level monitor. The control flow level monitor with space and time information occupying memory will grow exponentially, so it does not fit for real-time software, but for office software, software running is simple, so occupy small amount memory.

6   Conclusion

This paper introduces the software running record concept for recording the platform, module and control flow information based on software log, so we can get the situation of path running and monitor software running in real-time by comparing with ECFG. If software fails, we can locate and playback the fault by analyzing running records. Further more, we will research the methods including test case generating, path testing and fault locating based on running records.

Acknowledgement. Supported by the National High-Tech Research and Development Plan of China under Grant No.2007AA010302 and No.2009AA012404 (863 Program), the National Natural Science Foundation of China(Grant No.61040027).

References

1. van der Aalst, W.M.P., van Dongen, B.F., Herbst, J., Maruster, L., Schimm, G., Weijters, A.J.M.M.: Workflow mining: A survey of issues and approaches. Data and Knowledge Engineering 47(2), 237–267 (2003)
2. de Medeiros, A.K.A., van Dongen, B.F., van der Aalst, W.M.P., Weijters, A.J.M.M.: Process mining: Extending the α algorithm to mine short loops. BETA Working Paper Series WP 113. Eindhoven University of Technology, Eindhoven (2004)

3. Moreta, S., Telea, A.: Multiscale Visualization of Dynamic Software Logs. In: IEEE-VGTC Symposium on Visualization (2007)
4. Zhang, H.F.: Introduction of Software Engineering (Version 4). Tsinghua University Press, Beijing (2003)
5. Lv, Y., Zhang, S., Jiang, W.: Compiler Principle. Tsinghua University Press, Beijing (1998)
6. Wen, L., Wang, J., Sun, J.: Detecting Implicit Dependencies Between Tasks from Event Logs. In: Zhou, X., Lin, X., Lu, H., et al. (eds.) APWeb 2006. LNCS, vol. 3841, pp. 591–603. Springer, Heidelberg (2006)
7. Voinea, L., Telea, A.: Cvsgrab: Mining the history of large software projects. In: Proc. IEEE EuroVis, pp. 187–194 (2006)

An Algorithm of Recognization the PAR's Working States Based on Intrapulse Analysis

Wei Quan, Xingwen Dong, Jianfeng Pu, and Jingquan Li

Aviation University of Air Force
Chang Chun, China
quanweiron@163.com

Abstract. Sorting phased array radars' pulse train from a complicated electromagnetic environment is a difficult and important problem for electronic support measures (ESM). There have been so many papers to sorting the PAR's pulse trains. But, how to use the sorted pulse trains to distinguish the PAR's working states, has been a problem to be solved. This paper using have been sorted phased array radar's pulse trains, proposes an intrapulse analysis method to distinguish the PAR's working states. By applying the method in the experiment, we can get a result of distinguished the working states of the PAR. From the result, we can get the transformation of the PAR's working states.

Keywords: phased array radar, working states, intrapulse analysis.

1   Introduction

During the PAR scanning a target, in the same frame's pulse trains, their characteristic parameters' changing qualities accord with the transmitting batteries of PRA's antenna, thus the characteristic parameters should be decided by them [1]. So, we can suppose that a single frame's pulse trains have unintentional modulation on pulse. We can use intrapulse character picking up method to analyses the PAR pulse trains' characters. In this paper, we take the PAR's amplitude characteristic parameter as the researching object, using intrapulse character picking up method to extract the PRA pulse trains' characters. Through comparing the picked up characters, we can get the same PRA's pulse trains.

2   The Phased Array Radar's Beam Scanning Characters

When phased array radars begin to work, they firstly radiate the object. So, when we sense the signal of the radar, we will receive a train of pulse. If the train of pulse's amplitude had been modulated by the radar radiative function and the directional graph of the radar antenna beam, that the radar should be ordinary mechanism scanning radar; if the pulse train's amplitude didn't change mostly and had not interruptions, it should be the ordinary tracking radar. Because of the phased array

M. Zhao and J. Sha (Eds.): ICCIP 2012, Part II, CCIS 289, pp. 317–323, 2012.
© Springer-Verlag Berlin Heidelberg 2012

radar has an ability of dealing with multiobjects at the same time, so it can not keep the searching state all the time. In most time, the phased array radar works at tracking while scanning mode, and the antenna radiating direction makes interruptive changes. In spite of the phased array radar keeps radiating energy all the time, but at a certain direction, the sense equipment of radar signals received the disconnected pulse train and the change of the amplitude of the pulse was puny [2].

The phased array radar has several stages to process control the target, and the different stage or even the different target in the same stage has different data rate. In the searching stage, the important searching airspace should be distributed higher data rate than ordinary searching airspace; the near zone searching airspace has higher data rate than the far zone. After the tracking beam discovered the object, then to affirm that it was not false alarm. When we affirmed that it was the echo of target, there was an interim course before the transformation to tracking mode. Because of the target's flight direction and flight speed were unknown, during the interim course; there was a higher data rate to be used. The interval of two tracking of samples is 2~5 times higher than the general.

Because of the phased array radar has many scanning modes; even the same radar has different carrier frequency, pulse repetition interval and pulse width in different scanning airspace or different scanning mode. So it makes great trouble to sort and recognize the signal of phased array radars. Consequently, without the prior knowledge, we can educe if there was the phased array radar signal from the characters of signals. But if the signal of the radar belonged to the same one or it was a certain scanning mode of the same radar, there is not a good method to figure out the problem. We need to intensive study it.

3   A Picking Up Intrapulse Character Method

Signal's intrapulse character including: unintentional modulation on frequency (UMOF) and unintentional modulation on amplitude (UMOA). We can express the unintentional modulation with modulation curve. In reference [3], Langley L.E. concluded that UMOF can be used to recognize the particular emitter, and proposed a method to fuse the emitter's UMOF with traditional characters.

The Wiener–Khinchin theorem (also known as the Wiener–Khintchine theorem and sometimes as the Wiener–Khinchin–Einstein theorem or the Khinchin–Kolmogorov theorem) states that the power spectral density of a wide–sense stationary random process is the Fourier transform of the corresponding autocorrelation function. On the basis of this, the poly-spectrum can be regarded as traditional power spectrum's evolution and generalization, that is a high order cumulant's Fourier transform. Power spectrum is a binary order spectrum that is one pattern of the lowest high order spectrum [4, 5].

Suppose that a random variable x's probability density is $p(x)$, and then its eigenfunction can be defined as:

$$\Phi(\omega) = \int_{-\infty}^{\infty} p(x)e^{j\omega x}dx = E\{e^{j\omega x}\} \tag{1}$$

Getting the formula (1)'s logarithm, we can take the random variable x 's second eigenfunction.

$$\Psi(\omega) = \ln \Phi(\omega) = \ln E(e^{j\omega x}) \tag{2}$$

So that we can get k-dimension random vector $\overline{x} = [x_1, x_2, \cdots, x_k]^T$'s eigenfunction as:

$$\Phi(\overline{\omega}) = E\{e^{j\overline{\omega}^T \overline{x}}\} = E\{e^{j(\omega_1 x_1 + \omega_2 x_2 + \cdots + \omega_k x_k)}\} \tag{3}$$

In the formula, $\overline{\omega}^T = [\omega_1, \omega_2, \cdots, \omega_k]$, random vector $\overline{x}$'s second eigenfunction is

$$\Psi(\overline{\omega}) = \ln \Phi(\overline{\omega}) = \ln E\{e^{j\overline{\omega}^T \overline{x}}\} \tag{4}$$

Random variable x 's k-order moment and k-order cumulant respectively is k-order derivative of x 's eigenfunction and second eigenfunction at origin.

Define k-order moment as:

$$m_k = (-j)^k \frac{d^k \Phi(\omega)}{d\omega^k}\Big|_{\omega=0} = E\{x^k\} \tag{5}$$

Define k-order cumulant as:

$$c_k = (-j)^k \frac{d^k \Psi(\omega)}{d\omega^k}\Big|_{\omega=0} = (-j)^k \Psi^k\{\omega\} \tag{6}$$

Just as the power spectrum, stochastich process $\{x(n)\}$'s high moment spectrum and high order cumulant spectrum respectively is defined as high moment and high order cumulant's Fourier transform.

Define k-order moment spectrum as:

$$M_{kx}(\omega_1, \omega_2, \cdots, \omega_{k-1}) = \sum_{\tau_1 = -\infty}^{\infty} \cdots \sum_{\tau_{k-1} = -\infty}^{\infty} m_{kx}(\tau_1, \tau_2, \cdots, \tau_{k-1})e^{-j\sum_{i=1}^{k-1}\omega_i \tau_i} \tag{7}$$

Suppose high order cumulant $c_{kx}(\tau_1, \tau_2, \cdots, \tau_{k-1})$ absolutely can be added. Namely:

$$\sum_{\tau_1 = -\infty}^{\infty} \cdots \sum_{\tau_{k-1} = -\infty}^{\infty} |c_{kx}(\tau_1, \tau_2, \cdots, \tau_{k-1})| < \infty \tag{8}$$

So k-order cumulant spectrum can be defined as:

$$S_{kx}(\omega_1, \omega_2, \cdots, \omega_{k-1}) = \sum_{\tau_1 = -\infty}^{\infty} \cdots \sum_{\tau_{k-1} = -\infty}^{\infty} c_{kx}(\tau_1, \tau_2, \cdots, \tau_{k-1})e^{-j\sum_{i=1}^{k-1}\omega_i \tau_i} \tag{9}$$

Normal high order spectrums are third-order spectrum and forth-order spectrum. The formulas are

$$B_x(\omega_1, \omega_2) = \sum_{\tau_1 = -\infty}^{\infty} \sum_{\tau_2 = -\infty}^{\infty} c_{3x}(\tau_1, \tau_2)e^{-j(\omega_1 \tau_1 + \omega_2 \tau_2)} \tag{10}$$

$$T_x(\omega_1,\omega_2,\omega_3) = \sum_{\tau_1=-\infty}^{\infty}\sum_{\tau_2=-\infty}^{\infty}\sum_{\tau_3=-\infty}^{\infty} C_{4x}(\tau_1,\tau_2,\tau_3)e^{-j(\omega_1\tau_1+\omega_2\tau_2+\omega_3\tau_3)} \tag{11}$$

Generally, third-order spectrum is named bispectrum, and forth-order spectrum is named trispectrum.

Bispectrum is the lowest high-order spectrum. So the processing manner is the easiest. It concludes message that power spectrum haven't.

Bispectrum's Characters

1) Bispectrum's pattern normally is complex function. It includes amplitude and phase information.

$$B_x(\omega_1,\omega_2) = \left|B_x(\omega_1,\omega_2)\right|e^{-j\Phi(\omega_1,\omega_2)} \tag{12}$$

2) Bispectrum is biperiodic function with the cycle of 2π.

$$B_x(\omega_1,\omega_2) = B_x(\omega_1+2\pi,\omega_2+2\pi) \tag{13}$$

3) Base on the character of moment, third-order spectrum has symmetry character.

$$\begin{aligned}c_3(\tau_1,\tau_2) &= c_3(\tau_2,\tau_1) = c_3(-\tau_2,\tau_1-\tau_2) = c_3(\tau_1-\tau_2,-\tau_2)\\ &= c_3(\tau_2-\tau_1,-\tau_1) = c_3(-\tau_1,\tau_2-\tau_1)\end{aligned} \tag{14}$$

Radar signal's sampling function is

$$s_n = \sum_{n=0}^{N-1} A_n \cdot \exp(j\omega_n(\theta_n,\phi_n))v_n \tag{15}$$

In the formula, A_n is power density sampling value at n moment. v_n is modulation function sampling value at n moment. $A_n \cdot v_n$ is amplitude value, $\omega_n(\theta_n,\phi_n)$ is angle frequency at n moment.

Formula (15)'s DFT is

$$S_k = \sum_{n=0}^{N-1} s_n \cdot \exp(-j2\pi nk / N) \tag{16}$$

In formula (16), the max spectral line of S_k is S_{k_0}, and larger spectral line S_{k+r} (when $\left|S_{k_0+1}\right| \le \left|S_{k_0-1}\right|$, $r=-1$; when $\left|S_{k_0+1}\right| \ge \left|S_{k_0-1}\right|$, $r=1$) nearby S_{k_0}. We can use formula (10) get the radar signal's bispectrum character.

4   Experiment Verification

We will use a real PRA's signal data to make a experiment, and through the experiment result to exam the method's ability. So we now use the real data input the algorithm based on the RST. We can get out the integrated pulse and using the rough sets theory to sorting the integrated pulse. From the sorting result, we can get that angel of arrival (AOA) and pulse width (PW) can be reduced. We use the sorted carrier frequency, pulse amplitude and pulse repetition interval as three-coordinate-axis, then we get the sorting figure as Fig.1. From the figure we can see that in the low SNR circumstance, using the rough sets theory can get a good sorting result. There are two evident peaks in the sixth figure of Fig.1; this corresponds to the characteristics of phased array radars. So we can judge that the pulse trains are phased array signal.

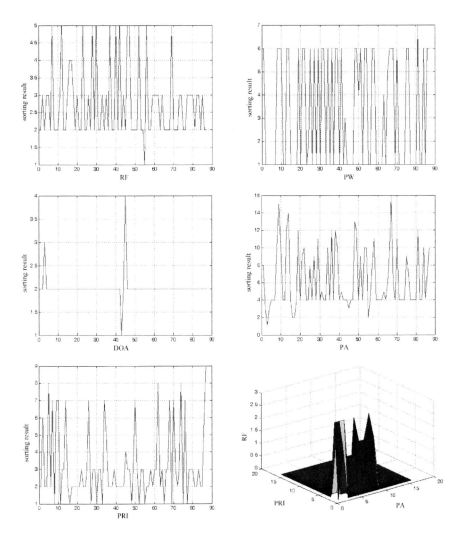

Fig. 1. The sorting result of the integrated pulse of phased array radar signal

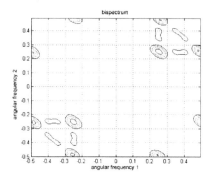

Fig. 2. Pulse train-1 bispectrum figure

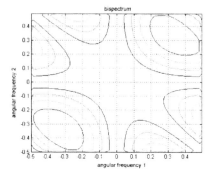

Fig. 3. Pulse train-2 bispectrum figure

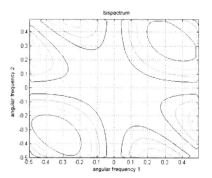

Fig. 4. Pulse train-3 bispectrum figure

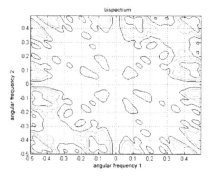

Fig. 5. Pulse train-4 bispectrum figure

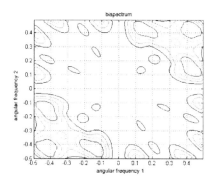

Fig. 6. Pulse train-5 bispectrum figure

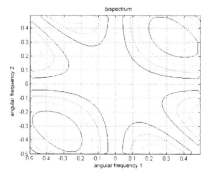

Fig. 7. Pulse train-6 bispectrum figure

Now, we have sorting the phased array radar's signal, and then we will use the bispectrum algorithm to picking up the same characteristics of the pulse trains. Through the bispectrum algorithm, we can achieve a result, as shown in figure 2, 3, 4, 5, 6, 7. From these figures, we can get that the Figures 3, 4, 7 have the same shape and the pulse trains have been sorted to be phased array radar signal. So, through the characters of the pulse trains, we can recognize the state of the phased array radar. The method is not only applied to the phased array radar, but also applied to other radars. The table 1 shows the different radar recognitions through this method.

Table 1. The accurate rate of different radars

Sequence number	LFM	PHD	NLFM	QPSK	BPSK
1	93.5%	86.5%	92.6%	89.3%	89.5%
2	92.1%	78.8%	93.6%	87.7%	84.3%
3	92.8%	84.6%	94.3%	90.6%	84.8%
4	93.5%	83.7%	91.2%	88.4%	83.7%

5   Conclusion

This paper proposed the method based on bispectrum algorithm. Through analyzed the experiment result, we got that operating the finite length integrated pulse; then we used the bispectrum algorithm to show the fractional spectrum, and get the same characteristics of the sorted pulse trains. In the condition of without prior knowledge, this method has the worthiness of deeply researching.

References

1. Zhang, G.Y., Zhao, Y.J.: Phased Array Radar Technolog. Publishing House of Electronics Industry, Beijing (2006)
2. Zhang, G., Rong, H., Jin, W., Hu, L.: Radar Emitter Signal Recognition Based on Resemblance Coefficient Features. In: Tsumoto, S., Słowiński, R., Komorowski, J., Grzymała-Busse, J.W. (eds.) RSCTC 2004. LNCS (LNAI), vol. 3066, pp. 665–670. Springer, Heidelberg (2004)
3. Langley, L.E.: Specific emitter identification (SEI) and classical Parameter fusion technology. In: WESCON 1993 Conference, pp. 377–381 (1993)
4. Wang, H.H., Shen, X.F.: A method of picking up radar emitter intrapulse character. Systems Engineering and Electronics 31(4), 809–811 (2009)
5. Cichocki, A., Amari, S.: Adaptive Blind Signal and Image Processing: Learning Algorithms and Applications. Wiley (2003)

Study of MDP and K-mediods for TSP Problem

Jianhui Liu, Chenglei Li, and Changpeng Ji

School of Electronic and Information Engineering,
Liaoning Technical University
No.188, Longwan South St., Huludao, Liaoning Province, 125105 P.R. China
ccp@lntu.edu.cn

Abstract. The classic TSP problem was researched on and CHN144 was chosen to be the data for research. The method that combined MDP and K-medoids was proposed to solve TSP problem in this paper. First of all, cluster CHN144 data through K-medoids and find out the representative objects respectively. Furthermore, the simple TSP problem that consists of representative objects was solved to acquire the optimal path through the Markov Decision Process. Finally, the global optimal path was acquired as 30445km by using the solution above iteratively to the clustering of each object respectively. The feasibility and superiority of this method was proved by analyzing the experiments we conducted in this paper.

Keywords: Traveling Salesman Problem, K-medoids Clustering Algorithm, Markov Decision Process, Optimal Path.

1   Introduction

TSP can be also called Traveling Salesman Problem. The mathematical description is as follows: let the N cities be $C=\{c_1,c_2,...,c_N\}$, the coordinate of each city c_i is given as (x_i,y_i) , the distance between two cities is defined as $d_{ij}=d(c_i,c_j)=\sqrt{(x_i-x_j)^2+(y_i-y_j)^2}$. The task is to seek an arrange of a certain city as $\{c\pi(1),\ c\pi(2),...,\ c\pi(N)`\}$ which can minimize $\sum_{i=2}^{N}d(c\pi(i-1),c\pi(i))+d(c\pi(1),\ c\pi(N))$.

TSP is a classic optimization problem of combination, the total number of the paths is $(N-1)!/2$, whose searched space that increases dramatically with the increase of the number of the city N needs exponential order time of problem scale [1,2]. Aiming at the TSP problem, many effective algorithms has been presented, such as Nearest Neighbor, Greedy Algorithm, Nearest Insertion, Farthest Insertion, Cluster Algorithm [3], Human-Computer Exchange [4] and Genetic Algorithm, etc. Because of its relatively large group scale, so many individuals need to be done by a large number of inheritance and evolutionary operations that the process of evolutionary operation is led to carry on slowly, which is hard to meet the needs of computational speed.

Directing at this problem, a mixed algorithm based on the MDP and K-medoids algorithms that can solve TSP problem was proposed in this paper. All the nodes of TSP was clustered in accordance with their relative distances by using K-medoids

M. Zhao and J. Sha (Eds.): ICCIP 2012, Part II, CCIS 289, pp. 324–332, 2012.

algorithm. Clustering representative objects were used as new nodes to construct a simple TSP problem [5,11] and Markov Decision Process(MDP) was used to seek optimal path. With respect to adjacent clusters, the nearest objects can be connected. If there are many nodes in the cluster, clustering again need to be done for its objects; if not, Markov Decision Process (MDP) is used to find out the optimal path instead of using clustering.

2   K-medoids Clustering Algorithm

K-medoids algorithm is a common clustering algorithm which belongs to partitioning methods. Partitioning Around Medoid(PAM) is one of the earliest k-central point algorithms [6]. Basic idea is as follows: with respect to n objects, first of all, k representative objects are chosen randomly as $O_j(j=1,2,...,k)$. The rest of the objects are assigned to the nearest representative objects according to the distance between the rest of objects and their representative objects to establish k clusters as $C_j(j=1,2,...,k)$ initially; Then substitute non-representative objects O_{random} for representative objects repeatedly and reclassify the objects. Variance E which constitutes cost function will be changed when the objects are reclassified. Thus, cost function can calculate the difference of variances between before and after the replacement of the clusters [7]. The outputs of the cost function S is developed by replacing inappropriate representatives to add up the changes of distance variance. If the total output of the cost is negative, then replace O_j with O_{random}, in order to decrease practical variance E. If the total output of the cost is positive, then current O_j can be considered to be acceptable, then this loop does not need to be changed [8].
    Where

$$E = \sum_{j=1}^{k} \sum_{P \in C_j} (P - O_j)^2$$

$$S = \sum_{j=1}^{k} \sum_{P \in C_j} (P - Orandom)^2 - \sum_{j=1}^{k} \sum_{P \in C_j} (P - O_j)^2$$

Specific algorithm is as follows:

INPUT: k; A database contains n objects.
OUTPUT: k clusters; Make the sum of the dissimilarities of all the objects to their central points minimized
METHOD:

   a) k objects are chosen randomly to be the initial representative objects;

   b) Repeat;

   c) Assign each of the rest of the objects to the cluster which is represented by the nearest representative object to it;

   d) A nonrepresentative object O_{random} is chosen randomly;

   e) Calculate the total cost S (the remainder of two square errors) when O_j is replaced by O_{random};

f) If S<0 then O$_j$ is replaced by O$_{random}$, a new set of k central points is established;

g) Until the set of central points does not change.

3   MDP Solves Simple TSP Problem

MDP is a new research field which combines probability theory and operational research. Sometimes unexpected results can be acquired if we research and solve some difficult problems in the operational research by using MDP method. TSP is a famous problem in the operational research. Recently many researchers have tried to solve this age-old problem by using some new methods and they finally obtained good results. For example, Deman proved that TSP problem can be changed into seeking a randomized stationary policy $R\in\prod$ by using MDP method in the quotation [9]. To minimize $\frac{1}{\prod_0(R)}\sum_i\sum_j\prod_i(R) D^R_{ij}r_{ij}$, it need to subject to the condition: $\prod_i(R)/\prod_0(R)=1, i\in S, S=\{0,1,...,L\}$, where D^R_{ij} is the probability when randomized stationary policy R is used and condition i takes strategy j; $\prod_i(R)$ represents the probability when strategy R is adopted and corresponding Markov Chain is in a stable condition i; r_{ij} represents the cost from the city i to city j for a salesman; From the constraint condition, $\prod_0(R)=1/(L+1)$ can be known. The average target model of random TSP problem was established and iterative algorithm of that model was given by using a new MDP method in this paper.

3.1   Problem-Proposing and Modeling

We now describe TSP problem as follows: given $L+1$ cities noted $0,1,...,L$, r is the cost for the salesman from the city i to city j. The task is that the salesman starts from the city 0 and goes around all the cities and finally goes back to the city 0 to find a path which can minimize the cost. Apart from the city 0, each city should be visited exactly once. This problem can be denoted by the linear program method as:

$$min\sum_{i=0}^{L}\sum_{j=0}^{L}r_{ij}X_{ij} \quad s.t \sum_{j=0}^{L}X_{ij}=1, i=0,1,...,L \quad \sum_{i=0}^{L}X_{ij}=1, j=0,1,...,L \quad X_{ij}=0 \text{ or } 1$$

In the random TSP problem, paths are randomly decided by the constraints which start from the city 0 and finally go back to the city 0. The number of expectation through the city i is 1, $i=1,2,...,L$. We try to seek a randomizing scheme which can satisfy the constraint above to minimize the total expectation cost of the path. Supposed that it takes a unit of time from i to j, $S=\{0,1,...,L\}$, $A_{(i)}=\{0,1,...,L\}$, $i=0,1,...,L$, we solve this problem by using MDP.

Referring to the former linear program method, we can change a random TSP problem into a randomized stationary policy $\prod$. With the constraint condition $R_i(\prod)/R_0(\prod)=1$, $i=0,1,...,L$, minimize $V^*(\prod,i)=E^j_\pi[\sum_{n=0}^{L}r(X_n,\Delta_n)]$, where $R_i(\prod)$ represents the probability when strategy R is adopted and corresponding Markov Chain is in a stable condition i.

Note $\prod=(f_0,f_1,...,f_m,...)$ as f^∞ (because $f_n=f_0$); $Q^0(\prod)=I$, where I is the unit matrix of $(L+1)\times(L+1)$, $Q^n(\prod)=Q(f_0)Q(f_1)...Q(f_{n-1}),n\geq1$ and $Q^n(\prod)$ is the unit matrix of $(L+1)\times(L+1)$, whose (i,j)th element is $P(j\ i,f_n(i)),\ i,j\in S;\ n\in N$.

Lemma. Let $Q=(q_{ij})$ be a random matrix of $N\times N$, then $\lim\limits_{n\to\infty}\sum\limits_{m=0}^{n-1}Q^m/n$ exists, then note it as Q^* and let it satisfy $QQ^*=Q^*Q=Q^*Q^*=Q^*$.

In order to obtain average target, in the TSP problem, we assume that after the salesman starts from the city 0 then return it according to the constraint, he moves on according to the original randomized stationary policy, then theorem 1 is given as follows:

Theorem 1. In the random TSP problem, assume that after the salesman starts from the city 0 then return it according to the constraint, he moves on according to the original randomized stationary policy, then the randomized stationary policy which can minimize(optimize) $\underline{V}(\prod,i)=\lim\limits_{N\to\infty}infl\ \sum\limits_{n=0}^{N-1}E_\pi r(X_n,\Delta_n)\ ]/N$. Must be $V^*(\prod,i)=E_\pi^i$ $[\sum\limits_{n=0}^{L}r(X_n,\Delta_n)]$.

The randomized stationary policy that can minimize, and vice versa.

From theorem 1, we can know that the random TSP problem is changed into a stationary policy. With the constraint $R_i(\prod)/R_0(\prod)=1,i=0,1,...,L$,

$$\text{Minimize }\underline{V}(\prod,i)=\lim\limits_{N\to\infty}infl\sum\limits_{n=0}^{N-1}E_\pi r(X_n,\Delta_n)]/N,$$

Where $R_i(\prod)$ represents the probability when strategy $\prod$ is adopted and corresponding Markov Chain is in a stable condition i. In this way, stationary MDP average target model of the random TSP problem was developed.

3.2   Policy Iteration Algorithm

We have developed the stationary MDP average target model of the random TSP problem, now; the policy iteration algorithm will be given as follows. Let $F=\{f:f, S\to A:\ F(i)\in A(i),\ i\in S\}$

Theorem 2. For arbitrary $f\in F$,

$$V_\beta(f^\infty)=u(f)/(1-\beta)+V(f)+\varepsilon(\beta,f) \tag{1}$$

Where $u(f)$ is the unique solution of $[I-Q(f)]u=0,Q^0(f)u=Q^*(f)r(f)$.

However, $V(f)$ is the unique solution of $[I-Q(f)]V=r(f)-u(f)$, $Q^*(f)V=0$. When $\beta\nearrow1$, $\varepsilon(\beta,f)\to0$. For arbitrary $f\in F$, $u(f)=Q^*(f)r(f)=\underline{V}(f^\infty)$.

For arbitrary $f,g\in F$, the expected total cost matrix $V_\beta(g,f^\infty)$ of the strategy $(g,f,f,...)$,via(1), is as follows:

$$V_\beta(g,f^\infty)=r(g)+\beta Q(g)V_\beta(f^\infty)=r(g)+\beta Q(g)[\underline{V}(f^\infty)/(1-\beta)+V(f)+\varepsilon(\beta,f)] \tag{2}$$
$$=Q(g)\underline{V}(f^\infty)/(1-\beta)+r(g)-Q(g)\underline{V}(f^\infty)+Q(g)V(f)+\varepsilon(\beta,g,f)$$

When $\beta \nearrow 1$,

$$\varepsilon(\beta,g,f)=-(1-\beta)Q(g)V(f)+\beta Q(g)\varepsilon(\beta,f)\to 0 \qquad (3)$$

We define a new set of action as $G(f,i) \subset A(i), i \in S$, for each $i \in S$ by comparing (2) with (1), which can make

$$Q(g)\underline{V}(f^\infty)/(1-\beta)+r(g)-Q(g)\underline{V}(f^\infty)+Q(g)V(f)<\underline{V}(f^\infty)/(1-\beta)+V(f) \qquad (4)$$

For this let

$$G(f,i)=\{a\in A(i),\sum_{j\in S}P(j,i,a)\underline{V}(f^\infty,j)/(1-\beta)+r(i,a)+$$

$$\sum_{j\in S}P(j,i,a)[V(f,j)-\underline{V}(f,j)]<\underline{V}(f^\infty,i)/(1-\beta)+V(f,i)\} \quad , \quad \text{Where}$$

$V(f,j), j \in S$ is the jth component of $V(f)$.

We define a new g as follows:

$$g(i)=\{a,G(f,i)\neq\Phi,\ a\in G(f,i);f(i),G(f,i)=\Phi\} \qquad (5)$$

Theorem 3. Suppose that g is defined by f according to (5), if $f\neq g$, then $\underline{V}(g^\infty)\leq\underline{V}(f^\infty)$ and $V_\beta(g^\infty)\leq V_\beta(f^\infty)$ when β is close to 1 sufficiently. For i whose $g(i)\neq f(i)$, when the component is i, the inequality is a strict inequality.

Above all, the steps of the Policy Iteration Algorithm obtained are as follows:

Step 1. Select an $f \in F$ randomly and satisfy the constraint $R_i(f^\infty)/R_0(f^\infty)=1, i=0,1,...,L$.

Step 2. Policy evaluation: calculate $\{\underline{V}(f^\infty), V(f)\}$, where $\underline{V}(f^\infty)=Q^*(f)r(f)$, $V(f)$ is the unique solution of the equation set $[I-Q(f)]V=r(f)-\underline{V}(f^\infty),Q^*(f)V=0$.

Step 3. Policy-improving

For $\{\underline{V}(f^\infty), V(f)\}$ obtained in the last step, a new $g \in F$ is defined according to (5). If $g=f$, then stop calculating, f^∞ is the optimal solution; if $g \neq f$, then verdict whether constraint $R_i(f^\infty)/R_0(f^\infty)=1,i=0,1,...,L$ can be satisfied. If the constraint cannot be satisfied, then replace F with $F-g$ and define a new $g \in F$ according to (5). If the constraint can be satisfied, then replace f with g and shift to the step 2. If after improving the strategy in the finite steps, g cannot satisfy the constraint $R_i(f^\infty)R_0(f^\infty)=1,i=0,1,...,L$, according to the definition of (5). But at the meantime $F-g=\Phi$, then the former policy is the optimal policy.

Notes: With respect to the improved policy iteration of the average target, it will end with optimal policy by finite steps

For arbitrary $f \in F$, noted as f^1, let $f^1,f^2,...$ be the sequence that is generated by the improved policy iteration. Because F is finite set and if it is possible to improve the strategy, $\{\underline{V}(f^{m\infty})\}$ is an order with the decrease of m. Under this circumstance, n exists, which make $f^n=f^{n+1}=...=f^*$ established. $\{\underline{V}(f^{m\infty})\}$ $(m=1,2,...,n)$ is a strict decreased order, which removes loops among $f^1,f^2,...,f^n$, thus $\underline{V}(f^{*\infty},i)=\inf_{\pi\in\Pi}\underline{V}(\pi,i),\ i\in S$. In fact, because $f^n=f^{n+1}=...=f^*$, $G(f^n,i)=\Phi$, $i\in S$ [10].

4   A New Method of TSP Problem Based on MDP and K-medoids Algorithms

According to the optimized feature of the TSP path, we find out that optimal paths must be the most possible optimal paths that are obtained by connecting the nearest points. This demand accords with the spirits of clustering and Markov Decision Process algorithm. Furthermore, the K-medoids algorithm of clustering algorithm is able to allocate global TSP to simple TSP problem with a few clustering objects. In this way, we only need to reflect on and solve the problem with respect to clustering representative objects and small clusters respectively. Thus, TSP problem can be solved better by mixed use of MDP and K-medoids algorithms.

Specific algorithm is as follows:

INPUT: A dataset C with $L+1$ objects as $P_1, P_2, ..., P_{L+1}$;
OUTPUT: Optimal directed path chain $P_1' \rightarrow P_2' \rightarrow ... \rightarrow P_{L+1}' \rightarrow P_1'$;
METHOD:
a)   Firstly, K-medoids algorithm flow is carried on the dataset C, which can generate clusters C1,C2,...,Ck and representative objects O1, O2,...,Ok.. for respective cluster.
b)   *MDP flow is carried on $O_1, O_2, ..., O_k$, which can generate an optimal directed path chain $O_1' \rightarrow O_2' \rightarrow ... \rightarrow O_k' \rightarrow O_1'$ for each representative object, whose corresponding order of the clusters is $C_1', C_2', ..., C_k'$.*
c)   *Connect the nearest objects in the adjacent clusters.*
d)   *If the object in C_i' is a simple TSP problem, then conduct MDP flow to the object in C_i' directly; if not, repeat steps* a) b) c) d) *until each cluster obtain its optimal path chain.*

The flow chart is shown as Fig. 1.

5   Experimental Analyzed Comparison and Conclusion

CHN144 is a classic TSP problem, which is a symmetrical TSP case that consists of 144 cities of China. Because of the unbalanced distribution of the city nodes, irregular paths and lots of convex and concave, it is more difficult to seek its shortest path. It is commonly used to test TSP evolutionary algorithm.

The experimental steps in this paper are as follows: Firstly, in the stage of K-medoids cluster, select the number of cluster and let the maximal number of iteration be 100, then construct simple TSP problem by utilizing the centers of the clusters. Secondly, acquire shortest paths of clustering representatives by using MDP algorithm, where each node represents a cluster. Thirdly, with respect to the shortest paths which consider clusters as nodes, calculate the distance between two adjacent clusters. For each cluster, seek the point which is nearest to its former cluster and is farthest to its latter cluster and iterate the procedure above in this cluster. In this way, a relatively optimal path of the original problem can be acquired.

In the experiments of CHN144, 10 groups of experiments were done. Each group evolves for 20 times and the results are given in Table 1. The results are shown as Table 1 and the paths are shown as Fig. 2.

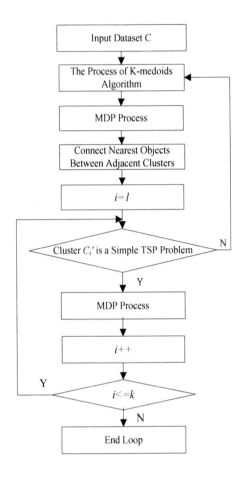

Fig. 1. The Flow Chart of the Algorithm

Table 1. The Result of Evolution of Each Group for 20 Times

Number of Times	Cluster number	Average Solution	Optimal Solution	Average Time
1	26	31665	30695	47.847
2	27	31779	31008	48.316
3	28	31941	30827	48.788
4	29	31943	30643	47.923
5	30	31259	30588	41.7
6	31	31336	30445	41.915
7	32	31379	30660	42.503
8	33	31666	30752	43.8733
9	34	31332	30482	44.317
10	35	31352	30855	44.875

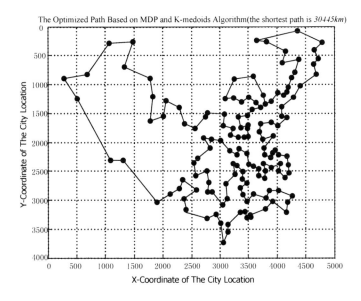

Fig. 2. The Path of CHN144(L=30445km)

From the table, we can see that the best result acquired by the algorithm mentioned in this paper id 30445km. The optimal result that has been known is 30353km [11] so far. The relative error between the experimental result acquired by calculating in this paper and the optimal solution so far is only (30445-30353)/30353=0.003.

Improved genetic algorithm was used to solve TSP problem in the literature [12] and the evolutionary algorithm of fuzzy C-mean clustering was used to solve TSP problem in the literature[13]. The experimental results of these two algorithms that are compared with the results of the algorithm mentioned in this paper are shown as Table 2.

Table 2. Comparison of the Algorithmic Experimental Results

Algorithm	Optimal Solution	Average Solution	Relative Error to Optimal Solution
Literature[11]	30628	30695	0.009
Literature[12]	30912	34182	0.018
This Paper	30445	31336	0.003

From the Table 2, we can see that the optimal solution and average solution acquired by the algorithm mentioned in this paper are both superior to the results in the literature [12] and the literature[13], and their errors are less when compared to the optimal solution so far. A new method was proposed to solve TSP problem in this paper.

References

1. Johnson, D.S., Papadimitriou, C.H., Yannakakis, M.: How easy is local search? Journal of Computer and System Science 37(1), 79–100 (1988)
2. Papadimitfiou, C.H., Yannakakis, M.: Optimization, approximation and complexity classes. Journal of Computer and System Science. 43(3), 425–440 (1991)
3. Xiong, S., Li, C.: Distributed Evolutionary Algorithms to TSP Based on Cluster of PC. Microcomputer System 24(6), 959–961 (2003)
4. Sun, H.-C., Wang, Y.-F.: A Method of Artificial Intelegence-Human-Computer Exchange for Solving Traveling Salesman Problem. Systems Engineering–Theory & Practice 20(5), 1–10 (2000)
5. Hu, X., Huang, X.: Solving Traveling Salesman Problem with Characteristic of Clustering by Parallel Genetic Algorithm. Computer Engineering and Application 35(1), 66–68 (2004)
6. Park, H.S., Jun, C.H.: A simple and fast algorithm for K-medoids clustering. Expert Systems with Applications 36(2), 3336–3341 (2009)
7. Xia, N.-X., Su, Y.-D., Qin, X.: Efficient K-medoids clustering algorithm. Application Research of Computers 27(12), 4517–4519 (2010)
8. Zhu, M.: Data Mining. Press of Science and Technology, University of China, Hefei (2002)
9. Derman: Finite state markov decision processes. Academic Press, New York (1970)
10. Liu, K.: Practical Markov Decision Process. Press of Tsinghua University, Beijing (2004)
11. Cai, Z.-H., Peng, J.-G., Gao, W., Wei, W., Kang, L.-S.: An Improved Evolutionary Algorithm for the Traveling Salesman Problem. Chinese Journal of Computers 28(5), 823–828 (2005)
12. Tao, L.-M., Guo, J.-E.: Application of solving TSP based on improved genetic algorithm. Computer Engineering and Application 45(33), 45–47 (2009)
13. Liu, H., Xiong, S.: Evolutionary Algorithms of TSP Based on Fuzzy C-Means Clustering. Computer Engineering and Applications 42(8), 53–55 (2006)

Simulation of Improving Commutation on Low-Voltage High-Current Vehicle Generators

Yuejun An, Limin Zhou, Wenrui Li, Hui An, and Dan Sun

School of Electrical Engineering
Shenyang University of Technology
Shenyang, 110870 China
anyj_dq@sut.edu.cn

Abstract. Aiming at finding a way to improve commutation and decrease the level of the spark for low-voltage high-current vehicle generators, using asymmetric pole structure, non-uniform commutating pole, single wave windings and oblique brush. This paper concludes the distribution of the flux line and the wave of the air gap magnetic field, analysis on the loading and no loading inner magnetic field with the method of finite element. The results reveal that although the asymmetric structure, the magnetic field created by the main poles is still symmetric and uniform, thus it ensures the provision of suitable medium space for mechanical and electrical energy conversion. It concludes that the commutating pole decreases the magnetic induction contrast to the generator without commutating pole, according to the curve of the gap magnetic field and the distribution of the inner magnetic field. It shows that the EMF has decrease on average by 58.25% under the influence of commutating pole, it have a demonstrable effect on improving commutation. The results show that it can provide the key technical program to the development of low-voltage high-current generator, improve commutation, decrease the level of spark, and inhibit the electromagnetic interference; it will help improve the generator run stability and reliability.

Keywords: modeling and simulation, vehicle generator, electrical apparatus on vehicle, magnetic field of commutating zone, commutating electromotive force.

1   Introduction

With the development of automobile technology [1], the vehicles are equipping with a variety of high-tech electrical equipments to improve their performance, thus this will increase the load of generator. Because of the limited installation space, the power of the generator is required to be developed without increasing its size. For special purposes and occasions, generator has so many features such as simple structure, high stability, low cost and it still plays an irreplaceable role in many fields nowadays. However, the stability, extreme power, and maximum speed of the generator depend mostly on the performance of its commutation; that is to say, commutation is an important indicator of the generator's quality.

M. Zhao and J. Sha (Eds.): ICCIP 2012, Part II, CCIS 289, pp. 333–342, 2012.

The common method to improve commutation is to install commutating pole and compensation winding. However, most installation space of the generator on vehicle is too small to place conventional commutating pole, neither nor the compensation winding.

According to the situation of the limited installation space, the paper introduces a generator which has the structures of non-uniform main magnetic pole, the number of commutating pole is not equal to the number of main magnetic pole, asymmetric main magnetic pole shoe, asymmetric commutating pole shoe, single wave winding playing a role of the pressure line and tilt brush to decrease commutating electromotive force and improve commutation. These non-uniform, non-isometric and non-symmetric structures of the generator will not affect the electromechanical energy conversion. This paper made a simulation on the distribution of magnetic field, especially on wave and characteristics of the air-gap which are the medium between the mechanical and electrical energy, and reveal the commutating zone precisely to achieve the quantitative evidence.

2   The Basic Structure and Characteristics of Generator

The major technical indicators of the generator on vehicle introduced in this article: Rated power of 6.5kW, rated voltage of 28V, and rated speed of 2800r/min.

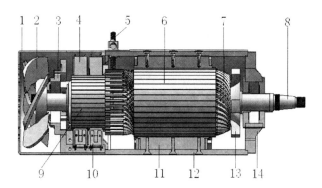

Fig. 1. Basic schematic diagram of the generator

1 fan cover, 2 External fan, 3 bearing, 4 brush, 5 terminals, 6 armature, 7 armature winding, 8 shaft, 9 commutator, 10 brush holder, 11main pole, 12 case, 13 internal fan, 14 cover

The basic structure of low-voltage high-current generator on vehicle is shown in Fig. 1. The stator consists of base, main poles, commutating poles, cover, brush devices and other components. The rotator armature consists of the armature shaft, armature core, windings, commutators, bearings and other components.

Fig.2 shows the cross section of the generator, It has six main poles, and the pole shoes on both side are asymmetric, thus the angle between the axis of six main pole is no longer 60°. According to the electrical magnetic finite element calculation, it will be defined that the angle between two main poles with commutating pole is 73°, and the angle without commutating pole is 47°under the premise of the symmetry distribution of the air-gap magnetic electrical field. Restricted by the installation space, there are only 3 commutating poles on the generator which is half of the main poles. The commutating poles are installed right in the geometry neutral line of the main poles. The angle between the main pole and commutating pole is 36.5°.

Armature winding of a single wave with the role of pressure line is designed; it can solve the problem of commutation brought by without installing pressure line which restricted to the limited space.

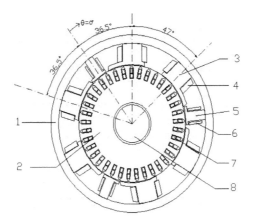

Fig. 2. Cross section view

1 case, 2 armature core, 3 main pole, 4 main pole windings, 5 commutating pole, 6 commutating pole windings, 7 armature windings, 8 shaft

3   Simulation of Electromagnetic Field in Generator

3.1   Description of Electromagnetic Field in Generator

To simplify the analysis, following assumptions are made on the generator [2]:

(1) do not consider the end effect;
(2) do not take the eddy current effect;
(3) the core permeability is isotropic.

Select the outer circumference of the stator as the boundary. This boundary satisfies Dirichlet boundary conditions, therefore, the magnetic vector potential of all points defined on the boundary are equal to zero ($A_z = 0$). Thus, the electromagnetic field of the internal generator can be described by the nonlinear Poisson equation, solver regional and boundary condition.

$$\frac{\partial}{\partial x}\left(\frac{1}{\mu}\frac{\partial A_z}{\partial x}\right) + \frac{\partial}{\partial y}\left(\frac{1}{\mu}\frac{\partial A_z}{\partial y}\right) = J_z \tag{1}$$

Solution region Ω : the entire subdivision areas.

Boundary conditions Γ : $B_n = 0$ at sell of stator.

Where μ is the magnetic permeability, J_z, Γ and B_n are the magnetic vector potential component along the Z-axis, component of source current density along the Z-axis, first boundary condition, normal component of the stator magnetic flux density on the outer boundary.

The finite element method applied in electromagnetic field is to solve problem by the means of dividing the continuous problem into discrete, while generator model discrete can be achieved through the mesh. The subdivision of this generator is shown in Fig. 3.

Fig. 3. Subdivision of the generator

3.2   Analysis of Electromagnetic Field on No-Load

Since the asymmetry of pole structure, for which overall structure of generator model and electromagnetic field analysis. The flux line distribution of generator by no-load is shown in Fig. 4.

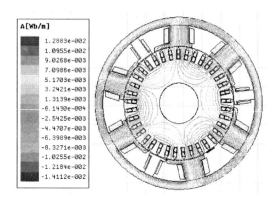

Fig. 4. Distribution of flux line by no-load

It is apparently that the angle between the air-gap magnetic flux density neutral lines is still 60°by observing the distribution curve of the air-gap magnetic flux density, namely each main pole covers 60°, as shown in Fig. 5. Although the six main poles arranged non-uniform, but the structure of asymmetric in mechanical does not result in the asymmetric in electromagnetic, and the electromechanical energy conversion of the generator is not affected.

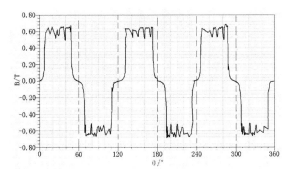

Fig. 5. Curve of air magnetic induction by no-load

3.3   Analysis of Electromagnetic Field on Load

To improve the commutation and reduce spark, the commutating pole is needed [3],[4]. Restricted by the limited space, only three commutating poles are installed. The installation location is shown in Fig.1. The flux line of the air-gap in the position of commutating pole with and without load is shown in Fig. 6 and Fig. 7 by setting the rated current in the way of finite element simulation.

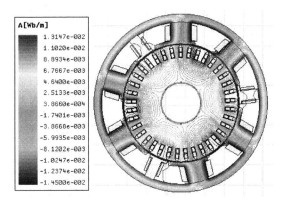

Fig. 6. Distribution of the loading flux line without action of commutating pole

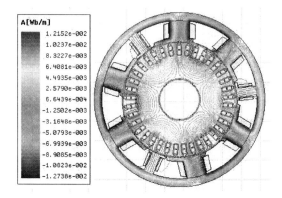

Fig. 7. Distribution of the loading flux line with action of commutating pole

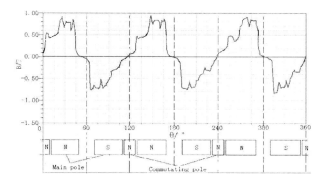

Fig. 8. Curve of the loading magnetic induction without action of commutating pole

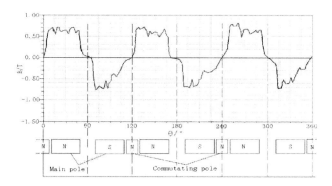

Fig. 9. Curve of the loading magnetic induction with action of commutating pole

Fig. 8 and Fig. 9 show the air-gap magnetic field curve without commutating poles effect and with commutating poles effect. It is clear that the air-gap magnetic field curve with the commutating poles is very close to the curve with no load. However, it is difficult to explain the commutation is improved, so precise division of the commutating zone and quantitative analysis of the commutating electromotive force is needed.

4   Simulation on Commutating Zone

The commutating zone width is proposed to further illustrate the effect of the improvement of the commutation [5],[6]. Commutating zone width is an arc length that one trough rotates along the surface of the armature during the time from the beginning commutation of the first component in it to the end.

Typically, the commutating zone width b_k can be calculated as follow:

$$b_k = t_k \frac{D_a}{D_k}(U + \beta + |\varepsilon_k| - \frac{a}{p}). \tag{2}$$

Where, D_k is the diameter of commutating pole, D_a is the external diameter of armature, U is the Number of components per slot, β is the number of commutating bar which the brush covers, a is the half of the number of parallel branches, p is the half of the number of main poles, ε_k is the pitch shorten factor of generator winding, t_k is the length of the commutating bar.

According to the calculation, the commutating zone width angle is $18.9°$. There are six commutating zones in the six main poles generator, three of them have commutating pole installed in between the two main poles and the rest are not installed.

Under the condition of running with load, in order to observe the electromagnetic field change in commutating zones where installed commutating pole under the action of commutating pole and without the action of commutating pole. An arc of length b_k is taken on the surface of the armature which named commutating zone a. As the precise division, Fig. 10 shows the magnetic induction B_{kp1} of the commutating zone a without the action of commutating pole, and the magnetic induction B_{kp2} of the commutating zone a with the action of commutating pole.

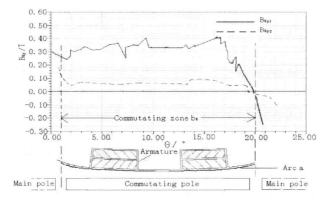

Fig. 10. Curve of the loading magnetic induction in commutation range a without action of commutating pole

The rotating electromotive force of the commutating components e_k can be achieved as:

$$e_k = 2N_y B_k l v_a .$$ (3)

Where, N_y, B_{kp}, l, v_a are turns of commutating components, average magnetic induction of commutating zone, edge length of the components, surface speed of the armature.

Assuming rotating electromotive force with the action of commutating pole is e_{k2}, while the one without the action of commutating pole is e_{k1}, the ratio of them is shown as:

$$\frac{e_{k2}}{e_{k1}} = \frac{2N_y B_{k2} l v_a}{2N_y B_{k1} l v_a} .$$ (4)

Here, B_{kp1} is the average magnetic induction of the commutating zone without action of commutating pole, B_{kp2} is the average magnetic induction of the commutating zone with action of commutating pole.

These parameters which N_y, l, v_a are same with the action of commutating pole and without the action of commutating pole under same running speed. The equation (4) can be reduced to （5）due to the same speed.

$$\frac{e_{k2}}{e_{k1}} = \frac{B_{kp2}}{B_{kp1}} .$$ (5)

Based on the calculation of Figure 10, the average magnetic induction B_{kp1} without the action of commutating pole is 0.31T, while magnetic induction B_{kp2} with the action of commutating pole is 0.048T, according to (5) obtained, $e_{k2} / e_{k1} = 15.5\%$. It is means that the commutating electromotive force decrease 84.5% with no commutating pole effects.

Similarly, under the condition of running with load, in order to observe the difference of electromagnetic field in commutating zones where not installed commutating pole under the action of commutating pole and without the action of commutating pole. An arc of length b_k named commutating zone b on the surface of the armature is taken. As the precise division, the magnetic induction B_{kp3} of the commutating zone b without the action of commutating pole and the magnetic induction B_{kp4} of the commutating zone b with the action of commutating pole are shown in Fig. 11.

The average magnetic induction B_{kp3} without the action of the commutating pole is 0.338T, while magnetic induction B_{kp4} with the action of commutating pole is 0.23T. It can be calculated by (3), $e_{k4} / e_{k3} = 68\%$; the commutating electromotive force reduces 32%. It is apparently that the magnetic induction with the action of commutating pole has reduced compare to the one without commutating pole. The commutating electromotive force decrease 58.25% with the action of commutating pole.

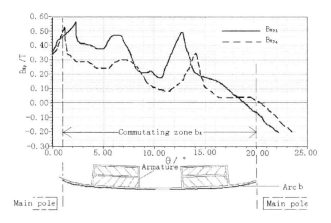

Fig. 11. Curve of the loading magnetic induction in commutation range b without action of commutating pole

5   Conclusion

According to the simulation on the unique generator of high-current low-voltage on vehicle, obviously, although the installation of six main poles arranged non-uniform in the inner circle of the case, namely between the mechanical axis of six main poles to each other angle is not 60 °uniform, but the coverage area of each pole flux density is still 60 °,   that is means each main pole field cover angle is still 60 °. Despite the structure of the main pole and the angel between axis of the neutral lines are asymmetric, it can be concluded that the asymmetric structure doesn't result in the asymmetric structure of the magnetic filed, thus electromechanical energy can be converted normally.

It shows that the commutating electromotive force of the generator with load has decreased on average by 58.25% under the influence of commutating pole compared to without commutating pole according to the simulation especially the exhibition of precise division, therefore, the commutation has been improved.

The result of this research provides key technology programs to the low-voltage high-current generator on vehicle. Meanwhile, the design can improve the commutation of generator effectively, lower spark level, suppress the electromagnetic interference, and enhance the stability and reliability of the electrical system on vehicle.

Acknowledgments. The first author would like to express his thanks to the Science and technology plan project of Liaoning (No.2010220011) and the Science and technology plan project of Shenyang (No.F11-190-7-00) for financial supported. At the same time, thank my collaborators for their cooperation.

342   Y. An et al.

References

1. Li, Z.: Study on Development of Automobile Electrical Equipment control technology. Automobile Technology 5, 37–40 (2011)
2. Hou, X., Zhou, G., Lian, Y.: Application of Finite Element Method for Electromagnetic Field on Optimized Design of Large and New Type Generators. Dong Fang Electric Review 24(96), 44–47 (2010)
3. Yang, K.: Research on the Commutation of DC Motor. Marine Electric & Electronic Engineering (1), 13–16 (2003)
4. Lin, D.: A New Way to Improve Performance of Permanent Magnet Motor to the Research of Supporting Pole. Household Appliance (6), 13–16 (1997)
5. Gu, C., Chen, Q., Xiong, Y.: Electric Machinery, pp. 99–100. Press of Huazhong University Science and Technology (2010)
6. You, S., Zhu, M.: Electromagnetic program of small DC motor. Electric Machines & Control Application (1), 1–14 (1981)

A Study Based on Markov Chain in Fuzzy Control System Stability

Minzhi Jia and Fei Guo

College of Information Engineering
Taiyuan University of Technology
Taiyuan, China
tutjmz666@sina.com,
276399445@qq.com

Abstract. Stability is one of the important quota of control system. For fuzzy control system, there are many troubles in analysis and correction of stability. Because of its nonlinear feature, and it is difficult to define the precise description of dynamic performance. Lyapunov founded the general stability theories, but now systematic methods based on the theories have not been found in application of fuzzy control system stability and adjustment. The paper aims to found a special model which do not depend on its precise mathematical description and get useful information by analyzing system output, and then adjust relevant fuzzy rules to achieve the goal of regulating system stability speed. This method has some reference value in engineering applications and theory.

Keywords: Fuzzy control, Stability, Markov chain.

1   Introduction

In dealing with some control systems which could be found mathematical model hardly and have strong nonlinear feature, fuzzy control is a very efficacious strategy. However, there are no mature and consummate theories in adjusting stability speed of fuzzy control system, and it is difficult to design and adjust the system. To solving this problem, the paper raises a Markov chain probability model and analyzes the system output for improving the stability speed by this model.

2   Fuzzy Control System

Fuzzy control belongs to a special Expert Control essentially, and one of the important missions of founding fuzzy control system is designing a suitable fuzzy controller. Fuzzy controller includes: knowledge base, fuzzification, defuzzification and fuzzy inference [1]. Its block diagram is followed:

M. Zhao and J. Sha (Eds.): ICCIP 2012, Part II, CCIS 289, pp. 343–350, 2012.
© Springer-Verlag Berlin Heidelberg 2012

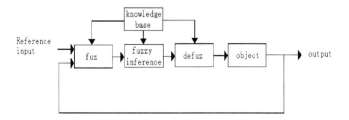

Fig. 1. Parts of fuzzy system

Fig. 1 suggests that we have to focus on the following work. First, choosing the basis style of fuzzy control system(Mandani or T—S) and founding the fuzzy rules. Second, determining the number of fuzzy language names based on the degree of precision. Third, determine membership function and related parameters. It can be seen in the conditions of fuzzy membership functions and their parameters fixed, the stability of fuzzy control system stability is mainly affected by the fuzzy rules.

In order to give the mathematical description of the relationship between them, let us introduce several important concepts before start.

3   Markov Chain

We consider a stochastic process $\{Xn, n = 0, 1, 2, \ldots\}$ that takes on a finite or countable number of possible values. Unless otherwise mentioned, this set of possible values of the process will be denoted by the set of nonnegative integers $\{0, 1, 2 \ldots\}$. If $Xn = i$, then the process is said to be in state i at time n. We suppose that whenever the process is in state i, there is a fixed probability Pij that it will next be in state j . That is, we suppose that

$$P\{Xn+1 = j \,|Xn = i, Xn-1 = in-1, \ldots, X1 = i1, X0 = i0\} = Pij \qquad (4.1)[2]$$

For all states i0, i1. . . in−1, i, j and all n≥0. Such a stochastic process is known as a Markov chain. Equation (4.1) may be interpreted as stating that, for a Markov chain, the conditional distribution of any future state Xn+1 given the past states X0,X1, . . . , Xn−1 and the present state Xn, is independent of the past states and depends only on the present state.

The value Pij represents the probability that the process will, when in state i, next make a transition into state j. Since probabilities are nonnegative and since the process must make a transition into some state, we have that pij≥0   i,j≥0;=1, i=0,1,2.......

Let P denote the matrix of one-step transition probabilities Pij , so that

$$P = \begin{bmatrix} p_{11} & p_{12} & \cdots \\ p_{21} & p_{22} & \cdots \\ \cdots & \cdots & \cdots \end{bmatrix}$$

We have already defined the one-step transition probabilities Pij. We now define the n-step transition probabilities to be the probability that a process in state i will be in state j after n additional transitions. That is,= P{Xn+k = j |Xk= i}, n≥0, i,j≥0.

Of course $P_{ij}^l = P_{ij}$. The Chapman–Kolmogorov equations provide a method for computing these n-step transition probabilities. These equations are

$$P_{ij}^{n+m} = \sum_{k=0}^{\infty} P_{ik}^n P_{kj}^m \quad \text{for all n, m≥0, all i, j} \tag{4.2}[2]$$

And are most easily understood by noting that   represent the probability that starting in i the process will go to state j in n + m transitions through a path which takes it into state k at the nth transition. Hence, summing over all intermediate states k yields the probability that the process will be in state j after n+ m transitions.

A homogeneous Markov chain and the state transition matrix P = (pij), if exist a probability distribution {j}, it satisfies j=Σijpij, call the {pj} is stationary distribution for the Markov chain.

Theorem 1 [3]: For the state space is finite-homogeneous, irreducible, aperiodic Markov chain, exist a unique stationary distribution, and it satisfies the following equations:

$$\begin{cases} \Pi_j = \sum_i \Pi_i \cdot p_{ij} \\ \\ 1 = \sum_i \Pi_i \end{cases} \qquad *$$

4   Control Strategy

Now, let us discus Mamdani fuzzy control systems, and form of rules is followed:

R1:if x1 is a1 and y1 is b1 ,then z1 is c1
also R2:if x2 is a2 and y2 is b2 ,then z2 is c2
                      …
also Rn:if xn is an and yn is bn ,then zn is cn
Assume that the system of fuzzy rules is given in the table:

Table 1. Initial fuzzy rule table

output c / de	NB	NS	ZR	PS	PB
NB	PB	PB	PS	PS	ZR
NS	PB	PS	PS	ZR	ZR
ZR	PS	PS	ZR	ZR	NS
PS	PS	ZR	ZR	NS	NS
PB	ZR	ZR	NS	NS	NB

In the table, e and de as a fuzzy controller input fuzzitificated into five levels: negative large NB, negative small NS, Zero ZR, positive small PB, positive large PS. e indicates deviation. Use "+","0","−" three symbols to represent positive deviation, zero deviation, negative deviation respectively. The three symbols could be constituted a state set S, and then S={"+"," 0 ","−"}.As the deviation only has positive, zero and negative three cases, so S is a closed set, and all the members of S can communicates with each other.

Matrix P

P Matrix is the state transition matrix of the system, and derives from experimental data. Its form is followed:

$$P = \begin{bmatrix} a_1 & a_2 & a_3 \\ b_1 & b_2 & b_3 \\ c_1 & c_2 & c_3 \end{bmatrix}$$

The matrix P is a stochastic matrix, i.e, $\sum_{i=1}^{3} a_i = 1$, $\sum_{i=1}^{3} b_i = 1$, $\sum_{i=1}^{3} c_i = 1$.

In the P, a1 is the probability of moving one step from "+" to"+".
a2 is the probability of moving one step from "+" to"0".
a3 is the probability of moving one step from "+" to"−".
b1 is the probability of moving one step from "0" to"+".
b2 is the probability of moving one step from "0" to"0".
b3 is the probability of moving one step from "0" to"−".
c1 is the probability of moving one step from "−" to"+".
c2 is the probability of moving one step from "−" to"0".
c3 is the probability of moving one step from "−" to"−".

Then we can get the state transition diagram followed:

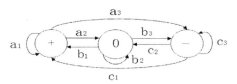

Fig. 2. State transition diagram

Fig.2 tells us the "+","−","0"represent a system of three deviation states. Arrows indicate the transfer relationship between the states. The letter above the arrow indicates the probability of transition. From the above diagram, we can be more intuitive to know the meaning of the P matrix.

As the input signal is the deviation state of the fuzzy system, the essence of the algorithm is based on deviation state, and finding corresponding fuzzy control rules, giving the output. So that, the output of the system in the next time is mainly based on the current state, the previous state of the system does not affect next output deeply, that is no after-effect. So the system meets the Markov chain model. As demonstrated before S is a closed, irreducible set, so the system model is a non-periodic Markov chain. By the Theorem: The model has a unique stationary distribution and satisfies equations:

$$\begin{cases} \Pi_j = \sum_i \Pi_i \cdot p_{ij} \\ 1 = \sum_i \Pi_i \end{cases}$$

According to the theorem, we can write the system stationary distribution of equations:

$$\begin{cases} \Pi_1 = a_1 \Pi_1 + b_1 \Pi_2 + c_1 \Pi_3 \\ \Pi_2 = a_2 \Pi_1 + b_2 \Pi_2 + c_2 \Pi_3 \\ \Pi_3 = a_3 \Pi_1 + b_3 \Pi_2 + c_3 \Pi_3 \\ 1 = \Pi_1 + \Pi_2 + \Pi_3 \end{cases}$$

Π_1, Π_2, Π_3 are the stationary distribution of the system states "+"," 0 ","$-$", Π_1 means that when $n \to \infty$, probability of system state in positive deviation.Π_2 means that when $n \to \infty$, probability of system state in zero deviation.Π_3 means that when $n \to \infty$, probability of system state in negative deviation. Better system stability and the transition process, the more $\Pi_2 \to 1$. Based on the above equations we can solve the formulas of Π_2, Π_1, Π_3.

$$\Pi_2 = \cfrac{1}{\cfrac{b_1 - b_1 \cdot c_3 + c_1 \cdot c_2}{(1-a_1) \cdot (1-c_3) + c_1 c_1} \cdot \cfrac{1 - c_3 + c_1}{1-c_3} + \cfrac{1 - c_3 + c_2}{1-c_3}}$$

$$\Pi_1 = \cfrac{1}{\cfrac{b_1 - b_1 \cdot c_3 + c_1 \cdot c_2}{(1-a_1) \cdot (1-c_3) + c_1 c_1} \cdot \cfrac{1 - c_3 + c_1}{1-c_3} + \cfrac{1 - c_3 + c_2}{1-c_3}}$$

$$* \quad \cfrac{(1-b_2) \cdot (1-c_3) + c_2 c_2}{b_1 \cdot (1-c_3) + c_2 c_1}$$

$$\Pi_3 = 1 - \Pi_2 - \Pi_1$$

Thus, the stability quota "0" ,of which the stationary distribution Π_2 determined by the matrix P, and by the same token, Π_1, Π_3 determined by matrix P. It concluded that: in the sense of probability, P matrix can reflect the stability of the system. Moreover, when we adjust the fuzzy rules, as long as $\Pi_2 \to 1$, then Π_1, $\Pi_3 \to 0$, so that the stability of the system and the transition process has been optimized.

In summary, the idea of control strategies: fuzzy rules determine the system deviation, deviation collection determine P matrix, P matrix determines the deviation of the stationary distribution. Hence establishing a relationship between fuzzy rules and the states stationary distribution, we can adjust the fuzzy rules to change the stationary distribution of the states. Through a diagram to illustrate it:

Fig. 3. Control strategy connection diagram

5   Simulation

In order to illustrate the correctness of the method, let us have a test: One industrial object can be equivalent to second-order pure delay part, its Transfer function is followed:

$$G(s) = \frac{20e^{-0.02s}}{1.6s^2 + 4.4s + 1}$$

And the system has dead zone with 0.07 and saturation zone with 0.7. Sampling time T=0.01s.

System adopts fuzzy control strategy. Fuzzy rules come from Table 1. Use Matlab to simulate model system, the unit of x axis is TIME(s).Its response curve as shown below:

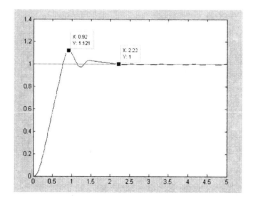

Fig. 4. Unadjusted response curve

Fig.4 indicates that the system output is stable in the 2.22s.
Because of

$$\Pi2 = \frac{1}{\dfrac{b_1 - b_1 \cdot c_3 + c_1 \cdot c_2}{(1-a_1) \cdot (1-c_3) + c_1 c_1} \cdot \dfrac{1 - c_3 + c_1}{1 - c_3} + \dfrac{1 - c_3 + c_2}{1 - c_3}}$$

And $\Pi2$ is "0" stationary distribution of the system. So when $\Pi2 \to 1$, the adjusting time will decrease. Because "$\Pi2 \to 1$" indicates the number of sampling points of zero deviation increase from system stability to the end of simulation, and the system just is in the zero deviation state in the same time. Zero deviation sampling point is more, and then the time is longer. For a fixed sampling time, only reducing the adjusting time can appear above-mentioned situation. Hence, $\Pi2 \to 1$ will make the system more quickly into a stable state. According to the expression of $\Pi2$, we can know that, by reducing the value of a1, c3 can make $\Pi2 \to 1$. Choose a1, c3 for the adjustment of parameters because a1 is the probability of moving one step from "+" to "+". This parameter can easily correspond with the fuzzy rule: if we want to reduce the a1, we should increase output slightly in way of modifying related fuzzy rules. Similarly deals with c3.

But blindly by adjusting the fuzzy rules to change the a1, c3 may be damage to the original expertise, resulting in unstable output. Therefore, adjusting appropriate rules should follow the principle of stability first. Hence, change the fuzzy rule "ZR" in the second line and the fourth column to "PS"; Change the fuzzy rule "NS" in the fourth line and the fourth column to "ZR". According to the above principle, adjusted fuzzy rules table is followed:

Table 2. Adjusted fuzzy rule table

output \ e de	NB	NS	ZR	PS	PB
NB	PB	PB	PS	PS	ZR
NS	PB	PS	PS	**PS**	ZR
ZR	PS	PS	ZR	ZR	NS
PS	PS	ZR	ZR	**ZR**	NS
PB	ZR	ZR	NS	NS	NB

The original rules have been replaced by new rules with underline. Adjusted system output is shown below:

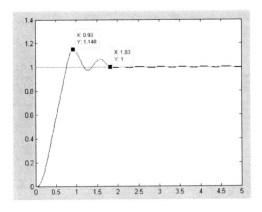

Fig. 5. Adjusted response curve

Fig.5 indicates that system is stable in the 1.83s. Comparing the two response curve, the output curve of Fig5 converges faster than the output curve of Fig4, it just proved the correctness of the method: by modifying the related fuzzy rules, the "0" of the stationary distribution will be closed to 1.That leads to the number of sampling points which is in the "0"state increase during the fixes sampling time. Hence the system is going to stability quickly. Above all, the method has a certain effect in convergence speed of the system. The only deficiency is that overshoot increase slightly.

6   Conclusion

Fuzzy control is a control strategy based on expert experience. Whether or not experts experience are completed and can be Optimized, it can not accurately measure, so these uncertain factors bring some difficult to correct the output of fuzzy system.

In this paper, though establishing the system of Markov chains to analyzes the stability and convergence speed, then this method has been verified through simulation. However, thinking of expertise could ensure the system requirements generally, so the method only consider the properties of positive and negative of deviation, do not give further quantitative deviation; Fuzzy set membership functions and their parameters, fuzzy partition of the system will also affect the stability and the transition process. These are all starting points to next step for research.

Although the effect of the method is not very satisfied in the aspect of theory and experiment, Markov chain model have some effect and provide a way to research in future. The method has some enlightening meaning in theory of fuzzy systems and the method of stability.

References

1.   Zadeh, L.A.: Fuzzy set. Information and Control (August 1965)
2.   Lawler, G.F.: Stochastic Processes, 1st edn. Chapman & Hall (1995)
3.   Ross, S.M.: Probability Models, 9th edn. (2007)

The Research on User Model
for the Network Intrusion Detection System

Lei Shang

Department of Information Science and Technology,
Shandong University of Political Science and Law
Jinan, China
leilishang@163.com

Abstract. Internet has become one of the most important tools in the people's lives with the rapid development of the Computer Science and Technology. It is important for everyone to ensure the safety of computer networks. Intrusion Detection System can be helpful for people to use computer network safely. Traditional intrusion detection technologies are based on the behavior of users. The content browsed by intruders is also an important clue for the Intrusion Detection System. In this paper, based on analyzing the traditional user profile, a user model named AVSM (Advanced Vector Space Model) which combined with user's browsing content and behavior is proposed. The experimental results show that, using this model, Intrusion Detection System can analyze both the content and behavior of intruder, and detect the intruder more effectively.

Keywords: vector space model, AVSM, IDS, intruder.

1 Introduction

With the rapid development of the Computer Science and Technology, Internet has become one of the most important tools in the people's lives. People are increasingly using computer network, while recognizing it is important to ensure the safety of it. Therefore, it is particularly urgent and important to study how quickly detect network intrusions. Intrusion Detection System (IDS) can be defined as a system that can identify malicious behavior and use of the computer or network resources, and give the appropriate treatment. Intrusion Detection System can be helpful for people to use computer network safely. There are two mainly technologies used in the Intrusion Detection System. One is Anomaly Detection Model, which detects the deviation between the behavior and the acceptable behavior. If you can define acceptable behavior for each, then each of the unacceptable behavior should be an intrusion. The other one is Misuse Detection Model, which detects the deviation between the behavior and the unacceptable behavior. If you can define all of the unacceptable behavior, then the behavior of each match will be able to cause the alarm.

We can see that all traditional intrusion detection technologies are based on the behavior of users. It is not reliable that only to analyze the behavior of users. Sometimes, the content browsed by intruder is also an important clue for the Intrusion

M. Zhao and J. Sha (Eds.): ICCIP 2012, Part II, CCIS 289, pp. 351–358, 2012.

Detection System. User model is widely used in the field of Information Retrieval. The user profile in personalized recommendation system can be taken to help for our user model. In Section 2, the traditional weighted vector space model in Information Retrieval System is introduced. And a user model named AVSM (Advanced Vector Space Model) for Intrusion Detection System is proposed in Section 3, the modeling and updating algorithm is also proposed in this section. In Section 4, we give the framework of the Network Intrusion Detection System using AVSM. Section 5 gives the experiment and analysis of the results. And in the last section, we conclude our works and point out the works we will do in the future.

2   Traditional Vector Space Model

The diversity and complexity of the information browsed by users make it difficult to obtain a standard form of characterizing the content. At present, many kinds of information processing system is used VSM (Vector Space Model) widely. The main idea of the traditional weighted vector space model is that: first, represent the content browsed by users and the documents by vector format, and then the information retrieval problem is change into the problem how compare two vectors are similar or match. More formally, we give the following definitions:

Definition 1: Document: refers to the general literature, or literature piece, usually refers to an article, denoted by d.

Definition 2: Keyword: refers to the fundamental language unit which can represent the document or the user, denoted by k.

Definition 3: Weight of the keyword: refers to the importance of the keyword k_j for the document d_i denoted by w.

Definition 4: The weighted vector model V_{ci}: Document d can be represented as one set of vectors, in which each dimension of the vector refers to the weight of each keyword, $V(d) = \{w_1, w_2, w_3, \ldots w_n\}$, in which w_i refers to the weight of the i-th keyword. There are many calculation methods for the weight; more is used TF-IDF formula as follow:

$$W(t,d) = \frac{tf(t,d) \times \log(N/n_t + 0.01)}{\sqrt{\sum_{w \subset d} [tf(w,d) \times \log(N/n_w + 0.01)]^2}} \tag{1}$$

Definition 5: Vector similarity: refers to the similarity of two vectors between V_j and V_i.

$$sim(V_i, V_j) = \frac{V_i \cdot V_j}{|V_i| \times |V_j|} \tag{2}$$

The traditional model of weighted vector is only based on content browsed by user, and ignores the behavior of user. IDS require the user's behavior to detect.

For example, one user has browsed a document which is not he needed, he soon end the view and then spend considerable time to browse another document. In this process, the traditional vector model does not distinguish the weights between two documents. In addition, as users are usually interested in a wide range of content, some long-term interests rarely change, while the short-term interest may often change, the traditional model can not effectively distinguish weights of vectors of long-term interest and short-term user interest, so unexpected for users' interest in search results is not obvious.

3   Modeling and Updating the Users Behavior

3.1   The Definitions of AVSM Model

The traditional Vector Space Model has been proposed in last section. Athough the traditional model of weighted vector is only based on content browsed by user, and ignores the behavior of user. IDS require the user's behavior to detect. The VSM also can give a helpful idea for the IDS. The traditional model can not effectively distinguish long-term interest and short-term user interest. Based on both the behavior and content of the user, we propose a new user model for the Network Intrusion Detection System, which named AVSM (Advanced Vector Space Model). And some definitions are as follow.

Definition 6: AVSM (Advanced Vector Space Model): In this model, each user profile contains multiple content and behavior categories, and each category is constituted by the following quintuple:

$$(V_{ci}, I_{ci}, F_{ci}, M_{ci}, T_{oci})$$

In which, V_{ci} is the i-th categorie of the content defined with the Definition 4.

Definition 7: Interestingness I_{ci}: refers to the degree of the user's interest in the i-th category, calculated by the following formula:

$$I_{ci} = \frac{n \cdot t}{T} \tag{3}$$

In Formula 3, n which is the number of documents viewed by user, and t which is the total time of viewting the documents, is proportional to I_{ci}. And T which refers to the time interval from the last visit is inversely proportional to I_{ci}.

Definition 8: Shot term attention F_{ci}: refers to the user's attention to the category, calculated by the following formula:

$$F_{ci} = \frac{n}{T} \tag{4}$$

In Formula 4, n which is the number of documents viewed by user is proportional to F_{ci}. And T which refers to the time interval from the last visit is inversely proportional to F_{ci}.

Definition 9: The Set of the documents M_{ci}: refers to the set of documents which are evolved the i-th category.

Definition 10: Modification time for the i-th category T_{oci}

3.2   The Modeling Algorithm

In this section, we give the algorithm for modeling the user. The input is the documents browsed by user, and the starting time of the behavior. The output is the user profile with the form of U (V_{ci}, I_{ci}, F_{ci}, M_{ci}, T_{oci}).

Step 1: Set the user profile with the form of vector set U, and initially empty.

Step 2: Get the contents browsed by the user. First, parse out the words of the document, the associated process, such as stop word table according remove stop words processing. And then, calculate the *tf-idf* using the Formula 1, expressed as a vector d_i.

Step 3: Get the user browsing behavior information. Record the start time *TDB* and the end time *TDE* when the user is browsing. Get the total time of this view $t = TDE-TDB$.

Step 4: Build the user model.

  1) Obtain the vector d_i expressed in Step2 as V_{ci}
  2) Because it is the first time for the user visits, it is not needed for considering the time between the last visit from this visit. Put the $I_{ci}=1$, $F_{ci\ i}=1$.
  3) Modify the the T_{oci} as the end of time user browsing. $T_{oci}=TDE$.

Step 5: Output and storage the user model U (V_{ci}, I_{ci}, F_{ci}, M_{ci}, T_{oci}).

3.3   The Updating Algorithm

In this section, we give the algorithm for updating the user model. The input is also the documents browsed by user, and the starting time of the behavior. And the output is the updated user model.

Step 1: Input the user model U (V_{ci}, I_{ci}, F_{ci}, M_{ci}, T_{oci}).

Step 2: When a user browses a document d, record the visit start time and end time *TDB* and *TDE*, calculate the *tf-idf* using Formula 1, expressed as a vector $V(d)$. $V(d) = \{w_1, w_2, w_3, \ldots w_n\}$.

Step 3: Calculate the similarity between $V(d)$ and each category in the users profile with the Formula 5. Record the highest similarity value R and the category C_z which has the highest similarity.

$$R = SIM(V,U) = \cos(V,U) = \frac{\sum_{i=1}^{n} V_i * U_i}{\sqrt{\sum_{i=1}^{n} V_i^2 * \sum_{i=1}^{n} U_i^2}} \tag{5}$$

If R is smaller than R_z which is the pre-set threshold value, in other words, this document is not similar to any category in the user profile. It is needed to create a new category with the method proposed in last section.

Else, update the category using the next formula:

$$Wi(C) = \begin{cases} Wi(C)(1-a)+Wj(D)a & Ki(C) = Kj(D) \\ Wi(C)(1-a) & Ki(C) > Kj(D) \\ Wj(D)a & Ki(C) < Kj(D) \end{cases} \tag{6}$$

In Formula 5, a is the learning rate, and with the range of values form 0 to 1.

Step 4: Update I_{ci}:

$$I_{ci} = \frac{(N_{ci}+1)(T_{ci}+TDE-TDB)}{T_{ici}} \tag{7}$$

Update F_{ci}:

$$F_{ci} = \frac{N_{ci}+1}{T_{ici}} \tag{8}$$

Step 5: Output the updated user model.

4   The Framework of the IDS Using AVSM

Traditional Intrusion Detection System can not be applied to other users profile, can not identify potential behavior. In this paper, the framework of Network Intrusion Detection System with AVSM model is shown in Figure 1.

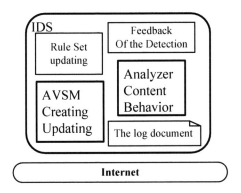

Fig. 1. The Framework of the IDS Using AVSM

With this framework, in the monitoring stage, if the detector found a pattern emerging, then the model reaction system may be compromised. This system can automatically take the appropriate measures. Meanwhile, the detector can complete its analysis of whether the user is an intruder, based on the user's current operation and its historical behavior with the AVSM model. Judgments based on the data source can be from the user and system audit log data; also can be including data packets from the network. Intrusion Detection Process is based on these data and analysis, to detect whether the occurrence is of intrusion.

5   Analysis of Experimental Results

The experiment uses the data from KDD CUP99 intrusion data set. To evaluate IDS system, the KDD CUP99 data set provides more than 480 million data, and each line of data also has several special data feature. The intrusion data set is divided into four categories, they are: a) denial of service DOS, such as SYN Flood; b) system exploits Probing, such as port scanning; c) remote root access by U2R, such as remote buffer overflow; and d) remote access services for R2L, such as password cracking.

In order to meet the experimental needs, we used 1000 data records from KDD CUP99 data set, including 100 records of normal behavior data and 900 records of abnormal behavior data. In addition, we use the Detection Rate and the False Alarm Rate to evaluate the system. The Detection Rate is defined as the ratio of the number of intrusion identified correctly and the total number of all data records. The False Alarm (missed detection or incorrect detection) Rate is defined as the ratio of the number of normal data which are incorrectly identified as the intrusion data and the total number of all data records. The experimental results are shown in Figure 2 and 3.

In the experiment, we used different thresholds from 10 to 70. When the value of threshold is 40, the Decoction Rates of Probing and U2R are higher, and the False Alarm Rate are lower. When the threshold is 10, all kinds of the categories have the higher False Alarm Rates. When the threshold is 70, the False Alarm Rates of all categories are lower. The results of the experiments show that using this model, Intrusion Detection System can analyze both the content and behavior of intruder, and detect the intruder more effectively.

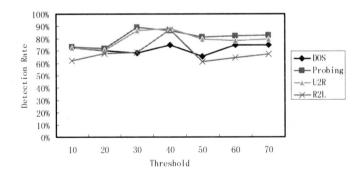

Fig. 2. The Detection Rate of Every Threshold

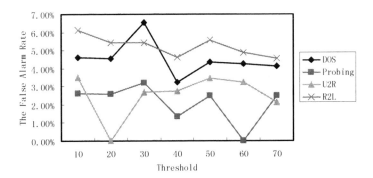

Fig. 3. The False Alarm Rate of Every Threshold

6   Conclusions and Future Works

Traditional intrusion detection technologies are based on the behavior of users. The content browsed by intruders is also an important clue for the Intrusion Detection System. In this paper, based on analyzing the traditional user profile, a user model named AVSM (Advanced Vector Space Model) which combined with user's browsing content and behavior is proposed. The results of the experiments show that using this model, Based on data mining and intrusion detection system characteristics, Intrusion Detection System can analyze both the content and behavior of intruder, and detect the intruder more effectively.In this article, AVSM model only takes into account the time which the users browse the documents, but not concluding some other behaviors, such as print, save, quote, reply, mark, add favorites. How to use this information is the problem for our future work.

Acknowledgment. This work was supported by Shandong Province National Science Foundation of China (Youth Fund) under Grant No. ZR2011FQ019.

References

1. Smith, T.F., Waterman, M.S.: Identification of Common Molecular Subsequences. J. Mol. Biol. 147, 195–197 (1981)
2. Zeng, C., Xing, C.-X., Zhou, L.-Z.: A Survey of Personalization Technology. Journal of Software 13(10) (2002)
3. Kabiri, P., Ghorbani, A.: A Research in intrusion detection and response-a survey. International Journal of Network Security 1(2), 84–102 (2005)
4. Linden, G., Smith, B.Y.: Amazon.com recommendations: item-to-item collaborative filtering. IEEE Internet Computing 7, 76–80 (2003)
5. Shaft, K., Abbass, H.A.: An adaptive genetic-based signature learning system for intrusion detection. Export Systems with Applications 36(10), 12036–12043 (2009)

6. Ali Aydin, M., Halim Zaim, A., Goldmn Ceylan, K.: A hybrid intrusion detection system design for computer network security. Computers & Electrical Engineering, 517–526 (2009)
7. Wu, Y.-H., Chen, Y.-C., Arbee, L., Chen, P.: Enabling Personalized Recommendation on the Web based on User Internets and Behaviors. In: 11th International Workshop on Research Issues in Data Engineering. IEEE (2001)
8. Kaski, S.: Dimensionality Reduction by Random Mapping: Fast Similarity Computation for Clustering. In: Proceedings of International Joint Conference on Neural Networks (IJCNN 1998), pp. 413–418. IEEE Service Center, Piscataway (1998)
9. Crimmins, F., Smeaton, A., Dkaki, T., et al.: Information discovery on the Internet. IEEE Intelligent Systems and Their Applications, 55–622 (1999)

The Algebraic-Hyperbolic Polynomial Ferguson Curve and Coons Patch

Juncheng Li, Lian Yang, Yue-e Zhong, and Chun Xie

Department of Mathematics, Hunan Institute of Humanities, Science and Technology,
417000 Loudi, China
lijuncheng82@126.com

Abstract. The algebraic-hyperbolic polynomial Ferguson curve and Coons patch analogous to the corresponding normal cubic Ferguson curve and bicubic Coons patch, with shape parameters, are presented in this work. The shapes of the proposed curve and the patch can be adjusted by altering the values of the shape parameters while the boundary conditions are kept unchanged. As the shape parameters approach to zero, the limit of the algebraic-hyperbolic polynomial Ferguson curve and Coons patch are the corresponding normal cubic Ferguson curve and bicubic Coons patch.

Keywords: computer aided geometric design, algebraic-hyperbolic polynomial, Ferguson curve, Coons patch.

1 Introduction

It is well known that curves and surfaces are general established based on polynomial functions in Computer Aided Geometric Design (CAGD). However, trigonometric or hyperbolic curves and surfaces have gained very much interest within CAGD. For instance, Zhang constructed the C-Ferguson curve, C-Bézier curve and C-B-spline curve in the space $\{1, t, \sin t, \cos t\}$ [1]. Mainar and Chen defined the C- Bézier curves of higher order in the space $\{1, t, \ldots, t^{k-3}, \cos t, \sin t\}$ [2, 3]. In the same space, Wang constructed the non-uniform algebraic trigonometric B-splines [4]. Han presented a cubic trigonometric Bézier curve with two shape parameters in the space $\{1, \sin t, \cos t, \sin^2 t\}$ [5]. In the same space, Li defined a family of quasi-cubic trigonometric curves [6]. Yan discussed a class of algebraic-trigonometric blended splines in the space $\{1, t, \sin t, \cos t, \sin^2 t, \sin^3 t, \cos^3 t\}$ [7]. Lü presented the hyperbolic polynomial B-splines in the space $\{\sinh t, \cosh t, t^{k-3}, t^{k-4}, \ldots, t, 1\}$ [8], and Li extended these hyperbolic spines to the case of non-uniform knot vector [9]. Liu studied a kind of hyperbolic polynomial uniform B-spline surface with shape parameter in depth [10]. These curves and surfaces constructed by trigonometric or hyperbolic polynomials inherit most properties of the corresponding polynomial curves and surfaces, and some of them have other excellent abilities such as the character of shape adjustment and the exactly representation of some conics or transcendental curves and surfaces.

M. Zhao and J. Sha (Eds.): ICCIP 2012, Part II, CCIS 289, pp. 359–367, 2012.

As useful interpolation models, the normal cubic Ferguson curve and bicubic Coons patch as, established in the spaces $\{1, t, t^2, t^3\}$, have gained widespread application. However, up to now, trigonometric or hyperbolic polynomial curves and surfaces like those of Ferguson curve and Coons patch have been studied scarcely. The purpose of this work is to present the practical algebraic-hyperbolic polynomial Ferguson curve and Coons patch, analogous to the corresponding normal cubic Ferguson curve and bicubic Coons patch, with shape parameters.

The present work is organized as follows. In Section 2, the algebraic-hyperbolic polynomial Hermite functions, called AH-Hermite functions, of the corresponding Ferguson curve and Coons patch are established and the properties of AH-Hermite functions are shown. In Section 3, the algebraic-hyperbolic polynomial Ferguson curve, called AH-Ferguson curve, is given and some properties are discussed. In Section 4, the algebraic-hyperbolic polynomial Coons patch, called AH-Coons patch, is given and some properties are shown. A short conclusion is given in Section 5.

2   Definition and Properties of AH-Hermite Functions

For $t \in [0,1]$, the normal cubic Hermite functions ([11]) can be expressed as

$$\begin{cases} H_0(t) = 2t^3 - 3t^2 + 1 \\ H_1(t) = -2t^3 + 3t^2 \\ I_0(t) = t(t-1)^2 \\ I_1(t) = t^2(t-1) \end{cases} \tag{1}$$

When using $\{1, t, \sinh t, \cosh t\}$ to replace the basis $\{1, t, t^2, t^3\}$ in the normal cubic Hermite functions, the algebraic-hyperbolic polynomial Hermite functions called AH-Hermite functions can be defined as follows.

Definition 1.   For an arbitrary real number α, where $\alpha \in (0, \pi]$, the following four polynomials are defined as AH-Hermite functions,

$$\begin{cases} F_0(t) = \dfrac{1}{2 - 2C + \alpha S}((1 - C + \alpha S) - St + S \sinh t + (1 - C)\cosh t) \\ F_1(t) = \dfrac{1}{2 - 2C + \alpha S}((1 - C) + St - S \sinh t - (1 - C)\cosh t) \\ G_0(t) = \dfrac{1}{2 - 2C + \alpha S}(-(S - \alpha C) + (1 - C)t + (1 - C + \alpha S)\sinh t + (S - \alpha C)\cosh t) \\ G_1(t) = \dfrac{1}{2 - 2C + \alpha S}(-(\alpha - S) + (1 - C)t - (1 - C)\sinh t + (\alpha - S)\cosh t) \end{cases} \tag{2}$$

where $C := \cosh \alpha$, $S := \sinh \alpha$, $0 \le t \le \alpha$.
    Eq. (2) can be rewritten to

$$\begin{bmatrix} F_0(t) & F_1(t) & G_0(t) & G_1(t) \end{bmatrix} = \begin{bmatrix} 1 & t & \sinh t & \cosh t \end{bmatrix} M \tag{3}$$

where

$$M = \frac{1}{2-2C+\alpha S} \begin{bmatrix} 1-C+\alpha S & 1-C & -(S-\alpha C) & -(\alpha-S) \\ -S & S & 1-C & 1-C \\ S & -S & 1-C+\alpha S & -(1-C) \\ 1-C & -(1-C) & S-\alpha C & \alpha-S \end{bmatrix}, \quad C := \cosh\alpha,$$

$S := \sinh\alpha$, $0 \le t \le \alpha$.

By simply calculating, AH-Hermite functions have the following properties,

$$F_0(0) = 1, \quad F_1(0) = 0, \quad G_0(0) = 0, \quad G_1(0) = 0,$$
$$F_0(\alpha) = 0, \quad F_1(\alpha) = 1, \quad G_0(\alpha) = 0, \quad G_1(\alpha) = 0,$$
$$F_0'(0) = 0, \quad F_1'(0) = 0, \quad G_0'(0) = 1, \quad G_1'(0) = 0,$$
$$F_0'(\alpha) = 0, \quad F_1'(\alpha) = 0, \quad G_0'(\alpha) = 0, \quad G_1'(\alpha) = 1.$$

The above results show that AH-Hermite functions have the some endpoint properties to the normal cubic Hermite functions.

By letting $t = u\alpha$, the AH-Hermite functions can be redefined as

$$F_0^*(u) := F_0(t), \quad F_1^*(u) := F_1(t), \quad G_0^*(u) := \frac{1}{\alpha}G_0(t), \quad G_1^*(u) := \frac{1}{\alpha}G_1(t). \qquad (4)$$

Then the new AH-Hermite functions are defined on a fixed interval $u \in [0,1]$ and have the following relation with the normal cubic Hermite functions.

Theorem 1. As $\alpha \to 0$, the limit of AH-Hermite functions defined on $[0,1]$ is the normal cubic Hermite functions.

Proof. Let $\sinh t, \cosh t$ expand as power series, *i.e.*

$$\sinh t = \frac{1}{2}(e^t - e^{-t}) \approx t + \frac{1}{6}t^3, \quad \cosh t = \frac{1}{2}(e^t + e^{-t}) \approx 1 + \frac{1}{2}t^2.$$

By putting the above result into Eq. (3), we have

$$\begin{bmatrix} F_0(t) & F_1(t) & G_0(t) & G_1(t) \end{bmatrix} = \frac{1}{2-2C+\alpha S}\begin{bmatrix} 1 & t & t^2 & t^3 \end{bmatrix} \times$$

$$\begin{bmatrix} 2-2C+\alpha S & 0 & 0 & 0 \\ 0 & 0 & 2-2C+\alpha S & 0 \\ \frac{1}{2}(1-C) & -\frac{1}{2}(1-C) & \frac{1}{2}(S-\alpha C) & \frac{1}{2}(\alpha-S) \\ \frac{1}{6}S & -\frac{1}{6}S & \frac{1}{6}(1-C+\alpha S) & -\frac{1}{6}(1-C) \end{bmatrix} \qquad (5)$$

Eq. (4) can be rewritten as

$$\begin{bmatrix} F_0^*(u) & F_1^*(u) & G_0^*(u) & G_1^*(u) \end{bmatrix} = \begin{bmatrix} F_0(t) & F_1(t) & G_0(t) & G_1(t) \end{bmatrix}\begin{bmatrix} 1 & 0 & 0 & 0 \\ 0 & 1 & 0 & 0 \\ 0 & 0 & \frac{1}{\alpha} & 0 \\ 0 & 0 & 0 & \frac{1}{\alpha} \end{bmatrix}$$

By putting Eq. (5) to the above formula and letting $t = u\alpha$, we have

$$\left[F_0^*(u) \quad F_1^*(u) \quad G_0^*(u) \quad G_1^*(u)\right] = \frac{1}{2 - 2C + \alpha S}\left[1 \quad u \quad u^2 \quad u^3\right] \times$$

$$\begin{bmatrix} 2 - 2C + \alpha S & 0 & 0 & 0 \\ 0 & 0 & 2 - 2C + \alpha S & 0 \\ \frac{1}{2}(1 - C)\alpha^2 & -\frac{1}{2}(1 - C)\alpha^2 & \frac{1}{2}(S - \alpha C)\alpha & \frac{1}{2}(\alpha - S)\alpha \\ \frac{1}{6}S\alpha^3 & -\frac{1}{6}S\alpha^3 & \frac{1}{6}(1 - C + \alpha S)\alpha^2 & -\frac{1}{6}(1 - C)\alpha^2 \end{bmatrix}$$

As $\alpha \to 0$, the above formula can be transformed to

$$\left[F_0^*(u) \quad F_1^*(u) \quad G_0^*(u) \quad G_1^*(u)\right] = \left[u^3 \quad u^2 \quad u \quad 1\right]\begin{bmatrix} 2 & -2 & 1 & 1 \\ -3 & 3 & -2 & -1 \\ 0 & 0 & 1 & 0 \\ 1 & 0 & 0 & 0 \end{bmatrix} \tag{6}$$

Eq. (6) is the matrix expression of the normal cubic Hermite functions defined as Eq. (1) exactly.   □

3   AH-Ferguson Curve

3.1   Definition and Properties of AH-Ferguson Curve

The normal cubic Ferguson curve ([11]) can be expressed as

$$r(t) = H_0(t)r(0) + H_1(t)r(1) + I_0(t)r'(0) + I_1(t)r'(1)$$

where $r(0)$, $r(1)$, $r'(0)$ and $r'(1)$ are position and derivative vectors on both ends of the segment $[0,1]$.

The normal cubic Ferguson curve interpolates the position and derivative vectors on both ends of the segment, which is convenient to construct interpolation curve in engineering. However, the shape of the normal cubic Ferguson curve cannot be adjusted when the position and derivative vectors on both ends of the segment are specified, which limit its applications.

Similar to the normal cubic Ferguson curve, the algebraic-hyperbolic polynomial Ferguson curve called AH-Ferguson curve can be defined as follows.

Definition 2. For $0 \le t \le \alpha$, $\alpha \in (0, \pi]$, given the position vectors $r(0)$, $r(\alpha)$ and the derivative vectors $r'(0)$, $r'(\alpha)$ on both ends of a curve, the following curve is defined as AH-Ferguson curve,

$$r(t) = F_0(t)r(0) + F_1(t)r(\alpha) + G_0(t)r'(0) + G_1(t)r'(\alpha) \tag{7}$$

where $F_i(t)$ and $G_i(t)$ $(i = 0,1)$ are AH-Hermite functions defined as Eq. (2).

By letting $t = u\alpha$, AH-Ferguson curve can be redefined as

$$r(u) = F_0^*(u)r(0) + F_1^*(u)r(1) + G_0^*(u)r'(0) + G_1^*(u)r'(1) \qquad (8)$$

Then the new AH-Ferguson curve is defined on a fixed interval $u \in [0,1]$ and has the following relation with the normal cubic Ferguson curve.

Theorem 2. As $\alpha \to 0$, the limit of AH-Ferguson curve defined on $[0,1]$ is the normal cubic Ferguson curve.

Proof. From theorem 1 and Eq. (8), theorem 2 can be educed easily. □

AH-Ferguson curve interpolates the position and derivative vectors on both ends of the curve, which is the same to the normal cubic Ferguson curve. However, the shape of AH-Ferguson curve can be adjusted by altering value of the free parameter α when the position vectors and derivative vectors on both ends of the segment are fixed, see Fig. 1.

Remark 1. In order to discuss the limit properties of AH-Ferguson curve, the curve is redefined to the new form on the fixed interval $[0,1]$. However, for the same position and derivative vectors on both ends of the segment, both the old and new curves are exactly the same in shape for AH-Ferguson curve. Therefore, the curve is redefined only when it is necessary.

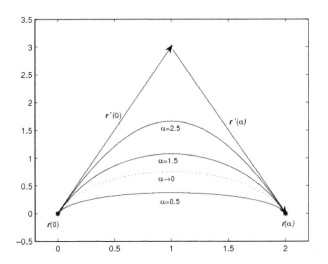

Fig. 1. The effect on the shape of AH-Ferguson curve of altering the value of α

3.2   Some Applications of AH-Ferguson Curve

1) Representation of a Segment of Catenaries. Given a segment of catenaries $r(t) = (t, \cosh t)$, $0 \le t \le \alpha$, $\alpha > 0$, the matrix form of $r(t)$ can be written as

$$r(t) = \begin{bmatrix} 1 & t & \sinh t & \cosh t \end{bmatrix} \begin{bmatrix} 0 & 0 \\ 1 & 0 \\ 0 & 0 \\ 0 & 1 \end{bmatrix} \tag{9}$$

According to Eq. (7), the matrix form of AH-Ferguson curve can be expressed as

$$r(t) = \begin{bmatrix} 1 & t & \sinh t & \cosh t \end{bmatrix} M \begin{bmatrix} r(0) \\ r(\alpha) \\ r'(0) \\ r'(\alpha) \end{bmatrix} \tag{10}$$

where

$$M = \frac{1}{2 - 2C + \beta S} \begin{bmatrix} 1 - C + \beta S & 1 - C & -(S - \beta C) & -(\beta - S) \\ -S & S & 1 - C & 1 - C \\ S & -S & 1 - C + \beta S & -(1 - C) \\ 1 - C & -(1 - C) & S - \beta C & \beta - S \end{bmatrix}, \quad S := \sinh \beta,$$

$C := \cosh \beta$, $0 \le t \le \beta$, $0 < \beta \le \pi$.

According to Eq. (9) and Eq. (10), AH-Ferguson curve can represent a segment of catenaries when the position and derivative vectors on both ends are chosen as

$$\begin{bmatrix} r(0) \\ r(\alpha) \\ r'(0) \\ r'(\alpha) \end{bmatrix} = M^{-1} \begin{bmatrix} 0 & 0 \\ 1 & 0 \\ 0 & 0 \\ 0 & 1 \end{bmatrix}$$

By simply calculating, we have

$$r(0) = (0,1), \quad r(\alpha) = (\alpha, \cosh \alpha), \quad r'(0) = (1,0), \quad r'(\alpha) = (1, \sinh \alpha).$$

2) Representation of a Segment of Hyperbola. Given a segment of hyperbola $r(t) = (a\cosh t, b\sinh t)$, $0 \le t \le \alpha$, $\alpha > 0$, $a,b > 0$, the matrix form of $r(t)$ can be written as

$$r(t) = \begin{bmatrix} 1 & t & \sinh t & \cosh t \end{bmatrix} \begin{bmatrix} 0 & 0 \\ 0 & 0 \\ 0 & b \\ a & 0 \end{bmatrix} \tag{11}$$

According to Eq. (10) and Eq. (11), AH-Ferguson curve can represent a segment of hyperbola when the position and derivative vectors on both ends are chosen as

$$\begin{bmatrix} r(0) \\ r(\alpha) \\ r'(0) \\ r'(\alpha) \end{bmatrix} = M^{-1} \begin{bmatrix} 0 & 0 \\ 0 & 0 \\ 0 & b \\ a & 0 \end{bmatrix}$$

By simply calculating, we have

$$\boldsymbol{r}(0) = (a,0), \quad \boldsymbol{r}(\alpha) = (a\cosh\alpha, b\sinh\alpha),$$
$$\boldsymbol{r}'(0) = (0,b), \quad \boldsymbol{r}'(\alpha) = (a\sinh\alpha, b\cosh\alpha).$$

4   Definition and Properties of AH-Coons Patches

The normal bicubic Coons patch ([11]) can be expressed as

$$\boldsymbol{r}(u,v) = \begin{bmatrix} H_0(u) & H_1(u) & I_0(u) & I_1(u) \end{bmatrix} \times$$
$$\begin{bmatrix} \boldsymbol{r}(0,0) & \boldsymbol{r}(0,1) & \boldsymbol{r}_v(0,0) & \boldsymbol{r}_v(0,1) \\ \boldsymbol{r}(1,0) & \boldsymbol{r}(1,1) & \boldsymbol{r}_v(1,0) & \boldsymbol{r}_v(1,1) \\ \boldsymbol{r}_u(0,0) & \boldsymbol{r}_u(0,1) & \boldsymbol{r}_{uv}(0,0) & \boldsymbol{r}_{uv}(0,1) \\ \boldsymbol{r}_u(1,0) & \boldsymbol{r}_u(1,1) & \boldsymbol{r}_{uv}(1,0) & \boldsymbol{r}_{uv}(1,1) \end{bmatrix} \begin{bmatrix} H_0(v) \\ H_1(v) \\ I_0(v) \\ I_1(v) \end{bmatrix}$$

where $H_i(t)$ and $I_i(t)$ ($i = 0,1$; $t = u,v$) are the cubic Hermite functions defined as Eq. (1), and

$$\boldsymbol{B} = \begin{bmatrix} \boldsymbol{r}(0,0) & \boldsymbol{r}(0,1) & \boldsymbol{r}_v(0,0) & \boldsymbol{r}_v(0,1) \\ \boldsymbol{r}(1,0) & \boldsymbol{r}(1,1) & \boldsymbol{r}_v(1,0) & \boldsymbol{r}_v(1,1) \\ \boldsymbol{r}_u(0,0) & \boldsymbol{r}_u(0,1) & \boldsymbol{r}_{uv}(0,0) & \boldsymbol{r}_{uv}(0,1) \\ \boldsymbol{r}_u(1,0) & \boldsymbol{r}_u(1,1) & \boldsymbol{r}_{uv}(1,0) & \boldsymbol{r}_{uv}(1,1) \end{bmatrix}$$

is the boundary information matrix.

The normal bicubic Coons patch interpolates every element of the boundary information matrix, which is convenient to construct interpolation surface in engineering. However, the shape of the normal bicubic Coons patch cannot be adjusted when the boundary information matrix are specified, which limit its applications.

Similar to the normal bicubic Coons patch, the algebraic-hyperbolic polynomial Coons patch called AH-Coons patch can be defined as follows.

Definition 3. For $0 \le t \le \alpha$, $0 \le s \le \beta$, $\alpha, \beta \in (0,\pi]$, the following patch is defined as AH-Coons patch,

$$\boldsymbol{r}(t,s) = \begin{bmatrix} F_0(t) & F_1(t) & G_0(t) & G_1(t) \end{bmatrix} \boldsymbol{B} \begin{bmatrix} F_0(s) & F_1(s) & G_0(s) & G_1(s) \end{bmatrix}^{\mathrm{T}} \quad (12)$$

where $F_i(w)$ and $G_i(w)$ ($i = 0,1$; $w = t,s$) are the AH-Hermite functions defined as Eq. (2), and

$$\boldsymbol{B} = \begin{bmatrix} \boldsymbol{r}(0,0) & \boldsymbol{r}(0,\beta) & \boldsymbol{r}_s(0,0) & \boldsymbol{r}_s(0,\beta) \\ \boldsymbol{r}(\alpha,0) & \boldsymbol{r}(\alpha,\beta) & \boldsymbol{r}_s(\alpha,0) & \boldsymbol{r}_s(\alpha,\beta) \\ \boldsymbol{r}_t(0,0) & \boldsymbol{r}_t(0,\beta) & \boldsymbol{r}_{ts}(0,0) & \boldsymbol{r}_{ts}(0,\beta) \\ \boldsymbol{r}_t(\alpha,0) & \boldsymbol{r}_t(\alpha,\beta) & \boldsymbol{r}_{ts}(\alpha,0) & \boldsymbol{r}_{ts}(\alpha,\beta) \end{bmatrix}$$

is the boundary information matrix.

By letting $s = v\beta$ $(0 \le v \le 1)$, AH-Hermite functions in direction of s can be redefined as

$$F_0^*(v) = F_0(s), \quad F_1^*(v) = F_1(s), \quad G_0^*(v) = \frac{1}{\beta}G_0(s), \quad G_1^*(v) = \frac{1}{\beta}G_1(s)$$

Then, Eq. (12) can be redefined as

$$r(u,v) = \begin{bmatrix} F_0^*(u) & F_1^*(u) & G_0^*(u) & G_1^*(u) \end{bmatrix} \times$$

$$\begin{bmatrix} r(0,0) & r(0,1) & r_v(0,0) & r_v(0,1) \\ r(1,0) & r(1,1) & r_v(1,0) & r_v(1,1) \\ r_u(0,0) & r_u(0,1) & r_{uv}(0,0) & r_{uv}(0,1) \\ r_u(1,0) & r_u(1,1) & r_{uv}(1,0) & r_{uv}(1,1) \end{bmatrix} \begin{bmatrix} F_0^*(v) \\ F_1^*(v) \\ G_0^*(v) \\ G_1^*(v) \end{bmatrix} \tag{13}$$

Then the new AH-Coons patch can be redefined on a fixed interval $[0,1] \times [0,1]$ and has the following relation with the normal bicubic Coons patch.

Theorem 3. As $\alpha, \beta \to 0$, the limit of AH-Coons patch defined on $[0,1] \times [0,1]$ is the normal bicubic Coons patch.

Proof. From theorem 1 and Eq. (13), theorem 3 can be educed easily.   □

AH-Coons patch has the same interpolation properties to the normal bicubic Coons patch. However, the shape of AH-Coons patch can be adjusted by altering values of the free parameter α and β when the boundary conditions are kept unchanged, see Fig. 2.

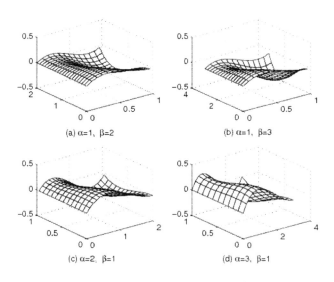

(a) α=1, β=2

(b) α=1, β=3

(c) α=2, β=1

(d) α=3, β=1

Fig. 2. The effect on the shape of AH-Coons patch of altering the value of α and β

Remark 2. In order to discuss the limit properties of AH-Coons patch, the patch is redefined to the new form on the fixed interval [0,1]×[0,1]. However, for the same boundary conditions, both the old and new curves are exactly the same in shape for AH-Coons patch. Therefore, the patch is redefined only when it is necessary.

5   Conclusions

As mentioned above, AH-Ferguson curve and AH-Coons patch have all the properties that the corresponding normal cubic Ferguson curve and bicubic Coons patch have. However, they have more expressive ability because of the free parameters. Also, because there are no differences in structure between an AH-Ferguson curve and a normal cubic Ferguson curve, an AH-Coons patch and a normal bicubic Coons patch, it is not difficult to adapt AH-Ferguson curve and AH-Coons patch to a CAD/CAM system that already uses the corresponding normal cubic Ferguson curve and bicubic Coons patch.

For practical applications of AH-Ferguson curve and AH-Coons patch, it is clear that some special algorithms are needed. Some interesting results in this area will be discussed in the following papers.

Acknowledgments. This work is supported by the Scientific Research Fund of Hunan Provincial Education Department of China (11C0707).

References

1. Zhang, J.W.: C-Curves: An Extension of Cubic Curves. Computer Aided Geometric Design 13, 199–217 (1996)
2. Mainar, E., Pena, J.M.: A Basis of C-Bézier Splines with Optimal Properties. Computer Aided Geometric Design 19, 291–295 (2002)
3. Chen, Q.Y., Wang, G.Z.: A Class of Bézier-Like Curves. Computer Aided Geometric Design 20, 29–39 (2003)
4. Wang, G.Z., Chen, Q.Y., Zhou, M.H.: NUAT B-Spline Curves. Computer Aided Geometric Design 21, 193–205 (2004)
5. Han, X.-A., Ma, Y.C., Huang, X.L.: The Cubic Trigonometric Bézier Curve with Two Shape Parameters. Applied Mathematics Letters 22, 226–231 (2009)
6. Li, J.C., Zhao, D.B., Li, B.J., Chen, G.H.: A Family of Quasi-Cubic Trigonometric Curves. Journal of Information and Computational Science 7, 2847–2854 (2010)
7. Yan, L.L., Liang, J.F.: A Class of Algebraic-Trigonometric Blended Splines. Journal of Computational and Applied Mathematics 235, 1713–1729 (2011)
8. Lü, Y.G., Wang, G.Z., Yang, X.N.: Uniform Hyperbolic Polynomial B-Spline Curves. Computer Aided Geometric Design 19, 379–393 (2002)
9. Li, Y.J., Wang, G.Z.: Two kinds of B-Basis of the Algebraic Hyperbolic Space. Journal of Zhejiang University (Science) 6A, 750–759 (2005)
10. Liu, X.M., Xu, W.X., Guan, Y., Shang, Y.Y.: Hyperbolic Polynomial Uniform B-Spline Curves and Surfaces with Shape Parameter. Graphical Models 72, 1–6 (2010)
11. Farin, G.: Curves and Surfaces for Computer-Aided Geometric Design, 4th edn. Elsevier Science & Technology Books, Maryland (1997)

An Algorithm for Maximum Flow Analysis
in Traffic Network Based on Fuzzy Matrix

Feng Zhao[1] and Yundong Gu[2,*]

[1] School of Mathematics Science, Liaocheng University,
Liaocheng, 252059, P.R. China
[2] School of Mathematics and Physics, North China Electric Power University,
Beijing, 102206, P.R. China
zhaofenglch@163.com, guyund@126.com

Abstract. The problem of traffic network analysis is studied in this paper. Firstly, the traffic flows in a traffic network is modeled by fuzzy matrix. Then the maximum flow in the traffic network is transformed to the transitive closure of the fuzzy matrix. By discussing the relations between the transitive closure of an arbitrary fuzzy matrix and that of its corresponding reflexive matrix, the squaring algorithm for computing the transitive closure of a fuzzy reflexive matrix is extended to the arbitrary case in the following. Lastly, the feasibility and effectiveness of the given algorithm is verified by an example.

Keywords: maximum flow, traffic network, fuzzy matrix, transitive closure, squaring algorithm.

1   Introduction

Network flow theory is an important branch of Graph Theory, and it is the theory of studying optimization problems upon network. In 1956, L.R. Ford and D.R. Fulkerson propound the algorithm to solve the problem of seeking maximal transportation quantity between two nodes on the network. From then on, network flow theory was founded and developed. Network flow theory now has been widely applied to communication, transportation, power transmission, engineering programming and other fields. In order to solve the practical problem better, some new network flow theory were presented, such as assignment and matching, Lagrangian relaxation of network optimization, multi-commodity flow, network flow's decomposition and combination and so on [1-6].

Distinguish from other studies, Zhou [7, 8] and Yao [9] describe the network flow in terms of the fuzzy matrix, and the flows between the paths are transformed to the compositions of the fuzzy matrix. Based on their works, the transitive closure of a fuzzy matrix is introduced to analyze the maximum flow in the traffic network.

It is well-known that fuzzy clustering is one of the most useful tools in data analysis and the transitive closure of a fuzzy matrix plays an important role in

---

* Corresponding author.

M. Zhao and J. Sha (Eds.): ICCIP 2012, Part II, CCIS 289, pp. 368–376, 2012.
© Springer-Verlag Berlin Heidelberg 2012

constructing fuzzy equivalence matrix, which is essential for similarity matrix based clustering analysis. Actually, fuzzy equivalent matrix is widely used in many fields, such as fuzzy recognition, fuzzy decision making, the computer science, information science, automatic control, flexible manufacturing systems, architecture and archaeology etc [11-16].

The transitive closure of an $n \times n$ fuzzy matrix A is represented as $t(A) = \bigcup\limits_{k=1}^{\infty} A^k$ and it can be simplified as $t(A) = \bigcup\limits_{k=1}^{n-1} A^k$ for fuzzy similar matrix. To calculate the transitive closure with this representation, the algorithm's time complexity is $O(n^4)$. As for fuzzy reflexive matrix A, we have $A^k \subseteq A^{k+1}$ and $t(A) = A^{n-1}$, thus the squaring algorithm is presented to calculate the transitive closure and its time complexity is $O(n^3 \ln n)$. This fast algorithm is widely used for its efficiency and convenience. However this algorithm is relied on the reflexivity while many matrices such as the representation matrix of traffic network and debt relation are not reflexive. So, find an algorithm for computing the transitive closure of a fuzzy matrix without reflexivity is important.

With an extensive study on the relations between the transitive closure of an arbitrary fuzzy matrix A and that of its corresponding reflexive matrix $I \cup A$, where I denotes the unit matrix, the squaring algorithm for computing the transitive closure of fuzzy reflexive matrix is extended to the arbitrary case.

As the background and the raise of the question, we first describe the traffic network in terms of fuzzy matrix, and discuss the relations between the maximum flow in the traffic network and the transitive closure of the fuzzy matrix.

2   Modeling of the Path Capacity in Traffic Network

Definition 1. Given a traffic network $G = (V, E)$ with $|V| = n$. The traffic flows of the path from node V_i directly to V_j is denoted by a_{ij} if $i \neq j$. The value of a_{ii} could set flexibly based on the consideration of the need of operation or blocking cases. Then fuzzy matrix $A = (a_{ij})_{n \times n}$ is called the representation matrix of a traffic network.

Definition 2. Let $L(x_{i_0}, x_{i_1}, \cdots, x_{i_k})$ be the path from node x_{i_0} to x_{i_k} with the length k. The capacity of the path will be denoted as $W(L) = a_{i_0 i_1} \wedge a_{i_1 i_2} \wedge \cdots \wedge a_{i_{k-1} i_k}$.

Actually, the capacity of the path is equal to the minimum capacity of every adjacent pair nodes, which indicates the status of the traffic network.

Definition 3. Let Ω_k be the set of the paths with length k from x_i to x_j.

(1) $\max\limits_{L\in\Omega_k} W(L)$ is called the maximum flow of Ω_k;

(2) If $L_0 \in \Omega_k$ and $W(L_0) = \max\limits_{L\in\Omega_k} W(L)$, then L_0 is called the maximum path

with length k from x_i to x_j;

(3) $\max\limits_{k\in N}\max\limits_{L\in\Omega_k} W(L)$ is called the maximum flow from x_i to x_j;

(4) If $W(L_0) = \max\limits_{k\in N}\max\limits_{L\in\Omega_k} W(L)$, then L_0 is called the maximum path from x_i

to x_j.

The maximum flow is one of the most important parameters in the traffic network, since it truly implies the status of the traffic network. Hence it is the key concept to study the maximum flow.

Theorem 1 [7]. If the fuzzy matrix $A = (a_{ij})_{n\times n}$ stands for a traffic network, then

the maximum flow of all the path with length k from x_i to x_j is equal to a_{ij}^k,

where a_{ij}^k is the entry element in the cell in row i and column j of A^k.

Theorem 1 shows that the maximum flow in the traffic network could be obtained by calculating the powers of A. Thus, the maximum flow in the network is transformed to the composition of the matrix.

Theorem 2 [7]. For any positive integer k, L is the maximum path with length k of

$A \Leftrightarrow L_\lambda$ is $k-$length path of A_λ, where $\lambda = a_{ij}^k$ and L_λ is the corresponding

path of L in A_λ.

In fact, theorem 2 proposes a simple algorithm to get the maximum path in the traffic network. It transforms the maximum path in the traffic network to the path in the Boolean matrix, and the latter has been well resolved in graph theory. It must be pointed out that when we look for the maximum path in the network with A_λ, the

value of λ is nothing else but a_{ij}^k. This fact indicates the specific significance of a_{ij}^k.

3   Relations between Maximum Flow and Transitive Closure

Theorem 3. If $t(A) = (t_{ij})_{n\times n}$ is the transitive closure of A, then the maximum

flow from x_i to x_j is equal to t_{ij}.

Proof. Since $t(A) = \bigcup\limits_{k=1}^{\infty} A^k$, from definition 1 and 3, we get

$$t_{ij} = \bigvee\limits_{k=1}^{\infty} a_{ij}^k = \max\limits_{k\in N}\max\limits_{L\in\Omega_k} W(L).$$

It is of great significance to calculate the maximum flow in the traffic network since it usually implies the optimization path. Theorem 3 implies that the maximum flow could be obtained by calculating the transitive closure of the fuzzy matrix. If the traffic network is asymmetric and irreflexive, then its fuzzy matrix is asymmetric and irreflexive. The known algorithms for calculating the transitive closure is constructed for similar fuzzy matrix or the reflexive fuzzy matrix, so it is a challenge to find a good algorithm for calculating the transitive closure of an arbitrary fuzzy matrix. With an extensive study on the relations between the transitive closure of an arbitrary fuzzy matrix A and that of its corresponding reflexive matrix $I \cup A$, the squaring algorithm for computing the transitive closure of fuzzy reflexive matrix is extended to the arbitrary case, where I denote the unit matrix.

Theorem 4. Let $A = (a_{ij})_{n \times n}$ be a fuzzy matrix and $I_{n \times n}$ be a unit matrix.

Let $t(A) = (t_{ij})_{n \times n}$ and $t(I \cup A) = (\bar{t}_{ij})_{n \times n}$ be the transitive closure of A and $I \cup A$

respectively, then we have $t_{ij} = \bar{t}_{ij}$ for $i \neq j$.

Proof. For an arbitrary fuzzy matrix A and a positive integer k, by mathematics induction, it is obvious that $(I \cup A)^k = I \cup A \cup A^2 \cup \cdots \cup A^k$.

Since $t(A) = A \cup A^2 \cup \cdots \cup A^n$ and $t(B) = B^n$, if B is reflexive, then

$t(I \cup A) = (I \cup A)^n = I \cup A \cup A^2 \cup \cdots \cup A^n = I \cup t(A)$.

So $t_{ij} = \bar{t}_{ij}$ if $i \neq j$.

From theorem 3 and 4, one can easily find the following corollary:

Corollary 1. The maximum flow of A is equal to that of $I \cup A$ when $i \neq j$.

Theorem 4 shows the elements of $t(A)$ and $t(I \cup A)$ are equal except the diagonal elements. Then it is possible to extend the squaring algorithm for the transitive closure of a reflexive fuzzy matrix to arbitrary case.

Corollary 2. If $i \neq j$, then the maximum path of A is the maximum path of $I \cup A$.

Proof. Suppose L is one of the maximum path of A and $\bar{L}$ is the corresponding

path of L in $I \cup A$, we have $t_{ij} = W(L) \leq W(\bar{L}) \leq \bar{t}_{ij} = t_{ij}$, thus $W(\bar{L}) = \bar{t}_{ij}$.

This means $\bar{L}$ is the maximum path in $I \cup A$.

But the reverse proposition of corollary 2 is not true. If $A = \begin{pmatrix} 0 & 1 & 1 \\ 1 & 0 & 1 \\ 1 & 1 & 0 \end{pmatrix}$, then

$\bar{L}(x_1, x_2, x_2, x_3)$ is one of the maximum path in $I \cup A$, but $L(x_1, x_2, x_2, x_3)$ is not the maximum path in A.

The preceding conclusion shows the maximum flow from x_i to x_j in A could be get by calculating the maximum flow of $I \cup A$ if $i \neq j$. Then is there a similar result for $i = j$?

Theorem 5. Let $A = (a_{ij})_{n \times n}$ be a fuzzy matrix and $I_{n \times n}$ be a unit matrix, $t(A) = (t_{ij})_{n \times n}$, $t(I \cup A) = (\bar{t}_{ij})_{n \times n}$. Then

$$t_{ii} = a_{ii} \vee (\bigvee_{j \neq i} (\bar{t}_{ij} \wedge \bar{t}_{ji})), 1 \leq i, j \leq n.$$

Proof. We first show that $t_{ii} \leq a_{ii} \vee (\bigvee_{j \neq i} (\bar{t}_{ij} \wedge \bar{t}_{ji}))$.

Since $t_{ii} = \bigvee_{k-1}^{n} a_{ii}^{k}$, then there exist a positive integer m, such that $t_{ii} = a_{ii}^{m}$ and $m = \min\{s \mid a_{ii}^{s} = \bigvee_{t-1}^{n} a_{ii}^{t}\}$. If $m = 1$, the conclusion is obviously true. If $m > 1$, then there exist a nature number j satisfying $t_{ii} = a_{ii}^{m} = a_{ij} \wedge a_{ji}^{m-1}$ and $j \neq i$. Otherwise $a_{ii}^{m} \leq a_{ii}$, which is a contradiction with $m > 1$. Taking into account that $a_{ij} \leq t_{ij}, a_{ji}^{m} \leq t_{ji}$, we have $t_{ii} \leq t_{ij} \wedge t_{ji} = \bar{t}_{ij} \wedge \bar{t}_{ji} \leq \bigvee_{j \neq i} (\bar{t}_{ij} \wedge \bar{t}_{ji}))$. Therefore,

$$t_{ii} \leq a_{ii} \vee (\bigvee_{j \neq i} (\bar{t}_{ij} \wedge \bar{t}_{ji})).$$

On the other hand, $\bigvee_{j \neq i} (\bar{t}_{ij} \wedge \bar{t}_{ji}) = \bigvee_{j \neq i} (t_{ij} \wedge t_{ji}) \leq t_{ii}^{2} = t_{ii}$ and $a_{ii} \leq t_{ii}$ is easily proved, hence $a_{ii} \vee (\bigvee_{j \neq i} (\bar{t}_{ij} \wedge \bar{t}_{ji})) \leq t_{ii}$.

Combining with theorem 4 and 5, we can deduce:

Theorem 6. Let $A = (a_{ij})_{n \times n}$ be a fuzzy matrix and $I_{n \times n}$ be unit matrix. If $t(A) = (t_{ij})_{n \times n}, t(I \cup A) = (\bar{t}_{ij})_{n \times n}$, then $t_{ij} = \begin{cases} \bar{t}_{ij}, & i \neq j, \\ a_{ii} \vee t_{ii}^{2}, & i = j. \end{cases}$

The squaring algorithm is proposed in [10] for calculating the transitive closure of a reflexive fuzzy matrix. With theorem 6, this algorithm could be extended to calculating the transitive closure of an arbitrary fuzzy matrix.

4   Squaring Algorithm for Calculating the Transitive Closure of an Arbitrary Fuzzy Matrix

Let $A = (a_{ij})_{n \times n}$ be an arbitrary fuzzy matrix and $t(A) = (t_{ij})$ be the transitive closure of A. Then the squaring algorithm for calculating the transitive closure will be proposed as follows:

Step 1. Set $A = (a_{ij})_{n \times n}$.

Step 2. Let $B = I \cup A = (b_{ij})_{n \times n}$. Then compute

$$B^2 = B \circ B = (\bigvee_{k=1}^{n} (b_{ik} \wedge b_{kj})) = (b_{ij}^2).$$

Step 3. If $B = B^2$, turn to step 5. Otherwise let $B = B^2$.

Step 4. Compute $B^2 = B \circ B = (\bigvee_{k=1}^{n} (b_{ik} \wedge b_{kj})) = (b_{ij}^2)$. Return to step 3.

Step 5. Compute $t(A) = (t_{ij})$, where $t_{ij} = \begin{cases} b_{ij}, & i \neq j, \\ a_{ii} \vee (\bigvee\limits_{j \neq i}(b_{ij} \wedge b_{ji})), & i = j. \end{cases}$

To calculate the transitive closure with the squaring algorithm, we will at most perform $\log_2(n-1) + 1$ times the max-min composition of the fuzzy matrix, so the time complexity is $O(n^3 \ln n)$.

Example 1. Suppose that there are five factories, denoted as x_1, x_2, x_3, x_4, x_5 in a city, and each two factories are connected with the road. Taking into account the bridge and the ascent or the downhill path, the limited carrying capacity of the roads between the factories is given as follows:

Carrying capacity (unit: ton)	x_1	x_2	x_3	x_4	x_5
x_1	0	4	5	2	3
x_2	2	0	4	4	5
x_3	4	5	0	3	2
x_4	3	4	5	0	3
x_5	5	4	2	2	0

Find the limited carrying capacity of any two factories.

Solution: The representation matrix of the traffic network is asymmetric and irreflexive, and the matrix is written as

$$R = \begin{pmatrix} 0 & 4 & 5 & 2 & 3 \\ 2 & 0 & 4 & 4 & 5 \\ 4 & 5 & 0 & 3 & 2 \\ 3 & 4 & 5 & 0 & 3 \\ 5 & 4 & 4 & 2 & 0 \end{pmatrix}.$$

It's easy to find that the greatest element of R is 5, so we transform the traffic network by setting $a_{ij} = \dfrac{1}{5} r_{ij}$, thus we get a fuzzy matrix A.

$$A = \begin{pmatrix} 0 & 0.8 & 1 & 0.4 & 0.6 \\ 0.4 & 0 & 0.8 & 0.8 & 1 \\ 0.8 & 1 & 0 & 0.6 & 0.4 \\ 0.6 & 0.8 & 1 & 0 & 0.6 \\ 1 & 0.8 & 0.8 & 0.4 & 0 \end{pmatrix}.$$

To calculate the transitive closure of A, let

$$B = I \cup A = \begin{pmatrix} 1 & 0.8 & 1 & 0.4 & 0.6 \\ 0.4 & 1 & 0.8 & 0.8 & 1 \\ 0.8 & 1 & 1 & 0.6 & 0.4 \\ 0.6 & 0.8 & 1 & 1 & 0.6 \\ 1 & 0.8 & 0.8 & 0.4 & 1 \end{pmatrix}.$$

Obviously, B is a reflexive fuzzy matrix. Then, getting long with the squaring algorithm, we have

$$B^2 = \begin{pmatrix} 1 & 1 & 1 & 0.8 & 0.6 \\ 1 & 1 & 0.8 & 0.8 & 1 \\ 0.8 & 1 & 1 & 0.8 & 1 \\ 0.8 & 1 & 1 & 1 & 0.8 \\ 1 & 0.8 & 1 & 0.8 & 1 \end{pmatrix}, B^4 = B^8 = \begin{pmatrix} 1 & 1 & 1 & 0.8 & 1 \\ 1 & 1 & 1 & 0.8 & 1 \\ 1 & 1 & 1 & 0.8 & 1 \\ 1 & 1 & 1 & 1 & 1 \\ 1 & 1 & 1 & 0.8 & 1 \end{pmatrix}.$$

Thus, the transitive closure $t(B) = \begin{pmatrix} 1 & 1 & 1 & 0.8 & 1 \\ 1 & 1 & 1 & 0.8 & 1 \\ 1 & 1 & 1 & 0.8 & 1 \\ 1 & 1 & 1 & 1 & 1 \\ 1 & 1 & 1 & 0.8 & 1 \end{pmatrix}.$

Since the diagonal elements of $t(A)$ is not the same as those of $t(B)$, we have to calculate the diagonal elements of $t(A)$. By theorem 5, we get

$$t_{11} = t_{22} = t_{33} = t_{55} = 1, t_{44} = 0.8.$$

Therefore, $t(A) = \begin{pmatrix} 1 & 1 & 1 & 0.8 & 1 \\ 1 & 1 & 1 & 0.8 & 1 \\ 1 & 1 & 1 & 0.8 & 1 \\ 1 & 1 & 1 & 0.8 & 1 \\ 1 & 1 & 1 & 0.8 & 1 \end{pmatrix}.$

The matrix $t(A)$ implies that the maximum flow between any two factories is 5 tons except that the maximum flow of the path from any other factories to x_4 is 4 tons.

5   Conclusion

The traffic network could be represented by fuzzy matrix, and then the computing of the maximum flow in the network is transformed to the calculating of the transitive closure of the fuzzy matrix. By discussing the relations between the transitive closure of A and that of its corresponding reflexive matrix $I \cup A$, we extend the squaring algorithm for calculating the transitive closure of the fuzzy reflexive matrix to the arbitrary case.

Acknowledgements. This paper is supported by the National Natural Science Foundation of China (Grant No. 71171080) and the National 973 Basic Research Program of China (2009CB-320602).

References

1. Yin, J., Wu, K.: Graphtheory and It's Algorithm. China Science and Technology University Press, Beijing (2003)
2. Gui, L., Gong, J.: Path-based and sa-based algorithm for transportation network design problem. Geomatics and Information Science of Wuhan University 33(4), 388–392 (2008)
3. Li, X., An, S.: A closed frequent subgraph based containment query algorithm. Acta Electronica Sinica 38(12), 2937–2943 (2010)
4. Zhong, S., Deng, W.: Path travel time reliability-based stochastic system optimum congestion pricing model. Systems Engeering—Theorem & Practice 30(12), 2297–2308 (2010)
5. Qin, J., Shi, F., Deng, L., Xiao, L.: Quantitative evaluation method for road transportation network efficiency and its application. Journal of Jilin University(Engineering and Technology Edition) 40(1), 47–1 (2010)

6. He, D., Yan, Y., Guo, S., Hao, G.: Optimal Routing algorithm for public traffic network based on matrix analysis. Journal of Southwest Jiao Tong University 42(3), 315–319 (2007)
7. Zhou, Z.: Maximum path analysis by the fuzzy matrix in the traffic network. Periodical of Ocean University of China 33(2), 324–328 (2003)
8. Zhou, Z., Ding, X.-Q., Liu, W.-B.: Fuzzy matrix analysis of the maximum road in traffic network. In: 22nd International Conference of the North American Fuzzy Information Processing Society-NAFIPS, pp. 283–286 (2003)
9. Yao, Z.-S., Liu, W.-B., Zhou, Z.: Maximum road analysis of traffic network. Advances in System Science and Application 4(4), 618–621 (2004)
10. Dunn, J.C.: Some recent investigations of a new fuzzy portioning algorithm and its application to pattern classification problems. J. Cybernet. 4, 1–15 (1974)
11. Li, G.-X.: Fuzzy cluster analysis on provenance of ancient Yaozhou porcelain bodies. Chinese Science Bulletin 23, 1781–1783 (2002)
12. Lemström, K., Hella, L.: Approximate pattern matching and transitive closure logics. Theoretical Computer Science 299(4), 387–412 (2003)
13. Penner, M., Prasanna, V.K.: Cache-Friendly implementations of transitive closure. Journal of Experimental Algorithmics (JEA) 11, 283–286 (2003)
14. Li, H.-X., Li, X.-F., Wang, J.-Y., Mo, Z.-W., Li, Y.-D.: Fuzzy decision making based on variable weights. Mathematical and Computer Modelling 39(1), 163–179 (2004)
15. Lee, J., Lee Jin, S.: Heuristic: search for scheduling flexible manufacturing systems using lower bound reachability matrix. Computers & Industrial Engineering 59(4), 799–806 (2010)
16. Pan, T.-T., Lin, S.-S., Qiu, K.: The transitive closure and related algorithms of digraph of the reconfigurable architecture. Parallel Processing Letters 21(1), 27–69 (2011)

Solving the 0-1 Knapsack Problem
with Polynomial-Time Quantum Algorithm

Hongying Liu[1] and Shuzhi Nie[2]

[1] Dept. of Computer Science and Engineering,
Guangzhou Vocational & Technical Institute of Industry & Commerce
510850 Guangzhou, China
327147616@qq.com
[2] Dept. of Electronics & Information Technology, Jiangmen Polytechnic
529090 Jiangmen, China
sznie778@163.com

Abstract. In this paper, Proposed a algorithm based on quantum, to solve the 0-1-knapsack problem on a hypothetical quantum computer. Utilized the especial characteristics of the quantum environment, constantly split up into the state of vector space, reduced the probability of state vector which don't meet the conditions of magnitude, increased the probability amplitude to meet the conditions, found a larger probability of obtaining the solution. Owing to the problem of solving the time complexity by traditional exponential is too complicated, turned it into the other problem which is relatively easy, then solving polynomial time with quantum computer, can reduce the difficulty of solving the problem. Analysis of the complexity of the algorithm and implementation results showed that the designed algorithm is effective and feasible. The designed algorithm can be extended to solve other NPC problems.

Keywords: Quantum computation, NPC problem, 0-1-kiapsack problem.

1   Introduction

Quantum mechanical computers were proposed in the early 1980s and the description of quantum mechanical computers was formalized in the late 1980s [1-3]. Many efforts on quantum computers have progressed actively since the early 1990s because these computers were shown to be more powerful than classical computers on various specialized problems, especially for the NPC problem. There are well-known quantum algorithms such as Shor's quantum factoring algorithm [3-4], and Grover's database search algorithm. But the difficulty in this field is that there are as yet only a few known techniques for designing quantum algorithms. Other known algorithms are essentially based on these methods [4-6].

Knapsack problem is a kind of combinatorial optimization problem of NP complete. Problems can be described as: given a set of items, each item has its own weight and price, in limited within the total weight of, how we choose, can make the total price of goods is the highest. The name of the problem comes from how to select

M. Zhao and J. Sha (Eds.): ICCIP 2012, Part II, CCIS 289, pp. 377–384, 2012.

the most suitable items placed in a given in the backpack. Similar problems often appear in the business, combinatorial mathematics, computational complexity theory, cryptography and applied mathematics, etc. Also can be described as decisive knapsack problem, that is not the total weight more than W, under the premise of total value whether can achieve V [7-9] ?

Supposed there is n kind of goods, articles of the weight of the j for W_j, price for P_j. Assumed all the weight of the goods and the price is negative. Backpack could take maximum weight for W.

If each item can choose only limited 0 or 1, the problem is called 0-1 knapsack problems. Can use the equation is expressed as follows:

$$\text{maximize } \sum_{j=1}^{n} P_j X_j \tag{1}$$

$$\text{subject to } \sum_{j=1}^{n} W_j X_j \leq W, \quad X_j \in \{0,1\} \tag{2}$$

If didn't limit the number of each item, the problem is called unbounded knapsack problem. All kinds of complex knapsack problem can always transformation for simple 0-1 knapsack problem solving [10-12].

The 0-1 Knapsack problem belongs to the NP-complete problems. The previous quantum algorithms research about the 0-1 Knapsack problem based on Grover's search algorithm are still exponential-time [13-16].

0-1 knapsack problem is the most basic knapsack problem, it contains a knapsack problems in design of the state, the equation the basic thought, in addition, other types of knapsack problem also often can be converted into 0/1 knapsack problem solving. So must experience carefully basic idea of above that method, transfer the meaning of state equation, and finally how to optimize the space complexity of [17-20].

In this paper, we consider quantum algorithms for the 0-1 Knapsack problem which have a Special partition method that can be exploited to design significantly faster quantum algorithms than what a direct application of Grover's search algorithm would yield. The 0-1-knapsack problem is closely related to the change counting problem and can be described as follows: Give a set of n items from which we are to select a number of items to be carried in the knapsack problems. Each item has both a weight and a profit. The objective is to choose the set of items that fit in the knapsack and maximize the profit.

2   Problem Description

0-1 Knapsack problem mathematical model is shown as follows: Assuming there are n objects, Its weight is expressed in ω_i, the value is $p_i (i = 1,2,...,n)$, the maximum weight of Knapsack problem is c, when the object i was elected into the Knapsack, defined the variable $x_i = 1$, else $x_i = 0$. Now consider the n objects choice or not,

The total weight of n objects within Knapsack is $\sum_{i=1}^{n} \omega_i x_i$, the total value of n objects

is $\sum_{i=1}^{n} p_i x_i$, how to determine the value of the variable $x_i (i = 1,2,...,n)$, then the

total value of objects in the backpack is the largest. Its mathematical model is expressed as follows:

$$\begin{cases} Maxinize \sum_{i=1}^{n} p_i x_i \\ Subject \quad to \quad \sum_{i=1}^{n} \omega_i x_i \leq 0 \end{cases} \tag{3}$$

Set w_i ($w_i > 0$) to be the weight of the item and v_i ($v_i > 0$) to be the profit, which must be accrued when the ith item is carried in the knapsack, and C is the capacity of the knapsack. Set $x_i \in \{0,1\}, 1 \leq i \leq n$ to be a variable the value of which is either zero or one. The variable x_i has one value when the ith item is carried in the knapsack. Then the problem is stated as follows:

$$W = (w_1, w_2 \cdots w_n) \tag{4}$$
$$V = (v_1, v_2 \cdots v_n) \tag{5}$$

In formula (4) and formula (5), W and V separately stand for the vectors.

$$g(x) = \sum_{i=1}^{n} v_i x_i \tag{6}$$

$$f(x) = \sum_{i=1}^{n} w_i x_i \tag{7}$$

In formula (6) and formula (7), $g(x)$ and $f(x)$ separately stand for the functions.

Find a binary vector x, $x = (x_1, x_2 \cdots x_n)$, that maximize the objective function (profit) $\max g(x)$, While satisfying the constraint $f(x) \leq C, C > 0$.

Clearly, we can solve this problem by exhaustively enumerating the feasible solutions and select the one with the highest profit. However, since there are 2^n possible solutions, the running time required for the brute-force solution becomes impossible when n gets large.

3   Algorithm Design

The 0-1 knapsack problem require whether it is to find any combination of n binary variables that satisfies a certain set of clauses C, the crucial issue in NP-completeness is whether it is possible to solve it in time polynomial in n [17-18]. So there are $N = 2^n$ possible combinations which have to be searched for any that satisfy the specified property and the question is whether we can do that in a time which is polynomial $O(n^k)$, Thus if it were possible to reduce the number of steps to a finite power of $O(n^k)$, it would yield a polynomial time algorithm for NP-complete problems [18-20].

Set a system have two registers $|R_1 >$ and $|R_2 >$, the two registers have n qubits independently, and which are labeled $x_1, x_2 \cdots x_n$. These are 2^n states which is represented as n bit strings after the Walsh-Hadamard transformation for the registers $|R_1 >$. The object is to find a unique state $|x >= (x_1, x_2 \cdots x_n)$ which satisfied the condition of the 0-1knapsack problem. The quantum algorithms design described as follow:

Step 1: Start with two registers $|R_1 >$ and $|R_2 >$ in the state $|S >= |0^n >| 0^n >$.

Step 2: Perform the Walsh-Hadamard transformation H in $|R_1 >$ on each bit independently in sequence, H:

$$H : | s > \rightarrow | s_1 >= \frac{1}{\sqrt{2^n}} \sum_{x=0}^{n-1} | x > | 0 > \tag{8}$$

Here, $|x >$ is n bit binary strings, $|x >= (x_1, x_2 \cdots x_n)$, $x_i \in \{0,1\}$, $1 \le i \le n$. The result of performing the transformation H on each bit will be a superposition of states described by all possible n bit binary strings with amplitude of each state having a magnitude equal to $2^{-n/2}$. There are 2^n possible solutions for 0-1 knapsack problem.

Step 3: Apply g to get

$$| R_1 >| \varphi_1 >= P_a U_a | s_2 > \tag{9}$$

Step 4: Perform the unitary transformation operation in $|R_1 >$

$$U_a : | s' >= \frac{(-1)^{a(x)}}{\sqrt{2^n}} \sum_{x=0}^{2^n-1} | x > \tag{10}$$

Use U_a to classify according to the capacity C of packsack,

$$U_a : | s' >= \frac{(-1)^{a(x)}}{\sqrt{2^n}} \sum_{x=0}^{2^n-1} | x > \tag{11}$$

Where the function $a(x) = \begin{cases} 1 & C > f(x) \\ 0 & C \le f(x) \end{cases}$, to any state $|x >$: In case $C > f(x)$, rotate the phase by π radians; In case $C \le f(x)$, leave the system unaltered.

After apply the transformation matrix P_a, the probability amplitude of the state that unsatisfied the condition is zero, and equally magnify the probability amplitude of the state that satisfied the condition. The transformation P_a is defined as follow:

$$P_a =< \varphi_1 | s' > \tag{12}$$

Here, the first register $|R_1>$ remained the states which satisfied the capacity of the knapsack as a result of quantum entanglement. The unitary transformation operation UP will formally proved in the section 4.

Step 5: Repeat the following unitary operations j times (the precise number of repetitions is important as discussed the paragraph of section 3.1)

$$| \varphi^{j+1} >= P_b^j U_b^j \cdots P_b^1 U_b^1 | \varphi_1 > \qquad (13)$$

Before the iteration every time, calculate the average value $c1$ in $|R_2>$, $b(x) = \begin{cases} 1 & c1 > g(x) \\ 0 & c1 \le g(x) \end{cases}$, The purpose of unitary operator U_b is to classify according to the value $c1$, rotate the phase of state in $|R_1>$ by π radians that the condition is; The phase of state is unaltered that the condition is $c1 > g(x)$.

$$U_b : (-1)^{b(x)} | x > \qquad (14)$$

The effect of transformation matrix P_b is the same as P_a, the probability amplitude of the state that unsatisfied the condition is zero, and equally magnify the probability amplitude of the state that satisfied the condition, and is defined as follows:

$$P_b^{(i+1)} =< \varphi_{i+1} | \varphi_i > \qquad (15)$$

Step 6: Repeat step 5 j times until the system is a basic state. The unitary transformation operation UP will formally proved in the next section as theorem 1.

In a practical implementation of this algorithm would involve one portion of the quantum system sensing the state and then deciding whether or not to rotate the phase. It would do it in a way so that no trace of the state of the system will be left after this operation (so as to ensure that paths leading to the same final state were indistinguishable and could interfere). The implementation does not involve a classical measurement.

The loop in 6 steps above is the heart of the algorithm. It is clear that the search in step 4 become a binary tree, the time of the iteration is the depth of this binary tree, and is decided by the value $c1$. The average value $c1$ in $|R_2>$ can be computed efficiently using only $n \log_2 n$ operations as well. The iterate equation can be constructed

$$T(2^n) = \begin{cases} C_1, & n = 1 \\ 2T(2^{n/2}) + C_2 n \log_2 n & n > 1 \end{cases} \qquad (16)$$

The answer is

$$T(2^n) = O(n^2 \log_2 n) \qquad (17)$$

The desired answer can be obtained in only $O(n^2 \log_2 n)$ steps.

4   Experimental Results

In this quantum algorithm of the 0-1 knapsack problem, the operations required are, first, the Walsh-Hadamard transforms, and second, the conditional phase shift operation both of which are relatively easy as compared to operations required for other quantum mechanical algorithms.

The implementation of the quantum transform UP is very similar to the diffusion transform D of the Grover's algorithm, and can be express from one representation to the other. Let A as input representation before the transformation and B as representation after the transformation, $\{|a_m>\}$ is the basic vector of the representation A and $\{|b_n>\}$ is the basic vector of, it was discussed in the previous section that the representation A satisfies the complete condition. Now we discuss the contact of the unitary state vector $|\phi>$ in this two representation.

$$<b_n|\phi>=\sum_n<b_n|a_m><a_m|\phi> \tag{18}$$

Expression (18) can be written as $\phi(B) = S\phi(A)$, the $\phi(B)$ and $\phi(A)$ are respectively expressed the representation A and B. the matrix S is defined as follows:

$$S_{mn} =<b_n|a_m> \tag{19}$$

The matrix S is a transformation matrix from the representation A to the representation B. because:

$$<a_m|b_n>=<b_n|a_m>^*= S_{mn}^* = S_{nm}^+ \tag{20}$$

So $S^{-1} = S^+$.

It is clear that the transformation keep unitary from one representation to the other representation B. The dimensionality of the matrix S can be identical also can be different; the effectiveness of the designed algorithm has been proved.

It is important to calculate the average value $c1$ in the register $|R_2>$ before the iteration every time. In order to get the average value $c1$, we firstly use the algorithm in [8] to sum the quantum data in $|R_2>$, and then we can calculate the average value $c1$. The addition algorithm in uses an approximate quantum Fourier transforms.

5   Conclusions

The designed algorithm combined the principles of the Grover's quantum mechanical algorithm and the approximate quantum Fourier transforms. The implementation of the quantum transform UP used the principle of Grover's quantum mechanical algorithms and calculation of the average value $c1$ in $|R_2>$ used the principle of the quantum Fourier transform Alternatively, it might combine other quantum algorithms to develop a fast algorithm for other NP-search problem in general. The algorithm for the 0-1 Knapsack problem is an example of such an application.

Acknowledgment. This project is supported by National High-Tech Research and Development Program of China under grant No. 2007AA04Z111.

References

1. Buhrman, H., de Wolf, R., Durr, C., Heiligman, M., Hoyer, P., Magniez, F., Santha, M.: Quantum Algorithms for Element Distinctness. In: 16th Annual Conference on Computational Complexity, pp. 131–137 (2001)
2. Aaronson, S.: Quantum Lower Bound for the Collision Problem. In: Proceedings of the 34th Annual ACM Symp. on Theory of Computing, pp. 635–642 (2002)
3. Ambainis, A.: Quantum lower bounds by quantum arguments. Journal of Computer and System Sciences 64, 750–767 (2002)
4. Shi, Y.: Quantum lower bounds for the collision and the element distinctness problems. In: Proceedings of Symposium on the Foundations of Computer Science (2002)
5. Vergis, A., Striglitz, K., Dickinson, B.: The complexity of analog computation. Math. Comp. Simul. 28, 91–113 (1986)
6. Nie, S.: Research on Collaborative Manufacturing Resources Optimization Deployment based on DNA genetic algorithm. Doctoral Dissertation of South China University of Technology, pp. 34–66 (2010)
7. Zhong, Y., Yu, X.: Quantum Associative Memory based on Entanglement. Chinese Journal of Quantum Electronics 6, 873–878 (2005)
8. Zhong, Y., Yu, X.: A Quantum Algorithm to Resolve TSP. Computer Engineering & Design 6, 1032–1033 (2004)
9. Lian, G.Y., Huang, K.L., Chen, J.H., Gao, F.Q.: Training algorithm for radial basis function neural network based on quantum-behaved particle swarm optimization. International Journal of Computer Mathematics 87(3), 629–641 (2010)
10. Yang, J.-P., Chen, Y.-J., Huang, H.-C., Tsai, S.-N., Hwang, R.-C.: The Estimations of Mechanical Property of Rolled Steel Bar by Using Quantum Neural Network. Advances in Intelligent and Soft Computing 56(6), 799–806 (2009)
11. McElroy, J., Gader, P.: Generalized Encoding and Decoding Operators for Lattice-Based Associative Memories. Neural Networks 20(10), 1674–1678 (2009)
12. Trugenberger, C.A., Diamantini, C.M.: Diamantini Quantum Associative Pattern Retrieval. Quantum Inspired Intelligent Systems 12(1), 103–113 (2008)
13. Sun, W., He, Y.J., Meng, M.: A Novel Quantum Neural Network Model with Variable Selection for Short Term Load Forecasting. Applied Mechanics and Materials 20(3), 612–617 (2010)
14. Liu, Y., Ma, L., Ning, A.-B.: Quantum competitive decision algorithm and its application in TSP. Application Research of Computers 27(2), 586–589 (2010)
15. Oskin, M., Chong, F., Chuang, I.: A practical architecture for reliable quantum computers. IEEE Computer 35(1), 79–87 (2002)
16. Shi, Y.: Quantum lower bounds for the collision and the element distinctness problems. In: Proceedings of Symposium on the Foundations of Computer Science (2002)

17. Zhu, J.B., Yao, T.S.: FIFA-based Text Classification. Journal of Chinese Information Processing (9), 20–26 (2003)
18. Yang, J.: Research of quantum genetic algorithm and its application in blind source separation. ACTA Electronic Sonica 20(1), 62–68 (2003)
19. Xie, G., Fan, H., Cao, L.: A quantum neural computational network model. Journal of Fudan University (Natural Science) 43(5), 700–703 (2004)
20. Han, K.H.: Genetic quantum algorithm and its application to combinatorial optimization problem. In: IEEE Proc. of the 2000 Congress on Evolutionary Computation, pp. 1354–1360. IEEE Press, San Diego (2000)

The Application of Improved Quantum Self-organizing Neural Network Model in Web Users Access Mode Mining

Fan Yang[1] and Shuzhi Nie[2]

[1] Dept. of Computer Science and Engineering,
Guangzhou Vocational & Technical Institute of Industry & Commerce
510850 Guangzhou, China
yfyf9@126.com
[2] Dept. of Electronics & Information Technology, Jiangmen Polytechnic
529090 Jiangmen, China
sznie778@163.com

Abstract. In this paper, Put forward a model of web users access mode mining, which is based on improved quantum self-organizing neural network, solved a series of interest problems of web users mining, used related superposition features of quantum states, accomplished the operations of automatic classification and statistical analysis, output some neurons whose membership grade is greater than threshold value. Testing results show that the improved model is feasible, has stronger model generalization ability and generalization ability in the case of sufficient training samples, can better perform clustering operations for web users, dynamically generate personalized web pages for different classes web users.

Keywords: quantum computation, self-organizing neural network, data mining.

1 Introduction

Web mining is the research focus and frontier of current computer science, application of neural network technology can enhance the intelligence of web mining [1-2]. Self-organizing neural network is a non-supervision, self-organizing feature map network, learns and trains parameters through competition, automatically obtain the clustering center, therefore, it has been widely used in pattern recognition, pattern control and other fields [3-5]. User's access patterns represent the interest of users access websites, by mining users access patterns, can improve web server performance, improve the site structure, identifies potential customers in e-commerce, and increases the quality of customer service [6-7]. Self-organizing neural network for users access pattern mining has some shortcomings, self-organizing neural network can only output the neurons of minimum Euclidean distance between input samples and output neurons, in other words, it is the output neurons of optimal matching, applies to the users access pattern mining, merely reflect a interest of users, ignores other interest of users, it is not suitable for users diverse interest mining [8-10].

M. Zhao and J. Sha (Eds.): ICCIP 2012, Part II, CCIS 289, pp. 385–393, 2012.

In this paper, proposed quantum self-organizing neural network algorithm, used a automatic classification and statistical analysis method of self-organizing neural network based on quantum, utilized related superposition features of quantum states, output some neurons whose membership grade is greater than threshold value, solved a variety of interest problems of users mining.

2   Model Design

A neuron can be described as a tetrad: input, weighted values, transferring functions and output; input and output are external features of neurons, weighted values and transferring functions are intrinsic properties of neurons, changes the characteristics of these four, can construct different types of neurons [11-12]. Based on the above ideas, quantum bits expressed input and weighted values of proposed quantum neurons in this paper, at the same time, this quantum neurons have a group of single-bit quantum gates, used to correct phase position of own weighted values quantum bits [13-14], it is shown in Figure 1.

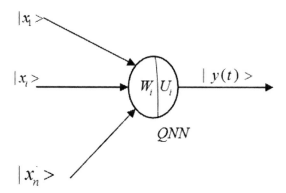

Fig. 1. The model of quantum neurons

Quantum bits sum express input and weighted values in quantum neurons model, the state of a quantum bit can be expressed as:

$$| \varphi_i >= \alpha_i |0> + \beta_i |1>, (i = 1, 2, \cdots, n) \qquad (1)$$

In formula (1), α_i and β_i are complex numbers, and meet the following normalization conditions:

$$| \alpha_i |^2 + | \beta_i |^2 = 1, (i = 1, 2, \cdots n) \qquad (2)$$

A pair of complex numbers m and n that satisfies formula (1) and formula (2) is called the probability amplitude of a quantum bit, so quantum bit also can be expressed as $[\alpha_i \ \beta_i]^T$, $| X >= [| x_1 >, | x_2 >, \cdots, | x_n >]^T$ is quantum input vector,

$|W> = [|w_1>, |w_2>, \cdots, |w_n>]^T$ is quantum weights vector, input-output relationship of quantum neurons can be shown as follows:

$$y = f(<W \mid X>) = \left| \sum_{i=1}^{n} <w_i \mid x_i> \right| \qquad (3)$$

In formula (3), f is modulo operator, as a transferring function, can map the input of quantum neurons to a real number, single-bit quantum gates U_i use the correction phase by phase rotation gates W_i.

Map network model of quantum self-organizing feature is a two-layer network, includes input layer and competitive layer, it is different from map network of general self-organizing feature, which is formed by quantum neurons, it is shown in Figure 2.

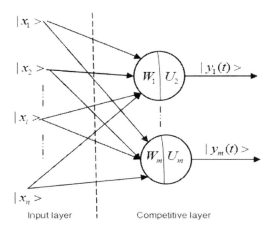

Fig. 2. The model of map network

The model is a two-layer structure, input layer and competitive layer contains n and m quantum neurons respectively, the input and output relationship of network can be shown as follows:

$$y_j = f(<W_j \mid X>) = \left| \sum_{i=1}^{n} <w_{ji} \mid x_i> \right| \qquad (4)$$

3   Clustering Algorithm Design

Set up clustering sample sets is $|X^1, X^2, \cdots X^n|$, $X^k = (x_1^k, x_2^k, \cdots x_n^k)(k = 1, 2, \cdots P)$, these samples belong to the class of d mode, recorded $M_j(j = 1, 2, \cdots, d)$ is the collection of each type survey samples, $D_j(j = 1, 2, \cdots d)$ is a collection corresponds to competitive and victorious neurons serial number in M_j model.

To achieve quantum states description of Euclidean space real vector clustering sample $X = (x_1, x_2, \cdots x_n)$, defined conversion formula is shown as follows:

$$| X >= [| x_1 >, | x_2 >, \cdots | x_n >)]^T \tag{5}$$

$$| x_2 >= \cos\left(\frac{2\pi}{1+e^{-x_i}}\right) | 0 > + \sin\left(\frac{2\pi}{1+e^{-x_i}}\right) | >=$$

$$\left[\cos\left(\frac{2\pi}{1+e^{-x_i}}\right), \sin\left(\frac{2\pi}{1+e^{-x_i}}\right)\right]^T \quad (i = 1,2,\cdots,n) \tag{6}$$

Defined $| X >= [| x_1 >, | x_2 >, \cdots | x_n >)]^T$, $| Y >= [| y_1 >, | y_2 >, \cdots | y_n >)]^T$ are n-dimensional quantum states vector, defined the similarity coefficient of $| X >$ and $| Y >$ are shown as follows:

$$r =< X | Y >= \left| \sum_{i=1}^{n} \frac{< x_i | y_i >}{\sqrt{< x_i | x_i >< y_i | y_i >}} \right| \tag{7}$$

In formula (7), the similarity coefficient of input samples $| X^k >$ and connection weight vector $| W_j >$ of competitive layer neurons j are shown as follows:

$$r_j^k =< X^k | W_j >= \left| \sum_{i=1}^{n} \frac{< x_{ki} | w_{ji} >}{\sqrt{< x_{ki} | x_{ki} >< w_{ji} | w_{ji} >}} \right| \tag{8}$$

Supposed the node j^* with the largest similarity coefficient win in the competition, and then j^* meet the following conditions:

$$r_{j^*}^k = \max_{j \in \{1,2,\cdots m\}} \left\{ r_j^k \right\} \tag{9}$$

Then adjusted $| W_{j^*} >$ to make the weight vector $| W_{j^*} >$ moving to the direction of sample $| X^k >$, finally get model categories that represented by the output $| X^k >$ of the node j^*.

The main steps of quantum weighted values clustering algorithm include: coarse adjustment of learning phase, refined learning phase, and application phase.

In coarse adjustment of learning phase, the detailed steps of are shown as follows:

1) Initialize the network weighted values $| w_{ij} >= \cos(\theta) | 0 > + \sin(\theta) | 1 >$, $\theta = 2\pi \times rnd$, rnd is a random number between 0 and 1. Input new vector $| X >= [| X_1(t) >, | X_2(t) >, \ldots, | X_m(t) >]^T$, $| X_i(t) >$ is the i-dimensional component of samples in time t(i=1,2,...,m), supposed the total study times is T=T1+T2.

2) Calculate the distance between sample vector and weighted value, it is shown as follows:

$$| d_j >= | X - W_j | = \sqrt{\sum_{i=1}^{m} (| x_i > - | W_{ij}(t) >)^2} \quad (j = 1,2,\ldots,n) \tag{10}$$

3) Search the minimum distance, found competitive layer nodes j^* of the most suited input sample vector, it is shown as follows:

$$d_{j^*} = \min d_j \quad (j = 1,2,\ldots,n) \tag{11}$$

4) Adjust weighted values in coarse adjustment of learning phase, set T1=100, η_0 =0.4, σ_0 =3m/2, m is the amount of competitive layer neurons, Calculate the neighborhood function value according to formula (10), the adjustment of Weighted value is shown as follows:

$$| w_{ij}(t+1) >=| w_{ij}(t) > +\eta(t)N_{ic}(t)(| x > -| w_{ij}(t) >) \qquad (12)$$

5) Gradually descending the learning rate and neighborhood width according to formula (10) and formula (11).

6) Return to Step (3), until learn all learning samples again.

7) Set t=t+1, until t>T1. In refined learning phase, the detailed steps of are shown as follows:

8) Set T2=500, η_0 =0.03, $\sigma(0)$ =1, repeat step 2) to step 6), train the easy confusing points in the second time, decrease neighborhood width and learning rate according to the following formulas:

$$\eta(t) = \eta_0(1-t/T_2) \qquad (13)$$

$$\sigma(t+1) = \sigma_0(1-t/T_2) \qquad (14)$$

9) Select another set of samples vector to provide network input, return to step 3) until the sample input is end or the value of plus item is reduced to zero, until excitatory neurons corresponded with input samples steadily.

10) Set t=t+1, learning phase is completed when t>T2.

11) Store and output connecting weight coefficients of all the output neurons. In application phase, the detailed steps of are shown as follows:

12) Normalize weighted coefficient vector of input samples and connected output neurons, to ensure the Euclidean distance of input samples and output neurons is between zero and two, it is shown as follows:

$$| x'_{ij} >= \frac{| x_{ij} >}{\sqrt{< x_{1j} | x_{1j} > + < x_{2j} | x_{2j} > + ... + < x_{nj} | x_{nj} >}} \qquad (15)$$

$$| w'_{ij} >= \frac{| w_{ij} >}{\sqrt{< w_{1j} | w_{1j} > + < w_{2j} | w_{2j} > + ... + < w_{nj} | w_{nj} >}} \qquad (16)$$

13) Read a new vector as the input sample of network.

14) According to the Euclidean distance d_j and the above defined membership function, calculate the membership degree of input samples to each neuron, according to formula (11), it is shown as follows:

$$\mu(C_j(X)) = \mu(d_j(X),0,\sqrt{0.2}) = e^{-\frac{d_j(X)^2}{0.4}} \qquad (17)$$

In output classification phase, the detailed steps of are shown as follows:

15) Set threshold value, consider its characteristic of Gaussian function, set it as 0.6 in this paper, Output neuron is the class of input samples when $\mu(C_j(X))$ is bigger 0.6, output this class and its membership degree of input samples.

16) Return to step 13), until haven't new input samples.

4   Training Results

Quantum self-organizing neural network model is a two-layer neural network model, include input layer and competitive layer, input layer has twenty-two neurons, represented the twenty-two site pages that can respond user accessing interest, output layer has ten neurons, it is mean that divide web users into 10 categories. $|W_{ij}>$ is connection weighted coefficient between input layer and output layer, can initialized to a small random number, after a period of training, connected with one output neuron $|W_{ij}>$ that represents the characteristics of such neurons. $\mu_1, \mu_2, ..., \mu_n$ is output of the model, represent the various degree belong to input samples, its value is between zero and one. The use of site structure is come from Jiangxi Xinhua Bookstore in this paper, and appropriately changed it according to the need. Used $|X>=[|x_1>,|x_2>,\cdots|x_{22}>)]^T$ represent twenty-two pages of input layer, which represented the definite pages in sites is shown in Table .1:

Table 1. Classification table

Item	Category Name	Item	Category Name
X1	humanity	X2	social sciences
X3	management	X4	economic
X5	mathematic	X6	physics/ mechanics
X7	Chemistry/ chemical engineering/ material	X8	geosciences/ astronomy
X9	biology	X10	agriculture/ foodstuff
X11	medicine	X12	electric
X13	Computer /network	X14	mechanical
X15	building/ construction	X16	circumstances/ energy
X17	communication /aviation /aerospace	X18	music
X19	movie	X20	TV
X21	cartoon	X22	synthesis

We didn't set the whole site page as a model input in this paper, because there are too many pages in the sites, but there are only a few pages can respond to user accessing interest. Classified the page in this paper, all of the pages shown in Table .1 is divided into 22 directions, for example, X13 represents books of accessing computer and network, when users access   a computer class book "Java programming ideas", added 1 count of X13 would not make the model scale too large, also helpfully adjust website structure.

Selected the number of user sessions more than five users log mining, which made the access mode of mining more effective. After preprocessed the data are shown in Table 2, the data show users viewing number of $|X>=[|x_1>,|x_2>,\cdots|x_{22}>)]^T$ pages since each user registration, for example, the first data of User1 is four, indicated the user visited X1 page and its link pages four times, and display data in the form $|X>=[|x_1>,|x_2>,\cdots|x_{22}>)]^T$, about $|X>=[|x_1>,|x_2>,\cdots|x_{22}>)]^T$ meaning please refer to Table .2.

Table 2. Pre-processed data

User	Data
user1	[4015000200010002212700]
user2	[1500100302302000300204]
user3	[3500000001100000100103]
user4	[1200100302100000200000]
user5	[0000100101000000300002]

After the training steps are 50 and 1000, the model output results are shown in Table .3.

When the training steps is 50, because the training sample is too small, cannot identified some users' access behavior, therefore, these users did not meet the conditions of data output. Analyzed the output of user data, the output of user 2 and user 3 both are X[2], indicates the two users both are interested in the social sciences; when training steps is 1000, user 1, user 2 and user 3 both have more interest, for example, user 1 has wide interest, likes to see books on the humanities, also likes economy and TV, so can be accurately divided into three categories: X[1],X[4] and X[20]. Through analysis of all data can get a conclusion, whether user has single interest or wide interest, after 1000 steps training, always can cluster users accurately.

Table 3. Training results

Input			Steps(50)	Steps(1000)	
group	item	value		item	value
1	X[2]	0.6248		X[1]	0.5731
				X[4]	0.5062
				X[20]	0.5208
2	X[2]	0.64504		X[2]	0.6155
				X[8]	0.5442
				X[11]	0.4565
				X[22]	0.4662
3	X[2]	0.7023		X[1]	0.4528
				X[2]	0.3453
				X[22]	0.2348
4	X[2]	null		X[8]	0.3430
5	X[2]	null		X[17]	0.5651
6	X[2]	0.9238		X[1]	0.8703
				X[4]	0.6016
				X[20]	0.7727
7	X[2]	0.8437		X[2]	0.7137
				X[8]	0.8937
				X[11]	0.6308
				X[22]	0.6159
8	X[2]	0.8343		X[1]	0.6010
				X[2]	0.6238
				X[22]	0.6021
9	X[2]	null		X[8]	0.8375
10	X[2]	null		X[17]	0.8058

5   Conclusions

Based on the above experiments and analysis, concluded the model of quantum self-organizing neural networks based on users access pattern mining is effective, can better cluster user in the case of sufficient training samples, thus for different categories of users dynamically generate personalized web pages, provides personalized service. Compared with other models, the correctness and correct rates of the model of clustering have improved to varying degrees in this model, it is due to introduce the quantum computing mechanism, so the model has more stronger pattern general ability and generalization ability.

Acknowledgment. This project is supported by National High-Tech Research and Development Program of China under grant No. 2007AA04Z111.

References

1. McElroy, J., Gader, P.: Generalized Encoding and Decoding Operators for Lattice-Based Associative Memories. Neural Networks 20(10), 1674–1678 (2009)
2. Trugenberger, C.A., Diamantini, C.M.: Quantum Associative Pattern Retrieval. Quantum Inspired Intelligent Systems 12(1), 103–113 (2008)
3. Sun, W., He, Y.J., Meng, M.: A Novel Quantum Neural Network Model with Variable Selection for Short Term Load Forecasting. Applied Mechanics and Materials 20(3), 612–617 (2010)
4. Lian, G.Y., Huang, K.L., Chen, J.H., Gao, F.Q.: Training algorithm for radial basis function neural network based on quantum-behaved particle swarm optimization. International Journal of Computer Mathematics 87(3), 629–641 (2010)
5. Zhang, D., Wang, D., Zheng, W.: Chinese text classification system based on VSM. Journal of Tsinghua University (Science and Technology) (9), 1288–1291 (2003)
6. Zhu, J.B., Yao, T.S.: FIFA-based Text Classification. Journal of Chinese Information Processing (9), 20–26 (2003)
7. Xie, G.J., Zhuang, Z.Q.: Research on Quantum Neural Computational Models. Journal of Circuits and System 7(6), 83–88 (2002)
8. Li, C.Z.: Quantum Communication and Quantum Computation. The National University of Defense Technology Press (2000)
9. Yang, J.-P., Chen, Y.-J., Huang, H.-C., Tsai, S.-N., Hwang, R.-C.: The Estimations of Mechanical Property of Rolled Steel Bar by Using Quantum Neural Network. Advances in Intelligent and Soft Computing 56(6), 799–806 (2009)
10. Yang, J.: Research of quantum genetic algorithm and its application in blind source separation. ACTA Electronic Sonica 20(1), 62–68 (2003)
11. Xie, G., Fan, H., Cao, L.: A quantum neural computational network model. Journal of Fudan University (Natural Science) 43(5), 700–703 (2004)
12. Xie, G., Zhuang, Z.: A quantum competitive learning algorithm. Chinese Journal of Quantum Electronics 20(1), 42–46 (2003)
13. Lu, M., Li, F., Pang, S., Lu, Y., Zhou, L.: Improved text classification methods based on weighted adjustments. Journal of Tsinghua University (Science and Technology) (4), 513–515 (2003)
14. Li, P., Yan, Y., Jia, W.-J., Bai, J.-F.: Short-term load forecasting based on quantum neural network by evidential theory. Power System Protection and Control 38(16), 49–53 (2010)

Design and Implementation of High Frequency Weakly-Radiative Wireless Power Charging System

Linlin Tan, Jiaming Zhao, Xueliang Huang,
Wei Wang, Hao Qiang, and Yingjun Sang

College of Electrical Engineering, Southeast University
210096 Nanjing, China
linsky@seu.edu.cn

Abstract. As the rapid development of electrical equipment, more and more mobile portable devices rely on battery power supply. If the energy can be provided wirelessly, the device can greatly reduce the dependence on the battery. In this paper, mutual inductance theory was used to analyze the system and a wireless charging system was designed which can achieve maximum 300W power transmission and the efficiency is up to 80% at the distance of 50cm. Finally we proposed a method based on adjusting the duty cycle of the DC/DC switch tubes to achieve stable voltage output of the system which can solve the issue that output voltage is sensitive to transmission distance. Theoretical and experimental results show that the system has good transmission characteristics and output voltage stability, suitable for resistive and battery load.

Keywords: wireless charging, rectifier, transmission distance, transmission efficiency.

1   Introduction

Magnetically coupled resonance wireless power transfer technology is research focus in power transmission area at present. This technology can realize power energy transmission at meter class and high transmission efficiency which was applied in implanted medical devices, small robots, and portable mobile devices, wireless charging electric vehicles areas etc[1-3]. German branch of Sony Corporation of Japan introduced a magnetic resonance wireless power TV in October 2009, which can achieve 60W power transmission at the distance of 50cm[4]. Subsequently, Haier launched the concept of "no-tail TV" based on this technology, whose safety has passed certification like FCC, IEEE, CCC[5] and other standards. Although the technology of magnetic coupling in the medium-range wireless transmission has a good advantage and has the conceptual product be launched, but there is a long way to go for practical application.

   MCRWPT (magnetically coupled resonant wireless power transmission) system makes use of near-field ($R \ll \lambda$, R is the radius of transmit and receive coil, λ is wavelength) magnetic resonance techniques[6], compared with traditional ICPT

M. Zhao and J. Sha (Eds.): ICCIP 2012, Part II, CCIS 289, pp. 394–402, 2012.

system (inductively coupled power transmission) the transmission distance has been greatly improved, but the system control complexity and difficulty of implementation have increased correspondingly. In order to achieve the purpose of effective transmission namely energy exchange between the two resonance coils, MCRWPT system needs to set parameters of transmit and receive coils reasonably to make transmit and receive coils achieve their own self-resonant state at certain frequency.

Through the analysis, it is not difficult to find that to make MCRWPT system operate stably and efficiently. It must meet the followings:

1) Transmit and receive coils have good symmetry of physical structure and electrical parameter, especially the match of electrical parameters is a prerequisite to ensure the system work efficiently.

2) To make transmit and receive coils with high quality factor, the inherent loss parameters of them must be minimized. In literature [7], it proposed that the use of superconducting materials (minus the inherent loss of the coils) can increase the transmission distance nearly 50 times under the same conditions.

3) Set resonance frequency of the system reasonably according to the transmission distance and coil parameter to make the system work in the best near-field conditions.

Based on the above analysis, this paper designs a MCRWPT system shown in Figure 1. High-frequency power supply is connected with single-turn drive coil, The energy of the drive coil is coupled to the transmitter coil by "electromagnetic coupling", on the one hand, this method can reduce the impact of the power to the transmitter coil effectively to play the role of isolation, on the other hand because most of the power system using oscillation theory produce high-frequency power, the drive coil participate in the oscillation of power system at the same time (reducing the number of turns can help to improve the system's output oscillation frequency). Transmit coil and receive coil are designed with the same topology (mechanical and electrical), which can achieve the resonance of physical and electronic structure easily. In order to reduce the effect of the introduction of the load has on the receive coil parameters, a single-turn load coil leads out power on the receive coil by inductive coupling approach. Through the above design can maximize guarantee the independence of transmit and receive coils to achieve the system resonant better.

The system schematic diagram is shown in Figure 1, the energy can be efficiently transmitted depends on the design of transmit and receive coils. The frequency of high-frequency power supply is generally in the range of MHz, therefore, the wavelength λ is ten meters to several hundred meters when the system is working. In the near-field conditions as we known, electric field is limited inside the capacitance, the energy is mainly passed out through the coils magnetic field. As a result, there are two kinds of consumption patterns when energy transfer in space, radiation loss and ohmic loss. At low frequency, the energy is mainly consumed by internal loss (ohmic loss) of the resonator, in the case of high frequency, mainly through the scattering consumption (radiation loss) of space. Therefore, to ensure system exchange energy in the near-field, the size parameters of transmit and receive coils should satisfy $\lambda/R \geq 70$, which is generally considered to be the optimum range for energy exchange under the near-field.

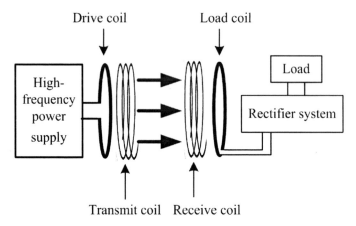

Drive coil   Load coil

Transmit coil   Receive coil

Fig. 1. Schematic diagram of the system transfer model

We use mutual inductance theory study the transmission model of the system in the system modeling analysis. In this paper, a wireless charging system based on magnetically coupled resonance technology is researched, and a method to stabilize the output voltage under the mode of vary distance transmission is proposed, the results show that the system has stable output voltage under this control method. It is worth saying that although electromagnetic environment and electromagnetic compatibility (EMC) problems of MCRWPT system are not mentioned in this paper, but it is still one of the main issues to consider in the process of system design later.

2   Theoretical Analysis and Modeling

2.1   Theoretical Analysis of MCRWPT System

This paper uses mutual inductance theory analyze the MCRWPT system[8], a system schematic is established as shown in Figure 2 according to the diagram shown in Fig.1. Assume the high-frequency power supply is U_s, the output frequency is ω, the equivalent resistance is R_s. L_1, L_t, L_r, L_2, respectively, for the equivalent inductance of the drive coil, the transmit coil, the receive coil and the load coil, R_1, R_r, R_t, R_2, respectively corresponding to the equivalent resistance of each coil, C_t, C_r are the compensation capacitors of transmit and receive coils. R_L is the equivalent load. M_{mn} is the mutual inductance between coils m and n. For a more intuitive analysis of the power transfer system as a whole as well as simplify the calculations, this paper focuses on analysis of energy exchange between the transmit coil and receive coil (This section is a major part of energy loss which determines the overall transmission efficiency). In a real system, M_{1r}, M_{12}, M_{2t} are ignored.

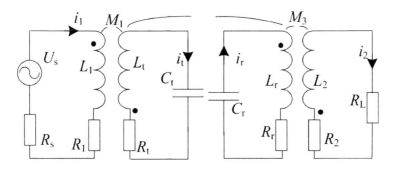

Fig. 2. System schematic

According to KVL and KCL, expression equations of the system shown in Fig.2 are listed as below:

$$
\begin{cases}
\left(j\omega L_1 + R_1 + R_s \right)i_1 + j\omega M_{1t}i_t = U_s \\[2mm]
\left(j\omega L_t + R_t + \dfrac{1}{j\omega C_t} \right)i_t + j\omega M_{t1}i_1 + j\omega M_{tr}i_r = 0 \\[2mm]
\left(j\omega L_r + R_r + \dfrac{1}{j\omega C_r} \right)i_r + j\omega M_{rt}i_t + j\omega M_{r2}i_2 = 0 \\[2mm]
\left(j\omega L_2 + R_2 + R_L \right)i_2 + j\omega M_{2t}i_r = 0
\end{cases}
\tag{1}
$$

By equation(1), when use mutual inductance theory analyzes the system model, the mutual inductance is a link between the two coils. Therefore, the solution of mutual inductance between two coils is one of the key to build an accurate model of the system. Currently, there is a variety of methods for solving mutual inductance between two spiral coils. Equation (2) gives a common method for solving the mutual inductance, assuming the horizontal displacement between the two coils is h. The mutual inductance between transmit and receive coils according to the Neumann formula is [9]:

$$
M = \frac{\mu_0}{4\pi} \int_{L_r} \int_{L_t} \frac{d\mathbf{l}_t d\mathbf{l}_r}{\mathbf{r}}
\tag{2}
$$

Where,

$$
\mathbf{r} = \sqrt{\begin{array}{l}\left[R\cos(\theta+\phi) - R\cos\theta \right]^2 + \\ \left[R\sin(\theta+\phi) + h - R\sin\theta \right]^2 + d^2\end{array}}
$$
, $dl_t dl_r = R\cos\varphi\, d\varphi\, d\theta$, therefore, the equation

(2) can be simplified as $\pi/2\mu_0 R^2/d^3$ [10] under the condition of $R \ll d \ll \lambda$ ($d/R=3\sim10$)[11]. Because in the medium-range distance, the mutual inductance between two coils is only influenced by the coils radius and the distance, the small-scale change of horizontal displacement does little influence on the mutual inductance parameter.

2.2   Rectifier Circuit Modeling

The power transfer process of the system is described above, we can see the system's transmission efficiency is inversely proportional to the distance of six times, and therefore it is more sensitive to changes of the distance. In order to make the system meet the requirements of the load. The system need to be AC/DC conversion to achieve constant voltage or constant current output under change distance. As a result, in this paper we design a charge control circuit shown in Fig.3.

Bringing high-frequency output voltage of load coils into the full-bridge rectifier to obtain DC voltage whose amplitude changes with distance, and then use DC / DC converter circuit regulate voltage, in which sample the output current or load voltage as a feedback signal of control circuit. Assume that the output voltage of load coil circuit is $U_L e^{(j\omega t + \delta)}$, so the average voltage after the full bridge rectified is $E_L = 0.9 U_L$, suppose if the make-and-break ratio of switching tube $\alpha = t_{on}/T$, here the conduction time of Chopper switch is t_{on}, T is chopping period. The output voltage through the chopper is approximately $V_0 = E_L \alpha / (1-\alpha) = 0.9 U_L \alpha / (1-\alpha)$.

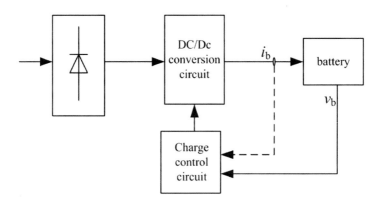

Fig. 3. Charge control circuit diagram

The charging circuit diagram of system is shown in Fig.4, in order to ensure stable output voltage $V_0 = 0.9 U_L \alpha / (1-\alpha)$ in the case of changes in transmission distance. We induct a new variable $\xi(d)$, the introduction of the impact coefficient $\xi(d)$ denotes the output voltage variation coefficient with distance and input voltage, clearly ξ is a function of d, in order to meet the output voltage V_0 stable, the parameter $\xi(d) t_{on}/t_{off}$ should be constant. Therefore, if we know the changing regularity of $\xi(d)$, the stability of voltage V_0 can be achieved by controlling α.

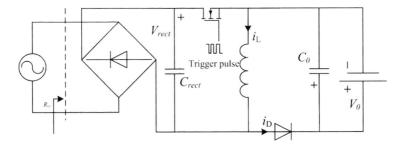

Fig. 4. Control circuit diagram

3   Experimental Study

The system overall transmission efficiency is determined by the power wireless transmission efficiency, but the power wireless transmission efficiency will change dramatically with different resonant frequency, coils size, load resistance and transfer distance. And the system transmission power is associated with mutual inductance between the coils and the input voltage, In order to further validation the above theoretical analysis and design process, this paper designed a set of 25 cm of the coils radius of wireless power supply system, and coils wire for 5 mm copper pipe. Use high frequency rectifier diodes for rectification, and through the DC/DC transformation to realize the stable output voltage, the experimental system is shown in Fig.5.

Fig. 5. Experimental devices of the system

In order to study intuitively, the main parameters of the experimental system are shown in Table 1.

By contrast, what can be seen from Table 1 is the internal resistance of the coil L_1 and L_2 is much smaller than R_t, R_r and can be neglected. By equation (2), the mutual inductance between the coils is related with transmission distance, horizontal

Table 1. Main parameters of the system

Name	Value
N_1, N_t, N_r, N_2	1,3,3,1
L_1, L_t, L_r, L_2	1.59μH,8.64μH, 8.64μH, 1.59μH
R_1, R_t, R_r, R_2	10.93mΩ, 214mΩ, 214mΩ, 10.93mΩ
f	2.25MHz

displacement, deflection angle etc. The mutual inductance of the system is only associated with the coil radius and the transmission distance when deflection angle is zero namely the two coils are parallel and the horizontal displacement $h=0$. The mutual inductances between the coils by calculated are $M_{1t} \approx 1.47$e-6H, $M_{tr} \approx 3.97$e-7H, $M_{r2} \approx 1.47$e-6H when the transmission distance is 50cm.

When the system transmission distance is around 50cm the output voltage can be at 140 ± 5V by adjusting α dynamically (as Fig.6(b) shown) and the Receiving coil output voltage as Fig.6(a) shown, the transmission power and efficiency achieve maximum value when the horizontal displacement of the coil $h = 0$.

Assume the maximum received power for the load is P_0 when the transmission distance is 50cm, Fig.7 shows when the horizontal displacement between transmit coil and receive coil h ranges from -30cm to 30cm ,the curve of system output power and efficiency change with the horizontal displacement.

It can be seen that received power and efficiency of the system tends to be the basically same after system horizontal displacement changes for quite a long distance, which indicates that the MCRWPT system with weak direction. It is a beneficial character for power transmission system, which can be considered as the distance increases, the system requirements for the direction is lower.

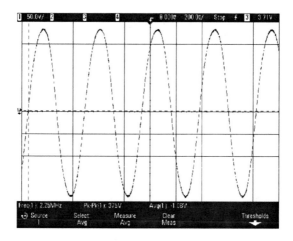

Fig. 6(a). Receiving coil output voltage

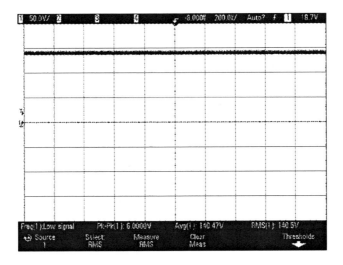

Fig. 6(b). Voltage of the load after DC/DC conversion

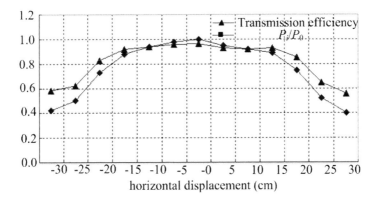

Fig. 7. Curve of system output power and efficiency change with the horizontal displacement

4   Conclusion

This paper presents a method for wireless power supply system design, and the system can achieve maximum 300W power transmission and stable voltage output at the distance of 50cm. By using mutual inductance theory to analyze the system model and do experimental verification. The results show that the system has good stability, we propose a method to achieve stable system DC output voltage by adjusting the duty cycle. But in this paper, the DC / DC converter circuit has a large overshoot, it is the shortcomings of this system design and the next job to improve.

Acknowledgment. This work was supported by Scholarship Award for Excellent Doctoral Student granted by Ministry of Education, the Sustentation Fund of the Excellent Doctoral Dissertation, the Research Innovation Program for College Graduates of Jiangsu Province (No.CXZZ11_0150) and the National Natural Science Foundation of China (No.51177011), the National Key Technology R&D Program (2011BAA07B02 &2011BAA07B05).

References

1. Guozheng, Y., Dongdong, Y., Peng, Z., et al.: Micro-robot for endoscope based on wireless power transfer. In: Proc. IEEE International Conferrnce on Mechatronics and Automation, Harbin, China, August 5-8, pp. 3577–3581 (2007)
2. Ning Low, Z., Andres Chinga, R., Tseng, R., et al.: Design and test of a high-power high-efficiency loosely coupled planar wireless power transfer system. IEEE Trans. Ind. Electron. 56, 1801–1812 (2009)
3. Jang, Y., Jovanovic, M.M.: A contactless electrical energy transmission system for portable-telephone battery chargers. IEEE Trans. Ind. Electron. 50, 520–527 (2003)
4. http://www.cnbeta.com/articles/94812.htm
5. http://digi.it.sohu.com/20100905/n274715175.shtml
6. Aristeidis, K., Joannopoulos, J.D., Soljačic, M.: Efficient wireless non-radiative mid-range energy transfer. Ann. Phys. 323(1), 34–38 (2008)
7. Sedwick Raymond, J.: Long range inductive power transfer with superconducting oscillators. Ann. Phys. 325(2), 287–299 (2010)
8. Huang, H., Huang, X.L., Tan, L.L.: Study of transmit and receive devices of wireless power transmission based on magnetic resonance. Electrical Engineering and Energy Technology 30(1), 32–35 (2011)
9. Tan, L.L., Huang, X.L., Huang, H., Zou, Y.W., Li, H.: Transfer efficiency optimal control of magnetic resonance coupled system of wireless power transfer based on frequency control. Science in China Series E: Engineering & Materials Science 54(6), 1428–1434 (2011)
10. André, K., Aristeidis, K., Robert, M., Joannopoulos, J.D., Peter, F., Soljačić, M.: Wireless power transfer via strongly coupled magnetic resonances. Science Express 317(5834), 83–86 (2007)
11. Hamam, R.E., Aristeidis, K., Joannopoulos, J.D., Soljačić, M.: Efficient weakly-radiative wireless energy transfer: An EIT-like approach. Ann. Phys. 324, 1783–1795 (2009)

Research and Realization of Digital Recognition Based on Hopfield Neural Network

Xiaofeng Wang

Computer Science and Technology School
Wuhan University of Technology
Wuhan, China
freewxf@21cn.com

Abstract. Digital recognition is an important aspect of computer model recognition. It has a very good prospect, as well as basis for post-processing. Discrete hopfield neural network simulates memory mechanism of biological neural network. Specifically, it first learns memory samples, then associates original figure according to noise figure to be identified. The paper identifys figure which have sufferd noise pollution with the use of discrete hopfield neural network. Finally, the issue puts forward certain important proposals.

Keywords: Digital recognition, Hopfield neural network, Noise.

1   Construct Network Security Risk AHP Evaluation Model

Digital recognition is an important aspect of computer model recognition. Array identification as an integral part of digital recognition has a very high application value in management factor such as commercial paper. Recently, there are many methods for digital recognition, such as fuzzy recognition, probabilistic identification and neural network recognition. Discrete Hopfield neural network with self-learning, self-organization and other excellent characteristics can be used in digital recognition and has the irreplaceable advantages which other methods cannot be replaced.

In our daily life, we often encounter many identification problems with noise character such as vehicle license plate number and vehicle license in transport system. Vehicles in use withstand wind and the sun, resulting in blurred fonts of license which is difficult to identify. Therefore, how to extract complete information from incomplete character is a key issue of character recognition. Array identification as an integral part of character recognition has a very high application value in postal, transport and commercial paper. Recently, there are many methods for digital recognition, such as fuzzy recognition, probabilistic identification and neural network recognition. The traditional methods of digital identification cannot properly identified on the digital in the case of interference, while discrete hopfield neural network has functions of associative memory and optimization, and also have fast convergence of the calculation. In this paper, I will use these features of discrete Hopfield neural network

M. Zhao and J. Sha (Eds.): ICCIP 2012, Part II, CCIS 289, pp. 403–410, 2012.
© Springer-Verlag Berlin Heidelberg 2012

to identify digit. At the same time, I will identify figure sufferd noise pollution under interference situation through simulation experiment and prove the effect of discrete hopfield neural network. [1-2].

2   The Principle of Discrete Hopfield Neural Network

2.1   Basic Structure of Discrete Hopfield Neural Network

Discrete Hopfield neural network has associative memory function. Recently, more and more researchers try to apply Hopfield neural network to fault diagnosis, classification, risk assessment of project, pattern recognition and other fields. Hopfield network is a fully connected model of neural network which open up a new avenue of research for development process of artificial neural network. It uses its features and learning method which are different from level neural networks to simulate memory mechanism of biological neural networks. So it can be used for associative memory, function optimization, pattern recognition and other important areas. The structure of Hopfield network is very simple, which is a single level feedback of non-linear network. That is, the output of each node entirely feedback to the input of other node and the entire network does not exist feedback. [3].

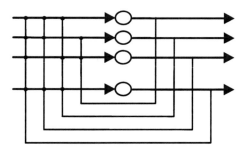

Fig. 1. Basic structure of discrete hopfield neural network

2.2   Learning Process of Discrete Hopfield Neural Network

In fact, the learning process of Hopfield network is weight adjustment process. Its purpose is to adjust connection weights, then to make the stable equilibrium state of the network to reach agreement with the expected state.. Hopfield network often use Hebb learning rule. The weight adjustment rule: if the i-th and j-th neuron at the same time in the excited state, the connection between them should be increased, hence weight increased.

$$\Delta\omega_{ij} = a y_i y_j \qquad\qquad (a > 0)$$

Suppose there are p orthogonal required steady-state network

$$V^s = (V_1^s, V_2^s, ... V_n^s), \quad s = 1, 2, ..., p,$$

then

$$\omega_{ij} = \sum_{s=1}^{p} V_i^s V_j^s$$

If increase new steady state, then:

$$\omega_{ij}' = \omega_{ij} + V_i^{p+1} V_j^{p+1}$$

If the steady-state is a memory, then the process from the initial state to convergence steady-state is the process of finding the memory. Specifically, the initial state can be considered given part of information and the convergence process can be considered as the process of finding fully information from partial information. As the network can converge to a stable state, it achieves the associative memory function. An important feature of associative memory is training mode reflected by the noise input mode.

2.3   Operation Steps of Discrete Hopfield Neural Network

- Set the network weights. Generally use the outer product method. When the calculation is completed, it remains unchanged.

- Initialize the network state. The mode is set to the initial state of the network status, which is noise figure after adding a certain probability.

- Iterative convergence. Randomly select a certain neurons state, iteratively until all the neurons in the same sate.

- Network output.

3   Used in Digital Identification

3.1   The Establishment of Relevant Data and Program Files

Following design a Hopfield network using MATLAB, make it have associative memory function and could correctly identify Arabic numbers which polluted by noise.

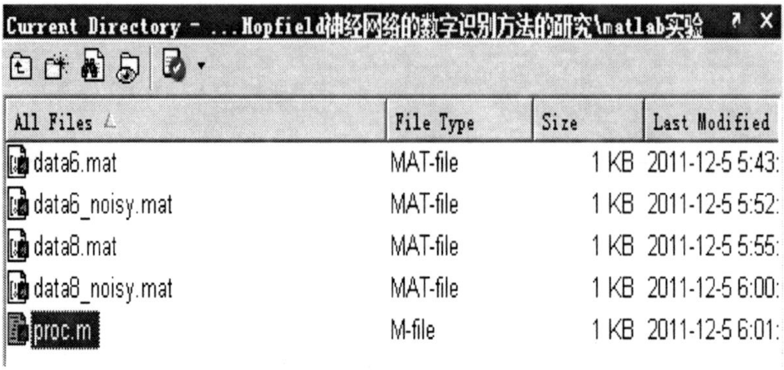

Fig. 2. Matlab experiment

According to figure 2, there are some relevant documents in MATLAB workplace. For example, mat files data6 and data8 are stored in the Arabic numerals 6 and 8 of the matrix, respectively; mat files data6_noisy and data8_noisy are stored in contaminated Arabic numerals 6 and 8 of the matrix; mat file proc is stored in the complete code.

3.2   Number of Matrix

Assume that the network consists of 10 initial state values from 0 to 9. That is, you can remember 10 kinds of figures. Each steady-state is formed by 10*10 bits matrix, which is used to simulate Arabic numerals lattice. Digital lattice, that is, the digital is divided into many small boxes and each small box corresponds to part of number. There are some figures divided into a 10*10 guidelines, which a digital box represented by 1 and space place represented by -1. Due to space reason in this issue, it only lists number 6, 8 and the corresponding pollution matrix shown in figure3 and

	1	2	3	4	5	6	7	8	9	10
1	-1.0	1.0	1.0	1.0	1.0	1.0	1.0	1.0	1.0	-1.0
2	-1.0	1.0	1.0	1.0	1.0	1.0	1.0	1.0	1.0	-1.0
3	-1.0	1.0	1.0	-1.0	-1.0	-1.0	-1.0	-1.0	-1.0	-1.0
4	-1.0	1.0	1.0	-1.0	-1.0	-1.0	-1.0	-1.0	-1.0	-1.0
5	-1.0	1.0	1.0	1.0	1.0	1.0	1.0	1.0	1.0	-1.0
6	-1.0	1.0	1.0	1.0	1.0	1.0	1.0	1.0	1.0	-1.0
7	-1.0	1.0	1.0	-1.0	-1.0	-1.0	-1.0	1.0	1.0	-1.0
8	-1.0	1.0	1.0	-1.0	-1.0	-1.0	-1.0	1.0	1.0	-1.0
9	-1.0	1.0	1.0	1.0	1.0	1.0	1.0	1.0	1.0	-1.0
10	-1.0	1.0	1.0	1.0	1.0	1.0	1.0	1.0	1.0	-1.0

(a)

Fig. 3. (a) matrix of 6   (b) matrix of noised 6

	1	2	3	4	5	6	7	8	9	10
1	-1.0	-1.0	1.0	1.0	1.0	1.0	1.0	1.0	1.0	-1.0
2	-1.0	-1.0	1.0	1.0	1.0	1.0	1.0	1.0	1.0	-1.0
3	-1.0	-1.0	1.0	-1.0	1.0	1.0	-1.0	-1.0	-1.0	-1.0
4	-1.0	-1.0	1.0	-1.0	1.0	1.0	-1.0	-1.0	-1.0	-1.0
5	-1.0	-1.0	1.0	1.0	1.0	1.0	1.0	1.0	1.0	-1.0
6	-1.0	-1.0	1.0	1.0	1.0	1.0	1.0	1.0	1.0	-1.0
7	-1.0	-1.0	1.0	-1.0	1.0	1.0	-1.0	1.0	1.0	-1.0
8	-1.0	-1.0	1.0	-1.0	1.0	1.0	-1.0	1.0	1.0	-1.0
9	-1.0	-1.0	1.0	1.0	1.0	1.0	1.0	1.0	1.0	-1.0
10	-1.0	-1.0	1.0	1.0	1.0	1.0	1.0	1.0	1.0	-1.0

(b)

Fig. 3. (*continued*)

	1	2	3	4	5	6	7	8	9	10
1	-1.0	1.0	1.0	1.0	1.0	1.0	1.0	1.0	1.0	-1.0
2	-1.0	1.0	1.0	1.0	1.0	1.0	1.0	1.0	1.0	-1.0
3	-1.0	1.0	1.0	-1.0	-1.0	-1.0	-1.0	1.0	1.0	-1.0
4	-1.0	1.0	1.0	-1.0	-1.0	-1.0	-1.0	1.0	1.0	-1.0
5	-1.0	1.0	1.0	1.0	1.0	1.0	1.0	1.0	1.0	-1.0
6	-1.0	1.0	1.0	1.0	1.0	1.0	1.0	1.0	1.0	-1.0
7	-1.0	1.0	1.0	-1.0	-1.0	-1.0	-1.0	1.0	1.0	-1.0
8	-1.0	1.0	1.0	-1.0	-1.0	-1.0	-1.0	1.0	1.0	-1.0
9	-1.0	1.0	1.0	1.0	1.0	1.0	1.0	1.0	1.0	-1.0
10	-1.0	1.0	1.0	1.0	1.0	1.0	1.0	1.0	1.0	-1.0

(a)

	1	2	3	4	5	6	7	8	9	10
1	1.0	1.0	1.0	1.0	1.0	1.0	1.0	1.0	1.0	-1.0
2	1.0	1.0	1.0	1.0	1.0	1.0	1.0	1.0	1.0	-1.0
3	1.0	1.0	1.0	-1.0	-1.0	-1.0	-1.0	1.0	1.0	-1.0
4	1.0	1.0	1.0	1.0	-1.0	-1.0	-1.0	1.0	1.0	-1.0
5	1.0	1.0	1.0	1.0	1.0	1.0	1.0	1.0	1.0	-1.0
6	-1.0	1.0	1.0	1.0	1.0	1.0	1.0	1.0	1.0	-1.0
7	-1.0	1.0	1.0	1.0	-1.0	1.0	1.0	1.0	1.0	1.0
8	-1.0	1.0	1.0	1.0	-1.0	1.0	-1.0	1.0	1.0	-1.0
9	-1.0	1.0	1.0	1.0	1.0	1.0	1.0	1.0	1.0	-1.0
10	-1.0	1.0	1.0	1.0	1.0	1.0	1.0	1.0	1.0	-1.0

(b)

Fig. 4. (a) matrix of 8   (b) matrix of noised 8

3.3   The Complete Code

Complete matlab code in File proc.m:

```
clc
clear
%% Data import
    load data6 array_six
    load data8 array_eight
%% Training sample(target vector)
    T=[array_six;array_eight]';
```

```
%% Create a network
    net=newhop(T);
%% Numbers 6 and 8 dot matrix with noise figure
    load data6_noisy noisy_array_six
    load data8_noisy noisy_array_eight
%% digital identification
    noisy_six={(noisy_array_six)'};
    identify_six=sim(net,{10,10},{},noisy_six);
    identify_six{10}';
    noisy_eight={(noisy_array_eight)'};
    identify_eight=sim(net,{10,10},{},noisy_eight);
    identify_eight{10}';
%% Show result
    Array_six=imresize(array_six,20);
    subplot(3,2,1)
    imshow(Array_six)
    title('Standard(number 6)')
    Array_eight=imresize(array_eight,20);
    subplot(3,2,2)
    imshow(array_eight)
    title('Standard(number 8)')
    subplot(3,2,3)
    Noisy_array_six=imresize(noisy_array_six,20);
    imshow(Noisy_array_six)
    title('Noise(number 6)')
    subplot(3,2,4)
    Noisy_array_eight=imresize(noisy_array_eight,20);
    imshow(Noisy_array_eight)
    title('Noise(number 8)')
    subplot(3,2,5)
    imshow(imresize(identify_six{10}',20))
    title('Identify(number 6)')
    subplot(3,2,6)
    imshow(imresize(identify_eight{10}',20))
    title('Identify(number 8)')
```

Finally, the results are shown below:

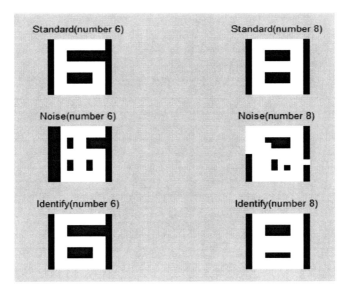

Fig. 5. The recognition effect

4   Conclusion

The results show that discrete hopfield neural network applied in digital identification achieve good effect. The method is simple and easy to utilize, especially have a high application value.

If the method could be improved, then applied to handwritten character recognition, it will lead to greater application prospects. In addition, this method assume the steady-state network with p orthogonal, however the facts often not. How to solve this problem? In my opinion, Schimidt method will help us. Schimidt orthogonal can enable any set of linearly independent vectors into their equivalent of the standard orthogonal vectors. Therefore, pretreat the memory sample through Schimidt method will change the network weights and then improve the network performance. In other words, after Schimidt orthogonal, we could design weights according to the outer product method. Then when we enter a mode, the program will encounter several iterations and the network will finally reach a steady state which is the sample of network recognition. It is also be studied in the future.

References

1. Ma, X.: Hopfield network case study. Computer Simulation (2003)
2. Bai, C.: Global Stability of Almost Periodic Solutions of Hopfield Nueral Networks with Neutral Time-Varying Delays (2008)
3. Wang, Y.: Improvement of image restoration for Hopfield networks. Computer Engineering (2007)

4. Zhang, Y.: Feedback-type associative memory neural network. Computer Engineering (2009)
5. He, H.: Offline handwritten numeral recognition theory and algorithms based on Hopfield. Communication Technology (2009)
6. Zhang, C.: Training of associative memory neural network. Journal of Automation (2006)

Wavelet-Contourlet Retrieval Algorithm
Using Four Statistical Features

Jing Ge, Chunfeng Fan, and Xinwu Chen

College of Physics and Electronic Engineering, Xinyang Normal University,
Xinyang, 464000, China
chenxinwu@126.com

Abstract. Contourlet is superior to wavelet in representing complex texture and structure lines images for its multi-directional ability and have been demonstrated the effectiveness in texture retrieval applications. Aiming to improve the retrieval rate of contourlet transform retrieval system and reduce the redundancy of contourlet which consume two much time in building feature vector database, a new wavelet-contourlet transform retrieval system was proposed. The feature vectors of this system were constructed by cascading the energy, standard deviation, absolute mean and kurtosis of each sub-band contourlet coefficients and the similarity measure used here was Canberra distance. Experimental results on 109 brodatz texture images show that the new system can lead to a higher retrieval rate than several contourlet transform retrieval systems which utilize the combination feature of standard deviation and absolute mean which is most commonly used today under same dimension of feature vectors.

Keywords: content based image retrieval, wavelet-contourlet transform, energy, kurtosis, standard deviation, absolute mean.

1   Introduction

For human beings, the process of study to classify different categories of objects mostly depends on the vision system which can differentiate the texture, shape and color characters. Content-based image retrieval (CBIR) system from un-annotated image databases for texture recognition has been a fast growing research area recently [1]. The two important procedures in typical CBIR systems are feature extraction (FE) and similarity measurement (SM). Typically, the features used in CBIR systems are low-level image features such as color, texture, shape and layout. In this work, we focus on the use of texture information for image retrieval. Some of the most popular texture extraction methods for retrieval are based on filtering or wavelet-like approaches [2,3,4] during the last twenty years. Other transforms are wavelet packets, wavelet frames and Gabor wavelet transforms [5], and the following one is contourlet transform proposed by Minh Do and Martin Vetterli due to its ability of capturing even more directional information in digital image [6]. Yet, this transform is shift

M. Zhao and J. Sha (Eds.): ICCIP 2012, Part II, CCIS 289, pp. 411–418, 2012.

sensitive and aliasing in both space and frequency domains. To alleviate these defects, Cunha and Zhou proposed a modified version called Non-subsampled contourlet transform which was constructed by combining a non-subsampled Laplacian pyramid and a non-subsampled directional filter bank [7]. The defect of this transform is higher redundancy which makes the transform much more time consuming and much larger memory needed.

To overcome the limitation of high redundancy, Cunha presented a compromise transform which was a cascade of non-subsampled Laplacian pyramid and critical subsampled directional filter banks, and made the redundancy decay to S+1, where S is the decomposition scale in the transform.

To further reduce the redundancy of the transform and make sure that the transform anti-aliasing and shift insensitive, Yue Lu modified the Laplacian pyramid filters in the band transition and subsampled rate, and followed by the original directional filter banks, got more localized time-frequency characteristics [8]. According to the difference of the redundancy, the new transform can be classified into 3 different versions named Contourlet-1.3, Contourlet-1.6 and Contourlet-2.3.

Ever since the contourlet transform was proposed, many literatures reported the application approaches in many different areas including CBIR systems [9-12]. We have constructed some texture image retrieval systems based on the above different versions of contourlet transform [10-12].

Yet, each of the contourlet transforms has a redundant factor above 1 which makes the transform domain data expanded, the feature sometimes affect its applications at some situations like compression and code. On the other hand, the directional information is always not rich; hence the coarse scales don't need too much directional sub-bands. We can use wavelet transform for coarse scales and contourlet transform for fine scales and name the mixture transform wavelet-contourlet transform. For short, we call it WCT. And we will use it in the retrieval system.

As we have known, the methods to improve the retrieval rate not only limited to improve the characteristics of multiscale transform. At least, we can utilize new feature or new combination of old features to build retrieval systems with higher retrieval rate. From statistical view, Wouwer et al. employed generalized Gaussian density functions to represent texture images in the wavelet domain [13]. The model parameters are estimated using a method of moment matching (MM), and the similarity function is defined as weighted Euclidean distances on extracted model parameters. Do and Vetterli developed a new frame that combine FE and SM together and got a promising result in wavelet-based texture image retrieval rate comparing with traditional methods [2]. Yang extended this idea to contourlet domain [14]. We have compared GGD model method and features composed of absolute mean energy and standard deviation with Canberra distance and experimental results show that the latter has higher retrieval rate using same length feature vector, hence we will ignore GGD parameter.

There are several other statistical values for the sub-bands coefficients, including mean, energy, absolute mean, and kurtosis, etc. And, each of them can be used as retrieval feature. In this paper, we will give a new combinational feature of energy, standard deviation, absolute mean and kurtosis to make satisfied retrieval rate under

Canberra distance measure metric. Further, we will show how to construct the new texture image retrieval system and some special points which should be paid attention.

The remaining parts of this paper are organized as follows: key techniques of the new contourlet texture image retrieval system will be covered in section 2 and experimental method and results will be shown in section 3 and in the section 4, the last section, we will conclude the whole paper.

2   Key Techniques

2.1   Feature Vectors

From statistical view, there are many parameters can be used as feature, including mean, absolute mean energy, energy, standard deviation, absolute mean, kurtosis, generalized Gaussian model parameters, etc. For convenience, we will index the features and some combinations as shown in table 1, and we can index other feature combinations by analogy. The features listed in table 1 can be calculated by (1)-(6).

Table 1. Index of features and some combinations

F1	F2	F3	F4
mean	standard deviation	absolute mean energy	energy
F5	**F6**	**F14**	**F45**
skewness	kurtosis	mean and energy	energy and skewness

$$F1(s,k) = \mu(s,k) = \frac{1}{MN} \sum_{m=1}^{M} \sum_{n=1}^{N} W_{s,k}(m,n) \tag{1}$$

$$F2(s,k) = \sigma(s,k) = [\frac{1}{MN} \sum_{m=1}^{M} \sum_{n=1}^{N} | W_{s,k}(m,n) - \mu_{s,k} |^2]^{1/2} \tag{2}$$

$$F3(s,k) = \frac{1}{MN} \sum_{m=1}^{M} \sum_{n=1}^{N} | W_{s,k}(m,n) | \tag{3}$$

$$F4(s,k) = \frac{1}{MN} \sum_{m=1}^{M} \sum_{n=1}^{N} | W_{s,k}(m,n) |^2 \tag{4}$$

$$F5(s,k) = \frac{1}{MN} \sum_{m=1}^{M} \sum_{n=1}^{N} \frac{(W_{s,k}(m,n) - \mu(s,k))^3}{\sigma(s,k)^3} \tag{5}$$

$$F6(s,k) = \frac{1}{MN} \sum_{m=1}^{M} \sum_{n=1}^{N} \frac{(W_{s,k}(m,n) - \mu(s,k))^4}{\sigma(s,k)^4} \tag{6}$$

Where s and k denote the index of scale and direction, M, N stand for the row and column number of the sub-band coefficients, W is the coefficient of row M and column N in sub-band indexed by s and k, μ and σ represent mean and standard deviation, respectively.

In retrieval systems, we hope to get high retrieval rate using short feature vectors. But, in reality, long feature vector means high retrieval rate, we should often make a compromise between retrieval rate and the length of feature vectors. In this paper, we argue that F2346 and Canberra distance can lead to higher retrieval rate under relatively short feature vectors.

2.2   Similarity Measure

The similarity measure is used to calculate the distance between different feature vectors. Up to now, at least there are 10 different types of distance measure, they are: Manhattan (L1), Weighted-Mean–Variance (WMV), Euclidean (L2), Chebychev (L), Mahalanobis, Canberra, Bray-Curtis, Squared Chord, Squared Chi-Squared and Kullback Leibler. Kokare compared the nine measures except Kull-back distance (KLD) and declared that Canberra and Bray-Curtis are superior to others [15], and we compared Canberra and Kull-back distance, the result is that Canberra is more suitable in such kind of situation. So in this paper, we directly choose Canberra distance as distance measure. The   Canberra distance is defined as (7), where $d(\mathbf{x},\mathbf{y})$ means the distance between vector $\mathbf{x},\mathbf{y}$, D denotes the dimension of the feature vectors, x_i, y_i are the i-th components of $\mathbf{x}$ and $\mathbf{y}$, respectively.

$$d(\mathbf{x},\mathbf{y}) = \sum_{i=1}^{D} \frac{|\mathbf{x}_i - \mathbf{y}_i|}{|\mathbf{x}_i| + |\mathbf{y}_i|} \tag{7}$$

2.3   Wavelet-Contourlet Transform (WCT)

Contourlet transform is superior to wavelet transform at several conditions including sparse representing texture characters and contours in complex digital images but not better than wavelet for smooth areas. We noticed that textures always present in detail sub-bands but not rich in approximation ones, hence we can represent images contour segment by wavelet.

In this work, we denote the decomposition parameters using data structure like [X1 X2 X3 0 0], here Xi (i=1,2,3…) stands for some particular digit which means the levels we decomposes for i-scale using directional filter banks, for example, 3 means we can get 2^3 sub-bands at that scale. And the number sequence imply the scale from detail to approximation ones, 0 means wavelet at this scale and we can get 3 different directional sub-bands.

WCT can represent digital images with a little less redundancy than contourlet and can improve the retrieval rates than contourlet retrieval system under same structure and demand less memory and computing times.

3   Experiment and Results

In this section, we will introduce the implementation approach of the new texture image retrieval system, and evaluate the retrieval rate of the system. Furthermore, we will study the factors which influence the retrieval rate and how to improve the retrieval rate of the system.

3.1   Experimental Objects

The experimental objects are the 109 texture images coming from Brodatz album [16]. For each 640×640 pixels image, we cut them into non-overlapped 16 sub-images and each one is 160×160 pixels size, then we can obtain an image database with 109×16=1744 sub-images. The 16 sub-images come from the same original image can be viewed as the same category.

3.2   Experimental Approach

The experimental approach can be divided into 4 steps:

Step 1: For each sub-image in the database, we used WCT to transform it into WCT domain. In WCT domain, for each image, we calculated the absolute mean energy and kurtosis of each directional sub-band using (1) to (6) or their combinations, respectively. Then we cascaded them together as the feature vector of that image.

Step 2: Select the first sub-image in the database, using (4), calculate the Canberra distance between its feature vector and every one in the feature vector database. Then find the N=16 nearest images as the retrieval result. Examine how many images belong to the corresponding group, and divided the value by 16 to get the retrieval rate;

Step 3: For next image feature vector in the 1744 sub-image vector database, using the same method as in step 2, calculate the average retrieval rate R, and repeat the procedure until all the feature vectors have been processed.

Step 4: For $N \in$ {16, 20, 30, 40, 50, 60, 70, 80, 90, 100}, repeat step 2 and 3, calculate the average retrieval rate for each N.

Step 2 to Step 4 can be described by (5) as follows, where q=1744, R(p) denotes the average retrieval rate for each $p \in$ {16, 20, 30, 40, 50, 60, 70, 80, 90, 100}. S(p, i) is the number of images belong to the correct group when the i-th image used as query image.

The procedure above can be described by (8) as follows, where q=1744, R(p) denotes the average retrieval rate for each $p \in$ {16, 20, 30, 40, 50, 60, 70, 80, 90, 100}, hence 10 retrieval results can be acquired. S(p, i) is the number of images belong to the correct group when the i-th image used as query image.

$$R(p) = \frac{1}{q}\sum_{i=1}^{q} R(p,i) = \frac{1}{q}\sum_{i=1}^{q}\frac{S(p,i)}{16} \tag{8}$$

3.3   Experimental Results

Using the approach above, we can get the average retrieval rate of different features of WCT texture image retrieval system as shown in table 2 using decomposition parameter [3 2 0 0]. It should be noted that [3 2 0 0] means directional number of each scale should be 8, 4, 3 and 3 from fine to coarse scale respectively, and 0 means wavelet transform at this scale.

From table 2, we can see that F3 performs better than other features under every decomposition parameter. F1, F5 and F6 are not suitable for retrieval system under single feature condition. It should be noted that for other decomposition parameters, almost same laws can be drawn. In order to improve the retrieval rate, we can use combination features. In the earlier work, researchers always use the combination of F2 and F3, namely F32. And it should be noted that situation is in contourlet and modified contourlet versions texture retrieval systems. From table 2, we can draw a conclusion that F3 is superior to others. Intuition tells us we can combine other feature with F3 to get a higher retrieval rate. We can see that F2346 can perform better than others.

Table 2. WCT retrieval rate using different features and combinations

	16	20	30	40	50	60	70	80	90	100
F1	17.0	17.7	19.0	20.1	21.1	21.9	22.8	23.7	24.5	25.5
F2	67.2	72.2	78.0	80.7	82.8	84.4	85.7	86.9	88.0	88.9
F3	66.8	71.8	77.7	81.1	83.1	84.6	86.1	87.2	88.2	89.0
F4	67.5	72.1	78.0	80.9	82.9	84.3	85.6	86.8	87.7	88.7
F5	26.9	28.7	32.5	35.9	38.6	40.8	42.8	44.8	46.7	48.3
F6	50.0.	53.9	60.3	64.6	67.7	70.2	72.2	74.0	75.5	76.8
F23	68.5	73.3	79.0	81.8	83.6	85.1	86.4	87.5	88.6	89.6
F36	70.2	75.5	80.9	83.9	85.8	87.3	88.4	89.3	90.0	90.8
F2346	72.0	77.0	81.6	84.2	86.0	87.5	88.7	89.8	90.6	91.4

Also, we give the comparison of retrieval rates between the new algorithm and some other old ones in table 3. The old systems used F23 futures and the corresponding version of contourlet transform. From table 3 we can see that the new system is superior to those earlier ones not only with higher retrieval rates, but also low dimension (dim in table 3) of feature vectors which means faster retrieval speed. And it should be noted that the new system has no redundancy makes it fastest in building feature vector database.

It should be noted that we can't decompose images using too many scales, for robust reason, we recommend that each sub-band should have at least 100 numbers.

Table 3. Comprasion of four different retrieval systems (%)

		16	20	30	40	50	60	70	80	90	100	dim
	CT	68.5	74	79.4	82.7	84.7	86.3	87.6	88.7	89.6	90.4	
[4 4 3 3]	NSCT	67.8	72.8	78.4	81.2	83.1	84.7	86.3	87.5	88.5	89.2	96
	CT23	68.4	73.8	79.0	82.2	84.2	85.8	87.1	88.4	89.4	90.2	
[3 2 0 0]	WCT	72.0	77.0	81.6	84.2	86.0	87.5	88.7	89.8	90.6	91.4	76
	CT	67.7	72.8	78.4	81.6	83.6	85.2	86.4	87.5	88.4	89.3	
[4 3 3]	NSCT	66.6	72.0	77.6	80.6	82.7	84.3	85.7	87.0	88.0	88.8	64
	CT23	67.3	72.5	78.1	81.1	82.9	84.4	85.7	86.9	87.9	88.8	
[3 2 0]	WCT	71.1	75.8	80.5	83.1	85.0	86.6	87.8	88.9	89.9	90.7	64

4   Conclusions

A wavelet-contourlet based texture image retrieval system was proposed in this paper which utilized the WCT combined with the Canberra distance and the features including absolute mean, standard deviation, energy and kurtosis of each sub-band coefficients. The new retrieval system has higher retrieval rate than the old systems which use absolute mean energy and standard deviation combined with the corresponding version of contourlet transform. It has faster retrieval speed and short time for building feature vector database.

Acknowledgment. This paper is supported by the High Level Science Research Starting Fund of Xinyang Normal University and Project of The Education Department of Henan Province (2010B120009).

References

1. Smeulders, A., Worring, M., Santini, S.: Content- based image retrieval at the end of the early years. IEEE Trans. Pattern Recognit. Machine Intell. 22(12), 1349–1380 (2000)
2. Minh, N.D., Vetterli, M.: Wavelet-based texture retrieval using Generalized Gaussian density and kullback-leibler distance. IEEE Transactions on Image Processing 11(2), 146–158 (2002)
3. Laine, A., Fan, J.: Texture classification by wavelet packet signatures. IEEE Trans. Pattern Recognit. Machine Intell. 15, 1186–1191 (1993)
4. Chang, T., Kuo, C.: Texture analysis and classification with tree-structure wavelet transform. IEEE Trans. on Image Processing 2, 429–441 (1993)
5. Smith, J.R., Chang, S.F.: Transform features for texture classification and discrimination in large image databases. In: Proceedings of IEEE Int. Conf. on Image Processing, Texas, pp. 407–411 (1994)
6. Do, M.N., Vetterli, M.: Contourlets: a directional multiresolution image representation. In: International Conference on Image Processing, New York, pp. 357–360 (September 2002)
7. Cunha, D., Zhou, J., Do, M.N.: The nonsubsampled contourlet transform: theory, design, and applications. IEEE Transactions on Image Processing 15, 3089–3101 (2006)

8. Mahyari, A., Yazdi, M.: Panchromatic and multispectral image fusion based on maximization of both spectral and spatial similarities. IEEE Transactions on Geoscience and Remote Sensing 49, 1976–1985 (2011), doi:10.1109/TGRS.2010.2103944

9. Arun, K.S., Hema, P.M.: Content Based Medical Image Retrieval by Combining Rotation Invariant Contourlet Features and Fourier Descriptors. International Journal of Recent Trends in Engineering 2, 35–39 (2009)

10. Chen, X., Li, X., Ma, J.: Contourlet-1.3 and generalized gaussian model texture image retrieval. In: Proc of ICEIT, pp. 458–462 (September 2010)

11. Chen, X., Yu, G., Gong, J.: Contourlet-1.3 texture image retrieval system. In: Proc of ICWAPR, pp. 49–54 (July 2010)

12. Chen, X., Ma, J.: Texture image retrieval based on contourlet-2.3 and generalized Gaussian density model. In: Proc of ICCASM, vol. 9, pp. 199–203 (October 2010)

13. Wouwer, G., Scheunder, V., Dyc, D.: Statistical texture characterization from discrete wavelet representations. IEEE Trans. Image Processing 8, 592–598 (1999)

14. Yang, J., Xu, C., Wang, Y.: Texture image retrieval based on contourlet transform using generalized Gaussian model. J. of Image and Graphics 12, 691–694 (2007)

15. Kokare, M., Chatterji, B.N., Biswas, P.K.: Comparison of similarity metrics for texture image retrieval. In: IEEE TENCON Conference, Bangalore, pp. 571–575 (2003)

16. Trygve, R.: Brodatz texture images,
    http://www.ux.uis.no/~tranden/brodatz.html

A Mathematical Model for Predicting Turbulence Variation in Air-Particle Two Phase Flows

Fusheng Yan[1,*], Weijun Zhang[2], and Ruquan Liang[3]

[1] Research Institute, Northeastern University, P.O. Box 318, Shenyang, China 110004
[2] School of Materials & Metallurgy, Northeastern University, Shenyang, China 110004
[3] Key Laboratory of National Education Ministry for Electromagnetic Process of Materials, Northeastern University, Shenyang, China 110004
Fusheng_Yan@mail.neu.edu.cn

Abstract. This research deals with development of a mathematical model which may account for the phenomenon of turbulence variation in dilute air-particle turbulent flows. The underlying formulation scheme adopts an Eulerian-Lagrangian reference frame, i.e. the carrier phase is considered as a continuum system, while the trajectories of individual particles are calculated using a Lagrangian frame work. A random walk model is employed to simulate the turbulence velocities. The new developed model as well the selected models from the literature is used to simulate a particle-laden vertical pipe flow. The calculated results show that the new model provides improved predictions of the experimental data.

Keywords: simulation, two phase flow, turbulence variation, gas-solid flow, mathematical model.

1   Introduction

Gas particle flows have found wide applications in both industry and natural processes, such as the pneumatic conveying of solid materials, spray drying, combustion of pulverized coal, dispersion of pollutants, to name a few. In these applications, the turbulence of the carrier phase plays an important role in the transport or mixing particles. The process of the particle dispersion or mixing can be enhanced by increased turbulence, where the interaction between the carrier phase and the particle phase is complex. The degree of coupling (i.e. one-way or two-way) between the particulates and the gaseous phase is dependent on the amount of particles present [1]. For dilute flows, the particle motion is only driven by the air phase, but the presence of particle phase does not affect the carrier phase. At volume fraction greater than 10^{-3}, the flow is no longer considered dilute and the collisions between particles become important. This is classified as the dense flow regime. It is well documented that the presence of even small amounts of particles may cause a

---

* Corresponding author.

M. Zhao and J. Sha (Eds.): ICCIP 2012, Part II, CCIS 289, pp. 419–426, 2012.
© Springer-Verlag Berlin Heidelberg 2012

modification (an increase or a decrease) in the turbulence level or structure of the carrier phase [2]. Experimental data has shown that the ratio of particle diameter to turbulent integral length scale was a crucial parameter for determining turbulence modulation by the presence of particles. The particles suppress turbulence if the ratio is less than 0.1 and the opposite effect is observed if the ratio is greater than about 0.1 [3].

During the last two decades, many researchers have presented "source term models" to predict turbulence modulation [4][5][6]. For these models, an extra term is included in the fluid momentum equation to account for the effect of particles on the fluid phase. The resulting additional source terms to the turbulent kinetic energy and the dissipation rate equations are responsible for turbulence modulation. However, the deficiencies of the conventional source term models lie in two areas: (i) Inability to predict an increase in the turbulence intensity of the carrier phase (ii) Failure to consider the particle crossing trajectory effect. This remains a motivation for the present study.

In this study, the following three mechanisms are considered: (i) Energy transfer through the drag force: this interaction normally results in a decrease in the turbulence intensity of the carrier's phase. (ii) The extra turbulence production due to the wake effects behind particles. (iii) Crossing Trajectory Effect (CTE): It refers to the phenomenon that a particle may fall through the eddy due to a large relative mean velocity between the particle and the turbulent eddy.

2   Governing Equations

In this study, the particle trajectories are computed based on the Lagrangian reference frame; the carrier phase equations are solved based on the Eulerian reference frame. Details on the modelling of the two phases are provided below.

2.1   Particle Phase

Particle trajectories are calculated through solution of the particle motion equation. Under the assumptions of dilute flow and very low gas-to-particle density ratios (on the order of 10^{-3}), the particle equation of motion reduces to:

$$\frac{d\vec{u}_p}{dt} = \frac{f}{\tau_p}\left(\vec{u}_g - \vec{u}_p\right) + \vec{g} \tag{1}$$

Where $\vec{u}_g$ and $\vec{u}_p$ are the instantaneous velocities for the gas phase and particle phase, respectively; $\vec{g}$ is the acceleration of gravity; and f is a correction factor to account for the effect of the drag force for flows beyond the Stokes' regime; the symbol τ_p denotes the particle response time. Since the instantaneous gas-phase velocities along the particle trajectories are required to render Eq. (1) solvable, the

Stochastic Separated Flow (SSF) model [7] was employed in this work to account for the fluid turbulence through random sampling of the instantaneous gas-phase velocity.

2.2   Air Phase Equations

Assuming that the mean flow of the gas phase is steady, incompressible, isothermal, and Newtonian with constant properties, then the time-averaged equations for conservation of both mass and momentum have the form in tensor notation below:

$$\frac{\partial U_{gi}}{\partial x_i} = 0 \tag{2}$$

$$\rho_g U_{gj} \frac{\partial U_{gi}}{\partial x_j} = -\frac{\partial \overline{P}}{\partial x_i} + \mu \frac{\partial^2 U_{gi}}{\partial x_j \partial x_j} - \rho_g \frac{\partial \overline{u'_{gi} u'_{gj}}}{\partial x_j} - \overline{F}_{pi} \tag{3}$$

Where the over-bar denotes a time-average quantity; ρ_g is the density of the gas phase; P is the static pressure; U_{gi} and u'_{gi} are the mean and fluctuating gas-phase velocities in the x_i-direction ($i = 1, 2, 3$) respectively; and F_{pi} represents the force exerted by the fluid on the particles per unit volume of mixture. Note that the solid volume fraction is not included since the particulate flow involved in this work is dilute. The two-equation $k-\varepsilon$ model is used to solve for the gas-phase turbulence due to its simplicity and robust performance. In addition, the effect of the particles on the turbulent characteristics can be incorporated into the modified $k-\varepsilon$ model with relative ease. The particle source terms to the turbulent kinetic energy and the dissipation rate equations can be obtained by starting with the instantaneous gas-phase momentum equation with the extra term included and following the standard procedure for deriving the k and ε equations in a single phase flow. It is noted that the extra particle source terms to the k and ε equations usually appear as a sink, and thus can normally account for the turbulence reduction mechanism due to the drag force between the two phases. To reflect the extra turbulence production mechanism which is attributed to the particle wake effects in this investigation, additional particle source terms must be added to the k and $\mathcal{E}$ equations.

2.3   Modelled Forms for Particle Source Terms

As previously mentioned, in order to reflect the effect of presence of the particles on turbulent flow, an extra term must be added to the two equation model. The first particle source term was modelled based on the model developed by Lightstone and Hodgson where the particle crossing trajectory effect was accounted for [4].

The formulation of the second particle source terms is essentially based on the following two physical observations: (i) the source of the turbulent kinetic energy is supplied via the mean flow field; (ii) the wake formation only occurs for the non-Stokes' regime. It is, thus, assumed that the actual mean force exerted by the particles on the gas phase ($\overline{F_p}$) may be divided into two components such that the first component stands for the particle Stokes' drag force, and the second one represents the difference between the actual mean force exerted by the particles on the gas phase and the particle Stokes' drag force, which contributes to the generation of particle turbulent wakes. It is thus conjectured that the work done by the latter force acting over a distance may account for the energy consumed to produce turbulent wakes behind particles. The resulting second particle source term to the turbulent kinetic energy equation has the form below:

$$S_{kp2} = \left| U_{gi} \frac{\alpha}{\tau_p} (U_{gi} - U_{pi})(f-1) \right|$$

(4)

$$S_{\varepsilon p2} = C_{\varepsilon w} \frac{\varepsilon}{k} \left| U_{gi} \overline{F_{pi,net}} \right|$$

(5)

Where $C_{\varepsilon w}$ is a model constant determined through optimizing predictions with experimental data (the subscript "w" implies wake).

3   Test Cases

The experiment of Hosokawa et al [8] is employed for the validation of the simulation results. In their experiment three types of particles (polystyrene, glass, ceramic) with different densities were used. Air was supplied from a blower and moved in the upward direction in a vertical pipe of 5.0m in length and 30.0mm in diameter. Spherical solid particles were released into the flow at the bottom of the pipe. The measurements were made in the fully developed region of the pipe by using Laser Doppler Velocimeter (LDV). Three test cases were selected in this investigation as detailed in Table 1.

Table 1. Test cases for pipe flow (Hosokawa et al, 1998)

Quantity	Case #1	Case #2	Case #3
Particle Diameter (μ m)	900	910	990
Loading Ratio	4.6	4.6	4.6
Particle Density (kg/m^3)	2500	980	3600
Particle Mass Flow Rate (kg/s)	3.9×10^2	3.9×10^2	3.9×10^2
Particle Volum Fraction	2.3×10^{-3}	5.8×10^{-3}	1.6×10^{-3}

4   Numerical Techniques

To take advantage of the geometric flexibility of the finite element method as well as at maintaining the physics of the flow by using the finite volume approach, a finite element based finite volume method was used to solve the gas-phase equations in a Cartesian coordinate system using a collocated grid. Initially, the flow field is calculated without the presence of the particulate phase until a converged solution is obtained. Then a large number of particles are tracked and the source terms to the gas-phase equations are calculated. Thereafter, the gas-phase equations are solved with the particle source terms included. This procedure is repeated until final convergence (a residual of 10^{-4} or less was imposed for this investigation).   It is noted that when particles are injected into the flow, the source terms are calculated and retained in memory. Then, the fluid coefficients are computed with the source terms applied. In this way, the flow fields adjust for the presence of particles and then the particles are injected again. After each injection the particles will follow a slightly different path through the new flow field. This cycle is repeated until a converged solution obtained, i.e. the source term ceases to change from injection to injection. The simulation was carried out using the commercial CFD code CFX-TASCflow, where a modifiable source code subroutine was used to implement the particle source terms to the k and ε equations.

A wedge-shaped grid was used to simulate this axisymmetric flow as shown in Fig.1, where a significant reduction in the number of nodes results and a decrease in the computational cost was realized. The wedge has an internal angle of $15°$. The radius of the wedge is 15.0mm, and the length of the physical domain is 3m which is long enough to obtain fully developed conditions. The simulation results were taken from the outlet region. A total of 300 nodes are distributed along the axial direction, 20 nodes along the radial direction with more nodes located near the wall, and 3 nodes in the azimuthal direction. To establish grid independence, the number of nodes distributed in the original grid was refined by doubling the number of nodes in the axial and radial directions (600x40x3). The predicted mean axial velocity radial profiles as well as the turbulent kinetic energy radial profiles are virtually identical for the two grids.

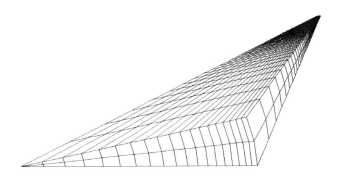

Fig. 1. Computational grid (300x20x3)

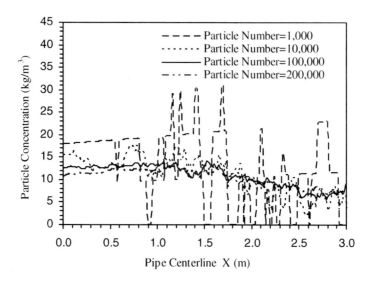

Fig. 2. Predictions of particle concentration along pipe centreline for Case #1

The boundary conditions for the gas phase are described as follows: a no-slip condition is assigned to the curved wall. On the axis and the radial planes, perfectly reflecting symmetry boundary conditions are imposed. The inlet velocity was specified as constant across the inlet plane. The inlet turbulence intensity was specified as 6%; and the eddy length scale was set to 5% of the inlet characteristic length scale. The reference pressure was set to 0 at a single control volume face on the outlet plane. In addition, scalable wall functions were used to resolve the large gradient in velocity near the wall region. The particles were injected with a constant mass flux across the inlet plane. The particle initial velocities were specified to be the same as the gas velocity at the inlet. A uniform particle concentration, consistent with the experiments, was applied. The particles are assumed to perfectly reflect at the walls with a coefficient of restitution equal to 1. The total number of particles injected was 100,000, which was tested to ensure statistical significance by comparing to the results with 200,000 particles as shown in Fig.2.

5   Results and Discussion

The first case, Case #1, considers the polystyrene particles of 900 μm in diameter with a density equal to 2500 kg/m3. The loading ratio is 4.6. With the mean velocity profile, the experimental data suggests that the radial velocity distribution of the gas phase should become flatter and the velocity gradient in the vicinity of the pipe wall become larger when the particles are introduced into the flow (Fig.3). These tendencies were predicted well by the new model, while the models by CW, MM, LH (short for Chen and Wood, Mostafa and Mongia, Lightstone and Hodgson, respectively) predict a velocity profile which is indistinguishable from that of the clean flow.

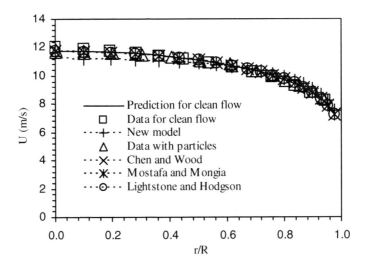

Fig. 3. Predictions of axial mean velocity for Case #1

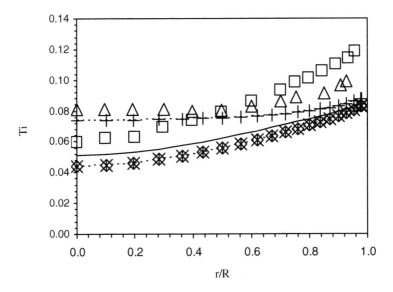

Fig. 4. Predictions of turbulence intensity for Case #1

For the turbulence intensity profile shown in Fig.4, the experimental data shows that the turbulence intensity is increased near the central region of the pipe and decreased away from the inner region with the presence of particles. The prediction given by the new model is seen to be in reasonable agreement with the experimental data in the center of the pipe, but underpredicts near the wall. The other models (CW, LH, MM) significantly under-predict the data since they predict a decrease in the turbulence intensity relative to the clean flow and again give nearly the same predictions. This results from the new model are encouraging because the new model is able to reflect the extra turbulence production with the introduction of large particles.

The similar trends were seen for Case#2 and Case#3. The results were omitted here due to the length of this article.

6   Conclusions

A new mathematical model was presented to account for the turbulence modulation by the presence of relatively large particles in dilute particulate flows. The model together with existing models in the literature was tested against the experimental data of Hosokawa [8]. The results have demonstrated that the new model is able to capture the turbulence enhancement occuring for particle laden flows with relatively large particles. This represents an improvement over predictions obtained using existing models from the literature.

Acknowledgements. The authors wish to thank ANSYS-CFX for providing the CFX-TASCflow computational fluid dynamics code for this research. The financial support from the Northeastern University Research Funding is also acknowledged with gratitude.

References

1. Elghobashi, S.: On Predicting Particle-Laden Turbulent Flows. Applied Scientific Research 52, 309–329 (1994)
2. Chen, C.P., Wood, P.E.: A Turbulence Closure Model for Dilute Gas Particle Flows. Can. J. Chem. Engr. 63, 349–360 (1985)
3. Crowe, C.T.: On Models for Turbulence in Fluid-Particle Flows. Int. J. Multiphase Flow 26, 719–727 (2000)
4. Lightstone, M.F., Hodgson, S.M.: Turbulence Modulation in Gas-Particle Flows: Comparison of Selected Models. Canadian J. of Chem. Eng. 82, 209–219 (2004)
5. Mostafa, A.A., Mongia, H.C.: On the Interaction of Particles and Turbulent Fluid Flow. Int. J. Heat Mass Transfer 31(10), 2063–2075 (1988)
6. Yan, F., Lightstone, M.F., Wood, P.E.: Numerical Study on Turbulence Modulation in Gas-Particle Flows. Heat and Mass Transfer 43, 243–253 (2007)
7. Shuen, J.S., Chen, L.D., Faeth, G.M.: Evaluation of a Stochastic Model of Particle Dispersion in a Turbulent Round Jet. AIChEJ 29, 167–170 (1983)
8. Hosokawa, S., Tomiyama, A., Morimura, M., Fujiwara, S., Sakaguchi, T.: Influence of RelativeVelocity on Turbulence Intensity in Gas-Solid Two-Phase Flow in a Vertical Pipe. In: Third International Conference on Multiphase Flow, Lyon, France (1998)

Validation of a Proposed Model for Computing Turbulence Variation in Air-Particle Flows

Fusheng Yan[1,*], Weijun Zhang[2], and Ruquan Liang[3]

[1] School of Materials & Metallurgy, Northeastern University, Shenyang, China 110004
[2] Research Institute, Northeastern University, P.O. Box 318, Shenyang, China 110004
[3] Key Laboratory of National Education Ministry for Electromagnetic Process of Materials, Northeastern University, Shenyang, China 110004
Fusheng_Yan@mail.neu.edu.cn

Abstract. This investigation aims to validate the former developed model by simulating another set of experimental data. The model was formulated to account for the process of turbulence variation in dilute air-particle turbulent flows. The Eulerian-Lagrangian reference frame was adopted for this study. A random walk model was employed to simulate the turbulence velocities. The calculated results show that the proposed model also agrees reasonably well with the experimental data of Tsuji et al.

Keywords: validation, simulation, two phase flow, turbulence variation, mathematical model.

1 Introduction

Computational Fluid Dynamics (CFD) has become an important tool for studying multiphase engineering flows. An important and relevant area where CFD is emerging is in particle-laden turbulent flows which have found wide applications in both industry and natural processes such as circulating fluidized bed reactors, spray fuel combustion, dispersion of pollutants and so on. In these applications, the turbulence of the carrier phase plays an important role in the transport or mixing particles. Increased turbulence leads to increased heat transfer and enhanced particle dispersion and mixing. To improve the efficiency of these processes and the quality of the final products, it is necessary to understand and be able to predict the mechanisms that influence the flow field. The interaction between the air phase and the particle phase is a complicated issue. This is not surprising, as turbulence itself has still remained a challenging problem for classical mechanics after Osborn Reynolds originally formulated the well known closure problem in the late 1800s, the addition of particles to a turbulent flow further enhances its complexity. Elghobashi (1994) proposed that the degree of coupling (i.e. one-way or two-way) between the particulates and the gaseous phase is dependent on the amount of particles present [1].

---

[*] Corresponding author.

M. Zhao and J. Sha (Eds.): ICCIP 2012, Part II, CCIS 289, pp. 427–434, 2012.
© Springer-Verlag Berlin Heidelberg 2012

It is well documented that the presence of even small amounts of particles may cause a variation (an increase or a decrease) in the turbulence level or structure of the carrier phase [2]. Experimental data has shown that the ratio of particle diameter to turbulent integral length scale was a crucial parameter for determining turbulence variation by the presence of particles. The particles suppress turbulence if the ratio is less than 0.1 and the opposite effect is observed if the ratio is greater than about 0.1 [3].

During the last two decades, many researchers have presented "source term models" to predict turbulence modulation [4][5][6]. For these models, an extra term is included in the fluid momentum equation to account for the effect of particles on the fluid phase. The resulting additional source terms to the turbulent kinetic energy and the dissipation rate equations are responsible for turbulence modulation. However, the deficiencies of the conventional source term models lie in two areas: one is the inability to predict an increase in the turbulence intensity of the carrier phase; the other one is the failure to consider the particle crossing trajectory effect. This remains a motivation for the present study.

The new proposed model may account for the following mechanisms:, the following three mechanisms are considered: one is the energy transfer through the drag force where the interaction normally results in a decrease in the turbulence intensity of the carrier's phase; next one is the extra turbulence production due to the wake effects behind particles; the last mechanism is the particle crossing trajectory effect which refers to the phenomenon that a particle may fall through the eddy due to a large relative mean velocity between the particle and the turbulent eddy.

2   Control Equations

In this study, the particle trajectories are computed based on the Lagrangian reference frame; the carrier phase equations are solved based on the Eulerian reference frame. Details on the modelling of the two phases are provided below.

2.1   Soild Phase

Particle trajectories are calculated through solution of the particle motion equation. Under the assumptions of dilute flow and very low gas-to-particle density ratios (on the order of 10^{-3}),   the particle equation of motion reduces to:

$$\frac{d\vec{u}_p}{dt} = \frac{f}{\tau_p}\left(\vec{u}_g - \vec{u}_p\right) + \vec{g} \tag{1}$$

Where $\vec{u}_g$ and $\vec{u}_p$ are the instantaneous velocities for the gas phase and particle phase, respectively; $\vec{g}$ is the acceleration of gravity; and f is a correction factor to account for the effect of the drag force for flows beyond the Stokes' regime; the symbol τ_p denotes the particle response time. Since the instantaneous gas-phase velocities along the particle trajectories are required to render Eq. (1) solvable, the

Stochastic Separated Flow (SSF) model [7] was employed in this work to account for the fluid turbulence through random sampling of the instantaneous gas-phase velocity.

2.2   Air Phase Equations

Assuming that the mean flow of the gas phase is steady, incompressible, isothermal, and Newtonian with constant properties, then the time-averaged equations for conservation of both mass and momentum have the form in tensor notation below:

$$\frac{\partial U_{gi}}{\partial x_i} = 0 \tag{2}$$

$$\rho_g U_{gj} \frac{\partial U_{gi}}{\partial x_j} = -\frac{\partial \overline{P}}{\partial x_i} + \mu \frac{\partial^2 U_{gi}}{\partial x_j \partial x_j} - \rho_g \frac{\partial \overline{u'_{gi} u'_{gj}}}{\partial x_j} - \overline{F}_{pi} \tag{3}$$

Where the over-bar denotes a time-average quantity; ρ_g is the density of the gas phase; P is the static pressure; U_{gi} and u'_{gi} are the mean and fluctuating gas-phase velocities in the x_i-direction ($i = 1, 2, 3$) respectively; and F_{pi} represents the force exerted by the fluid on the particles per unit volume of mixture. Note that the solid volume fraction is not included due to dilute flow. The k–ε model is used because of its simplicity and robust performance. In addition, the effect of the particles on the turbulent characteristics can be incorporated into the modified k–ε model with relative ease. The particle source terms to the turbulent kinetic energy and the dissipation rate equations can be obtained by starting with the instantaneous gas-phase momentum equation with the extra term included and following the standard procedure for deriving the k and ε equations in a single phase flow. It is noted that the extra particle source terms to the k and ε equations usually appear as a sink, and thus can normally account for the turbulence reduction mechanism due to the drag force between the two phases. To reflect the extra turbulence production mechanism which is attributed to the particle wake effects in this investigation, additional particle source terms must be added to the k and ε equations.

2.3   Modelled Forms for Particle Source Terms

The first particle source term was modelled based on the model developed by Lightstone and Hodgson where the particle crossing trajectory effect was accounted for [4].

The formulation of the second particle source terms is essentially based on the following two physical observations: (i) the source of the turbulent kinetic energy is supplied via the mean flow field; (ii) the wake formation only occurs for the non-Stokes' regime. It is, thus, assumed that the actual mean force exerted by the particles on the gas phase ($\overline{F}_p$) may be divided into two components such that the first component stands for the particle Stokes' drag force, and the second one represents the difference between the actual mean force exerted by the particles on the gas phase and the particle Stokes' drag force, which contributes to the generation of particle turbulent wakes. It is thus conjectured that the work done by the latter force acting over a distance may account for the energy consumed to produce turbulent wakes behind particles. The resulting second particle source term to the turbulent kinetic energy equation has the form below:

$$S_{kp2} = \left| U_{gi} \frac{\alpha}{\tau_p} (U_{gi} - U_{pi})(f-1) \right| \tag{4}$$

$$S_{\varepsilon p2} = C_{\varepsilon w} \frac{\varepsilon}{k} \left| U_{gi} \overline{F_{pi,net}} \right| \tag{5}$$

Where $C_{\varepsilon w}$ is a model constant determined through optimizing predictions with experimental data (the subscript "w" implies wake).

3   Experimental Data

The experiment of Tsuji et al [8] is employed for the validation of the simulation results. In their experiment, the polystyrene particles were released into an upward flow of air in a vertical pipe with an inner diameter of 30.5mm. Similar particle densities were used. The air was supplied from a blower and moved in the upward direction in a vertical pipe of 5.11m in length and 30.5mm in diameter. The spherical solid particles were released into the flow at the bottom of the pipe. The measurements were made in the fully developed region of the pipe by using Laser Doppler Velocimeter (LDV). Three test cases were selected in this investigation as detailed in Table 1.

Table 1. Test cases for pipe flow (Tsuji et al, 1984)

Quantity	Case #1	Case #2	Case #3
Particle Diameter (μ m)	200	500	1000
Loading Ratio	3.2	3.4	3.0
Particle Density (kg/m^3)	1020	1020	1030
Particle Mass Flow Rate (kg/s)	2.64×10^2	2.83×10^2	2.95×10^2
Particle Volum Fraction	3.68×10^{-3}	3.91×10^{-3}	3.42×10^{-3}

4   Numerical Scheme

A finite element based finite volume method was used to solve the gas-phase equations in a Cartesian coordinate system using a collocated grid to ensure the coupling between the pressure and velocity fields in the discretized form of the linear equations. The method takes advantage of the geometric flexibility of the finite element methods, and at the same time, maintains the physics of the flow by using the finite volume approach. Initially, the flow field is calculated without the presence of the particulate phase until a converged solution is obtained. Then a large number of particles are tracked and the source terms to the gas-phase equations are calculated. Thereafter, the gas-phase equations are solved with the particle source terms included. This procedure is repeated until final convergence (a residual of 10^{-4} or less was imposed for this investigation).   The simulation was carried out using the commercial CFD code CFX-TASCflow, where a modifiable source code subroutine was used to implement the particle source terms to the k and ε equations.

A wedge-shaped grid was used to simulate this axisymmetric flow as shown in Fig.1. This symmetry may allow a three dimensional problem to be solved on a two dimensional basis. Thus, a significant reduction in the number of nodes results and a decrease in the computational cost was achieved. The wedge has an internal angle of 15°. The radius of the wedge is 15.0mm, and the length of the physical domain is 3.0m which is long enough to obtain fully developed conditions. The simulation results were taken from the outlet region. A total of 300 nodes are distributed along the axial direction, 20 nodes along the radial direction with more nodes located near the wall, and 3 nodes in the azimuthal direction. To establish grid independence, the number of nodes distributed in the original grid was refined by doubling the number of nodes in the axial and radial directions (600x40x3). The predicted mean axial velocity radial profiles as well as the turbulent kinetic energy radial profiles are virtually identical for the two grids.

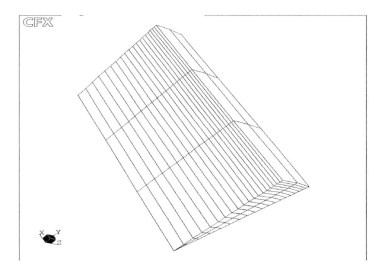

Fig. 1. Computational grid (300x20x3)

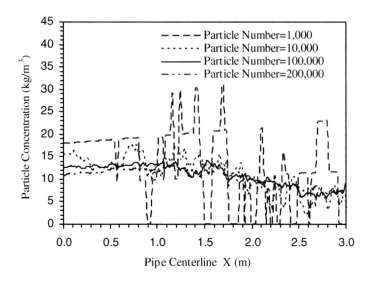

Fig. 2. Predictions of particle concentration along pipe centerline for Case #1

The boundary conditions for the gas phase are described as follows: a no-slip condition is assigned to the curved wall. On the axis and the radial planes, perfectly reflecting symmetry boundary conditions are imposed. The inlet velocity was specified as constant across the inlet plane. The inlet turbulence intensity was specified as 6%; and the eddy length scale was set to 5% of the inlet characteristic length scale. The reference pressure was set to 0 at a single control volume face on the outlet plane. In addition, scalable wall functions were used to resolve the large gradient in velocity near the wall region. The particles were injected with a constant mass flux across the inlet plane. The particle initial velocities were specified to be the same as the gas velocity at the inlet. A uniform particle concentration, consistent with the experiments, was applied. The particles are assumed to perfectly reflect at the walls with a coefficient of restitution equal to 1. The total number of particles injected was 100,000, which was tested to ensure statistical significance by comparing to the results with 200,000 particles as shown in Fig.2.

5   Results and Discussion

Case #3, considers the polystyrene particles of 1000 μm in diameter with a density equal to 1030 kg/m^3. The loading ratio is 3.0. For the mean velocity profile as shown in Fig.3, the experimental data suggests that the radial velocity distribution of the gas phase should become flatter and the velocity gradient in the vicinity of the pipe wall become larger when the particles are introduced into the flow (Fig.3). These tendencies were predicted well by the new model, while the selected models by Chen and Wood, Mostafa and Mongia, Lightstone and Hodgson all predict a velocity profile which is indistinguishable from that of the clean flow.

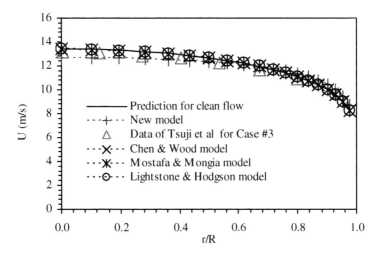

Fig. 3. Predictions of axial mean velocity for Case #3

For the turbulence intensity profile as shown in Fig.4, the experimental data shows that the turbulence intensity is increased significantly by the presence of large particles across the pipe except near the wall. The prediction given by the new model is seen to agree well with the experimental trends, while the selected models significantly under-predict the data and yield the same predictions. The results from the new model are encouraging because the new model is validated to be able to reflect the extra turbulence production with the introduction of large particles.

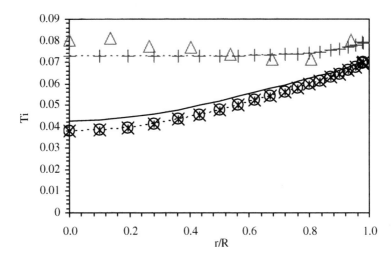

Fig. 4. Predictions of turbulence intensity for Case #3

The similar trends were seen for Case#1 and Case#2. The results were omitted here due to the length of this article.

6   Conclusions

A new mathematical model was presented to account for the turbulence modulation by the presence of relatively large particles in dilute air-particle two phase flows. The model together with existing models in the literature was tested against the experimental data of Tsuji et al [8]. The results have demonstrated that the new model is able to capture the turbulence enhancement occurring for particle laden flows with relatively large particles where the particle wake effects play an important role in causing an enhancement of the turbulent kinetic energy of the air phase. This represents an improvement over predictions obtained using existing models from the literature.

Acknowledgements. The authors wish to thank ANSYS for providing the computational fluid dynamics code for this research. The financial support from the Northeastern University Research Funding is also acknowledged with gratitude.

References

1. Elghobashi, S.: On Predicting Particle-Laden Turbulent Flows. Applied Scientific Research 52, 309–329 (1994)
2. Chen, C.P., Wood, P.E.: A Turbulence Closure Model for Dilute Gas Particle Flows. Can. J. Chem. Engr. 63, 349–360 (1985)
3. Crowe, C.T.: On Models for Turbulence in Fluid-Particle Flows. Int. J. Multiphase Flow 26, 719–727 (2000)
4. Lightstone, M.F., Hodgson, S.M.: Turbulence Modulation in Gas-Particle Flows: Comparison of Selected Models. Canadian J. of Chem. Eng. 82, 209–219 (2004)
5. Mostafa, A.A., Mongia, H.C.: On the Interaction of Particles and Turbulent Fluid Flow. Int. J. Heat Mass Transfer 31(10), 2063–2075 (1988)
6. Yan, F., Lightstone, M.F., Wood, P.E.: Numerical Study on Turbulence Modulation in Gas-Particle Flows. Heat and Mass Transfer 43, 243–253 (2007)
7. Shuen, J.S., Chen, L.D., Faeth, G.M.: Evaluation of a Stochastic Model of Particle Dispersion in a Turbulent Round Jet. AIChEJ 29, 167–170 (1983)
8. Hosokawa, S., Tomiyama, A., Morimura, M., Fujiwara, S., Sakaguchi, T.: Influence of RelativeVelocity on Turbulence Intensity in Gas-Solid Two-Phase Flow in a Vertical Pipe. In: Third International Conference on Multiphase Flow, Lyon, France (1998)

Research on Finding Elementary Siphon in a Class of Petri Nets

Feng Wang[1,2], Keyi Xing[1], Xiaoping Xu[3], and Libin Han[1]

[1] State Key Laboratory for Manufacturing Systems Engineering and Systems Engineering Institute, Xi'an Jiaotong University, Xi'an 710049, China
[2] School of Mathematics and Statistics, Xi'an Jiaotong University, Xi'an 710049, China
[3] School of Sciences, Xi'an University of Technology, Xi'an 710054, China
wangf@mail.xjtu.edu.cn

Abstract. This paper develops an algorithm to find a set of elementary siphons for a linear simple sequential process with resources. A graph-based technique is used to achieve elementary resource transition circuits (RTCs) initially. Then, some maximal perfect resource-transition circuits (MPCs) can be derived from elementary RTCs. Next, MPCs are used to developed T-characteristic vectors according to their correspondence relation. Finally, the set of elementary siphons can be established through computing a maximal set of linear independent rows of the characteristic T-vector matrix using the Gauss elimination. An example is included to validate the effectiveness of the proposed method.

Keywords: Petri net, elementary siphon, resource-transition circuit, T-character vector.

1   Introduction

Effective approaches for deadlock control in resource systems have received significant attention in the past two decades [1, 2, 5-10]. Petri nets as a mathematical tool are well suited for modeling and analyzing systems So many researches use Petri nets as a formalism to develop appropriate deadlock control methods. There are two special structural objects related to the liveness properties of Petri net models: siphon [11, 12] and resource-transition circuit [6-8].

Ezpeleta et al. [1] proposed a special class of Petri net, called system of simple sequential processes with resources (S^3PR), to describe an automated manufacturing system (AMS). Deadlock prevention method can be implemented by adding a control place and related arcs to each strict minimal siphon (SMS) so that no SMS can be emptied, which guarantees the liveness of the controlled system. Elementary siphons was first proposed by Li et al. [2] , which are a subclass of SMSs. Obviously, their number is smaller the set of all SMSs. They used the method to control only elementary siphons and proved that the controlled system is live under some conditions.

M. Zhao and J. Sha (Eds.): ICCIP 2012, Part II, CCIS 289, pp. 435–442, 2012.

An algorithm is proposed to find a set of elementary siphons for a linear simple sequential process with resources (L-S^{3}PR) in this paper. Firstly, a graph-based technique is used to achieve RTCs. Then, some MPCs can be derived from RTCs. Next, MRCs are used to developed T-characteristic vectors according to their correspondence relation. Finally, the set of elementary siphons can be established through computing a maximal set of linear independent rows of the characteristic T-vector matrix using the linear algebra method.

2   Preliminarise

2.1   Basic Notations on Petri Nets

A Petri net is a 3-tuple $N = (P, T, F)$, where P and T are finite, nonempty and disjoint sets. P is a set of places and T is a set of transitions. $F \subseteq (P \times T) \cup (T \times P)$ is called flow relation. Given a Petri net $N = (P, T, F)$ and a vertex $x \in P \cup T$, the preset of x is defined as $^\bullet x = \{y \in P \cup T \mid (y, x) \in F\}$, and the post set of x is defined as $x^\bullet = \{y \in P \cup T \mid (x, y) \in F\}$. The notation can be extended to a set. For example, let $X \subseteq P \cup T$, then $^\bullet X = \cup_{x \in X} {}^\bullet x$ and $X^\bullet = \cup_{x \in X} x^\bullet$. A Petri net is called a state machine if $\forall t \in T, |^\bullet t| = |t^\bullet|$.

A marking or state of N is a mapping $M: P \rightarrow IN$, where $IN = \{0, 1, 2, \cdots\}$. Given a place $p \in P$ and a marking M, $M(p)$ denotes the number of tokens in p at M. Let $S \subseteq P$ be a set of places, the sum of tokens in all places of S at M is denoted by $M(S)$, that is, $M(S) = \Sigma_{p \in S} M(p)$. A Petri net N with an initial marking M_0 is called a marked Petri net, denoted as (N, M_0). A transition $t \in T$ is enabled at a marking M, denoted by $M[t >$, iff $\forall p \in {}^\bullet t, M(p) > 0$. $M[t >$ means that transition can be fired under M. An enabled transition t at M can be fired, resulting in a new marking M', denoted by $M[t > M'$, where $M'(p) = M(p) - 1, \forall p \in {}^\bullet t \backslash t^\bullet$; $M'(p) = M(p) + 1, \forall p \in t^\bullet \backslash {}^\bullet t$; and otherwise $M'(p) = M(p)$, for all $p \in P - \{ t^\bullet \backslash t, {}^\bullet t \backslash t^\bullet \}$. A sequence of transitions $\alpha = t_1, t_2, \cdots, t_k \in T^*$ is feasible from a marking M if there exist $M_i[t_i > M_{i+1}, i = 1, 2, \cdots, k$, where $M_1 = M$ and T^* is the set of all sequences of transitions in T.

The incidence matrix of N is a matrix $[N]: P \times T \rightarrow IN$ indexed by P and T such that $[N](p, t) = -1$ if $p \in {}^\bullet t \backslash t^\bullet$; $[N](p, t) = 1$ if $p \in t^\bullet \backslash {}^\bullet t$; and otherwise $[N](p, t) = 0$ for each $p \in P$ and $t \in T$. A nonzero P-vector is a column vector $I: P \rightarrow Z^+ = \{0, 1, 2, \cdots\}$. Where, every entry equals 0 or 1. I^T and $[N]^T$ are the transposed versions of a vector I and a matrix $[N]$. I is a P-invariant if and only if $I \neq 0$ and $I^T[N] = 0^T$. The support of a P-invariant I is the set of places: $\| I \| = \{p \in P \mid I(p) \neq 0\}$.

2.2   L-S^{3}PR

A Linear S^{3}PR (L-S^{3}PR) is an ordinary Petri net $N = (P, T, F)$ such that[4]

(1) $P \cup P^0 \cup P_R$ is a partition such that

(1.1) $P^0 = \{ p_1^0, p_2^0, \cdots, p_k^0 \}$ is the set of process idle places;

(1.2) $P = \cup_{i=1}^{k} P_i$ is the set of operation places, where $P_i \cap P_j = \varnothing$ for all $i \neq j$;

(1.3) $P_R = \{r_1, r_2, \cdots, r_n\}$ is the set of resource places, where $n > 0$.

(2) $T = \cup_{i=1}^{k} T_i$ is the set of transitions, where $T_i \cap T_j = \varnothing$ for all $i \neq j$.

(3) $\forall i \in Z_k = \{1,2,\cdots, k\}$, the subnet N_i generated by $P_i \cup \{p_i^0\}$ and T_i is a strongly connected state machine, and every cycle of N_i contains p_i^0 and $\forall P \in P_A^i$, $|P^{\bullet}|=1$

(4) $\forall i \in Z_k$, $\forall p \in P_A^i$, $\exists r \in P_R$, $^{\bullet\bullet}p \cap P_R = p^{\bullet\bullet} \cap P_R = \{r\}$ and $|^{\bullet\bullet}p \cap P_R|=1$.

(5) For $r \in P_R$, $H(r)=(^{\bullet\bullet}r) \cap P_A$, the operation places that use r are called the set of holder of r.

(6) N is strongly connected.

2.3   Siphons and RTCs

A siphon is a non-empty subset of places such that $^{\bullet}S \subseteq S^{\bullet}$, i.e. every input transition also belongs to the set of output transition of S. $S \subseteq P$ is a trap if and only if $S^{\bullet} \subseteq ^{\bullet}S$ holds. A siphon is minimal if there does not exist a siphon contained in it as a proper subset. Specially, a minimal siphon is strict if it does not contain a marked trap in N, which is called strict minimal siphon denoted by SMS in short. Let Π denote the set of all SMSs of N.

$S \subseteq P$ be a siphon of N, P-vector λ_S is called the characteristic vector of S iff $\forall p \in S$, $\lambda_S(p) = 1$; otherwise, $\lambda_S(p) = 0$. η_S is called the characteristic T-vector of S, if $\eta_S^T = \lambda_S^T[N]$, where $[N]$ is the incidence matrix of N. Let $N= (P, T, F)$ be a net with $|P|=m$, $|T|=n$, which has k siphons $S_1, S_2, \cdots$, and S_k, m, $k \in IN$. Define $[\lambda]_{k \times m}=[\lambda_1\ \lambda_2\ \cdots\ \lambda_k]^T$ and $[\eta]_{k \times n}=[\eta_1\ \eta_2 \ldots \eta_k]$ is called the characteristic P-vector matrix and T-vector matrix of the siphons in N, respectively.

A path in N is a sequence of vertices and arcs $\alpha=x_1 x_2 \cdots x_n$, where $x_1, x_2, \cdots, x_n \in P \cup T$. The numbers of arc are $n-1$, which is the length of the path. A circuit is a path in which the first vertices and the last vertices are identical. A circuit is elementary if no vertex but the first and last appears twice. Two circles are the same if the sets of their vertices and arcs are the same. Obviously, a circuit is a strongly connected subnet. A path $\alpha=x_1, x_2, \cdots, x_n$ is elementary if $\forall i \neq j$, $1< i, j<n$ $x_i \neq x_j$. A circuit $\alpha=x_1, x_2, \cdots, x_n$ is elementary if $\forall i \neq j$, $1< i, j<n$ $x_i \neq x_j$, furthermore $x_1=x_n$. Thus, the union of some elementary circuits construct another circuit contained each of the part.

θ be a directed circuit in S^3PR of N. θ is called a resource-transition circuit (RT) if it contains only resource places and transitions. Let $\Re[\theta]$ and $\Im[\theta]$ denote the sets of resource places and transitions in θ, respectively. Then, a RTC θ does not contain any operation or processing places and is uniquely determined by its resource set $\Re[\theta]$ and transition set. Hence, it can be written as $\theta= N [\Im[\theta] \cup \Re[\theta]]$.

3   Elementary Siphon and MPCT-Circuit

The concepts of elementary siphons and maximal perfect resource-transition circuits (MPCs) are proposed in [2] and [8], respectively.

Definition 1: Let η_α, η_β, $\cdots$, $\eta_\gamma (1 \le \alpha, \beta, \gamma \le k)$ are a linearly independent maximal set of $[\eta]_{k \times n}$, then S_α, S_β, $\cdots$, and S_γ are called elementary siphons of N. Let Π_E denote the set of elementary siphons, here, $\Pi_E = \{S_\alpha, S_\beta, \cdots, S_\gamma\}$.

Definition 2: An RT-circuit θ is a perfect RT-circuit (PRT) if it satisfies $(^{(A)}\Im[\theta])^\bullet = \Im[\theta]$, where, $^{(A)}\Im[\theta]$ denotes the input operation of $\Im[\theta]$.

Definition 3: Let θ_1 and θ_2 be two RTC-circuits with the same resource set R_1, then the union of θ_1 and θ_2 is a RTC-circuit with R_1. Therefore, there exists a unique maximal PRT-circuit (MPC) with the resource set R_1. Let Ξ denotes the set of all MPCs in N.

Definition 4: Let $\Lambda = \{p \in P | |p^\bullet| > 1\}$, a place p in Λ is called a split place

Lemma 1: Given an RTC θ, if $\forall p \in \Lambda \cap {}^{(A)}\Im[\theta]$, $p^\bullet \subseteq \Im[\theta]$, then θ is perfect.

Definition 5: Let θ be an RTC in N, then, $\langle \Re[\theta], \Re[\theta]^\bullet \cap {}^\bullet\Re[\theta] \rangle$ is RTC, denoted by $\gamma(\theta)$.

Lemma 2: if $\gamma(\theta)$ is perfect, then $\gamma(\theta)$ is a MPC.
Although SMSs and MPCs are different structural objects, Xing et al. have already proved that there exists a one-to-one correspondence between them in S³PRs.

Lemma 3: Let $N = (P_A \cup P^0 \cup P_R, T, F)$ be an S³PR, then there exists a one-to-one relationship g between Σ and Π, where g: $\Sigma \to \Pi$, and $g(\theta) = \Re[\theta] \cup (H(\Re[\theta])\backslash^{(p)}\Im[\theta])$, $\theta \in \Sigma$.

4   An Algorithm for Computing Elementary Siphons in LS3PR

In this section, we will give our algorithm of computing the elementary siphons. Firstly, some definitions and theorems are given as follows:

Theorem 1: Let $N = (P_A \cup P_0 \cup P_R, T, F)$ be an L-S³PR, and RTC and split(N) denote the set of PCTs in N_R and split transition in N, respectively, then $\forall \theta \in$ RTC, θ is perfect.

Proof: $N = (P_A \cup P_0 \cup P_R, T, F)$ be an L-S³PR, then split $(N) = \emptyset$, and $\forall \theta \in$ RTC, $(^{(A)}\Im[\theta])^\bullet = \Im[\theta]$, thereby $\forall \theta \in$ RTC, θ is perfect.

Theorem 2: In an L-S³PR, $\gamma(\theta)$ is a MPC.

Proof: By the definition of $\gamma(\theta)$, we can get $\gamma(\theta)$ is the maximal RTC with the set of resource $\Re[\theta]$, on the other hand, from the Theorem 1, $\gamma(\theta)$ is perfect, hence $\gamma(\theta)$ is a MPC.

Theorem 3: Let $N = (P_A \cup P_0 \cup P_R, T, F)$ be an L-S³PR, and MPC(N) and RTC(N) denotes the set of all the MPCs and RTCs in N_R, then $\forall \theta_1$, $\theta_2 \in$ RTCs(N), if satisfies two conditions: (i) $\Re(\theta_1) \cap \Re[\theta_2] \ne \emptyset$; (ii) $\theta_1 \cup \theta_2 = \gamma(\theta_1 \cup \theta_2)$, then $\theta_1 \cup \theta_2 \in$ MPCs(N).

Proof: $\Re(\theta_1) \cap \Re[\theta_2] \ne \emptyset$, and $\theta_1 \cup \theta_2 = \gamma(\theta_1 \cup \theta_2)$, then by the Theorem 2, $\theta_1 \cup \theta_2 \in$ MPCs(N).

Definition 6: A resource-transition circle is called an elementary RTC (ERTC) iff it is also an elementary circle.

Definition 7: $\forall \theta_1$, $\theta_2 \in$ RTC, if $\Re(\theta_1) \cap \Re[\theta_2] \neq \varnothing$, then we call the operation of $\theta_1 \cup \theta_2$ is feasible.

Algorithm A (Elementary Siphon Enumeration):
Input: N_R, a resource-transition net of an L- S^3PR N;
Output: Π_E, the set of elementary siphons of N;
Step 1: Find all the elementary circuits by using Circuits-Finding- Algorithm in [4]. Let Ξ_1 be the set of all elementary circuits in N_R.
Step 2: For each $\theta \in \Xi_1$, do the following process:
Step2.1: Construct $\gamma(\theta)$.
Step2.2: If $\gamma(\theta) \neq \theta$, then add $\gamma(\theta)$ into Ξ_1 and delete all the θ' in Ξ_1 with $\Re[\theta']=\Re[\theta]$.
Step 3: For each $\theta \in \Xi_1$, recursively construct the set of Ξ_C as follows:
Step 3.1: Let $\Xi_C := \Xi_1$.
Step 3.2: For each $\theta_1 \in \Xi_1$ and each $\theta_2 \in \Xi_C$ if $\Re[\theta_1] \cap \Re[\theta_2] \neq \varnothing$, and $\theta_1 \cup \theta_2 \notin \Xi_C$, then add $\theta_1 \cup \theta_2$ into Ξ_C.
Step 3.3: Add $\gamma(\theta_1 \cup \theta_2)$ into Ξ_C, and delete all $\theta \in \Xi_C$ with $\Re[\theta]=\Re[\theta_1 \cup \theta_2]$, let $\Xi_C=\{\theta_1, \theta_2, \cdots, \theta_l\}$ at the end of Step 3.
Step 4: According to the one to one correspondence between MPCs and SMSs, compute the correspondence set $\Pi =\{ S_i \mid S_i = g(C_i), C_i \in \Xi, i =1, 2, \cdots, l\} = \{S_1, S_2, \cdots, S_l\}$.
Step 5: For each $S_i \in \Pi$, compute the characteristic vector of S_i denoted by λ_i.
Step 6: Compute the characteristic T-vector matrix of Π, $[\eta]_{l \times n} =[\lambda_1|\lambda_2 \cdots |\lambda_l]_{l \times m}^T \times [N]_{m \times n} = [\eta_1| \eta_2| \cdots |\eta_l]_{l \times n}^T$, where, $n = |T|$, $m = |P|$ and $[N]_{m \times n}$ is the incidence matrix of N.
Step 7: Using the Gauss elimination method, compute a set of maximal linear independent rows in $[\eta]_{l \times n}$, and let Π_E be the set of the corresponding SMSs with the same subscript as the maximal linear independent rows.
Step 8: output Π_E.

Lemma 4: At the end of Step 2 of Algorithm A, for each $\theta \in \Xi_1$, θ must be a MPC.

Proof: At the Step 2, for each $\theta \in \Xi_1$, we do the two operations: step2.1 is constructing $\gamma(\theta)$, step2.2 add $\gamma(\theta)$ into Ξ_1 and delete all the θ' in Ξ_1 with $\Re[\theta']=\Re[\theta]$. There are two cases in constructing $\gamma(\theta)$: (i) $\gamma(\theta)=\theta$; (ii) $\gamma(\theta) \neq \theta$. From the Theorem 2, if $\gamma(\theta)=\theta$, then θ must be a MPC, θ is kept in Ξ_1; otherwise, θ is deleted as well as all the $\theta' \neq \theta$ in Ξ_1 with $\Re[\theta']=\Re[\theta]$. So in Step 2.1 all θ which is not a MPC can be deleted. Thereby, at the end of Step 2, for each $\theta \in \Xi_1$, θ must be a MPC.

Lemma 5: Let $\Xi_1=\{\theta_1, \theta_2, \cdots, \theta_m\}$, here, Ξ_1 denotes the set of some RTCs at the end of step2 of Algorithm A, then, $\forall \theta \in$ MPCs, there exists $\theta_1^*, \theta_2^*, \cdots, \theta_k^*$, where, $\theta_i^* \in \Xi_1$, such that θ can be express the union of these RTCs, i.e., $\theta=\gamma(\bigcup_{i=1}^{k} \theta_{i=1}^*)$.

Proof: From Lemma 4, we can conclude $\forall \theta \in \Xi_1$, where, Ξ_1 denotes the set of some RTCs at the end of step2, θ must be a MPC, nevertheless, $\forall \theta_1^*, \theta_2^*, \cdots, \theta_k^*$, where,

$\theta_i^* \in \Xi_1$, $\bigcup_{i=1}^{k} \theta_{i=1}^*$ not always a MPC, e.g., when $\bigcup_{i=1}^{k} \theta_{i=1}^* \neq \gamma$ ($\bigcup_{i=1}^{k} \theta_{i=1}^*$), $\bigcup_{i=1}^{k} \theta_{i=1}^*$ is not a MPC. Thereby, we can get a MPC by two steps: one is by union of some RTCs; the other is maximized the unions by constructing $\gamma(\bigcup_{i=1}^{k} \theta_{i=1}^*)$. Thereby, $\forall \theta \in$ MPCs, there exists θ_1^*, $\theta_2^*, \cdots, \theta_k^*$, where, $\theta_i^* \in \Xi_1$, such that θ can be express the union of these RTCs, i.e., $\theta = \gamma(\bigcup_{i=1}^{k} \theta_{i=1}^*)$.

Lemma 6: $\forall 1 \le k \le l$, the feasible union of θ_1^*, $\theta_2^*, \cdots, \theta_k^*$ can be obtained through Step 3.1 and Step 3.2 of Algorithm A, where, Ξ_1 denotes the set of some RTCs at the end of step2, $k=|\Xi_1|$, and $\theta_i^* \in \Xi_1$, $i=1,2,\cdots,k$.

Proof: In Step 3.1 and 3.2, the arbitrarily two feasible unions can be obtained, i.e., $\forall \theta_1 \in \Xi_1$ and $\theta_2 \in \Xi_C$, if $\Re[\theta_1] \cap \Re[\theta_2] \neq \varnothing$, and $\theta_1 \cup \theta_2 \notin \Xi_C$, then add $\theta_1 \cup \theta_2$ into Ξ_C. Obviously, here, $\theta_1 \cup \theta_2 \notin \Xi_C$ is the new RTC which is not in the set Ξ_C at the beginning. Thereby, by recursively construct the set of Ξ_C in Step 3.1 and 3.2, as a new RTC in Ξ_C, $\theta_1 \cup \theta_2$ can be to repeatedly do the arbitrarily feasible union with θ in Ξ_1. Thereby, when Step 3.2 is over, all the feasible union of θ_1^*, $\theta_2^*, \cdots, \theta_k^*, 1 \le k \le l$, can be obtained.

Lemma 7: At the end of Step 3 of Algorithm A, for each $\theta \in \Xi_C$, θ must be a MPC.

Proof: At the Step 3, for each $\theta \in \Xi_C$, we do the three steps: in step3.1, let $\Xi_C := \Xi_1$; in step3.2, recursively construct arbitrary unions which is feasible.

Theorem 5: For an L-S³PR N, let Ω be the set elementary RTC of N, then $\forall \theta \in \Omega$, if $\theta = \gamma(\theta)$, then θ is an elementary MPC, i.e., θ is an EMPC.

Proof: By theorem 2, for an L- S³PR N, $\gamma(\theta)$ is a MPC. Thereby, $\forall \theta \in \Omega$, if $\theta = \gamma(\theta)$, then θ must be an elementary MPC, i.e., θ is an EMPC.

Theorem 6: For an L-S³PR N, $\Xi_C = \{\theta_1, \theta_2, \cdots, \theta_l\}$ obtained at the end of Step 3 of Algorithm A is the set of all MPCs of N.

Proof: From Lemma 5-7, we can get that $\Xi_C = \{\theta_1, \theta_2, \cdots, \theta_l\}$ obtained at the end of Step 3 of Algorithm A is the set of all MPCs of N.

Theorem 7: For an L-S³PR N, $\Pi = \{S_1, S_2, \cdots, S_l\}$ obtained from Algorithm A is the set of all SMSs of N.

Proof: It is obvious that the set of $\Pi = \{S_1, S_2, \cdots, S_l\}$ obtained from Algorithm A in an L-S³PR N is the set of all SMSs of N according to the one to one correspondence between the MPCs and SMSs.

Theorem 8: For an L-S³PR N, then Π_E obtained from Algorithm A is a set of elementary siphons of N (MPCs(N)).

Proof: From Theorem 7, we can conclude that the set of $\Pi = \{S_1, S_2, \cdots, S_l\}$ obtained from Algorithm A in an L- S³PR N is the set of all SMSs of N. Let Π_M denotes the set of all SMSs of N, by the definition of elementary, for each $S \in \Pi_M$, η_S can be expressed as a linear combination of the characteristic T-vectors of SMSs in Π_E. Thereby, by Step 6-7, Π_E obtained in Algorithm A is a set of elementary siphons of N.

5   Illustrative Example

Example: AN L-S^3PR model is considered shown in Fig.1, and its relevant resource-transition N_R of N is shown in Fig.2.

In Fig.2, all elementary RTCs in N_R is Found by using Circuits-Finding-Algorithm presented in [4]. Let Ξ denote all elementary RTCs in N_R, $\Xi=\{c_1,c_2\}$, where, $c_1=r_1t_{12}r_2t_{23}r_1$; $c_2=r_2t_{22}r_3t_{13}r_2$. $r(c_1)=c_1$, $r(c_2)=c_2$; c_1, c_2. $r(c_1)$ and $r(c_2)$ are perfect, so in Step2 of Algorithm A, $r(c_1)$ and $r(c_2)$ are added into $\Xi 1$. $\Xi 1=\{r(c_1), r(c_2)\}=\{c_1, c_2\}$. In Step3 of Algorithm A, $r(c_1\cup c_2)=c_1\cup c_2= r_2t_{12}r_1t_{23}r_2t_{22}r_3t_{13}r_2$. Accordingly, Ξ_C which denoted the set of all MPCs of N can be obtained at the end of Step3 of Algorithm A, here, $\Xi_C=\{c_1, c_2, c_1\cup c_2\}$. In Step4 of Algorithm A, the set of all SMSs denoted by Π According to the one to one correspondence between MPCs and SMSs is found, $\Pi =\{S_1, S_2, S_3\}$, wherer, $S_1=\{r_1, r_2, p_{12}, p_{23}\}$, $S_2=\{r_2, r_3, p_{13}, p_{22}\}$, $S_3=\{r_1, r_2, r_3, p_{13}, p_{23}\}$. In Step 5 of Algorithm A, compute the characteristic vector of S_i. Finally, By Step 6-7 of Algorithm A, the set of elementary siphon is obtained, i.e., $\Pi_E=\{S_1, S_2\}$.

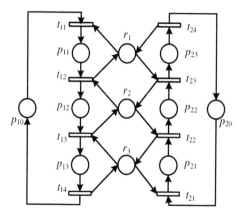

Fig. 1. A S^3PR N

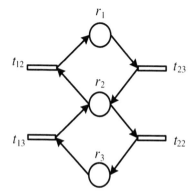

Fig. 2. Resource-transition net N_R of N

6   Conclusions

In this paper, we develop an algorithm in an algebraic fashion for the computation problem of the elementary siphons in an L-S^{3}PR. A graph-based technique is used to achieve all elementary RTCs. Then, some maximal perfect resource-transition circuits (MPCs) can be derived from elementary RTCs. MPCs are used to developed T-characteristic vectors according their correspondence relation. The set of elementary siphons can be established through computing a maximal set of linear independent rows of the characteristic T-vector matrix using the Gauss elimination. The correctness of this algorithm is proved finally.

Acknowledgments. This work is supported by the National Nature Science Foundation under Grant 50975224, the Scientific Research Program Funded by Shaanxi Provincial Education Department (Program No. 2010JK708), and the Ph. D. Scientific Research Start-up Funds of Teachers of Xi'an University of Technology of China (Grant No. 108-211006).

References

1. Ezpeleta, J.J., Colom, M., Martinez, J.: A Petri Net Based on Deadlock Prevention Policy for Flexible Manufacturing Systems. IEEE Trans. Robot. Automat. 11, 173–184 (1995)
2. Li, Z.W., Zhou, M.C.: Elementary Siphons of Petri Nets and Their Application to Deadlock Prevention in FMSs. IEEE Trans. Syst. Man, Cybern. A, Syst. Humans 34, 38–51 (2004)
3. Johnson, D.B.: Finding All the Elementary Circuits of a Directed Graph. SIAM J. Comput. 4, 77–84 (1975)
4. Ezpeleta, J., Garcia-Vallés, F., Colom, J.M.: A Class of Well Structured Petri Nets for Flexible Manufacturing Systems. In: Desel, J., Silva, M. (eds.) ICATPN 1998. LNCS, vol. 1420, pp. 64–83. Springer, Heidelberg (1998)
5. Huang, Y., Jeng, M., Xie, X., Chung, S.: Deadlock Prevention policy Based on Petri Nets and Siphon. Int. J. Prod. Res. 39, 283–305 (2001)
6. Xing, K.Y., Hu, B.S., Chen, H.X.: Deadlock Avoidance Policy for Petri-net Modeling of Flexible Manufacturing Systems with Shared resources. IEEE Trans. Automat. Contr. 41, 289–296 (1996)
7. Xing, K.Y., Zhou, M.C., Liu, H.X., Tian, F.: Optimal Petri Net-based Polynomial-complexity Deadlock Avoidance Policies for Automated Manufacturing Systems. IEEE Trans. Syst. Man, Cybern. A, Syat. Humans 39, 188–199 (2009)
8. Xing, K.Y., Zhou, M.C., Wang, F., Liu, H.X., Tian, F.: Resource Transition Circuits and siphons for Deadlock Control of Automated manufacturing Systems. IEEE Trans. Syst. Man, Cybern. A, Syst. Humans 41, 74–84 (2011)
9. Hruz, B., Zhou, M.C.: Modeling and Control of Discrete Event Dynamic Systems. Springer, London (2007)
10. Hu, H.S., Li, Z.W.: Efficient Deadlock Prevention Policy in Automated Manufacturing Systems Using Exhausted Resources. Int. J. Adv. Manuf. Technol. 40, 566–571 (2009)
11. Chao, D.Y., Li, Z.W.: Structural Conditions of Systems of Simple Sequential Processes with Resources Nets without Weakly Dependent Siphons. IET Control Theory Appl. 3, 391–403 (2009)
12. Huang, Y.S., Jeng, M.D., Xie, X.L., Chung, D.H.: Siphon-based Deadlock Prevention Policy for Flexible Manufacturing Systems. IEEE Trans. Syst. Man, and Cyber. 36, 2152–2160 (2006)

The Design of Grain Temperature-Moisture Monitoring System Based on Wireless Sensor Network

Shifeng Qi and Yanhua Li

Institute of Computer, Panzhihua University,
Panzhihua 617000, China
{qeverest,liyanhua5566}@163.com

Abstract. China is a large agricultural country, the safe storage of grain is a major question related to the national economy and the people's livelihood in our country. In the daily custody of grain, the major factor affecting the security storage of grain is the temperature and moisture of grain. So, in order to ensure the security storage of grain, the monitoring of grain temperature and moisture is essential. In this paper, the focused research of the grain temperature-moisture monitoring system based on wireless sensor network technology overcomes the current disadvantages of our country's grain information monitoring system, and gives the design scheme of its hardware and software system. The sensor node in the hardware system is a digital sensing device based on two-wire, which can measure the temperature and moisture of the multilayer grain on line. Verified by several tests and analyzed the test results, which shows stable work performance, high-precision measurement capability and low cost of the system, and that the system is suitable to large-scale popularize. The results will give the important help on development of the technique of the grain monitoring in China.

Keywords: wireless sensor network, grain, monitoring, temperature-moisture sensor.

1 Introduction

The agriculture of china occupies an important position in national development, so grain problem is the most important. On-line measurement for the temperature and moisture of the grain is absolutely necessary [1, 2], whether in daily storage, or in precipitation ventilation, cooling ventilation, regulating quality ventilation. On-line measurement demands the horizontal spacing of the monitoring point is less than 5 meters, the vertical spacing is less than 2 meters, and the less is the repetitive error of the temperature and moisture, the better. The repetitive error of the temperature less than or equal to 0.1°C is the best, and the repetitive error of water less than or equal to 0.02% is the best. With these conditions, even minimal change of the grain statement in storage can be detected. Due to technical and cost reasons, most of the on-line

M. Zhao and J. Sha (Eds.): ICCIP 2012, Part II, CCIS 289, pp. 443–450, 2012.

measurement system, existing so-called "The Grain Information Monitoring System", can only measure the grain temperature, the granary temperature and the granary humidity. Very few of on-line measurement system which are used in Laboratory can not be mass production and put into use, because of sophisticated technique, high cost, large systematic error and repetitive error. The insertion sensor for quick measuring moisture of grain is usually used in grain purchasing, but this method is neither suitable for measuring the depth of 6 m or deeper grain bulk nor on-line measurement. Grain moisture sensing device which is used in grain drying device is not suitable for the on-line measurement of the grain bulk because of structure and large repetitive error. That is to say, the existing "Grain Information Monitoring System" can not suitable for on-line measurement for the temperature and moisture at the same time.

The monitoring system studied in this paper is based on Wireless Sensor Network Technology, the digital sensing device, which can measure the temperature and moisture of the multilayer grain on line, is used to solve the above problems. It has the advantages of simple production process and low cost, and is suitable for mass production.

2   System Overall Design

There are three kinds of nodes in the system, they are acquisition node, routing node and management node [3]. The acquisition node is responsible for field data collection, that is to convert the analog signal such as temperature and moisture to digital signal, and then the transceiver retransmits the recognizable digital signal to the router. The routing node is responsible to retransmit the local node data or the retransmitted data from the other router to the next higher level, plays the role of data routing and relaying, and the sink node in the grain bulk. The management node is responsible for converting the format of the data from the wireless network and retransmitting to the host computer, while, retransmits the task published by the host computer to the wireless network, and plays the role of protocol conversion.

The entire network can be divided into two layers, the network composed of routers and the network composed of acquisition nodes in the granary and routers. Because of the far distance among routers, low distribution density, and showing chainlike distribution, the tree network is used to connect routers. The distribution density of acquisition nodes in the granary is large, and the acquisition nodes exchanges data with routers, so star network is used in the granary.

Because of the particularity of the design of the granary top, the wireless signal attenuation is relatively large. A router is set both inside and outside each granary top to strengthen the wireless signal. The overall structure is shown in figure 1.

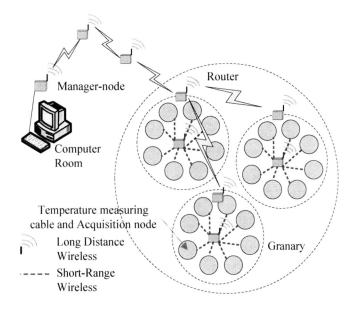

Fig. 1. Overall structure of wireless grain temperature-moisture monitoring system

3   Design of the Sensor Node

3.1   Architecture of the Node

The sensor node [4] is composed of three parts: sensor module, processing module, wireless communication module. The system structure is shown in Figure 2.

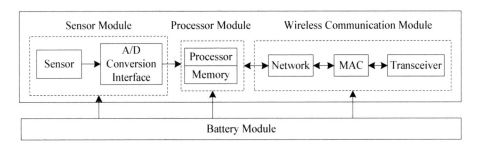

Fig. 2. Architecture of the sensor node

The sensor module is mainly responsible for collecting the grain temperature-moisture information in the monitoring area, for converting the information into electrical signals, then, the A/D converter interface converts from the analog data collected by the sensor to the digital information which can be recognized by the processor.

The processor module is responsible for manipulating the operation of the whole sensor node, storing and processing the digital information which is collected and converted by the local node and the data which is retransmitted from the other router.

The wireless communication module is responsible for communicating with other sensor nodes, exchanging control information and transceiving the data collected by the sensor module.

The battery module respectively provides the required energy which each module runs. It is usually a miniature battery.

3.2   Design of the Temperature-Moisture Sensor

The grain temperature-moisture sensor [5,6] can measure temperature and moisture at the same time, it uses a thermistor or other temperature sensor to measure the grain temperature changing, and uses two detection electrodes to measure the grain moisture value. In practice, the grain filling around the detection electrode becomes the dielectric, the change of grain moisture content causes the difference of dielectric constant, which to cause the change of the capacitance value of the detecting electrode to measure the grain moisture. The measured value of the moisture also needs to be calibrated by the different varieties of grain, and also to be corrected by the grain density and the grain temperature. The equivalent circuit of the sensor is shown in Figure 3.

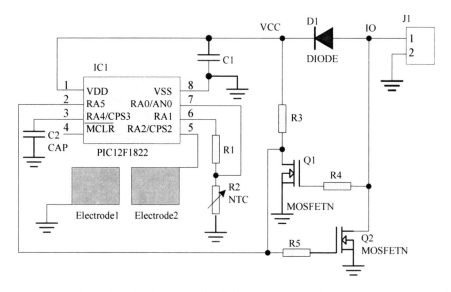

Fig. 3. Circuit principle of the Grain temperature-moisture sensor

In the temperature-moisture measurement circuit, there is a microcontroller PIC 12F1822, which has the function of capacitance detection and temperature detection, or other microcontroller. And two moisture detection electrodes are respectively connected to the ground wire of the detection circuit and one capacitance detection pin of the microcontroller, then, a standard capacitor C2 is respectively connected to the ground wire of the detection circuit and another one capacitance detection pin of the microcontroller, the difference value of the capacitance value of the moisture detection electrodes and the standard capacitor C2 is just the measured value of the grain moisture. The microcontroller supplies power to the series circuit of the thermistor NTC (R2) and the resistor R1. The connection side of the R1 and R2 is connected to the A/D conversion pin of the microcontroller, which is used to measure temperature. The measured temperature value is just the grain temperature value, and this temperature value is used to correct the final measured grain moisture value. The microcontroller is connected to the multiplex circuit of the power line and data line of the sensor, so as to provide the power energy.

The temperature detection component of the sensor is a thermistor, which can also use a pure digital component 18b20, but the cost of 18b20 is high, and the volume is large, which will increase the cost and the production difficulty of the whole sensor cable.

3.3 Design Principle of the Nodes

The sensor node is a digital sensing device based on two-wire [7], which can measure the temperature and moisture of the multilayer grain on line. We use two tensile steel ropes as wire, and the PIC12F1822 microcontroller, which has the advantages of low cost and capacitance detection function, instead of the original circuit composed of microcontroller and capacitive detection device. The sensor node, studied in this paper, has the advantages of simple production process and low cost, and is suitable for mass production. The production process: the first is mass production of the flat cable composed of two tensile steel wires, one is multiplex wire of power line and digital signal transmission line, and another is ground wire of the sensing device. Second, remove a small plastic cladding from a position which needs to install the sensor, the two steel wire show, then weld the two-wire digital grain temperature-moisture sensor to the wire, and then the polymer protective material is deposited on the sensor, adhere to the plastic cladding. Then we insert the two-wire sensor into the grain heap to collect the grain temperature-moisture information. The appearance structure of the node is shown in Figure 4.

Fig. 4. Appearance graph of the sensor nodes

4   Software System Design

The system software [8] is mainly used to control and manage each sensor node in the wireless sensor network. The system uses each sensor node to collect the grain temperature-moisture data from in granaries, and the data are sent to the sink node by the wireless communication module, and then transmitted to the computer through the wireless network, so as to get the real-time data of the grain temperature-moisture. Then, the system detailedly analyses and processes the data, and visually displays the data to the users, in the form of chart or table. The user sends an order to each node, such as cooling or ventilation precipitation order, and to regulate the temperature and moisture of grain heap. The system's control flow chart is shown in Figure 5.

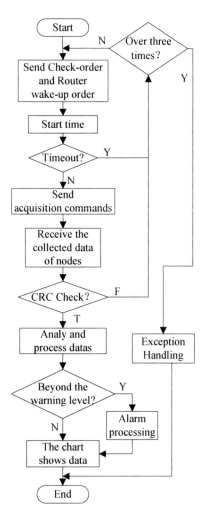

Fig. 5. The flow chart of the system software

5   Experimental Results

Now, according to the design plan, the comparative experiments [7, 9] are conducted between the product and the standard instrument. The experimental environment's temperature is 25°C, relative humidity is 46%, and atmospheric pressure is 91.8Kpa. The experimental data are shown in table 1.

Table 1. Grain Temperature-Moisture Experimental Data

Inspection Items	Temperature / °C		moisture / %	
Serial number	Standard instrument	Product	Standard instrument	Product
1	21.5	21.8	13.22	13.42
2	21.5	21.8	13.22	13.42
3	21.5	21.8	13.22	13.42
4	21.5	21.8	13.22	13.42
5	21.5	21.8	13.22	13.42

According to the experimental data in the table, we find that, the product and the standard instrument, the temperature error is 0.3°C, the moisture error is 0.2%. Moreover, the repetitive error of the temperature is 0.0°C, the repetitive error of the moisture is 0.0%. According to the related technical requirements, the systematic error of the temperature between the product and the standard instrument should not be inferior to ±0.5, moisture systematic error should not be inferior to ±0.5%. The repetition error of the temperature should not be inferior to ±0.1°C, the repetitive error of the moisture should not be inferior to ±0.02%. The experimental results show that, the product can accurately measure grain temperature-moisture values, stable work, high reliability, is an ideal product, and can meet the requirements of practical applications.

6   Conclusion

With the development of science and technology, The sensor technology is increasingly used in people's lives. The grain temperature-moisture measuring device designed in this paper has several characteristics such as stable performance, high accuracy, low cost and so on. Through several experiments and debugging, the monitoring system can well realize to monitor and manage the whole wireless sensor network. The system can run in good condition and high stability, and be promoted in a large-wide. The design plan be given in this paper can also be well applied to other wireless sensor network monitoring system.

Acknowledge. This work is supported by The Ministry of Science and Technology Fund of China (No.06c26211400735).

References

1. Akyildiz, I.F., Su, W., Sankarasubramaniam, Y., Cayirci, E.: A survey on sensor networks. IEEE Communications Magazine 40, 102–114 (2002)
2. Gilbert, J.M., Balouchi, F.: Comparison of Energy Harvesting Systems for Wireless Sensor Networks. International Journal of Automation and Computing 05, 334 (2008)
3. Zhang, X., Wei, P.: A temperature-humidity control system in archives. Industrial Instrumentation & Automation 01, 36–38 (2002)
4. Sun, L., Li, J., Chen, Y., et al.: Wireless Sensor Network, pp. 4–6. Tsinghua University Press, Beijing (2010)
5. Hu, Z.H., Peng, C.W., Xia, Y.X.: A New Kind of Intellectualized Temperature and Humidity Sensor in Measurement and Control System. Sensor World 02, 39–42 (2001)
6. Zhang, R., Zhao, C., Chcn, L., et al.: Design of wireless sensor network node for field information acquisition. Transactions of the CSAE 25, 213–218 (2009)
7. Shi, G., Zhang, B.: Research of A New Soil Moisture Sensor. Agricultural Equipment & Vehicle Engineering (11), 25–27 (2009)
8. Tang, X., Wen Wang, B., Qiang Tan, G., et al.: Health Monitoring of Bridge Using W ireless Sensor Networks. Computer Technology and Development 21, 174–177 (2011)
9. Liu, J., Xie, S.: Development of Intelligentized Water Stage Real Monitoring System. Manufacturing Automation 33, 111–112 (2010)

Study of Improved Genetic Algorithm Based on Neural Network

Xin Chan[1], Baiming Liu[2], and Guoyan Yang[1]

[1] School of Information Science and Technology, Heilongjiang University
Harbin, 150001, China
cheng224@163.com
[2] Department of Computer and Information Engineering, Beijing Science Technology
Management College, Beijing, 102206, China
netbaimingliu@sina.com

Abstract. In order to overcome these disadvantages such as low rate of convergence in neural network back propagation (BP) algorithm, the likeliness to fall into local minima, the absent foundations for selecting initial weight values and threshold values as well as great randomness, the neural network optimization method is developed based on adaptive genetic algorithm. This technique combines advantages on both neural network BP algorithm and neural network optimization method. However, it proves to be unsatisfactory due to the slow evolution of population in early stage. The proposed algorithm is applied in the optimized design of weight values and threshold in neural network. The algorithm model is employed to make forecasts about unfathomable SVI parameters in a sewage plant in one city. The simulation experiment suggests that the aforesaid algorithm can not only eliminate shortcomings in BP algorithm, but also can improve remarkably convergence speed and precision through the comparison of its model with BP and GA-BP network models, obtaining good results.

Keywords: genetic algorithm (GA), neural network, error back propagation algorithm, sewage parameter, soft measurement.

1   Introduction

The artificial neural network (ANN) has excellent nonlinear approximation ability, parallel distributed structure, fairly good tolerance and also adaptive learning and inductive abilities, which all make it to be applied extensively in many aspects e.g. modeling, time sequence analysis, pattern recognition, signal processing and industrial control. Being the primary learning method for feed forward network (FFN), back propagation network algorithm, in short of BP algorithm, is simple and flexible together with small amount of computation and strong parallelism. BP algorithm has been so far one of the most widely used and mature algorithms for neural network training. However, it's quite necessary to improve or optimize it due to the slow rate of convergence and being easy to fall into local minimal values.

M. Zhao and J. Sha (Eds.): ICCIP 2012, Part II, CCIS 289, pp. 451–458, 2012.

In the 1970s, American scholar Holland designed genetic algorithm, which is a kind of optimization searching method based on natural selection and the theory of genetics. By introducing the principle of biological evolution-"Survival of the fittest" to encoding string groups which are produced by to-be-optimized parameters, GA selects out every single individual as per a given fitness function and a series of genetic operations, so as to retain those individuals with higher fitness and form new groups. The fitness of each individual in new groups is continuously increased until it meets some extreme conditions. At the moment, the individual with the highest fitness is considered the optimal solution for such parameters to be optimized. It's on the account of unique working principle of GA that it's probable to search quickly and efficiently for the global optimal solution in a complicated, multimodal and non-differentiable large-scale vector space with strong robustness[1].

In this work, by making use of the improved adaptive genetic algorithm in the optimized design of neural network, recognition and simulation abilities are enhanced against nonlinear problems; and meanwhile, the speed for solving problems is advanced and also the generalization precision in the predictions.

2   Neural Network Optimization Method Based on Improved GA

As far as the features of neural network BP and GA are concerned, the training of BP algorithm depends on the weight modification principle of downward error gradient so that it's inevitable to fall into local minima. Genetic algorithm is suitable for global search but disabled for the accurate local search. Nevertheless, the combination of by taking advantage of GA to optimize initial weight and threshold values in neural network and neural network algorithm to complete network training makes their respective advantages complementary to each other and helps to settle practical problems.

2.1   Steps in the Optimization Neural Network Based on Improved GA

An ANN model can be described by limited parameters like, neuron, layer, the number of neuron in each layer, interconnecting way, weight of each connection, transfer function and so forth. Therefore, it's possible to encode an ANN model and fulfill the whole learning process of neural network through genetic algorithm.

1) Parameters setting. Import population size, layer (exclusive of input layer), the number of neuron in each layer. GA shows very good robustness against the setting of such parameters, so the result will not be affected a lot only by changing those parameters.

2) Initialization and evaluation. Generate randomly the initial population P= { x1 , x2 , ., xn }, set any xi ∈P a weight of neural network, which consists of a weight vector and a threshold vector. The former is an n-dimension real vector, where n is the number of all connection weights. The latter is also an n-dimension real vector, to the exclusion of neurons in the input layer. Each network weight xi is just like a chromosome. The number for such chromosome is N, which is also the size of population. Neurons are numbered in a bottom-up and left-right way, the same case for the input of neurons.

Calculate the global error of each neural network for particular input and output set in accordance with the corresponding neural network to both weight and threshold vectors which are randomly derived. Since GA evolves only towards the way where the fitness can be promoted, the fitness function can be formulated as per the expression (1):

$$f_i = 1/E_i \qquad E_i = \sum_{p=1}^{m}\sum_{k=1}^{n}(V_{pk}-T_{pk}) \qquad (1)$$

where, fi is the adaptive value for the ith individual (i = 1, .,). N is the number of chromosome. k = 1, .. n is the node in output layer. p = 1, .. m stands for learning sample. Vpk means the output value of the kth node when inputing the pth training sample. It is an expected output value.

3) Selection of operator. In the paper, it exerts roulette wheel method and the elitist strategy to integratively select operator. The procedure of such selection is based on roulette wheel [2]. It is a playback random sampling technique. All selections are made against good individuals from the existing population by according to their respective fitness and a standard. The basic theory is: the selective possibility of each individual is equal to the fitness against the summation of that of all individuals in the whole population. The higher the individual fitness is, the bigger possibility there is for it to be selected and the more likely it goes to the next generation. However for the reason of random operation, there are bigger errors in the option of such kind of method. Sometimes individuals with higher fitness are not selected. In order to improve GA's convergence, the elitist strategy is utilized to select individuals with the highest fitness as seeded players to retain in the next generation. Each time when a new group is produced, its worst individuals are substituted by the best individuals in the last generation to prevent the individual with the best fitness in the current population from being damaged[2].

4) Crossover operator and mutation operator. Probability of improved adaptive crossover and mutation Among parameters of genetic algorithm, the selection of crossover probability Pc and mutation probability Pm is the key to influencing GA's behavior and performance, impacting directly the convergence of a method. In simple GA, as Pc and Pm are constant values, in addition to problems like pre-maturity and non-convergence, it's not efficient for solving the complex optimization problems in multivariate. Then, Srinivas et al. proposed adaptive GA algorithm. The basic idea is: consider both smaller crossover possibility Pc and mutation possibility Pm for individuals in a group with higher fitness than the average fitness of the group, for the purpose of keeping individuals with sound structures going to the next generation while from being destroyed. For individuals with lower fitness than the average value, bigger Pc and Pm are adopted as to speed up eliminating individuals of such kind. Problems still occur despite the method is improved against simple GA[3]. To be specific, the more approximate the fitness is to the maximum, the smaller the crossover and mutation possibility become. When the fitness is the maximum, both crossover and mutation possibility are 0. AGA is not so desired in the initial stage of evolution as in the group in a preliminary stage, the best individual lies in a state without changes, which is in this case not really the global optimal solution,

increasing the possibility for the evolution towards the local convergence. Hence, on the basis of the method, it applies an improved adaptive algorithm to make both crossover and mutation possibility of the individual with the maximum fitness not zero, as indicated in formulae (2) and (3):

$$
P_c = \begin{cases} P_{c1} - \dfrac{(p_{c1} - p_{c2})(f' - f_{max})}{2}, & f \geq f_{avg} \\ p_{c1}, & f \leq f_{avg} \end{cases} \tag{2}
$$

$$
P_m = \begin{cases} P_{m1} - \dfrac{(p_{m1} - p_{m2})(f_{max} - f)}{2}, & f \geq f_{avg} \\ p_{m1}, & f \leq f_{avg} \end{cases} \tag{3}
$$

where, favg is the average fitness of each group; fmax is the maximum fitness in a group; f means the bigger fitness for two individuals to be crossed; f means the fitness of individuals to be mutated. Pc1, Pc2, Pm1 and Pm2 are design parameters, respectively equal to 0.9, 0.6, 1.0 and 0.001. The improved AGA not only preserves adaptive advantages in AGA and also gets over the slow evolution of a group in the early stage, being optimized quite well.

Crossover operator First of all, choose randomly in a population a certain amount of chromosomes as parents based on the crossover possibility Pc which is derived in ①. Then randomly select a breaking point and exchange gene chains in the right/upper side of parents to produce new generations. Finally, replace parent chromosomes with offspring ones to obtain new population.

Mutation operator Similar to the selection of parents in the crossover operation, select every good chromosome to go for mutation and allow for many times so as to get better results. During the mutation, a vector is randomly generated with the same dimension to that of each weight value and threshold of those chromosomes, which then sums up with vectors that are selected for mutation. Use the result of each mutation to restore neural network and carry out performance evaluation. If offspring precedes parent, stop the mutation; otherwise, the mutation continues till a generation superior to the parent appears[4].

5) *Immigration operator.* As demonstrated in the experimental test, in search process of genetic algorithm, the individual with the highest fitness in the existing population may also engage in crossover and mutation operation even if it is very small; whereas the possibility is bigger for individuals with lower fitness to be selected for crossover and mutation. The fitness of resultant individuals is lower and global search ability against the method is not significantly promoted. For this reason, it introduces immigration operator, which is a good way for avoiding pre-maturity. During the immigration, it not only stimulates the removal of bad individuals and also enables the diversity of solution, more in conformity with evolution mechanism. Immigration operator eliminates the worst individuals at some rate (about 15%-20%) during each evolution and some outstanding immigrants are derived to be added to the group. Here excellent immigrants are formed by performing several times of

crossover on individuals to die out. Thus, the parent's gene pattern which proves good is saved. The variety of group is guaranteed and the searching performance of GA is improved.

If network error meets the condition or it reaches a certain number of evolution generations, stop it and output the result; otherwise, turn back to 3[5].

2.2   Primary Process of the Algorithm

Initialize the population and encode them, including the initialization of its size and each weight value pursuant to what's adopted by neural network for producing initial weight;

Calculate the selective possibility of each individual and put in a sequence;

Take roulette wheel method to pick out good individuals to the next population;

From the new population, adaptive individuals are selected based on their adaptive crossover probability and mutation probability for respectively crossover and mutation operation as to create new individuals;

Insert new individuals into the population and compute the fitness;

Operation of immigration operator: determine whether it's premature. If yes, take immigration strategy and return to 2;

If desired individuals are found, end it. Or else, return to 2. If the required performance standard is lived up to, the best individual in the final group is decoded and that the optimized network connection weight is obtained.

3   Application and Analysis

In the activated sludge process, sludge volume index (SVI) is one of the major indices for measuring the quality of activated sludge. It displays sludge flocculation and settling ability. Moreover, it can indicate the abnormal occurrences like sludge bulking as early as possibly. In practical use, SVI can not be measured online in real time. Instead, it's measured and calculated manually. It takes at least over two hours for each measurement. Were it possible to measure SVI in real time, it's meaningful for the operation management of sewage treatment system (STS), the improvement of water quality, as well as the prevention from the emergence of sludge bulking[6].

What's used for the test is collected from the real data relating to a Chongqing wastewater disposal plant. The first nine variables are considered measurable auxiliary variables, i.e. input variables. SVI is immeasurable variable, i.e. output variable. 15 nerve cells are extracted from the hidden layer for setting up a BP neural network in a 9-15-1 structure. The input and output of the first eight samples are selected for learning and training. Then the recent four groups of information are employed for testing the network[7].

SVI measured by the improved AGA-BP algorithm, GA-BP algorithm and BP algorithm are respectively 277, 275, 231, 247; 280, 270, 235, 252 and 250, 290, 263, 222. In comparison with the desired output in Table. 1, it displays that both the improved AGA-BP algorithm and GA-BP algorithm have better convergence precision than BP algorithm.

Table 1. Operating A Sewage Treatment Plant Measured The Number Of Training Samples

COD /N	TN /TP	DO (po)	T(po)	F /M	NH4	turbid	ORP
4. 53	10. 54	2. 1	16.4	0.36	28.23	278	1.6
6. 90	8. 99	1. 9	18.8	0.764	48.25	256	1.1
6. 39	9. 60	3. 5	17.4	0.19	34.86	355	1.4
5. 28	10. 04	0.6	17.4	0.368	32.87	403	1.3
7. 20	8. 67	3.1	18.3	0.159	35.24	373	0.6
8. 18	8. 45	3.2	18.8	0.235	53.10	176	0.9
7. 38	8. 70	4.9	19.2	0.125	21.25	157	1.2
4. 59	14. 73	3.2	19.8	0.254	18.23	147	0.9
6. 36	11. 76	1.5	19.2	0.562	16.58	88	2.3
4. 62	10. 81	0.6	18.0	0.042	25.15	69	2.5

Table 2. BP Algorithm, GA – BP   Algorithm and AGA – BP Algorithm   Comparison Of Training

	Standard deviation	Convergence times	Average income convergence Time / s	Convergence rate
BP Algorithm	0.025	8	20.24	Slower
GA – BP Algorithm	0.02	24	14.52	Faster
AGA – BP Algorithm	0.03	25	10.25	Fast

As the experimental comparisons between BP algorithm and GA-BP algorithm as well as the improved AGA-BP algorithm demonstrate, both GA-BP algorithm and the improved AGA-BP algorithm have faster convergence rate and the running time is shorter. In addition, the softsensing model established by the improved AGA-BP algorithm or GA-BP algorithm displays not only the superiority in the global convergence and also the local searching capability owned by BP algorithm. The convergence performance is far better than that of the pure BP algorithm. Also through the comparison, AGA-BP algorithm confirms a faster convergence rate than GA-BP algorithm (Fig. 2).

Figures 1 and 2, respectively, to improve the error of the AGA - BP algorithm and adaptation curve.

Figure 1 and Figure 2 shows that after about 200 generations of search, improved AGA - BP algorithm error of the average fitness of the smallest chromosomes stabilized.

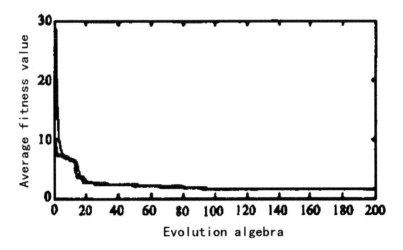

Fig. 1. Error curve

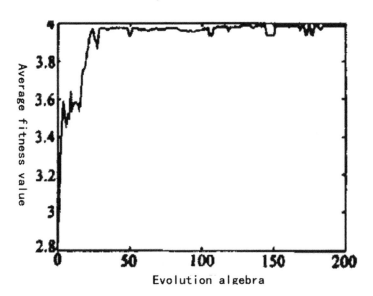

Fig. 2. Adapt to the curve

4   Conclusion

The improved AGA-BP algorithm can perform optimal selection simultaneously on many points within the solution space. After the optimized point is sought out, BP algorithm searches in a negative gradient. As a result, it avoids falling into local minima and a low rate of convergence. Further, shortcomings are overcome, e.g. long-time and slow search, which is caused when GA is seeking for the optimal solution in the method of exhaustion. It's a fast and dependable technique. Besides, the improved AGA-BP algorithm increases further the rate of convergence on the basis of that in GA-BP algorithm.

The optimization method of taking neural network softsensing model based on improved genetic algorithm provides inspirations about promoting the research on the soft measurement of sewage parameters, which is based on intelligent optimization algorithms.

References

1. Holland, J.H.: Adaptation in Natural and Artificial Systems, pp. 99–102. The University of Michigan Press (2005)
2. Srinivas, M., Patnaik, L.M.: Adaptive Probabilities of Crossover and Mutation in Gas. IEEE Trans. on SMC, 656–667 (2004)
3. Niu, X.-Y.: Research Progress on Problems of Neural Network Optimization. Journal of Fuyang Teachers College, 34–42 (2008)
4. Xue, F.-Q., Ge, L.-D., Wang, B.: RBF equalizer based on adaptive niche hierarchy genetic algorithm. Journal of Computer Applications, 102–112 (2009)
5. Ei, Z.C., Yang, L.X.: Optimize the Weight Distribution and Topology of Neural Network by Using The Genetic Algorithm (GA). Journal of Guangxi Normal University, 32–38 (2003)
6. Feng, S.-H., Zhou, P., Qian, F.: A new method of determining the initial weights of a neural network. Industrial Instrumentation & Automation, 65–76 (2006)
7. Zhao, Q., Guo, Y., Mei, Q., Qi, Z.: A Survey on Determination Methods of RBF Neural Network Centers. Guangdong Automation & Information Engineering, 85–93 (2002)

The Application of Improved DNA Genetic Algorithm in Solving Multi-objective Optimization Problem

Hua Huang[1], Yanhua Zhong[2], and Shuzhi Nie[2]

[1] Dept. of Information Science and Technology, Qingyuan Polytechnic
511510 Qingyuan, China
qyhuanghua@126.com
[2] Dept. of Electronics & Information Technology, Jiangmen Polytechnic
529090 Jiangmen, China
{zhflowers,sznie778}@163.com

Abstract. In this paper, set up a mathematical model on multi objective optimization problem, raised a RNA genetic algorithm based on DNA computing to solve multi objective optimization problem. Carried out RNA four digit system encoding method based on DNA computing and RNA computing operator in genetic algorithm. Solved the encoding scheme and convergence problem. Under some constraint conditions, the designed algorithm got simulated; Simulation results showed that this algorithm has a better optimum searching and seeking abilities, made the scheduling results comparatively reasonable and enlarged the application of DNA computing.

Keywords: DNA computation, RNA computation, genetic algorithm, multi objective optimization.

1 Introduction

Multi-objective flexible scheduling is one of the representative problems of uncertain polynomial hard problems, which seek optimum solutions of multi-objects. Now there are many answers for the flexible scheduling actuality. This study is of practical and theoretical significance. It has a role in guiding production and practice [1-3].

In recent years, some intelligent calculation methods such as genetic algorithm, neural networks etc... They are being successively used to solve scheduling problems. These optimization methods have made certain application effects on scheduling problems [3-4]. It has large latent abilities for solving the complex optimization, which has been successfully applied to some industrial projects. Genetic algorithms have attracted wide attention and concern. It was considered to be a very worthwhile research method of intelligent optimization, particularly in the areas of application, development, and production, planning and scheduling [5-7].

DNA computation and genetic algorithm exist certain similarities in ideological, DNA computation is a method of molecular biology information coding, used the double-helix structure of DNA and the rule of complementary base pairing [7-9]. DNA

M. Zhao and J. Sha (Eds.): ICCIP 2012, Part II, CCIS 289, pp. 459–467, 2012.

is an important material, carried ample genetic information. It can promote genetic algorithm simulate biological rule, improve the performance of genetic algorithm. Genetic algorithm can be a breakthrough in the limits of DNA computation [9-10]. Scholars have put forward some algorithms based on DNA computation to solve various complex problems [10-11]. Researchers have divided the DNA molecular sequence into two classes: neutral and harmful. They pointed out that genetic manipulation in molecular sequences can cause different evolutionary results. The same DNA sequence exist hot spots and cold spots in different locations; the mutation probability of the base in the cold spots is far less than the base in hot spots [7-8, 11].

2   Problem Description

Flexible scheduling problems means to give each work-piece optional path solutions, to find a workable scheduling solution for each group of work-piece, and to optimize some of these given performance index. Details are as follows: to process N work-pieces on M machine tools, each work-piece J_i is made up by n_i working procedures, among these n_i working procedures, there is a kind of order restricts relations in arts and crafts, each working procedure of work-piece can be processed by many machine tools out of M machine tools, and the processing time differs from performance to performance of these machine tools.   In view of the different surroundings of manufacturing system, make the following assumption: each machine tool can process only one work-piece at one time; the processing time was given ahead of time; all machine tools are perfect and workable at time of $t=0$; all work-pieces can be processed at time of $t=0$; the machine damage is ignored [5-7].

   The hybrid scheduling objectives of flexible scheduling are as follows: In every possible way, to shorten the period of production and boost working efficiency; to shorten general time of delivery and improve customers' satisfaction; to decrease load of machine tools and increase utilization rate of available resources. In that case, production period f_1, general deferred time f_2, largest load of machine tool f_3 and general load of machine tool f_4 can be expressed as follows:

$$f_1 = \max C_i \tag{1}$$

$$f_2 = \sum_{i=1}^{N} \max\{C_i - d_i, 0\} \tag{2}$$

$$f_3 = \max \sum_{i=1}^{N} \sum_{j=1}^{n_i} t_{ijk} X_{ijk} \tag{3}$$

$$f_4 = \sum_{k=1}^{M} \sum_{i=1}^{N} \sum_{j=1}^{n_i} t_{ijk} X_{ijk} \tag{4}$$

Among them, $i = 1, 2, \ldots, N$; $k = 1, 2, \ldots, M$; C_i is the completion time of the work-piece J_i ; d_i is the delivery time of job J_i ; t_{ijk} is the processing time of the process j for work-piece J_i on No. k Machine; X_{ijk} is the decision variable, if the process j of the work-piece J_i can be processed by No. k Machine tools, then $X_{ijk} = 1$, otherwise $X_{ijk} = 0$.

In the following hybrid genetic algorithm based on DNA computation is used to solve multi-objective scheduling optimization problems.

3   Algorithm Design

From the calculation angle of view, single strands of DNA chain become a string, can use four characters alphabet $\sum = \{A, T, G, C\}$ to represent information encoding. Give every DNA element a binary code, set A=00, T=01, G=10, C=11, can easily realize the interchange between DNA base and binary code. At the same time, maintain the complementary corresponding relations between DNA bases. That is, the calculation model of DNA coding can also be built based on two binary numbers---0, 1. The different coding characters are equivalence one-to-one mapping.

Further, sometimes DNA double-strand structure isn't suitable for direct combining with the chromosomes of genetic algorithm. However, the unique single-strand RNA structure, and the vertical inheritance of genetic information Adenine, Guanine, Cytosine and Uralic, combine RNA computation and genetic algorithm is possible, Which make a great development for RNA computation.

In a standard genetic algorithm, the initialization of chromosome is usually conducted through a random generation, which produced unlawful chromosome easily. In this paper, first, the RNA population initialization produced a number M of $N \times M$ matrices at random. Then, used the chromosome of natural numbers coding of $[1, N]$ as RNA colonies formed by initial populations, the numbers of RNA populations are just M, which is different from the standard genetic algorithm. To prevent producing unlawful chromosome, used random numbers to produce the natural numbers between $[1, N]$ in turn, recorded the times of each production, set each random number only appeared M times in chromosome, otherwise, reinitialized the population. In this way, unlawful chromosome can be prevented.

The solutions space of RNA sequences are $E = \{A, U, G, C\}^L$. That is, RNA sequences used A, U, G, C four bases to encode a length of L RNA sequences, which composed by four kinds of bases: Uralic, Cytosine, Adenine, Guanine. Used 0(00), 1(01), 2(10), 3(11) to encode A, U, G, C with four-digit-system, then, the spaces of the L length RNA molecule sequences are $E = \{0, 1, 2, 3\}^L$.

Adopt coding ways based on an improved process. First, arrange scheduling code corresponding to working procedure, thus, each gene in the sequences of RNA population stand for one process. Can appoint all processes of a work-piece with the same symbol, compile these symbols according to which appeared in the order of the sequences, scan the sequences from left to right. The serial-number of a work-piece appeared i times stand for the number S_i process of the work-piece. So, for number N processes and number M machines, one RNA sequence includes a number $N \times M$ of genes, each work-piece appears M times in the sequence. To distinguish from the standard genetic algorithm, each gene doesn't stand for the specific process S_i of a work-piece i, but indicates the upper and lower dependency process. This way can overcome the possible process incompleteness in a work-piece process, make the random arrangement of RNA sequences always can produce feasible scheduling.

The strategy for preserving elites is: first, if the elite individuals participate and the new solutions dominate part of the elite population solutions, wipe off the dominated solutions and add some new solutions. After reservation elite, the individuals in preserved colonies are all non-dominated individuals, their Pareto sorting values both are 1. When there are excessive preserved individuals, under the restriction of density grid, should delete high grid density to ensure only one individual for one grid. The objective function as dimensionality of the cell width is shown as follows:

$$g_{wi} = \frac{\max f_i(x) - \min f_i(x)}{K_i} \tag{5}$$

In formula (5), parameter g_{wi} is the width of the i-dimension cell. Parameter K_i is the quantity of the i-dimension cell, for the different evolutionary algebra. The largest and smallest values of objective function are quite different. The width of cell depends on the evolutionary algebra, but the quantity of cell will never change. Get the grid information, select the individuals in the same grid, and delete the dense individuals.

Through operation of elite reservation, the reserved colonies obviously are the best parents' colonies, can directly regard them as genetic operation of the parents. If the reserved colonies quantity is $N' < N$, according to the fitness value of the remaining colonies, use the championship method to choose the excellent individuals as the parents.

Document [8-9] divides the DNA molecular sequence into two classes of neutral and harmful, and points out to carry out the genetic manipulation in different molecular sequence can result in different evolutionary results. Inspired by this, we can define the best $N/2$ individuals as neutral individuals, the remaining as harmful ones. Crossover operator is always implemented in neutral individuals, which the probability of replacement operation is 1 and transposition operation is 0.5. R_2 is the random son-sequence within the scope of the current sequence [1, L], R_2' is the random son-sequence within the other neutral sequence, but the sequence length of R_2' are the same as R_2. When transposition operation is to be carried out, R_2 is accessed randomly from the former half part of the current sequence, then the new location of R_2 will generated randomly from scope of $[R_{2h}+L/2, L]$, in which R_{2h} is the son-sequence location in the latter half part corresponding to the location of R_2 in the former half part. If transposition operation is not to be carried out, then replacement operation will be implemented. In replacement operation, son-sequence R_2 will generated randomly from the former half part of the current sequence, son-sequence R_4 will generated randomly from the latter half part, which with the same length of R_2. According to cross operation, N/2 neutral father sequences will generate N son sequences, i.e., the son sequences will be twice as the father sequences.

In order to maintain the diversity and generate new genotypes, mutation operation will be carried out among the harmful father sequences, and among son sequences which produced by cross operation, so at the beginning there are 3N/2 mutation operators. In the study of DNA sequence model, Document[8] points out at the same DNA sequence exists hot spot and cold spot in different locations, the mutation probability of the base in clod spot is far less than the base in hot spot. In terms of RNA-GA, RNA sequence should have a different hot spot and cold spot in different stages of evolution. So, mutation probability should be a dynamic process. If we set the [1, $L/2$] RNA sequence as the law position, [$L/2$, L] as the high position, accordingly, we can define two kinds of mutation probability, i.e. high mutation probability p_h and law mutation probability p_l , respectively showed as follows:

$$p_h = a + b / \{1 + \exp[c(g_1 - g_2)]\} \tag{6}$$

$$p_l = a + b / \{1 + \exp[-c(g_1 - g_2)]\} \tag{7}$$

In these two formulas, a is the ultimate mutation probability of p_h and the initial mutation probability of p_l, b is the range of mutation probability, g_1 is the current evolutionary algebra, g_2 is the turning point of hot spot and cold spot, c is the change rate. Upon the completion of the above-mentioned mutation probability calculation will create a random L number between [0, 1]. When compared it with the mutation probability, if the mutation probability is greater than the corresponding random number, then the mutation operation will be implemented.

The steps of designed algorithm are shown as follows:

Step 1: Set N as the genotype scale, G as the biggest evolutionary algebra, and k_i as the grid number of the No. i target function;

Step 2: Randomly generate initial quaternary sequences, calculate the fitness value of individual;

Step 3: Elite-reservation and individual-safeguard;

Step 4: Retain the individual as the paternal sequence of the genetic manipulation. If the reservation number of individuals is less than N , then use the Championship methods in the remaining individuals to complement the shortage.

Step 5: Implement the RNA crossover and mutation operator based on DNA computation;

Step 6: Of the produced sequences in Step 5, select the best $N/2$ sequences and the worst $N/2$ sequences as the next initial generation, calculate the fitness of them. If the result meets the quit condition, then out; if not, go back to Step 3, repeat until it meet.

4   Experiment and Analysis

To verify the above designed algorithm, use the following simulation test conditions: there are six machine tools to process four work-pieces, each work-piece has three processes, each process can select more than one machine tool for processing. The processing time of each process is different on different machine tools. The processing time of a work-piece in each process on different machine tools are shown in Table 1.

Table 1. Processing schedule

Work-piece	Process	M1	M2	M3	M4	M5	M6	Delivery date
J_1	0	2	3	4				
	1		3		2	4		14
	2	1	4	5				
J_2	0	3		5		2		
	1	4	3			6		17
	2			4		7	11	
J_3	0	5	6					
	1		4		3	5		13
	2			13		9	12	
J_4	0	9		7	9			
	1		6		4		5	12
	2	1		3			3	

Successively use standard genetic algorithm and DNA genetic algorithm to resolve the scheduling problem. From several times of simulation optimization process, we found that the convergence rate and optimizing performance of RNA-GA algorithm were more sensitive to a and b, but not to c. Set up a larger a and b can speed up the convergence rate. However, if a and b parameters were too large, it will lead algorithm into a random search algorithm and reduce the convergence rate of algorithm; similarly, if a and b parameters were too small, it will lead algorithm into a local minimum point, also affect the performance of algorithm. After many times of simulation optimization, set the RNA-GA parameters respectively between [0.01, 0.05] and [0.10, 0.30].

When doing the simulation optimization, we took the largest evolutionary algebra G as 50, population number N as 50, sequence length L as 40, a as 0.02, b as 0.2, g_2 as $G/2$, c as $20/G$, and suppose k_i as 50, λ as 0.9. Pareto optimal solution sets obtained by these two methods as shown in Table 2.

After analyzed the dates in Table 2, we know that under the same conditions, optimal solutions obtained by DNA genetic algorithm are apparently better than the standard genetic algorithm. We chose the two former optimal solution sets to make analysis; the results obtained by scheduling Gantt will show in Fig.4. From Fig.4, we know that the parallel processing machines were equally assigned the tasks, and all machines remained continuously in the processing time. It indicates that the scheduling results were reasonable. Although the processing orders of each work-piece were different, the two optimal solution groups can exactly get the same target. So this algorithm has its realistic meaning for flexible scheduling optimization, and it also expanded the application of DNA computation.

Table 2. Optimal solution sets

	SGA				DNA-GA			
No.1	17	5	11	46	17	5	11	44
No.2	17	5	11	46	17	5	11	44
No.3	17	6	11	48	17	6	11	45
No.4	17	6	11	48	17	6	11	45
No.5	18	10	10	54	18	10	10	48
No.6	18	10	10	54	18	10	10	48

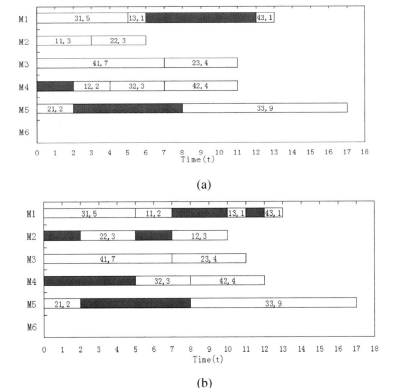

(a)

(b)

Fig. 1. Optimal solutions

From the algorithm and simulation analysis, we knew that in the process of RNA-GA realization been replaced by biological RNA molecules computation, even the better solution calculation of RNA molecules was deleted unconsciously, by reorganizing and mutating RNA molecules, we can still get a better optimal solution in the next step. Through the limited duplication of operation, the best optimal solution or sub-optimal solution will be greatly increased.

5   Conclusions

For the multi-objective optimization problem, we put forward an improved genetic algorithm based on DNA computation. Used elite-reservation strategy, at the same time adopting quaternary encoding based on DNA computation and RNA genetic operator, designed subsection crossover and dynamic mutation operation. Ensured the diversity of solution and meet the multi-objective flexible scheduling. Simulation results prove the feasibility of the algorithm. The algorithm provides a better optimum searching and higher seeking abilities.

Acknowledgment. This project is supported by National High-Tech Research and Development Program of China under grant No. 2007AA04Z111.

References

1. Altiparmak, F., Gen, M., Lin, L., Paksoy, T.: A genetic algorithm approach for multi-objective optimization of supply chain networks. Computers & Industrial Engineering 51(1), 196–215 (2006)
2. Pezzella, F., Morganti, G., Ciaschetti, G.: A genetic algorithm for the Flexible Job-shop Scheduling Problem. Computers & Operations Research 35(10), 3202–3212 (2008)
3. Gonçalves, J.F., Mendes, J.J.M., Resende, M.G.C.: A genetic algorithm for the resource constrained multi-project scheduling problem. European Journal of Operational Research 189(3), 1171–1190 (2008)
4. Mendes, J.J.M., Gonçalves, J.F., Resende, M.G.C.: A random key based genetic algorithm for the resource constrained project scheduling problem. Computers & Operations Research 36(1), 92–109 (2009)
5. Zhu, S., Wang, Y.-M., Hu, X.-Q.: Application of immune genetic algorithm to back analysis for parameters in model of rockfill dam coarse grain material. Yantu Lixue (Rock and Soil Mechanics) 31(3), 961–966 (2010)
6. Huang, B.: The Research on Several Theoretic Problems of DNA Computer. Doctoral dissertation of Huazhong University of Science & Technology, pp. 43–51 (2005)
7. Nie, S.: Research on Collaborative Manufacturing Resources Optimization Deployment based on DNA genetic algorithm. Doctoral dissertation of South China University of Technology, pp. 75–92 (2010)
8. Zhang, G., Shao, X., Li, P., Gao, L.: An effective hybrid particle swarm optimization algorithm for multi-objective flexible job-shop scheduling problem. Computers & Industrial Engineering 56(4), 1309–1318 (2009)

9. Moslehi, G., Mahnam, M.: A Pareto approach to multi-objective flexible job -shop scheduling problem using particle swarm optimization and local search. International Journal of Production Economics 129(1), 14–22 (2010)
10. Karimi, N., Zandieh, M., Karamooz, H.R.: Bi-objective group scheduling in hybrid flexible flowshop: A multi-phase approach. Expert Systems with Applications 37(6), 4024–4032 (2010)
11. Dudas, C., Frantzén, M., Ng, A.H.C.: A synergy of multi-objective optimization and data mining for the analysis of a flexible flow shop. Robotics and Computer Integrated Manufacturing 27(4), 687–695 (2011)

Study on High-Sensitivity Detection System of Aromatic Hydrocarbons

Gang Sun, Zhiming Zhou, Mengzhong Zhu, and Wei Quan

Basic Department, Air Force Aviation University, Changchun, China
sundazui@gmail.com

Abstract. In order to meet the requirement of oil pollution detecting, a study on the detection system of oil in water is initiated in this paper. According to the fluorescence characteristics of aromatic hydrocarbons in oil, an optical system is made to produce UV and to detect fluorescence, and then we use a PMT to collect the fluorescence and transform it into current signal, which can be processed by the system composed of hardware and software. We take C8051F020 MCU as the core of hardware; also the system can complete the data acquisition, storage, and communicate with PC via interface software. After implementation of software, we take experiments to test the effectiveness of system. Experimental results show that whole system performed well in detection of aromatic hydrocarbons.

Keywords: aromatic hydrocarbons, fluorescence, piecewise linear interpolation.

1 Introduction

With the large exploitation and wide application of oil, oil pollution is becoming an increasingly serious problem, detection and resolution of oil pollution is very important[1]. Generally speaking, oil has many ingredients in water, but the proportion of the aromatic hydrocarbons is stable, therefore, determining the content of oil in water by detecting Aromatic hydrocarbons has been widely recognized in the environment detecting [2].

2 Measuring Principle

Lambert- Beer's Law indicates the relationship among the absorbance, the concentration and the thickness of solution, which is given by the formula

$$A = \varepsilon L C \tag{1}$$

Where A is the absorbance; ε is a characteristic constant of the substance; L is the thickness of solution; and C is the density of the solution.

M. Zhao and J. Sha (Eds.): ICCIP 2012, Part II, CCIS 289, pp. 468–475, 2012.

The fluorescence intensity of the solution is determined by absorbance of the solution and fluorescence efficiency of the substance, that is:

$$F = \varphi(I_0 - I)$$

(2)

Where F is the fluorescence intensity; φ is the fluorescence efficiency of the substance; I_0 is the incident intensity; and I is the transmitted intensity.

According to Lambert-Beer's Law, we can make the conclusion that

$$I = I_0 \times 10^{-\varepsilon LC} = I_0 \times e^{-2.3\varepsilon LC}$$

(3)

$$F = \varphi I_0 (1 - e^{-2.3\varepsilon LC})$$

(4)

Combined with Taylor formula

$$e^x = \sum_{n=0}^{\infty} \frac{x^n}{n!}$$

(5)

$$F = \varphi I_0 (2.3\varepsilon LC - \sum_{n=2}^{\infty} \frac{x^n}{n!})$$

(6)

Formula (6) implies that if the solution is thick enough (εLC <0.05), the above formula can be simplified as

$$F = \varphi I_0 \times 2.3\varepsilon LC$$

(7)

If the solution is thin enough (εLC <0.05), the density and the fluorescence intensity of the solution is linear. Under the ultraviolet irradiation (wavelength: 253.7 nm), only aromatic hydrocarbons will produce fluorescence of 352 nm wavelength[1], so we can detect the fluorescence intensity of 352 nm wavelength in order to determine the density of aromatic hydrocarbons in water, which is the detection principle of this system.

3   Hardware Design

This system takes C8051F MCU (Micro Control Unit) as its core, keyboard, LCD and printer as its human-machine interface, EEPROM was used as data storage, this system can also communicate with PC. And most important it must equip an optical system, which can produce UV and detect fluorescence. The hardware structure can be described in the form of the block diagram in Figure 1.

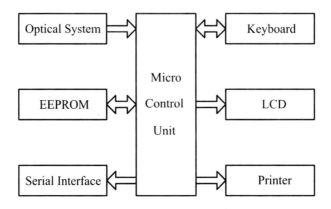

Fig. 1. Block diagram for hardware structure

3.1   MCU

The C8051F single chip computer manufactured by Silicon Laboratories is a completely integrated system-level chip, fully compatible with the instruction set of MCS-51[3-4].

The C8051F020 family utilizes Silicon Labs' proprietary CIP-51 microcontroller core. The CIP-51 employs a pipelined architecture that greatly increases its instruction throughput over the standard 8051 architecture. By contrast, the CIP-51 core executes 70% of its instructions in one or two system clock cycles, with only four instructions taking more than four system clock cycles.

The most unique enhancement is the Digital Crossbar. The on-chip counter/timers, serial buses, HW interrupts, comparator outputs, and other digital signals in the controller can be configured to appear on the Port I/O pins specified in the Crossbar control registers.

The C8051F020 has an on-chip 12-bit SAR ADC (ADC0) with a 9-channel input multiplexer and programmable gain amplifier. With a maximum throughput of 100 ksps, the ADC offers true 12-bit accuracy. The internal voltage reference circuit consists of a 1.2 V, 15 ppm/°C (typical) band gap voltage reference generator and a gain-of-two output buffer amplifier. So using the internal voltage requires that the input current must be lower than 2.4V.

3.2   Optical System

The structure of optical system is shown in figure 2.

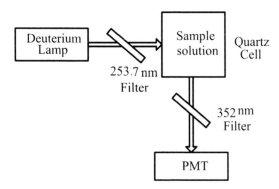

Fig. 2. Structure of optical system

The deuterium lamp is used to radiate UV, the UV then irradiates quartz cell filled with sample solution through a filter of 253.7 nm. The aromatic hydrocarbons in quartz cell would produce fluorescence of 352 nm, we use another filter of 352nm to filter out the rest of the wavelength, a photomultiplier tube(PMT) is used to collect the fluorescence and transform fluorescence into current signal.

To solve the detection problem of photomultiplier tubes incepting weak photo-electric signal, the method of detecting weak photo-electric signal is proposed based on the H7712 photomultiplier tubes.

The current signal emitted by the photomultiplier is so weak that the MCU can not detect exactly. The amplifier circuit contains a low-pass filter and an integrated operational amplifier ICL7650. The out voltage from the amplifier circuit and the signal ground are connected to the differential input ports of a instrumentation amplifier AD623 which is configured for unity gain ($G = 1$) in order to eliminate the common-mode interference.

3.3   Human-Machine Interface

The system employs a LCM240128 made by XINHUALONG Corp. to display the results. LCD can display the Chinese characters, numbers and letters, and it also can display cursor blinking and real time data. So LCD has been widely used in the display of intelligent instruments and meters. The module contains LCD display, driving circuit, controlling module T6963C made by TOSHIBA, PCB main board, RAM, and backup light.

A 4*5 matrix keyboard is used and its nine controlling lines are all linked to the I/O ports of the MCU. Keyboard is the most common input device in computer systems. A connection matrix is used especially when too many keys are needed; namely each key is placed at the intersection point of N I/O lines and M I/O lines. Set N equal to 4 and M equal to5, so totally 20 keys are placed on the system.

A serial printer made by WEIDA is used. The application of single-chip micro-printer is very wide, such as intelligent instrument, medical equipment, fire alarm printing, etc. It almost becomes a standard system configuration. It makes that the result can not only be stored in the EEPROM, but also be printed out for people to check out.

3.4   Other Interface

The system has the capability of storing results by using an EEPROM AT24C512 even when it is not powered. The SMBus0 I/O interface between AT24C512 and MCU is a two-wire, bi-directional serial bus. It is compatible with the I2C serial bus.

It is convenient for users to confirm and record the time by using a real time clock chip SD2303. In this system users could get or modify the time at any time. The interface between SD2303 to MCU is also a two-wire serial bus.

The system employs a portable switch power. Other internal voltages can be got by using some DC-DC converters.

4   Software Design

The system is programmed with C language under the development environment of Keil C51 μVision 2. Software platform is master-slave model, in which the main program and subroutine debugged in their own separate environment with top-down approach. With the function of application development process, and have been the perfect combination debugging. Main program of the role is to finish by setting the CPU of the whole system integration and between modules of coordination. The main program flowcharts see Figure 3.

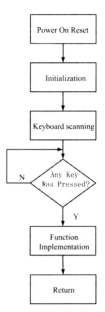

Fig. 3. Main program flowcharts

Function implementation consists of: multi-Chinese character menu, displaying and modifying time, measuring and storing the result, querying and printing the history data, connecting to PC and calibration algorithm.

When it comes to the calibration of system, such measurement is widely accepted. Serials of different density(x_i) standard solution would be tested, the corresponding voltage(y_i)would be recorded as well at the beginning, then the relationship between x_i and y_i would be established, further more, we can get the working curve of the system, to which we can get any aromatic hydrocarbon density of sample solution according. According to the above mentioned relationship between concentration of solution and the fluorescence intensity, If the solution is thick enough (εLC <0.05), they are linear, so we apply piecewise linear interpolation as the calibration curve of this system.

At the given interval, we choose n+1 knots as $x_0< x_1<...<x_n$, and the corresponding function value $y_i=f(x_i)(i=0,1,2...n)$. If we want to compute any function value $f(x)$ of any knot $x \neq x_i$, only the subinterval x belongs to$[x_i, x_{i+1}]$ is known, can we apply linear interpolation at this subinterval. And, the piecewise linear interpolation formula is given as

$$P(x) = \frac{x-x_i}{x_{i+1}-x_i} y_{i+1} + \frac{x-x_{i+1}}{x_i - x_{i+1}} y_i \quad x \in [x_i, x_{i+1}] \tag{8}$$

The advantage of piecewise linear interpolation is that we only take two knots, left and right, no all the knots. Thus, this can highly avoid accumulative errors. The implementation flowcharts are given as figure 4(N knots).

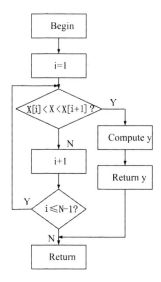

Fig. 4. Piecewise linear interpolation flowcharts

5   Experiment and Results Analysis

To test the reliability and effectiveness of the system, diesel is used as a testing object, ultrasonic oscillator is used to mix diesel and water, the solution of different density would be tested by system. The test results are shown in table 1.

Table 1. Different density & different voltage

Density (mg/L)	Voltage (V)
1	0.01220
2	0.02562
5	0.06344
10	0.12688
20	0.25620
50	0.67954
100	1.57014

According to the above mentioned piecewise linear interpolation formula, the calibration curve of system is given as figure5.

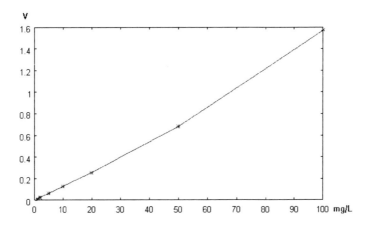

Fig. 5. Calibration curve of system

In order to test the errors of this system, we test 3 samples of different density 15 mg/L, 30mg/L and75 mg/L; we take V_s as the results for system measuring, take V_c as the results for calibration curve computing, and define errors E_v as

$$E_v = |V_s - V_c|$$

(9)

The testing results is given as table 2. Results indicate that when the solution is thin enough($\leq$20mg/L), the voltage and the density is linear, but this linear relationship becomes bad when the solution is thicker($\geq$50 mg/L).

Table 2. Comparison of system measuring &calibration curve computing

Density(mg/L)	Vs(V)	Vc(V)	Ev(V)
15	0.18910	0.19154	0.00244
30	0.39162	0.39730	0.00568
75	1.11386	1.12484	0.01098

6   Conclusion

The results obtained from this study indicate that the detection system based on C8051F is appropriate for further application and for characterization of simple designed, easy operated. Giving full consideration to the design of the system functionality and flexibility, the system was designed around the C8051f microcontroller and applied for any physical signals. In the hardware circuit design comprehensively considered the present as well as the future will be possible to expand the function. The system can also be improved into on-line measuring system.

References

1. Cao, Z., Dong, X.D.: Fluorescence analysis of mineral oil in water. Journal of Northeast Normal University (Natural Science Edition) 37(3), 64–68 (2005)
2. Shi, L.J., Wang, L.R.: Online system of examing oil-in-water using ultraviolet fluorescence. Journal of Changchun University 17(08m), 37–40 (2007)
3. Pan, Z.J., Shi, G.J.: The priciple and application of C8051Fxxx high speed SOC, pp. 55–70. Beihang University Press, Beijing (2002)
4. Mei, J.: The embedded system designing. Journal of Guizhou University of Technology(Natural Science Edition) 36(1), 13–14 (2007)

Algebraic-Trigonometric Cubic Hermite Curve with a Shape Parameter

Yue-e Zhong, Juncheng Li, Chun Xie, Lian Yang, and Chunying Liu

Department of Mathematics
Hunan Institute of Humanities, Science and Technology
Loudi, 417000, China
yuezye@163.com

Abstract. A class of algebraic-trigonometric cubic Hermite interpolating curve with a shape parameter is presented, which shares the same properties of the classical cubic Hermite interpolating curve. The shape of the proposed curve can be adjusted by taking different values of the shape parameter. And the proposed curve also can be C^2 continuous and represent some transcendental curves exactly.

Keywords: Algebraic-trigonometric cubic Hermite interpolating curve, shape parameter, C^2 continuous, archimedes spiral, conical spiral.

1 Introduction

Curve and surface design are one of the important scientific research subjects in computer aided geometric design (CAGD) and computer graphics (CG). The spline curves and surfaces are usually based on the polynomial function space in early studies, such as the traditional Ferguson curve, Bezier curve, and B-spline curve. In recent years, many non-polynomial bases are presented in other new space. For instance, Pena [1] constructed trigonometric polynomial basis in the space $\{1, \cos t, \cos 2t, \cdots, \cos mt\}$, which was similar to Bernstein basis. Some quasi-cubic triangle curves with parameters were investigated based on the space $\{1, \sin u, \cos u, \sin^2 u\}$, and this kind of curves not only had the same properties of the traditional cubic polynomial curve, and also could accurately represent some quadratic curves [2-3]. Han [4-5] discussed the segmented quadratic trigonometric polynomial spline curve and cubic trigonometric polynomial spline.

In some papers, mixed basis functions were constructed with polynomial and trigonometric functions. Zhang[6-8] put forward the C-Ferguson curve, C-Bézier curve and C-B-spline curve in the space $\{1, t, \sin t, \cos t\}$. Mainar [9-10] gave the normal B-basis in the spaces $\{\sin t, \cos t, t^2, t, 1\}$ and $\{1, t, \cos t, \sin t, t \cos t, t \sin t\}$. A class of quasi-Bézier curve was presented based on the space $\{\sin t, \cos t, t^{n-3}, t^{n-4}, \cdots, t, 1\}(n \geq 3)$ [11].

M. Zhao and J. Sha (Eds.): ICCIP 2012, Part II, CCIS 289, pp. 476–483, 2012.

The traditional polynomial splines can not represent some transcendental curves precisely, such as the cycloid, conical spiral, Archimedean spiral, which limits the range of its applications. In order to overcome the defects of the standard cubic interpolating splines, this paper establishes a new algebraic-trigonometric cubic C^2 continuous Hermite interpolating curve with a shape parameter in the space $\{1, t, t\cos t, t\sin t\}$, which shares the same properties of the traditional cubic Hermite interpolating curve. And the shape of the interpolating curve defined by algebraic-trigonometric functions can be adjusted easily by using the shape parameter α. With the appropriate control points and shape parameters, the new C^2 continuous quasi-cubic spline can be used to exactly represent circular arcs and some transcendental curves, such as Archimedes spiral, conical spiral lines.

2 Algebraic-Trigonometric Hermite Basis

Definition 1. For a given parameter $\alpha \in (0, \pi)$, and $0 \le t \le \alpha$, the following four functions

$$
\begin{cases}
F_0(t) = 1 + \dfrac{\sin\alpha + \alpha\cos\alpha}{\alpha^2(\cos\alpha - 1)}(t\cos t - t) - \dfrac{\alpha + \sin\alpha + \alpha\cos\alpha}{\alpha^2\sin\alpha}t\sin t \\[2mm]
F_1(t) = \dfrac{\sin\alpha + \alpha\cos\alpha}{\alpha^2(\cos\alpha - 1)}(t - t\cos t) + \dfrac{\alpha + \sin\alpha + \alpha\cos\alpha}{\alpha^2\sin\alpha}t\sin t \\[2mm]
G_0(t) = \dfrac{t}{\cos\alpha - 1}(\cos\alpha\cos t - 1) - \dfrac{1 + \cos\alpha}{\sin\alpha}t\sin t \\[2mm]
G_1(t) = \dfrac{\sin\alpha}{\alpha(\cos\alpha - 1)}(t\cos t - t) - \dfrac{1}{\alpha}t\sin t
\end{cases}
\tag{1}
$$

are called algebraic-trigonometric Hermite basis, where α is called the shape parameter.

From Eq. (1), the new Hermite basis functions have the following properties:

1) Properties of the Endpoints. By calculating, the algebraic-trigonometric Hermite basis functions have the similar properties to the classical Hermite basis functions, i.e.

$$
\begin{cases}
F_0(0) = 1, F_0(\alpha) = 0, F_0'(0) = 0, F_0'(\alpha) = 0 \\
F_1(0) = 0, F_1(\alpha) = 1, F_1'(0) = 0, F_1'(\alpha) = 0 \\
G_0(0) = 0, G_0(\alpha) = 0, G_0'(0) = 1, G_0'(\alpha) = 0 \\
G_1(0) = 0, G_1(\alpha) = 0, G_1'(0) = 1, G_1'(\alpha) = 1
\end{cases}
\tag{2}
$$

2) Monotonicity about the Shape Parameter α. For the fixed t, $F_0(t)$ and $G_0(t)$ are monotonically decreasing about α, $F_1(t)$ is monotonically increasing about α, and $G_1(t)$ is non-monotonic about α.

Given $\alpha = 0.5, 1, 1.5$, the algebraic-trigonometric Hermite basis functions are showed in Figure 1, where the long-dashed line, solid line, short-dashed line correspond to the shape parameter 0.5, 1, 1.5 respectively. From Figure 1, we can find that $F_0(t)$, $F_1(t)$ and $G_0(t)$ are monotonous about α except for $G_1(t)$.

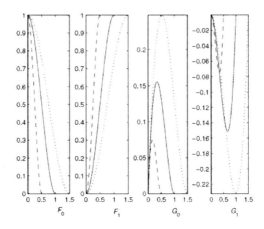

Fig. 1. The figure of algebraic-trigonometric Hermite basis with different shape parameters

3   Algebraic-Trigonometric Ferguson Curve

3.1   Definition of Algebraic-Trigonometric Ferguson Curve

Definition 2. For $0 \leq t \leq \alpha$ ($\alpha \in (0, \pi)$), the algebraic-trigonometric Ferguson curve is defined as

$$r(t) = F_0(t)r(0) + F_1(t)r(\alpha) + G_0(t)r'(0) + G_1(t)r'(\alpha) \tag{3}$$

where $r(0)$ and $r(\alpha)$ are the point vectors in two endpoints, $r'(0)$ and $r'(\alpha)$ are the tangent vectors in two endpoints. $F_i(t)$ and $G_i(t)$ $(i = 0,1)$ are algebraic-trigonometric Hermite basis functions defined as Eq. (1).

From Eq. (3), we know that the algebraic-trigonometric Ferguson curve has the same interpolating properties to the classical Ferguson curve, and the shape of the classical Ferguson curve cannot be adjusted under the interpolation conditions. However, the graphic shape of the proposed algebraic-trigonometric Ferguson curve can be easily adjusted by altering the value of shape parameter α .

For example, taking the point vectors and tangent vectors:

$$r(0) = (0,0), \ r(\alpha) = (2,0), \ r'(0) = (1,2), \ r'(\alpha) = (1,-1).$$

when the shape parameters are of different values, the different shapes of the algebraic-trigonometric Ferguson curves are shown in Figure 2, where the long-dashed line, solid line, short-dashed line correspond to the shape parameter 0.5, 1, 1.5 respectively.

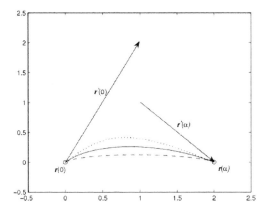

Fig. 2. The figure of algebraic-trigonometric Ferguson curve with different shape parameters

3.2   Application of Algebraic-Trigonometric Ferguson Curve

1) The Accurate Representation of Archimedes Spiral. In the plane coordinate system, taking the point vectors and tangent vectors:

$$r(0) = (0,0), \quad r(\alpha) = (\alpha\sin\alpha, \alpha\cos\alpha),$$

$$r'(0) = (0,1), \quad r'(\alpha) = (\sin\alpha + \alpha\cos\alpha, \cos\alpha - \alpha\sin\alpha),$$

the expression of the algebraic-trigonometric Ferguson curve defined as Eq. (3) can be converted to

$$r(t) = (t\cos t, t\sin t)$$

which represents a part of Archimedes spiral.

Figure 3 shows the representation of a part of archimedes spiral with $t \in [0, 4\pi]$, and the solid line corresponds to the parameter $\alpha=3$.

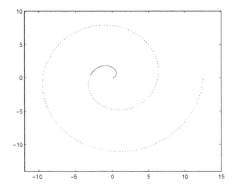

Fig. 3. Archimedes spiral represented by algebraic-trigonometric Ferguson curve

2) The Accurate Representation of Conical Spiral. In the spatial coordinate system, taking the point vectors and tangent vectors:

$$r(0) = (0,0,0), \quad r(\alpha) = (2\alpha \sin \alpha, 2\alpha \cos \alpha, \alpha),$$

$$r'(0) = (0,2,1), \quad r'(\alpha) = (2(\sin \alpha + \alpha \cos \alpha), 2(\cos \alpha - \alpha \sin \alpha), 1),$$

the expression of the algebraic-trigonometric Ferguson curve defined as Eq. (3) can be converted to

$$r(t) = (2t \cos t, 2t \sin t, t)$$

which represents a part of Conical spiral.

Figure 4 shows the representation of a part of Conical spiral with $t \in [0, 4\pi]$, and the solid line corresponds to the parameter $\alpha = 3$.

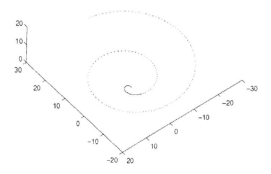

Fig. 4. Conical spiral represented by algebraic-trigonometric Ferguson curves

4   Algebraic-Trigonometric Cubic Hermite Interpolation Spline Curve

Definition 3. For $0 \le t \le \alpha$ ($\alpha \in (0, \pi)$) and $\{(x_i, y_i, m_i), \ i = 0, 1, 2 \cdots, n\}$, set $h_i = x_i - x_{i-1}$, $t = \alpha(x - x_{i-1})/h_i$, the algebraic-trigonometric cubic Hermite interpolation spline curve is defined as

$$r_i(x)\big|_{[x_{i-1}, x_i]} = y_{i-1}F_{i-1}(t) + y_i F_i(t) + h_i m_{i-1}G_{i-1}(t)/\alpha \qquad (4)$$
$$+ h_i m_i G_i(t)/\alpha, \qquad i = 1, 2 \cdots, n$$

where the node x_i satisfies $a = x_0 < x_1 < \cdots < x_n = b$, m_i is the tangent vector for the point (x_i, y_i), $F_{i-1}(t)$, $F_i(t)$, $G_{i-1}(t)$ and $G_i(t)$ are algebraic-trigonometric Hermite basis functions defined as Eq. (1).

From Eq. (4), we can get

$$r_i(x_i^-) = r_{i+1}(x_i^+) = y_i, \quad r_i'(x_i^-) = r_{i+1}'(x_i^+) = m_i \ (i = 1,2,\cdots,n-1).$$

If the proposed quasi-cubic curve has continuous second derivative vector in the adjacent curve segments, *i.e.*

$$r_i''(x_i^-) = r_{i+1}''(x_i^+) \ (i = 1,2,\cdots,n-1),$$

We have the continuity equation:

$$\lambda_i m_{i-1} + k_i m_i + u_i m_{i+1} = C_i, i = 1,2\cdots,n-1 \tag{5}$$

where

$$\lambda_i = \frac{-\alpha^3}{\cos\alpha - 1}h_{i+1}^2,$$

$$k_i = [\frac{\alpha}{2} + \cot\frac{\alpha}{2}]\alpha^2 h_{i+1}^2 + 2\cot\frac{\alpha}{2}\cdot\alpha^2 h_i^2,$$

$$u_i = 2\alpha h_i^2,$$

$$C_i = h_{i+1}^2[-2 + \frac{\alpha(\sin\alpha + 1) + (\alpha^2 - \alpha)\sin^2\alpha}{\cos\alpha - 1}]y_{i-1}$$

$$-[2h_i^2 l_\alpha + h_{i+1}^2 \frac{2 + \alpha^2 + \alpha\sin\alpha - 2\cos\alpha}{\sin\alpha(\cos\alpha - 1)}]y_i + 2h_i^2 l_\alpha y_{i+1}$$

and

$$l_\alpha = \frac{\alpha + \sin\alpha + \alpha\cos\alpha}{\sin\alpha}$$

Therefore, when the parameters satisfy the Eq. (5), algebraic-trigonometric cubic Hermite interpolation spline curve (4) is C^2 continuous.

In the following, we compare our method with the classical Hermite interpolating spline curve.

Suppose $y(x) = x\sin x$, the corresponding data is listed in Table 1.

Table 1. $y(x) = x\sin x$

x_i	1.0000	2.0000	3.0000	4.0000	5.0000	6.0000
y_i	0.8415	1.8186	0.4234	-3.0272	-4.7946	-1.6765
m_i	1.3818	0.0770	-2.8289	-3.3714	0.4594	5.4816

For $\alpha=1$, these interpolation curves and original curve are plotted in Figure 5, where short-dashed line is the original curve. In order to facilitate observation of the difference, the algebraic-trigonometric cubic Hermite curve (solid line) increases by 0.2 units as a whole, and the traditional cubic Hermite curve (long-dashed line) decreased by 0.2 units as a whole. Apparently, the new Hermite interpolation is the high accuracy approximation of smooth curves.

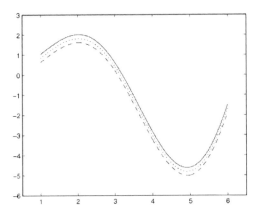

Fig. 5. The original curve,cubic Hermite curve and quasi-cubic Hermite curve

5   Conclusions

In this paper, a new algebraic-trigonometric cubic Hermite interpolation spline curve with shape parameters is constructed in the space $\{1,t,t\sin t,t\cos t\}$ .Compared with the classical Hermite interpolation; the new Hermite interpolation has a great superiority since it can adjust the graphic shape by altering the free parameter. And the new interpolation spline curve, which reaches to C^2 continuous, can accurately represent the transcendental curves, such as archimedean spiral and conical spiral.

Acknowledgments. This work was supported by Scientific Research Fund of Hunan Institute of Humanities, Science and Technology, China (2011QN12) and Scientific Research Fund of Hunan Provincial Education Department, China (11C0707).

References

1. Pena, J.M.: Shape preserving representations for trigonometric polynomial curves. Computer Aided Geometric Design 14, 5–11 (1997)
2. Li, J., Song, L.: A class of quasi-cubic parametric curves based on trigonometric functions. Computer Engineering and Design 29, 2702–2704 (2008) (in Chinese)
3. Li, J.: Method for constructing arbitrary quasi-cubic trigonometric curves. Journal of Chinese Computer Systems 32, 1441–1445 (2011) (in Chinese)

4. Xuli, H.: Piecewise quadratic trigonometric polynomial curves. Mathematics of Computation 72, 1369–1377 (2003)
5. Xuli, H.: Cubic trigonometric polynomial curves with a shape parameter. Computer Aided Geometric Design 21, 535–548 (2004)
6. Zhang, J.: C-curves: An extension of cubic curves. Computer Aided Geometric Design 13, 199–217 (1996)
7. Zhang, J.: C-Bézier curves and surfaces. Graphical Models and Image Processing 61, 2–15 (1999)
8. Zhang, J.: Two different forms of C-B-splines. Computer Aided Geometric Design 14, 31–41 (1997)
9. Mainar, E., Pena, J.M.: A basis of C-Bézier splines with optimal properties. Computer Aided Geometric Design 19, 291–295 (2002)
10. Mainar, E., Pena, J.M.: A basis of C-Bézier splines with optimal properties. Computer Aided Geometric Design 19, 291–295 (2002)
11. Chen, W., Wang, G.: Algebraic-Trigonometric Spline. Journal of Computer Research and Development 43, 679–687 (2006) (in Chinese)

A Robust Image Zero-Watermarking Algorithm Based on DWT and PCA

Xiaoxu Leng, Jun Xiao, and Ying Wang

Graduate University of Chinese Academy of Sciences, 100049 Beijing, China
lengxiaoxu@163.com, {xiaojun,ywang}@gucas.ac.cn

Abstract. Zero-watermarking which doesn't modify the original image but constructs zero watermarks from it, is a useful technique for resolving the contradiction between robustness and invisibility. In this paper, a robust image zero-watermarking algorithm that based on Discrete Wavelet Transformation (DWT) and Principal Component Analysis (PCA) is proposed. In the proposed algorithm, the original image is first transformed with DWT, and its LL band is divided into nonoverlapping image blocks with each image block transformed into a vector, and then it performs a PCA on the set of vectors. Finally, it constructs the zero-watermark sequence by judging the positive and negative polarity of the coefficient which has the maximal absolute value in each analyzed vector. The robustness of the proposed algorithm to given image processes is analyzed, and the results show that the proposed algorithm is very robust to conventional signal processing, such as noise, filtering, JPEG compression, and cropping etc.

Keywords: Robustness, Arnold, Principal component analysis (PCA), Discrete wavelet transformation (DWT).

1   Introduction

With the rapid development of digital multimedia and the Internet, the pirating phenomenon aiming at the digital product is becoming more and more serious. In order to protect the copyright of digital images, the conventional watermarking has to modify them so as to embed watermarks. But this leads to a contradiction between robustness and imperceptibility [1]. To solve this problem, Wen, Sun and Wang proposed the zero-watermarking schema which doesn't embed watermark but constructs zero watermark from the original image [1]; and the zero watermark must be kept in a third party agency, for example, the Intellectual Property Rights (IPR) information database.

The most important part of a zero-watermarking algorithm is the image feature detection method. The detected image feature should have properties of stability and otherness, the stability means that the image feature can still be detected after the image is attacked; and the otherness means that different images have different features. Generally, the image feature detected from the original image can be used

M. Zhao and J. Sha (Eds.): ICCIP 2012, Part II, CCIS 289, pp. 484–492, 2012.
© Springer-Verlag Berlin Heidelberg 2012

straightforwardly as a zero watermark in copyright protection application, but it cannot reflect information of stakeholders due to its unmeaning bit stream. Some zero-watermarking algorithms use encryption method to embed meaningful information into image features.

In recent years, zero-watermarking has gained great development, and many zero-watermarking algorithms have been proposed. For example, Wen constructs zero watermarks on the basis of the high order cumulat [2]; Gao, Luo and Liu construct zero watermarks on the basis of the Most Significant Bit (MSB) of the original image [3]; Wen, Sun and Wang construct zero watermarks on the basis of the low frequency coefficients in DCT domain [1]; Ma and He construct zero watermarks on the basis of the LL band in Discrete Wavelet Transformation (DWT) domain [4]; Hu and Zhu construct zero watermarks on the basis of Principal Component Analysis (PCA) [5]; Ye, Ma and Niu etc. construct zero watermarks on the basis of singular values of the image matrix [6]; Wu and Sun construct zero watermarks on the basis of the image moments [7]. These algorithms have very good performances resisting conventional signal processing, but existing zero-watermarking algorithms use somewhat single methods to detect image features, and the robustness is still can be improved by combination of several methods.

In this paper, a new zero-watermarking algorithm is proposed based on the theory of DWT and PCA. The rest of this paper is organized as follows. Section 2 describes the detailed design of the proposed algorithm. Section 3 presents the experimental results. The paper is concluded in section 4.

2   Proposed Algorithm

The image zero-watermarking algorithm proposed by Hu and Zhu [5] is one of the most typical algorithms. In the algorithm proposed by [5], the original image is first subdivided block by block and PCA is used to decorrelate the image pixel to obtain the principal components of an image. Then a chaotic sequence is generated based on Renyi mapping and the principal components are thrown into confusion. Finally, the zero watermark sequence is generated by comparing the confused principal components. The robustness of this algorithm depends largely on the magnitude relationship of the confused principal components.

Based on the above algorithm, this paper proposes an improved algorithm by introducing DWT and constructing zero watermark sequence in accordance with the positive and negative polarity of the principal components. For the first improvement strategy, PCA is performed on the transform domain instead of the spacial domain, which could improve the performance of the algorithm resisting conventional signal processing. For the second improvement strategy, the positive and negative polarity is more stable than the magnitude relationship of the principal components when the image is attacked. Furthermore, a binary meaningful watermark image is embedded into the image feature with XOR operation and the Arnold scrambling method is used to encrypt the watermark image in the proposed algorithm.

Fig.1 shows the zero watermark construction diagram of this algorithm, while Fig.2 shows the zero watermark detection diagram of this algorithm. Because the construction procedure and the detection procedure use identical method to extract image features, they both have the same central process. The main difference is that the detection method adds the similarity calculation between the extracted watermark image and the original watermark image.

2.1   Zero Watermark Constructing Method

Suppose the original image I is a gray image with size of $W \times H$, and choose db1 as the wavelet. Then the zero watermark constructing process can be described as the following six steps.

Step 1: pre-process the watermark image W. Scramble the watermark image W with Arnold transformation taking K as the number of scrambling times. The chaotic watermark image is indicated by W'.

Step 2: extraction of the low frequency components in DWT domain. The original image I is transformed with DWT at level c, and its LL band of level c is indicated by LL.

Step 3: block LL. Divide LL into nonoverlapping blocks with size of $s \times s$. Convert each block into column vectors $\vec{x}_i$, where $i = 1, ..., count$ and $count = (W/4s) \times (H/4s)$. The matrix $X_{m \times n}$ is constituted by the set of these vectors, where $m = s \times s$ and $n = count$, as shown in (1).

$$X = \left[\vec{x}_1, \vec{x}_2, \cdots, \vec{x}_n \right] \tag{1}$$

Step 4: construct the covariance matrix C_x. Calculate the covariance σ_{pq}^2 between row vectors $X_{p\bullet}$ and $X_{q\bullet}$ of matrix X according to (2), then construct C_x according to (3).

$$\sigma_{pq}^2 = \frac{1}{n-1} X_{p\bullet} X_{q\bullet}^T \tag{2}$$

$$C_x = \begin{bmatrix} \sigma_{11}^2 & \sigma_{12}^2 & \cdots & \sigma_{1n}^2 \\ \sigma_{21}^2 & \sigma_{22}^2 & \cdots & \sigma_{2n}^2 \\ \vdots & \vdots & \ddots & \vdots \\ \sigma_{m1}^2 & \sigma_{m2}^2 & \cdots & \sigma_{mn}^2 \end{bmatrix} \tag{3}$$

Step 5: diagonalize the covariance matrix C_x, and then get the eigenvector V and the eigenvalue D. According to the magnitude of diagonal elements, sort D in descending order, and at the same time transform synchronously the corresponding eigenvector V into P.

Step 6: construct the zero watermark sequence EW. Generate the matrix Y according to (4). Then the image feature C is produced by (5). Finally, utilize XOR operation to embed W' in C, and get the zero watermark EW which is kept in the IPR information database.

$$Y = (PX)^T \tag{4}$$

$$c_i = \begin{cases} 1, Y_{i1} > 0 \\ 0, Y_{i1} \le 0 \end{cases}, \ i = 1, 2, ..., n \tag{5}$$

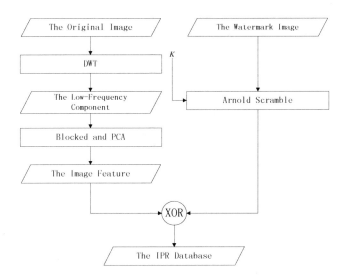

Fig. 1. The zero watermark constructing diagram

2.2   Zero Watermark Detecting Method

The zero watermark detecting method is similar with the constructing method. For the convenience of description, P is used to represent the image to be authenticated with the same size as I. The detecting process can be described as the following four steps.

Step 1: image feature extraction. According to the 2-6 steps in the constructing process, extract the image feature C^P from P.

Step 2: extract the watermark sequence DW. Generate the chaotic watermark image DW' by performing XOR operation on C^P and EW fetched from the IPR database. And then extract DW from DW' with Arnold transformation according to K.

Step 3: calculate the similarity degree between DW and W. Since the original watermark and the extracted watermark are both binary sequences, calculating the bit error rate is a simple and effective way to measure robustness. Define $BER = A / B$, where A indicates the number of different elements between them, and B indicates the total number of elements.

Step 4: given a watermark detection threshold T, if $BER < T$, then there is watermark in the detected image, otherwise there isn't.

According to the above detection procedure, the proposed algorithm does not require the inverse transformation of DWT and PCA, thus avoids the numerical errors while converting.

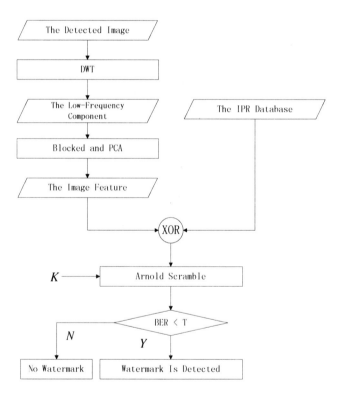

Fig. 2. The zero watermark detecting diagram

3   Experimental Results

Since the robustness to given processes and attacks is a crucial issue in the design of zero-watermarking algorithms, the validity of the proposed algorithm is studied in this section.

In the experiments, BER is used to measure the robustness, and the threshold T is set to be 0.4. The 8-bit gray scale image 'Lena' is used as the original image, the size of which is 256×256. The level of DWT is set to be 2, and the size of blocks is set to be 2×2. According to the above parameters, the original image can generate a binary sequence of 1024 bits. A binary image with size of 32×32 is used as the meaningful watermark image. Fig. 3 (a) shows the original image; Fig.3 (b) shows the binary watermark image; Fig.3 (c) shows the zero watermark constructed by the proposed algorithm; Fig.3 (d) shows the watermark detected without being attacked, and its BER is 0.

(a) The original image   (b) The binary watermark image

(c) The zero watermark   (d) The detected watermark

Fig. 3. Results of the availability test

Comparative experiments of robustness resisting typical kinds of conventional signal processing between the proposed algorithm and the Hu algorithm [5] are tested. Results are described below.

(1) Noise

Add salt and pepper noise to the original image, with mean 0 and variance from 0.01 to 0.10, 10 testing images in total, from which extract watermarks to test this algorithm's robustness resisting such noise. Fig. 4 shows the comparison of experimental results between the two algorithms. According to the experimental results, the highest BER of the proposed algorithm is lower than 0.04, while the BER of Hu is lower than 0.05, both are lower than the threshold 0.4, and can easily detect the watermarks, but the proposed algorithm has lower bit error rate.

Add gaussian noise to the original image, with mean 0 and variance from 0.01 to 0.10, 10 testing images in total, from which extract watermarks to test this algorithm's robustness resisting such noise. Fig. 5 shows the comparison of experimental results between the two algorithms. From the experimental results, the highest BER of this algorithm is lower than 0.07, while the BER of Hu is lower than 0.09, both are lower than the threshold 0.4, and can easily detect the watermarks, but the proposed algorithm has lower bit error rate.

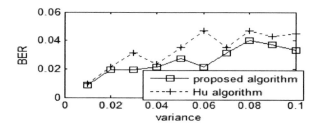

Fig. 4. Comparison of two algorithms resisting salt & pepper noise

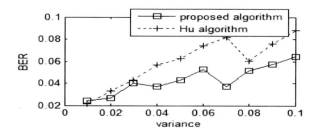

Fig. 5. Comparison of two algorithms resisting gaussian noise

(2) Filtering

Tab.1 shows the comparison of experimental results between the two algorithms resisting filtering attacks. Under the same attack parameters, the BER of the proposed algorithm is lower than that of Hu, except the first attack.

Table 1. Comparison of two algorithms resisting filtering

Filtering types	Size of template	Proposed algorithm	Hu algorithm
Mean filtering	3*3	0.0176	0.0176
Mean filtering	5*5	0.0215	0.0293
Median filtering	3*3	0.0049	0.0117
Median filtering	5*5	0.0127	0.0156

(3) Shearing

Tab.2 shows the comparison of experimental results between the two algorithms resisting shearing attacks. The BER of the proposed algorithm is a bit higher than that of Hu when the shearing degree is small (cut 1/8), and is smaller when the shearing degree is large (cut 1/4 and 1/2).

Table 2. Comparison of two algorithms resisting cropping

Shearing degree	Proposed algorithm	Hu algorithm
cut 1/8 of the upper left	0.0762	0.0625
cut 1/4 of the upper left	0.1963	0.2227
cut half of the left	0.2549	0.2871

(4) JPEG Compression

Tab.3 shows the comparison of experimental results between the two algorithms resisting JPEG compression, in which the greater the quality factor is, the better the compressed image quality has or vice versa. Both algorithms can extract intact watermarks when the compression quality factor is 75 or 90. When the compression quality factor is reduced to 50, the BER of the proposed algorithm is lower than that of Hu. The proposed algorithm can extract the intact watermark when the compression quality factor drops to 5 while the Hu algorithm cannot. Thus the performance of the proposed algorithm is superior to the Hu algorithm.

Table 3. Comparison of two algorithms resisting JPEG compression

the quality factor	Proposed algorithm	Hu algorithm
90	0.0000	0.0000
75	0.0000	0.0000
50	0.0001	0.0020
5	0.0000	0.0605

(5) Translation

Tab. 4 shows the comparison of experimental results between the two algorithms resisting translation attacks. This algorithm has robustness of a certain degree resisting translation, and its performance is superior to the comparison algorithm under the same attack parameters.

Table 4. Comparison of two algorithms resisting translation

translation parameters	Proposed algorithm	Hu algorithm
[5 0]	0.1416	0.1660
[0 5]	0.0850	0.1270
[5 5]	0.1797	0.2324

4   Conclusions

In this paper, an optimized zero-watermarking algorithm based on DWT and PCA has been presented. The proposed algorithm makes full use of properties of DWT and PCA. Experimental results show that the proposed algorithm can resist typical conventional image attacks, such as noise, filtering, cropping and JPEG compression attacks etc., and has lower BER compared with Hu algorithm in most cases. Namely, the proposed algorithm has very good robustness to conventional image attacks.

Acknowledgments. This work is supported by National Natural Science Foundation of China (No. 61003275) and President Fund of GUCAS.

References

1. Wen, Q., Sun, T.F., Wang, S.X.: Concept and Application of Zero-Watermark. Acta Electronica Sinica 31(2), 214–216 (2003)
2. Wen, Q.: Research on Robustness and Imperceptibility of Multimedia Digital Watermarking. Jilin University, Jilin (2005)
3. Gao, S.Q., Luo, X.Y., Liu, B., et al.: A Robust Zero-Watermarking Algorithm Based on Chaotic Array. Computer Science 32(9), 76–81 (2005)
4. Ma, J.H., He, J.X.: A Wavelet-Based Method of Zero-Watermark. Journal of Image and Graphics 12(4), 581–585 (2007)
5. Hu, Y.F., Zhu, S.A.: Zero-watermark algorithm based on PCA and chaotic scrambling. Journal of Zhejiang University(Engineering Science) 42(4), 593–597 (2008)
6. Ye, T.Y., Ma, Z.F., Niu, X.X., et al.: A Zero-Watermark Technology with Strong Robustness. Journal of Beijing University of Posts and Telecommunications 33(3), 126–129 (2010)
7. Wang, Z., Sun, Y.: Zero watermarking algorithm based on Zernikemoments. Computer Applications 28(9), 2233–2235 (2008)

REML: Rock Engineering Markup Language

Zhenya Shen[1], Jun Xiao[1], Ying Wang[1], and Hongjian Sui[2]

[1] Graduate University of Chinese Academy of Sciences, 100049 Beijing, China
[2] Beijing Branch of Chinese Academy of Sciences, 100190 Beijing, China
zjdpszy@qq.com, {xiaojun,ywang}@gucas.ac.cn, hjsui@cashq.ac.cn

Abstract. REML is presented for the rock engineering data exchange and sharing, which is a markup language based on Geography Markup Language (GML). In this paper, the scope and content of REML are discussed, and the features of rock engineering data are summarized. According to the results of the discussions, a 4-tier architecture is proposed for REML. The tiers and the modules in the architecture are introduced respectively. Furthermore, some typical XML schema code fragments from REML and their relative XML instance document are demonstrated in this article.

Keywords: Data exchange, Rock engineering, XML, GML, REML.

1   Introduction

Masses of data that different by content, type, style and so on from variety data sources are produced and processed in every stage of rock engineering. Under these circumstances, if absents the data exchange and sharing standards for this domain, the data quality and the data processing efficiency must be low. Especially with rock engineering software and models related, most of them have the own private formats, and data exchange between them in a state of disorder. Representation and standardization of rock engineering data have become the focus issue in the process of rock engineering informationizing [1]. Several markup language solutions about rock engineering, e.g., GeotechML [2], AGSML, GeoSciML [3], have been proposed from different disciplines and perspectives. However, their ability of expression is comparatively insufficient while they are describing the rock engineering objects, e.g., some has no definitions for nondeductible objects in this domain, some lacks of self-contained descriptions for the objects (especially for spatial information properties).

So the Rock Engineering Markup Language (REML) is presented in this paper. On the basis of analyzing data in the rock engineering field and concluding the features of them, it is built upon the Geography Markup Language (GML) [4]. REML tries to propose a rock engineering oriented data encoding specification with consistent semantic descriptions, and services as a hub for the data exchange and sharing (see Fig. 1).

M. Zhao and J. Sha (Eds.): ICCIP 2012, Part II, CCIS 289, pp. 493–501, 2012.
© Springer-Verlag Berlin Heidelberg 2012

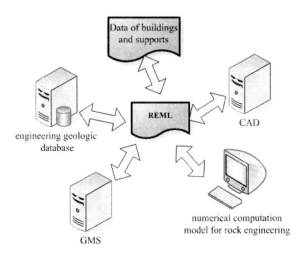

Fig. 1. REML as the center of Hub-and-Spoke structure for data exchange and sharing

2   Analysis of Rock Engineering Data

Rock engineering is the multi-dimensional knowledge integration involved with engineering geology, rock mechanics, civil engineering, etc. So, covering multiple disciplines, the rock engineering data have a wide range from data sources to contents, and the scope and content of REML must meet the data request. The main data objects in REML are categorized as follows:

1) Metadata of the rock engineering project: project name, data sources and other attributes describing the project itself;

2) Geological data: rock types, geological structures, drillings, bore holes and so on;

3) Rock test data: the physical and mechanical properties of rock measured in-situ tests, laboratory tests and other tests;

4) The data of building and facilities involved with rock engineering: tunnels, slopes, foundations, reinforcements and supportings, etc.;

5) About rock engineering model: constitutive equations, calculation parameters, grid descriptions from meshing, the computing results;

6) Data from monitoring of rock engineering: data obtained from the monitoring of rock engineering, includes videos, photographs and so on.

As the result of the analysis of the rock engineering data, its features are summarized and shown in the following:

1) Diverse: the data objects involved are quite different, which are in the structured, semi structured or unstructured formats, even between the properties of the same data object;

2) Changeful: the scope and content of the data concerned to have been changing at different rock engineering stages, and the same object also needs different representations;

3) Temporal: all data are in a close relationship to the time and need to express the temporal concept by variety ways;

4) Spatial: how to express the objects' spatial information is not only a key point, but also a difficult one. Their complex mathematical descriptions require the knowledge of geometry and topology;

5) Multi-source: the data are from multiple sources, and the sources need to be clearly identified;

6) Integrative: there are complex relationships between the data items, such as transformations, constraints, etc.

Rock engineering is an integration of diverse knowledge, so it needs the data specifications that can cover all involved fields throughout its whole life cycle. In order to fulfill the request, REML will give full consideration to the features while being designed.

3   Design of REML

REML is developed for data exchange and sharing in the rock engineering domain, and we hope it can serve as a data specification in the field. To achieve the objective, REML accepts the technical proposal based GML. GML is a powerful tool and has naturally obvious advantages in describing the similar data from rock engineering to GIS [5]. It provides a set of basic tags, a generic data model and a mechanism of extension. Therefore, for full use of its advantages, GML is adopted as to develop the "Application Schema" for rock engineering, and REML directly uses the GML tags or defines new tags by extending them. The relationships between REML, GML and XML Schema are shown in Fig. 2.

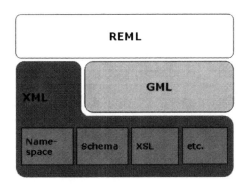

Fig. 2. The relationship between REML, XML and GML

Some XML schema design methods are evaluated, and the object-oriented methods are finally adopted to design and implement REML. In order to match the design pattern of GML, REML also uses the Garden of Eden schema, the "object-property model" and the same coding rules to the lexical conventions with GML. Thus, REML is constructed with a 4-tier architecture (see Fig. 3).

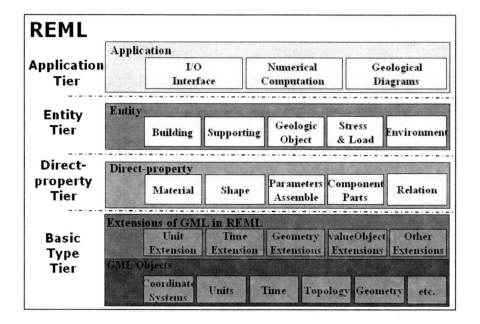

Fig. 3. The 4-tier architecture of REML

The Basic-Type Tier. In the basic-types tier there are two sub-tiers: the GML objects sub-tier and the extensions of GML sub-tier. The objects in this tier come from the different sources - GML's core schema and application schema user defined, which do not affect the arrange of placing them in the same tier, since they are all the basic and reused types and just server as the component parts of the objects in the direct-property tier not the direct components of the feature objects in REML.

The GML Objects Sub-Tier. It is made up of the GML objects in the schemas of coordinate systems, units of measure, temporal objects, geometry, topology and others but the Feature type, because they fit for describing the basic data content and all of them have already been excellently defined by GML.

The Extensions of GML Sub-Tier. This sub-tier contains the REML's extensions from GML specifically for the rock engineering domain, e.g., the pressure unit added for the units schema, the engineering classifications value types for rocks, and the degree enumeration values for weathered rock.

The Direct-Property Tier. This tier is designed to reduce the complexity of the classes derived from GML Feature. The feature objects for rock engineering in REML generally have large numbers of properties, thereby they require a well structured form to organize the data. An object in this tier puts together some properties of the same facet for a Feature object, and its composition mirrors an arrangement of the data. They act as the only direct properties of the objects in the upper tier, which separates the Feature classes from the large number of the basic types. This approach reduces the flexibility but increases the encapsulation of GML

Feature, and it makes a REML instance document more understandable in business without exceeding the "object-property model" of GML. They are derived from the AbstractGML. Based on the different perspectives of the rock engineering they are divided into the five modules: Material, Shape, ParametersAssemble, ComponentParts and Relation.

The Entity Tier. The entity tier contains geologic structures, supportings, buildings and other entities in the rock engineering domain. "An entity can comprise a number of elements that are 'fitted together' to provide a full representation of all the component parts of the entity."[2]. The concept of objects of the entity tier is almost equivalent to GML's feature, and actually the entities are the subclass of GML's "AbstractFeature" in REML's implement. Nevertheless, these objects are named "entity" not "feature" here. First, there is a subtle difference between the "entity" and the "feature", and the latter means an "abstraction of real world phenomena"[6] that focuses on the field of GIS. Second, the "entity" has already been generally used in the rock engineering data exchange and sharing. And lastly but most importantly, the "entity" is a restricted "feature" whose direct components are limited to the objects in the direct-property tier. In the same way, this tier is named "the entity tier".

The Application Tier. The application tier is closely related to a particular scene of the application of REML. Each object of this tier is a set of the recognized specific entities from REML for a specific scene, and its component parts and structures are a reflection of the scope and content of the corresponding application. At the same time, the entities are fully reused in the different applications with the same semantics. Currently, this tier consists of the scenes of the I/O interface, the numerical computation model and the geological diagrams three kinds of application.

In a word, depending on the 4-tier architecture, REML will be more flexible and reusable. Considering both the business and the technology, the framework of REML emphasizes the balance in the reusability, flexibility and structure while developing the GML application schema for rock engineering. The architecture and the implied design method could be worthwhile to apply in the other fields' GML extensions.

4   Implementation and Instance of REML

According to the aforementioned framework, REML is developed following the order of the tiers in the overall structure. The REML objects of the same tier are split into the modules by their content, and the detailed information can be found in Table 1.

Due to the limit of space, only the StructuralPlane as a representative object of REML will be demonstrated here. The design and implementation of the class for structural planes are shown in Fig. 4.

The class StructuralPlane is a member of the geologicObject module in the entity tier, and it inherits from the class GeologicalStructure. GeologicalStructure is derived from class RockEngineeringFeature which is the subclass of the gml:AbstractFeature class. The class StructuralPlane is expressed in the following XML schema code fragment:

```
<xs:complexType name="StructuralPlaneType">
  <xs:complexContent>
    <xs:extension base="GeologicalStructureType">
      <xs:sequence>
        <xs:element
ref="structuralPlaneParametersAssembleProperty"
maxOccurs="1"/>
        <xs:element
ref="structuralPlaneComponentPartsProperty"
maxOccurs="1"/>
        <xs:element ref="structuralPlaneShapeProperty"
maxOccurs="1"/>
        <xs:element
ref="structuralPlaneRelationProperty" maxOccurs="1"/>
      </xs:sequence>
    </xs:extension>
  </xs:complexContent>
</xs:complexType>
```

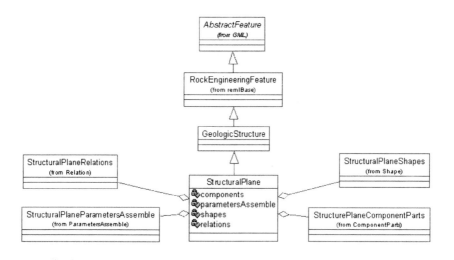

Fig. 4. The structural plan class

The direct properties of StructuralPlane include the "componets" (StructuralPlaneComponentParts), the "parametersAssemble" (StructuralPlane ParametersAssemble), the "shapes" (StructuralPlaneShapes) and the "relations" (StructuralPlaneRelations). They are all from the direct-property tier and derived by extension from gml:AbstractGML.

The following XML fragment from a REML instance document describes a structural plane:

```xml
<StructuralPlane gml:id="ID_1">
   <structuralPlaneParametersAssembleProperty>
      <StructuralPlaneParametersAssemble gml:id="ID_3">
        <structuralPlaneCategorization>
            <category>IV</category>
            <length uom="m">13.4</length>
        </structuralPlaneCategorization>
        <geneticCategory>tectonic</geneticCategory>
        <tensileStrength uom="MPa">33.8</tensileStrength>
     </structuralPlaneParametersAssembleProperty>
     <structuralPlaneComponentPartsProperty>
        <StructuralPlaneComponentParts gml:id="ID_4">
          <wall xlink:href="#ID_7"/>
          <filling xlink:href="#ID_8"/>
    ...
     </structuralPlaneComponentPartsProperty>
   <structuralPlaneShapesProperty>
   <StructuralPlanesShape gml:id="ID_5">
       <attitude>
         <azimuth>
           <dip>
              <direction>SW</direction>
              <angle uom="deg">205</angle>
           </dip>
  <dipDirection uom="deg">25</dipDirection>
  <description>SW205°•25°</description>
<quadrantalAngle>
         <strike>
            <from>N</from>
            <angle uom="deg">295</angle>
            <to>W</to>
         </strike>
         <dipDirection uom="deg">25</dipDirection>
         <dipQuadrant>SW</dipQuadrant>
         <description>N295°W/25SW</description>
       ...
       <shape1D>
           <gml:OrientableCurve gml:id="ID_6"
  orientation="+">
              <gml:baseCurve>
                <gml:Curve gml:id="ID_12">
                   <gml:segments>
                     <gml:ArcString
  numDerivativesAtStart="0" numArc="3"
  interpolation="circularArc3Points"
  numDerivativesAtEnd="0" numDerivativeInterior="0">
              <gml:pos srsDimension="2">2</gml:pos>
              <gml:pos srsDimension="2">3</gml:pos>
              <gml:pos srsDimension="2">4</gml:pos>
                       . . .
                  </gml:ArcString>
```

```
        . . .
      </gml:baseCurve>
    </gml:OrientableCurve>
  </shape1D>
  ...
<structuralPlaneRelationsProperty>
<StructuralPlaneRelations gml:id="ID_15">
      <geologicStructureFrom xlink:href="#ID_17" />
        <structuralBlockCutBy xlink:href="#ID_18"/>
  </StructuralPlaneRelations>
 </structuralPlaneRelationsProperty>
</StructuralPlane>
```

Table 1. The modules of REML

Module name	Content	Tier name
basic	The extensions of GML objects, pressure units, stratigraphic time, geometric descriptions of cross section, etc.	basic type
material	Defines tags for minerals and some material properties used in rock engineering, e.g., rock structures, rock texture	direct-property
shapes	The subclasses of AbstractGML describing the geometric information of the feature objects as direct feature propertes, e.g., StructuralPlaneShapes, RockBlockShapes	direct-property
parameters Assemble	Each object in this module has a set of attributes from physics, mechanics, etc. for the features, derived from AbstractGML, e.g., SupportingParametersAssemble	direct-property
component Parts	Tags to describing the composition of each feature, derived from AbstractGML, e.g., RockMassComponentParts	direct-property
relations	The subclasses of AbstractGML describing the relations between the features objects as direct feature properties	direct-property
building	Representations of the four rock engineering types: underground, cavern, tunnel, slope and foundation	entity
support	Contains the tags for the bolts, retaining structures, shotcrete, piles	entity
geologic Object	The abstract parent class and its derived classes for geological objects, for example, geologic structure, geologic units, etc.	entity
environment	The abstract parent class and its derived classes for environment objects, for example, topography, climate	entity
stress & load	Tags for the stresses and loads, the definitions for mechanic entities, concentrated load, line load, effectives stress, etc.	entity
I/O interface	Tag in this module means a set of specific entities requested for exchange in specific scene	application
numerical computation	Numerical computation models used in rock engineering can be described by the tags in this module, the content of each tag covering input/output data, parameters, meshing, etc.	application
geological diagrams	Tags for a geological diagram, which made up of the diagram's features, meta data and their graphic expressions, etc.	application

5   Summaries

REML proposed in this paper provides a new solution for data exchange and sharing in the rock engineering domain. Benefiting from GML's comprehensive infrastructure, REML can well describe complex objects covering a wide range of data in rock engineering. Fully considering the combination of business and technology, the 4-tier architecture of REML is present, and this framework can be a reference for designing the GML application schema in other fields.

References

1. Toll, D.G.: Geo-Engineering Data: Representation and Standardisation. Electronic Journal of Geotechnical Engineering, http://www.ejge.com/2007/Ppr0699/Ppr0699.html (accessed August 19, 2010)
2. Toll, D.G., Cubitt, A.C.: Representing geotechnical entities on the World Wide Web. Advances in Engineering Software 34(11-12), 729–736 (2003)
3. Sen, M., Duffy, T.: GeoSciML: Development of a generic GeoScience Markup Language. Computers & Geosciences 31(9), 1095–1103 (2005)
4. Portele, C. (ed.): Geography Markup Language v3.2.1. OGC 07-036. Open Geospatial Consortium, Inc. (2007)
5. Lake, R.: The application of geography markup language (GML) to the geological sciences. Computers & Geosciences 31(9), 1081–1094 (2005)
6. International Organization for Standardization (ISO): ISO 19101:2002. Geographic Information-Reference Model (2002)

Modeling a Web-Based Bearing Fault Diagnosis System Using UML and Component Technology

Jie Shi[1,*], Yijie Zhang[1], Xiuying Tang[1], and Jun Shi[2]

[1] Faculty of Engineering and Technology, Yunnan Agricultural University,
Kunming, Yunnan 650201, P.R. China
km_shijie@126.com
[2] Yunnan Design Institute of Chemical Engineering Co., Ltd.,
Kunming, Yunnan 650041, P.R. China
1120368374@qq.com

Abstract. With the increasing complexity of the architecture and web applications of the fault diagnosis software, the original CGI, ISAPI and other technologies have been difficult to meet the requirements to access and operate distributed objects. The best way to manage the risk is to build a distributed object framework of web design. Therefore, this paper presents a method of modeling Web-based Bearing Fault Diagnosis System (WBFDS) with Unified Modeling Language (UML), which includes ranging from demand model, static model, and dynamic model to physical model. This paper, which studies the full life cycle visual modeling of a specific areas system, aims to achieve the goal of a reuse system, combining component technology and web technology. Finally, a highly reusable WBFDS was developed and proved to be effective in the actual project.

Keywords: Web application, UML, Fault diagnosis, Component technology.

1 Introduction

After nearly 20 years of development, Mechanical Equipment Fault Diagnosis System (MEFDS) has been gotten a wide range of application in the domestic petrochemical, metallurgical and other industries. Several hundred kinds of MEFDS system have been successively released at home and broad, including off-line or on-line single machine systems, master-slave and distributed, network-based fault diagnosis system. Bearing, which plays a key role in rotating machinery, is the most commonly used as a machinery and equipment parts. Therefore, building a distribute Web-based Bearing Fault Diagnosis System (WBFDS) has practical significance. In order to manage effectively the software life cycle, the most direct way is to build the software system model.

---

* Corresponding author.

M. Zhao and J. Sha (Eds.): ICCIP 2012, Part II, CCIS 289, pp. 502–511, 2012.
© Springer-Verlag Berlin Heidelberg 2012

With the rapid development of web technologies and applications, the complexity of its application has been increasingly. Traditional web technologies such as CGI, ISAPI have been difficult to meet the requirements to access and manipulate distributed objects. However, component technology has improved reusability, portability and interoperability. Meanwhile, UML which includes the components of thinking and visual modeling provides a good support for distributed system construction. This paper is to study how to model the architecture modeling of WBFDS using UML in the web-based system to make better web components into WBFDS system, thereby enhancing the efficiency of system development WBFDS and web components can be reusable and modifiability.

2   Related Background and Research

2.1   UML (Unified Modeling Language)

The Unified Modeling Language (UML) that is a standard language for designing software blueprints is appropriate for modeling systems ranging from enterprise information systems to distribute web-based applications and even to hard real time embedded systems. As a part of method of software-development, the UML is only a language and process independent; it is not difficult to understand and to use. Learning to apply the UML effectively starts with forming a conceptual model of the language, which requires learning three major elements: the UML's basic building blocks, the rules that dictate how these building blocks may be put together, and some common mechanisms that apply throughout the language.

2.2   Component Technology

Component can be considered a binary code which is to be reused. It has a feature of plug and play. It follows a standard of the binary external interface, the details of component's internal implementation open to user, and it is interacted with each other by the "software bus". In addition, component can also be considered as a software code which includes a clear identification, but also includes requirement documents of software development and software framework.

Currently, there are many main technical standards, including Microsoft's COM/DCOM (Distributed Component Object Model), the OMG`s CORBA (Common Object Request Broker Architecture), SUN launched Java Beans, EJB (Enterprise Java Bean) and OpenDoc technology, these technologies, mentioned above, have their own characteristics.

2.3   Web-Based Bearing Fault Diagnosis System

Rolling Bearing Fault Diagnosis (RBFD) in foreign countries commenced in the 1960s. In subsequent decades of development, continue to produce a variety of methods and techniques, development and improvement of applications continue to expand and improve. RBFD has experienced from using the general-purpose spectrum analyzer to using shock pulse meter developed by the Swedish SPM, but also experienced from the "Resonance Demodulation Analysis System" invented by Boeing Company to computer-centric monitoring and fault diagnosis system. It achieved precise diagnosis and artificial diagnostic across.

With the rapid development of detection technique, computer technique, digital signal processing and artificial intelligence technology, bearing fault diagnosis has become a comprehensive subject. Increasingly reflect the distributed, networked, intelligent features.

3   Modeling WBFDS with UML

UML will be used to implement the following visual modeling of WBFDS.

3.1   Domain Analysis

The WBFDS consists of some Data Acquisition Workstations (DAW), a Web Diagnosis Center (WDC) and a Remote Collaboration Diagnosis Center (RCDC). The main role of DAW is responsible for the collection and preliminary analysis of bearing vibration signals, and collects data uploaded to the database server; In support of signal processing and artificial intelligence component, WDC is responsible for intelligence and precision diagnosis; At the same time, WDC has been capable of management and maintenance the Database Server and Web server; RCDC provides remote diagnostic services for domain expert together, including such as: electronic whiteboards, net meeting and other functions.

3.2   Model Architecture of the WBFDS

According to the description of the problem domain of the WBFDS, and taking into account the analysis of running structure and hierarchy, the topology model of WBFDS is presented. Fig. 1 is the topological graph diagram of the system.

This model shows that the Data Acquisition Workstation (DAW) accesses to the Internet by a network device, connects with Database Server and Web Server of WDC. Remote domain experts can use WBFDS to diagnose a fault only by local IE browser. The center of fault diagnosis consists of Database Server, Web Server, System Management and Remote Experts. Workstation is used to store uploaded data, diagnosis data and other information of the bearing.

This topology structure is a full use of inherent features of the Internet, such as opening architecture, simple information exchanging and sharing of information and so on.

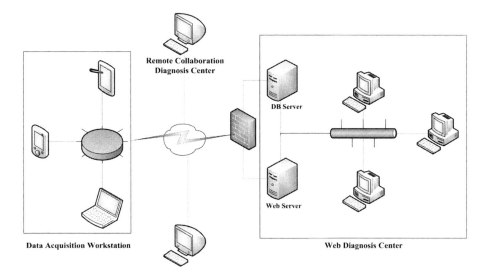

Fig. 1. Topological graph diagram of WBFDS

3.3   Requirement Model of the WBFDS

Use case modeling is a formal process used to capture the scene of a system, becomes an increasingly popular method of requirement definition. Requirement modeling is a process of use case acquiring and achieves trough use case diagram with UML.

Fig. 2 is a use case model of WBFDS, which describes the user roles of WBFDS and use cases that can be used. The roles include: System Administrator, Test Points User, Equipment Manager, Field Expert and Equipment Manager. All roles need to be registered, so Register User is an abstract of those roles. As can be seen from the Fig. 2, the different roles can use independent cases, and have a relationship between user cases.

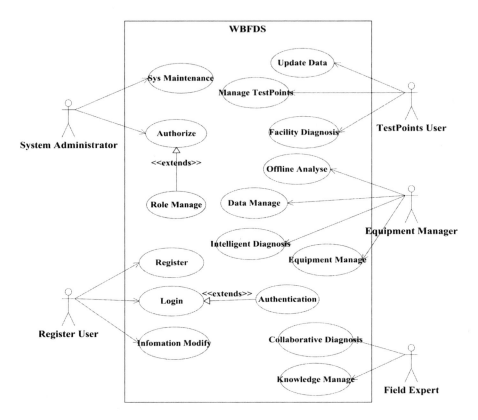

Fig. 2. Use case diagram of WBFDS

3.4   Static Class Model of the WBFDS

Class diagram is the most commonly used in UML, showing the classes, interfaces, their static   structure and   relationships; it   is used   to   describe   the structure   of system design. Fig. 3 shows a simplified model of static structure of WBFDS. Using UML's extension mechanism, WBFDS is divided into eight prototype class.

The <<Browser>> And <<Web Server>> are the client and server abstraction of static behavior; The <<Entity>> represents the application abstraction in the sensor, monitoring , collecting cards, collecting system; The <<Algorithm >> is an algorithm class which includes signal processing and an artificial intelligence algorithms; The <<Database>> represents an abstraction class of database system and data structure ; The <<ActiveX>> is an abstraction of the graphical control providing a description of ActiveX control object; The <<Control>> manages the communications among instances of classes; The <<table>> models tables as classes. It visualizes the persistent data model.

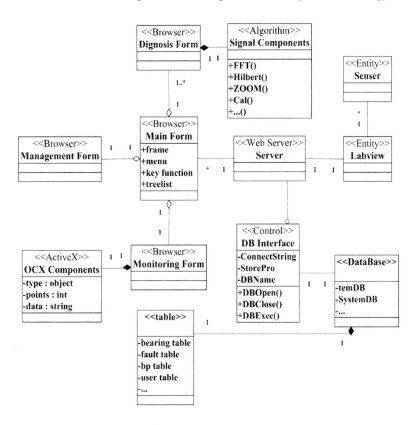

Fig. 3. Class diagram of WBFDS

3.5   Dynamic Behavior of the WBFDS

Sequence diagram shows time sequence of sending message between objects, is often used to describe the system's dynamic structure. Fig. 4 is the sequence diagram of a troubleshooting use case. It reflects the behavior of an equipment manager during the fault diagnosis process, it events flow in the system.

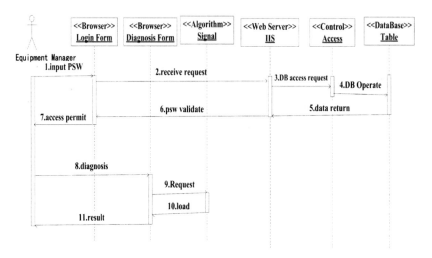

Fig. 4. Sequence diagram of fault diagnosis case

3.6   Physical Model of the WBFDS

Configuration diagram describes run-time hardware nodes, and static views of software component running on these nodes. Configuration diagram displays the system hardware, software installed on the hardware, as well as connecting middleware between heterogeneous machines. Fig. 5 is the system configuration diagram of WBFDS, as shown: the database server and the web server connect with each other and provide data services. Through the network, web server respectively connects with data-acquisition workstation, business users and experts, and provides applications of fault diagnosis.

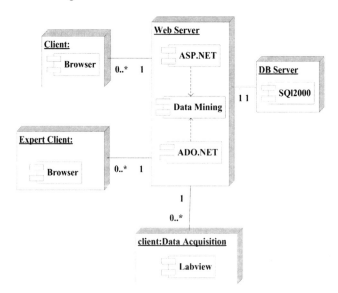

Fig. 5. Configuration diagram of WBFDS

4   The Use of Component Technology

To guarantee reusability and maintainability, the system must be designed and developed using component technologies. The COM and ActiveX component technology is adopted in WBFDS system. COM is an executable binary code which is issued in the form of Dynamic Link Library (DLL) or executable (EXE) file. It is extremely easy to build scalable applications. ActiveX is an Object Linking and Embedding (OLE) technology following the COM/DCOM protocols. For web-based applications, it provides to extend the feature of interactive.

WBFDS contains three components packages: Graphic Controls Package based on ActiveX, Data Operation Package based on COM, and Algorithms Package based on COM. The Graphic Controls Package is a Graphic Interface Component in the client-side for user to interact with the system and monitor various data. The Data Operation Component lies in the server-side, separates the application service tier from the Database Service Tier in order to easily extend the database. The Algorithms component includes several signals processing algorithms. Fig. 6 displays the application of components in WBFDS.

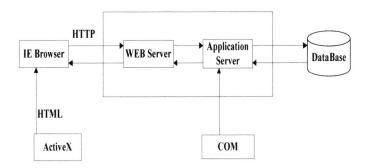

Fig. 6. B/S structure based on component technology

5   Implementation of the WBFDS

According to the theory of software architecture and component structure based on UML, the prototype system of WBFDS was implemented by using ASP.NET, ActiveX and COM technologies. Fig. 7 is the prototype system diagram. Through program development, software debugging, software testing, the effectiveness of the prototype system was verified.

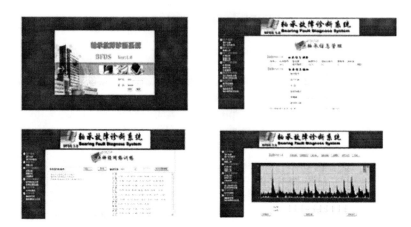

Fig. 7. Prototype system of WBFDS

6   Conclusion

In this paper, a method of WBFDS visual modeling is presented, which uses UML to model the whole system. It facilitates the management of complexity in the development of WBFDS. Using this visual model, a new project must shorten the period of analysis, design and development. Moreover, using component technology, we achieved a highly maintainable system. WBFDS has a good practical significance, especially for the software development of specific areas.

Acknowledgments. Firstly, I would like to show my deepest gratitude to my supervisor, Prof. Wu Xing, a respectable, responsible and resourceful scholar, who has provided me with valuable guidance in every stage of this project. His keen and vigorous academic observation enlightens me not only in this thesis but also in my future study. Furthermore, the thanks go to my colleague for support and feedback during the project.

References

1. Shi, J., Huang, Y.Y., Wu, X., Shi, J.: Design and Implementation of Bearing Fault Diagnosis System Based on Web. Development & Innovation of Machinery & Electrical Products 20, 105–107 (2007)
2. Booch, G., Rambaugh, J., Jacobson: The unified modeling language user guide, Beijing (2001)
3. Booch, G., Rambaugh, J., Jacobson: The unified modeling language reference manual, Beijing (2001)
4. Boggs, W., Boggs: Mastering UML with Rational Rose, Beijing (2000)

5. Repenning, A., Ioannidou, A., Payton, M., Ye, W., Roschelle: Using components for rapid distributed software development, pp. 38–45. IEEE Press, New York (2001)
6. Wu, X., Chen, J., Li, R.Q.: Web-based remote monitoring and diagnosis system model with UML. Computer Engineering 30, 27–29 (2004)
7. Wu, X., Chen, J., Li, R.Q.: Study of equipment remote monitoring and fault diagnosis system architecture. Computer Engineering and Application, 192–196 (2005)

A Survey on Localization Algorithms for Wireless Ad Hoc Networks

Yanlin Pei

Department of Telecommunication Engineering and Management,
International School Beijing University of Posts and Telecommunications
Beijing, China
jp092791@bupt.edu.cn

Abstract. In wireless ad hoc networks, location service is used to confirm geographical position and data information of a specific node for efficient routing. However, since in some specific circumstances ad hoc network localization cannot just rely on global positioning system (GPS), self-localization algorithm is a focus during wireless ad hoc research process and supplies solution for the problem. This paper integrates some existing prevalent self-localization algorithms and introduces some representative algorithms, then evaluates the algorithms and makes a comparison, at last educes a conclusion.

Keywords: wireless ad hoc networks, localization algorithm, non-GPS.

1   Introduction

In wireless ad hoc networks, the location information of a node is necessary for the node to communicate with other nodes. The transmitter can transmit data to the receiver only when it knows the location information of the receiver. Generally, nodes in the wireless ad hoc networks use global positioning system (GPS) to localize all nodes. However, in some special situations, the GPS signal can be very weak and even cannot be received, thus the localization cannot just rely on GPS. On the other hand, installing GPS receivers for all nodes needs expensive cost, enormous power consumption, and extra volume. Therefore, nodes need self-localization in wireless ad hoc networks. Several localization algorithms are suggested in the literature basing on advanced mathematics. This paper gives an overview of some localization algorithms.

This paper introduces existing representative algorithms, all the algorithms have their own characteristics, including advantages and disadvantages. Obviously, the algorithms have solved some problems, however, more problems exist, for example, power consumption, imprecision, large equipment cost.

This paper is organized as follows. Section 1 is a brief introduction of this paper. Section 2 gives the category of the localization algorithms for wireless ad hoc networks. Section 3 introduces the specific introductions of typical algorithms. Section 4 educes the conclusion.

M. Zhao and J. Sha (Eds.): ICCIP 2012, Part II, CCIS 289, pp. 512–519, 2012.
© Springer-Verlag Berlin Heidelberg 2012

2   Localization Algorithms for Ad Hoc Networks

As illustrated in Fig. 1, According to the efficiency of localization and the application conditions, localization algorithms can be categorized into three types: centralized localization method, distributed localization method, and local-style localization method.

In the centralized localization method, the information of all nodes is gathered into one central node (such as the server). The central node uses the information to calculate the location of each node, and then sends appropriate location information back to the corresponding nodes. The advantage of this method is that it has high precision whereas the disadvantage is that the central node and its surrounding nodes suffer excessive traffic pressure and serious power consumption. When the central node's power wears out, no nodes in the entire network can exchange information any more. In addition, the central node has to process large amounts of data, which is extremely heavy burden for one single node.

Since the wireless ad hoc networks are non-infrastructure and terminal-mobile networks, if the central node is selected and replaced frequently, it will lead to network instability or even paralysis.

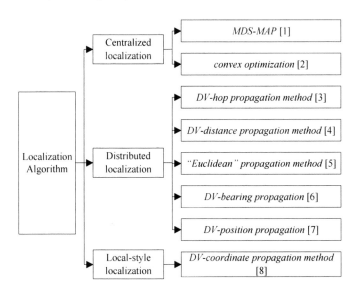

Fig. 1. Localization algorithms for wireless ad hoc networks

In the distributed localization method, each node confirms its own location information by exchanging information with other nodes in the networks. This method avoids information flooding so that it can reduce network transmission traffic. The procedure of information processing and calculation is carried out on every node in the network, which avoids the selection of central node, and thus improves the efficiency of localization.

In the local-style localization method, a node that owns the higher degree of connection is selected as an original point of one specific local area, and then a local rectangle coordinate system basing on this original point is established. All adjacent nodes of the original point are located in coordinate system. In this way, all nodes can be unified into one global coordinate system by coordinate transformation. This method is based on distributed localization algorithm and makes some improvements synchronously, which utilizes local resources in ad hoc network.

3   Specific Introductions of Typical Algorithms

3.1   DV-Hop Localization Algorithm

DV-hop localization algorithm is a basic method among all self-localization method for the wireless ad hoc networks.

In the DV-hop localization algorithm, firstly some specific nodes are selected as anchors. Every anchor broadcasts its location information to all of its adjacent nodes. The format of the broadcast packet is $\{ID_i, x_i, y_i, h_i\}$, where ID_i represents the identification of the anchor i, $\{x_i, y_i\}$ represents the coordinates of the anchor node i, and h_i represents the number of hops. The initial value of h_i is 0. The receiving node, which accepts the location information of anchor node, records a new number of hops (increasing by 1) in a diagram and then broadcasts the location information to the new adjacent nodes. By the flooding mode, the location information of all anchors will be broadcast to the whole network. The numbers of hops from every anchor to all nodes are known; synchronously one anchor acquires other anchors' location information. Then the average hop distance of node i can be calculated: (j represents other anchors, and h_{ij} represents the number of hops between anchor i and anchor j.)

$$C_i = \frac{\sum_1^n \sqrt{(x_i - x_j)^2 + (y_i - y_j)^2}}{\sum_1^n h_{ij}}, i \neq j \tag{1}$$

Every anchor broadcasts the average hop distance, the format of packet is $\{\{ID_i, C_i\}$, and the unknown nodes receive every anchor's packet information and then broadcast to other adjacent nodes. Once the information broadcast is finished, the local network average hop distance is calculated by counterpoising the average hop distance of different anchors, represented by c_c. Thus, the unknown nodes calculate the distance to every anchor by formula $d_i = h_i \times c_c$ and then these unknown nodes are localized in the networks.

3.2   DV-Distance Localization Algorithm

The DV-distance localization algorithm is similar with the DV-hop localization algorithm, and the difference is that this method calculates the distance between the adjacent nodes based on meter unit. This method estimates the distance using cumulative single hop distance, which must lead to the measured shortest distance larger than the actual result. The calculation error is often reduced by adding the number of anchors. Comparing with DV-hop localization algorithm, this method has less information exchange quantity, higher localization accuracy, but the results are more easily influenced by measuring error.

3.3   "Euclidean" Propagation Method

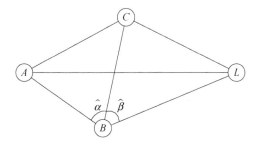

Fig. 2. "Euclidean" propagation method

As illustrated in Fig. 2, anchor A has at least two adjacent nodes, and the distances between these nodes and A are known. For anchor A, the length of AC, AB and BC are all known. There are two ways to acquire the value of BC. One is that B and C are adjacent nodes and BC can be measured directly. The other is that anchor A establishes a local coordinate system and localizes all adjacent nodes in the system, then calculates the value of BC.

For quadrangle $ACLB$, the lengths of side AC, AB, CL, BL and one diagonal line BC are known, and then the length of the other diagonal line can be calculated.

For $\triangle ACB$, by cosine theorem:

$$\cos \alpha = \frac{AB^2 + BC^2 - AC^2}{2 \times AB \times BC} \tag{2}$$

For $\triangle ABL$, by cosine theorem:

$$\cos \beta = \frac{BL^2 + BC^2 - CL^2}{2 \times BL \times BC} \tag{3}$$

For $\triangle BCL$, by cosine theorem:

$$AL^2 = AB^2 + BL^2 - 2 \times AB \times BL \times \cos(\beta + \alpha) \tag{4}$$

Hence, the length of AL can be calculated.

3.4   DV-Bearing Localization Algorithm

Before introducing the DV-bearing localization algorithm, several definitions are given first.

Bearing: The angle is measured by counterclockwise rotation from the self-defined reference direction of transmitter to the direction of transmitted signal.

Radial: The angle is measured by counterclockwise rotation from the self-defined reference direction of receiver to the direction of received signal.

Heading: The angle is measured by counterclockwise rotation from the self-defined reference direction to terminal to the north.

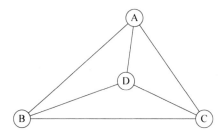

Fig. 3. DV-bearing localization method

Triangulation method: As illustrated in Fig. 3, for $\triangle ABC$, the coordinates of nodes A, B and C are known, the magnitudes of $\angle ADC$, $\angle BDC$ and $\angle BDA$ are known, then the location of node D can be confirmed.

The process can be described as follows. the coordinates of A and B are known, the magnitude of $\angle BDA$ is known, then two possible positions of node D can be confirmed. Similarity, node A, node C and $\angle ADC$ can also confirm two possible positions of node D. node B, node C and $\angle BDC$ can confirm two possible positions of D. Then the interaction node of all these possible positions is the actual position of node D, i.e. The position of D is confirmed.

Node A knows the bearings to B, C, recorded as $\hat{b}$ and $\hat{c}$. and the bearings from node B, C to anchor L are also known already. Then the $\angle BAL$ can be got by using cosine theorem in $\triangle ABC$, $\triangle BCL$. Thus node A to anchor L's bearing is $\hat{b} + \angle BAL$. then by triangulation method, the position of node A can be confirmed.

3.5   DV-Position Localization Algorithm

Nodes in the DV-position localization algorithm require higher ability and they must have the ability to process the distance and measure the angle. Therefore, each anchor needs a compass synchronously.

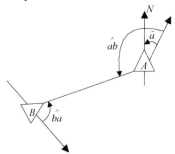

Fig. 4. DV-position localization method

As illustrated in Fig. 4, the heading of anchor A is $\hat{a}$, the bearing from node A to node B is $\widehat{ab}$, and the radial from node B to node A is $\widehat{ba}$, then the heading of node B is: $\hat{b} = 2\pi - (\widehat{ab} + \pi - \widehat{ba}) + \hat{a}$. If the distance between A and B is known, then the position of B can be confirmed.

3.6   DV-Coordinate Localization Algorithm

Three steps are used to elaborate the rectangular coordinate system method.

Step 1: A local rectangular coordinate system is set up centralizing the node A, as illustrated in Fig. 5.

If node A can gauge the distances to all adjacent nodes, then all the sides and angles of the triangle consisted by node A and adjacent node pair can be calculated. The direction from A to D is chosen as a positive direction of x-axes, the direction from A to E is the positive direction of y-axes. Adjacent nodes of A can be localized in the rectangular coordinate system uniquely. Similarity, other nodes in the network can use the same method to set up rectangular coordinate system, localize the adjacent nodes in coordinate system uniquely.

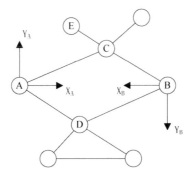

Fig. 5. DV-coordinate localization method

Step 2: The process is to acquire transfer matrix from one coordinate system to another. The inputs of this process are the coordinates of nodes overlapping in two systems. Every node can use the transfer matrix to transform the coordinates from one system to another.

Table 1. Corresponding diagrams of transformation

Type of information	Transfer modes
Distance	transformation, rotation, mirroring
Angle	transformation, rotation, scaling
Distance and angle	transformation, rotation

Noted that mirroring is needed only the direction of axes is reverse after rotation.

Step 3: The transfer matrix from node B to node A is

$$M_{ba} = \begin{bmatrix} sr_1 & sr_2 & t_x \\ sr_3 & sr_4 & t_y \\ 0 & 0 & 1 \end{bmatrix} \tag{5}$$

r_n represents rotation and mirroring, s represent scaling factor, t_n represents transformation, r_n is a orthogonal matrix, possessing the following attributes:
$|r_1|=|r_4|, |r_2|=|r_3|$

$$\det\{r_n\} = \begin{cases} -1, \text{mirroring} \\ 1, \text{otherwise} \end{cases} \tag{6}$$

When solving a problem, if some transfer modes are unwanted, the corresponding parameters are set to 1. For instance, utilizing a distance information to localize, scaling is unwanted, then s=1 in this circumstance.

$c_a = [x_a^c \, y_a^c \, 1]^T$ represents the parameters of node C in o_a, c_b represents the parameters in o_b .equation $c_a = M_{ba} \times c_b$ is used to transform nodes from one system to another.

4   Conclusion

In ad hoc network, the self-localization algorithm has tremendous influence on its practical application, thus it is imperative to establish rational criterion. Four indexes are used to judge whether an algorithm is proper or not.

Index one: Localization precision, which is a basic evaluation standard, usually defined as the ratio of calculation error to node telecommunication scope.

Index two: Node density, which is defined as average connectivity degree of network. Larger node density may aggravate difficulty to dispose distribution of nodes, and may also cause collisions telecommunication process.

Index three: Power assumption, since the energy resource of mobile nodes is limited, the power would be assumed when nodes execute telecommunication and calculation, thus power assumption is also a criterion.

Index four: Additional hardware, whether it is necessary to use external hardware to obtain data when conducting telecommunication. Additional hardware would not only affect the volume of nodes scope, but also increase the expense of nodes.

References

1. Bachrach, J., Taylor, C.: Localization in Sensor Networks. In: Handbook of Networks: Algorithms and Architectures
2. Costa, J.A., Patwari, N., Hero, A.O.: Distributed weighted-multidimensional scaling for node localization in sensor networks. ACM Trans. Sen. Netw. 2(1), 39–64 (2006)
3. Doherty, L., Pister, K., Ghaoui, L.E.: Convex position estimation in wireless sensor networks. In: Proceedings of IEEE Infocom, vol. 3, pp. 1655–1663 (2001)

4. Niculescu, D., Nath, B.: Position and Orientation in ad hoc networks. Ad Hoc Networks 2, 133–151 (2004)
5. Girod, L., Bychovskiy, V., Elson, J.: Locating in time and space: a case study. In: Proc. of the 2002 IEEE Int'l Conf. on Computer Design, Freiburg, pp. 214–219 (2002)
6. Langendoen, K., Reijers, N.: Distributed Localization in wireless sensor networks: a quantitative comparison. Computer Networks 43(4), 499–518 (2003)
7. Shang, Y., Shi, H., Ahmed, A.A.: Performance study of localization methods for ad-hoc sensor networks. In: Proc. 2004 IEEE International Conference on Mobile Ad-hoc and Sensor Systems, Fort Lauderdale, Germany, October 25-27, pp. 184–193 (2004)
8. Lu, G., Edwards, R.M., Ladas, C.: Mobile node positioning in mobile ad hoc network. In: Proc. the London Communications Symposium 2003, London, pp. 165–168 (2003)

An Approach to Scene Segmentation Based on Energy and Uncertainty Distribution of Velocity Field

Guoqiang Zhou and Rongyi Cui[*]

Intelligent Information Processing Lab.,
Dept. of Computer Science & Technology
Yanbian University, Yanji, China
cuirongyi@ybu.edu.cn

Abstract. A new scene segmentation method based on the distribution of motion intensity was proposed in this paper. Firstly, the motion foreground was extracted by fusing time and spatial information. Furthermore, noise was eliminated after motion vectors were extracted via pyramid-style Lucas-Kanade optical flow method. Finally, a frame scene was divided into blocks by proposed pyramid-style division method and the intensity mask generated by computing the motion intensity for each block was used to scene segmentation. The experimental results show that the motion intensity measurement is easy to compute and it has an outstanding performance on region segmentation and scene discrimination.

Keywords: Scene segmentation, image energy, direction entropy, pyramid-style optical flow, motion intensity.

1   Introduction

Scene analysis based on video is a hot research topic in the field of computer vision [1]. By extracting and analyzing the scene characterization information (e.g., crowd density, motion distribution), the scene surveillance could be implied effectively. In the process of scene analysis, segmentation is the significant foundation. Therefore, research on scene segmentation is very significant and has realistic value.

Recently, the main works for scene analysis focus on the crowd density estimation and crowd abnormal detection. Reference [2] combined optical flow and DCT to detect abnormality in different scenes. The energy and mutual information were used to analyze crowd motion variation in [3]. A custom energy function for crowd assessment and abnormal detection was discussed in [4].

An approach to scene segmentation based on the distribution of motion intensity is proposed in this paper. We extract the motion area by employing the detection method which fuses the time and spatial information , and velocity field was computed by Lucas-Kanade (L-K) optical flow. After eliminating the noise, the scene

---

[*] Corresponding author:

M. Zhao and J. Sha (Eds.): ICCIP 2012, Part II, CCIS 289, pp. 520–528, 2012.

is divided into blocks by proposed pyramid-style division method and intensity mask is computed by calculating motion intensity for each block. The proposed method, with reasonable theoretical foundation, can achieve effective result for segmentation.

2   Motion Estimation

2.1   Motion Detection

Motion detection is the foundation work for movement analysis. The common methods are background subtraction and frame difference. The former has been widely used in recent years, and the key problem is how to generate background model and update the background real-timely. The latter method, which uses the continual inter-frame difference to pick up the moving area, is simple and it can adapt to the changes of illuminations.

We detect object motion by the method of combining frame difference and background subtraction method [5]. Images in Fig. 1 show the results of motion detection for a frame.

(a) Original frame   (b) Detected result

Fig. 1. Motion detection

2.2   Optical Flow Computation

We use the pyramid-style L-K optical flow approach to extract the velocity field [6]. In most motion analysis applications, the first step of optical flow computation is feature extraction. But in our approach, we did not use any feature extraction methods because that none of these methods can provide an equally distributed feature set. We use all of the points as feature set of each frame. The optical flow computation result for one frame is as shown in Fig. 2.

It can be seen from Fig. 2(b) that a lot of noise exists in the optical flow computation result because of the influence of luminosity and shadow. Therefore denoising is necessary and we will take the corresponding processing in the following section.

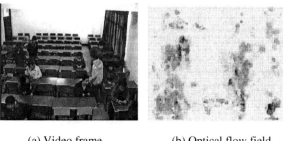

(a) Video frame   (b) Optical flow field

Fig. 2. Optical flow computation

3   Segmentation Based on Motion Intensity Distribution

3.1   Preprocessing

In order to reduce the affection of noise, we refine the feature set by using motion foreground as a mask. All the motion vectors outside the foreground mask are excluded from the feature set to emphasize the motion area. We also consider that the noise features are those features which motion is less than two pixels and have a large angle and magnitude difference with their neighbor features. Therefore, we apply a 3×3 median filter to smooth the motion field. As shown in Fig. 3, the noise features are effectively removed.

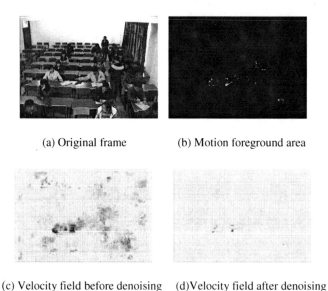

(a) Original frame   (b) Motion foreground area

(c) Velocity field before denoising   (d)Velocity field after denoising

Fig. 3. Velocity field preprocessing

3.2   The Measurement of Motion Intensity

The energy, direction histogram and entropy, etc. are often used to represent the motion characteristics [7-9].

Energy is the magnitude for objective assessment of motion intensity. The energy of each frame is defined as:

$$E_i = \sum_{j=1}^{n} m_j v_j^2 \tag{1}$$

where E_i denotes the energy of the i-th frame in a video sequence, and v_j is the magnitude of the j-th motion vector in the i-th frame, and n is the total number of motion vectors in the i-th frame respectively. We assume that $m_j = 1$ to mean the equivalent value of each direction.

Direction histogram can be used to present the motion direction distribution, and it can be expressed as follow:

$$h(i) = \{k_i, 0 < i \le n\} \tag{2}$$

where n denotes the number of histogram bins, k_i implies the number of motion vectors at a certain angle range which is related to the i-th bin for each frame.

Entropy is a magnitude for systematic randomness. It can be used to describe the dispersion of direction probability distribution, and it is defined as:

$$Entropy = \sum_{i=1}^{N} p(x_i) \log(\frac{1}{p(x_i)}) \tag{3}$$

where p is the direction probability distribution, N denotes the number of different values. In our work, we divide 2π into 8 bins, which means each bin recovers the angle interval of 45 degrees.

Considering both energy and direction distribution are important for motion description of a scene, we combined them and proposed a new magnitude to describe the motion intensity. The definition can be formulated as:

$$Lvalue = ME + Entropy \tag{4}$$

where ME is the modified motion energy and $Entropy$ is the motion direction entropy defined by (3) .

The modified motion energy is defined as:

$$ME = \frac{fn}{tn} \sum_{i=1}^{m} m_i v_i^2 \tag{5}$$

where fn is the number of foreground pixels, tn is the total number of pixels in the given region. The ratio between fn and tn is used to emphasize the motion area and avoid computation inconvenience with large values.

It can be seen from (4) that the more energy or direction entropy, the more motion intensity. When the movement is in order, the intensity mainly depends on the energy, and in contrast, the intensity mainly depends on the direction entropy.

3.3   Scene Segmentation

Scene segmentation refers to dividing the scene into different areas according to certain criterion. In our work, the scene of each frame was divided into blocks at first, then the intensity of each block was calculated, and the scene was segmented based on intensity at last.

The common method for scene division is equisection method, which can be simply implemented [10]. But the perspective effect, which refers that the objects with different distance from camera are different in size on the image, is completely ignored in this method. To cut down perspective effect, we propose a pyramid-style method for scene division. We assume that size of image is $M \times N$ pixels, the initial size of block side is *mbsize*, and the number of the use of the same block size is *count*. Steps to scene division are as follows:

Step1: Initialize *count*=1, *i*=*M-mbsize*;

Step2: Let X be the matrix with the size of *mbsize*×*N*. Divide X into blocks with the size of *mbsize*×*mbsize*, and regard the rest size as the last block.

Step3: Reset *M=i*, and reset *mbsize* according to (6).

$$mbsize = mbsize - sizethresh \ (for \ count > 2) \tag{6}$$

Step4: If *count*>2, then reset *count*=1, and go step2. otherwise, *count*= *count*+1;

Step5: Iterate step2~step4 until the whole image have been processed.

The value of *sizethresh* in (6) is determined according to shooting angle and the minimum size of objects on the image. In our work, the *sizethresh* equal to 8, and *mbsize* equal to 64. An example of scene division is shown in Fig. 4.

After scene division, the intensity of each block can be calculated according to (4), and the scene can be segmented at last. The complete steps for segmentation are presented as follows:

Step1: Compute velocity field between continuous frames.

Step2: Divide scene into blocks and calculate intensity of each block based on (4).

Step3: Map the intensity of each block into different gray values, and generate the intensity mask after normalizing intensity values.

Step4: Product the original frame with intensity mask.

Step5: Stretch the contrast of the image generated in step4.

Fig. 5 is an example of scene segmentation. Fig. 5(a) shows the original frame, Fig. 5(b) shows the computed velocity field, Fig. 5(c) shows the intensity mask in which the brightness represents the motion intensity and Fig. 5(d) illustrates the result of segmentation in which the motion area has been labeled hierarchically.

(a) Original frame   (b) Sub-block image

Fig. 4. Blocking diagram

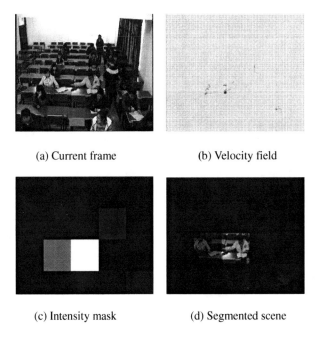

(a) Current frame	(b) Velocity field

(c) Intensity mask	(d) Segmented scene

Fig. 5. Example of scene segmentation

4   Experiments and Analysis

We use a set of videos provided by a stationary camera in a topdown view, to monitor the examination situation in a classroom. The original video frame size is 240 × 320 *pixels* and frame rate of video is 15 *fps*.

Experiment 1: The Initial Block Size Selection. The initial block size directly determines the quality of segmentation. It is easy to cause the lack of representability with large block size, and can't reflect scene semantics with small block size. In order to get the appropriate initial size, we randomly select five frames from video sequence to compute intensity levels with different initial block size. The results for different initial block sizes are shown in Table 1.

From Table 1, we can find that the number of intensity levels decreases gradually with the increase of initial block size. We choose the size of 64×64 as the initial size for trade-off between representability and semantics.

Table 1. Intensity levels of different block size

Typical Frames	Initial Block Size				
	8×8	*16×16*	*32×32*	*64×64*	*128×128*
F1	5	5	4	4	4
F2	9	9	7	8	5
F3	3	3	3	3	3
F4	7	7	5	6	4
F5	10	10	10	7	6

Experiment 2: Motion Fierce Region Detection. The motion fierce regions are detected by using the segmentation algorithm proposed in this paper. Images in Fig. 6 show the diagram of fierce region detection.

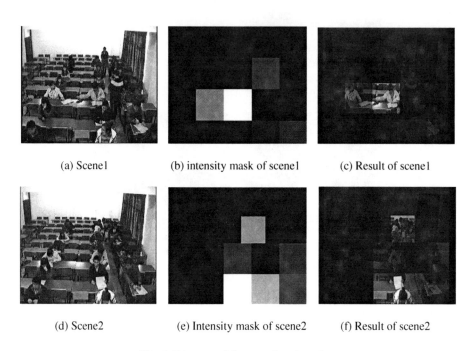

(a) Scene1   (b) intensity mask of scene1   (c) Result of scene1

(d) Scene2   (e) Intensity mask of scene2   (f) Result of scene2

Fig. 6. Diagram of fierce region detection

Fig. 6(a) is a scene in which two students are delivering their papers to each other, Fig. 6(d) is another scene in which several students are gathering together and two students are peeking at the others' paper, Fig. 6(b) and Fig. 6(e) show the intensity mask of each scene, Fig. 6(c) shows the detected result of scene1, and Fig. 6(f) shows the result of scene2. We can find that the proposed segmentation method has a good performance on motion fierce region detection in both simple and complex situation.

Experiment 3: Scene Discrimination. The distribution of intensity is used to evaluate and discriminate the scene in this experiment. Three typical scenes are extracted from video sequence as shown in Fig. 7. Fig. 7(a) shows the test scene with little movement, Fig. 7(b) shows the test scene in which a few people gather together, and Fig. 7(c) shows the test scene without any order.

Modified energy, direction entropy and intensity of each of the three scenes are calculated and curves are as shown in Fig. 8 (solid line for intensity, dashed line for entropy and dotted line for modified energy). We can find that the change of intensity value is faster than others and it is more suitable for scene evaluation.

Therefore, we can use some criterion based on intensity to discriminate scenes. In our work, the criterion is defined as:

$$condition = \begin{cases} 1, & Lvalue < \gamma \\ 0, & otherwise \end{cases} \tag{7}$$

where γ is threshold, which is determined according to practical conditions. If the intensity value is greater than γ, we consider that the scene condition is unacceptable because of possible violent contained in the part of scene.

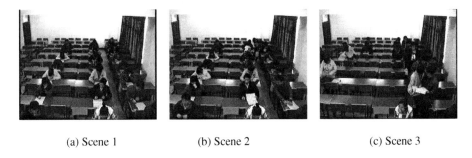

(a) Scene 1   (b) Scene 2   (c) Scene 3

Fig. 7. Typical scenes

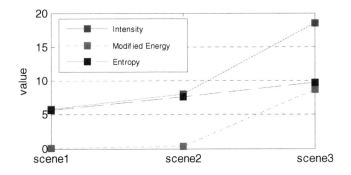

Fig. 8. Curves of modified energy, entropy and intensity

5   Conclusion

A new measurement for motion intensity, which combines motion energy and motion randomness, is discussed in this paper, and it is used to segment and evaluate scenes.

The experimental results show that the proposed intensity measurement is easy to compute and realize, furthermore the intensity measurement has an outstanding performance on fierce region detection and scene discrimination, which can be applied to many practical areas such as traffic surveillance, public order monitor, and examination surveillance and so on.

The selection of initial block size, which is determined based on the practical situation, is a complex problem. For a scene, different segmentation results can be achieved with different initial block size. Meanwhile the scene is only evaluated in overall view. Therefore, the future work includes the design for self-adaptive initial size of block and the analysis on details of a scene.

Acknowledgments. Our work was supported by Education Department of Jilin Prov. of China under Grant No. [2011]8. We would like to thank editor and anonymous referee for their careful reading and valuable comments on improving the original manuscript.

References

1. Varadarajan, J., Odobez, J.M.: Topic models for scene analysis and abnormality detection. In: 12th IEEE International Conference on Computer Vision Workshops (ICCV), pp. 1338–1345. IEEE Press, Kyoto (2007)
2. Wu, X.Y., Ou, Y.S., Qian, H.H., Xu, Y.S.: A detection system for human abnormal behavior. In: 2005 IEEE/RSJ International Conference on Intelligent Robots and Systems, pp. 1204–1208. IEEE Press, Edmonton (2005)
3. Ihaddadene, N., Djeraba, C.: Real-time crowd motion analysis. In: 19th International Conference on Pattern Recognition (ICPR), pp. 1–4. IEEE Press, Florida (2008)
4. Zhong, Z., Xu, Y.S., Shi, W.R.: Crowd abnormality surveillance. Chinese Journal of Scientific Instrument (Chinese Edition with English Abstract) 28, 614–620 (2007)
5. Niu, W.Z., Shi, L.S., Jin, G.Z., Li, X.L., Bai, X.F.: Moving object detection algorithm with fusion of time and spatial information. Computer Engineering (Chinese Edition with English Abstract) 37, 170–173 (2011)
6. Gan, S., Temiz, M.S., Kulur, S.: Real time speed estimation of moving vehicles from Side View Images from an uncalibrated video camera. Sensors 10, 4816–4824 (2010)
7. Zhou, Z.N., Chen, X.: Activity analysis, summarization, and visualization for Indoor Human Activity Monitoring. IEEE Transaction on Circuits and Systems for Video Technology 18, 1489–1505 (2008)
8. Cao, T., Wu, X.Y., Guo, J.N., Yu, S.Q., Xu, Y.S.: Abnormal crowd motion analysis. In: Proceedings of the 2009 IEEE International Conference on Robotics and Biomimetics, pp. 1709–1714. IEEE Press, Guilin (2009)
9. Pei, G.J., Li, F., Zhou, H.Q.: Real-time anomaly detection in crowd scenes using CP-GMM model. Electronic Technology (Chinese Edition with English Abstract) 38, 7–9 (2011)
10. Lin, S.F., Chen, J.Y., Chao, H.X.: Estimation of number of people in crowded scenes using perspective transformation. IEEE Transaction on System, Man, and Cybernetics A31, 645–654 (2001)

Method of Formation Cooperative Air Defense Decision Based on Multi-agent System Cooperation

Chao Wang, Bo Wang, Guo Zhang, and Yizhi Liang

Department of Research, Dalian Naval Academy, Dalian, China
{naval_wang,Wang_bo,Zhang_guo,Liang_yizhi}@yahoo.com.cn

Abstract. In order to solve the problem of cooperative air defense for warship formation in complicated battlefield situation, a method of formation cooperative air defense decision based on multi-agent was proposed using technology of agent. The principle of the method and the design of agent were introduced in detail, aimed at the key problem of how to develop the cooperative among multi-agent of warship decision effectively and how to eliminate the conflict during the cooperative decision process, a method of combat troops cooperation and conflict elimination were proposed based on multi-agent cooperation, which could help commander of the formation establish the combat scheme scientifically and accurately facing complex battlefield environment, and realize the whole formation of cooperative air defense operations.

Keywords: multi-agent cooperation, formation cooperative air defense, decision method.

1   Introduction

The modern sea war in the condition of high technology, because the long-range and precision-guided weapons are equipped largely on warships, submarines and battle planes, the threat of the air increases greatly, which brings huge challenges to warship formation air defense operation, the air anti-ship missiles "saturated attack" has become a serious threat to the survival of the formation. Facing the challenge, air defense resources of the warship formation must be integrated, using all kinds of efficient air defense means, constructing tight, multi-level air defense system and multilayer phase of intercept defense nets, to get the best out of the whole of the warship formation operational efficiency, and realize the cooperative air-defense of the warship formation [1].

The decision is the core of the operation command [2]. Air defense decision of the warship formation cooperative is a kind of dynamic decision in the command of formation command organization, which is to achieve the goal of against the air threat cooperatively. The formulation of cooperative air defense decision plan for warship formation needs to fully consider the cooperation of internal formation, both consider being able to reach each other of cooperation and fully consider the possible conflict.

M. Zhao and J. Sha (Eds.): ICCIP 2012, Part II, CCIS 289, pp. 529–538, 2012.
© Springer-Verlag Berlin Heidelberg 2012

2   Principle of Formation Cooperative Air Defense Decision Method

Agent is now a widely used concept, which can be considered as a certain decision ability of independent entity. Multi-agent system (MAS) can be regarded as an agent group in which agent interacts with each other to achieve a global target [3].

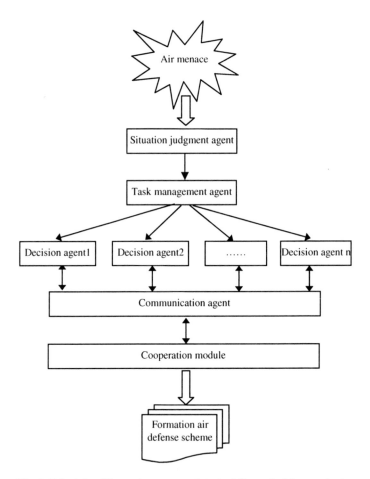

Fig. 1. Principle of formation cooperative air defense decision method

Decision method of formation cooperative air defense based on MAS cooperation was proposed in this paper, in which agent was used as the basic unit of abstract, and the related role in warship formation cooperative decision process were abstracted as situation judgment agent, task management agent, warship decision agent and communication agent. The decision agent includes not only the ordinary warship decision members, but also the formation command members. Formation decision scheme of air defense was formulated by warships decision agent together cooperatively, based on the processing of situation judgment agent and task management agent. The principle of the method is shown in figure 1.

During the process of task executing for warship formation, if threat target was detected by sensors of warship, first, according to the target's type, position, course, speed, situation judgment agent analyses threat level of the target, ascertains target's relative threat degree to the formation, and build the threatening target table sorted by the threatening degree. Second, according to the threat the target's campaign elements, task management agent judges the target's attacking goal, distributes one or more warship to oppugning the target according to the threat level. Third, after delivery of the oppugning mission, warship decision agent formulates air defense plans of oppugning threatening target, according to the situation and weapons equipment.

In the formulating process of air defense plan, warship decision agents realize real-time information interaction with each other through communication agent, and implement collaborated decision through the cooperation module. On one hand, the task which is difficult for single warship to carry out could be cooperated by others. On the other hand, through the uninterrupted communications, each warship could exchange combat plan to eliminate the conflict appeared in plans in time.

3 Design of Formation Cooperative Air Defense Decision Agents

According to principle of the formation cooperative air defense decision method, agents of the decision process mainly include situation judgment agent, task management agent, warship decision agent, communication agent.

3.1 Situation Judgment Agent

The task of situation judgment agent is to sense and process battlefield information, set up the enemy target list sorted by threatening degree, which provide a basis for the command and decision of warship decision agents.

When establishing enemy targets threat linked list, first, according to the basic situation and the movement elements of enemy target, the threat level of target should be determined, mainly according to the type of goal, carrying weapons and equipment, the orientation of the target, distance, side angle, course, speed and other information. And then, the targets should be sorted by the threatening degree according to the grade of target threat and the pressure degree of target attacking. At the same time, agent uses artificial neural network and adaptive method to analyze target's movement state and issuing other agents in time once that information changes.

3.2 Task Management Agent

The function of task management agent is decomposing the general task of formation cooperative air defense, generating a series of tasks in the composition of the son task list, and then distributing to the warship decision agents.

The model of task management agent is shown in figure 2. Task decomposition module and task allocation module accomplish the task of decomposition and distribution respectively. Task decomposition is mainly reasoned according to knowledge database, in which the general task of formation cooperative air defense was decomposed according to combat phase, combat aspect and combat target. The results of task decomposition form a task list, which was written in the blackboard.

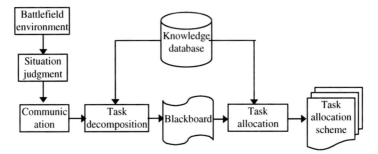

Fig. 2. Model of task management agent

Task allocation is mainly realized through judging the attacking attempt of enemy threaten target according to the movement of the enemy and own formation situation, and then distributing the task to the right warship decision agent according to target's attacking attempt and the information of weapon equipment. Thereby, the plan of formation task allocation was formed.

3.3   Warship Decision Agent

Warship decision agent is the most important category in the system, whose task is to establish the combat scheme according to the distribution of air defense task and the current battlefield situation. The model of warship decision agent is shown in figure 3.

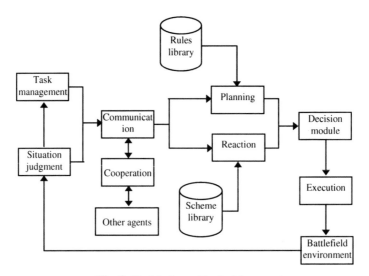

Fig. 3. Model of warship decision agent

First, warship decision agent gets the distributed combat mission and the information of situation respectively through communication agent, and then, establishes its own decision plan according to combat targets and the operational rules. For task which is difficult to accomplish by its own ability, implements through the cooperation with other warship agents. In the process of formulating air defense plan, warship decision agent could make a rapid response to emergencies according to its own knowledge and experience of the existing scheme library, or make decision through reasoning, behavior planning according to combat rules in normal condition. After that, the decision would be sent to execution and action in battlefield environment.

3.4   Communication Agent

The function of communication agent is realizing data exchange among other kinds of agent as agency of information interaction, in which blackboard is used to store global information database, which records public information of system component agent, and can share with all the other agents [4]. If all information of system component agent run at any moment is released in blackboard, the storage capacity of blackboard would be increased greatly and the burden of the blackboard would be very heavy. So, considering the problem of storage capacity, only the necessary public information and certain information are released in blackboard, such as the moving track of enemy threat the target, the information of weapons using, etc.

Communication agent uses mechanism of message to realize information alternation, the syntax of message is:

$$\langle messagename \rangle [(p_1, p_2, \cdots, p_n)]$$

The syntax of message sending is:

$$send \langle receiver \rangle \langle messagename \rangle [(p_1, p_2, \cdots, p_n)]$$

Communication agent is responsible only for news of transmission, not for processing.

4   MAS Planning for Formation Cooperative Air Defense Decision

How to realize the cooperation of warships decision agents is the key problem of the method for formation cooperative air defense decision.

4.1   MAS Cooperation Based on Behavior Planning

Agent cooperation is the core of the research work for MAS system [5]. At present, according to the research of agent, cooperation can be divided into two types [6]: the first kind use method and technology of entity behavior, such as game theory, classical mechanics theory, etc. The second kind study from the goals, intentions, planning and other mental attitude of agent, such as FA/C model, combined intentions framework, sharing planning etc.

Planning means a sequence of operations formulated by agent, in order to complete the distributed task and achieve a goal; it describes a path from given initial state to target state. At present, MAS planning has two ways [7]: centralized planning and distributed planning. In centralized planning, a central coordination agent constructs a plan which is to be done by several agents, and then the plan would be sent to every agent, each agent executes the plan in distribution, all the agents finish the task cooperatively together. The central coordination agent is also responsible for the resolution of conflict. In distributed planning, the whole planning task is assigned to each application agent, the agent makes out its own goal respectively, and communicates with other agent to solve the conflict among them, and there exists no central coordination agent.

4.2   MAS Planning Algorithm

According to the characteristics of formation cooperative air defense decision, the decision scheme is formulated through sufficient negotiation by the entire warship decision agents, organized by formation command post. So, first, each warship decision agent makes out distributed according to its combat task, cooperate with other agents in need. After the initial combat scheme finished, agent eliminates the conflict in the scheme by distributed negotiation. Formation command post is responsible for the arbitrage when there is conflict existed which could not be reached to an agreement through consultation.

Thus, in allusion to the cooperative question of warship decision agent during the process of formation cooperative air defense, a kind of "center control" MAS planning algorithm was proposed. The main steps are as follows:

Step1: Received distributed combat task from task management agent, decision agent sorts the task and construct their task set.

Step2: Decision agent gets current processing task from task sets. When all the tasks are processed, the planning has been completed and exited successfully.

Step3: Decision agent analyzes whether cooperation is needed to accomplish the current task. If need other agent's cooperation, turn to the Step5, otherwise, move on to the next step.

Step4: Decision agent formulates the action plan based on its own operational resources for the current task, and then turns to Step7.

Step5: According to the requirements analysis of cooperation and the ability of other agent, decision agent determines the cooperative partners set in allusion to the current task and the priority order. Then move on to the next step. If no partner can provide cooperation, turn to Step4.

Step6: Decision agent send application of cooperation to agent according to the order in cooperative partners set. Partners assess the application after receiving it, develop cooperative plan according to the cooperative goal and their own operational resources situation if it is approved. Move on to the next step after the work is completed. If it is not approved, agent makes a choice from the following three options:

(1) Sending application of cooperation to other agent in partners set, turn to the Step6;

(2) Reporting to formation command agent for arbitration, return to Step4 or Step6 according to the arbitration;

(3) Giving up this cooperative application, turn to the Step4.

Step7: After the combat plan was generated, decision agent sends the plan to all the other agents for conflict examination. If there is no conflict, this scheme becomes a official scheme, if not, decision agents eliminate the conflict using conflict eliminate algorithm. After that, move on to the next step.

Step8: Current task of decision agent has been finished; turn to Step2 for planning of the next task.

This planning algorithm combines the advantage of distributed planning and centralized planning; the scheme is formulated by decision agents distributed. As the central coordinator, the work of formation command agent is reduced evidently, which makes the size of formation not limit by the computing power of central coordinator. At the same time, the leading role of formation command is assured during the process of combat, which is in line with the basic model of formation operation command. So it can be a very good solution to resolve the cooperative question of formation cooperative air defense.

5   Conflict Elimination of Formation Cooperative Air Defense Decision

Conflict is a kind of inevitable phenomenon in cooperative decision process. A conflict eliminate method was proposed based on multi-agent cooperation aimed at how to eliminate the conflict among sub-schemes of decision agent.

5.1   Basic Definition

To realize the formalization of conflict eliminating process, based on theory of extension [8], some concepts were given first including scheme element, constraint condition, conflict question, etc.

Definition 1: Scheme element

Decision scheme is consist of several parameters; each parameter of the scheme has a definite value, the name, parameters and values of scheme constitute the basic unit of the description are referred to as scheme element, described as $R = \langle N, C, V \rangle$, N express scheme name, C express scheme characteristics, V express value of C .These three numbers are called three elements of scheme element. Their relationship could be expressed as $V = C(N)$.

Definition 2: Constraint condition

To avoid conflict, the requirements of scheme element values that must be satisfied are called constraint condition, which are described as a binary group $CQ = \langle X, D \rangle$. In the group, $X = \{X_1, X_2, \cdots, X_n\}$ which is a set of variables, $D = \{D_1, D_2, \cdots, D_n\}$, which is a group of domain, each element is s set of possible values corresponding to the variable.

Definition 3: Question

The expression consists of scheme element R1, scheme element R2 and CQ is called a question, expressed as $P_{12} = (R_1 \otimes R_2) * CQ$.

Definition 4: Conflict examination

The behavior of judging whether scheme element R1 and R2 can be realized simultaneously in CQ is called conflict examination.

Definition 5: Conflict question

For the given problem of $P_{12} = (R_1 \otimes R_2) * CQ$, if after conflict examination, scheme element R1 and R2 could not realized simultaneously in CQ, P is called a conflict question, expressed as $P_{12} = (R_1 \uparrow R_2, CQ)$.

Definition 6: Compatible question

For the given problem of $P_{12} = (R_1 \otimes R_2) * CQ$, if after conflict examination, scheme element R1 and R2 could be realized simultaneously in CQ, P is called a compatible question, expressed as $P_{12} = (R_1 \downarrow R_2, CQ)$.

Definition 7: Related

For any two scheme element R1 and R2, if they don't oppugn the same target, don't using electromagnetic resources simultaneously and have no requirement for ship moving, they are called unrelated scheme element, otherwise, they are called Related.

Definition 8: Conflict characteristics set

For the given question of $P_{12} = (R_1 \uparrow R_2, CQ)$, the set consist of characteristics leading to conflict is called a conflict characteristics set, expressed as $CA = \{C_i, \cdots, C_n\}$.

Definition 9: Conflict set

For the given question of $P_{12} = (R_1 \uparrow R_2, CQ)$, the set consist of conflict characteristic, corresponding values and dissatisfied CQ is called a conflict set, expressed as $CS = \{CA, V, CQ\}$.

5.2   Algorithm

In case of a system of formation cooperative air defense that includes m decision agents, among which n decision agents have formulated their schemes already, expressed as $AS = \{A_1, A_2, \cdots, A_n\}$. The conflict examination and the elimination among agent i and AS about combat scheme after agent i has finished its own plan is discussed below.

Step1: AS construct scheme elements according to their own combat schemes, expressed as $\{R_1, R_2, \cdots, R_n\}$.

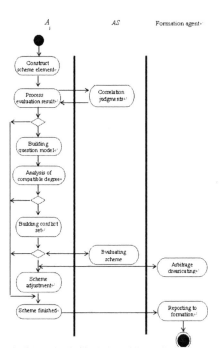

Fig. 4. Process of conflict examination and elimination

Step2: A_i constructs scheme elements according to its own combat plan and sends to AS .Other agents judge the correlation of the scheme elements based on constraint conditions after receiving it and make feedback to A_i .

Step3: If the relationship of the scheme elements is unrelated, that means no conflict exists. Otherwise, for the agents whose scheme elements are related, build the question model according to their scheme elements and constraint conditions.

Step4: Decision agent actualizes conflict examination respectively according to the question model, to determine question type, analyze the degree of compatible and make a judgment whether it is a conflict question or a compatible question. If it is a compatible question, determines conflict characteristics set and constructs conflict set.

Step5: If all the questions are compatible, which means the conflict doesn't exist, move to the next decision-agents. Else, according to the constraint condition, A_i eliminate conflict uniformly through adjust its own combat scheme; If the conflict can not be eliminated by itself, A_i send adjustment suggestion to correlative agents.

Step6: After correlative agents receive adjustment suggestion of scheme, if they could accept the suggestion, then adjust their own scheme and inform A_i that the conflict is eliminated, else inform A_i the message that they refuse to adjust.

Step7: According to the negotiations results with all the other agents, A_i decides whether to give up its own scheme or report to formation command agent for arbitration.

Step8: Formation command agent sends the final opinion to A_i after arbitration.

The process of conflict examination and elimination for formation air defense decision is shown in figure 4.

6   Conclusions

Along with the development of information technology, the pattern of air defense operation in the sea has been changed from traditional single-warship combat to formation cooperative air defense. How to make reasonable cooperative scheme of air defense for formation is a question needed by formation commander urgently. This paper imports technology of agent to the research of the cooperative air defense decision, proposes a method of formation cooperative air defense decision based on multi-agent system cooperation, which provides important reference basis for the implement of formation cooperative air defense operation. It can effectively help formation commander formulate decision scheme scientifically facing complex battlefield environment, and realize the whole formation of cooperative air defense operations, which has the important practical significance.

References

1. Wu, C.H., Chen, W., Luo, Y.C.: CGF Technique of Navy Ship Cooperation Aerial Defence Based on Role Mapping. Journal of System Simulation 22, 1528–1530 (2010)
2. Cheng, Q.Y.: Operational Analysis of command. Publishing House of Military Science (2006)
3. Li, Y., Ma, S.F.: Modelling of simulation system based on agent. Journal of System Engineering 21, 225–231 (2006)
4. Xu, R.P., Wang, S.Z., Gu, J.: Agent based action planning method of the fight unit. Systems Engineering and Electronics 27, 844–847 (2005)
5. Wooldridge, M.: Introduction of multi-agent system. Publishing House of Electronics, Beijing (2003)
6. Pan, Y., Li, D.H., Liang, J.Z., Wang, J.Y.: Multi-agent cooperative reinforcement learning algorithm based on practical reasoning. J. Huazhong Univ. of Sci. & Tech (Natural Science Edition) 38, 54–57 (2010)
7. Wang, C., Jing, N., Li, J., Wang, J., Chen, H.: An Algorithm of Cooperative Multiple Satellites Mission Planning Based on Multi agent Reinforcement Learning. Journal of National University of Defense Technology 33, 53–58 (2011)
8. Cai, W.: Introduction of Extenics. System Engineering and Practice 18, 76–84 (1998)

Object Location and Tracking
in Binocular Vision System

Kai Liu, Renjie Hu, and Zhiyong Ma

Southeast University
Nanjing, China
liukai@seu.edu.cn

Abstract. A framework of detecting and tracking object is given by binocular vision system approach. Selecting the image in one frame of video stream from camera, instead of modeling object's features, the framework finds out the given object's position and pose, and then starts the tracking. There are three research points in the framework. First of all, online learners and detectors using object's image from different visual angle is built. Secondly, integrating with object's location calculation, a method of image matching is defined. Finally, based on the previous velocity, position and pose, object's tracking strategy is proposed. At the end of this paper, a vehicle tracking experiment is given and the result shows that the framework is robust and fast.

Keywords: object detection and tracking, image matching, computer vision.

1   Introduction

In the traditional transportation system, to detect red light runner and other illegal acts, sensors must be buried underground in the road, which usually damage the road surface and hard to maintain. With the development of computer vision theory, researchers has used object detection and tracking in intelligent transportation system. For example, detecting red light runners by using video analysis is used by Nelson H. C. Yung [1]. Most of those applications use one camera[2-5] which is easy to get videos and to retrieve information. But in single camera system, it is hard to rebuild 3-dimensional information and cannot calculate the distance of targets. So, in this paper, a framework using two cameras is proposed in the study of object detection and tracking.

The proposed framework is based on the constraint that target's acceleration is limited and the target's velocity will not change sharply in each inspection cycle. Obviously, in the real application, such constraint is easily met. Figure 1 illustrates the process of tracking an object. At the first state, object's image library is empty. The first image of given object, which is selected from a frame of one camera, is matched in the image from other camera at the same time spot. Then using the distance measurement algorithm, target object's position and relative angle can be calculated. Further more, in next inspection time, assuming the unchanged of target's velocity, the interesting range in each image from two cameras is set. Setting an operating window which size equals to template image size and moving operating

M. Zhao and J. Sha (Eds.): ICCIP 2012, Part II, CCIS 289, pp. 539–546, 2012.
© Springer-Verlag Berlin Heidelberg 2012

window throughout the interesting range, object's image location can be found with the matching of image library. If it still does not work, match interesting ranges from two cameras and rebuild the 3-D information, then using the position constraint, target can be found. At this situation, new image of target is obtained and can be update to object's image library. The main advantage of this framework is that stereo vision and template library are used at the same time which can accelerate the process of finding object and can increase the recognition accuracy.

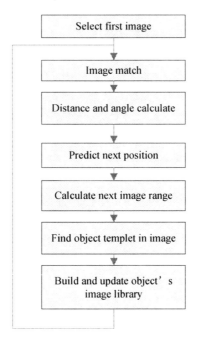

Fig. 1. One Process of object detection and tracking

The reset of this paper is organized as follows: section 2 illustrates the algorithm of stereo vision, the method of image matching and template library learning is given at section 3. In section 4, prediction and correcting of target object's position is discussed. Section 5 gives an experiment to test this framework. Conclusions and future work are given at the end of this paper.

2   Bincular Distance Measurement Algorithm

To measure the distance and relative angle between target object and two-camera system, we use two types of coordinate systems which are image coordinate (UV) and camera coordinate (XYZ). In image coordinate system, the coordinate value [u, v] can be given by the digital image's pixel values [px, py] and camera's intrinsic calibration parameters K as

$$\begin{bmatrix} p_x \\ p_y \\ 1 \end{bmatrix} = K \begin{bmatrix} u \\ v \\ 1 \end{bmatrix}$$

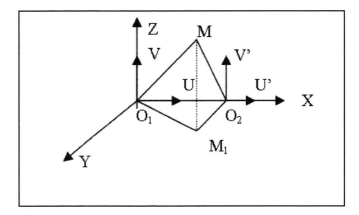

Fig. 2. The camera coordinate and image coordinate. O1 and O2 are camera centers. V and V' are optical axis of cameras. M is target object. M1 is Projection on plan XO1Y of M.

As figure 2 shows, two cameras are fixed in a same plane and the optical axis parallel to the plane normal vector. We denote the left optical center (O1) as axis origin, and the direction of connect line of two optical center (O1O2) as axis X, the optical axis as axis Z, and the normal direction of plan (XO1Z) as axis Y. Target M is at coordinate position [x, y, z]. We transform rectangular coordinate system to polar coordinate as

$$\begin{bmatrix} x \\ y \\ z \end{bmatrix} = r \begin{bmatrix} \cos(\theta) & 0 & 0 \\ 0 & \cos(\theta) & 0 \\ 0 & 0 & \sin(\theta) \end{bmatrix} \begin{bmatrix} \cos(\alpha) \\ \sin(\alpha) \\ 1 \end{bmatrix} \qquad (1)$$

Where r is distance between M and coordinate origin O_1 and$\theta$is the angle between line (O_1M) and plane $(X O_1Y)$.

In the left camera's image coordinate(UO$_1$V),there are

$$\begin{bmatrix} u \\ v \end{bmatrix} = \begin{bmatrix} Ku & 0 \\ 0 & Kv \end{bmatrix} \begin{bmatrix} \cos(\alpha) \\ \sin(\alpha) \end{bmatrix} \cot(\theta) \qquad (2)$$

Where Ku and Kv are parameters of camera and can be calculated by camera calibration.

Also, In the right camera's image coordinate(U'O$_2$V'), there are

$$\begin{bmatrix} u' \\ v' \end{bmatrix} = \begin{bmatrix} Ku' & 0 \\ 0 & Kv' \end{bmatrix} \begin{bmatrix} \cos(\alpha') \\ \sin(\alpha') \end{bmatrix} \cot(\theta') \tag{3}$$

While set O$_2$ as coordinate origin, we get

$$\begin{bmatrix} x-d \\ y \\ z \end{bmatrix} = r' \begin{bmatrix} \cos(\theta') & 0 & 0 \\ 0 & \cos(\theta') & 0 \\ 0 & 0 & \sin(\theta') \end{bmatrix} \begin{bmatrix} \cos(\alpha') \\ \sin(\alpha') \\ 1 \end{bmatrix} \tag{4}$$

From (2) , (3) and (4) , αandθcan be obtained as

$$\begin{cases} \alpha = \arctan(\dfrac{v * Ku}{u * Kv}) \\[2mm] \alpha' = \arctan(\dfrac{v'*Ku'}{u'*Kv'}) \\[2mm] \theta = arc\cot(\dfrac{u}{Ku * \cos(\alpha)}) \\[2mm] \theta' = arc\cot(\dfrac{u'}{Ku'*\cos(\alpha')}) \end{cases} \tag{5}$$

In triangle M$_1$ O$_1$O$_2$, we can find $\alpha = \angle MO_1O_2$ and $\alpha' = \pi - \angle MO_2O_1$. So, from sine theorem we can get

$$\frac{|O_1M_1|}{\sin(\pi - \alpha')} = \frac{|O_1M_1|}{\sin(\alpha)} = \frac{|O_1O_2|}{\sin(\pi - (\pi - \alpha') - \alpha)} \tag{6}$$

We denote the distance between camera's optical center as d. There are

$$\frac{r * \cos(\theta)}{\sin(\alpha')} = \frac{r'*\cos(\theta')}{\sin(\alpha)} = \frac{d}{\sin(\alpha'-\alpha)} \tag{7}$$

From (5) and (7), we can get

$$\begin{aligned} r &= \frac{d * \sin(\alpha')}{\cos(\theta) * \sin(\alpha'-\alpha)} \\[2mm] r' &= \frac{d * \sin(\alpha)}{\cos(\theta') * \sin(\alpha'-\alpha)} \end{aligned} \tag{8}$$

Now we get the distance and relative angle between target object and two cameras.

We have assumed that two camera's optical center axis is parallel and is in the same plane. Unfortunately, in real system, cameras can not be equipped so ideally, but the coordinate rotation and translation of the camera coordinates can transform the question to the ideal mode, and the only difference is that there is a transform matrix between camera-coordinates which should be calibrated.

3   Image Matching and Template Library Building

In the two cameras system, ignoring the time delay of camera's catching picture, $I_l(t)$ and $I_r(t)$ can express the target's visual projection at same time. The process of image matching is that to build a function to find the region where exists the max value of image calculation with given image template. Assume the two cameras have nearly same parameters, $I_l(t)$ and $I_r(t)$ can subtract directly.

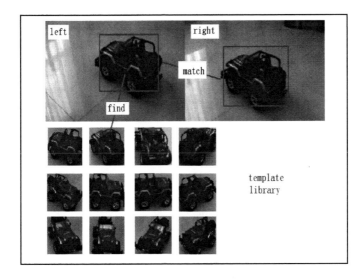

Fig. 3. The image matching and template library

As shown in Figure 3, image matching and template library building can be down at the same time. At time t, match the left and right image to find the most likelihood region. If find the sub image in template library, the suspect region is the target and can be tracking, otherwise discard the region. If such finding cycle can not locate the target image, separate left into sub images and find them in right image, then using the distance and angle calculation method described in section 2, find the most possibly region and if this result match target's kinematics' constraints, add this region two image template library.

Define the evaluation function as

$$F(x, y) = \frac{\sum_{x',y'}[T(x', y') - I(x + x', y + y')]^2}{\sqrt{\sum_{x',y'}T(x', y')^2 * \sum_{x',y'}[I(x + x', y + y')^2}}$$

Where T(x, y) means the image to be located, I(x, y) means the searching image. Obviously, the value of F(x, y) has the range of [0,1], and when I equals to T the value reaches 1. Selecting a suitable threshold for function F can adjust the performance speed and accuracy of locating.

In many cases, there will be similar images in one scene. For example, there are always many vehicles on road and in one frame of picture. So, position restriction is used at that situation. When multi region R(i) is found that mach a same template image look up those region in the image from other camera and the result is R'(j). Calculate the distance and angle between i and j as D(r, θ, i, j) .

Define a difference function as

$$Dif\,(D(r1,\theta 1),D(r2,\theta 2)) = (r1-r2)^2 + (\theta 1-\theta 2)^2$$

Find the min   value of each D(i, j) with   previous object location (r, θ). If the result is greater than lower threshold, the target is out of range and tacking is failed, otherwise, set the selected region as target position.

Each image matching process is time consuming, to reduce the time elapse, searching strategy is set as nearby first rule. The template library is built as tree nodes. Each template image sets as a node and the connection means that in target is found in adjacent scene. The template image sequence is ordered by the distance to current template image with increasing. At the template library building thread, new template image is inserted according to this rule too.

4   Prediction and Relocation Target

In section 1, the position and angle of target is obtained at each sample time. As formula 1 shows , when r andθ is calculated, the coordinate [x, y, z] can be received. At time t, mark the coordinate XYZ as $P_w(t)$, and camera coordinate as $P_c(t)$ and $P_{c'}(t)$.

Velocity of target can be set as $V(t) = d\mathrm{Pw(t)}\,|\,/\,dt$. With the linear character of optical Projection, in image coordinate, velocity can be calculated by V(t) too. Define current visual coordinate is (u,v). After detecting cycle T, at time t+1, the implicit region can be referred as $(u+\Delta u,v+\Delta v)$. So, the method of image matching in section 3 can reduce the full image range to a region which center at $(u+\Delta u,v+\Delta v)$ and the radius as w. At the first time, w is set as image width. When the object's position is calculated at time t+1, adjust the w as substance of image position in time t and t+1. Then in the next detecting cycle, reasonable search range and size of search image can be set.

5   Experiment

Using the OpenCV library, testing software is implemented by visual studio 2005 in C++ language. The camera calibrate that be built in OpenCV are used to calculate the inherent parameters of cameras. The testing environment is build on windows XP operating system and run on a personal computer which has 2G hz Intel CPU and 1G bytes memory.

Setting a vehicle with unknown speed as the tracking target, we get a set of values. Four example of sample picture are given in figure 4. The position and angle of four time point is given in table 1.

Table 1. Distance and angles of each sample time

Distance(R) and angle(θ)	Time 1s	Time 100s	Time 150s	Time 200s
R(m)	2.458	3.423	2.354	1.496
θ (rad)	1.501	1.588	1.745	1.919
R'(m)	2.455	3.44	2.424	1.623
θ '(rad)	1.623	1.675	1.867	2.094

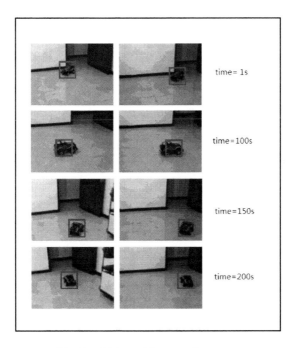

Fig. 4. vehicle tracking experiment

6   Conclusion

Within this framework, object's tracking can work well in real application. The combination of stereo vision and image template match enhance the detection qualify and efficiency. At a detecting period of 10 frames per second, the speed of object, which can be robust tracking, is up to 80km/h. So, this framework is reliable to used in ITS systems. But, all of this calculation is based on the assume that cameras are not moving, when cameras are rotation, the calculate model is to be changed and that is our future research point.

References

1. Yung, N.H.C., Lai, A.H.S.: An effective video analysis method for detecting red light runners. IEEE Transactions on Vehicular Technology 50(4), 1074–1084 (2001)
2. DuPont, E., et al.: Frequency response method for terrain classification in autonomous ground vehicles. Autonomous Robots 24(4), 337–347 (2008)
3. Viola, Jones: Rapid object detection using boosted cascade of simple features. Computer Vision and Pattern Recognition (2001)
4. Wang, S.-P., Ji, H.-B.: A new appearance model based on object sub-region for tracking. Wavelet Analysis and Pattern Recognition (2007)
5. Murata, M., Taniguchi, Y., Hasegawa, G., Nakano, H.: An Object Tracking Method based on Scenario-Type Hypothesis Tracking in Segmented Multiple Regions. In: 2010 Sixth International Conference on Networking and Services, ICNS (2010)
6. Gemeiner, P., et al.: Real-Time SLAM with a High-Speed CMOS Camera. In: Image Analysis and Processing (2007)

A Dynamic Peers Maintenance Method Based on the SuperPeer Stability

Lu Gao[1], Zhen Xu[1], and Zhongmin Li[2]

[1] School of Electrical & Electronic Engineering, Wuhan Polytechnic University
430023 Wuhan, Hubei, China
gaoluwh@gmail.com, albert_xu@tom.com
[2] School of Electronic and Information Engineering, Nanchang Hangkong University
330063 Nanchang, Jiangxi, China
zhongmli@gmail.com

Abstract. Due to the dynamic nature of P2P systems, it is difficult to keep load balance among SuperPeers (SPs) in the hybrid Peer-to-Peer system. An important source of SP's load is to process the peers' joining and departing frequently. In the paper a new strategy is proposed to reduce the impact on the SP's load when new peers join the system. Messages received by SP are classified into maintenance messages, update messages and query messages, of which the first two is produced by peers' churn. Every SP has an attribute, *stability*, to describe its state. New peers selects a SP to link based on the information from many SPs. Through the simulation, the result shows the strategy can be efficient and the load unbalance among SPs produced by new peers adding is relieved.

Keywords: distributed system, hybrid Peer-to-Peer system, superpeer stability, peer churn.

1 Introduction

In the past decade, new generation of large-scale Internet applications such as Facebook, YouTube and Taobao based on the cloud environment has produced many demands on the network, of which the most important one is how to manage and allocate resource [1]. Peer-to-Peer (P2P) has been widely applied in the Internet since it can effectively resolve the network resource assignment problems [2]. So it should help to address some issues to balance servers load, improve the response time for online applications and reduce the system overhead that P2P is applied in the clouding environment. According to the topology, P2P overlay network is divided into three classes: unstructured, structured and hybrid. Because the hybrid P2P system is more efficient than others in resource sharing, it has recently received considerable attention from the networking research community.

In the hybrid P2P SP acts as a centralized sever to a subset of Ordinary-Peers (OP), which can improve the system performance on resource management [3]. So it could still prove to be a productive effort to discuss issues related SP. In the hybrid P2P the

M. Zhao and J. Sha (Eds.): ICCIP 2012, Part II, CCIS 289, pp. 547–555, 2012.
© Springer-Verlag Berlin Heidelberg 2012

efficiency of SP is mainly affected by two factors: one is the capacity of SP, which depends on the SP selection strategy; the other one is the load of SP, which lies on the system operation strategy. The discussed in this paper is mainly the latter. The peer load comes from processing all kinds of messages. The load of SP over its capability will lead to SP failure, which affects system performance, even brings down an entire system. In order to avoid the overload of the SP, Currently, all kinds of methods are put forward by researchers at home and abroad. These methods are classified into two types. One is to focus on how to select the SP with better performance; the other is to reduce message number accepted by SPs. The method researched in the paper belongs to the last.

In the system OPs can join in or leave from the system at any time to form dynamic network environment, which is main source of system message and update message. So in this paper, we propose a new strategy to reduce OPs churn impact for the SP load.

The idea is to set a weight for every SP, and to compute the value of every SP's weight in a cycle. The weight consists of three parts: current load, peer ratio and file ratio. The peer ratio is the number of peers in the cluster, where the SP is located, to the number of peers in the system. And the file ratio is the number of files stored in the cluster, where the SP is located, to the number of files stored in the system. And the system can get the information about peers and files from the SP tables and the OP tables of all SPs.

The rest of the paper is organized as follows: Section 2 reviews some related work briefly. Section 3 analyzes message types and adding strategy; Section 4 presents the system structure and simulation. And it analyzes the performance evaluation of proposed strategy. We conclude the work in Section 5.

2   Related Work

In the hybrid P2P systems, SPs serve as servers for the OPs and constitute a separate SP network by connecting to other SPs. All peers send query messages to SPs, and the SPs received messages forwarded them throughout the SP network until the SP storing the requested data is found. In the system the efficiency of SP directly impact on the system performance. Reducing the SP load is always a hot problem in the research field.

Structured SP overlay can reduce the number of average transmission of query messages. [4] combines the use of DHT to messages transmission, such as Kazaa [5]. [6] presents a distributed algorithm for SP overlay and the new peer selects and link with the SP based on the network delay between them. [7] presents three general purpose SP selection protocols, which we have developed, for the three basic types of overlay networks used by P2P applications, of which one is to measure its distance, processing power and content similarity of the OPs in its cluster. OPs can consider capacity and similarity when they join a SP and the SP can use the content profile to improve searches.

However, current approaches only have simple static strategies for new peers adding. A better way of linking new peer with a suitable SP will further improve the system performance. So in this paper we consider three groups of factors in the process of selecting SP: the size of cluster, the number of sharing files stored in the cluster and its load in the last cycle.

3   Selection Strategy

3.1   System Model

Structure. The paper assumes that only OPs' state may change and SP's state will remain sable when the system runs.

In this paper, each SP is connected to a set of OPs and every ordinary-peer is connected to a single SP only. We call a SP and its OPs a cluster, where cluster size is the number of peers in the cluster, including the SP itself. All SPs construct an SP overlay by means of connection. SPs in the overlay exchange their information with each other to realize the function of resource lookup. SP stores indexes of all file sharing by all OPs in the same cluster, and these indexes will be updated in cycles. Besides data indexes, SP must possess state information of all OPs in the cluster. In every cycle, SP must update all information it stores by message exchange between OPs and SPs.

Message. These messages are classified into three categories: (1) Maintenance Messages (MM), which are from the operation maintaining the integrity of the system topology; (2) Update Messages (UM), which are used to update data index stored in the SPs when data saved in the peers changes; (3) Query Messages (QM), which are used to find the information users require.

Maintainance Message. The hybrid P2P system is a logical view of the network on the application layer. MM is used to maintain the logical topology of the system. Some MMs come from the OPs in the same cluster with it; the others are from the neighboring SPs logically. The number of the latter is thought of as a constant because the topology structure of SP layer can keeps stable in a relatively long period of time When an OP joins a SP-based system, it broadcasts MMs to try to link with a SP. Also, when an OP leaves normally, it sends a MM to the SP.

Update Message. When OP's state, joining or leaving, changes, SP must update its index data which is directly bound with data stored in the OP.

After OP has connected with a SP, it will upload sharing data information by UMs. The two things are certainly relevant with the amount of UMs that the SP receives in a cycle. The first is how many new OPs to join the system in a cycle; and the second is the number of sharing files stored in these OPs. When SP receives a MMs sending by the departed OP, it will delete relevant index data based on the MM.

Whatever joining or leaving, both operations are to update index data stored in the SP.

Query Message. Query message comes from any peer in the system. For all QMs received by a SP, some are from OPs in the same cluster and the others are from SPs adjacent to the SP. All QMs will be transmitted based on a strategy by SPs until termination condition stopping transmitting has been met. More files are there in a cluster, more QMs are the SP receives, which cause load increasing.

3.2   Load Analysis

In the hybrid system a SP connects with n_{leaf} OPs and with n_{super} SPs; every OP connects only with a SP and with no any other OP. A cluster is composed of a SP and n_{leaf}OPs linked with the SP. And the SP has n_{super} SPs connected. Based on the cluster state, the paper shall discuss the two cases respectively.

Stable Environment. Stable environment means that no peer joins in or leaves from the cluster. All kinds of information are exchanged by messages among logically adjacent peers periodically. For the function of MM is to judge whether the peer is online or not, the SP spends the same number of resource, recorded as M_s, on process all MMs. Costs of resource processing an update message and a maintenance message between SP and OP_i is β_i and α respectively. And Costs processing the two type of message between SP and SP_i is β_i and α respectively. So the variable W denotes the total resource cost spending on processing system messages and update messages receiving by the SP in a cycle, whose computing method is (1).

$$M_s = \sum_{i=1}^{n_{leaf}} (\alpha + \beta_i) + \sum_{i=1}^{n_{super}} (\alpha + \beta_i) \tag{1}$$

For all sharing files stored in the OPs don't change in the stable state, the SP won't receive any UMs from the OPs in the same cluster. Similarly, the SP won't receive any UMs from the SPs. So in every cycle the SP only receive MMs to maintain the topology structure of the system. Equation (1) turns into (2).

$$M_s = \sum_{i=1}^{n_{leaf}} \alpha + \sum_{i=1}^{n_{super}} \alpha = (n_{leaf} + n_{super}) \times \alpha \tag{2}$$

Whatever from the Ops in the cluster or from the other SPs the QMs are considered to same. The number of resource that is needed for processing a QM is defined as γ. In every cycle every OP in the cluster sends a QM to the SP with the probability of ε, and the SP received r QMs from the other SPs. The cost of total resource processing QMs in a cycle is defined as Q_s.

$$Q_s = (r + \varepsilon \times n_{leaf}) \times \gamma \tag{3}$$

The total of resource SP using in each cycle is (4), called as P.

$$\begin{aligned} P_{stable} &= M_s + Q_s \\ &= (n_{leaf} + n_{super}) \times \alpha + (r + \varepsilon \times n_{leaf}) \times \gamma \end{aligned} \tag{4}$$

Unstable Environment. Unstable environment is defined that there are some OPs joining in or leaving randomly from the system in a cycle. In the environment the SP in the cluster must be update operations increasing its indexes about sharing files stored in the new OPs in each cycle, which result some Ums from new OPs to SP. And if an OP in the cluster leave, SP will update operations deleting some indexes about sharing files stored faulty Ops. The objects of both operations are indexes, so the cost of resource processing an update message is related with the number of indexes.

The cost of operation on an index is α. The number of resources spent on processing an UM depends on n_{super}, the number of related indexes in the SP. During a cycle there are k OPs leaving from and j OPs join in the cluster. In this process, the OPs send $(j+k+n_{leaf})$ MMs and $(j+k)$ UMs, so the calculating formulas about U_u, M_u and Q_u are :

$$U_u = \sum_{i=1}^{k+j} n_i \beta$$

$$M_u = \sum_{i=1}^{k+j+n_{leaf}} \alpha + \sum_{i=1}^{n_{super}} \alpha$$

$$Q_u = (r + \varepsilon \times n_{leaf}) \times \gamma$$

In the unstable environment the total resource cost is (5), called $P_{unstable}$.

$$P_{unstable} = M_u + Q_u + U_u \tag{5}$$

In the two environments, the load of SP comes from two aspects, OP state change and query operation. From (4) and (5), a conclusion is found that the number of new peers is relating directly or indirectly with SP's resource consumptions. How to dispose state change of peers is a crucial point to maintain the load balance among SPs in the system.

3.3   Stability Analysis

When many new peers want to join the system, it should be avoided that most of them linked with the same SP. In this paper SP stability is used to describe the change of SP's load. The value of SP stability maintains a reasonable level of comfort can guarantee the reasonable load on the SP.

If all peers in the system always keep stable, the global state of the system will be obtained, which means that it is easy to keep load balance among all SPs. But in any time any OP could join in or leave from the system, so it is difficult to obtain the global state. In the hybrid P2P system the most important standard judging SP's efficiency is how many query messages it can process in a cycle. Based on the selection method, the state of SP can be maintained relatively stable so that we can predefine the maximum of various messages that every SP can accept in a cycle to keep SP's efficiency desirable. In order to make the SP's efficiency stable, it is necessary to make Ops' churn a minimal impact on the SP. We use stability to describe the impact. The resource cost ratio of processing query messages to non-query messages in a cycle is called SP's stability, which is recorded as φ.

The value of the SP's stability is defined as follows.

$$\varphi = \frac{U+M}{Q} = \frac{\sum_{i=1}^{k+j} n_i \beta + \sum_{i=1}^{k+j+n_{leaf}} \alpha + \sum_{i=1}^{n_{super}} \alpha}{(r + \varepsilon \times n_{leaf}) \times \gamma} \tag{7}$$

3.4   Adding Algorithm

In the system, the number of QMs received by SP can be controlled by query algorithm, and the capacity of SP is certain so that the number of UMs and MMs would affect directly the efficiency of the system. Peers can leave randomly from the system or join the system after getting the permission from the SP. So a method is raised that new peers select a SP based on its stability φ.

Every SP has a threshold *th* which is used to describe SP's resource allocation proportion between processing non-query messages and query messages. When φ is greater than or equal to *th*, new peer won't be linked with the SP. On the contrary, new peer might contact with the SP.

A sketch of the Stability-Based Peer Adding Algorithm (SPAA) is given as the following:

1) *New peer np sends MMs, whose content must include new peer's ID pid and the number of its sharing files f_{num}, to SP sp_i ($1 \leq i \leq n$);*
2) *The sp_i receives all MMs, and counts resource cost based on f_{num} and the information in the last cycle;*
3) *The sp_i count the value of φ;*
4) *if its φ is more than th, the sp_i refused the peer whose f_{num} is the biggest in all new peers, and continues to 3);*
5) *the sp_i collecting the sum of sharing files, $fileNum_{sp}$, and the number of peers $peerNum_{sp}$, in the cluster respectively and return the two results with φ to the corresponding peer;*
6) *The np receives   response messages from SPs, and computes these SPs' peer proportion θ_1 and file proportion θ_2 using (8) and (9);*

$$\theta_1 = \frac{peerNum_{sp_i}}{\sum_{j=1}^{n} peerNum_{sp_j}} \tag{8}$$

$$\theta_2 = \frac{fileNum_{sp_i}}{\sum_{j=1}^{n} fileNum_{sp_j}} \tag{9}$$

7) The np calculates the weight value, w_i of sp_i based on the strategy , using (10);

$$w_j = \omega_1 \times \theta_1 + \omega_2 \times \theta_2 + \omega_3 \times \varphi_i$$
$$(0 \le \omega_i \le 1, \sum_{i=0}^{3} \omega_i = 1) \tag{10}$$

8) The np selects the SP whose value of w_i is the smallest to contact.

4   Simulation-Based Experiments and Results

4.1   Simulation Environment

The performance of the proposed system was analyzed based on a simulation using Peersim[8], with a 2.93GHz CPU, 2G RAM, and Windows XP environment as the hardware. We choose newscast, a gossip protocol that maintains an approximately random topology. The test uses files and capacity randomly arranged to every peer in the system. The duration of the simulation was set at 100 cycles; the initial number of OPs is 30000 and the number of SP is 100. And the times allowed for the OP to search for the SP is set at 8. From 20th cycle to 80th Cycle, some peers join in or leave from the system in each cycle randomly. Each OP broadcasts self-information every cycle, and no peer mobility is set. The performance evaluation compares the results when using the SP selection method with and without file distribution in the system.
Equations should be punctuated in the same way as ordinary text but with a small space before the end punctuation mark.

4.2   Result Analysis

Figure 1 shows in the unstable environment the mean resource cost of every SP processing all kinds of messages received by it. From the 21th cycle to 80th cycle, 10% OPs are in an unstable state.   The resource cost processing UMs is 20% of total resource, which denote that the load of a fraction of SPs will change remarkably if new OPs link with these SPs.

   Figure 2 shows the number of SPs which are in the overload state in the two environments using or not using SPAA. In the simulation the standard of SP overload judgment is whether the resource SP spends on processing messages is more than 80% to its total resource or not. From the graph, we can find that OPs's churn result that some SPs are overload. After the system uses the SPAA, the overload problem is relieved to a certain extent.

   The result comparing with the two cases shows that the SPAA has some influence on reduce the SPs load.

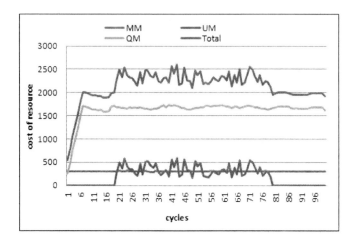

Fig. 1. The statistics of the SP load in the unstable environment

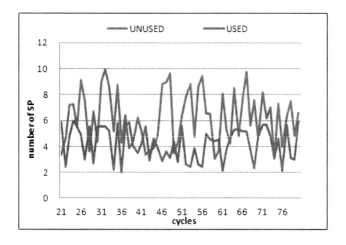

Fig. 2. Comparison of overload SP number in two cases

5   Conclusion

This article proposes a new method to lighten the load of SPs in the hybrid P2P system, which can enhance the efficiency of the system. In this paper stability is used as a SP's property whose value is depends on the size of cluster, the number of sharing files stored in the cluster and its load in the last cycle. When a peer joins the hybrid P2P system, it will select a SP based on the stabilities of accessible SPs. In simulations using Peersim, the performance of improved method is compared with that of the conventional method. The simulation result shows the proposed method is a better performance than the conventional method.

Acknowledgment. We're grateful to the anonymous reviewers whose valuable comments helped us improve this article. This paper is supported by the PHD fund of Wuhan Polytechnic University (5321005), National Natural Science Foundations under Grant 61075015 of china, Hubei Provincial Science Foundation under Grant 2010CDB06601, and Education Commission of Hubei Province of China Q20111707.

References

1. Rimal, B.P., Choi, E., Lumb, I.: A Taxonomy and Survey of Cloud Computing Systems. In: Fifth International Joint Conference on INC, IMS and IDC, pp. 44–51. CPS Press, Korea (2009)
2. Park, H., Yang, J., Park, J., Kang, S.G., Choi, J.: A survey on peer-to-peer overlay network schemes. In: 10th International Conference on Advanced Communication Technology, pp. 986–988. Institute of Electrical and Electronics Engineers Inc., IEEE Press, Korea (2008)
3. Beverly, Y., Garcia-Molina, H.: Designing a super-peer network. In: Proceedings 19th International Conference on Data Engineering, pp. 49–60. IEEE Press, India (2003)
4. Project JXTA: A Loosely-Consistent DHT Rendezvous Walker, http://www.jxta.org/project/www/docs/jxta-dht.pdf
5. Kazaa, http://www.kazaa.com
6. Merz, P., Priebe, M., Wolf, S.: Super-Peer Selection in Peer-to-Peer Networks Using Network Coordinates. In: Third International Conference on Internet and Web Applications and Services, pp. 385–390. IEEE press, Greece (2008)
7. Lo, V., Zhou, D., Liu, Y., GauthierDickey, C.: Scalable supernode selection in peer-to-peer overlay networks. In: Second International Workshop on Hot Topics in Peer-to-Peer Systems, pp. 18–25. IEEE Press, USA (2005)
8. Peersim, http://peersim.sourceforge.net

An Efficient VLSI Architecture and Implementation of Motion Compensation for Video Decoder

Chao Cao[1], Li-zhen Yu[1], and Yanjun Zhang[2]

[1] Department of Electronic of Information Engineering Academy,
NanChang University
NanChang, 330031, China
caochao131@126.com,
yulli1zhen1@163.com
[2] School of Information and Electronics,
Beijing Institute of Technology
Beijing, 100081, China
nextsecond@gmail.com

Abstract. Motion compensation calculation of video decoder frequently access the video data which are stored in external memory, thus efficient memory access is critical in the design of decoder. An advanced parallel multi-pipe line architecture of Motion compensation is proposed in this paper, which fulfilled different of picture prediction modes employed by multi standard video decoder. In this architecture, buffering mechanism for the reference data is used to reduce external memory access, and DMA is used to control data transformation between modules. Compared with traditional memory fetch module, the proposed architecture reduces 30%~40% video decoding cycle in H.264 decoding. Synthetically result shows that timing and the area of this design are both satisfied the requirement of video decoder.

Keywords: component, Video decoder, Reference data fetch, Motion Compensation.

1   Introduction

In design of video decoder, technology based on hardware has become more and more important, especially in the demand of high efficient performance and low power consume[1]. MC is the most frequently access the external memory of all the video decoder modules and it has high data throughputs. Optimal design of memory are very important for improving the performance of video decoder. At the normal station, there are two typical ways to reduce requirement of compensation calculation: one is to reduce the access times of memory, another is to reduce the delay of memory access. Buffering mechanism for reducing frequently access external memory are proposed in this paper, and some special sizes pixel buffers are used to reduce access delay. the whole module adopt parallel multi-pipeline, compare with normal design, it can save 30%~40% cycles and makes more efficient.

M. Zhao and J. Sha (Eds.): ICCIP 2012, Part II, CCIS 289, pp. 556–563, 2012.

2   Principle of Motion Compensation

The whole structure of motion compensation is shown in figure 1, there are two main modules, one is MC which used for motion calculation, it include a frame memory unit which are used to store reference frames and reconstructed frames and DMA controller. Besides, MC unit include reference data buffer, half pixel filter, data buffer from IDCT and residual coefficient calculation module.The process of motion compensation are as following shows.

Step1 search the matched block at the reference frame, then compare every blocks of current frames and reference frames in given regions, find the smallest difference block as optimal matching one. this named motion estimate.

Step2 use the optimal matching block as the reference of current block, the current block subtract reference block could get the residual block, this progress named motion compensation. Then, the residual value will implement quantization, DCT transform, entropy encoder, also the reference location between the reference and current blocks are encoded.

3   Hardware Structure of Motion Compensation

The whole structure of motion compensation is shown in figure 1, there are two main modules, one is MC which used for motion calculation, it include a frame memory unit which are used to store reference frames and reconstructed frames and DMA controller. Besides, MC unit include reference data buffer, half pixel filter, data buffer from IDCT and residual coefficient calculation module.

Every blocks of motion compensation adopt parallel multi-pipeline, their timing controlled by some control signals. Besides ,motion vector decoder unit are used to decode motion vector and calculate the address of frame memory of reference macro block of reference frame picture, then the addresses will be transmit by bus; address maker send instruction to SDRAM instruction maker to get the physical address for accessing external memory. For the design of frame memory architecture, "Ping Pong" mechanism are normally proposed, this mechanism use two same sizes memory to separately store reconstruction frame and reference frame[2] , after every times of frame motion compensation, reconstruction frame memory and reference frame memory exchanged. At the same time, the data of current frame memory will be used to next compensation as reference frame. But in real scene, not all the information are changed between neighbor frame. So, we adopt combination frame memory architecture   similarly   with literature[3], although it increase complexity, but this can save half memory spaces, and reduced power consume.

3.1   Hardware Structure of Reference Buffer

Traditional half pixel filter are designed to direct read the reference data from reference data memory which used to half pixel filtering, but not use reference data buffer, this module need to access external memory each half pixel calculation. For solve this question, in this paper proposed reference data buffering mechanism as show in figure2, reference data buffer receive reference data from external memory by bus, fetched data are stored in internal SRAM, there are two pieces SRAM in internal of reference data buffer, SRAM0 is used to store forward reference data, and SRAM1 store backward reference data. Every SRAM include four different size SRAM, those SRAM are used to store one macro block data for half pixel calculation, reference data buffer could dispose forward and backward data at the same time. Store, export selected, data transmission and other multi pipeline manipulate, then pass the data to next module. There are two types of memory formats, half and full which are used in different prediction. Two memory formats are show in figure 2. Finally, two reference data would output by multi selector for next half pixel prediction calculation. Whole reference data buffer are serial input and parallel output, input signals send 8 pixels (one row data of each block) data at every clock cycle, then those data are stored in corresponding SRAMX. In this design, the memory reference position of luminance and chrominance are the same as displayed, this design is convenient for after luminance and chrominance filtering calculation. Additional adders are used in this design for satisfaction high data process.

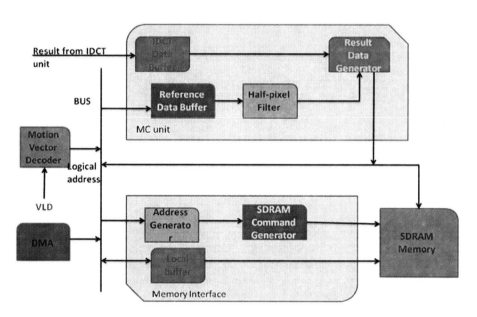

Fig. 1. Whole structure of motion compensation calculation

3.2   Hardware Structure of Half Pixel Filter

In video decoder, motion vector can be used in half pixel calculation. The distance between two neighbor pixels can be indicated by motion vector. In this situation, the true values of reference pixels are the average of these two pixels. If the current location is belong to both horizontal and vertical half pixels point. Then the real values are the average of its four neighbor pixels as figure 3 shows. Data path of MC unit deal with 8 pixels row for each clock cycle (one pixel value need 9 bits). For manage 8 pixels output, there need 9 pixels to satisfy horizontal half pixels process. Vertical half pixel calculation is then process, it use a 8 pixels sizes buffer, so, the data of rows of signed nth and nth+1 can concurrently pass the vertical half pixels filter, if there is no need to deal with vertical half pixels filter, the row of nth 8pixels data are direct output.

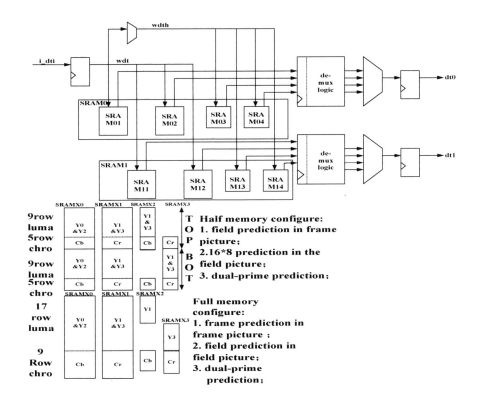

Fig. 2. Hardware structure of reference buffer

During motion compensation calculation, the parameters of half pixels are transmitted by parameter controller, these parameters can be used to control open or close half pixel calculation during the whole motion compensation path. The fetched reference data include one horizontal and one vertical pixels which are used to half-pixel calculation, half-pixel filter unit would receive the data which are transferred from data buffer, then all these data would pass the whole pipe line as following: horizontal half pixel filter, vertical half pixel filter, average calculation and export selected controller. The mechanism of half- pixel is shown in figure 4.

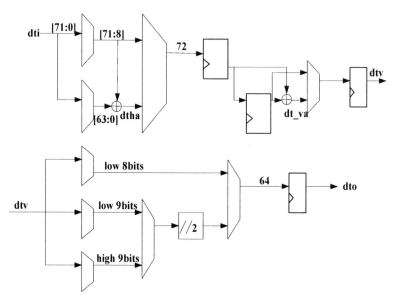

Fig. 3. Hardware structure of half pixel filter

3.3   Forward/Backward Reference Data and Residual Calculation

When the data from forward and afterward reference are disposed by half pixel addition, then two reference data should be used for average calculation ((A+B)//2); the last step of motion compensation is to add average value of reference data value on residual value and last saturated calculation.

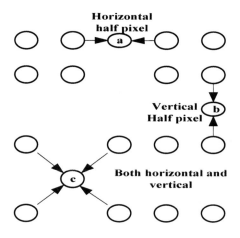

Fig. 4. Half pixel mechanism

The hardware structure of motion compensation is shown in figure 5, there are two half pixel units which have the same function, they are used for forward and backward reference data calculation. Half pixel calculation element include three types: horizontal half pixel, vertical half pixel and both. Corresponding forward and backward prediction data would be get by average of three modes' data. Then handle these forward and backward prediction data by "//2", after that we can get the prediction data of reconstructed frame picture. If only have one mode of prediction, then those pixel data would directly send to residual calculation unit but not through "//2", last step of motion compensation calculation is to add prediction data on residual data which are transmitted from IDCT module, the result is the reconstructed picture data. So, the whole motion compensation path can divide into two parallel multilevel pipelines, forward and backward reference data would separately through horizontal half pixel calculation, vertical half pixel calculation, export selected and average calculation in turn, then average forward and backward reference data, the calculation result is prediction data, finally, the reconstructed data can be get by the processing of adding predicted data on residual data which from IDCT module.

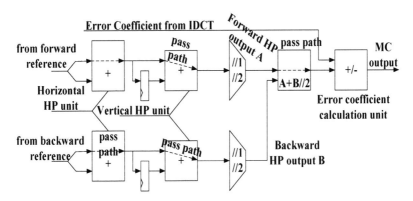

Fig. 5. Hardware structure of motion compensation data path

In 4:2:0 format, one macro block include 384 pixels data: including 16*16=256 luminance pixels data and 16*8=128 chrominance pixels data. Because, each cycle of MC data path can deal with 8 pixels, so, each macro block need at least 48 cycle to complete. MC firstly deal with the most left 16(chrominance is 8)*8 pixel row, then from left to right in turn. These 16 (chrominance is 8)*8 pixel row's data's read/write are controlled by different predicted modes, For example: field prediction in field picture, 16*8 prediction in field picture, frame prediction in frame picture, field prediction in frame.

4   Synthetically Results and Contrast

The design proposed in this paper, are described by RTL level using Verilog language. this design is synthesized using 0.09um COMS cells library by Synopsys

Design Compiler. Synthetically result shows that this design has lower resource consume and higher clock frequency compared with literature [4][5]. Compared with literature [6], dealing with one macro block element can save 33% clock cycle.

Table 1. Resource degradation and performance comparison

(a)   Each modules of resource degradation

Function	Total area	Total gates
Half-pixel filtering	37800	9.67K
Forward/backward data buffer	9100	3.25K
Reference data buffer fetch	3864	1.28K
Data path controller	1596	0.57K

(b)   Resource and performance contrast

	[4]	**[5]**	**In paper**
Clockfrequency	100M	125M	135M
Logical gate	20.686k	21.506k	14.77k
Technology	UMC0.18	TSMC0.18	SMIC0.09

(c)   Design of this paper and literature[6]constrast

	[6]	In paper	Saved
Process one MB	492	330	33%

5   Conclusion

A motion compensation architecture is proposed in this paper, adopting parallel multi-pipeline and combinatorial frame memory mechanism, it achieves high efficient access and compensation calculation. Compared with traditional design, this design can save half memory resource, disposing one macro block (including read reference data from SDRAM to external memory interface and MC calculation element) are need 330 clock cycles, compared with literature [5], this design can save 33% clock cycle, experiment results show, this design not only improve the speed of memory access, but also enhance the performance of motion compensation.

References

1. Meribout, M., et al.: A new embedded hardware architecture for global motion estimation in MPEG4. In: Proceeding of ICM 2004, pp. 59–62 (2004)
2. Wu, M., Guo, J., Zhang, C.: High Efficient Memory Fetch Architecture for Motion Compensation of Video Decoding. In: Proceedings of IC-NIDC 2010 (2010)
3. Chang, N.Y.-C., Chang, T.-S.: Combined Frame Memory Architecture for Motion Compensation in Video Decoding. IEEE (2005)
4. Tsai, C.-Y., Chen, T.-C., Chen, T.-W., Chen, L.-G.: Bandwidth optimized motion compensation hardware design for H.262 HDTV decoder. In: Circuits and Systems on 48th Midwest Symposium, August 7-10, vol. 2, pp. 1199–1202 (2005)
5. Wang, S.Z., Lin, T.A., Liu, T.M., Lee, C.Y.: A new motion compensation design for H.264/AVC decoder. In: Proc. of Int. Symposium on Circuits and Systems (ISCAS 2005), pp. 4558–4561 (2005)
6. Wang, R., Li, M., Li, J., Zhang, Y.: High throughput and low memory access sub-pixel interpolation architecture for H.264/AVC HDTV decoder. IEEE Trans. Consumer Electron. 51(3), 1006–1013 (2005)

Web Service Selection Based on Improved Genetic Algorithm

Yi Lin[1,*], Yi Yang[1], Lian Li[1], Junling Wang[2],
Chenyang Zhao[2], and Wenqiang Guo[2]

[1] School of Information Science & Engineering
[2] School of Mathematics and Statistics,
Lan Zhou University
yy@lzu.edu.cn

Abstract. Nowadays, Web services are becoming more and more population, and the challenge brought by Web services is dynamic selection of services. In this paper, an Improved Genetic Algorithm is proposed to solve QoS-aware service selection problem, which mainly imports an adaptive crossover, mutation strategy and also imports a terminal condition by computing variance value of the fitness of population. Experiment results show that the approach proposed in this paper can improve the efficiency of Web service selection. Although it can not only find an optimal solution, it has a better convergence speed than that of the Simple Genetic Algorithm.

Keywords: Web services, service selection, Genetic Algorithm, QoS.

1   Introduction

Nowadays Web services are becoming more and more population, the Web services framework has evolved to become the software foundation for next generation enterprise and Web-based systems. Web services can be deployed, located and invoked using standard protocols (such as SOAP, WSDL and UDDI)[1-2]. Also atomic services from different providers can be integrated into a composite service regardless of their locations, platform and speed. As more and more services are deployed, many of them may have the same functionalities but with different non-functional attributes, such as price, response time, reputation, etc. So the problem is how to select a composite service when there is not an existing service can meet the user's request[3-4], this problem is also called quality-driven services selection problem. Since finding a solution for this problem is NP-hard[5], and various optimal Web service selection problems have been intensively studied and different approaches have been proposed in the past few years [7-17], the study on the optimal Web service selection problem with constraints remains open.

In this paper only think about Genetic Algorithm, other algorithms will be considered in future work. Genetic Algorithm is an optimal solution search method which simulates natural Darwinian evolution and was first proposed by J. Holland Professor

---

* Corresponding author.

M. Zhao and J. Sha (Eds.): ICCIP 2012, Part II, CCIS 289, pp. 564–574, 2012.

from the United States Michigan University in 1975 [6]. A new crossover strategy is used in this paper, the crossover locations in two parent individuals relay on their average QoS value and the QoS value in each abstract Web services. This paper also proposed a dynamic mutation strategy to prevent the population from falling into local solutions. Different from other papers, the condition in this paper to end the executing of algorithm is by computing variance of fitness of population.

The rest of paper is organized as follows. Section 2 formulates the service selection model and defines some key concepts used throughout the paper. An improved Genetic Algorithm is proposed to solute the problem in section 3. Section 3 presents several experiments comparing improved Genetic Algorithm with Simple Genetic Algorithm. Finally, Section 4 discusses some related work and draws some conclusions.

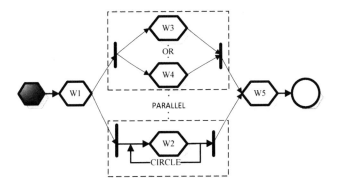

Fig. 1. An instance of workflow for Web service selection

2   Problem Formulation

When a new composite Web service is built, the following process is usually being followed. First, a workflow should be selected, and then all information about available implementations for each Web service in the workflow should be obtained. Fig1 is an example of workflow, which consists of 5 Web services $W_1, W_2,..., W_5$. This can be done by using a Web service discovery tool or by querying Knowledge repository. The information includes URL, functionality, non-functional attributes about each Web service, etc. Thus how to select a usable path and specify a concrete Web service (a simple Web service with concrete function and non-functional attributes) for each abstract service (a collection of some Web services with the same function but different non-functional attributes) is the most work of this paper. This can be done by using a Web service discovery tool or a Web service broker [18]. In this paper, only five non-functional attributes are involved, but as the algorithm is extended, when other attribute is needed, it can be added to the algorithm easily.

2.1   Some Conception of Web Service

Workflow of Composite Web Services. A workflow of a composite Web service, which contains some abstract Web services $W = W_1, W_2, ..., W_n$, where n is the total number of the abstract Web services in the workflow.

All   the   concrete   Web   services   for   abstract   Web   services
$W = \{(W_{11}, W_{12}, \ldots, W_{1m_1}), \ldots, (W_{n1}, \ldots, W_{nm_n})\}$. Here W_{im_j} represents the jth concrete Web service for the ith abstract Web service and m_j is the total number of the ith abstract Web service.

The QoS of Each Concrete Web Service. When each concrete Web service is selected, the non-functional attributes are also known. In this paper, only price(p), response time(t), availability(a), reliability(rl) and reputation(rp) are discussed. Firstly, all the attributes should be normalized. But with the increasing of each attribute, the influence of the QoS is different. When p and t increase, the QoS will decrease, and when a, rl, rp increase, the QoS will grow up. So p and t arenormalized follow the formula (1), and the other attributes follow the formula (2).

$$attri_{norm}(i) = \frac{attri_{max} - attri_i}{attri_{max} - attri_{min}} \tag{1}$$

$$attri_{norm}(i) = \frac{attri_i - attri_{min}}{attri_{max} - attri_{min}} \tag{2}$$

After all the attributes have been normalized, the QoS of each concrete service can be computed then. Before this, the weight of each attributes also should be known. W_1, W_2, W_3, W_4, W_5 are the weight of each attributes and following formula (3).

$$W_1 + W_2 + W_3 + W_4 + W_5 = 1 \tag{3}$$

In the end, the QoS is computed as $QoS = \sum_{j=0}^{5} a_k \cdot W_j$, here a_k is the attribute of the Web service and W_j is the weight of each attribute.

The Average QoS of Each Abstract Web Service. The attributes of every concrete service is known from above and average attributes of each abstract can be computed follow the Equation(4).

$$Attri_i(W_j) = \begin{cases} \dfrac{\sum_{k=1}^{m} Attri_{ik}(W_j)}{m} & i = 1,2 \\ \dfrac{\sum_{k=1}^{m} e^{Attri_{ik}(W_j)}}{m} & i = 3,4,5 \end{cases} \tag{4}$$

Where m is the total number of the concrete services in the jth abstract service, $Attri_i$ is the attribute of the concrete services, $Attri_i(W_j)$ is the attribute of the jth abstract service, where $i = 1,2$ represents the attribute price and response time, and $i = 3,4,5$ represents the attribute availability, reliability and reputation. By the above steps, the average attributes of the abstract services are computed, thus the average QoS can be computed like the concrete ones multiplied by each weight and attribute value. From the average QoS, the weight of each abstract service can be seen. But why is the concept of average QoS proposed in this paper? This is used for the crossover of Genetic Algorithm. By computing the average QoS of each abstract service, we will know that some Web services are more important than others. In this paper, only talking about QoS value, if you would like to talk about other values (such as price, time, etc), you can change QoS with your own values.

Most important abstract Web service are put into set M_1 and more important Web services into set M_2. These two concepts are proposed as the reason of average QoS.

Before the operator of crossover, M_1 and M_2 should be formed. After the computing of average QoS, the contribution to fitness value of every abstract Web services is different. So in this paper, it is supposed that the average QoS value of each abstract Web services represents its contribution to the fitness. If one of the abstract Web service's average QoS is greater than another's, it is thought that the former is more important than the latter. And all the abstract Web services will be divided into two sets M_1 and M_2. This supposes that abstract Web services in M_1 are more important than these in M_2. The size of M_1 and M_2 is identified to m_1 and m_2, where m_1 and m_2 is fixed in the experiment and follows $m_1 + m_2 = n$, n is the total number of abstract Web services.

In particular, you can see that there are four complex workflow structures (such as parallel, switch, sequence and circle) in fig 1. As the others can be changed into sequence structure, so in this paper only refers to sequence structure.

2.2   The Final Objective

Find a path $P = \{x_1, x_2, ..., x_n\}$, where x_i is a concrete Web service of the abstract Web service W_i, and $1 \ll i \ll n$. Such that the total number of selected abstract Web services in the path is $F(x) = \sum_{i=1}^{n} QoS_{ij}$, where i represents the ith abstract service and j is the jth concrete Web service of the ith abstract Web service.

3   Services Selection with GA

3.1   Genetic Encoding

An individual in the population of this genetic algorithm represents a Web service selection plan and it is encoded in an array of n integers $x_1, x_2, ..., x_n$, where n is the total number of abstract Web services in the workflow of composite Web service. In the genetic encoding scheme, each gene represents an abstract Web service in the composite Web service and the value of the gene represents a concrete Web service of the abstract Web service. Fig 2 illustrates the encoding scheme.

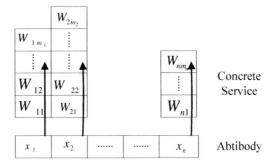

Fig. 2. Antibody Encoding

3.2   Fitness Function

It is known to all that when a user requests a Web service, he always has some constraints belongs to himself. For example, when a user request a travel plan service, it contains airplane ticket booking, hotel reservation, traffic selection between airport and the hotel, he wants the QoS of the composite service to be the best and he also wants the cost and the total time to be the least. So when use the Genetic Algorithm, it is impossible that all individuals in the population is available. Some people always remove the infeasible individuals, but some genes in the infeasible individual may be better than the available ones, so it is not the best choice to remove the infeasible individuals. In this paper, a penalty is given to the fitness of the infeasible ones. Equation (5) gives the definition of the fitness function.

$$Fitness(X) = \begin{cases} 0.5 + 0.5 \times F(x) & V(x) = 0 \\ 0.5 \times F(x) - \frac{V(x)}{V_{max}} & V(x) \neq 0 \end{cases} \tag{5}$$

Where X represents an individual in the population, $F(x)$ is the total QoS of the concrete Web services in X, $V(x)$ is the number of constraints that the X is not in accord with and V_{max} is the total number of constraints that X should be in accord with. It can be seen from the Equation(5) that when an individual is infeasible its fitness is less than 0.5; otherwise its fitness is between 0.5 and 1.0. It can be guaranteed that an infeasible individual has less fitness value than any feasible individual.

3.3   Genetic Operators

From the above, the QoS of each abstract service has been known, and the weight of each abstract service also can be computed. Different from other crossover operators, the crossover operator used in this paper is a knowledge-based one. The knowledge-based crossover operator has two parents P1 and P2 (this suppose that the fitness of P1 is greater than that of P2), and this operator generate only one child C.

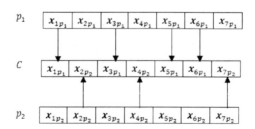

Fig. 3. Crossover Operation

When producing C, two sets M_1 and M_2 should be identified. Then the operator copies the genes from p_1 to C that the abstract Web services of these genes of concrete services are come from M_1, and the rest genes in C are copied from p_2. Fig 3 illustrates the ideas. In this figure, total size of individual is 7, the number of the most important abstract Web services in individual is assumed to be 1, 3, 5, 6. Thus, those genes in next generation individual C are copied from p_1. Now, C has the genes that represent the concrete Web service selection for abstract Web services W_1, W_3, W_5 and W_6. For the rest genes for concrete Web services of abstract Web services W_2, W_4 and W_7 are copied from p_2. This algorithm in crossover operator helps Genetic Algorithm to convergent faster than Simple Genetic Algorithm.

The mutation operator is also not the same as normal genetic algorithm. To prevent the last result getting in the local solution, this paper proposes a self-adapting algorithm. It firstly identifies a probability constant value P_m (it is fixed by experiments), and the operator follows the equation(6). Here in_i is the ith individual of the population, $Fitness(x)$ is the fitness of the ith individual, $Fitness_{max}$ and $Fitness_{min}$ is the max and min value of the fitness of the individuals in the population. P_m represents the initial crossover probability. This operator helps the Genetic Algorithm to take the better genes to the next generation more easily.

$$P_m(in_i) = P_m \times \frac{Fitness_{max} - Fitness_i}{Fitness_{max} - Fitness_{min}} \tag{6}$$

3.4   Convergent of the Algorithm

When the Genetic Algorithm is convergent, it may not find the best solution of the result and it maybe find a local solution. So when talking about Genetic Algorithm, it is always relative to the local solution. The problem here is how to judge the algorithm is trapping into the local solution and how to solution the problem when the algorithm coming with the local solution. As is known to all that when the genetic is convergent, the individuals in the population are mostly the same, so we can judge whether the algorithm is trapping into the local solution by comparing the fitness of the individuals. This paper judges the fitness of the individuals whether the fitness of them is mostly the same by computing their variance, and the operator follows equation(7).

$$E(Fitness) = \frac{\sum_{i=1}^{n} Fitness(X_i)}{n}$$

$$D(Fitness) = \frac{\sum_{i=1}^{n}(Fitness(X_i - E(Fitness)))^2}{n} < \delta \tag{7}$$

Where $Fitness(X_i)$ is the fitness of the X_i^{th} concrete service of the ith abstract service and $E(Fitness)$ is the average value of the fitness of the individuals in the population, $D(Fitness)$ is the variance of the individuals in the population, δ is a constant value. When $D(Fitness)$ is less than δ it means that the individual have been convergent, and δ is fixed by the experiment. After the algorithm is convergent, it will jump out of this state and roll back to the initial population, repeat above operators for several times and after all get the greatest value of these solutions, it may be the nearest one to the real solution.

3.5   Algorithm Description

This paper initials the population randomly and Select individuals from Population using roulette selection strategy. Having defined our fitness function, genetic operator, the improved genetic algorithm for Web service selection is now present as Algorithm 1.

Algorithm 1. An improved genetic algorithm for Web service selection problem.

1: Randomly create an initial population of PopSize individuals, Population:

2: **for** each individual in population **do**

3:     Calculate its fitness using the fitness function

4: **end for**.

5: Find the best individual in the initial population and store it into best and store its fitness value into $Best_{fitness}$

6: **while** current times is less than total times **do**

7:     **If** First time population = initial population

8:         **While** D(Fitness) is less than δ**do**

9:For$\forall$x $\in$ Population**do**

10: Calculate its fitness value Fitness(x)

11:**If** fitness(x) is greater than best_fitness

            then

12:                $Best_{fitness} = Fitness(x)$

13:                Best=x

14:        **end if**

15:        **end for**

16:        Select individuals from Population using roulette
            selection strategy

17:            **For** Randomly select two parents from all the selected parents
            do

18: **if** the number children individuals is not less than the PopSize**then**

19:                    Probabilistically use the crossover operator
                    to produce one child

20:                    Probabilistically use the mutation operator
                    to mutate one child

21:                **end if**

22:            **end for**

23:        **end while**

24:    **end if**

25: **end while**

26: Output best.

---

4   Experiments

The algorithm proposed in this paper improves simple Genetic Algorithm. Through the improves the algorithm have more faster search ability, more quicker convergence speed and the smaller acceleration as the number of the abstract services increases. Follows the capacity and efficiency of the proposed algorithm will be tested and analyzed.

In order to test the two algorithms fairly, they would run in the same hard and software operating environment, including CPU, memory, OS, develop language and IDE, etc.

Besides, the two Genetic Algorithms used initialization parameters as following. The population size is 100. The mutation probability P_m is 0.15 and the crossover probability P_c is 0.7.

Based on the preparation of test data above, the two genetic algorithms were run respectively. The test results were analyzed from convergence speed, search capabilities and acceleration rate.

4.1   Convergence Speed

Algorithm convergence speed refers to the number of population generation to reach the final solution. In order to confirm the improved genetic algorithm is better than simple genetic algorithm, both of them were run for 100 times respectively. As shown in table 1, the average running generation was taken.

As described in Table 1, comparison of data can fully verify that the improved Genetic Algorithm has faster convergence speed than the simple Genetic Algorithm. The reason is that the improved algorithm has an adaptive crossover convergence strategy   and when the algorithm convergences, improved algorithm can be observed more earlier.

Table 1. Comparison of average generation

Number of abstract services	Simple GA	Improved GA
10	240	78
20	306	188
30	320	218

As can be seen from Table 2, when the number of tasks increases, the running time will increase. For the same number of tasks, the improved GA has less running time than the simple GA. This means that a genetic algorithm will have less running time when it has a dynamic and adaptive crossover probability and dynamic termination conditions.

Table 2. Comparison of average running time

Number of abstract services	Simple GA(s)	Improved GA(s)
10	1.56	1.20
20	2.71	1.66
30	3.14	2.01

4.2   Search Capability

Search capability is that the algorithm can find the optimal solution in a solution space. It can be measured by the quality of the solution that the algorithm searches. Improved Genetic Algorithm took an adaptive crossover and mutation to improve Genetic Algorithm. In order to verify these strategies, both of the two algorithms were run for 100 times respectively.

As shown in Table 3, when in the face of the selection problem with the same size of combination services, the improved Genetic Algorithm can get higher average final solution value than the simple Genetic Algorithm. In the test conditions of this article, the improved Genetic Algorithm clearly has stronger search capabilities. This shows that the adaptive Genetic Algorithm has better search capabilities.

Table 3. Comparison of the search capability

Number of abstract services	Simple GA	Improved GA
10	0.862	0.876
20	0.845	0.870
30	0.766	0.787

4.3   Acceleration

Acceleration can defined as the increasing trend of running time as the scope of abstract service increases. It can't be measured by experiments, but it can be seen from the picture drawn by running time and scope of abstract services. Improved Genetic algorithm took and an adaptive crossover and terminal condition to improve Genetic Algorithm. In order to verify these strategies, both of the two algorithms were run for 100 times respectively.

As shown in fig 4, the acceleration of improved Genetic Algorithm is smaller than Simple Genetic Algorithm. This means that when the scope of abstract service increases, the rate of running time increasing rate of Improved Genetic Algorithm is smaller than Simple Genetic Algorithm. So it is confirmed as the scope of abstract service becomes, the running time of Improved Genetic Algorithm will always less than that of Simple Genetic Algorithm.

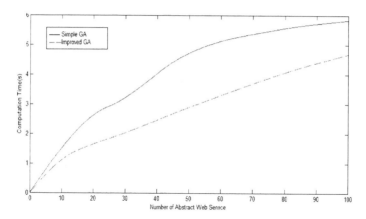

Fig. 4. Acceleration of two algorithm

5   Conclusions

This paper presents a services selection algorithm based on an Improved GA. The improvements include that the design of a population diversity and an adaptive crossover, mutation strategy and terminal condition. In the result, the searchability and convergence speed can be improved at the same time. Through the realization of the above-mentioned algorithm, testing and analyses of test results, some strong validations of the proposed algorithm in capacity and efficiency effects were done.

As talked above, the structure of the workflow has four types, but in the above experiments, only sequence type was come true. If all the four types can be added to this improved Genetic Algorithm, the efficiency of the algorithm will be greatly improved. Therefore, the next study is to add all the types into the algorithm and see if other algorithms can work together with Genetic Algorithm.

Acknowledgment. The authors would like to thank to the Natural Science Foundation of P. R. of China (90912003, 90812001, 61073193), the Key science and technology Foundation of Gansu Province (1102FKDA010), Natural Science Foundation of Gansu Province (1107RJZA188) for supporting this research.

References

1. Yu, T., Lin, K.-J.: Service Selection Algorithms for web services with End-to-end QoS Constraints. ACM Transactions on the Web 1(1), 6 (2007)
2. Yu, T., Lin, K.-J.: Service Selection Algorithms for Composing Complex Services with Multiple QoS Constraints. In: Benatallah, B., Casati, F., Traverso, P. (eds.) ICSOC 2005. LNCS, vol. 3826, pp. 130–143. Springer, Heidelberg (2005)
3. Zeng, L., Benatallah, B., Ngu, A.H.H., et al.: QoS-Aware Middleware for Web Services Selection. IEEE Transactions on Software Engineering 30(5), 322–327 (2004)
4. Zeng, L., Benatallah, B., Dumas, M.: Quality Driven Web Services Selection. In: 12th International Conference on World Wide Web, Budapest, Hungary, pp. 411–421 (2003)

5. Canfora, G., Di Penta, M., Esposito, R., Villani, M.L.: A lightweight approach for QoS-aware service selection. In: Proc.2nd International Conference on Service Oriented Computing (ICSOC 2004) – Short Papers, New York, USA (November 2004)
6. Whitley, D.: A Genetic Algorithm Tutorial. In: Statistics and Computing. Springer (1994)
7. Aggarwal, R., Verma, K., Miller, J., Milnor, W.: Constraint driven web service selection in METEOR-S. In: Proc. 2004 IEEE International Conference on Services Computing, pp. 23–30 (September 2004)
8. Jaeger, M., Rojec-Goldmann, G., Muhl, G.: QoS aggregation for web service selection using workflow patterns. In: Proc. the 8th IEEE International Conference on Enterprise Distributed Object Computing Conference, pp. 149–159 (September 2004)
9. Maximilien, E., Singh, M.: A framework and ontology for dynamic Web services selection. IEEE Internet Computing 8(5), 84–93 (2004)
10. Verma, K., Akkiraju, R., Goodwin, R., Doshi, P., Lee, J.: On accommodating inter service dependencies in web process flow selection. In: Proc. AAAI Spring Symposium on SWS, pp. 37–43 (2004)
11. Canfora, G., Di Penta, M., Esposito, R., Villani, M.L.: An approach for QoS-aware service selection based on genetic algorithms. In: Proc. the 2005 Conference on Genetic and Evolutionary Computation, pp. 1069–1075. ACM, New York (2005)
12. Ardagna, D., Pernici, B.: Adaptive service selection in flexible processes. IEEE Transactions on Software Engineering 33(6), 369–384 (2007)
13. Yu, T., Zhang, Y., Lin, K.-J.: Efficient algorithms for web services selection with end-to-end qos constraints. ACM Trans. on Web 1(1), 6 (2007)
14. Ai, L., Tang, M.: QoS-based web service selection accommodating inter-service dependencies using minimal-conflict hill-climbing repair genetic algorithm. In: Proc. IEEE Fourth International Conference on e-Science, pp. 119–126 (December 2008)
15. Srinvas, M., Patnaik, L.M.: Adaptive Probabilities of Crossover and Mutation in Genetic Algorithms. IEEE Tran. on Systems, Man and Cybernetics 24(4) (1994)
16. Aiello, M., El Khoury, E., Lazovik, A., Ratelband, P.: Optimal QoSawareweb service selection. In: IEEE International Conference on E-Commerce Technology, pp. 491–494 (2009)
17. Tang, M., Li, F.A.: A Hybrid Genetic Algorithm for the Optimal Constrained WebService Selection Problem in Web Service Selection. IEEE (2010)
18. Menasce, Casalicchio, Dubey: A Heuristic Approach to Optimal Service Selection in Service Oriented Architectures. In: The 7th ACM International Workshop on Software and Peiformance (WOSP 2008), USA (2008)
19. Menasce, Casalicchio, Dubey: On optimal service selection in service oriented architectures. Performance Evaluation Journal, 34 pages (2009)
20. Zhang, L.J., Li, B.: Requirements Driven Dynamic Services Selection for Web Services and Grid Solutions. Journal of Grid Computing 2(2), 121–140 (2004)

Protein Folding Shape Code Prediction Based on PSI-BLAST Profile Using Two-Stage Neural Network

Chong Yu[1], Jiaan Yang[2], Juexin Wang[1], Wei Du[1], Yan Wang[1,3,*], and Yanchun Liang[1,*]

[1] College of Computer Science and Technology, Jilin University
[2] Sundia MediTech Company, Shanghai, China
[3] College of Mathematics, Jilin University
wy6868@hotmail.com, ycliang@jlu.edu

Abstract. Protein Folding Shape Code (PFSC) is a symbolic definition of protein structure, which defines the details of protein structure between second structure and tertiary structure. In this article, we build a two-stage neural network model based on PSI-BLAST profile to predict Protein Folding Shape Code. First of all, we use PSI-BLAST to generate the position specific scoring matrices, and then use the slicing window to encode the PSI-BLAST profile information, which is the input of the whole module. The output is the existing PFSC code which presented by 27 orthogonal vectors. 128 unique protein folds were picked out for both testing and training. (No similar folds were presented in both the testing and training sets). Those folds were chosen by structural similarity criteria rather than similarity criteria of sequence. After evaluated by the three-fold cross-validation, our model can reach the accuracy about 65% while considering the top 3 predicted PFSCs. Although the results are not high enough for applications, the PFSC method could also provide a breakthrough of the tertiary structure prediction.

Keywords: Protein Folding Shape Code, Artificial Neural Network, Profile.

1 Introduction

With the increased knowledge of protein, scientists have realized that the protein structures have great relationship with biological process, such as function and property. So the protein structure determination is a key step to quest from genome to life. As we known, determined protein structure in laboratory mainly used X-Ray and NMR (Nuclear Magnetic Resonance) methods. As of Tuesday Nov 29, 2011, there are 77546 structures have been solved by X-ray crystallography and NMR in PDB. Due to the inherently time-consuming and complicated nature of structure determination techniques, each result will cost of more than $150000 and half a year. And these experiments results are only made up less 1% of the known protein sequence information (Genomics projects leave us with millions of protein sequences, currently $\approx 6 \times 106[1]$). The goal of high- throughput protein structure determination has cost

---

* Corresponding authors.

M. Zhao and J. Sha (Eds.): ICCIP 2012, Part II, CCIS 289, pp. 575–583, 2012.

billions of dollars internationally but still the gap between the number of determined proteins and the number of determined protein structures continues to widen rapidly. Therefore, protein structures prediction by computational methods are essential to solve this problem.

Generally, there are two essential types of computational methods to predict the protein 3D structure [2]:

Template-based protein structure modeling techniques rely on the study of principles that dictate the 3D structure of natural proteins from the theory of evolution viewpoint. The well known methods to predict protein structures, such as FB5-HMM [3], PROSPECT [4], ROSETTA [5], TESSER [6-7], RAPTOR [8], MUFOLD [9] and many other programs.

In the viewpoint of that the new folds suggest novel clues to be emphasized for understanding protein folding mechanism [10]. ROSETTA [5] uses structural fragments of size 9 to assembly a Protein structure. FALCON [11-12] uses these fragments to train a position specific HMM to model the structure. TESSER [6-7] uses more flexible fragments.

These methods are all at a relatively low resolution (3-4 Å from the native structure and most of them manual intervention is at least helpful. To achieve a high resolution (within 1° A RMSD), the refinement process, and an accurate energy function is a determined step to these methods to select the best structural models [13].

1.1   PFSC

Protein folding shape code (PFSC) is a new definition of protein structure which is between secondary structures and tertiary structure. PFSC is determined by using a pattern-recognition process, hydrogen-bonded, and geometrical features are extracted from protein 3D coordinates. They are able to cover the enclosed space systematically, and the structure characters are represented by a set which contains 27 vectors. The 27 vectors are represented by 26 alphabetic letters in upper case and the sign of "$". The 27 vectors stand for possible folding shapes, and each vector carries specific folding characteristics at N and C-termini as starting and ending points for the vector. It is more important to make the structural description with better assignment to reflect the nature of secondary structures. The concept of PFSC analogous vector provides the flexibility to describe the boundaries of secondary structures [14].

1.2   PSI-BLAST Profile

The BLAST programs are widely used tools for searching sequence similarities of protein and DNA databases. PSI-BLAST is an essential part of them. PSI-BLAST is used to find several new and interesting members of the DNA or protein sequences from family (super family) by iteration searching. It can also be used in detecting the similarities and homologies of the query sequences. In many cases, it is much more sensitive to weak but biologically relevant sequence similarities [15].

prot ein	Alignment						A	R	N	D	C	Q	E	G	H	I	L	K	M	F	P	S	T	W	Y	V
...	··	···	···	···	···	···																				
A	A	A	A	A	A	A	7	0	0	0	0	0	0	0	0	0	0	0	0	0	0	0	0	0	0	0
Y	Y	Y	Y	Y	Y	Y	0	0	0	0	0	0	0	0	0	0	0	0	0	0	0	0	0	0	7	0
I	I	I	I	E	E	E	0	0	0	0	0	0	3	0	0	4	0	0	0	0	0	0	0	0	0	0
A	A	A	A	A	A	A	7	0	0	0	0	0	0	0	0	0	0	0	0	0	0	0	0	0	0	0
K	K	K	K	K	K	K	0	0	0	0	0	0	0	0	0	0	0	7	0	0	0	0	0	0	0	0
Q	Q	Q	Q	Q	Q	Q	0	0	0	0	0	0	0	0	0	0	0	0	0	0	0	0	0	0	0	0
R	P	R	P	R	P	P	0	3	0	0	0	0	0	0	0	0	0	0	0	0	4	0	0	0	0	0
Q	Q	Q	Q	Q	Q	Q	0	0	0	0	0	7	0	0	0	0	0	0	0	0	0	0	0	0	0	0
I	I	L	I	L	E	E	0	0	0	0	0	0	2	0	0	3	2	0	0	0	0	0	0	0	0	0
S	S	S	S	S	S	S	0	0	0	0	0	0	0	0	0	0	0	0	0	0	0	0	0	0	0	0
F	E	K	A	S	F	P	1	0	0	0	0	0	1	0	0	0	0	1	0	2	1	1	0	0	0	0
V	V	V	V	V	V	V	0	0	0	0	0	0	0	0	0	0	0	0	0	0	0	0	0	0	0	7
S	S	S	S	S	S	S	0	0	0	0	0	0	0	0	0	0	0	0	0	0	0	7	0	0	0	0
H	H	H	H	G	G	G	0	0	0	0	0	0	0	3	4	0	0	0	0	0	0	0	0	0	0	0
...	··	···	···	···	···	···																				

Fig. 1. The generated method of raw profile

Based on a weighted average of BLOSUM62 matrix scores for the given alignment position, PSI-BLAST program will filler out the related sequences from the aimed database (we used the nr database) and generate a raw profile which calculate the percentage of the frequency of each amino acid, and record it in each position.(As the Fig. 1 shows us)

A Position Specific Score Metric (PSSM) which is a profile was generated based on the raw profile [16] during the circulating detecting process. PSI-BLAST uses a simple but effective matrix to record the weights which is about the local different numbers of sequences. And here no attempts have to make further adjust.

Comparing with the traditional analysis of sequences, analyzing by PSI-BLAST profile is of great advantage, as profile is a method to detecting the homology of related proteins. Profile is generated by aligning protein sequences which are filtered from one family (super family) or similar to each other. It contains variations which impact the 3D structure of protein significantly such as insertion, deletion or mutation at each amino acid site.

1.3 Artificial Neutral Network

The artificial neutral network (ANN) is widely used in structure prediction and feature selection, especially in secondary structure prediction, such as PSIPRED [17] program which can obtain 80% accuracy rate. As the BP network has been proved in mathematical theory that it could adapt any kinds of complexity nonlinearity mapping and it is the most widely used ANN. So in this article, we employed BP network to build the PFSC prediction model, and map the inputs to PFSC code as predicted results. The classical BP network contains three levels, including the input, the hidden and the output, and the different level may contain multiple layers. The nodes in the adjacent layers are connected each other with different weights.

2 The Prediction Process of Protein Folding Shape Code

Profiles are integrated as the inputs of the model to predict the PFSC code, rather than optimized sequence information. The generation of those profiles is a separated step.

In that way, we could reduce the process of PFSC prediction by eliminating the stage of multiple sequence alignment which is very time-consuming.

The prediction method (illustrated in Fig. 2) mainly consists of three steps: the first is generated PSI-BLAST profiles, the second is predicting the initial PFSC, and the last is using the initial PFSC results to predict the final PFSC results. In order to meet the PSI-BLAST profile requirement and get a much more optimal prediction result, we build the first level BP model which contains one input layer with 21*15 input nodes, one output layer with 27 output nodes which representing 27 PFSC codes, and two-hidden layers with 10 and 5 nodes respectively in this paper.

We detect the aimed sequences and get the profile by PSI-BLAST program. In order to ensure the far away relationship sequences can be found, PSI-BLAST search with 5 iterations. The use of iterated profiles greatly enhances the sensitivity of PSI-BLAST; using the sliding window to encode the metrics and used as the inputs of the network. We tried many times and found that the result is better when the sliding window length is 15 amino acid residues. The final input layer comprises 315 input units, divided into 15 groups of 21 units. The extra unit per amino acid is used to indicate where the window spans either the N or C terminus of the protein chain.

The output layer includes 27 units. The 27 PFSC are presented by 27 orthogonal vectors such as "A" is (1,0,0,0,0,0,0,0,0,0,0,0,0,0,0,0,0,0,0,0,0,0,0,0,0,0,0), "B" is (0,1,0,0,0,0,0,0,0,0,0,0,0,0,0,0,0,0,0,0,0,0,0,0,0,0,0) etc. and "$" is (0,0,0,0,0,0,0,0,0,0, 0,0,0,0,0,0,0,0,0,0,0,0,0,0,0,0,1). Two hidden layers of 10 and 5 units were used. As the two hidden layer network can simulate the curve surface which is closed to the natural results. There is not any effective method to determine the number of units of hidden layer right now, so we use Trial and Error Method [18] and decide the units of the 1st and 2nd hidden layers are 10 and 5.

Picking supervised or unsupervised learning algorithm is usually depends on the availability of external teaching signal and the tasks to be solved. As the prediction of the PFSC codes whose types have been known (27 kinds of folding shape code), we chose a supervised neural network. In order to optimize the design of network, selection of parameters is very essential. We used the dynamic gradient descent algorithm (learngdm) to make it converges rapidly. According to the error surface, the weights in the network were updated after each pattern presentation, though with a momentum term to prevent oscillation. And the dynamic method makes the net responsed in a wise way. A momentum term of 0.9 and a learning rate of 0.01 were found to be effective.

A 15-residue sequence window is presented to the network, and the PFSC of the central residue is chosen (e.g., the partially string 'ADDABBVJVJBBVJB' 15 codes mapping to the inputs, and the middle one that is 'V' used in the outputs to train the model), according to the output units with the largest signal. In order to improving the accuracy further, the outputs of the first level network are fed to the second level BP network. The hidden layer and outputs is exactly same as the first level network. So the first level network is a "sequence-to-structure" one, and then feeds its outputs into the second level network that is a "structure-to-structure" one. The error function to be minimized in training is the sum over the squared difference between current output and target output values. This two stage network training model could strengthen the whole prediction finally.

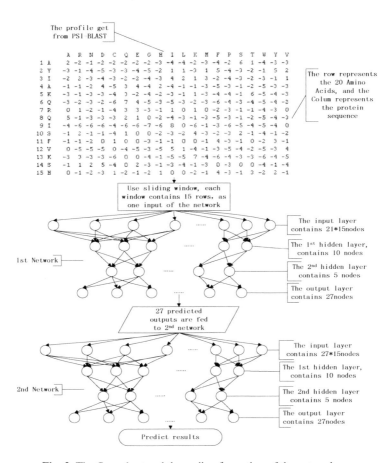

Fig. 2. The flow chart and the coding formation of the network

It has been known for a long time that poor cross-validation can produce overly favorable results. Up until now, secondary structure methods have been tested with training and testing sets screened for significant sequence similarity [17]. So we used the same method to evaluate our model. The data of the training and testing sets were all picked out from the CATH [19]. CATH classifies the protein sequences by domain, so we could filter them by family (super family) conveniently and accurately. Only highly resolved structures were chosen (resolution<1.8 $\overset{\circ}{A}$) [17], and any protein in the training set which comes from different families (super families) contains at least one domain. We could also collect the data from SCOP, but in that way would spend more time. A total of 128 protein sequences in the testing set, divided into four sets randomly, and each set contains 32 protein sequences. Three sets are used to train the network, the other one used to evaluate it. In this way we could prevent the problem of network over-training Results.

The results of prediction are shown in table 1. The lager the value is, the closer to the nature PFSC code it will be. The first row is the sequence of PFSC, the others are predicting results.Top1 is the largest value, Top2 is the 2nd largest value and the Top3 is the 3rd largest value.

Table 1. Predict results of PFSC

PFSC	Top1	Top2	Top3
B		B	
W			
A	A		
A	A		
J			J
B		B	
B		B	
V			V
J			J
...	...	...	...
B		B	
V			V
B		B	
A	A		
A	A		
B		B	
S			
P			

Usually, all of "A" are predicted quite well, all of "B" are predicted fairly well, all of "J" are predicted medium well and others are poorly. This imbalance is caused by the PFSC itself, as the frequency of each PFSC vector is not balance. Fig. 3 shows us the frequency of each PFSC code.

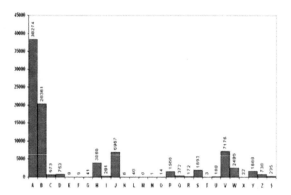

Fig. 3. The frequency of PFSC, the horizontal axis is labeled the PFSC, the vertical bar indicates frequencies [14]

The predicted accuracy of Top1 is 38.32 %, Top 2 is 16.91%, Top 3 is 9.91% and total is 65.14%. When we choose the top1, it is about 38-44%. If we use top1, top2 and top3 to predict, the accuracy is about 65%. Comparing with the equal proportion (Top1 is 3.7%, Top2 is 11.1%), it is much higher than random selection and is very constructive.

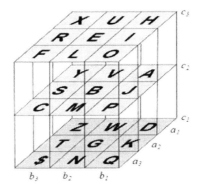

Fig. 4. The relationships of 27 PFSC vectors, three layers represent different pitch distance blocks [14]

The relationships of 27 PFSC vectors are presented as Figure 4. For example: X is closest to U, R and Y, represented by 1, is closer to H and F, represented by 2, and others are much far away, represented by ∞. In the results of prediction, as A, B, J are closer to each other (A, B and J, the distance is 1, they are similar to each other in the structure). The predicted results of PFSC would confuse them, because their structures are similar. If chosen top1-3 prediction results, we would avoid the error which is coursed by the similarity of PFSC itself.

PFSC can descript the loop area of the protein tertiary structure more clearly and provide an accurate description of protein folding shape of tertiary structure which is a breakthrough of the study of protein structure. So we can use this result for a further study of tertiary structure. However, to get accurate results of that still needs a deeper research and exploration.

3   Discussion

The prediction of tertiary structure by computational methods greatly depends on the accurate of secondary structure. Hence, the PFSC is a new definition of protein structure which is between secondary structures and tertiary structure. And the features of the PFSC model include [14]:

1) Offering a complete and reliable description of folding shape along the protein back bone.

2) It is able to reveal folding shape changes with soft or abrupt transitions in details.

3) It is able to expose similarity or dissimilarity for different protein structures and different conformers of the same protein.

4) Giving a one-dimensional finger print for the complex 3D protein folding structure.

5) Providing a meaningful description for individual protein folding structural assignments.

These features provide a new approach in tertiary structure prediction and a model for analysis of protein tertiary structure r.

The prediction of secondary structure is already mature and difficult to exceed, but the prediction of PFSC has not been proposed before. Here we provide a new perspective based on PFSC firstly. Though, the results of our PFSC prediction model are not good enough to get reasonable high accurate for scientist research in tertiary structure prediction and also a little far from being used in real applications right now, the model can be further exploration and improve in the future.

Acknowledgments. This work was supported by the support of the NSFC (61073075, 60903097 and 10872077), the PhD Program Foundation of MOE of China (20090061120094), and the Science-Technology Development Project from Jilin Province (20120730, 20121805), "985" and "211" Project of Jilin University and the Project from Jilin University (200904004, 20101030 and 20101031).

References

1. Chandonia, J., Brenner, S.: The Impact of Structural Genomics: Expectations and Outcomes. Science 311, 347 (2006)
2. Li, M.: Can we determine a protein structure quickly? Journal of Computer Science and Technology 25(1), 95–106 (2010)
3. Kim, D., Xu, D., Guo, J., Ellrott, K., Xu, Y.: PROSPECTII: Protein structure prediction program for genome-scale applications. Protein Eng. 16(9), 641–650 (2003)
4. Bradley, P., Misura, K.M.S., Baker, D.: Toward high-resolution de novo structure prediction for small proteins. Science 309(5742), 1868–1871 (2005)
5. Zhang, Y., Arakaki, A., Skolnick, J.: TASSER: An automated method for the prediction of protein tertiary structuresin CASP6. Proteins 61(S7), 91–98 (2005)
6. Zhang, Y.: Template-based modeling and free modeling by I-TASSER in CASP7. Proteins 69(suppl. 8), 108–117 (2007)
7. Xu, J., Li, M., Kim, D., Xu, Y.: RAPTOR: Optimal protein threading by linear programming. Journal of Bioinformatics and Computational Biology 1(1), 95–117 (2003)
8. Zhang, J., Wang, Q., Barz, B., He, Z., Kosztin, I., Shang, Y., Xu, D.: MUFOLD:A new solution for protein 3D structure prediction. Bioinformatics (2009), doi:10.1002/prot.22634
9. Li, S.C., Bu, D., Xu, J., Li, M.: Fragment-HMM:A new approach to protein structure prediction. Protein Science 17, 1925–1934 (2008)
10. Walsh, I., Bau, D., Martin, A., Mooney, C., Vullo, A., Pollastri, G.: Ab initio and template-based prediction of multi-class distance maps by two-dimensional recursive neural networks. BMC Structural Biology 9, 5 (2009), doi:10.1186/1472-6807-9-5
11. Li, S.C.: New approaches to protein structure prediction. (Ph.D.Dissertation). University of Waterloo, Waterloo, Canada (2009)

12. Park, S.-J.: A Study of Fragment-Based Protein Structure Prediction: Biased Fragment Replacement for Searching Low-Energy Conformation. Genome Informatics 16(2), 104–113 (2005)
13. Xu, W., Lu, K.: Brief review on the methods of protein secondary structure prediction based on neural networks. China Journal of Bioinformatics (January 2006)
14. Yang, J.: Comprehensive description of protein Structures using protein folding shape code. Proteins, 1497–1518 (July 2, 2007)
15. Altschul, S.F., Madden, T.L., Schäffer, A.A., Zhang, J., Zhang, Z., Miller, W., Lipman, D.J.: Gapped BLAST and PSI-BLAST: a new generation of protein database search programs. Nucleic Acids Research 25 (1997)
16. Kabsch, W., Sander, C.: Dictionary of protein secondary structure: pattern recognition of hydrogen-bonded and geometrical features. Biopolymers 22, 2577–2637 (1983)
17. Hamelryck, T., Kent, J.T., Krogh, A.: Sampling realistic protein conformations using local structural bias. PLoS Comput. Biol. 2(9), e131 (2006)
18. Goto, H., Hasegawa, Y., Tanaka, M.: Efficient Scheduling Focusing on the Duality of MPL Representatives. In: Proc. ASME Symp. Computational Intelligence in Scheduling (SCIS 2007), pp. 57–64. ASME Press (December 2007), doi:10.1109/SCIS.2007.3576
19. http://www.pdg.cnb.uam.es/cursos/hola/pages/Farmac_prac/ CATH/index.html

Optimized Tracking Method Using GPU Based Particle Filter

Wenfei Wang, Rui Zhao, Lili Jia, Yu Cai, and Lin Mei[*]

R&D Center of Cyber-Physical Systems,
The Third Research Institute of the Ministry of Public Security, Shanghai, China
wolfeiwang@gmail.com, zhaorui1@126.com,
{jia.li.li,cai309569029}@163.com, l_mei72@hotmail.com

Abstract. In this paper, we address the problem of object tracking with abrupt motion. In particular, a parallel particle filter processed on Graphic Processing Unit (GPU) with improved proposal distribution has been proposed to generate stable tracking results in real-time. Using maximum likelihood estimation, the observations are introduced into importance function to obtain accurate estimation of the proposal distribution. It reduces the algorithm demand for particle quantity and makes tracking object under unpredictable motion feasible. We transplant particle filter processing into GPU kernel, keeping all the computation on the video card. Paralleling techniques greatly improve the computational efficiency of our proposed algorithm. The experimental results demonstrate that optimized particle filter performances better than classic method, and GPU parallel scheme achieves a good speedup compared to the corresponding sequential algorithms.

Keywords: Particle filter, improved proposal distribution, GPU, object tracking.

1   Introduction

Tracking is very important in many areas such as image compression, robot localization, visual surveillance, etc. Tracking object under poor motion continuity in real-time is a hard problem in this research area. The difficulty is that solving this problem will ask for searching in large space, which will cost huge amount of computation. The practical requirement to solve this problem can be found in low frame rate (LFR) video tracking problem [1] and "kid-nap" problem [2] in robot localization. There are plenty of literatures in the research field of tracking, but most existing approaches are not suitable to overcome the problem above, either because of the slow computing speed or the heavy dependence on motion continuity.

Particle filter [3] is a traditional tracking approach, which uses a dynamic model to guide the particle propagation by a proposal distribution. The accuracy of the proposal distribution greatly affects the tracking result. Several researchers introduce detection

---

[*] Corresponding author.

M. Zhao and J. Sha (Eds.): ICCIP 2012, Part II, CCIS 289, pp. 584–591, 2012.

or online learning into particle filter to improve the performance of original method. Okuma et al. [4] use a boosted detector to form a mixture proposal distribution of particle filter. Zhang and Bhandarkar [5] propose a boosted adaptive particle filter to integrate face detection and face tracking. Li et al. [1] introduce a cascade particle filter to combine tracking and detection by discriminative observers of different lifespans. Song and Li [6] use an online multiple instance learning boosting algorithm in particle filter visual tracking framework to deal with the problem of target appearance model online learning.

The increasing programmability and computational power of the GPU present in modern graphics hardware provide a low cost way to accelerate conventional algorithms. Li and Xiao [7] introduce mean shift parallel tracking on GPU kernel. Liu et al. [8] propose a multi-cue based face-tracking algorithm based on GPU accelerator. There are also several parallel particle filter research papers on GPU.

In this paper, an optimized tracking algorithm is proposed, which uses improved proposal distribution and GPU-based parallel scheme to realize real-time tracking under unpredictable motion. We briefly describe particle filter in the next section, and introduce the method to improve proposal distribution. Section 3 is devoted to the parallel scheme based on GPU techniques. The experiment results in section 4 demonstrate the efficiency of our algorithm. Finally, a conclusion is made in section 5.

2   Particle Filter under Unpredicted Motion

The aim of a tracking system is to estimate p(xt|zt), where xt is the target state at time t and zt ={z1,...,zt} the observations up to time t. The sequential Bayesian estimation is the most popular method to solve this problem, which simulates the distribution by the two-step recursion:

$$Prediction : p(x_t \mid z^{t-1}) = \int p(x_t \mid x_{t-1}) p(x_{t-1} \mid z^{t-1}) dx_{t-1},$$
$$Update : p(x_t \mid z^t) = p(z_t \mid x_t) p(x_t \mid z^{t-1}). \tag{1}$$

The particle filter calculates the integral above by sampling from a proposal distribution π in the prediction step. And importance weighing and resampling are used to accomplish the update step and obtain the tracking results. The particle filter assumes that the true target state is in the proposal distribution $xt \in \pi$. When the target motion is predictable, the motion model p(xt|xt−1) is always used as the proposal distribution. But when the target motion becomes drastic, such distribution will result in gradual departure of the sample set from the true target state, which finally leads to tracking fail.

There are two optimization choices to remedy the problem. One is increasing samples in much bigger state space, the other is to introduce p(zt|xt) into π and form an accurate proposal distribution. Both methods will decrease the efficiency and probably loss the target when tracking in real-time. With the help of GPU computing, we can overcome the problem in huge computation consumption.

The common particle filter for tracking can be summarized by the following three steps:

- Sampling: generate the particles $\{x_t^{(i)}\}$ by sampling from the proposal distribution π.
- Importance Weighting: compute an individual weight $\omega_t^{(i)}$ for each particle to present the difference between proposal distribution and distribution of true target state.

$$\omega_t^{(i)} = \frac{p(x_t^{(i)} \mid z^t)}{\pi(x_t^{(i)} \mid z^t)} \tag{2}$$

- Resampling: redraw the particles according to their weights and replace the old ones.

According to Doucet et al. [10], if the proposal distribution fulfill the assumption in (3), we can obtain a recursive formulation to compute $\omega_t^{(i)}$.

$$\pi(x_t \mid z^t) = \pi(x_t \mid x_{t-1}, z^t)\pi(x_{t-1} \mid z^{t-1}) \tag{3}$$

The weights are computed as

$$
\begin{aligned}
\omega_t^{(i)} &= \frac{p(x_t^{(i)} \mid z^t)}{\pi(x_t^{(i)} \mid z^t)} \\
&\overset{Bayes}{=} \frac{p(z_t \mid x_t^{(i)}, z^{t-1}) p(x_t^{(i)} \mid z^{t-1})}{p(z_t \mid z^{t-1}) \pi(x_t^{(i)} \mid z^t)} \\
&\overset{Markov}{=} \frac{\eta\, p(z_t \mid x_t^{(i)}) p(x_t^{(i)} \mid x_{t-1}^{(i)})}{\pi(x_t^{(i)} \mid x_{t-1}^{(i)}, z^t)} \frac{p(x_{t-1}^{(i)} \mid z^{t-1})}{\pi(x_{t-1}^{(i)} \mid z^{t-1})} \\
&\propto \frac{p(z_t \mid x_t^{(i)}) p(x_t^{(i)} \mid x_{t-1}^{(i)})}{\pi(x_t^{(i)} \mid x_{t-1}^{(i)}, z^t)} \omega_{t-1}^{(i)}
\end{aligned}
\tag{4}
$$

Under unpredicted motion, the proposal distribution (xt(i) |xt-1(i),zt) have to be carefully selected. According to the two optimization mentioned above, increasing samples needs diffusing the proposal distribution in order to cover the expected range of possible state transition. In this situation, the importance weight can be computed by a simple way:

$$\omega_t^{(i)} = p(z_t \mid x_t^{(i)}) \cdot \omega_{t-1}^{(i)} \tag{5}$$

For the optimization of improving proposal distribution, p(zt|xt) is introduced into π by considering the most recent observation zt when generating samples. According to Doucet [8], the best choice of proposal distribution should be p(xt(i)|xt-1(i),zt). This probability is not easy to estimate directly, so we solve it as a maximum likelihood problem.

A Gaussian distribution $\mathcal{N}(\hat{x}_t, \Sigma_t)$ is used to approximate the improved proposal p(xt|xt-1,zt). We use the gradient descent search to calculate $\hat{x}_t$ and Σt, in which $\hat{x}_t$ is estimated by

$$\hat{x}_t = \arg\max_{x_t} \{ p(z_t \mid x_t) \cdot p(x_t \mid x_{t-1}) \}. \tag{6}$$

The gradient descent search will compute p(zt|xt)·p(xt|xt-1) in large search space, which cost huge amount of computation but get an accurate estimation. It makes the probability distribution of importance function more similar to the practical probability distribution, thus the demand on the number of particles is cut down. The importance weight is then computed as (7).

$$\omega_t^{(i)} = \omega_{t-1}^{(i)} \frac{\eta \, p(z_t \mid x_t^{(i)}) p(x_t^{(i)} \mid x_{t-1}^{(i)})}{\pi(x_t^{(i)} \mid x_{t-1}^{(i)}, z^t)}$$

$$\propto \omega_{t-1}^{(i)} \frac{p(z_t \mid x_t^{(i)}) p(x_t^{(i)} \mid x_{t-1}^{(i)})}{p(x_t^{(i)} \mid x_{t-1}^{(i)}, z^t)}$$

$$\overset{Bayes}{=} \omega_{t-1}^{(i)} \frac{p(z_t \mid x_t^{(i)}) p(x_t^{(i)} \mid x_{t-1}^{(i)})}{\dfrac{p(z_t \mid x_t^{(i)}) p(x_t^{(i)} \mid x_{t-1}^{(i)})}{p(z_t \mid x_{t-1}^{(i)})}} \tag{7}$$

$$= \omega_{t-1}^{(i)} p(z_t \mid x_{t-1}^{(i)})$$

$$= \omega_{t-1}^{(i)} \int p(z_t \mid x) p(x \mid x_{t-1}^{(i)}) dx$$

Another sampling method is used to calculate the integral in (7). According to (6), the gradient descent search makes the Gaussian distribution $\mathcal{N}(\hat{x}_t, \Sigma_t)$ covering most distribution probability of p(zt|xt)·p(xt|xt−1). Supposing J samples are drawn from the Gaussian distribution, the importance weight can be computed by the following closed form solution:

$$\omega_t^{(i)} \approx \omega_{t-1}^{(i)} \int_{x \in \mathcal{N}(\hat{x}_t^{(i)}, \Sigma_t^{(i)})} p(z_t \mid x) p(x \mid x_{t-1}^{(i)}) dx$$

$$\approx \omega_{t-1}^{(i)} \sum_{j=1}^{J} p(z_t \mid x_j) p(x_j \mid x_{t-1}^{(i)}) \tag{8}$$

The two common optimizations for particle filter are introduced in this section. Sampling and importance weighting are the most computation consuming steps. Transplanting them into GPU kernel can transfer most computation cost, which helps to realize object tracking under unpredictable motion in real-time.

3   Parallel Particle Filter

Our method in this paper employs maximum likelihood estimation in the step of sampling to find the most possible target state. Gradient descent search is adopted to solve the maximum likelihood estimation. But either the gradient descent algorithm that involves iteration searching or the importance weighting that involves the computation of probability estimation in large space is time consuming. To release the overload of CPU and ensure the object tracking running in real-time, we transplant our algorithm to GPU kernel. Benefiting from highly parallel structure, GPU is much more efficient than CPU. It can make the slow speed CPU method valid to process in real-time. For a computation with n similar procedure, calculating for each procedure in individual threads would be n times faster as with doing it sequentially. The key task of transplant is the process of parallelizing. Parallelization is a scheme to split a complex computation problem into multiple simple ones, which can be solved independently and concurrently.

Fortunately, the particle filter is very suitable for parallelization. Analyzing the three steps of particle filtering, it is straightforward to get the strategy of parallelization. In the steps of sampling and importance weighting, particles are able to run in parallel because they are independent from each other. But in the last step, resampling, a combined calculation is needed to get the weight distribution of the particle swarm. Therefore, the parallelization process for particle filter on GPU is shown as Fig.1 and Fig.2. Every time our algorithm executes to the sampling step, the particle swarm {xt-1(i)} is divided into individual particles and processes sampling and importance weighting simultaneously in n threads. After that, resampling is taken in main thread according to the weight distribution of the particles. This procedure iterates with the arriving sensor data and the state estimation of target xt can be obtained in real-time. In robot localization, the texture memory on GPU only needs to be initialized at the beginning to store the map of the environment. But for the object tracking in video, frames will be transmitted into the memory of GPU in each iteration.

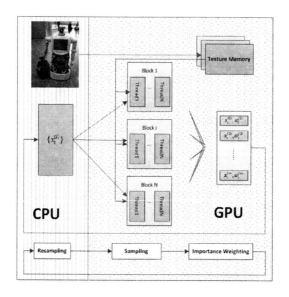

Fig. 1. The tracking algorithm using GPU based particle filter

To improve the computation efficiency of gradient descent search for the best target state guess in our proposed method, the parallelization ability of GPU is also utilized. We use a trade that spends extra memory for time saving, i.e. a probability space for each particle is allocated to store the temporary search results, and the gradient descent search is changed to paralleling probability estimation in large search spaces. This optimization significantly improves the efficiency. The details are as follows. When we use the improved proposal distribution in the sampling step, each particle will face to a maximum likelihood estimation. For each particle, the observation probability at several probable locations around the estimated target will be calculated to determine the descending direction. Then the calculation of importance function at each probable location is put into different threads in GPU kernel and the generated result is stored in the pre-allocated memory space. By comparing the results in this memory space, we can find the direction that the gradient of the importance function is descending. An extreme value indicates the descending direction is obtained from the comparing and a new search will be started from that location. This procedure iterates until no difference is obtained. In each gradient descent search iteration, a particle may have lots of hypotheses of its location, but the computation complexity under parallelization will be equivalent to that of a single hypothesis. The execution of this procedure on CPU is actually a process of circularly getting close to the optimal estimation. GPU parallelizes the sequential steps by concurrently searching on a large scale, which leads to a remarkable time saving.

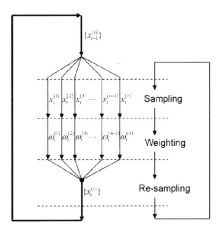

Fig. 2. The procedure of parallelization on particle filter

Using the parallelization proposed in this section, one can transplant classic particle filter from CPU to GPU. We also introduced the method to run the improved particle filter mentioned in the previous section on GPU kernel.

4   Experiment

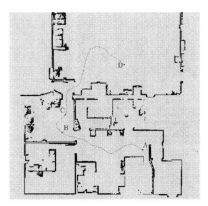

Fig. 3. The experiment system for kid-nap problem

We have tested the kid-nap problem in a robot localization system. And we will try our method in low frame rate video tracking problem in the future. The localization system has been developed with C++ code based on Compute Unified Device Architecture (CUDA) 4.0. The hardware configuration is as follows. CPU is Intel Core i5-2400@3.10GHz, memory is 2G, and graphic card is GeForce210 with a frequency of 589MHZ and 16 stream processors.

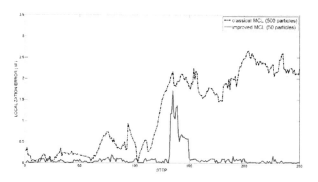

Fig. 4. The experiment results in kid-nap problem

A simulation platform is used to simulate the kid-nap action. Fig.3 shows the user interface and the procedures of our experiment. The curve from A to D is the moving trajectory of a robot, where the cluster of points around point D represents the particle estimations of robot location. In the experiment, the robot moves from A to D, when it moved to point B, it is kidnapped to C. Fig.4 shows the localization results comparison between classic particle filter and particle filter using improved proposal distribution. The method using particle filter to localize robot is also called Monte Carlo Localization (MCL) [11]. The result shows that the classical approach with 500 particles failed tracking the robot pose when it is kidnapped, but the improved approach with 50 particles is able to re-localize the robot within 20 execution cycles.

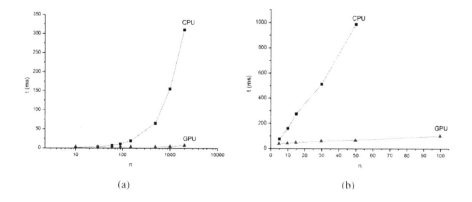

Fig. 5. Comparisons of time consumption between GPU and CPU

In our experiments, GPU is much faster than CPU. Fig.5 gives the comparisons of the algorithms' time consumption between GPU and CPU. The axis x denotes the number of particles, and y the computation time. Fig.5.(a) compares the time costs of the classical MCL algorithm. Fig.5.(b) compares the time costs of our improved algorithm. It is found that the time consumption on CPU average increases about 20x times longer than that on GPU.

5   Conclusion

A particle filter framework for object tracking under unpredictable motion is introduced in this paper. Using improved proposal distribution and GPU parallel processing, the problem can be solved in real-time. The kid-nap experiment for robot localization has been implemented. The experimental results demonstrate that our method can get good effect and significant speedup. In the future, we will test our algorithm in low frame rate video tracking problem.

Acknowledgments. This work was supported by the Science and Technology Commission of Shanghai Municipality (Grants No. 10511500700).

References

1. Li, Y., Ai, H., Yamashita, T., Lao, S., Kawade, M.: Tracking in low frame rate video: A cascade particle filter with discriminative observers of different life spans. IEEE Transactions on Pattern Analysis and Machine Intelligence 30(10), 1728–1740 (2008)
2. Engelson, S.P., McDermott, D.V.: Error correction in mobile robot map learning. In: Proceedings of the IEEE International Conference on Robotics and Automation, pp. 2555–2560. IEEE (1992)
3. Salih, Y., Malik, A.S.: 3d tracking using particle filters. In: Instrumentation and Measurement Technology Conference (I2MTC), pp. 1–4. IEEE (2011)
4. Okuma, K., Taleghani, A., de Freitas, N., Little, J.J., Lowe, D.G.: A Boosted Particle Filter: Multitarget Detection and Tracking. In: Pajdla, T., Matas, J(G.) (eds.) ECCV 2004, Part I. LNCS, vol. 3021, pp. 28–39. Springer, Heidelberg (2004)
5. Zheng, W., Bhandarkar, S.M.: Face detection and tracking using a boosted adaptive particle filter. Journal of Visual Communication and Image Representation 20(1), 9–27 (2009)
6. Song, Y., Li, Q.: Visual tracking based on multiple instance learning particle filter. In: International Conference on Mechatronics and Automation (ICMA), pp. 1063–1067. IEEE (2011)
7. Li, P., Xiao, L.: Mean Shift Parallel Tracking on GPU. In: Araujo, H., Mendonça, A.M., Pinho, A.J., Torres, M.I. (eds.) IbPRIA 2009. LNCS, vol. 5524, pp. 120–127. Springer, Heidelberg (2009)
8. Liu, K.Y., Tang, L., Li, S.Q., Wang, L., Liu, W.: Parallel particle filter algorithm in face tracking. In: IEEE International Conference on Multimedia and Expo., pp. 1817–1820. IEEE (2009)
9. Doucet, A., de Freitas, N., Gordon, N.: Sequential Monte Carlo Methods in Practice. Springer (2001)
10. Doucet, A.: On sequential simulation-based methods for bayesian filtering. Technical report, Signal Processing Group, Dept. of Engeneering, University of Cambridge (1998)
11. Dellaert, F., Fox, D., Burgard, W., Thrun, S.: Monte carlo localization for mobile robots. In: Proceedings of IEEE International Conference on Robotics and Automation, Detroit, MI, USA, vol. 2, pp. 1322–1328 (1999)

Real-Time Vehicle Detection and Tracking System in Street Scenarios

Lili Jia, Dazhou Wu, Lin Mei[*], Rui Zhao, Wenfei Wang, and Cai Yu

R&D Center of Cyber Physical Systems,
The Third Research Institute of the Ministry of Public Security,
Shanghai, China
shxmx@163.com

Abstract. The paper represents a framework for a vehicle detection, segmentation, and tracking system. The Challenge is to use a single monocular camera as input, in order to achieve a low cost final system that meets the requirements needed to undertake serial production in auto supervisory industry. We use a hierarchical method from the foreground region level to the vehicle level. The approach concerns stages of motion detection, edge detection, filtering, detection of the vehicle's position, and investigation into tracking cars by their appearance visual features. Color, which is one of the strongest cues, is used for the tracking step. The Continuously Adaptive MeanShift Algorithm (CamShift) is an adaptation of the Mean Shift algorithm, and we use it as a tracking method. Competitive performance results are provided using real video sequences in real traffic conditions.

Keywords: Segmentation and Recognition, transport information systems, edge detection, Camshift algorithm.

1 Introduction

Nowadays, the on-road flow of vehicles has already become people's primary concerns of intelligent transportation. In recent years, vehicle count and presence detection available from loops or other conventional traffic detectors have been widely used. Besides the traditional parameters, we can infer more information from the video than the loop such as the color of the car, which is an important parameter for tracking and recognition. However, the ability to analyses and process the surveillance video is still relatively limited, especially in the face of the current massive surveillance video data base.

Many related vehicle detection research has been done in recent years [1]. Most of the proposed approach can roughly be divided into three types: motion based [2]-[3], knowledge based [4]-[5] and appearance based [6]-[8]. While many of them have a good performance with real-time application or non-real-time application, they are either not accurate enough or computational expensive.

---

[*] Corresponding author.

M. Zhao and J. Sha (Eds.): ICCIP 2012, Part II, CCIS 289, pp. 592–599, 2012.

While tracking the moving vehicles, we can infer the trace of it, and get more information about the traffic situation. The MeanShift algorithm was originally proposed by Fukunaga and Hostetler for data clustering. CamShift is primarily intended to perform efficient head and face tracking in a perceptual user interface [10]. It is based on an adaptation of Mean Shift which is robust, and non-parametric. The primary difference between CamShift and the Mean Shift algorithm is that CamShift uses distributions that may be recomputed for each frame while Mean Shift is based on static distributions, which are not updated unless the target experiences significant changes in shape, size or color. The Intel Open Source Computer Vision Library (OpenCV) contains an implementation of the CamShift algorithm that tracks head and face movement using a single channel in the color model[11].

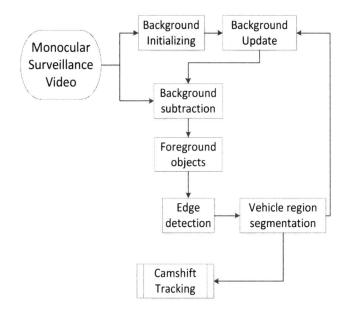

Fig. 1. The flowchart of the algorithm

In our paper, we segment the raw street scenarios video into the different regions use the motion based segmentation method. Based on the moving region, we get the hypothesis vehicle area, then we use Sobel operator to extract the edged contour for the ROI including both the horizontal and vertical edges to verify the area. We use the CamShift method to tracking the ROI of the video, then car detection and tracking system has been accomplished. A flowchart for illustrating the process of our system is depicted in Figure 1.

We have a review of the related work in Section 1 with the introduction of our proposed flowchart of the vehicle recognition system .In each of Sections 2 through 4 we describe the vehicle region detection, the feature extraction, and the tracking performance of the experiment results. The conclusion and future work are in Section 5.

2   Processing for Forground Update

In our system, our first goal is segmenting moving region in the raw region , then remove the non vehicle region , get the vehicles in our region of interests (ROI) to the camera from the background. This is difficult due to the complex nature of street scenes; it contains other moving region, for example the moving trees with the wind , complicated shape and texture of ever changing background. The presence of specular reflection and shadows on the metallic surfaces of cars make the detection unreliable. Cars with colors similar to the background meld into their surroundings and become indistinguishable [9].

Segementation is the first and key step in the traffic sence understanding system. The quality of tracking depends largely on the quality of the segmentation. We use a self-adaptive background subtraction method for segmentation as described in [7]. The used technique here can generate the background image of a scene without pre-evacuating the scene. The background image is progressively generated; its quality increases as the number of input images increases. A measure is associated with the background image generated at any instant, which indicates the degree of goodness of the image. The generated background image is later on continually updated in order to be consistent with the actual background at any moment.

2.1   Segmentation

We change the RGB image from the video into the gray image first by formula (1).

$$GRAY = (R * 19595 + G * 38469 + B * 7472) >> 16 \tag{1}$$

We set the fisrt input video frame as the background frame at first. Then we take the difference between the current image and the current background giving the difference image.

2.2   Adaptive Background Update

We update the background by taking a weighted average of the current background and the current frame of the video sequence.

The object mask is used as a gating function that decides which image to sample for updating the background.

2.3   Dynamic Threshold Update

Since the background I (x,y) changes dynamically, a static threshold T cannot be used to compute the object mask.

$$\left| I_t(x, y) - B_t(x, y) \right| > T \tag{2}$$

Different from method used in [7], we use the OTSU method to give a binary object mask. Otsu's thresholding T chooses the threshold to minimize the intraclass variance of the thresholded black and white pixels.

2.4   Automatic Background Extraction

The background and threshold updating described above is done at periodic update intervals. we compute a binary motion mask by subtracting images from two successive update intervals. Considering an input video image, foreground objects are first extracted from the image by means of background subtraction.

(a)   (b)   (c)

Fig. 2. (a) Original image   (b) Automatic extracted Background (c) Foreground segmentation mask with holes

But the subtraction result of this step is inevitably defective. We use connected component labeling followed by size filtering to remove the noise. And some morphological manipulations including both Erosion and Dilation techniques for both grouping broken vehicles and separating connected vehicles are used too.

3   Fine-Tuning Vehicle Region by Edged Contour

During our video foreground update tests, we found the region behind the vehicle along the moving direction always stays as the foreground. This phenomena is caused by the difference of the current image and later one. We adapt more operations to eliminate defects. Here we use the edge contour as the feature of the vehicles.

Edge detects the discontinuities which are abrupt changes in pixel intensity which characterize boundaries of objects in a scene. So the vehicle's edge is full of much more details than the road.

The Canny edge detection algorithm is known to many as the optimal edge detector. The canny edge detector first smoothes the image to eliminate noise. It then finds the image gradient to highlight regions with high spatial derivatives. The algorithm then tracks along these regions and suppresses any pixel that is not at the maximum (nonmaximum suppression). The gradient array is now further reduced by hysteresis. Hysteresis is used to track along the remaining pixels that have not been suppressed.

2	4	5	4	2
4	9	12	9	4
5	12	15	12	5
4	9	12	9	4
2	4	5	4	2

$\frac{1}{115}$

Fig. 3. Discrete approximation to Gaussian functin with σ =1.4 used

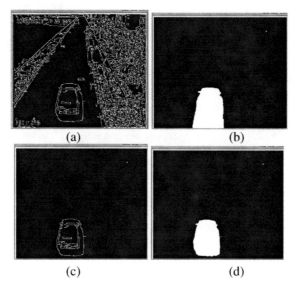

(a)   (b)

(c)   (d)

Fig. 4. (a) Canny edge image   (b) hole filled foreground image (c) image(a) add image (b) result (d)hole filled image from (c)

Hysteresis uses two thresholds and if the magnitude is below the first threshold, it is set to zero. If the magnitude is above the high threshold, it is made an edge. And if the magnitude is between the two thresholds, then it is set to zero unless there is a path from this pixel to a pixel with a gradient above high threshold.

We use the edge information to refine the region of the moving car segmentation. We can see the result from the Figure 4. The region has been reduced with the edge.

4   Moving Vehicle Tracking with Camshift Tracking

4.1   MeanShift Tracking

MeanShift is a non-parametric, iterative procedure to find the mode of a density function represented by a set of samples $\{x_i\}_{i=1,\ldots n}$ and a Kernel K :

$$\hat{f}(x) \;=\; \frac{1}{nh^d} \sum_{i=1} K(\frac{X - X_i}{h}) \tag{3}$$

With mean shift method, the kernel is recursively moved from the current location to the new location   until converge with:

$$\hat{y}_1 \;=\; \frac{\sum_{i=1}^{n_h} X_i W_i g\left(\left\|\frac{\hat{y}_0 - X_i}{h}\right\|^2\right)}{\sum_{i=1}^{n_h} W_i g\left(\left\|\frac{\hat{y}_0 - X_i}{h}\right\|^2\right)} \tag{4}$$

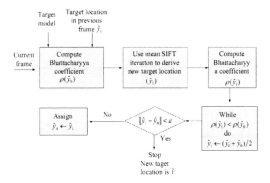

Fig. 5. The flowchart of the meanshift algorithm

The mean shift algorithm is designed to find modes (or the centers of the regions of high concentration) of data represented as arbitrary-dimensional vectors. The algorithm proceeds as follows.

• Choose the radius of the search window.
• Choose the initial location (center) of the window.
• Repeat computing the average of the data points over the window and translate the center of the window into this point.
• Until the translation distance of the center becomes less than a preset threshold.

4.2   CamShift Tracking

CamShift essentially climbs the gradient of a back projected probability distribution computed from rescaled color histograms to find the nearest peak with in an axis-aligned search window. These occur when objects in video sequences are being tracked and the object moves so that the size and location of the probability distribution changes in time. The CamShift. The primary difference between CamShift and the Mean Shift algorithm is that CamShift uses continuously adaptive probability distributions while Mean Shift is based on static distributions, which are not updated unless the target experiences significant changes in size, shape or color.

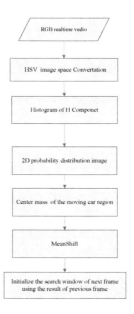

Fig. 6. The flowchart of the camshift algorithm

CamShift adjusts the size and angle of the target rectangle each time it shifts it. It does this by selecting the scale and orientation that are the best fit to the target-probability pixels inside the new rectangle location.

• Step 1. Choose the initial location of the 2D mean shift search window.

• Step 2. Calculate the color probability distribution in the region centered at the search window location in an ROI slightly larger than mean shift window size

• Step 3. Run Mean Shift algorithm to find the search window center. Set the search window size equal to a function of the zeroth moment found in Step 2.

• Step 4. For the next video frame, center the search window at the mean location stored in Step-3 and set the window size to a function of the zeroth moment $M00$ found there. Then go to Step 2.

We implemented our experiments for CamShift-based tracking using Intel's Open Computer Vision library .The black car being tracking is defined an ellipsoidal region in the image.

Fig. 7. The tracking result in different frames

5   Conclusion

We have described a new combined scheme for vehicle detection and tracking system in supervisory video. The system successfully detects and tracks vehicles in real time. The method effectively combines the motion information in the video and the image edge feature to locate the car region. The method is also reason-ably robust to orientation, changes in scale, and lighting conditions. The experimental results carried out show that the algorithm is very efficient. We are currently working on handling occlusions and multiple object tracking and detecting in different environments.

Acknowledgment. This work was supported by the Science and Technology Commission of Shanghai Municipality (Grants No. 10511500700).

References

1. Sun, Z., Bebis, G., Miller, R.: On-road vehicle detection: A review. IEEE, Trans. Pattern Analysis and Machine Intelligence 28(5), 694–711 (2006)
2. Di Stefano, L., Viarani, E.: Vehicle Detection and Tracking Using the Block Matching Algorithm. In: Proc. of 3rd IMACS/IEEE (1999)
3. Cai, B., Tan, F., Lu, Y., Zhang, D.: Knowledge Template Based Multi-perspective Car Recognition Algorithm. International Journal of Information Engineering and Electronic Business (February 2010)
4. Collado, J.M., Hilario, C.: Model Based Vehicle Detection for Intelligent Vehicles. In: IEEE Intelligent Vehicles Symposium (2004)
5. Moon, H., Chellappa, R., Rosenfeld, A.: Performance Analysis of a Simple Vehicle Detection Algorithm. Image and Vision Computing 20(1), 1–13 (2002)
6. Schneiderman, H., Kanade, T.: A statistical method for 3d object detection applied to faces and cars. In: Proc. CVPR (2000)
7. Gupte, S., Masoud, O., Martin, R.F.K., Papanikolopoulos, N.P.: Detection and classification of vehicles. IEEE Transactions on Intelligent Transportation Systems (March 2002)
8. Leung, B.: Component-based Car Detection in Street Scene Images. Master's Thesis, Massachusetts Institute of Technology (2004)
9. Jazayeri, A., Cai, H., Zheng, J.Y., Tuceryan, M., Blitzer, H.: An Intelligent Video System for Vehicle Localization and Tracking in Police Cars. In: SAC 2009, March 8-12 (2009)
10. Bradski, G.R.: Computer vision face tracking for use in a perceptual user interface. Intel. Technology Journal, 2nd Quarter (1998)
11. Intel Corporation: Open Source Computer Vision Library Reference Manual, 123456-001 (2001)
12. Bradski, G.R., Clara, S.: Computer Vision Face Tracking For Use in a Perceptual User Interface. Intel. Technology Journal Q2 (1998)
13. Xia, J., Wu, J., Zhai, H., Cui, Z.: Moving vehicle tracking based on double difference and camshift. In: Proceedings of the International Symposium on Information Processing, vol. 2 (2009)
14. Keselman, Y., Micheli-Tzanakou, E.: Extraction and characterization of regions of interest in biomedical images. In: Proceeding of IEEE International Conference on Information Technology Application in Biomedicine

Design and Implementation of 3D Graphics Rendering Engine with DirectX

Ping Guo, Yao Cheng, and Zhu-Jin Liu

School of Computer Science, Chongqing University, Chongqing, China
guoping@cqu.edu.cn

Abstract. Graphic Rendering, which is the core of three-dimensional (3D) graphic engine, is fundamental for further research of 3D graphic engine. Based on the study of 3D graphic engine pipelines, this paper designs and implements a simple graphic rendering engine with DirectX. The key parts of 3D rendering engine include lighting and color rendering, texture mapping, z-buffer and rasterization. In the paper, the coloring process, texture processing method, Z cache operation function and rasterization function are given. The experimental results show that the rendering engine can meet better the application needs.

Keywords: DirectX, Graphic Engine, Rendering.

1 Introduction

3D graphic technology which is widely used in the field of Virtual Reality, Real-time Emulation and Building Simulation has gained numerous attentions and got rapid development in recent years. Since DirectX-based virtual reality technology has a good prospect and considerable commercial value in industrial software, the related researches are significant.

Graphic rendering is the core of 3D graphic engine. So it is important for evaluating a 3D engine. The paper establishes a 3D graphic rendering engine on the basis of analyzing the architecture and working process of 3D graphic engine. The existing DirectX-based professional graphic engines are limited while the OGRE is one of them. OGRE is an open source rendering engine developed by fans of graph and is usually introduced as basic tool engine for computer graphics[1]. However, it's not easy to design scenes and manipulate objects by using OGRE. By analyzing structural features of 3D applications, China University of Geosciences proposed a 3D graphic engine architecture based on two kinds of 3D API, OpenGL and Direct3D[2]. Sichuan University implemented object-oriented 3D graphic engine which shields rock-bottom graphic operations and supports dynamic cutting technology[4]. However, the existing researches are lacking flexibility and interactivity. The solution proposed by the paper aims at improving flexibility and interactivity, and has done expansion to other issues as well.

The paper firstly analyzes the different steps of DirectX-based 3D graphic engine pipeline. And then, lightening and texture mapping which are two keys for rendering have been discussed. Lightening and texture mapping are important technologies for

M. Zhao and J. Sha (Eds.): ICCIP 2012, Part II, CCIS 289, pp. 600–607, 2012.

simulating real world, which directly determine efficiency and quality of graphic engine. Lastly, the engine realizes z-buffer which makes polygon could be rendered in correct sequence.

2   3D Graphic Engine Module

3D graphic engine module is not an independent module of 3D graphic engine. It cooperates with the other modules to fulfill tasks. Firstly, the architecture of graphic engine is introduced in Figure 1.

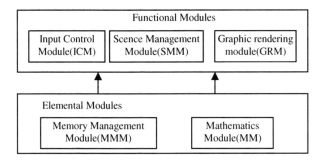

Fig. 1. Architecture of 3D graphic engine

MMM partly optimizes memory allocation in order to decrease memory fragmentation and page missing error of running program. During the whole running period, MMM monitors memory allocation and release, and check memory leak. The implementation slathers templates, which makes some finicky calculation and assigned judgment to be completed in compile time.

MM realizes basic 3D and 2D geometric algebraic operations. 2D and 3D vector, matrix, quaternion and relationship between them are defined in MM. The operations include vector operation (addition, subtraction, multiplication and division), matrix operation (addition, subtraction, multiplication, transposition, inversion, and matrix rank), operation between matrix and vector, quaternion operation (addition, subtraction, and dot product, modulo, calculating reciprocals). These operations mainly serve for vector conversion among different coordinate systems. The conversion is realized by multiplication between matrix and vector. In addition, rotation is realized by using quaternion. Generally, a plural contains real part and imaginary part. But quaternion expands plural to multi-dimension, which means a quaternion contains one real part (scalar quantity) and three imaginary parts (vector quantity). Above mentioned operations are the fundamental techniques for any 3D engine.

ICM abstracts all inputs received from mouse or keyboard into unified information. This module is responsible for processing inputs from keyboard or mouse, and managing output functionalities such as printing or saving documents. In general, we should keep input processing simple so as to make program get inputs with minimum delay. In ICM, inputs are received by data processing module in form of dataflow, and then the processed data are allocated to corresponding modules for future dispose. Output functionality should be executed by specialized program in the background, which can reduce users' waiting time.

The role of graphic rendering module is to display scenes in 3D coordinate system. These scenes can only be presented by computational data while could not be shown on computer screen directly. 3D rendering is just about transition from 3D scene related data to visible graph on 2D display panel.

As to implementing a 3D graphic engine, the effective processing of complex scenes is an important part. A common scene may contain thousands of objects while an object is comprised of thousands of polygons. So traditional pipeline render and scene object management is quite inefficient. The main task of SMM is to manage and organize the objects efficiently.

3   3D Graphic Rendering Engine

3.1   3D Pipeline

Actually, the display of a 3D graph is a three-step process. The first step is to put a discrete model and gate in a proper place. Then, they are projected to a correct planimetric position from the prospective of human eyes. The last step is filling pixels. The transitional process called 3D pipeline[5]is shown in figure 2.

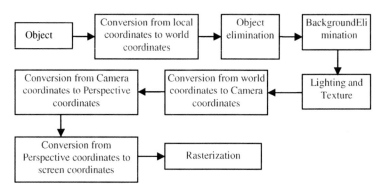

Fig. 2. Simple 3D Pipeline

Since the object which is the easiest to be rendered is triangle, we represent all models with triangles. In a model, one vertex may belong to several adjacent triangles. To save storage space, this engine organizes all vertexes of an object into an array. For every object, each triangle has a pointer points at the vertex array which contains vertexes of this triangle. The structure is shown in figure 3. V indicates vertex of triangle, P indicates vertex array. For each vertex, it contains information such as coordinates, normal, color, texture coordinates. One model corresponds with an object data type. Each object contains a list of polygons and a list of vertexes which are respectively pointed by two pointers.

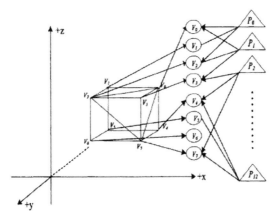

Fig. 3. Definition of geometry by a list of vertexes

Local coordinates is the coordinates of 3D entity in local coordinate system. In the beginning of establishing 3D entity, it usually has its own coordinate axis. Generally, the center of object is located in origin of local coordinate system. World coordinates indicate the actual position of object in virtual world. World coordinates is absolute coordinates which is fixed and does not respond to the change of observer directions. Conversion from local coordinates to world coordinates means moving the center of object to the needed position in the world coordinate system.

Object elimination eliminates object so as not to process it through the whole pipeline. Object elimination could be carried out in either world coordinate system or camera coordinate system. This step is the most important part in 3D pipeline. In most cases, there are only a few objects in the scene while the others locate either out of sight or behind observer. So there is no need to process them. Background elimination eliminates polygons which are back on to viewpoint. This step is usually executed in world coordinates rather than camera coordinates. This could eliminate lots of polygons without conversion from world coordinates to camera coordinates.

Camera coordinates are relative coordinates which refers to the operator's viewpoint and direction of observation. The viewpoint and direction of observation are changing when we are operating mouse or keyboard. Then observation coordinates in world coordinate system are changing as well. The space using camera coordinate system is called observation space. The conversion from world coordinates to camera coordinates means that, making camera locate in the origin of world coordinate system and the lens direct to +z-axis by moving world coordinate system. Translation and rotation are two kinds of conversion.

After the conversion from world coordinates to camera coordinates, the camera locates in the origin of camera coordinate system and the degree of view is zero. The conversion from camera coordinates to perspective coordinates means projecting the vertex of object to sight plane.

The conversion from perspective coordinates to screen coordinates maps the sight plane to screen. This is the last step of 3D pipeline. It scales coordinates of sight plane to turn them into screen coordinates.

3.2   Lighting and Coloring

To make the model look more real, lighting and coloring steps are brought in pipeline. The engine supports four types of illuminant, including directional illuminant, spotlight, focus lamp and surround light. The Init_Light() initiates illuminant when it is being established. The values of fields in the illuminant data structure are set by the initial function. According to the different values of fields, corresponding type of illuminant is created. All the illuminants are saved in a list. It is impossible to do lighting calculation for each pixel because of huge amount of calculation. So the lighting calculation is executed only for vertexes of triangles. Then, we use interpolation to smooth lighting of the surface. The coloring model — constant coloring model is introduced as follows [8][9].

Constant coloring colors the polygon according to lighting condition of a certain pixel (generally, we choose a vertex) of the polygon. The process is shown in the following steps.

Step 1: compute the face normal;
Step 2: compute the lighting intensity of each illuminant in the list;
Step 3: compute the sum of all the lighting intensity;
Step 4: write the results to color variables of polygon;
The prototype of constant coloring function is listed as follows.

```
int Light_OBJECT_Flat(OBJECT_PTR obj, CAMERA_PTR cam,
LIGHT_PTR lights, int max_lights);

int Light_RENDERLIST_Flat(RENDERLIST_PTR obj,
CAMERA_PTR cam,LIGHT_PTR lights,int max_lights);
```

We describe the workflow of this function in form of flow chart (Figure 4).

3.3   Texture Mapping

Texture is the graphic pattern of object's surface. In 3D scene, it greatly increases the vraisemblance of object. For example, we could draw a set of rectangles to represent a wall. But it is just a blank wall which looks not real. If we add some cracks, frays or slogans on this wall, it looks more real. So those are texture of the wall [3].

The graphic pattern of object's surface is saved in 2D graphs which are called texture. Texture is usually saved as BMP or JPG format. Each pixel in texture is named texture pixel. Theoretically, texture could be any size. But for the sake of efficiency, the square with 2n length on each side is the best form of texture. For instance, 16×16, 32×32, 64×64, 128×128 are the most efficiency size of texture. Moreover, the small size of texture is preferable if possible [10].

Generally, a texture is identified by texture coordinates which appoint a dot in texture. Since the texture is ZD, only two values U and V are needed. U stands for values of horizontal axis while V stands for values of vertical axis. The values of U and V are usually normalized between 0 and 1. The top left is (0,0) and lower right is (1,1). Figure 5 shows a texture and its several dots. In the scene, the process in which we apply the texture to 3D object is called texture mapping. During this process, texture coordinates will be mapped to vertexes. So the vertexes have got two additional values U and V. The vertex mapping effect of a cube is shown in Figure 5 and Figure 6.

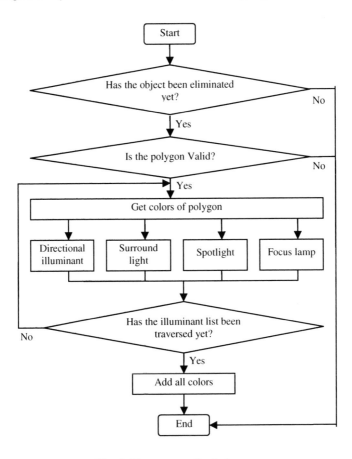

Fig. 4. The process of coloring

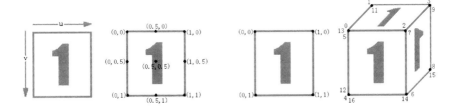

Fig. 5. Texture Coordinates   **Fig. 6.** Texture mapping to a cube

3.4   Z-order and Z-buffer

When a polygon list of an object is created and passed to rendering function, the sequence of polygons in the list depends on the order of inputs. Rendering function does not know the order of rendering which is quite important considering coloring and lighting steps. The incorrect rendering order will screw everything up.

Z-order is proposed to resolve the sequence of rendering polygon. The main idea of the algorithm is that, sorting polygons from rear to front according to the value Z of each polygon, and then rendering them in order. If the polygon is relatively small and not concave, the algorithm is easy to be realized and get good effect. To avoid exceptional situations, the pixel-level Z-order algorithm named Z-buffer[7] is adopted. The difference between Z-order and Z-buffer is that, Z-order sorts polygons according to their value Z while Z-buffer executes Z-order according to every pixel on the screen. As to Z-buffer, no order is incorrect.

The operations related to Z-buffer include create, clear and fill, delete, etc. Each operation is realized by a function.

```
int Creat_Zbuffer(ZBUFFER_PTR zb, int width, int
height);

void Clear_Zbuffer(ZBUFFER_PTR zb,UINT data);

int Delete_Zbuffer(ZBUFFER_PTR zb);
```

3.5   Rasterization

Rasterization is the last step of 3D pipeline. During the process of rasterization, the color values of vertexes of each polygon are written to corresponding display buffer of screen coordinates[6]. Before rasterization, lighting, coloring and texture mapping have been done. The relative information is saved in the rendering list. Rasterization is carried out with the help of Z-buffer system. The prototype of rendering polygon function is shown as follows.

```
void Draw_Triangle (float x1,float y1,float x2,float
y2,float x3,float y3,int color UCHAR*dest_buffer,int
mempitch)
```

3.6   Experimental Results

Graphic engine reads 3D model shown in Figure 7. The effect of rendering is shown in Figure 8.

Fig. 7. Model   **Fig. 8.** Rendering Effect

4   Conclusions

The paper analyzes architecture and workflow of 3D rendering engine, and then designs and implements a relatively complete 3D graphic rendering engine. The implementation of 3D module of this engine does not use any existing graphics supporting library. So the program of this part could be transplanted to different platforms conveniently. The engine could also read 3D model information from model documents generated by modeling tools.

References

1. Donald, H., Pauline Baker, M.: Computer Graphics. Electronic Industry Press, Beijing (2005)
2. Wang, Q.D., Yang, F.S.: The Creation of Virtual Experimental Station of Automobile with DirectX. Computer Applications and Software 24(5), 110–112 (2007) (in Chinese)
3. DirectX Documentation for C++. Microsoft Corp. (2007)
4. Ye, Z.J.: Visual C++/DirectX9 3D Game Development Guidance. Posts and Telecom Press, Beijing (2006)
5. Dunn, F., Parberry, I.: 3D Math Primer for Graphics and Game Development, pp. 1–67, 83–193. Wordware Publishing, Texas (2002)
6. Luna, F.: Introduction to 3D Game Programming with DirectX 9. Wordware Publishing, Inc., Texas (2003)
7. Watt, F.: Policarpo, 3D Game: Technology of Real Rendering and Software, vol. 1. Mechanical Industry Press (2005)
8. Zhou, Z.R., Deng, W., Qiu, Y.H., Lu, L.R.: A Grid Based Graphics Rendering Design. In: 2009 International Forum on Information Technology and Applications, vol. 3, pp. 75–78 (2009)
9. Tong, T.C., Chang, Y.N.: A low cost 2D graphics anti-aliasing rendering scheme. In: 2010 International Symposium on Next-Generation Electronics (ISNE), pp. 207–210 (2010)
10. Boulanger, K., Pattanaik, S.N., Bouatouch, K.: Rendering Grass in Real Time with Dynamic Lighting. IEEE Computer Graphics and Applications 29(1), 32–41 (2009)

Introduction and Computation of Longevity Risk Index Based on Mortality Rate Decomposition Model

Ning Zhang

China Insitute For Actuarial Science, School of Insurance
Central University of Finance and Economics
100081, Beijing, China
nzhang@amss.ac.cn

Abstract. The paper introduces an important conception "longevity risk index" in insurance and actuarial research. Based on the decomposition of mortality rate data, the paper gives the definition and computation of longevity risk index. Because of different focus, there are two ways to compute longevity risk index and both of them give the similar expression of faced longevity risk. And the paper also gives the application and the computation results for different countries which make sense for governments and insurance companies.

Keywords: Longevity risk, mortality decomposition, Lee-Carter model, longevity risk index.

1   Introduction

The improvement of mortality rate with time will give rise to longevity risk. In the other words, mortality is the most factors for longevity. So it makes sense to run over the mortality model. In fact, mortality risk is always the substitute word for longevity word when doing research in basic analysis.

It makes sense for an insurance company to give a longevity risk index which shows the level of longevity risk of products. In front of managers of company, there are many products whose profits are influenced by longevity. It is possible that every product is for some specific people group and the longevity risk of every group is different. Always, only the way the national mortality rate table is used for all groups will bring wrong result. And based on the past products data, the company can compute the mortality table for every group. So is there a good way to utilize the data to give a longevity risk index for the managers?

Also, it is important to show a country the index of longevity risk since many countries must be involved with aging society. Different department is concerned with different group. For example, the social security pays more attention to the whole nation people and the medical department will pay more attention to the group with illness. So is there a longevity risk index for the whole nation?

As the longevity risk index, it should satisfy the followings: 1) It can use a simple index show the longevity risk of the fixed group; 2) The different indexes are express the difference the longevity risk faced by different group; 3) It is normalized process to compute it.

M. Zhao and J. Sha (Eds.): ICCIP 2012, Part II, CCIS 289, pp. 608–615, 2012.

In this paper, a model to compute longevity risk index is constructed. We first introduce the basic theory for longevity and basic tools for computing longevity index in Section 2. We then introduce and discuss the framework to the longevity risk index in Section3. In section 4, we will use the mortality data from American to compute longevity risk model and naturally we give the longevity risk index of some main country.   And the conclusion is given in Section 5.

2   Models and Decomposition of Mortality Rate

2.1   Mortality Rate Models

Mortality rate is the basic factor for using pricing many insurance products, especially pension products. So many people want to use some models to describe mortality rate about some fixed group.

The most used method is life table. For a country, the basic model of the population mortality rate is whole national life table. And an insurance company also constructs life table based on its collection of products data. It makes sense that there is some difference between the above two.

Another way to model mortality is to find the laws for the force of mortality. The mortality force is defined as the following:

$$\mu_x \lim_{\{t \to 0\}} = \frac{P(T_x \le t)}{t} \lim_{\{t \to 0\}} = \frac{{}_t q_x}{t}$$

There are many laws for the mortality force like Gompertz law, Makebam law, Tbiele law and Weibull law.

The classical dynamic model for mortality over age and time is Lee-Carter model. The model has the following form:

$$\ln m_x(t) = \alpha_x + \beta_x k_t + \epsilon_{x,t}$$

Where x is about age and t is about time.   And α_x α_x describe the age-pattern of mortality and is the average of mortality over the time for any fixed age. The k_t describes the time pattern of mortality. And β_x describe the adjustment part according to time for any fixed age.

It is impossible to calibrate the Lee-carter model without other constraints. For example, so many researches choose the following constraints:

$$\Sigma k_t = 0, \Sigma \beta_t = 1$$

Other constraints can be adopted. But the constraints have no impact on the fitting and forecasting of the model.

Based on the above, we can calibrate the model and solve the result of α_x, β_x, k_t when given the matrix of mortality rate. Let $m_x(t)$ is the data. The data set is a matrix with t rows and x columns. And let T is the total number of years and M is the total number of ages. Then the result of α_x is the following:

$$\widehat{\alpha}_x = \frac{\Sigma \ln m_x(t)}{T}$$

That means α_x is the average on time. Then use the singular value decomposition for the matrix Z, and Z is defined as the following:

$$Z = \begin{pmatrix} \ln m_{x_1}(t_1) - \alpha_{x_1} & \cdots & \ln m_{x_1}(t_T) - \alpha_{x_1} \\ \vdots & \ddots & \vdots \\ \ln m_{x_M}(t_1) - \alpha_{x_M} & \cdots & \ln m_{x_M}(t_1) - \alpha_{x_M} \end{pmatrix}$$

The result is the followings:

$$Z \approx Z^* = \sqrt{\lambda_1} v_1 u_1^*$$

β_x, k_t are given as :

$$\beta = \frac{v_1}{\sum v_{1j}}, \text{ and } k = \sqrt{\lambda_1} \left(\sum v_{1j} \right) u_1$$

2.2   The Decomposition Model of Mortality Rate Data

But Lee-Carter model can't get enough information from the data set. So we construct the mortality decomposition based on Lee-Carter model. If we regard the factors as the different signals, then the kernel focus is to decompose into several level signals. The framework can be described by the followings:

$$M = L + H_1 + H_2 + \epsilon$$
$$L = \text{Lee} - \text{Carter Model}$$
$$H_1, H_2 \text{ are from EMD of HHT}$$

In fact, HHT can give more levels for decomposition. But in the analysis of mortality data, two levels are enough for the following computation. And the remainder is naturally regarded as the white noise.

3   The Longevity Risk Index and Modeling Computation

There are many papers to discuss longevity. But almost no one give a systematic measurement about it. But for any insurance company or any investor, what is be considered is how much is the longevity risk? Is there any explicit result for it? How should we do to get the explicit information about longevity risk? The paper will give the first work about it.   The work is to construct measurement of longevity.

Always, financial risk comes from uncertainty. But longevity risk, as a kind of financial risk, comes from more. Except uncertainty, longevity risk also comes from the certain trend that the mortality rate is improved as time. And in fact, the certain trend with time is the focus of longevity risk for researchers before.   The common situation for the insurance product is to use the fixed mortality rate for pricing. The fixed mortality means that the mortality is only changes with age and not changes as time. Of cause, mortality rate is not regarded as stochastic process.

So to measure the longevity, we must consider the trend risk and stochastic risk. We separate the longevity risk into two forms: trend risk and stochastic risk. And the trend risk is measured by Lee-Carter Model and the stochastic risk is measured by VaR which is introduced from financial risk management.

Let $m_{x,t}$ as the basic mortality rate data and $\{m_{x,t}\}_{0 \le x \le M, t_0 \le t \le t_T}$ is a matrix with M+1 columns and T+1 rows. Here M is the oldest age of the mortality rate data. For the sake of convenience we set the beginning year t_0 of the mortality rate data into the 0 year and set the t_T into the T year. So the mortality rate matrix can be denoted by $\{m_{x,t}\}_{0 \le x \le M, 0 \le t \le T}$.

Just like what we said, mortality data can be decomposed into three level data based on the mortality decomposition model. And every level data plays different important role in the change of mortality. And we use the different weights to change the original data into the new data set.

We choose the weights $\{0.5, 0.3, 0.2\}$ for three levels. There are two reasons for this weights set: the first reason is the fact that more definite trend should be given more weight; the second reason is that it is from optimization results of function with free weights.

We denote the new mortality data set as $\{m_{x,t}^*\}$. And define the longevity risk index function as the following map:

$$f_{index}: \{m_{x,t}^*\}_{0 \le x \le M, 0 \le t \le T} \times [0, +\infty] \to R$$

$[0, +\infty]$ is the time horizon for longevity risk index and it is understandable that the longevity risk index of different time horizon should different. Also, we can get that more accurate longevity risk index is for the shorter time horizon.

Here we give two kinds of definition of f_{index}, one of them is the following:

$$f_{index1} = E_x(E(\max\{0, \Delta m_{x,t}^*\}))$$

The other way is the following:

$$f_{index1} = E_x(VaR_t(m_{x,t}^*))$$

Here VaR is defined as its definition in financial risk management, VaR method takes the prominent role in the financial risk management. Its essence is to give a explicit idea about the faced risk and use a simple number to express it. For a given confidence level and time horizon, the probability for the portfolio loss to exceed the VaR will be the given confidence level over the given time horizon.

Let β is the confidence level like 5% and L is the loss for portfolio. Then,

$$VaR_\beta(L) = -\inf\{l \in R: F_L(l) \ge \beta\}$$

There are many methods to compute VaR value for portfolio like Delta-Normal method, historical data method and simulation methods. Because the delta-Normal method is limited to the normal distribution, we will use the other methods to computing VaR for mortality rate data.

Now for the first definition, the computing process is the following:

Step 1: Computing $\Delta m_{x,t}^{*}$ for fixed x age based on the mortality rate series;
Step 2: Removing the negative results for the computing results;
Step 3: Computing the expectation;
Step 4: Computing the expectation according to the population proportion and get the result.

Now for the other definition, the computing process is the following:

Step 1: Computing $VaR_t\left(m_{x,t}^{*}\right)$ for fixed x age based on the mortality rate series;
Step 2: Computing the expectation according to the population proportion and get the result.

Here, in the first step, we use the historical data to compute $\Delta m_{x,t}$ and $VaR_t\left(m_{x,t}^{*}\right)$. But in fact there are two other methods which can be used for computing: One method is statistical distribution and this method will give the distribution of the mortality rate; the other method is Monte-Carlo simulation. Both methods also must use the historical data. In practices, the results from three methods are similar.

4   The Longevity Risk Indexes of Different Countries

Our American mortality data is a 75×110 matrix which includes 75 years and 110 ages. The data is from official statistical data. The surface formed by the data set is just like showing in Figure 1.

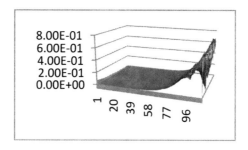

Fig. 1. The surface of American mortality rate

And based on it, we can compute the longevity risk index. The following computed the index based the first definition. Figure 2 gives the expectation of $\max\{0, \Delta m_{x,t}\}$ at different age.

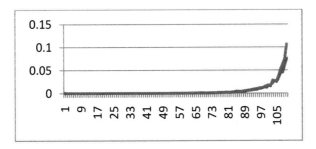

Fig. 2. $E(\max\{0, \Delta m_{x,t}\})$ with respect to different age

Then the final longevity risk index is 0.004757. This is for one year. Considering two years, the computing processing is just like above except the interval time is two year in step 1. And the result for 2 year is 0.005541. And so on. Figure 3 gives the longevity risk index with respect to year. It is understandable that there is more risk for more years.

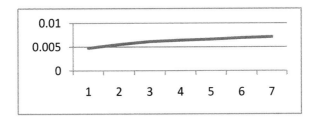

Fig. 3. The trend of American longevity risk with years

The following computed the index based the second definition (Fig.4).

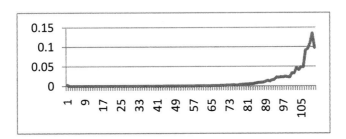

Fig. 4. The result of the first step of 2nd definition in different ages

And the longevity risk index is 0.01035. And the longevity risk index for different horizons is figured by the following (Figure 5).

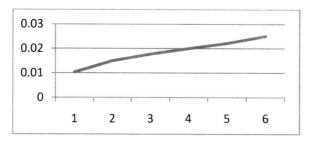

Fig. 5. The longevity risk index for different horizon by 2nd definition

Table 1 gives the longevity risk index of some different country of the world for one, two and three years. 95% is the confidence ratio.

Table 1. The longevity risk indexes of several countries

Longevity risk indexes of several Countries		
	1st Definition	2nd Definition
the United States	0.004757	0.01035
Canada	0.00392	0.00813
Austrilia	0.0046	0.00831
Japan	0.0053	0.01127
Germany	0.003795	0.00819
English	0.00365	0.00811
China	0.003417	0.006012

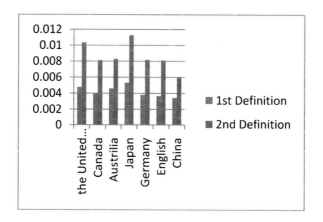

Fig. 6. The longevity risk indexes of several countries

5   Conclusion

The longevity risk index gives an explicit expression about longevity risk which a country must face. Governments can take computation results as important information to adjust their policy. The longevity risk index is not only used for the governments but also for the insurance companies. Our further steps are to finish its application for the portfolio correlated with longevity risk.

Acknowledgment. The paper was the research results of 2011 project "Mortality rate decomposition and its application in longevity risk measure" of The Insurance Institute of China. The work was finished under the support of the 2011 research grant from the China Institute for Actuarial Science and the program for Young Innovative Research Team of CUFE (leader Pro. Zhang Liqing). And it also was supported by MOE project of key research institute of humanities and social sciences in Universities (No2011JJD790004).

References

1. Alho, J.M.: Discussion of Lee. North American Actuarial Journal 4(1), 91–93 (2000)
2. Emms, P.H.C., Haberman, S.: Income drawdown schemes for a defined contribution pension plan. Journal of Risk and Insurance 75(3), 739–761 (2008)
3. Felipe, A., Guillen, M., Perez-Marin, A.M.: Rescent morality in Spanish population. British Actuarial Journal 8, 757–786 (2002)
4. Lee, R.D.: The Lee-Carter method for forecasting morality, with various extensions and applications. North American Actuarial Journal 4(1), 80–93 (2000)
5. Lundstrom, H., Qvist, J.: Mortality forecasting and trend shifts: an application of the Lee-Carter Model to Swedish mortality data. International Statistical Review 72, 37–50 (2004)
6. Olivieri, A.: Heterogeneity in survival models. Application to pension and life annuities. Application to pension and life annuities. Belgian Actuarial Bulletin 6, 23–29 (2006)
7. Renshaw, A.E., Haberman, S.: On simulation –based approaches to risk measurement in mortality with specific reference to poisson Lee-Carter modelling. Insurance: Mathematics and Economics 42, 797–816 (2008)
8. Wong-Fupuy, C., Haberman, S.: Projecting mortaltiy trends: recent developments in the United Kingdom and the United States. North American Actuarial Journal 8, 56–83 (2008)

Traffic Flow Time Series Analysis
Based on the Three-Phase Traffic Theory

Hang Yu[1] and Shi An[2]

[1] School of Management, Harbin Institute of Technology, Harbin, 150001, China
yuhang1101@gmail.com
[2] Harbin Institute of Technology, Harbin, 150001, China

Abstract. The string oscillation equation is proposed to model the pattern of traffic flow time series, based on three-phase traffic theory. Traffic flow time series analysis has many applications to various areas, such as intelligent transportation, signal control, routing guidance, and traffic safety. Traffic flow pattern recognition is focused under the transition between the three traffic flow phases. For this purpose, traffic flow status features are described in every phase and used for traffic flow model fitting as an empirical premise. The results demonstrate that traffic flow status pattern can be correctly recognized in 87 percent of situations using the presented equation.

Keywords: traffic flow, time series analysis, three-phase traffic theory, string oscillation equation.

1 Introduction

The status of a series of traffic flow data shows very complex spatial–temporal traffic patterns and these patterns would appear again sometime in a short term. Thanks to several types of detectors, like loop detectors, infrared, ultrasonic, radar, microwave, and video, measurements of traffic flow can be collected and interpreted, so that the information of classification and surveillance of traffic can be done and applied to make an online automatic recognition and tracking of traffic patterns. So pattern recognition of traffic flow time series could play an important role in making more efficient traffic control optimization strategy, by signal control, traffic assignment, routing guidance and etc., ultimately, a kind of fast, safe, comfortable, efficient operation of smart traffic service can be realized.

Traffic flow modeling and driving behavior analysis have many practices in different fields, such as Intelligent Transportation Systems (ITS), traffic safety, pollutant emissions dispersion and adaptive cruise control. A few studies in this field are related to the mathematical modeling of traffic flow (e.g., Mallikarjuna, Ch. and Ramachandra Rao, K.[1], 2009; Qiu, Y. and Chen, S.[2],2010; Kanai, M.[3], 2010). A few approaches and trials in traffic technology to estimate, track and predict traffic patterns were a kind of application of either microscopic (in particular, the car-following models), or macroscopic traffic flow models, which calculate the movement of individual vehicles, the average vehicle speed and the density spatial–temporal

M. Zhao and J. Sha (Eds.): ICCIP 2012, Part II, CCIS 289, pp. 616–624, 2012.

distributions in freeway networks (e.g., May and Keller[4], 1968; Gartner et al.[5], 1997; Kronjager and Konhauser[6], 1997; Kaumann et al.[7]). In other studies, a traffic flow management system based on case-based reasoning was proposed (Sadek et al.[8]), in which the defined case was actually equivalent to pattern. According to the analysis of the real traffic flow data the predicted data in next period, the different and typical traffic network was defined as different case (pattern), and then the case was solved and the optimal traffic assignment strategy was saved into the system. Traffic pattern was also applied in the field of traffic flow predicting. A method for predicting traffic flow velocity was proposed based on nonlinear time series analysis (Nair et al.[9], 2001), in which the truth that the traffic flow velocity time series pattern was similar and took place repeatedly was used to predict the speed. A forecasting method took the trend of increase and decrease of traffic flow volume in a period as a kind of pattern (Taehyung Kim[10],2007), and the method overcame the flaw of a mathematics model that was assumed to be ruled by a kind of function and the results would lose effectiveness unless the rule was followed exactly.

The algorithm presented in this paper is a supervised pattern recognition algorithm base on a k-means clustering procedure. It is a non-parametric pattern recognition technique which has been already applied on a number of pattern recognition problems successfully. The idea of Keller[11] that there were three traffic flow phases: (i) free traffic flow; (ii)synchronized traffic flow; and (iii) wide moving traffic jams was taken as the premise to find out the model fitting the traffic patterns more precisely in a more complex urban road network than the freeway network.

The remaining content of this article is organized into the following sections. Section 2 explains traffic flow status features. In Section 3, the model of string oscillation equation is presented to fit the traffic flow patterns and the process of the solution is depicted. Then in Section 4 the experimental setup will be depicted for pattern recognition of traffic flow status. Finally, in Section 5, the pattern recognition results are compared and analyzed, and the conclusions will be drawn.

2   Traffic Flow Phases

Based on some empirical findings, Kerner[12] developed a three-phase traffic theory: (i) free traffic flow, (ii) synchronized traffic flow and (iii) wide moving traffic jams, which can explain results of empirical observations of the phase transitions between these three traffic phases and the spatial–temporal features of patterns in congested traffic at freeway bottlenecks. Based on this theory, a model was proposed to approach to the spatial–temporal congested traffic pattern recognition, tracking and forecasting on freeways which has been realized in the models FOTO (Forecasting of Traffic Objects) and ASDA (Automatic Tracking of Moving Traffic Jams) [13].

According to the three-phase traffic theory, a wide moving jam is a localized congested pattern which is spatially restricted for the reason of a sharply propagation continuously upstream of the average vehicle speed and the density. Inside the wide moving jam each vehicle is in a stop-and-go or at least for a finite time which is long enough that the traffic upstream of the wide moving jam cannot influence the traffic downstream and vice versa. Free traffic flow is in a metastable status with respect to the jam occurrence. If the flow rate in a free flow is higher than the flow rate in the outflow from a wide moving jam, $q > q_{out}$, in this case, a wide moving jam can be excited in this free flow. In contrast, if the flow rate in a free flow is lower than the outflow, $q < q_{out}$, then the free flow is stable with respect to the wide moving jam formation[12,13]. Wide moving jams can neither exist for a long time nor be excited by a short time local perturbation in this free flow. Synchronized traffic flow is also separated spatially either from free flow or from a wide moving jam by the downstream front and by the upstream front where vehicle speed sharply changes. However, the flow rate in contrast to a wide moving jam can remain in synchronized flow almost constant inside these fronts. The transition for the measured values of vehicle speed and density can be interpreted as shown in Fig 1[11] and more detailed information is listed in Table 1.

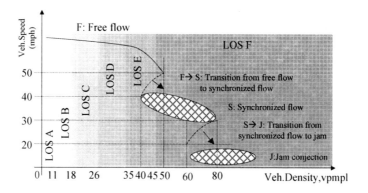

Fig. 1. Clarified phases of traffic flows(Kerner, 2008)

Table 1. Summarized traffic flows phase features form literature review

Traffic flow phases	described	Speed u mph	Density k vpmpl	Delays t spv
Free flow		≥ 50	≤ 40	≤ 10
Stable flow	Transition from free flow to synchronized flow (or oscillating dense traffic)	40-50	40-50	>10-35
Approaching unstable flow	Synchronized flow (or local clusters)	30-40	40-80	>35-55
Unstable flow	Transition from synchronized flow to jam congestion	20-30	60-80	>55-80
Forced flow	Wide moving jam congestion (stop-and-go)	≤ 20	≥ 60	>80

3   Mathematic Model

It is found that the traffic flow changing features most look like a sting oscillation, so we try to use the string oscillation to model and fit the observed changing trend with a time series of the traffic flow.

In this section, the string oscillation equation [14] is described. The typical linear second order partial differential equation is shown as following:

$$u_{tt} - a^2(u_{xx} + u_{yy} + u_{zz}) = 0 \ ,$$

and in which,

x, y, z -- spatial independent variables,

t -- temporal variable,

$u = u(x,t)$ -- unknown function of independent variables.

According to traffic flow features, the average speed u can be purposed as the function of the volume q and time t, which can be represented like $u = u(q,t)$.

Consider a little segment of the trend curve is a tight string with length-l fixed two end points, and affected by an external force F, which can be the weather condition, road face and infrastructure condition, and also the most important traffic demand considering transportation actual practices. Based on the following assumptions[14], we can obtain $u = u(x,t)$ of the string of traffic flow at any t-moment by initial perturbation.

(1)   The string is soft and elastic, and the tension direction is the same with its tangent.
(2)   Arbitrary small section is not stretched, and then the tension is constant by Hooke law.
(3) $\dfrac{Weight}{Tension} < 0.1$ (very small).
(4) $\dfrac{Displacement}{Length} < 0.1 \Leftrightarrow \dfrac{\max |u|}{l} < 0.1$.
(5)   The slope on any point after displacement is smaller than 0.1.
(6)   The string only has transverse vibration.

Suppose T is the tension on two end points as shown in Fig 2.

By Newton's second law, result force equals the product of mass and acceleration, and then there is

$$T \sin \beta - T \sin \alpha = \rho \Delta s \cdot u_{tt} \ ,$$

where ρ --density, Δs --arc length of this small section after displacement. After some simplification operations, we obtain the general equation:

$$u_{tt} = a^2 u_{xx} + f \ , \text{ where } f = \frac{F}{\rho}.$$

Then the partial differential equation is simplified with two fixed end points respectively and we obtain the solution of Cauchy problem:

$$u(x,t) = f_1(x+at) + f_2(x-at)$$

$$= \frac{1}{2}[\varphi(x+at) + \varphi(x-at)] + \frac{1}{2}\int_{x-at}^{x+at}\psi(s)ds,$$

which is called D'Alembert formula, where $\varphi \in C^2$, $\psi \in C^1$ are arbitrary.

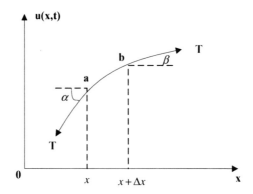

Fig. 2. Micro-Element on the string

Thus as long as we confirm the parameter a and the initial fixed end points condition, we can obtain the formulation and the curve fit for the traffic pattern.

4   Data Experiment and Solution

To validate the model fitness of the real status, we use the real data collected by a real location observation and investigation. The investigation was taken placed on a Tuesday day with sun, around the clock from 6:30am to 6:30pm. The data were collected on some typical and important intersections around the second circle route of the city of Changchun. The collected data include the basic information of sample intersections, the observation moment and time interval, consecutive 12hours' traffic flow volume and vehicle types on each direction, left, though, and right, the ratio of the traffic signal.

4.1   Set Up Experiment

Traffic data measured at some intersections on some urban arterial road can be used as some kind of "boundary conditions" for these mathematical traffic flow models which should calculate spatial–temporal distributions of traffic variables on a local urban network. Here the initial traffic volume of Jilin Street and Dongsheng Road intersection for a 12-hour daytime consecutively collected in a survey are showed in Table 2. The traffic volume was calculated per 10 minutes. The data should be treated by (1) to get the average speed (mph short for miles per hour) of vehicles passing a plane of the intersection.

$$u = \frac{Q \bullet L_v}{\lambda} = \frac{6 \bullet q \bullet L_v}{\lambda}$$ (1)

u --the average speed by mph,

q --traffic flow volume in 10 min,

Q --traffic flow volume in an hour,

L_v --the adjust length of a car by mile,

λ --the spilt green ratio which is equal to green time divided by the whole period.

Table 2. Traffic flow consecutive volume and average speed

Time	q veh	u mph	Pha	Time	q veh	u mph	Pha	Time	q veh	u mph	Pha
7:30	6100	35.38	Syn	-	6580	45.80	FtS	-	6617	46.06	FtS
-	6494	37.67	Syn	11:30	6679	46.49	FtS	-	6819	47.47	FtS
-	6857	39.78	Syn	-	6626	46.12	FtS	15:30	6870	47.82	FtS
8:00	6870	29.89	StC	-	6447	44.87	FtS	-	6997	29.15	StC
-	6788	29.53	StC	12:00	6353	44.22	FtS	-	7114	29.63	StC
-	6839	29.75	StC	-	6417	44.67	FtS	16:00	7293	30.38	Syn
8:30	6924	30.12	Syn	-	6392	44.50	FtS	-	7417	30.89	Syn
-	6908	30.06	Syn	12:30	6199	43.15	FtS	-	7393	30.80	Syn
-	6857	29.83	StC	-	6077	42.30	FtS	16:30	7523	31.34	Syn
9:00	6973	30.33	Syn	-	6209	43.22	FtS	-	7618	31.73	Syn
-	6979	30.36	Syn	13:00	6235	43.40	FtS	-	7740	32.24	Syn
-	6973	30.33	Syn	-	6201	43.17	FtS	17:00	7750	32.28	Syn
9:30	7035	30.61	Syn	-	6346	44.17	FtS	-	7753	32.29	Syn
-	7110	49.49	FtS	13:30	6462	44.98	FtS	-	7835	32.64	Syn
-	7213	50.21	Fre	-	6714	46.74	FtS	17:30	7839	32.65	Syn
10:00	7397	51.49	Fre	-	6760	47.06	FtS	-	7709	32.11	Syn
-	7311	50.89	Fre	14:00	6911	48.11	FtS	-	7687	32.02	Syn
-	7288	50.73	Fre	-	6927	48.22	FtS	18:00	7689	32.03	Syn
10:30	7109	49.48	FtS	-	6834	47.57	FtS	-	7691	32.04	Syn
-	7115	49.52	FtS	14:30	6817	47.45	FtS	-	7641	31.83	Syn
-	7037	48.98	FtS	-	6663	46.38	FtS	18:30	7654	31.88	Syn
11:00	6780	47.20	FtS	-	6610	46.01	FtS	-	-	-	-
-	6730	46.84	FtS	15:00	6527	45.43	FtS	-	-	-	-

Fre –free flow.

FtS -- from free flow to synchronized flow.

Syn – synchronized flow.

StC –from synchronized flow to congestion.

Con – congestion.

The metadata are shown in Table 2, and base on the three-theory traffic theory we attained three phases for the whole day traffic status, so we could get values of the two fixed points for each phase, and the parameter a could be estimated, so that the model could be confirmed.

4.2 Model Fitting

In the previous part, the string oscillation equation is described and the model fitting method is explained. In this section, the traffic flow status will be recognized by the proposed model using a real time series data and the effectives of the model will be validated. The total 67 cases will be grouped in two, 43 of them was used as a training dataset to issue the unknown or predicted parameters in the model, and the last 24 rows were took as a verification group.

The estimated a is shown as following for each changing phase:

$$a = \begin{cases} 0.083 & \text{from Fre to FtS} \\ 0.076 & \text{from FtS to Syn} \\ 0.066 & \text{from Syn to StC} \end{cases} \Rightarrow$$

$$u(x,t) = f_1(x+at) + f_2(x-at)$$

$$= \begin{cases} \dfrac{1}{2}[\varphi(x+0.083t) + \varphi(x-0.083t)] + \dfrac{1}{2}\int_{x-0.083t}^{x+0.083t} \psi(s)ds \\[2ex] \dfrac{1}{2}[\varphi(x+0.076t) + \varphi(x-0.076t)] + \dfrac{1}{2}\int_{x-0.076t}^{x+0.076t} \psi(s)ds \\[2ex] \dfrac{1}{2}[\varphi(x+0.066t) + \varphi(x-0.066t)] + \dfrac{1}{2}\int_{x-0.066t}^{x+0.066t} \psi(s)ds \end{cases}$$

By these initial data, the model fitness values are shown in the Table 3, and we obtain the curve to fit for these cases and a flow trend as shown in Fig 3, the fitting curve and the little oscillation can be seen in different phases according to the Kerner's three-phase theory.

Table 3. Model Statistics

Model	R-squared	Statistics	DF	Sig.
AveSpeed-Volume	.000	7.319	17	.979

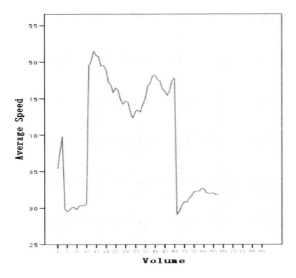

Fig. 3. Fitting curve for the relationship of average speed and volume

5   Conclusions

In this study, a new model for Traffic Flow Recognition (TFR) was presented based on the three-phrase theory. The string oscillation was utilized for modeling the traffic flow pattern and the space-temporal distributions of traffic variables. The results demonstrate that the one-dimensional wave equation can simply fit the traffic pattern in a good way. Take our limited knowledge and ability into account and the errors exit in the data and the process of the experiment, the results cannot be exactly precise, but we considered the idea and practice could be a novel interesting point and challenge in related field. Also we will continue to modify and improve our model and method to make it more reasonable and precise.

For further work, in order to use the traffic flow pattern to do short term prediction, signal control, traffic assignment and routing guidance, the controller parameters should be optimized for different traffic flow phases.

Acknowledgment. This research is supported by National Natural Science Foundation of China (Project No. 71073035, 70973032 and 70903018), People's Republic of China. This work was performed at Key Laboratory of Advanced Materials & Intelligent Control Technology on Transportation Safety, Ministry of Communications, People's Republic of China. Thanks to support of the Harbin Institute of Technology Doctoral Short-term Abroad Visiting Sponsor Project.

References

1. Mallikarjuna, C., Ramachandra Rao, K.: Cellular automata model for heterogeneous traffic. Int. J. Adv. Transport. 43(3), 321–345 (2009)
2. Qiu, Y., Chen, S.: A new nonlocal traffic flow model with anticipation dependent relaxation time, equilibrium velocity and variance. Int. J. Stat. Mech. Theory Exp., 12012 (2010)
3. Kanai, M.: Two-lane traffic-flow model with an exact steady-state solution. Int. J. Phys. Rev. E 82(6), 66107 (2010)
4. May, A.D., Keller, H.M.: Evaluation of single and two-regime traffic flow models. In: Proceedings of the 3rd International Symposium on Transportation and Traffic Theory, Karlsruhe, Germany, pp. 37–47 (1968)
5. Gartner, N., Messer, C., Rathi, A. (eds.): Special Report 165: Revised Monograph on Traffic Flow Theory. Transportation Research Board, Washington, DC (1997)
6. Kronjager, W., Konhauser, P.: Applied traffic flow simulation. In: Papageorgiou, M., Pouliezos, A. (eds.) Transportation Systems, IFAC, Kreta (Greece), pp. 777–780 (1997)
7. Kaumann, Froese, K., Chrobok, R., Wahle, J., Neubert, L., Schreckenberg, M.: On-Line Simulation of the Freeway Network of NRW. In: Helbing, D., Hermann, H.J., Schreckenberg, M., Wolf, D.E. (eds.) Traffic and Granular Flow, pp. 351–356. Springer, Berlin (2000)
8. Sadek, A.W., Demetsky, M.J., Smith, B.L.: Case Based Reasoning for Real Time Traffic Flow Management. Computer Aided Civil and Infrastructure Engineering 14, 347–356 (1999)
9. Nair, A.S., Liu, J.C., Rilett, L., Gupta, S.: Non Linear Analysis of Traffic Flow. In: Proceedings of IEEE Intelligent Transportation Systems Conference, pp. 683–687 (2001)
10. Taehyung, K., Hyoungsoo, K., Cheol, O., Bongsoo, S.: Traffic Flow Forecasting Based Pattern Recognition to Overcome Memoryless Property. In: International Conference on Multimedia and Ubiquitous Engineering, pp. 1181–1186 (2007)
11. Kerner, B.S.: A theory of traffic congested at heavy bottlenecks. Journal of Physics: Mathematical and Theoretical, Theor. 41, 215101 (2008)
12. Kerner, B.S.: Synchronized Flow as a New Traffic Phase and Related Problems for Traffic Flow Modelling. Mathematical and Computer Modelling 35, 481–508 (2002)
13. Kerner, B.S., Rehborn, H., Aleksic, M., Haug, A.: Recognition and tracking of spatial–temporal congested traffic patterns on freeways. Transportation Research Part C 12, 369–400 (2004)
14. Sobolev, S.L.: Partial Differential Equations of Mathematical Physics (February 2011)

The Advantages of RAW Format Image Post-processing

Pirong Yao[*]

Yibin University's School of Computer & Information Engineering
No. 8 Jiusheng Road Cuiping District Yibin City, Sichuan, China
458468255@qq.com

Abstract. Whether professional photographers or ordinary photography enthusiasts often forget to adjust the different camera settings when shooting a scene. For example, when they shoot portraits, they set landscapes in the camera. RAW image format is created and used because it is just a set of raw data. You can re-set output image quality that you want after you come back home. If you only save a JPG format, you will only accept the fait accompli of the images. RAW format images of digital camera is the original data that the optical signal captured by image sensor is changed into a digital signal .However, JPG format images is a common digital photo images format handled by the camera's image processor according to the image settings quality demands of the users . Therefore, it is a revolutionary reform to save RAW format in the digital camera. People can no longer spend much more about the image quality settings when shooting, because everything can be changed.

Keywords: Image format, RAW and JPG format, post-processing, advantages.

1 The Advantages in the Post-processing RAW Format

Now almost every digital SLR camera or some high-end consumer digital camera can save images in RAW format. What does RAW mean? Raw means "the original, raw, unprocessed things so on" in English. In fact, RAW image is the CMOS image sensor captures the light signal into a digital signal of the original data file. Strictly speaking, it can not be considered as an image file but a packet because it can not be previewed and opened in the computer unless we use the special software. RAW format is direct access from the raw sensor data. The packet is not converted and processed through the camera's image processor. So what the photographer sets the camera on many of the data packet is invalid. When shooting all the set parameters, only whether exposure data packet is correct or not works. The rest of the parameters have not been "set", color mode, white balance, contrast, sharpening and other special needs are done in RAW format conversion software. In other words, in addition to the focus, depth of field and exposure outside, everything can be changed later. RAW file contains all the photos of the original information. Documents are generated in the

---

[*] Pirong Yao (1966.9 -), male, Associate Professor, Ping Shan, Sichuan. Research Area: Visual Arts, Media Technology & Art, Educational Technology Research. Tel: 13990968024 or 0831-3545070. Email: 458468255@qq.com.

M. Zhao and J. Sha (Eds.): ICCIP 2012, Part II, CCIS 289, pp. 625–631, 2012.

sensor. The image processor goes into the camera before it is recorded by the camera produced some of the original data (Metadata, such as ISO settings, shutter speed, aperture, white balance, etc.) files. RAW is the raw and uncompressed formats. RAW can be conceptualized as "the original image coded data" or the image called "digital film."

The general format for digital photo images is JPG; JPG photo format is compressed by software coding an image format. It can adjust the compression rate and compression ratio in different software, which is not the same. Digital camera save photos in JPG format by selecting "image quality" in: Fine, good, fair and poor to get the file sizes of images. Although the digital cameras can save space in the memory card as a photo storage using the JPG format. But while shooting, such as adjusting brightness, color temperature, color balance, image sharpness and other parameters have been processed through the camera "locked" in the document. The latter can only be adjusted by image processing software, such as Adobe Photoshop to deal with. But after adjusting, the image quality will be lost. All the image processing software uses a different digital camera image processor is different from the encoding methods and compression ratio. So the amount of the image file will be smaller and the quality will deteriorate.

1.1   The Advantages of RAW Format

First: the advantage of RAW format is that it is not a real image but the image sensor captures the light signal into a digital signal of the original packet. In the latter part of the use of special image generation software to generate the actual image. In the use of computer imaging, you can within the ± 2 stops exposure compensation. White balance can be re-adjusted arbitrarily change the photo style, sharpness, contrast and other parameters. So when you judge those settings difficultly, you can shoot them on the computer screen and then fine-tune the output generated image. And these post-processing, all is without loss and reversible process. We processed a RAW file, as long as the preservation of the original RAW file format .Then we can adjust different settings producing different images. For example, I just output a color image that is generated as soon as I can, generating black and white images. RAW format is a true "electronic film". In the film shot in black and white negatives of different formulations and techniques can be washed and access to different levels of contrast. Slides can reduce or increase the development time to change the way the limited exposure, but the film can only be washed once, not repeated washing. RAW format, however, the original photo can be a multiple of the "wash". That uses different methods to convert the software to obtain more than one level, color, exposure of a completely different picture. Using one to create more than one such legend in the production of digital technology in reality Those who govern our traditional technology bottlenecks are broken New technologies bring us a new world [1].

Second: RAW format provided by camera manufacturers specialized software processing, the resulting picture is a lessee compression format that can be JPG format or lossless TIFF format (8-bit or 16-bit optional).A JPG format, in the case of the same pixel by software to convert from RAW format JPG format the resolution up to 350DPI, and camera images directly save the JPG format only 72DPI. Print or print out the picture, the minimum requirements of the resolution is 300DPI.

RAW and JPG compared to the greatest advantage lies in the color depth. RAW format, thanks to 12-bit, 14 or 22 to record information (has medium format digital back monochrome color depth to 22 bits). Conversion can be converted to 16-bit TIFF output, which means that there are at least 65,536 kinds of color RGB color record capability compared to the 256 8-bit JPEG is a great advantage. In some red, for example, only 256 8-bit JPEG can be used, and in the RAW format, whose color is up to 4096. So the level of the RAW format is much richer. Its practical significance is this: if we make drastic changes in color and brightness adjustments, we will find the same adjustments. When we use the JPEG format or TIFF format, the photos have been blurred, resulting in noise, damaging the image quality, and RAW format is also far from the "exhausted" with it. There can be room to explore this potential that is determined by the nature of the RAW format---- the largest color space, up to the level of record, and does not give you the most primitive processing over the raw materials, so you will adjust out the best image.

1.2   The Disadvantage of RAW Format

RAW format images and JPG files are different from the common image data. If you do not use the dedicated software for image processing, then it can not be as common image browsing. And RAW files because it usually does not save compressed or low compressed. So the file size is often the same resolution JPG files than two to three times larger for the memory card capacity requirements. Indirectly, the storage time after taking a picture, post-processed by the computer hardware requirements and processing time is more than high JPG files. Moreover, the various manufacturers of almost all of the different RAW format codes and even different versions of the same vendor code are different so in the post-processing RAW files are handled in software terms which are not universal.

2   The Technique of RAW Files Using

2.1   RAW Files Adjust the White Balance

Accurate white balance settings can make the pictures more pleasing color for the human eye. However, users are accustomed to using the automatic white balance. Auto white balance may often encounter the problem of inaccurate. Although the manual white balance can solve this problem, but every time when we meet a new scene or new lighting environment, we must re-define a white balance. Even professional photographers think this is quite tedious.

White balance is also known as color temperature balance, referring to the composition of the image corresponding to the three RGB color balance with the proportional relationship. Resulting image color cast for many reasons: exposure error, white balance errors, ambient color, etc. How to correct white balance? By 1802, Thomas Young proposed a RGB three primary colors (Three Primary Colors) concept: white = 228 R +228 G +228 B, black = 28 R +28 G +28 B, gray = 128 R +128 G +128 B, that is either black, white, ash, which constitutes three-color RGB should be equivalent [2]. RAW data file in this package has a considerable advantage.

The JPG files in the latter part of the white balance bias are often difficult and not necessarily accurate adjustment. To adjust the white balance of RAW files we usually use the various manufacturers of specialized software. Take Canon Digital Photo Professional as the following example.

Canon Digital Photo Professional (referred to as DPP) is introduced to deal specifically with Canon camera RAW files taken out of the software. To adjust the white balance Canon RAW files, just open the file in DPP, then the right of the "white balance adjustment" in the drop-down menu to select the appropriate settings to the screen there will be real change. You can also select "color temperature" mode and you can in 100K step, shown in Figure 1, set a specific color temperature value.

If a variety of preset white balance modes can not accurately restore the site colors, you can use the "Custom White Balance" (manual white balance) to set. Manual white balance, generally neutral gray screen location as the base as long as the right to restore the scene neutral colors. The light will restore the site colors. Canon DPP, select "click white balance", then click on the above "straw", and finally tap the screen in black and white gray block Manual white balance setting is completed [3]. Its essence is black and white gray block sampling and analysis by the RGB values,

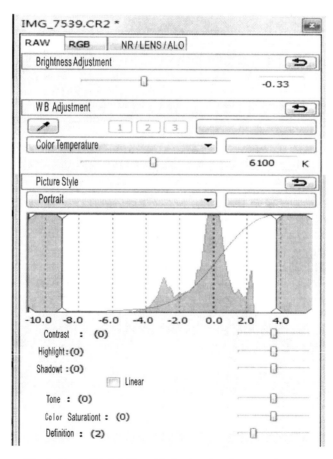

Fig. 1. Canon Digital Photo Professional software tool palette

for example, is: R180 G170 B150, drawn in black and white to make the screen the RGB value of the same gray block in the encoded output RGB JPG format the whole the proportion of the original data should be 0.83R: 0.88G: 1B. The white balance is adjusted. Digital Photo Professional window displays the status of files in real time the mouse position RBG pixel values for processing by reference, especially select "color temperature" mode when adjusting.

2.2 Adjust Exposure Compensation and Synthetic HDR Image with the Output of Different Stages of Exposure to Photos

Digital camera auto exposure when the exposure is based on measuring the reflection rate of 18% gray (skin color) brightness of the scene as a standard. When the brightness of the high reflectivity of 18% or less of the gray, we must restore the brightness of the correct use of exposure compensation is necessary. If you do not use exposure compensation, in many cases the transition will occur, such as exposure (the screen is too bright) or underexposed (too dark) situations, professional photographers as well. If you save a JPG format, post by image processing software to adjust the brightness, picture quality will be affected to some degree, such as increased noise, loss of image detail and so on. If you shoot RAW files, adjust the screen brightness of the late (post-exposure compensation), not only better, and reversible process, the original file will not cause any damage.

High-Dynamic Range HDR is the acronym for the high dynamic range. So what is Dynamic Range? Image's dynamic range is the reality of the scene to record the image of the brightest and darkest parts of the ratio of the size.

Scene to generate a dynamic range of ability by two constraints. The first limitation: imaging equipment. Images generated by digital cameras are generally considered as a low dynamic range. If the noise and other constraints into account the impact of the case, most of the camera sensor maximum dynamic is ranging of approximately 1000:1 or less. The second restriction - reproduction of the media, the standard computer screen can reproduce the dynamic range that is about 100:1. However, the real-world scene is much higher dynamic range (100,000:1 ratio of the natural world is common).

In digital photography, if we are to get together, including highlights and shadows of the real scene, we must use special software to different exposures of the same scene photo image photo synthesis, the so-called HDR photos. Require depends on the number of images and image series between the dynamic ranges of the exposure. If the image contains a very high dynamic range, such that there is a dark indoor scene also contains a sunny room location, to cover the entire dynamic range of at least two exposures. These photos, so produced, in the light and dark, color and other details are very rich, equivalent to increases in the camera (film, CCD) of tolerance, there is a surreal painting-like effect.

For images of moving objects in the scene is concerned, you have to shoot the same scene multiple photos of different exposure is not possible, because moving objects in the frame position change. However, you can by the same RAW file output by more than one photo at different stages of exposure to synthetic HDR image. Specific methods: such as Canon's DPP software, when other parameters are not changed after adjusting the premise, you adjust brightness, such as:-2EV,-1EV, 0, +1

EV, +2 EV output an image of the total exposure to get five different images of the same scene, you shoot the equivalent of five different exposure photos of the same scene, such as Adobe Photoshop CS4 by the "files - Automatic - merged to HDR" menu command, or specialized HDR software such as Photomatixpro so to get highlights and shadows blend high dynamic range images.

2.3   Adjust the Screen Color and Style of Picture Styles

Digital photo frame style and color tendencies can be adjusted later .It is well known that JPG image format is no exception. However, no matter how good the PS master is, if he used to adjust a landscape photo with "Portrait" mode shooting, never goes on landscape images better than the right of "landscape" mode shooting. This is why digital cameras generally must be properly set up, such as "Picture Style", "color space" and so on, tending to color options If you save a JPG format, these options can make the picture show tendency of different colors.

If you shoot JPG format to save the file, set these options once, shooting JPG files can not adjust these options. I believe that many users are using the camera's "portrait" mode to record the "landscape", which of course is not the result you want. If you still do it tomorrow, but you shoot using RAW format, it can be Digital Photo Professional software, after any necessary adjustments, such as the output processing.

Convert images in different color styles based on a model, we can individually adjust the RAW file contrast, saturation, sharpness, and etc. settings. Although these settings in the camera before shooting on the set we have, but usually can be set to "neutral", and its essence is to leave these settings to post-processing step further, you can take more time to pre-stay to the picture framing and other steps.

2.4   Amount of Light Surrounding the Lens Correction

Uniform brightness when you shoot the scene, you will find a darkened corner of the screen phenomenon called "blind", commonly known as "dark corners." Four weeks for any darker than the center of the lens is inevitable. Many camera manufacturers have kit lens at the factory on the surrounding light amount of the correction, so if you save the JPG format, it does not matter. But if you are not using the same manufacturers of the lens, you can not solve this problem. RAW files can only be used to correct their amount of light around the lens center and the gap between the light.

White balance correction principle is as the RAW data package .The original brightness uniformity by sampling and analysis after the actual non-uniform imaging through the lens of the screen the RGB values of different locations, in JPG format encoded output RGB raw data to adjust the ratio. Also be used directly for the hidden corners of the lens manufacturers test data to hidden corners of the screen calibration. We can not only eliminate the dark corners, but also artificially generated hidden corners by using RAW data packets, for example, in the Canon Digital Photo Professional, the vignette correction slider, in addition to positive regulation, the negative regulator, two corresponding to "eliminate the Dark Corners" and "increase the Dark Corners" two effects.

2.5   Differences in Color Correction and Image Noise Reduction

Color differences, also known as dispersion, is due to the camera lens which do not gather the different wavelengths of light to the same focal plane (the refractive index of light of different wavelengths is different), or due to the lens of different wavelengths of light to form different levels of magnification of. Color can be divided into "vertical component" and "lateral chromatic aberration."

RAW format can use the software to correct the color problem. The principle is the first manufacturer to detect differences in the color of the lens itself, and then make a configuration file, the software according to the configuration file for this lens taken out of the RAW file to correct. In general, the original lens can automatically correct color in the shooting, but if it is to use non-original lens or the lens manufacturer, which has no color detection. You can manually correct him. Of course, the original test results out of the correction are not good.

3   Summary

In short, in addition to digital SLR, more and more digital cameras can also shoot in RAW format. RAW is not just the thing that professional photographers have used. If used properly, a few simple steps can significantly improve the quality of photos, such as color cast, exposure, etc. are not allowed to frequently asked questions, almost all RAW formats can be used to solve.

If you have been accustomed to using the JPG format, the use of RAW format is not yet confident that when, as the first camera to save the format is set to RAW + JPG, then the camera will also save both formats. You first or the basis used method to adjust the JPG format, and then learn to use the camera manufacturers to give you a special deal with RAW format JPG format software to output JPG format images, by comparing directly save a JPG image and use the RAW format conversion out of JPG photos, you will understand the truth.

Acknowledgment. This paper is a key research project of the humanities and social science in Yibin University, as well as a project funded by the key subject of Education in Yibin University and the project number is 2011 Z18.

References

1. Applications and digital photo file format introduced, Jun Shang Color Film, http://wo.fengniao.com/117/article_116385.html
2. Yao, P.: On the color image processing teaching quantitative analysis. Shidai Wenxue 126, 150–151 (2008)
3. Soso baike, http://baike.soso.com/v6636262.htm?pid=baike.box

Anti-terrorism Anti-drug Terahertz Automatic Security Check Technology

Hong Zhu and Guang Ouyang

The Third Research Institute of Ministry of Public Security
Shanghai, 201204, China
zhzj339@163.com

Abstract. This paper introduces the characteristics of terahertz technology, discusses the terahertz detection and imaging of anti-terrorism in drug control automatic security technology in application of terahertz technology as a new generation of perception means undertook discussing, analysis of the automatic inspection of terahertz detection and imaging equipment, on the future of modular low cost terahertz detection imaging automatic security technology wide application is prospected.

Keywords: automatic security check, Terahertz ray, Time-domain and Frequency-Domain detection, Scanning imaging, Anti-terrorism, Contraband.

1 Summary

Now the world, terrorist attacks and drugs serious threat the life of people. The gunman walks carrying the gun, burst happened in many where, the bodies become the carrier of concealed carrying drugs, weapons, explosives. In this regard, countries attached great importance to security check as a means of prevention measure. Exploration in clothes weapons and contraband goods in one of the best means is the terahertz ray detection and the terahertz radiation imaging, this new type of sensing technology makes security into an automatic security check a brand new era. The terahertz radiation is harmless to people, the terahertz detection and terahertz imaging equipment is relied on finding masked things and don't worry there will be like the X-ray that damage.

2 The Application and Characteristic of the Terahertz Radiation

For frequencies in the 0.1 ~ 10THz range of THz wave, wavelength is 30um ~ 3mm range, in the microwave and infrared radiation. It serves as a kind of electromagnetic wave for non metal body penetrating, plastics, ceramics, paper and cloth and other nonpolar material dielectric absorption is very small, water and other polar materials on its absorption, reflection metal on it. Metal reflector and the ray high transmittance and refractive index of the polyethylene material for focusing the collimated lens operation, through the perspective or reflection detection mode of objects in non

M. Zhao and J. Sha (Eds.): ICCIP 2012, Part II, CCIS 289, pp. 632–638, 2012.

destructive nature analysis or the perspective imaging in THz band. It is common for the carton packaging, clothing in the terahertz radiation becomes transparent, detection of explosives, drugs THz band spectral feature can be found in contraband, showing the shape about a metal body and the other object in the weapon, on their camouflage becomes difficult, is the ideal means of automatic security perception. Terahertz radiation is non-ionizing, 1THz photon energy only 4meV, ratio of soft X ray small by six orders of magnitude, people can secure the acceptance and use of terahertz technology check[1].

Study of terahertz ray detection of contraband mechanism. On one hand it and physical molecular interaction energy absorption and scattering, although the photon energy is small, but the pulse frequency spectrum, explosives, drugs and other non-polar substances and the interaction of the molecular vibration-rotation motion as well as other energy conversion, in the THz band to produce some measurable, specific spectral features. When the THz pulse laser photons to the GHz ~ THz wide spectrum energy bombardment detection objects, allowing the detection of molecular structure of the micro structure to generate THz frequency changes and in the THz band has characteristic absorption peak, can test the absorption peak of spectral line frequency and intensity data to calculate the absorption rate of dielectric constant of photoconductive rate parameters to qualitative analysis of the measured object composition. On the other hand detection mechanism is when the computer control the dot probe for scanning a surface area at the time of detection, can obtain the area within the object shape and properties, using its penetrability and high signal to noise ratio, can be safely to the people of material security, security ideal sensing technology, as the important occasions automatic detection of the body or parcel of explosive drug weapon provides a new effective method[2].

3   Using Terahertz Technology Automatically Detects the Packaging of the Contraband

Accurate detection for packaging of the contraband, with terahertz spectroscopy analysis of the effect of no less than of Raman spectroscopy and infrared spectroscopy analysis, because the material THz pulse wave vibration spectrum of precision is better than ordinary light Raman scattering and infrared absorption spectrum and Raman spectroscopy, and infrared spectrum analysis can not penetrate the bags and clothes to telemetry analysis in which the explosive drugs. The terahertz spectroscopy of contraband detection using time-domain analysis of transmission spectrum detection, by pulsed THz ray in the packaging of the suspicious object to test its absorption peak position number and sample library absorption peak data contrast to determine whether contraband. Due to the time domain pulse sampling measurement, can greatly suppress background infrared noise interference, although the current technology can only get low terahertz ray average power limit the effect of distance, but as a result of terahertz pulsed high peak power, in coherent detection is used in terahertz pulse real-time power rather than the average power, can have 10^5 times a high signal to noise ratio.

THz time-domain automatic detection technology is composed of the following parts: a femtosecond laser pulse with terahertz ray generator, ray optical focusing lens, THz wave coherent spectroscopy detector, computer processing controller and automatic scanning mechanism (Figure 1). When the femtosecond pulsed laser by ray generator excitation nonlinear crystal THz ray generated by mirror convergent irradiation by security objects, through or reflecting information received by the THz ray contains security object molecular rovibrational THz spectrum and the system background noise. In the time domain coherent detection, THz ray with beam splitting device one divides into two. A beam is used to measure the object, the absorption spectrum, the other beam as a reference phase of the original spectra, measured information spectroscopy combined with the original spectra by the polarization light and computer calculation of two axis numerical changes. High-pass filtering method to get high frequency measured THz absorption spectrum of each wave number and strength, removing the pulse ray itself and background of the low frequency effects, a better method is to use a Michelson interferometer Fourier-transform method measuring terahertz spectroscopy section of each absorption peak, to make more accurate reading peak. Because of the absorption peak position by the molecular structure of the material in the corresponding energy level decisions, with similar light repeatability, through building sample database using computer matching, a variety of contraband detection[3].

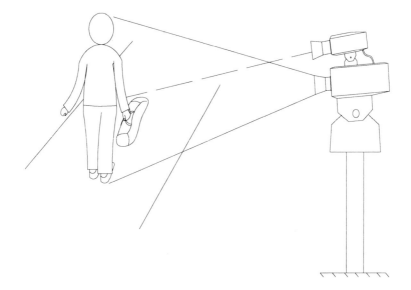

Fig. 1. A kind of the automatic security schemes of the terahertz radiation

Study of related components: ray generator is through the use of solid laser pumped Ti: sapphire and locking mechanism are femtosecond ultrashort laser pulses, relying on a photoconductive or optical rectification technology of THz ray; also available novel quantum cascade laser or THz field effect tube and so on to get the THz pulse; using nonlinear difference frequency process (DFG) and parametric process can produce a continuous THz ray; maximum power THz wave output is the free electron laser, when solve the miniaturization of electronic beam accelerator and vacuum undulator structure ,the miniaturization free electron laser will promote long-distance large-area terahertz security technology development.

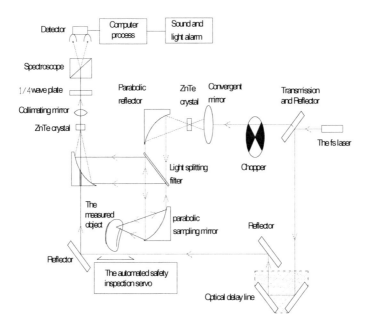

Fig. 2. Terahertz spectrum detection system diagram

Pulsed terahertz rays and time domain detection is dependent on the repetition frequency of more than tens of MHz fs laser pulse, after beam splitting mirror for detecting light and the reference light, the reference light, a detection beam path time delay and the detection of light will cooperate to provide baseline phase detector can realize the synchronous detection. Detection of light along the optical axis of the detection window converging mirror irradiated objects ahead, ray vertical focus on a target test object surface or internal, window receiving objective to collect objects reflecting THz information beam and the reference light and a polarization detector using balance method to detect THz spectral information, send computer detected objects and material parameters and terahertz spectrum sample library than for probabilistic analysis of whether contraband, terahertz detection in the database of the system get the support of the object on the qualitative analysis, security detection results are contraband alarm[4] [5].

The computer processing controller to control the THz ray generator by a femtosecond laser and pulse wavelength stabilization, controlling the lens focal plane position and the spectrometer receives, for terahertz absorption spectrum computation and sample library data comparison, the sample library data storage of explosives drug Thz band characteristic absorption peak position data and common goods packaging absorption peak data computer use, differential spectrum method to remove the interference of other items to calculate probability judgment is contraband to alarm.

The computer control of terahertz detection scanning mechanism according to the requirement, it is based on the detection of target shape recognition by computer control of objects launched fine scanning THz ray and receiving and transmitting or penetrate out of the terahertz information beam precision machinery mechanism, can be used for items for two-dimension scanning and longitudinal section scanning, automatic step focusing optical system so that the system has a search and detection function.

Automatic security mechanism is on important occasions entrances or on the way to the pedestrian passageways terahertz detection device, through a set of servo system on the detection region after people were scanning terahertz time domain property test. Since the dot probe scanning frequency is low, the larger the scan time need a few more minutes, the solution can be used in a number of points at the same time scanning for the detection of reducing time. Further, by using multiple beam pulses of terahertz ray generator and a linear array of THz spectroscopy detection, application of terahertz devices improve ray output intensity and pulse frequency, reducing the volume of the equipment, the production of multiple nonlinear crystal THz photoconductive sampling conversion while receiving multiple beam THz ray information, thus the area of terahertz time-domain detection terahertz spectrum information of objects, through fast terahertz automatic security.

4   Terahertz Imaging Security Technology

Along with the variety of high power terahertz lasers and ultrafast scanning detection technology for terahertz imaging, which provided reliable excitation light source and practical device. Terahertz imaging in two main aspects of the research, point-by-point scanning terahertz imaging and infrared focal plane array terahertz imaging technique, has made some progress, the best results have been achieved on twenty meters away from the people, the terahertz imaging shooting, now research increases ray power, hope for more for people in the distance, for terahertz imaging, to meet the needs of automatic inspection and other applications. Figure 2 is on the sidewalk, the terahertz imaging automatic security diagram[6].

Point by point scanning terahertz imaging is the basic principle of terahertz pulse laser beam through a collimated light path, the light beam is focused on the sample to be tested on a single point or arrays of multiple point detection area scan imaging. A computer controlled scanning linear stepping platform for samples or emission imaging device in optical Jiao Chu two-dimensional translational. The time domain method for terahertz pulsed imaging as ray, precise two-dimensional scanning, can test and record the image or reflection from the sample through the sample of terahertz electromagnetic wave intensity and phase and other parameters, composition of the terahertz image sample. Although this imaging modality in the long time, the large articles scanning imaging require tens of minutes above, but this imaging method to obtain a large amount of information, which can construct two and three images, and each pixel corresponding source of a terahertz time-domain spectroscopy, based on time domain spectrum FFT can be obtained in every the terahertz frequency response spectrum. In this way the human body and the security package can be used as precision security technology, can be used as the extension and supplement of X-ray method.

The focal plane array shot terahertz image on anti-terrorism drug security plays an important role, it can quickly shoot and found that the tested person carrying firearms and contraband shape, through active way of terahertz ray irradiation on THz band electromagnetic waves sensitive array sensor for terahertz photography or videography. Laser pumped by a nonlinear crystal frequency difference or parameter generating terahertz lasers or ray generator can emission reached watt level continuous THz ray, ray through the clothes by the lens focus, cases concentrated in people or things, with cryogenic infrared focal plane array uptake of terahertz optical reflection or transmission intensity, energy get all kinds of objects of different absorption and reflectivity of the pattern of security. But as a result of human blood on THz wave absorption, the body if the drug hidden explosives placed due to blood high decay rate and ray is difficult to penetrate into the interior through or reflected, for in vivo object security needs comprehensive detection technology[7][8].

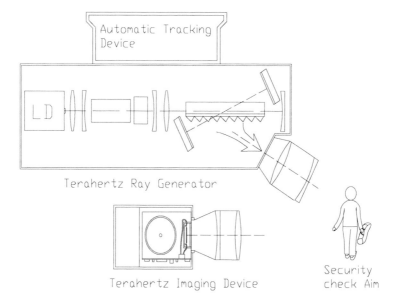

Fig. 3. The parameter terahertz radiation and pyroelectric face array THz camera diagram

Because of the far infrared focal plane array THz band response is very low still, with ultra low temperature refrigeration to reduce background noise for imaging. But the nonlinear pyroelectric array without refrigeration for THz imaging with promotion. Especially the use of lithium tantalate crystal thin film pyroelectric sensor array for THz band imaging, by thinning technique to achieve high sensitivity, is the future practical terahertz imaging device. The present continuous ray generator output energy is weak, is to further research and improvement. Future miniaturized free electron laser can produce high power THz electromagnetic wave output, for remote terahertz imaging to provide adequate security terahertz radiation emitter. Figure 3 is the use of parametric technology generation of terahertz ray with thin pyroelectric array for terahertz imaging structure sketch map.

5   Conclusion

Because the terrorists and drug dealers will be explosive drugs firearms hidden in the body, the inside of the package and goods, was a clever disguise, single eye is difficult to find, rely on terahertz technology penetration and perspective of physical analysis and shape detection, can be found inside the clothes and backpacks in contraband.Terahertz radiation is safe for people, with terahertz radiation efficiency and strength to further improve, terahertz time-domain detection from the point of scanning probe to the development of the line type multipoint beam rapid scan time of detection, but also for terahertz time-domain detection imaging security application provides practical techniques, is developing.

Terahertz automatic security technology is safe for people with new sensing technology, information processing technology and development of laser technology and new technology means. Combined with the city security network, forming a multi-layered perceptron network, is the public security network part. It will make the gangsters and criminals early exposure, compress their activity space, with intelligent perceptual significance. Terahertz detection with terahertz fluoroscopic imaging for automatic security provides applicable sense technology, promoted the city security development, has become the research hotspot of the field, will lead to a new stage of rapid development.

References

1. Siegel, P.H.: Terahertz technology. IEEE Transactions on Microwave Theory and Technology 50, 910 (2002)
2. Nagel, M., Bolivar, P.H., Brucherseifer, M., et al.: Integratated THz technology for label-free genetic diagnostics. Appl. Peys. Lett. 80, 154 (2002)
3. Jiang, Z.P., Zhang, X.C.: 2D measurement and spatio-temporal coupling of few-cycle THz pulses (November 1999)
4. Kawase, K., Ogawa, Y., Watanable, Y., et al.: Non-destructive terahertz imaging of illicit drugs using spectral fingerprints. Optics Express 11(20), 2549–2554 (2003)
5. Kawase, K., Hatanaka, T., Takahashi, H., et al.: Tunable terahertz-wave generation from DAST cystal by dualsignal-wave parametric oscillation of periodically poled lithiumniobate. Opt. Lett. 25(23), 1714–1716 (2000)
6. Sherwin, M.S., Schmuttenmaer, C.A., Bucksbaum, P.H., Editors: Opportunities in THz Science. Report of a DOE-NSF-NIHWorkshop, Arlington, VA, February12-14 (2004)
7. Redo, A., Karpowicz, N., Zhang, X.C.: Sensing and imaging with continuous-wave terahertz systems (October 2006)
8. Chiang, A.C., Wang, T.D., Lin, Y.Y., et al.: Enhancedterahertz-wave parametric generation and oscillation in lithiumniobate waveguides at terahertz frequencies. Optics Letters 30(24), 3392–3394 (2005); Published in Chinese Journal of Laser 33(10), 1349–1359 (2006)

Evaluation on the Regional Ecological Security Based on Support Vector Machine and GIS

Jingyi Tian[1] and Lihua Huang[2]

[1] Department of Environment Science and Engineering, Northeastern University
at Qinhuangdao, Qinhuangdao, China
[2] State Key Laboratory of Powder Metallurgy, Central South University, Changsha, China
tianjingyi135@163.com, huanglihuamzl@sina.com

Abstract. According to the basic concepts of ecological security, the evaluation index system with the health- service- risk framework has been established in this paper, and the standard values as well as the evaluation levels of ecological security has been also determined. At the same time, the simulation model of the ecological security evaluation based on the support vector machine has been also established in this paper. This model is based on the statistical theory, which has the rigorous theoretical and mathematical foundations as well as the good generalization ability. Meanwhile, the problem that the complexity of algorithm is closely related with the input vectors has been solved. Through the adoption of kernel functions, the nonlinear problem in the input space has been mapped to the high-dimensional feature space where the linear discrimination function has been constructed. It mainly refers to the limited sample trees, which has avoided the local minimum problems which can't be solved by neural network. In this paper, the support vector machine and the GIS technology have been employed to conduct the spatial and quantitative evaluation for the ecological security through taking Qinhuangdao in Hebei province as example.

Keywords: Ecological security evaluation, support vector machine, index system, GIS, Qinhuangdao.

1 Introduction

Being in the joint area of two geological units-north china and northeast china, located in middle part of western bank of Bohai Bay, Qinhuangdao is an important city in the economic zone around Bohai. Since the end of 1980s, Qinhuangdao quickened its urbanization process obviously, leading to decrease of regional environmental quality, facing with serious ecological safety, which began to affect its sustainable development. Meanwhile, this issue attracted high attention from Qinhuangdao municipal government. The evaluation on ecological safety is identification, judge and research on ecological system integrity and its sound and sustainable development faced with various risks; the evaluation on ecological safety is quantitative description of bad or good quality of ecological environmental system

M. Zhao and J. Sha (Eds.): ICCIP 2012, Part II, CCIS 289, pp. 639–646, 2012.

safety. the key contents of the evaluation on ecological safety is evaluation on ecological risk and health and the evaluation on ecological safety plays a leading role in human safety.

2   The Construction of the Index System of Regional Ecological Security

According to the interrelationships between the ecological security influence factors and the socio-economic sustainable development, the ecological security evaluation refers to the boundary to analyze the ecological security and the ecological insecurity based on the influence and the constraints of ecological environment on the socio-economic sustainable development. At the same time, it also employs a series of security evaluation indexes to distinct the degree of ecological security. This method contains the influence factor analysis, the evaluation index system and the evaluation method of ecological security, the ecological security threshold and some others[1-3].

Based on the concept of ecological security, the index system in this paper has combined the characteristics of complex ecosystem and selected the ecological health, the ecological risk and the ecosystem services to establish the evaluation index system. According to the relationships between the various components of evaluation objects, the multi-level evaluation index system has been established. Generally speaking, the index system of the regional ecological security evaluation can be summarized as the following hierarchy system, which can be shown in Table 1.

3   The Determination of the Evaluation Levels and the Standards of Ecological Security Index

As for the regional ecological security evaluation, the ecological security has been comprehensively evaluated. The evaluation levels can be divided into five levels: the security status, the safer status, the early warning status, the middle alarm status and the heavy alarm status.

I . Safe status: basically complete ecological environment service function. The ecological environment is basically not intervened and damaged; the ecological environmental structure is complete with strong function; the restoration capability of ecological system is strong; the ecological disaster is less and the damage to ecological system is not serious.

II . Relatively safe status: Relatively complete ecological environment service function. The ecological environment is seldom intervened and damaged; the ecological environmental structure is relatively complete with strong function; the restoration capability of ecological system is good; the ecological disaster is relatively less and the damage to ecological system is not serious.

III . Primary warning status: the service function of ecological environment is degenerated. The ecological environment is intervened and damaged to some extents;

the ecological system structure is changed a little bit, but can maintain its basic function; the restoration capability of ecological system is bad and is easy to deteriorate after interference; the ecological disasters happen sometime; the damage to ecological system is seeable;

IV. Medium warning status: the service function of ecological environment is seriously degenerated. The ecological environment is intervened and damaged to large extents; the ecological system structure is changed a lot and the system function is also degenerated; the restoration capability of ecological system is much bad and is difficult to deteriorate after interference; the ecological disasters happen frequently; the damage to ecological system is big;

V. High warning status: the service function of ecological environment is losed. The ecological process is very difficult to reversed; the ecological environment is damaged seriously; the ecological system structure is incomplete and the system function is also losed; the recovery and restoration capability of ecological system is very difficult; the ecological issue is huge and frequently evolved into ecological disaster;

It is required to determine the security standard values of each index in the ecological security evaluation. In other words, it is necessary to establish a quantitative reference frame to measure the ecological security. The security levels can be determined through the comparison of the reference frame so as to identify the development objectives.

The writer takes the following detailed methods to choose evaluation standard in this paper:

1、Standards regulated by the state, industry and local, including environment quality standard published by the state, evaluation specifications, regulations and design required by published by the environment industry and standards and environmental protection area target, protection requirements, water system protection requirements of rivers as well as protection requirements of special areas.

2、Background standard, take background value of ecological environment in the researched area as evaluation standard.

3 、Analogy standard. Take similar ecological environment not intervened seriously by human or raw and natural ecological system under similar natural conditions as analogy standard; take ecological gene and function of similar conditions as analogy standard.

According to the determination basis of evaluation standards, the security standards of the ecological security evaluation index in Qinhuangdao have been determined through referring the five levels, which can be shown in Table 1.

Table 1. The index system and the standards of ecological security evaluation in Qinhuangdao

Criterion level	Index	V	IV	III	II	I
Vitality	Normalized vegetation index	[0 0.2)	[0.2 0.4)	[0.4 0.6)	[0.6 0.8)	[0.8 1]
	High-ecological function composite index	[0 0.2)	[0.2 0.4)	[0.4 0.6)	[0.6 0.8)	[0.8 1]
	Per capita GDP(Ten thousand yuan/ person)	[0 0.8)	[0.8 1)	[1 3)	[3 15)	[15 50]
Organiza--tional structure	CONTAG	(0 20]	(20 40]	(40 60]	(60 80]	(80 100]
	Population density(person/Km²)	[6000 1000]	[500 1000]	(300 500]	[300 100)	[0 100]
	Area weighted average patch fractal index	[1 1.1)	[1.1 1.2)	[1.2 1.3)	[1.3 1.4)	[1.4 1.5]
Elasticity	Ecological elastic degree	[0 0.2)	[0.2 0.4)	[0.4 0.6)	[0.6 0.8)	[0.8 1)
	Proportion of environmental investment in GDP(%)	[0 1.0)	[1.0 1.5)	[1.5 2.0)	[2.0 2.5)	[2.5 5]
Services	Eco-environmental quality index	[0 20)	[20 35)	[35 55)	[55 75)	[75 100]
	Soil erosion (tons/Km²)	(8000 10000]	(5000 8000]	(2500 5000]	(500 2500]	[0 500]
	Urban pollution index good weather(%)	[0 50)	[50 70)	[70 80)	[80 90)	[90 100]
	Per capita water resources(m³/person)	[0 1000)	[1000 17000)	[1700 2200]	[2200 3000)	[3000 8000]
Risk	Human disturbance index	(0.8 1]	(0.6 0.8]	(0.4 0.6]	(0.2 0.4]	[0.2 0]
	Probability of drought	(0.59 1]	(0.35 0.59]	(0.24 0.35]	(0.12 0.24]	[0 0.12]
	Probability of flooding	(0.49 1]	(0.19 0.49]	(0.11 0.19]	(0.005 0.11]	[0 0.005]
	Fertilizer consumption (tons/km²)	(50 100]	(40 50]	(22.5 40]	(10 22.5]	[0 10]

4   The Establishment of the Regional Ecological Security Evaluation Model

4.1   The Establishment of the Model

According to the instance of ecological security evaluation

$$(x_i, y_i) \ (i = 1, 2, \cdots k)$$

$x_i \in R^n$ refers to the evaluation index of ecological security and $y_i \in R$ refers to the levels of ecological security.

As for the ecological security evaluation model based on SVM, it actually looks for the relationship between x_i and y_i. According to the SVM theory, there is

$$y_i = SVM(x_i, p) \qquad (i = 1, 2, \cdots k) \qquad (1)$$

In this formula, x_i refers to the 16 indexes of ecological security evaluation, which can be shown in Table 1. y_i refers to the levels of ecological security and there are five levels, namely the security status, the safer status, the early warning status, the middle alarm status and the heavy alarm status. p is the parameter of model, which includes the penalty parameter C and the kernel function parameter. This parameter can be obtained by the sample (x_i, y_i) $(i = 1, 2, \cdots k)$.

4.2   The Selection of the Training Samples and the Testing Samples

The training samples have employed the rand function of MATLAB and each index interpolates to form the training samples with the uniform and random distribution at all levels of evaluation criteria. There are 400 at all levels of standard ranges, which will form 2000 training samples.

The testing samples are generated by the same method. There are 80 randomly generated in each level range, which will form 400 testing samples.

4.3   The Tools

OSU-SVM is formed by JunshuiMa and Yi Zhao based on Lib SVM version 2.33 of Dr. Lin, which can be easily used above the MATLAB environment and that has the strong multi-class classification ability. There are also the instructions for use and the reference examples in the tool box, which has the features such as the versatility. The use steps of the tool box can be shown as follows:

Firstly, the preparation of data: it is required to introduce the sample data to MATLAB.

Secondly, the set of the model parameters: according to the theory of support vector machine, the set parameters should include the penalty parameter, the kernel function and the kernel function parameter. The default penalty parameter C=1, the default kernel function is the RBF kernel function and the kernel function parameter Gamma=1. As the model parameters don't have the theoretical solutions, the default parameter values are not necessarily the optimal parameters. In the actual calculations, the parameters are generally obtained through several adjustments and spreadsheets.

Thirdly, the learning: it is necessary to call the training function RbfSVM and a specific SVM model will be got in return.

Fourthly, the testing: it is required to call the testing function SVMTest. The SVM model established by this function has the results of the correct classification of testing samples, namely the correct rate. The reliability of the SVM model can be evaluated by the correct rate and then determine whether it is required to continuously adjust the model parameters.

Fifthly, the prediction: it is necessary to call the classification function SVMClass and use the established model to predict the given object data. The predicted results should be returned.

4.4   The Establishment of the Evaluation Model

In fact, the establishment of the evaluation model refers to the process in which the model parameter p is determined by the sample data. After determining the learning samples, the establishment of the ecological security evaluation model is mainly to select the appropriate parameters of support vector machine: the penalty parameter C, the kernel function and the kernel function parameter. They have greatly influenced the predicted results and their reasonable determination will directly affect the accuracy and the generalization ability of model. In this paper, through the test for the various kernel functions, it is ultimately determined that the kernel function of the ecological security evaluation model is the RBF kernel function and the parameter Gamma=2. C=100 can be determined through a large number of tests of C value so as to establish a specific ecological security evaluation model.

It is required to adopt the established model to test the testing samples and the accuracy rate is 90%. From the test results, we can find that the establishment of this model is reasonable and reliable[4].

5   The Determination of the Information Map Unit in Study Areas

According to the advantages and the disadvantages of vector information map unit and the grid information map unit, they have been combined in this paper, namely the grid is considered as the basic information map unit which has ensured the accuracy of the spatial distribution of data as the data carrier. The vector information map unit is regarded as the comprehensive information map unit and both of them should be coupled.

Firstly, the basic information map unit in study areas is gird. According to the range of study areas, the mapping scale and the spatial resolution, the grid unit in study areas is determined as 25m×25m.

Secondly, the comprehensive information map unit in study areas is the small watershed. The small watershed refers to the regional unit with the complete natural ecological process. Taking the small watershed as the comprehensive information map unit, the information can be integrated according to the evaluation results of grid information map unit, which can overcome the deficiencies of the above grid information map unit in applications. In this paper, the ArcGIS based on the digital terrain analysis function has been employed to conduct the small watershed segmentation in Qinhuangdao so as to establish the comprehensive evaluation information map unit of the ecological security evaluation.

The study areas can be divided into 84 small watersheds. The average area is below 100km^2 and the upper limit should be below 20km^2.

6   The Ecological Security Evaluation Based on SVM

Based on the above model SVM, the division of the levels of ecological security evaluation in Qinhuangdao has been achieved through running in MATLAB.

The ecological security of 84 small watersheds can be divided into five levels, namely the security status, the safer status, the early warning status, the middle alarm status and the heavy alarm status, which are respectively represented by 1, 2, 3, 4 and 5. The statistical results can be shown in Table 2.

Table 2. The statistical table of the ecological security levels in Qinhuangdao

Security levels	Number of watershed	Area (Km²)	Area percentage (%)
I	13, 15, 20, 30, 33, 37, 38, 43, 60, 61, 62, 69, 81	970	12.39
II.	12, 17, 22, 24, 31, 32, 35, 36, 44, 45, 46, 47, 51, 52, 56, 63, 64, 72, 74, 75, 76,	1589	20.35
III	1, 2, 4, 14, 18, 21, 28, 29, 34, 48, 49, 54, 55, 66, 67, 68, 71, 73, 80	2233	28.59
IV	3, 9, 10, 16, 19, 26, 27. 39, 40, 41, 50, 53, 65, 70, 78, 79, 84	1656	21.20
IV	5, 6, 7, 8, 11, 23, 25, 42, 57, 58, 59, 77, 82, 83	1366	17.49

Then the statistical results can be shown in ArcGIS and the spatial distribution can be shown in Figure 1.

The results have shown that we should pay more attention to the ecological security in Qinhuangdao: the area of security region and safer region accounts for 32.74% of the whole area and the area of early warning status accounts for 28.59%. However, the area of heavy alarm region and middle alarm region accounts for 38.69% of the whole area. These watersheds are mainly concentrated in County, the urban area of Qinhuangdao and the coastal zones.

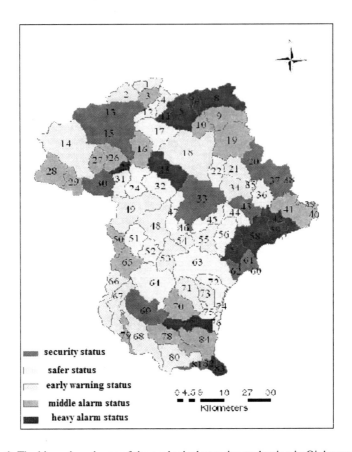

Fig. 1. The hierarchy scheme of the ecological security evaluation in Qinhuangdao

References

1. Xie, H., Li, B.: A Study on Indices System and Assessment Criterion of Ecological Security for City. Journal of Beijing Normal University (Natural Science) 40(5), 705–710 (2004)
2. Liu, Y., Liu, Y., Xu, P.: Evaluation on Ecological Security of Regional Land Resources: A Case Study of Jiaxing City, Zhejiang Province. Resources Science 26(3), 69–75 (2004)
3. Wang, M., Wang, J., Liu, J.: Research on Urban Eco-security Assessment—A Case Study of Changchun. Journal of Arid Land Resources and Environment 21(3), 72–76 (2007)
4. Gong, X., Kuh, A.: Support Vector Machine for multiuser detection in CDMA communications. In: at Manoa Source: Conference Record of the Asilomar Conference on Signals, Systems and Computers, Univ of Hawaii at Manoa Source, pp. 680–684, 1058–6393. IEEE (1999)

Analysis of Reducing the Harmonic Voltage of PM Wind Generator with Pole Width Modulation

Hao Yuan, Yuejun An, Hui An, Dan Sun, and Liping Xue

School of Electrical Engineering, Shenyang University of Technology
Shenyang, 110870 China
anyj_dq@sut.edu.cn

Abstract. The harmonic voltage is an important indicator to evaluate the power quality of permanent magnet(PM) wind generator. Voltage waveform is closely related to the degree of the air-gap magnetic field waveforms sinusoidal in the generator, so generator structure optimization to improve the degree of air-gap magnetic field sinusoidal is an effective method to improve the quality of generator voltage waveform. This paper presents a method called pole width modulation (PWM) method to reduce harmonic voltage of PM wind generator. Do respectively finite element analysis to traditional surface permanent magnet generator and a new very wide modulation permanent-magnet generator; and then develop two structure prototypes and build voltage waveform experimental equipment to study them. Finite element analysis and prototype experiments show that the pole width modulation method is one of the effective and feasible technologies on reducing the harmonic voltage of PM wind generator.

Keywords: wind generator, permanent magnet generator, pole width modulation, voltage waveform, harmonic Analysis.

1 Introduction

With energy and environmental issues become more prominent, as a clean, renewable energy, wind power develops quickly in the world and the power generation of grid operation increasing. However, the harmonics of the permanent magnet wind generator voltage waveform easily lead to capacitors and cables overheating, insulation aging, shorten life, even damaged; at the same time the harmonics will lead to the local utility grid parallel resonance and series resonance, so that it is magnified, greatly increase the danger, even cause serious accidents; In addition, the high harmonics will interfere with nearby communications systems, generate noise, lower communication quality, makes the communication system can not function properly.

Here depended on the air-gap magnetic field waveforms, we propose a new pole width modulation method to reduce the voltage harmonic of surface permanent magnet wind generator [1],[2],[3].

M. Zhao and J. Sha (Eds.): ICCIP 2012, Part II, CCIS 289, pp. 647–655, 2012.

2   Pole Modulation Method for PM Generator

The method is that air gap sinusoidal magnetic field waveforms under every pole are divided into N equal parts, with N same amplitude but different width rectangular magnetic field component waveforms to replace the sinusoidal air-gap magnetic field waveform so that the midpoint of the rectangle and the mid-point of divided part of the corresponding sine wave coincide, and the rectangular wave area and sine wave divided parts equal to determine the width of permanent magnet arrays and central angle parameters. Now we use novel magnet arrayed permanent magnet generator which has five permanent magnets of each pole to illustrate this new type of rotor structure reducing effect on the harmonic voltage, as shown in Fig. 1.

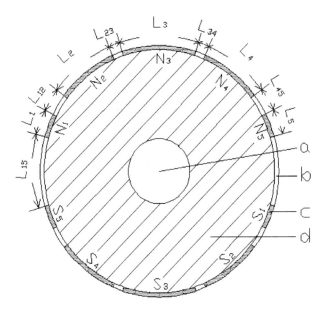

a-shaft b-padding c-permanent magnet d-rotor core

Fig. 1. PWM rotor by each pole from 5 arrays magnets

As shown in Fig. 2, sine wave amplitude and the modulated square wave have the same height in the equivalent, setting sine function expression for the $B = B_M \sin\theta$, B_M is flux density amplitude which can calculate the width and midpoint interval of the rectangular wave. Calculated the width and spacing of rectangular wave is a proportional relationship, when design specific rotor structure; we need according to this ratio to arrange each magnet pole corresponding central angle with the actual circumference of rotor.

According to this method, the proportional relationship of five permanent magnets each pole corresponding central angle is 1.9:5:6.2:5:1.9[4],[5].

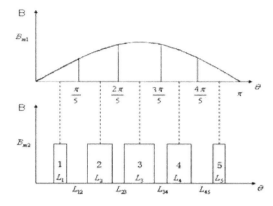

Fig. 2. Modulation permanent-magnet array schematic diagram

3 Finite Element Analysis of Generator

Using the relevant parameters given in the table 1 and 2 to establish the generator finite element model by ansoft.

Table 1. The main parameters of generator

parameter	value
P_N/kW	0.8
$n_N/r/min$	1000
gap/mm	0.3
poles and Slops	6 and 36
Stator diameter/mm	155
core length/mm	53

Table 2. The magnet specific actions of generator

permanent magnet	rotor with pole wide modulation(PWM)	rotor with traditional surface PM
magnet type	N35SH	N35SH
B_r/T	1.20	1.20
$H_c/A/m$	876000	876000
pm thickness /mm	2.5	2.5
outside arc length of magnet 1,5 /mm	4.9694	-
outside arc length of magnet 2,4/mm	12.9419	-
outside arc length of magnet 3/mm	15.9855	-
outside arc length of each pole /mm	51.81	60.60

The magnetic field distribution of two types of PM generator by no-load is show in Fig. 3.

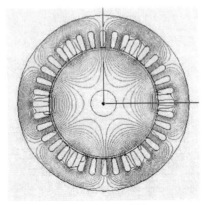

(a) Traditional surface PM generator

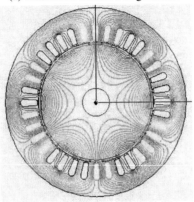

(b) PWM generator

Fig. 3. Model of the magnet arrayed permanent magnet generator

After calculation, we get the air gap flux density in Fig. 4, back EMF curve in Fig. 5.

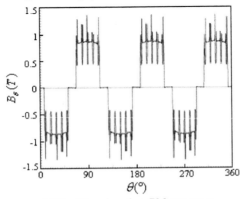

(a) Traditional surface PM generator

Fig. 4. Air gap flux density curve

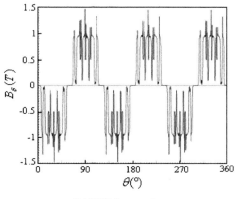

(b) PWM generator

Fig. 4. (*continued*)

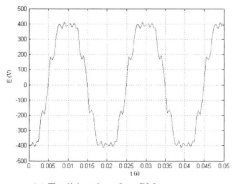

(a) Traditional surface PM generator

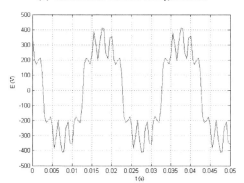

(b) PWM generator

Fig. 5. Simulation curve of potential

Fig. 4,5 visually show that the flux density waveform and voltage curve of the magnet arrayed permanent magnet generator are improved comparing with the traditional surface permanent magnet generator, it proves that modulation methods can reduce the voltage harmonic.

4 Prototype and Experiment

4.1 Prototypes

We design and develop two three-phase 380V, 800W permanent magnet synchronous generator as prototype. Stator is the same as shown in Fig. 6.

Fig. 6. Stator of PM wind generator (prototype)

For comparing and analyzing, the rotor were used to the traditional block rotor structure and the five permanent magnet pole width modulation rotor structure as shown in Fig. 7.

(a) Rotor with traditional surface PM

(b) Rotor with PWM

Fig. 7. Rotor of prototypes

4.2   Test for Voltage Waveform

The theoretical analysis and simulation show that the pole width modulation rotor structure can reduce voltage harmonics; voltage waveform is closer to sine wave. In order to verify the results we do experiment in the following. In this study we use the embedded detection coil to measure the voltage waveforms, it is that place a group of coils crossing a whole range on the stator openings, then we can get the voltage waveform by measuring the voltage of detection coil, apparatus and equipment shown in Fig. 8.

1 inverter 2 oscilloscopes 3 prime mover 4 tested generator

Fig. 8. Equipment for voltage waveform

For example, when the power frequency is 50Hz, the voltage waveforms of traditional rotor structure and pole width modulation rotor structure is shown in Fig. 9.

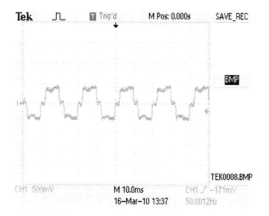

(a) Traditional surface PM rotor

Fig. 9. Voltage waveform at 50Hz

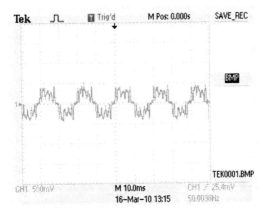

(b) PWM rotor

Fig. 9. (*continued*)

Use the discrete data sampled from the oscilloscope to write Matlab program for the preparation of Fourier harmonic analysis and compare with the simulation results, as shown in Fig. 10 and Fig. 11.

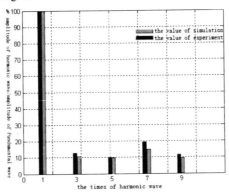

Fig. 10. Voltage harmonic analysis of traditional surface PM generator

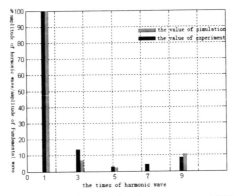

Fig. 11. Voltage harmonic analysis of magnet arrayed PM generator

From Fig. 10 and Fig. 11, both the simulation and experiment show in wind generator with pole width modulation (PWM) that sub-harmonic is significantly lower than the traditional surface permanent magnet wind generator.

5   Conclusion

Here presents a pole width modulation (PWM) method to reduce the voltage harmonics of wind permanent magnet generator.

Firstly, establishing finite element models to respectively analyze the traditional permanent magnet rotor structure and PWM rotor structure. The results show that the PWM rotor structure can reduce the voltage harmonic and improve the level of the sine wave; it proves PWM method has a theoretical possibility.

Then respectively develop the traditional block-type PM rotor structure and the PWM-type PM rotor structure prototypes, establish experimental system to sample and process the voltage waveform data and compared the experimental results with the theoretical results. It proves the method is correct and accurate.

The theoretical analysis and experimental comparison prove PWM method can significantly reduce the voltage harmonic and improve the level of the sine wave.

Acknowledgments. The first author would like to express his thanks to the Science and technology plan project of Liaoning (No.2010220011) and the Science and technology plan project of Shenyang (No.F11-190-7-00) for financial supported. At the same time, thank my collaborators for their cooperation.

References

1. Zhang, X.-F., Xu, D.-P., Lv, Y.-G.: Technical Development and Problems of Wind Turbines. Modern Electric Power (10), 29–34 (2003)
2. Zhu, G.-P., Wang, S.-M.: A Survey on Power Quality Control Technology. Automation of Electric Power Systems 26(19), 29–31 (2002)
3. Wang, X.-R., Wang, W.-S., Dai, H.-Z.: Present status and prospect of wind power in China. Electric Power 7(1), 81–84 (2004)
4. An, Y.-J., Sun, C.-Z.: A type of pole width modulation method of PMSM. China Patent: CN200720015431 (2007)
5. Popescu, M., Cistelecan, M.V., Melcescu, L.: Low Speed Directly Driven Permanent Magnet Synchronous Generator for Wind Energy Application, pp. 78–788. IEEE (2007)

Design and Implementation
of Embedded Forewarning System Based on GPRS

Heping Li and Yu Yi

Loudi Vocational & Technical College, Loudi Hunan, 417000, China
lhp13973812001@sina.com

Abstract. This paper presents a forewarning system of disastrous weather based on GPRS network. The upper computer is composed of a PC and a voice card for forewarning information distribution and the lower computer is composed of an embedded processor and a GSM /GPRS module as a forewarning terminal. The forewarning terminal can carry out sound and light alarm and voice broadcast, and it can control the rural broadcasting system according to the warning levels, thereby it can improve the efficiency of early warning.

Keywords: Forewarning system, GPRS, forewarning terminal, embedded system.

1 Introduction

China, with a vast territory and complicated natural conditions, is one of the few countries with world's worst natural disasters. In developed countries, advanced technologies and equipments have been applied to meteorological disaster prevention and mitigation. In the United States, the remote sensing technology of earth weather satellites and resource satellites have been used for meteorological disaster monitoring and warning. Even in remote mountainous areas, the local farmers can receive information through special FM radio receiver with RDS function. Even if in the closing state and upon receiving the warning information, the radio can automatically start up and broadcast. Radio, television, newspapers, Internet and other public media are mainly used to release weather broadcasting information in the domestic, but a common problem is the coverage of early warning information. The forewarning information released by the existing disaster warning system in urban and rural areas is not real-time, and worse still sometimes it cannot warn people effectively. The Meteorological Development Plan (2011-2015) notes that improving public meteorological service should be the main task of meteorological bureaus at all levels, and the time for releasing severe weather warning information will be in advance of 15 to 30 minutes during the Twelfth Five-year Program. Meteorological disaster prediction and warning as well as real-time monitoring of key, worth noting, severe and extreme weather events should be strengthened.

How to accurately convey the weather early warning information, the maximally reduce the disaster losses become an urgent need to solve major problems. The design under discussion in this paper, combined with the local broadcasting system, and the

M. Zhao and J. Sha (Eds.): ICCIP 2012, Part II, CCIS 289, pp. 656–662, 2012.
© Springer-Verlag Berlin Heidelberg 2012

existing mobile communication system, can provide early warning of disastrous weather events, especially in rural areas with frequent disasters and relatively backward communication networks, which is the solution to "last kilometer" problem of information early warning in the vast rural areas and remote mountainous areas.

2   Overall Structure of the Forewarning System

This system is mainly composed of a forewarning information distribution system and a forewarning terminal. In a province or a city, a forewarning information distributing system can be set, which is responsible for distributing forewarning information of disastrous weather events through text or audio messages. The forewarning terminal uses an ARM processor as the core, and the GSM/GPRS module is to receive warning information issued by the Information Center, and then send it to the ARM processor control center. The GSM module in the ARM processor controller is responsible to forward the forewarning information to turn on the broadcasting system and then broadcast the forwarding information. Meanwhile, it can display the forewarning information on the screen. System diagram is as shown in figure 1.

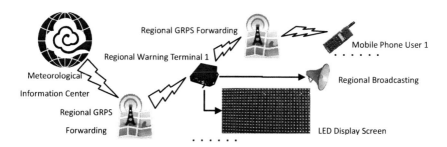

Fig. 1. Diagram of the System

3   Hardware Circuit Design

3.1   Structure of Forewarning Terminal

Embedded early warning terminal is as shown in figure 2. The ARM-Cortex-M3 processor (STM32F103) is used as the CPU; Flash memory is used for storing voice play list, a list of telephone numbers, user information (including user ID, user name, telephone number, the user address and other information), GB1232 Chinese characters dot matrix font and text message UCODE code and GB1232 table. Chip SRAM in the system works as space for program running, data storage and stack area. GSM/GPRS communication module is mainly responsible for voice communication and text message reception. In the remote mountainous area, people can use RDS radio to trigger the automatic boot for voice broadcast through the codes. Through the UART interface of the ARM processor, GSM/GPRS module can broadcast the forewarning information using a segmented mode. USB2.0 module connects forewarning terminal and PC machine, and updates the voice data (voice data stored in the TF card). Outdoor displaying module and liquid crystal displaying module are used for forewarning information display. Keyboard and state indicator light are mainly used to control and display the state of warning terminal. Users can set the name, phone number and other user information in the terminal through a PC. The embedded terminal store the above mentioned information as a format of file in the Flash Memory, while also record the standard font and text font GB1232.

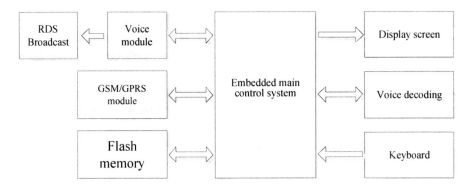

Fig. 2. Diagram of embedded forewarning terminal

3.2   Embedded Main Control System

The main control system is a hardware development platform established with the embedded ARM-Cortex-M3 processor, and loaded with the μc/os- II operating system. STM32F103VB is a high performance, low power 32 ARM processor. The system architecture of the processor in was modified, it has a single cycle multiplication, division of hardware and efficient Thumb2 instruction set, and will interrupt the delay between down to 6 CPU cycle. clock frequency of STM32 can be

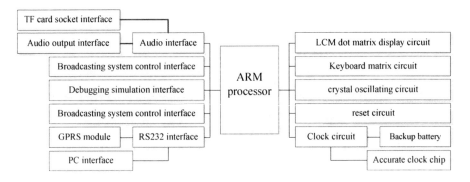

Fig. 3. Diagram of the embedded main control circuit

up to 72MHz per second, and can perform 2000000 times by add operation. The built-in Flash memory high up to 128K bytes and a SRAM of 20K bytes, have a wealth of general I / O port. In the standby mode, the current consumption is down to 2uA, and it has lower power consumption, which is fully applicable to the meteorological information monitoring and early warning.

ARM-Cortex-M3 is a popular embedded chip in the market, with mature technology and high portability. The μc/os-Ⅱ operating system is also widely used in all kinds of industrial control systems. It has open source codes, good real-time performance, portability, scalability, and is a fully preemptive multitasking real-time efficient kernel. The embedded main control circuit is as shown in figure 3.

3.3   GSM/GPRS Module Circuit

Siemens TC35i module is selected as the GSM/GPRS module. The TC35i module, with the features of small size, low power consumption and convenient integration, now become a more popular SMS module. TC35i and GSM2 / 2 + are compatible, and integrate RF with baseband, to provide users with the standard AT command interface, data, voice, short message provides fast, and reliable transmission. TC35i support GSM dual frequency, data, voice, fax and other short messages and short message data transmission, while short messages supports both PDU (Protocol Data Unit, protocol data unit) model, also supports the TEXT (text mode).

A standard RS232 interface is used between GSM/GPRS module and ARM processor, through which AT commands are sent for completion of the operation of the module. In the application design, when the processor needs communication between the RS232 serial port and the module, we only need to use the serial port of the two pins RX and TX, and the module also supports SIM card. The latest GSM/GPRS module has strong real-time performance in sending and receiving messages, and the module details are as shown in figure 4. Forewarning terminal uses an information processing system based on GSM/GPRS module, which can reliably receive forewarning information, and report back the state of real-time processing via the terminal to the forewarning center. The terminal can carry out sound and light alarm and voice broadcast, thus improving the efficiency of forewarning through the rural broadcasting system according to the warning levels. After the embedded terminal system receives messages from meteorological center, the system will send text messages to users according to user information in the Flash Memory, and read the user's feedback information to determine whether the messages are sent successfully. If the information cannot be received, the retransmission is progressing every 5 minutes, repeating 3 times.

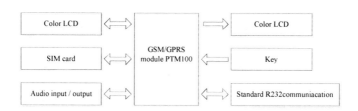

Fig. 4. Diagram of the GSM module

3.4   Voice Broadcasting Circuit

Voice Broadcasting Circuit can realize the repeated erasing of a great amount of speech content and can plug in a TF Card memory with a maximum capacity of 1GB by using the WTV020-SD module. Both WAV and AD4 format voice can be loaded, and speech content can be updated in PC directly through the TF card reader. The module supports FAT file system, AD4 voice of 6 KHz ~ 32 KHz and 36 KHz sampling rate and WAV audio of 6 KHz ~ 16 KHz sampling rate and it can also automatically recognize the voice sample rate and voice file format. The WTV020-SD module uses WTV020SD-20S voice chip as the main control core with second serial port controlling mode. The central controller sends data to controlWTV020-SD module via the CLK clock and DI data line; it can play the voice of any address and voice combination. The information output by the voice module is to be transmitted to the cable area broadcasting system and wireless data broadcasting system, and then the embedded processor sends control signals to control the two broadcasting systems reporting forewarning information. Specific module circuit is as shown in figure 5.

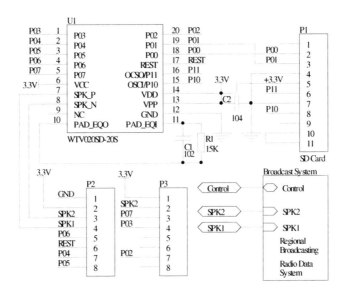

Fig. 5. Diagram of WTV020-SD circuit module

4   Software Design

μC / OS - II is a first-performed section of background process in the embedded system after starting the system and a user application program is to run on its various tasks. According to the requirement of each task, μC / OS - II will operate resource collocation, peripheral management, message management, task scheduling, and exception handling and so on.

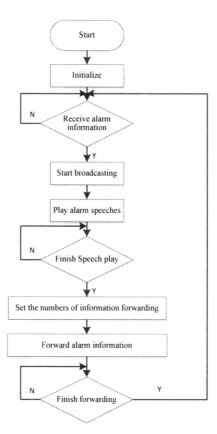

Fig. 6. Flow chart of program design

When developing application in the operating system transplanted with μC/OS- II, the document management system of μC/OS- II operating system is adopted to manage the FLASH memory reading and writing. This can not only ensure the reliability and stability of reading and writing FLASH, but also can greatly shorten the software development cycle. At the same time the FLASH data using the format of file is more convenient for computer management of data. In the PC computer, the corresponding statements and other documents can be directly generated with the alarm system data, which reduces the complexity of PC software, accelerates the speed of software development, and improves development efficiency.

This system adopts C language to program, and uses modular programming method in the preparation of programs. This increases the readability, portability, and makes the software more flexible in functional extension. Programming flow diagram is as shown in figure 6. According to the need of the forewarning system, the μC/OS- II is transplant. The embedded system communication program sends cycle commands and monitors forewarning information. If there is early warning information, the information will be immediately sent to each of the numbers stored in the phone. Then after the forewarning information being processed by the forewarning system, it will be broadcasted through radio. The software can also set time for the alarm information to be played, thus improving the reliability of the warnings.

5   Conclusion

The early warning system uses a 32-bit microprocessor as its core and a GPRS-based data transmission scheme, making the system real-time and more stable. Meanwhile, the system can also turn on the country's broadcasting system for early warning information dissemination and the information can also be displayed by LED dot matrix. The system has the advantages such as high efficiency, low cost, versatility, and 24/7 services. Not only can the system send out early warnings of disastrous weather events, but also work as a public information dissemination center in rural areas.

Acknowledgments. This work was supported by the Hunan Province Scientific and Technological Research Projects (2011SK3069, 08D108, 2011ZK003).

References

1. Wei, M., Yao, K.: Research and Design of Intelligent Transportation System of the Terminal Site Based on GPRS. In: 2011 Third International Conference on Intelligent Human-machine Systems and Cybernetics, pp. 174–177 (2011)
2. Yu, H., Liu, L.: Remote Health Monitoring System Using ZigBee Network and GPRS Transmission Technology. In: 2011 Fourth International Symposium on Computational Intelligence and Design, pp. 152–154 (2011)
3. Ma, C., Li, X., Li, Z.: Design of Gas Information Collection and Control System Based on GPRS. In: 2011 International Conference on Mechatronic Science, Electric Engineering and Computer, pp. 1222–1224 (2011)
4. Liu, S., Chundi, Zhao, M.M.: Human Oid Robot Controller Based on ARM Embedded System. Tsinghua Univ. (Sci. & Tech.) 48(4), 482–485 (2008)
5. Chen, Q., Ding, T., Li, C., Wang, P.: Low-power Wireless Remote Terminal Design Based on GPRS/ GSM. J. Tsinghua Univ. (Sci. & Tech.) 49(2), 223–225 (2009)
6. Maoshen, J., Changchun, B.: A Embedded Stereo Speech and Audio Coding Method Meeting the Requirement s of ITU-T Terms of Reference. Application of Electronic Technology 37(10), 2291–2297 (2009)
7. Cui, G., Chen, F., Zhang, H.: Design of Gateway Nodes of Wireless Sensor Network Based on ARM9. Application of Electronic Technology (11), 115–118 (2008)
8. Luo, W., Wang, L., Xiao, K.: Remote Monitoring and Software Upgrade of Embedded System Based on GPRS. Application of Electronic Technology (5), 159–162 (2010)
9. Jiang, D., Yang, H.: Design of Embedded Mobile GIS for Customizable Data Wireless Transmission. Journal of Computer Applications 30(9), 2538–2540

A Modal for Outlier Removal by MLBP Neural Network Based on Adaptive Performance Function

Yuhua Dong and Haichun Ning

College of Information & Communication Engineering, Dalian Nationalities University,
Dalian, China
dongyuhua@dlnu.edu.cn

Abstract. Based on the analysis of the back propagation (BP) algorithm, the application limitation of BP neural network mean square error (MSE) used in outlier removal is pointed out. An adaptive error performance function (AE) is proposed, and it is integrated into Levenberg-Marquardt algorithm (LM). Simulation results show that the three layer BP neural network model trained by the method have a certain ability of recognition for outlier with isolated type and spotted type, not knowing the theoretical true value.

Keywords: Performance function, BP algorithm, isolated outliers, spotted outliers.

1   Introduction

Outlier removal is an important step in the post process of spacecraft tracking data, and it plays a basic role. In the engineering practice, even it is high precision measurement equipment, because of comprehensive influence by many accidental factors, the sampled data set generally contains include of 1%-2% and up to 10-20% data which seriously deviate the true value, e.g. high elevation of radar. Literature [1] defined the outliers as the trend of a small portion of data points which seriously deviate from most of the data in set D. The outliers are generally divided into two kinds, one is isolated, and the other is spotted. The isolated outliers appear isolated, and there is no necessary link with the data quality before sampling or after. The spotted outliers appears in group, the outliers at sampling time may lead to several data at subsequent time seriously deviate from the true value [1]. The outlier removal methods for isolated type are mainly least square estimation, time polynomial extrapolation, differential detection, and so on [2]. The method for spotted type are Kalman filter, robust filter M estimation, least square B spline approximation, and so on[3]. The artificial intelligence method suitable for outlier removal is not much.

BP neural network is feed forward neural network adopting back propagation training algorithm, which has the advantages of structural property, robustness, parallelism, etc. and it has height ability of nonlinear fitting. It has been shown that BP neural network can approximate any interested function at arbitrary precision, in which S transfer function is used for the only hidden layer, and the linear transfer function used for the output layer [4]. Its disadvantage is that the supervised learning

M. Zhao and J. Sha (Eds.): ICCIP 2012, Part II, CCIS 289, pp. 663–671, 2012.

model is used, and it is required to use the "true value" to train the network and fit the function. While the aim of outlier removal is reverse of true value filter, so the existing research need the theoretical trajectory (assumed as true value) as training set[5,6], which limits the application BP neural network for testing data rationality to a great degree.

The paper analyzes the causes of the limitations, that is, the performance function of BP algorithm is sensitive to outliers. Then the adaptive error (AE) performance function is proposed, integrating into Levenberg-Marquardt algorithm to train BP neural network model with three layers. Simulations results verify the removal ability of outlier with isolated type and spotted type. The method extends the research scope of outliers removal using BP neural network. Meanwhile, because the performance function is the common part of all neural networks, so the method has a certain reference significance for artificial intelligent algorithm using in testing data rationality.

2   Adaptive Error Performance Function

BP is back propagation algorithm for short, refers to a series of algorithm which computes partial derivatives of sensitive factor from output layer reverse to the first hidden layer by use of chain method. Different feed forward neural network of BP training algorithms have different name, such as LMBP, MOBP(Momentum BP), to VLBP (Variable Learning rate BP) and so on. BP algorithm is numerous, but the algorithm structure is basically same, including of error forward propagation, back propagation of sensitive factor by chain rule, the iterative process of weight value update, shown in Figure 1.

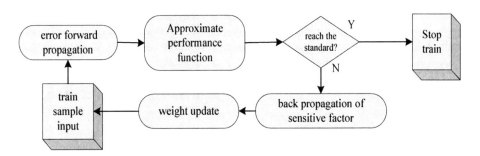

Fig. 1. The structure diagram of BP algorithm

The performance function is the core of BP algorithm, and its origin is the introduced Mean Square Error (*MSE*) function in single layer ADALINE network by Hoff, that is,

$$F(x) = \mathrm{E}(e^2) = \mathrm{E}[(t - a)^2] \tag{1}$$

where t is the output of the target, a is the actual output. The view of Hoff is that the kth iterative MSE is used instead of the expectation of *MSE*, that is

$$\hat{F}(x) = (t(k) - a(k))^2 = e(k)^2 \tag{2}$$

The estimation of every iterative gradient is $\hat{\nabla}F(x) = \nabla e^2(k)$, the first R elements of estimation value is the derivate value on the network weight, can be written as

$$[\nabla e^2(k)]_j = 2e(k)\partial e(k) / \partial w \tag{3}$$

Then the steepest descent method with fixed learning rate α is adopted to adjust weight as

$$w(k+1) = w(k) + \alpha 2e(k)\partial e(k) / \partial w \tag{4}$$

The so-called BP algorithm is to use chain rule to back propagate sensitive factors, solving the derivation $\partial \hat{F} / \partial w$ of multi-layer network. The weight update theory is consistent. So weight update scale is affected by performance function, the outliers with large errors will have a greater negative impact in the update process. The ultimate fitting function may deviate by outliers, which is the reason why the theory true value is needed in most researches.

The negative effects of outliers in the weight update process can be controlled according to performance function. Here performance function of the adaptive error is given as

$$F(x) = \frac{a|x|}{1 + e^{b|x|}} \tag{5}$$

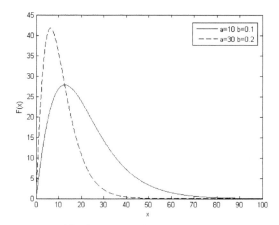

Fig. 2. The adaptive error function

where x is the error of target output and actual output, e is natural logarithm, parameter a is the amplitude regulatory factor, parameter b is error sensitive factor to control sensitive degree of performance function to error. The concrete value is determined by dimension of sampling sequence. The function of AE is shown in Fig.2. The error x is taken 0-100m. It can be seen that the curve width (error sensitivity) of AE is a decreasing function of b. The dashed line is sensitive within 10, and the solid line is sensitive within 20, and $\lim_{x \to \infty} F(x) = 0$, that is, the influence of maximal error for performance function is close to 0. The performance of the adaptive error function can be shown as Figure 2.

LM is the Levenberg-Marquardt algorithm for short, and itself is deformation of Newton method. Here the adaptive error function is integrated into LM algorithm. Remain LM algorithm unchanged, gradually increase parameter b according to the iterative step to gradient reduce the sensitive degree of AE function to error. It is sensitive to large error in the initial training stage, sensitive to small error in end stage, which furthermore decreases the impact to fitting by outliers as possible.

3   Modal Structure of AE-LMBP Neural Network

The BP neural network is made of an input layer, an output layer and a number of hidden layers in which neurons are connected to each other with modifiable weighted inter-connections. This modal uses three layers feed forward neural network with an input layer, a hidden layer and an output layer is shown as Figure 3.

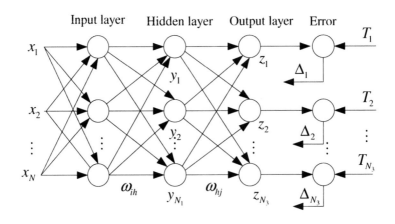

Fig. 3. The structure diagram of AE-MLBP

Where x_i is the input; y_h is the output of one node in the hidden layers; z_j is the output of one node in the output layer; T_j is the target output; ω_{ih} is the weight between the ith node in the input layer and the hth node in the hidden layers; ω_{hj} is the weight between the hth node in the hidden layers and the jth node in the output layer; N_1 is the number of nodes in the input layers; N_2 is the number of nodes in the hidden layers; N_3 is the number of the output layer. In this paper, we choose $N_1 = 1$ $N_2 = 15$ and $N_3 = 1$.

The BP neural network consists of two steps: the learning and the prediction. The first one is the forward phase where the activations are propagated from the input to the output layer. The second one is the backward phase where the error between the observed actual value and the desired nominal value in the output layer is propagated backward in order to modify the weights and bias values.

The performed function is expressed as the following equations:

The function of one node in hidden layers:

$$y_h = f\left(\sum_{i=1}^{N_1} \omega_{ih} x_i + \theta_h\right) \tag{6}$$

The function of one node in output layers:

$$z_j = f\left(\sum_{h=1}^{N_2} \omega_{hj} y_h + \gamma_j\right) = f\left(\sum_{h=1}^{N_2} \omega_{hj} f\left(\sum_{i=1}^{N_1} \omega_{ih} x_i + \theta_h\right) + \gamma_j\right) \tag{7}$$

Then according to the adaptive error function proposed in this paper, we can get the error E. and the transfer function between input layer and hidden layer we choose the logarithmic S function which can be written as

$$f(x) = \frac{1}{1 + e^{-x}} \tag{8}$$

The logarithmic function $f(x)$ has the same characterize as sigmoid function such as: smooth monotonicity, and its derived function also has a smooth properties. Logarithmic - S function and its derivative function is shown in Figure 4 and figure 5 respectively.

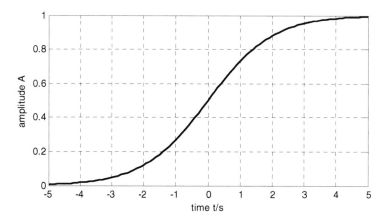

Fig. 4. The curve of logarithmic function $f(x)$

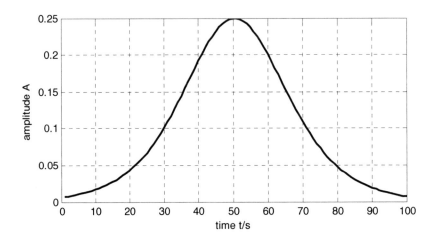

Fig. 5. The curve of derivative function of logarithmic function $f(x)$

And the purlin function is chosen as the transfer function between hidden layer and output layer, the purlin function is

$$f(x) = x \qquad (9)$$

The network input is sampling time; output is the spacecraft tracking data at the sampling time. Considering the input data and the output data is one dimension, the network is small, and the spacecraft tracking data does not have too much inflection points. So initially the number of hidden layer neurons is 15, the structure is 1-15-1.

Levenberg-Marquardt algorithm obtained the high precision of the results of the processing at the cost of increasing the computational complexity, at the same time, has faster convergence rate compare with the conjugate gradient algorithm and the quasi-Newton algorithm. As data post processing, computational complexity increase is not the additional hardware cost, so it is feasible. The LM gradient search algorithm has been introduced to MLP network training to provide better performance (Hagan and Menhaj, 1994). Basically, the LM gradient search is a Hessian-based algorithm for nonlinear least squares optimization without having to compute the Hessian matrix. Under the assumption that the error function is some kind of squared sum, then the Hessian matrix can be approximated as

$$H = J^{\mathrm{T}}J \qquad (10)$$

and the gradient information can be computed as follows:

$$g = J^{\mathrm{T}}e \qquad (11)$$

where J is the Jacobian matrix that contains first derivatives of the network errors with respect to weights and biases, and e is an error vector. The Jacobian matrix can be computed through a standard BP technique that is much less complex than computing the Hessian matrix.

The LM algorithm uses this approximation to the Hessian matrix in the following Newton-like update:

$$x_{k+1} = x_k - \left[J^T J + \mu I \right]^{-1} J^T e \tag{12}$$

where μ is a scalar controlling the behavior of the algorithm, the convergence behavior of the LM is similar to the Gauss-Newton method. Near a solution with small residuals, it performs well and gives a very fast convergence rate.

4   Simulations

Set sampling frequency 15 points per second, 1000 simulation points is generated by function

$$y(t) = 0.01 \times (t-15)^3 - (t-20)^2 + 450 \tag{13}$$

From 0.04 second to 40 second, and 40dB white noise random is used as random error. Suppose four points of y(80)=80, y(120)=465, y(200)=200, y(650)=450 as outliers with isolated type, and outliers with spotted type is added by e=0.1t-28 from point 451 to point 499, shown in Figure 6. LM algorithm is used to train BP neural network with three layers by 3000 iterations, the fitting results is shown in Figure 7. AE function is used, the AE parameter initially is set, a=30, b=0.05, and b increases by 0.01 every 50 iterations, the iterative times of training is 3000, and the fitting results is shown in Figure 8.

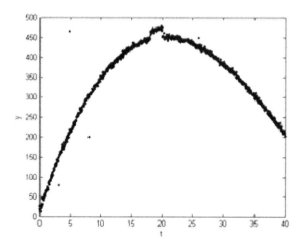

Fig. 6. The simulation trajectory

From the two figures, it can be seen that the fitting ability of traditional BP neural network is influenced by greater outliers of isolated type and spotted type, and the fitting curve is deviated by outliers, which is shown as glitch section and process section in Figure 7. In contrast, the influence by isolated outliers using AE-LMBP is small, that is, there are no glitches, and a certain influence by spotted outliers, but it can still be distinguished. Set the threshold $c=11$, the outliers removal of two model is shown in Figure 8 and Figure 9. The traditional BP network is no removal ability to spotted outliers, and can remove all isolated outliers, 9 points is mistaken to remove. The AE-LMBP network remove 37 spotted outliers (74%), and remove all isolated outliers, 6 points is mistaken to remove. Because BP neural network is sensitive to MSE, it cannot recognize spotted outliers in the absence of true training condition, and because the fitting is affected by large error, so the mistaken rate is high. AE-MLBP still has certain removal ability to spotted outliers in the absence of true value, and the mistaken rate is low.

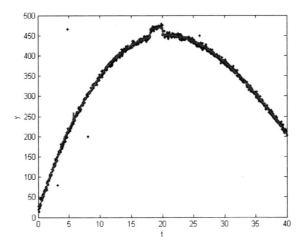

Fig. 7. Fitting curve of traditional BP network

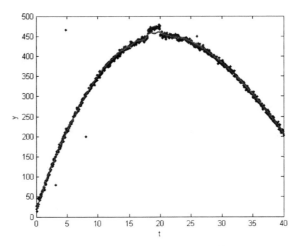

Fig. 8. Fitting curve of AE-LMBP network

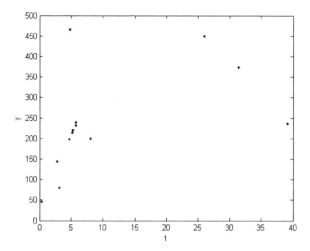

Fig. 9. The results of outliers removal by traditional BP network

5   Conclusions

At the absence of true value, using BP neural network, the feasibility of outliers removal is discussed in this paper, the aim is to give references for deeply research, and it does not involve the theoretical problems of local minimum point, network structure over-fitting, the generality of simulation experiments, and so on. The practical removal of outliers is a complex engineering problem, and it is hard to solve thoroughly by some theory or algorithm. The experience is important, and the specific problems need specific analysis. The drawback of this method is the strong empirical of AE parameters setting is required. And the research focus of next step is to give the theoretical models for parameters varying.

References

1. Shaolin, H., Guoji, S.: Statistical Diagnosis Method For Outliers From Spacecraft Tracking Data. Journal of Astronautics, China 20, 68–74 (1999)
2. Liu, L.: External trajectory measurement data processing. National Defence Industry Press, Beijing (2002)
3. Zhuo, N.: Study on Outlier Eliminating Method for Data Processing of Exterior Trajectory. Journal of Test and Measurement Technology, China 22, 314–316 (2008)
4. Hornik, K.M., Stinchcombe, M., White, H.: Multilayer feedforward networks are universal approximators. Neural Networks 2(5), 359–366 (1989)
5. Xue, Y.: Detection of Outliers from Spacecraft Tracking Data using GP-RBF Network. Journal of System Simulation 17, 286–289 (2005)
6. Liu, J.: Application of Back Propagation Neural Network in Handling of Abnormal Value of Radar Measurement Data. Journal of Spacecraft TT & C Technology 28, 32–35 (2009)

Patent Search Technology of Automobile Steering Gear Manufacturing Enterprises

Jun Chen[1,2], He Huang[1], Ting Wu[1], and Gangyan Li[1]

[1] School of Mechanical and Electronic Engineering,
Wuhan University of Technology, 122, Luoshi Road,
430070, Wuhan, Hubei Province, P.R. China
[2] Mechanical and Electronic Engineering College,
Hubei Polytechnic University, 16, Guilin North Road,
435003, Huangshi, Hubei Province, P.R. China
{Cjund,flying-0415}@163.com,
393840532@qq.com, gangyanli@whut.edu.cn

Abstract. Considering the characteristics of patent information of automobile steering gear manufacturing enterprises, the type of information is classified. Accordingly, the method of need representation and technology of feature extract is researched in searching patent information of automobile steering gear manufacturing enterprises, and a matching model of similitude cosine is built. Aiming to the example of searching patent information of automobile steering gear manufacturing enterprises, the searching process is implemented by helps of the method and strategy, which testifies the effectiveness and feasibility of the methods mentioned in the paper.

Keywords: Automobile steering gear, Patent information, Search, Matching model.

1   Introduction

Automobile steering gear is not only an important sub-assembly in the system of vehicle, but a high-demanded safety component. Nowadays, there are nearly 160 automobile steering gear manufacturing enterprises in China. Compared with foreign company, Chinese enterprise lacks of international competitiveness, due to its poor product development capability, too long period of product development, not very high production scale, narrow channel of international trade and low export rate [1]. Currently, Digestion and absorption of foreign advanced technology is the main approach to developing product in most Chinese enterprises, but the reliability and robustness are not satisfactory. With the development of intellectual property rights, Chinese enterprises have been aware patent is important to their survival, and the recent wars between international companies also give some warnings [2][3][4]. Therefore, the amount and proportion of patent application for new technologies in product manufacturing and development has been increased in many Chinese automobile steering gear manufacturing enterprises. However, it is not enough for Chinese enterprises to protect their interests only through patent application, and the

M. Zhao and J. Sha (Eds.): ICCIP 2012, Part II, CCIS 289, pp. 672–679, 2012.

formulation of patent strategy benefiting enterprise development becomes more and more important. Mastering much patent information is the prerequisite for the formulation of patent strategy, while the technology of patent information search is the necessary way of obtaining patent information from different enterprises [5].

2   The Classification of Patent Information for Automobile Steering Gear Manufacturing Enterprises

Classifying scientifically patent information is the guarantee of an effective search. According to the feature of automobile steering gear manufacturing enterprises, the patent information can be classified as six groups, that is, rack and pinion steering gear, recirculating ball steering gear, manufacturing tool, machining method or manufacturing process, electric power steering system (EPS) and other information type.

Generally, patent of electric power rack and pinion steering gear belongs to EPS patent information, detection tool patent in the process of production is the category of manufacturing tool, and measure method in production is patent information of machining method or manufacturing process.

As a special kind of product, electric power steering system mainly includes all components of the system, such as electric power steering device, electric engine, sensor, and controller etc. Other different type of EPS, for example, electric power rack and pinion steering system, also contains the whole system, machining and manufacturing tool, method and process of each component.

Besides the above groups, the rest patents belong to the category of other information type.

3   The Patent Search Technology of Automobile Steering Gear Manufacturing Enterprises

Patent information source of automobile steering gear manufacturing enterprises is mainly from Internet and some database. Faced with mass information, efficient searching technology is the guarantee of gaining necessary patent information. In the paper, patent search technology is chiefly composed of need representation, feature extraction and match model.

3.1   The Method of Need Representation

In patent information search of automobile steering gear manufacturing enterprises, need representation is a process of representing reasonably the needed information feature. It is described and implemented through need template, which exerts a direct influence on correlation degree of needed patent information.

Currently, there are many kinds of need templates, among which Vector Space Model is the most typical, that is,

$$\Pr ofile(i) = \{(x_{i1}, w_{i1}), (x_{i2}, w_{i2}), ..., (x_{ik}, w_{ik})\}$$

Where, the template is represent by Vector Space, profile(i) (i=1,2,3,…)is the n th template, x_{im} (m=1,2,3,…,k)is the m th feature item, and w_{im} is the weight corresponding to x_{im}. Figure 1 shows the common pattern of need template.

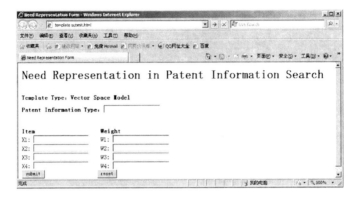

Fig. 1. The representation of need template in patent information search

The template has some advantages as follows when represented with Vector Space Model.

(1) Simple and clear structure, where feature item is in line with the content of needed information and weight reflects useful degree of the information;

(2) Convient to match with the searched information under the given match model;

(3) Easy to manage,maintain, correct and update, and no influence on the searching result due to the dynamic change of patent information.

For different kinds of patent information, the representation methods of feature item are as follows.

(1) Keywords. Mainly aiming at non-structured and half- structured patent information, a few keywords can describe the topic of the whole text;

(2) Keywords and Boolean expression. Boolean expression is a method of connecting a few keywords together through Boolean operator. For example, "rack and pinion steering gear" or "variable transmission ratio steering gear" has the same meaning and is the same item feature, while "rack" and "pinion" put into effect when appearing in the same patent information document. The method is used in the search of patent information where strong relevance exists among words, such as engagement and assemble information.

(3) Phrase and area expression. For some high-structured patent information, the type of information is usually shown in the initial location, so a phrase (such as "component of xx steering system") and its location (such as "in the xxth line") can be used as additional condition.

In addition, considering the need of patent information is uncertain to some extent, need template must update in terms of the type of changing patent information. Before template is submitted, it is necessary to predict the content of needed information, describe its feature, express the reasonable weight and give the right threshold. The process of need representation determines the recall of patent information to a great extent.

3.2 Feature Extraction

Feature extraction is one important part of patent information search. It is a process of converting information from searching source into feature vectors, which offers real time data to gain the need patent information. In a sense, Feature extraction is also a process of pretreatment of the searched patent information [6]. As shown in Figure 2, each traversed patent information document should be treated sequentially according to its number in feature extraction, the steps are as follows: first, feature items in need template are used as index for searching one by one in the patent information; second, weight of each feature item is determined and output in the form of item vector which will be used in the phase of similarity match; third, the second document of patent information begins to be extracted after the first and such circulation will not stop until all documents of patent information finish extraction.

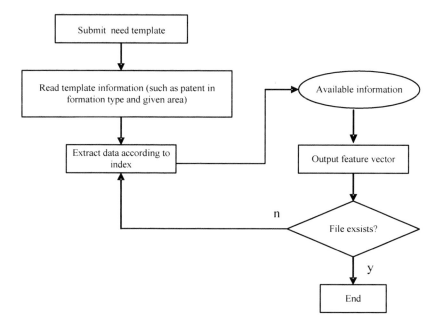

Fig. 2. The flow of feature extraction of patent information search

There are many computation methods of weight, some common are listed as follows.

(1) Single computation method of word frequency, where weight is computed according to the frequency of feature item in a patent information document, that is,

$$cw_{ji} = Feq_{ji} / \sqrt{\sum_{m=1}^{k} (Feq_{jm})^2} \qquad (1)$$

In formula (1), cw_{ji} is the weight of the i th feature item in the j th document information, Feq_{ji} is the frequency of the i th feature item appearing in the j th document information, k is the number of feature item in the need template. This computation method is simple, direct, and easy to be implemented by program, but it is just fit for the patent information described by nature language where word frequency reflects the topic of a document.

(2) Area computation method, where the weight value of feature item is given if it locates in the specified area, otherwise the weight is zero. The formula is as follows.

$$cw_{ji} = \sum_{n=1}^{c_i}(1-b_{in})w_{in} / \sqrt{\sum_{i=1}^{k}(\sum_{n=1}^{c}(1-b_{in})w_{in})^2}$$ (2)

Where, b_{in} is the Boolean value judging whether the i th feature item appears in the given n th area, it is 1 if the feature item appears, otherwise 0; w_{in} expresses what weight should be valued when the i th feature item appears in the given n th area, c_i is the number of area corresponding to the i th feature item, and k is the number of feature item in the need template. This method is fit for high-structured patent information such as text information.

(3) Word frequency and area computation method, that is, the weight of feature item is related not only to word frequency, but to the area, which is generally frequency times weighted coefficient,

$$cw_{ij} = \sum_{n=1}^{c_i}Feq_{in}.w_{in} / \sqrt{\sum_{i=1}^{k}(\sum_{n=1}^{c}Feq_{in}.w_{in})^2}$$ (3)

Where, Feq_{jn} is the frequency of the i th feature item appearing in the n th area, w_{in} is the weighted coefficient of the n th area, and k is the number of feature item in the need template. This method is fit for half-structured patent information.

Feature extraction in patent information search is different from that in information filtering. First, it needs no train document and only takes advantage of feature parameters delivered by need template, that is, it is a process of extraction according to the feature item in need template; Second, the computation of weight is determined by information type in the submitted template and the specified area.

3.3   Match Model

Match is an important technology in information search and used for judging what the correspondence degree is between the searching information and need template. In patent information search, the method of similarity match is applied, that is, feature item after feature extraction of the searching patent information is matched with the weight vector in need template, similarity is calculated by helps of the constructed algorithm, and judge is given if the searching information meets the demands.

Similitude cosine algorithm [7] is used as classification in patent information search.

$$SIM_{ij} = \cos(CW_j, W_i) = \left(\sum_{m=1}^{k} cw_{jm} \cdot w_{im} \right) \Big/ \left(\sqrt{\sum_{m=1}^{k} cw_{jm}^2} \cdot \sqrt{\sum_{m=1}^{k} w_{im}^2} \right) \qquad (4)$$

Where, SIM_{ij} is the similarity after the j th patent information (file) matches with the i th need template; CW_j is vector space of the j th file after feature extraction, that is, $CW_j = [cw_{j1}, cw_{j2}, cw_{j3}, ..., cw_{jk}]$; W_i is vector space of feature item weight in the i th need template, that is, $W_i = [w_{i1}, w_{i2}, w_{i3}, ..., w_{ik}]$.

Threshold is also called doorsill value and a valve determining the flowing direction of patent information. In patent information search, the final decision is made according to Threshold. Threshold is usually expressed by θ, which is given by helps of rule and experience and submitted with need template. It can be rectified in terms of search results, when $SIM_{ij} \geq \theta$, the patent information can be shown as a needed search result.

4   Case Study

Aiming to the feature and type of patent information of automobile steering gear manufacturing enterprises, searching strategy is formulated in terms of searching method and technical principle, as is shown in Table 1.

Table 1. Patent information searching stratagy

ID	Information type	Representing method	Computing method of weight	Searching language	Search source
1	Information of automobile steering gear enterprises	Keywords	Word frequency	Chinese and English	Internet and patent database
2	Rack and pinion steering gear	Keywords and boolean expression	Word frequency	Chinese and English	Internet and patent database
3	Recirculating ball steering gear	Keywords and boolean expression	Word frequency	Chinese and English	Internet and patent database
4	Manufacturing tool	Keywords and Boolean expression	Area computation or word frequency	Chinese and English	Internet and patent database
5	Machining method	Keywords and boolean expression	Area computation or word frequency	Chinese and English	Internet and patent database
6	EPS	Keywords and boolean expression	Area omputation or word frequency	Chinese and English	Internet and patent database
7	Other type	Synthesis	Experience	Chinese and English	Internet

In Table 2, A, B, C, D, E, F are respectively rack and pinion steering gear, recirculating ball steering gear, other information type, manufacturing tool, machining method or manufacturing process and electric power steering system (EPS).

According to the setting keywords and the related searching method, many needed patent information, such as the names of automobile steering gear manufacturing enterprises, the corresponding information type and number, can be found from Internet and patent database. As is shown in Table 2, five famous foreign and eight Chinese automobile steering gear manufacturing enterprises are listed and the amount of patent information related to steering system adds up to 593. Among the searching results, there are 350 patents from foreign enterprises; compared with 350 patents Chinese enterprises, the advantage is remarkable. There are 243 patents of applicants from Chinese enterprises which takes 40.98% of the total amount, while the amount of patents of applicants from foreign enterprises takes 40.98% of the total. The searched patents cover invention, utility model and appearance design, it can be seen from the searching results the search method and strategy is effective and feasible.

Table 2. The searched patent of automobile steering gear manufacturing enterprise

	Company Name	A	B	C	D	E	F	Sum Total
Chinese Enterprise	Henglong	13	8	49	31	3	4	108
	Siping			4	1			5
	Sanhuan			2	4			6
	Shibao	5	3	6		1	4	19
	Yudong	5	15	19			6	45
	Guangyang			11	11		1	23
	Jiangmen			11			5	16
	Huanqiu			19	1	1		21
	SumTotal	23	26	121	48	5	20	243
Foreign Enterprise	ZF	1		16	6	2		25
	Bosch			8		5	103	116
	Jtekt	4		36		3	85	128
	Showa	1			1	2	5	9
	Mando	7		26		2	37	72
	SumTotal	13		86	7	14	230	350

5   Conclusions

Aiming to the type of patent information of automobile steering gear manufacturing enterprises, patent search is realized by helps of the constructed search method and strategy, which is testified to be effective and feasible by the search results. However, the following aspects should be further researched.

(1) The diversity and pertinence of match model, that is, how to construct a targeted model according to the type and structure of patent information so as to improve searching results and enhance the precision.

(2) The extension of searching ways. Especially how to formulate the searching strategy according to latent semantic to widen the searching range and improve the recall.

(3) Deepen searching strategy, further mining the content of patent information, extend its types, refine patent information data in order to provide reasonable reference and basis to formulate patent strategy of enterprise.

Acknowledgment. The author gratefully acknowledges the support of the key project of Huangshi Institute of Technology (project ID: 10yjz05A) and Hubei provincial key discipline of Mechanical & Electronics in Huangshi Institute of Technology.

References

1. He, H.R.: Study on Characteristics of Vehicle Hydraulic Power Steering Gear and Its Test System Development. A Dissertation for the Degree of Master. Zhejiang University (2008) (in Chinese)
2. Bao, H.L., Zhu, D.H., Li, J.L.: Knowledge Discovery in Patent Literatures. Forecasting 22(4), 11–15 (2003)
3. Fu, Q.M.: Study on Patent Strategy of Chinese Enterprises under the Circumstance of Economic Globalization. A Dissertation for the Degree of Master. Suzhou University (2010) (in Chinese)
4. Hu, S.S.: The Researching for Enterprise Technological Innovation and Patent Strategy. A Dissertation for the Degree of Master. Wuhan University of Technology (2006) (in Chinese)
5. Han, J.W., Fang, B., Jian, B., Cang, G.L., Chen, H., Zhang, L.L.: How Do the Engineers Use the Existing Patents. Machine Design & Research 27(5), 1–5 (2011)
6. Yang, Z.Z., Han, X.: An Algorithm of Text Information Filtering Based on Feature Extraction. New Technology of Library and Information Service 163(4), 29–34 (2008) (in Chinese)
7. He, B.: Design and Reliability of Product Design Information Filter Based on Web. A Dissertation for the Degree of Master. Wuhan University of Technology (2005) (in Chinese)

A Network Coding Cipher
for Wireless Sensor Networks

Haifeng Lin[1], Suyun Wei[1], Yunfei Liu, and Di Bai[2]

[1] School of Information Science & Technology, Nanjing Forestry University, Nanjing, China
[2] College of Engineering, Nanjing Agricultural University, Nanjing, China
lhf31@hotmail.com

Abstract. Security features are to be a particular issue for wireless sensor networks. However, a wireless sensor network has constrained energy reserves. Data encryption in wireless sensor networks and energy consumption face a trade-off. In this paper, we propose novel efficient security architecture by network coding. The goal of the proposed security model is to provide security suites to each packet.

Keywords: WSN, Network Security, Network Coding, Scream Cipher, Energy Efficient.

1 Introduction

Wireless sensor networks (WSNs) are popular due to their potential applications in civil and military domains [1,2]. WSNs consist of many devices which can process data, store data and communicate with others via short range radio connections. They have no infrastructure, but they can configure themselves as a network and construct the routing table.

In WSNs, energy source is usually provided as battery power for sensors which gives a constrained life time for sensors without recharging. WSNs are typically deplored in remote or hostile environment, such as battlefield or desert. It is impossible for us to replace new battery for these sensors. For WSNs one of the most energy-expensive operations is data transmission. If there are number of sensors that are out of service, the wireless sensor networks become useless. Therefore, energy efficient design which is used to extending the lifetime without sacrificing system reliability is one important challenge to the design of a large wireless sensor network [3,4].

Security is a significant factor in any network, but particularly in WSNs, which are open to many forms of injection attacks that are much less likely traditional, wired networks. For the purpose of making WSNs secure, we should consider the following attributes: authentication, availability, confidentiality, freshness, integrity, and non-repudiation.

- Authentication: With authentication, sensors can ensure the identity of communication powers. Without authentication, an adversary could masquerade the real sensors, so it can gain unauthorized access to resource and sensitive information.

M. Zhao and J. Sha (Eds.): ICCIP 2012, Part II, CCIS 289, pp. 680–690, 2012.

Data authentication allows the receiver to verify that the data was really sent by the claimed sender [5].

- Availability: This means that we should ensure the survivability of network services *despite denial-of-service* (DoS) attacks. So all the sensors are available to authorized parties when needed [5].

- Confidentiality: A confidential message is resistant to disclose the meaning to unauthorized entities. As we know, one standard solution to keep sensitive data secret is to encrypt the data with a secret key that only the intended receivers possess, hence achieving confidentiality [5].

- Freshness: There are two types of freshness, data freshness and key freshness.

   - Data freshness guarantee that the data is recent, and it ensures that no adversary replayed old messages.

   - Key freshness means that a key used in one cryptographic association has not been reused in another association again. So the secret key for a session is always the new one.

- Integrity: With integrity, we can guarantee that the message being transferred is not altered, such as modification, insertion, deletion or replay, by any adversary [5].

- Non-repudiation: Provides protection against denial by one of the entities involved in a communication of having participated in all or part of the communication. It guarantees that both the message was sent by the specified party and the message was received by the specified party [5].

Although there are several security issues' WSNs, we only consider the confidentiality, authentication and freshness in this paper. We propose a data encryption scheme which only uses fundamental arithmetic operations and is energy friendly.

The rest of this paper is organized as follows. In Section 2, we introduce the concept of stream cipher. In Section 3, we propose our energy efficient model for data privacy in WSNs. The security analysis is also given in Section 3. At last, we conclude our results and describe some future work in Section 5.

2   Stream Cipher

In cryptography, a stream cipher is a symmetric cipher where plaintext bits are combined with a pseudorandom cipher bit stream (key stream), typically by an exclusive-or (xor) operation [5]. In a stream cipher the plaintext digits are encrypted one at a time, and in which the transformation of successive digits varies during the encryption. We use Fig. 1 to illustrate the idea. An alternative name is a state cipher, as the encryption of each digit is dependent on the current state. In practice, the digits are typically single bits or bytes.

In Fig. 1, key stream generator is a "pseudo random" sequence of bits which is unpredictable even given knowledge of some key stream bits. *IV* is the initial vector, which is typically used when block encrypting.

Stream cipher mimics one fine pad but still based on restricted key size such as 128 bits for AES in OFB mode. Therefore, it cannot be unconditionally secure [5].

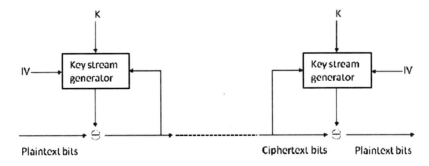

Fig. 1. Stream cipher

Stream ciphers represent a different approach to symmetric encryption from block ciphers. Block ciphers operate on large blocks of digits with a fixed, unvarying transformation. However, stream ciphers typically execute at a higher speed than block ciphers and have lower hardware complexity [5]. This nature makes it more suitable for WSNs, since it consumes little computing resource and energy.

3   Network Coding Cipher

In our approach, we mix the authentication and key management protocols together by using a simplified stream cipher. That is we use the linear combination of previous packets to generate the pseudo random key bits in stream cipher. To achieve this, we use one of clustering algorithms with the dominating set initially.

3.1   Clustering with Dominating Set

A dominating set of a graph $G = (V, E)$ is a subset $S \subseteq V$, such that every vertex $v \in V$ is either in S or adjacent to a vertex of S [6]. We call the vertex in set S cluster heads and those who are adjacent to a vertex of S cluster members.

Using dominating sets, each cluster can communicate with its cluster members directly. We will let each cluster member forward its sensing data to its cluster head directly in our proposal.

We divide the security procedure in two phases, inter-cluster and intra-cluster by the clustering algorithm.

3.2   Hash Function

We also assume that all the cluster heads and all the cluster members use the same hash function – $h(M)$, which is a function that take an arbitrary length message and produces a unique code of fixed length n [5]. This hash function is installed on any sensor node as manufactured. We list the properties of hash function as follows.

- $h(M)$ is easy to compute and we use β to represent the result of $h(M)$.
- For given β, it is computationally infeasible to find M such that $h(M)= \beta$. We call it "on way function."
- For given M, it is computationally infeasible to find $M' \neq M$, such that $h(M')=h(M)$. We call it "weak collision resistance."
- It is computationally infeasible to find any pair (M, M') so that $h(M')= h(M)$. We call it "strong collision resistance."

With the nature of the last three properties, if the configuration of this hash function is secret, then no others can impersonate the sensor node. Therefore, we can prevent from masquerading attack or impersonating attack.

Considering the properties of "weak collision resistance" and "strong collision resistance", we can detect the modification of the received messages.

Since the hash code is easy to compute, the sensors can ignore the energy consumption for computing hash function.

In order to prevent the replaying message attacks, we include the *Time_Stamp* in each message.

In our protocol, we only calculate partial hash code, which means the input for the hash function is the plaintext of the *packet* sent from cluster member to cluster head and *Time_Stamp*. With this partial hash function, we can detect packet loss and tolerate some packet loss, which is discussed later in this paper.

3.3   Inter-cluster Model

Since we do not need to consider the energy consumption of the data sink, we can use public key to achieve the data privacy.

Initially, the data sink will broadcast its public key to all the cluster heads. We use Table 1 to illustrate this procedure.

Table 1. The Procedure of Distributing the Public Key of Data Sink

Message 1. Data Sink $\rightarrow$ Cluster heads: $K_s^+ \mid Time\_Stamp \mid \beta'$
Message 2. Cluster heads $\rightarrow$ Data Sink: $E_{K_s^+}(packet) \mid Time\_Stamp \mid \beta'$

We depict this process as follows.

- Data Sink broadcasts its public key to all cluster heads. We use Message 1 to denote it.
- In Message 1, we use K_s^+ to represent the public key of the data sink.
- When the cluster heads receive Message 1, they first authenticate it by computing the β of the received message and comparing it with the received β'.
- If this verification is passed, they still need to check the freshness of this message.
- If it is a fresh message, the cluster heads will use the public key to encrypt the data they want to send to the data sink.

- We use Message 2 to denote the message sent by cluster heads.
- When the Data Sink receives Message 2, it first needs to authenticate it by computing the β of the received message and comparing it with the received β'.
- If this verification is passed, the Data Sink also need to check the freshness of this message.
- If it is a fresh message, the Data Sink stores the packet.

3.4   Intra-cluster Model

In our proposal, there are two steps for protecting intra-cluster data. They are the exchange of initial key packet and data collection.

1) *Initial Key Packet Exchange:* Initially, each cluster head and its cluster members need to exchange the key packet which is used for encrypting and authenticating the data in each session. We use Table 2 to illustrate this procedure.

Table 2. Exchange the initial key packet

Message 1. Cluster members $\rightarrow$ Cluster heads: $E_{K_{master}}(key\_packet) \mid Time\_Stamp \mid \beta$
Message 2. Cluster head $\rightarrow$ Cluster members: $ACK \mid Time\_Stamp \mid \beta$

We describe this procedure of exchanging the initial key packet as follows.

- Cluster members send Message 1 to the cluster head. This message is organized as

$$E_{K_{master}}(key\_packet) \mid Time\_Stamp \mid \beta$$

Here K_{master} is the master key which is stored in each sensor as manufactured and is the hash code of *key_packet|Time_Stamp*.

- Each cluster member still needs to store this *key_packet*, and use this *key_packet* to generate a *key* pool of size k by left shifting the *key_packet*. We use Fig. 2 to illustrate the *key* pool in a cluster member. The cluster member will use this key pool to code the packets sent from it to the cluster head. The *key* pool is a *first in first out* (FIFO) queue.

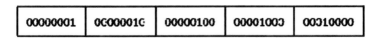

00000001	0C00001C	00000100	00001003	00010000

n this example, the key packet is 000C0001.
And the size of key pool is 5.

Fig. 2. The example of *key* pool in each sensor

- When the cluster head receives Message 1, which contains the initial key packet, the cluster head should authenticate it by computing the β for the received message and comparing it with the received β'.

- If this validation is passed, it still needs to check the *Time_Stamp*.
- If it is a fresh message, the cluster head will store it and use it to generate the *key* pool of the cluster member, which is shown in Fig.2. The cluster head also need to use the *key* pool to decode the packets sent from the corresponding cluster member.
- At last, the cluster head will reply Message 2 to notify the corresponding cluster member that the *key* pool is set correctly.

2) *Data Collection:* After the initial communication, cluster head will collect data from its cluster head will collect data from its cluster members. We use Table 3 to illustrate this procedure.

We describe this data collection procedure in details as follows.

Table 3. Data colletion

Message 1. Cluster members $\rightarrow$ Cluster head:
$$(g_1, g_2, ..., g_k) \mid packet \oplus \sum_{i-1}^{k} g_i \times key\_packet_i \mid Time\_Stamp \mid \beta$$

- Each cluster member will send the sense data *packet* by randomly coding of with the packets in the *key* pool.
- In this message, β is the hash code for

packet|Time_Stamp

and

$$(g_1, g_2, ..., g_k)$$

are the coefficients.

- When the cluster head receives this message, it first authenticates it by computing the β for the received message and comparing it with the received β'.
- If this verification is passed, the cluster head still needs to check the *Time_Stamp* for freshmen.
- If it is a fresh message, it can use the received coefficients and its own *key* pool to decode the *packet.*
- After decoding, it should store this *packet* in *key* pool.

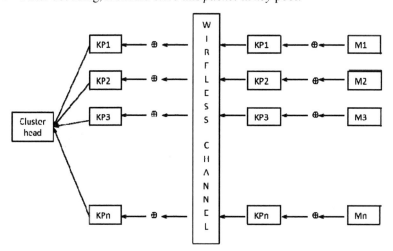

Fig. 3. The procedure of data collection

Fig.3 illustrates the procedure of data collection in our proposal. In this figure, we use M_i to represent the cluster member and *KP* to represent the *key* pool.

3.5   Security Analysis

1) *Inter-Cluster Security*: Since we use the public key of data sink to encrypt the data sent by each cluster head, these data is secure.

2) *Intra-Cluster Security*: We need to prove that we can achieve the confidentiality in each cluster.

Since we use the public key to encrypt the *key_packet* sent by each cluster member, we can protect this information due to the nature of public key.

The initial key packet is randomly generated by each cluster member, so the key space is 2^n and n is the length of the packet. To make our model more secure, we need the length of the packet to be more than 192-bit. Therefore, the initial key packet cannot be guessed by the attackers and the *key* pool is secret.

Consider that we randomly use the previous packets to code the packet by the operation $\oplus$ which is shown in Table 3. In this table, we use *packet* to represent the sensed data packet at the cluster member and use $packet \oplus \sum_{i-1}^{k} g_i$ to represent the packet sent by the cluster member. It is obvious that the key space is reduced to the packet space of the source.

Since the packet space is decided by the stochastic property of the source we monitored, we argue it in two cases as follows.

• If the source has a perfect stochastic property, our proposal can achieve perfect secrecy, which is defined as $\Pr[x \mid y] = \Pr[x]$ for all x in Plaintext and, y in Ciphertext. A posterior probability that plaintext is x given observed ciphertext y, is identical to a prior probability that plaintext is x.

Suppose the length of packet is n bits, the key space is $\dfrac{1}{2^n}$. Since we suppose that the source is a perfectly random source, the probability of each packet is equally likely. With this nature, we can prove our proposal achieves perfect secrecy as follows.

$$\Pr[y] = \sum_{k \in 2^n} \Pr[y,k] = \sum_{k \in 2^n} \Pr[k] \times \Pr[y \mid k] = \sum_{k \in 2^n} \Pr[k] \times \Pr[x = d_k(y)] = \frac{1}{2^n} \sum_{x \in 2^n} \Pr[x] = \frac{1}{2^n}$$

Consider

$$\Pr[y \mid x] = \Pr[k = (y+x)] = \frac{1}{2^n}$$

So

$$\Pr[x \mid y] = \Pr[x] \times \frac{\Pr[y \mid x]}{\Pr[y]} = \Pr[x] \times \frac{1/2^n}{1/2^n} = \Pr[x]$$

Now, we see that our technique archives the one time pad, which is the dream for all the cryptography system.

- Even if a source does not have a well stochastic property, we still can prove that our proposal is intra-cluster secure.

As shown in Table 3, we randomly use the previous packet to code the current packet. Therefore, we use diffusion to hide the statistical information of the source.

It is obvious that the attackers cannot map the coded packets to samples directly. The reason is that some coded packets will never exist in the set of samples of source.

If they want to map the coded packets to samples, they first need to estimate the parameters of the coded packets. The process is same as the one we discussed previously. We also can define a N' as the thresh hold and we call this strong secure condition of our protocol. If any application is satisfied with this strong secure condition, we can apply our model as the secure method.

We conclude that although the source do not have a good random property, we still can protect our data in secure.

3.6   Advantages of Our Model

There are several advantages of our model and we describe them as follows.

- Save communication

Since we randomly use the previous packets to encode the current packet, we do not need to exchange session key periodically.

Generally, if we need to exchange session key, we need 2 messages at least, which is shown in Table 4.

Table 4. Exchange of session key

Message 1. Cluster members → Cluster heads: $E_{K_h^+}(K_{sess}) \mid Time\_Stamp \mid \beta$
Message 2. Cluster head → Cluster member: ACK

We describe this process as follows.

-    The Cluster member will randomly generate a session and send it to cluster head. We use Message 1 to denote it.

-    In Message 1, we use the public key of cluster head to encrypt the session key, K_{sess}.

-    When the cluster head receives Message 1, it first need to authenticate it by computing β of the receive message and comparing it with the received β'.

-    If this verification is passed, it still needs to check the freshness.

-    If it is a fresh message, it will reply ACK to tell the cluster member that it got the new session key.

Therefore, we can save the exchanging messages in our protocol and reduce the energy consumption significantly.

- Save computing energy

It is obvious that we only need to encode the decode the packets by the operation $\oplus$. This operation consumes little energy compared with AES.

- Save computing resource

In our proposal, we only need to XOR the packets, so the hardware cost can be reduced significantly.

- Our protocol is open to any coding algorithm.

We can use any coding algorithm to encode the packet before sending it. It does not affect the security issues in our model. The reason is that coding algorithms can not affect the statistical information of the source. Therefore, our model is still in secure.

- Detect packet loss and tolerate some packet loss.
- Detect packet loss

We use Fig. 4 as an example for detecting packet loss.

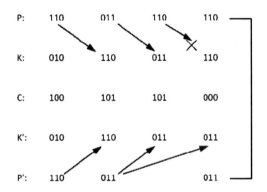

Fig. 4. Packet loss detection

In this example, we only use the previous packet to encode the current packet equaling to g=(000...1). We can observe that the third packet sent by the sensor node is lost, and then the cluster head will use the second packet to decode the packet. It can detect the packet loss by authentication. The reason is that the received β' is h(110), but the β of the received message is h(011). This verification is not passed and then the cluster head will ask this cluster member to re-set the communication as we discussed in III-D1.

- Tolerate some packet loss

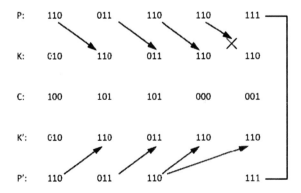

Fig. 5. Packet loss toleration

We use Fig. 5 to illustrate the scenario of how to tolerate some packet loss.

In this example, we also only use the previous packet to encode the current packet equaling to g=(000...1). We can see that the fourth packet sent by a sensor is lost, but the previous packet is same as the lost packet. Therefore, we still can decode the fifth packet correctly in cluster head. It is obvious that this lost will never affect the following decoding at cluster head.

4   Simulation Results

Fig. 6 shows a comparison of system lifetime using our model versus traditional AES. Our model has more than doubles the useful system lifetime compared with the alternative approaches.

We run similar experiments with different energy thresholds and found that no matter how much energy each node is given, it takes approximately 10 times longer for the first node to die and approximately 6 times longer for the last node to die in our model as it does in AES.

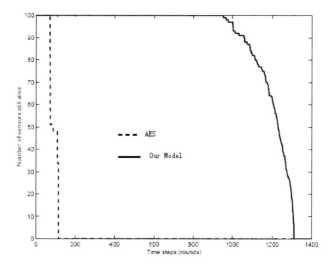

Fig. 6. System lifetime using AES and our model

5   Conclusion and Future Work

In this paper, we first introduce the challenge of security issues design in WSN and then we discuss the concepts of stream cipher and network coding briefly. Furthermore, we propose a data encryption scheme using stream cipher and network coding approach for efficient and secure data transmission. Through simulation results and security analysis, we showed that our model can significantly improve energy efficiency in providing a high level of data security.

Since the cluster heads will consume more energy than cluster members, we still need to design a new clustering algorithm which can balance the energy consumption and extend the lifetime. We also need to detect the fault of the cluster heads and fix this vulnerability in future.

References

1. Estrin, D., Govinda, R., Heidemann, J., Kumar, S.: Net century changes: Scalable coordination in sensor networks. In: Proc. Annual International Conference on Mobile Computing and Networks (MobiCom 1999), pp. 263–270. ACM Press, New York (1999)
2. Pottie, Kaiser, W.: Wireless integrated network sensors. Communication of the ACM 43, 51–58 (2000)
3. Wieselthier, J.E., Nguyen, G.D., Ephremides, A.: Algorithms for energy-efficient multicasting in static ad hoc wireless network. ACM Mobile Networks and Applications 6, 251–263 (2001)
4. Singh, S., Raghavendra, C., Stepanek, J.: Power-aware broadcasting in mobile ad hoc networks. In: Proc. IEEE PIMRC 1999 (1999)
5. Stallings, W.: Cryptography and Network Security: Principles and Practices, 4th edn. Prentice Hall (2003)
6. West, D.: Introduction to Graph Theory, 2nd edn. Prentice-Hall (2001)

A Base-Point Searching Algorithm
in the Digitization of Seismograms

Zhian Pan[1], Jilin Feng[1], Maofa Wang[1], Fangping Gao[1],
Lingling Zhao[2], Jing Yuan[1], and Ying Han[1]

[1] Department of Information Technology, Institute of Disaster Prevention
[2] Department of Basic Courses, Institute of Disaster Prevention
101601, Beijing, P.R. China
{Cidpza,lingling8383}@163.com, {fengjilin,gaofangping,yuanjing,
hanying}@cidp.edu.cn, wangmaofa2008@126.com

Abstract. History simulated earthquake records are important information for earthquake monitoring and prediction. The digitization of simulated seismograms is an important problem to be resolved. Auto extraction of earthquake waveform is the most key technology for the digitization of the simulated seismograms, and it can transform the original data into waveform data of earthquake records. Accurately determining the searching base-point of each curve in seismograms is the foundation for waveform extraction. In the paper, we present a filtering algorithm based on region of interest, applying in the selection of the searching base-point of each curve. The experimental results have shown the algorithm is effective.

Keywords: Simulated earthquake records, Waveform extraction, Region of interest.

1 Introduction

Historical simulated earthquake records are important information for earthquake monitoring and prediction. Although the construction of digital seismic stations has been undertaken in our country at present, those saved simulated seismogram over the past decades still have a great value, which is important original information for analyzing and studying earthquake and contain lots of valuable information associated with the earthquake-generating process. The digitization and its application for the huge amount of various seismograms is an urgent problem. With the development of computer and image processing technology [1], it is possible for extracting seismic precursory information associated with earthquake-generating process from seismogram, and is an important and urgent task for saving simulated seismograms. In this paper, we will do research on the key technology for the digitization of the simulated seismograms.

M. Zhao and J. Sha (Eds.): ICCIP 2012, Part II, CCIS 289, pp. 691–698, 2012.

2   General Architecture

The general architecture of the digital processing for the simulated seismograms is represented by a flowchart in Fig. 1.

The flowchart shows each module of the digital processing. The paper will focus on the module of seismic waveform extraction, in which we will do research on determining the searching base-point of each curve. The subsequent sections will describe specifically.

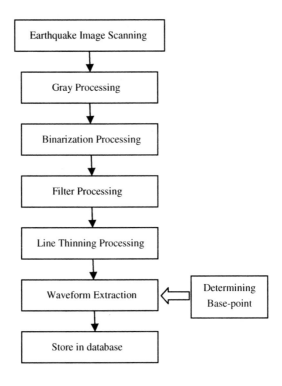

Fig. 1. Flowchart of the digital processing of seismograms

3   Image Preprocessing

3.1   Earthquake Image Scanning

Firstly, we will scan simulated earthquake image. In order to ensure the accuracy of acquisition of imaging data, we use high precision scanner to complete the image acquisition.

3.2   Gray Processing

It is necessary to transform the seismogram to gray pattern, because of that an available gray pattern image is essential preparation for binarization processing later.By Eq.(1), we can obtain the conversion relation.

$$G = 0.30r + 0.59g + 0.11b. \tag{1}$$

Where G is the brightness value of one pixel in the new gray image, whose three corresponding colour brightness (red, green, blue) values are r, g, b, separately.

3.3   Binarization Processing

Binarization[2] is an important digital image processing technique. We can divide one image into two parts: object part and background part, after doing the operation of binarization. To partition one image by magnitude of grayscale is the most popular binarization method. If one pixel value of original image is f(x,y), we can choose one grayscale value t as partition threshold by some certain algorithms, then determine one pixel point as object point and when its original pixel value is not less than the value of t and give the point a new pixel value of 1, or else determine all pixel point as backgroud point whose original pixel value is less than of t, and give it a new pixel value of 0. By Eq.(2), we can obtain the conversion relation between new and original pixel value.

$$g(x, y) = \begin{cases} 1......f(x,y) \geq t \\ 0......f(x,y) < t \end{cases} \tag{2}$$

3.4   Median Filter

In image processing, it is often desirable to be able to perform some kind of noise reduction on an image. The median filter is a nonlinear digital filtering technique, often used to remove noise. Such noise reduction is a typical pre-processing step to improve the results of later processing. Median filtering is very widely used in digital image processing. It can preserve edges while removing noise, under certain conditions.

Median filtering[3] is a classical nonlinear signal processing technology based on order-statistics theory. In image median filtering, the value of the target pixel in an image is replaced with the median value of its neighborhood, and then the isolated noise points will be eliminated. Median filtering algorithm can reserve the high frequency part of image to large extent, thus ensures the visual effect of the image. In case of image preprocess, median filtering is the preferred technology to eliminate the salt-and-pepper noise and random additive noise. Median value is the value in the middle position of a sorted sequence.

In application, the filter window or neighborhood may be chosen as rectangle, circle, cross or cirque. Suppose that the pixel values in neighborhood are put into a sequence and it becomes $x_{i1} \leq x_{i2} \leq x_{i3} \ldots \leq x_{in}$ after sorted in ascending order or $x_{i1} \geq x_{i2} \geq x_{i3} \ldots \geq x_{in}$ in descending order, then its median value is

$$
\begin{aligned}
x_{median} &= Med\{x_1, x_2, x_3, \ldots x_n\} \\
&= \begin{cases} x_{i(n+1)/2}, n \text{ is odd} \\ [x_{i(n/2)} + x_{i(n/2+1)}]/2, n \text{ is even} \end{cases}
\end{aligned}
\tag{3}
$$

To use median filtering algorithm, all pixel value in certain neighborhood need to be sorted in ascending or descending order, and then replaces the center pixel with the median value of the value in neighborhood. As the radius of the filtering window becomes larger, median filtering will becomes more and more slow. So this algorithm is only suitable for small filtering radius case or those cases where the timely request is not the very high.

3.5   Line Thinning Processing

Thinning is a morphological operation[4] that is used to remove selected foreground pixels from binary images, somewhat like erosion or opening. It can be used for several applications, but is particularly useful for skeletonization. Skeletonization is the process of peeling off of a pattern as many pixels as possible without affecting the general shape of the pattern. In other words, after pixels have been peeled off, the pattern should still be recognized. The skeleton hence obtained must have the following properties: as thin as possible, connected, centered. When these properties are satisfied, the algorithm must stop. Skeletonization is useful when we are interested not in the size of the pattern but rather in the relative position of the strokes in the pattern. In this mode it is commonly used to tidy up the output of edge detectors by reducing all lines to single pixel thickness. Thinning is normally only applied to binary images, and produces another binary image as output.

There are several algorithms which were designed for this aim. In the paper, we are concerned with one of them namely the Hilditch's Algorithm. We adopt Hilditch's algorithm which is the simplest and most common thining algorithm. It proceeds by progressively eroding the objects, while carefully preserving the original topology, when no further pixels can be eroded, the algorithm halts. The detail algorithm description is mentioned by Mr.Hildithch[5].

4   The Algorithm of Determining Base-Point

Accurately determine the searching base-point of each curve in seismograms is the foundation for accurately separating each curve and demarcating timer axis punctuation. Because there are some disconnected curves of landscape orientation in the top and bottom of the image, it is a key that how to use search algorithms for finding all such curves and determine the search base-point.

We present region of interest filtering algorithm based on domain distribution features. The concept of region of interest[6] (ROI) comes from human visual attention mechanism. The researches have shown that even if the observer was given a long time for observing an image, people will just show strong interest in one of the few areas in an image. In every stage of the process of digitalization of simulated seismogram, we search for useful information, remove noise and ultimately achieve the goal of complete digitalization, according to domain distribution features to be extracted.

The algorithm we use for selecting base-point of each curve is described as follows:

Step 1:
Now the number of rows and columns of the image is nx and ny.
Select 10 of y orientation to traverse base-points.
$y_i = \text{int} 16(ny/12) * k_i$ $k_i = 1, 2, \ldots, 10$ $i = 1, 2, \ldots, 10$
for $y_i = y_1$ to y_{10}
   for i=2 to nx
     if $C(i, y_i) == 1$

       if $C(i+1, y_i) == 0$
         choose this point as base-point
           if $C(i, y_i-4) == 1 \| C(i+1, y_i-4) == 1 \| C(i-1, y_i-4) == 1$
      choose this point as base-point
      $searchsum(y_i) = searchsum(y_i) + 1$
    $searchstarts1(y_i, i) = i$

After the above cycle operations, the total number of the base points in y_i orientation is stored in variable searchsum(data type of array).

Step 2:
The element of variable searchsum is sorted from small to large removing duplicates, the frequency of occurrence of each element is symbolized by n0. The number of base point is determined according to the priority of the frequency and the numerical value of n0.Finally the number of base-point is symbolized by variable key.

Step 3:
For i=1 to key
   For j=1 to 10
If the number of the base-point in j orientation is equal to the numerical value of variable key
    $sum = sum + searchstarts1(j, i+1)$
    $num = num + 1$
After the above cycle operations
    $searchstarts0(i) = sum/num$

Now after the above algorithm, the coordinate of the base-point has already been determined. The value is $(Searchstarts0(i), ny/2)$, $i = 1, 2 \ldots, key$.

5   Experimental Results

Now we apply the above algorithm to ditigal seismograms for verifying the effectiveness. The simulated seismogram is represented in Fig.2. First,we do the series of image preprocess operations: Gray Processing, Binarization Processing, Median Filter, and Line Thinning Processing. The result of binarization processing is represented in Fig.3. From Fig.4, we can see the result of median filter and Line Thinning Processing. Then we use the algorithm of searching base-point for determining base-point and the experimental result is represented in Fig.5.We can see that the white spots in the middle of figure 5 is corresponding to the searching base-point of each curve in figure 2.From the matching degree between the 5 base-points of the bottom and the corresponding curve in figure 5, we can see that the searching effect is good and the algorithm is effective.

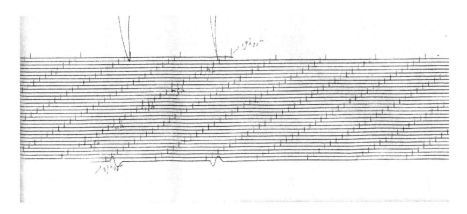

Fig. 2. Simulated seismogram

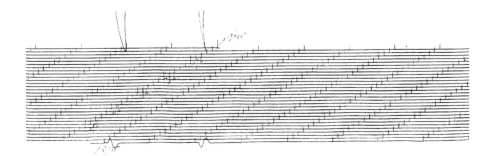

Fig. 3. The result of binarization processing

Fig. 4. The result of median filter and Line Thinning Processing

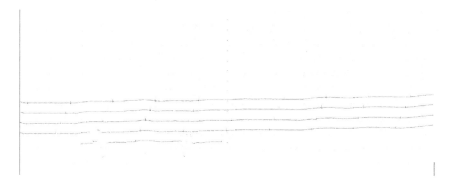

Fig. 5. The searching base-point of each curve

6 Conclusion

The paper focuses on a base-point searching algorithm, applying in the module of seismic waveform extraction of the digitization of the history simulated earthquake records. Auto extraction of earthquake waveform is the most critical technology for the entire digitization of the simulated seismograms. The original data of earthquake records is transformed into waveform data by waveform extraction. The success of waveform extraction is directly related to the subsequent analysis of earthquake waveform. Accurately determining the searching base-point of each curve in seismograms is the foundation for waveform extraction, and it has a very important role on earthquake waveform extraction. In the paper, we present region of interest filtering algorithm based on domain distribution features. The experimental results using the algorithm have shown the effectiveness of the method used in the paper. It also explore a new way for the research of seismic waveform extraction, and have a certain scientific research value.

Acknowledgment. This research is supported by Spark Program of Earthquake Sciences(No.XH12077). Two of Authors (Zhian Pan, Jilin Feng) thank the financial support from this funding program.

References

1. Patin, F.: An Introduction To Digital Image Processing. Graphics Programming and Theory (October 20, 2003)
2. Ntirogiannis, K., Gatos, B., Pratikakis, I.: An Objective Evaluation Methodology for Document Image Binarization Techniques. Document Analysis Systems (2008)
3. Zoican, S.: Improved median filter for impulse noise removal. TELSIKS Serbia and Motenegra, Ni 10(123), 681–684 (2003)
4. Haralick, R.M., Steinberg, S.R., Zhuang, X.: Image Analysis Using Mathematical Morphology. IEEE Trans. Pattern Analysis and Machine Intelligence, PAMI 9(4), 532–550 (1987)
5. Hilditch, C.J.: Proceedings of the 4th Annual Machine Intelligence Workshop, vol. 4, p. 403, Edinburgh University (1969)
6. Eldrdgem, H.G.: A Scalable Graphics System for Clusters. In: Proc. of ACM SIGRAPH 2001. ACM Press, Los Angeles (2001)

Analysis and Algorithm of Load Balancing Strategy of the Web Server Cluster System

Shaojun Zou

Dept. of Electronics and Information Technology, Jiangmen Polytechnic
Jiangmen, China
qvbitpl@qq.com

Abstract. In this paper, analyzed the main factors that influence the Web server cluster's performance and the load equilibrium strategy. Furthermore, Proposed an improved Weighted Round-Robin Scheduling strategy algorithm, which help to reasonably allocate the Web clients' request, in order to achieve a dynamic Web server clusters load balancing. Experimental results shown the algorithm for the weighted round-robin policy is feasible.

Keywords: Web server, Cluster, Load balance.

1   Introduction

Because of the rapid development of Internet, there are great challenges for network bandwidth and server. The exponential growth of Web request and booming development of e-commerce urgent need a higher performance, cost-effective and higher -availability Web server system. Web server cluster is widely adopted in today's Web site server architecture, where the load balancing cluster technology is one of the effective solutions to provide high-performance servers and effective means to solve the server overload problem. Load balancing cluster technology is balanced with a server cluster algorithm, the purpose is to provide and the number of nodes proportional to the load capacity. Load balancing cluster system improves overall system performance through the rational allocation of workloads between the nodes in the system [1-2].

The goal of the Web server cluster system load balances is providing the shortest average task response time based on the performance of each server processing capacity assigned with the task to match the amount of the request, through the appropriate request load scheduling algorithm and balancing cluster server workloads [3-4].

Requesting Web server load distribution is an important work in the system of distributor cluster, as the system's HTTP request will forward to the server on a server pool by the distributor in accordance with a certain load distribution strategy. Different load distribution strategies used, the load on each server to obtain the amount will be different, so the overall system performance may differ [5-6]. Overall, load distribution strategies and algorithms is one of the main ways to solve the Web server cluster system performance.

M. Zhao and J. Sha (Eds.): ICCIP 2012, Part II, CCIS 289, pp. 699–706, 2012.

In brief, this paper analyzed the main factors that influence the Web server cluster performance and the normal load- balancing strategy and proposed a dynamic load distribution strategies and algorithms, to achieve dynamic load balancing for the Web server cluster, Type Style and Fonts.

2   Main Factors That Affect the Performance of Web Server Cluster

There are so many factors that can affect the performance of Web server clusters, here mainly summarized in the following aspects:

2.1   Web Server and Application Processing Performance of Its Own Type of Service Affect the Performance of the Cluster

Processing performance of the server itself is a factor that must be considered first, as server processing performance differences cause the server to accept the same amount of tasks with varying load conditions. Since most of the existing network applications are based on TCP/IP protocol, then our main reference system to be in the TCP/IP protocol stack on the analysis of the network load balance. In layman's terms , TCP/IP traffic is characterized by many short and some long transactions that matters , which is due to the different types of applications connected to the server's request processing time is different , and this directly affects the performance of the server cluster .

2.2   The Error between the Record and Actual Load of Each Node, the Performance of Different Servers in Different Weight Handling Capacity and the Real Processing Power of Cluster Will Affect the Performance of the System

Load balancer exist errors between the record and the real load of each node, and accumulated over time, the error may be greater. To show the different treatment of different server performance, system administrators often need to experience a weight on the server settings. There must be an error in the real weights and server processing which will affect the real-time server load, while the error is not eliminated. This also directly affects the performance of the server cluster system.

2.3   Impact of the Restriction of Node Operating System to the Whole Cluster System

As can be extended , which makes the majority of cluster systems are heterogeneous, different vendors or different operating systems have different processing nodes, for the same network load, each server's processing time and resources spent are different . In Web applications, servers dwell time is the main factor affecting user access server time, it is the sum of linking delay (queuing time) and processing delay (service time), that is to say, it is the experienced time during establish a TCP connection from the front-end node to start receiving HTTP request until the acknowledge transferred to the transport layer protocol TCP connections. Some operating systems are limited in the processing speed for dealing with package, the number of connections and supporting the flow types, so the high-speed network in the new packet arrival will generate a large number of system interrupts, these over interrupt is simply a CPU disaster for the less well-designed system.

2.4   Heterogeneous Cluster System Affects the Performance of the System

Operating system handles the TCP/IP protocol stack architecture design components may also cause problems, perhaps due to a high degree of encapsulation. These components of different levels of data processing capability is limited, leading to not support the underlying network protocol data stream related operations. Thus, load-balancing algorithm for heterogeneous cluster support is very important.

Load balancer's limit load balancer in theory can be expanded with an infinite capacity. However, due to memory, CPU and other components present the maximum amount and speed, cannot indefinitely support the balancer process. In the network traffic load, the load balancer need to remain connected within a certain time and node status information, limiting the cluster size and flow processing speed. It is a direct impact on the cluster scalability and performance when handle complex protocol network load, as it requires the introduction of the protocol packet header parsing which will increase the burden on the CPU balancer.

2.5   The Characteristics of Network Traffic Affect the Cluster System

Network flow is a wavy happens, it means after occurring in a longer period of low flow, there will be a large flow of access, and then a small flow, such as with the waves occur periodically. Because of this feature, it requires a load- dynamic feedback mechanism, using the state of the server group to deal with access to self-similar flow. TCP/IP protocol data contains the necessary network information, and therefore the cache in the network or specific network load balancing algorithm, the packet of information is very important. Through the entire packet in the network flow analysis, you can see the network packet processing time and resources spent in the period, and thus avoid some of the cluster system bottlenecks. While the imperfect conversation function maybe the key consideration when design the network load-balancing technology in the TCP/IP.

3   Load Balancing Strategy of the Web Server Cluster

Web server clusters need to design and implement effective Load Balancing strategy and Request Dispatching system, so that the customer's request to be assigned to the cluster nodes in the most appropriate Web server for processing, to obtain the best Web QoS (Quality of Service) performance , and through the load- balancing strategy by each server in the cluster to be in an equilibrium state (that is, the request of the server load and its processing capacity is in a directly proportional), makes the whole cluster system most efficient. Now, at home and abroad, the Web server load balancing cluster strategy study carried out around the following three areas:

- Web server load balancing indicators and the choice of load balancing algorithm;
- Web server load balancing scheduling strategy's effectiveness;
- Web server cluster system of remote access efficiency of executable files.

The major factors that affect the Web server load balancing are load balanced scheduling algorithm, network topology and load balancing granularity (grained) and so on. Among them, the scheduling algorithm is the core of the Web server load balancing technology [4]. People has put forward a lot of load balancing scheduling algorithm [5-8], these algorithms can be divided into two categories: Static scheduling algorithm and Dynamic scheduling algorithms.

Static scheduling algorithm is the scheduling algorithm in scheduling without regarding to the backend state of the server's current load, but on a different principle to choose a uniform schedule before scheduling rules to complete the service request scheduling. Such algorithms typically have rotation (Round-Robin) algorithm, the weighted rotation (weighed Round-Robin) algorithm, the minimum number of connections (Least Connections) algorithm, weighted least connections algorithm and random algorithm etc [9-11].

Such as, Round-Robin (RR) is a typical static load balancing strategy, is a non-state scheduling strategy. The basic idea is to give each node server for 1-N number of N nodes forms a circular queue and the request will forward to team head node server to poll the way, while assign to each node in turn. As the polling method does not take the current load on the server node into account, thus after run for some time, some node server may have been overloaded with work, and some are still idle node server.

Dynamic scheduling algorithm is the scheduling algorithm before making a service request to consider some of the current back-end server dynamic index, based on these indicators to determine the dynamic scheduling of service requests. Such scheduling algorithms include least connections balanced, weighted rotation algorithm, the target address hashing algorithm etc. By the Dynamic scheduling algorithm, the Web server cluster achieve dynamic load balancing, and its goal is to have the best solution to the balance between the various nodes , while also ensuring cost minimization after long-range communication and load redistribution.

4   Analysis and Algorithms of the Dynamic Allocation Strategies

Web server cluster dynamic load balancing, refers to the cluster server nodes according to a certain point of load conditions and dynamically allocated task to the server node, so that the lightly loaded server can take on more new tasks [9]. Although dynamic load equilibrium can consider each server of the real-time load and responsiveness, mainly through connection number to determine the size of the server load. While in Web services, the service time and computing resources to be consumed are vastly different when the client access network via Tcp connection, such as it depends on the type of service requested, the current network bandwidth consumption, server resource utilization and the current situation. Some of the heavy load of requests need to be compute-intensive queries or responses with very long data streams ; and relatively light load of requests often only need to read a Web page or for a very simple calculation. In addition the service client connection requests on the server resource requirements vary widely; frequent collect information will result in additional costs, resulting in node server cluster load tilt.

Therefore, the number of connections to the server can not accurately reflect the actual load conditions, and then you need to seek other indicators to estimate the parameters of the server busy degree, usually some of the parameters are CPU load, disk usage, memory utilization, the current process service number and the response time to the server. In this one, the server response time can better reflect the request on the server request queue length and processing time. Here, it using server response time as the weights, combined with the weighted rotation algorithm (Weighted Round-Robin, referred to WRR), proposing an improved Weighted Round-Robin Scheduling algorithm to reasonably allocate Web clients' request, so as to realize the Web server cluster dynamic load balancing.

Weighted round-robin scheduling algorithm is based on weight and the level of allocation to delicate requests to the web server. Inside the group of load members, each of them is assigned a weight to indicate their data processing capabilities. The higher weight value servers will obtain service request earlier than lower weight value and their request volume is greater than the. Meanwhile, the equal weight servers hold the same service process level which in accordance with a method of balancing rotation algorithm.

The scheduling algorithm is based on a weighted round-robin scheduling , through a test on each Server page to access the test, according to their response time to get the server's current load conditions, thereby automatically adjust the weights in different servers. Therefore, from the Web servers, it can take a Web page's response delay to estimate the load conditions. This test of server response time should complete in the user space, carried out once every 6 seconds and the sum of the first 10 response time for each server once every minute((SUM (i) refers to sum of the response time to the i-th), and as a basis for the system to adjust the weights. In scheduling a new connection, Weighted Round-Robin will make the established number of connections and its weight value in positive proportional as possible.   The algorithm flow is as follows:

Suppose there is a set of server S = {S_0, S_1,... , S_{n-1}}, W (S_i) said the weights server S_i, a instructions I said a variable selection of the server, cw said the current scheduling instructions variable metric, Max (S) said all the server set S the most power value, GCD (S) said all set S the biggest companies weights server. Variable I initialized to-1, cw initialized to zero.

```
while(true)
{
i=(i+1)mod n;
if(i==0)
{
cw=cw-gcd(S);
if(cw<=0)
{
cw=max(S);
if(cw==0)
return NULL;
}
}
if(W(S_i)>=cw)
return S_i;
}
```

Also assumed $C(S_i)$ said the number of the current connection server S_i. The number of all the current server connection sum to $C_{SUM} = \sum C(S_i) (I = 0, 1,..., n-1)$. The current new connection request will be sent server Sm, when and only when the server Sm meet the following requirements: $(C(S_m) / C_{SUM}) / W(S_m) = \min \{(C(S_i) / C_{SUM}) / W(S_i)\}$ $(I = 0, 1,.., n-1)$, including $W(S_i)$ is not zero. Because C_{SUM} in this round of search is a constant, so the judge conditions can be simplified as $C(S_m) / W(S_m) = \min \{C(S_i) / W(S_i)\}$ $(I = 0, 1,.., n-1)$, including $W(S_i)$ is not zero. Because the division CPU cycles than multiplication, and in the Linux kernel don't allow floating point division, and server weights are greater than zero, so the judge condition $C(S_m) / W(S_m) > C(S_i) / W(S_i)$ can be further optimized for $C(S_m) * W(S_i) > C(S_i) * W(S_m)$. At the same time guarantee the right to zero value server, the server will not be scheduling. So, the algorithm as long as perform the following process:

```
for(m=0;m<n;m++)
{
  if(T(S_m)>0)
{
for(i=m+1;i<n;i++)
{
if  (C(S_m)*T(S_i)>C(S_i)*T(S_m))
m=i;
}
return S_m;
}
}
return NULL;
```

Next, system initialization, the administrator for each server, weights to set an estimated value (Default Weight). The system begins after the operation, obtain the server of the page to test response time, send a request in record the current time sendtime, when response message completely when received, in the current time recvtime record, and obtain the time difference, namely the request processing time. Process is as follows:

```
    rnt=gettimeofday(&sendtime,&tz);//When a request to the
current time
    GetTestPage();// get test page
    rnt=gettimeofday(&recvtime,&tz)//Take   the   time   after
the test page
    acttime.tv sec=recvtime.tv sec-sendtime.tv sec:
    acttime.tv usec=recvtime.tv usec-sendtime.tv_usec; //Get
the response time of the server
```

Then, every minute statistics once every server before 10 times the time and sum (I), with Si said the first I server, make the sum (j) = Max (sum (1.)... sum (n)); Sum (k) = min (sum (1)... sum (n)); In turn formula in the sum (j) and sum (k) makes the following treatment:

$$T_{max} = \frac{sum(j)}{\frac{1}{n}\sum_{i-1}^{n} sum(i)} - 1 \tag{1}$$

$$T_{min} = 1 - \frac{sum(k)}{\frac{1}{n}\sum_{i-1}^{n} sum(i)} \tag{2}$$

If Tmax is greater than a certain threshold, it said server Sj load is too large, need to adjust their weights, so the server can reduce the weight of 1; Similarly, if the Tmin is less than a threshold, it said Sk load is too small, thus can increase the weight of the server 1. Based on such processing, after the system running for some time , the adjusted weights will be able to more accurately reflect current service capabilities of each server to provide a reasonable load distribution .

5   Conclusion

In conclusion, this paper mainly analyzes the main factor that may affect the Web server cluster performance and the normal load- balancing strategy, put forward an improved Weighted Round-Robin Scheduling algorithm to achieve the Web client requests a reasonable allocation, in order to achieve Web server clusters dynamic load balancing. The scheduling algorithm used weighted rotation scheduling algorithm in the kernel and can estimate the current load on the server and server performance during the response time to select the server in user space. It is simple and effective, taking up less system resources, and ensures high-speed packet forwarding and reasonable adjust load distribution.

References

1. Rajkumar, B.: High Performance Cluster Computing Architecture and System. Prentice-Hall (2000)
2. Teo, Y.M., Ayani, R.: Comparison of Load Balancing Strategies on Cluster-based Web Servers. Transactions of the Society for Modeling and Simulation 77(5-6), 185–195 (2001)

3. Li, Y., Yang, Y., Ma, M., Zhou, L.: A hybrid load balancing strategy of sequential tasks for grid computing environments. Future Generation Computer Systems 25(8), 819–828 (2009)
4. Bertini, L., Leite, J.C.B., Mossé, D.: Power optimization for dynamic configuration in heterogeneous web server clusters. Journal of Systems and Software 83(4), 585–598 (2010)
5. Robinette, S.L., Zhang, F., Lei, B.-L., Brüschweiler, R.: Web Server Based Complex Mixture Analysis by NMR. Analytical Chemistry 80(10), 3606–3611 (2008)
6. Gao, A., Mu, D.-J., Hu, Y.-S.: Differentiated Service and Load Balancing in Web Cluster. Journal of Electronics & Information Technology 33(3), 555–562 (2011)
7. Wang, S., Xiu, B., Xiao, W.: Research on Dynamic Load-balancing Algorithm for Web-Service Cluster System. Computer Engineering and Applications 25, 78–80 (2004)
8. Crovella, M.E., Carter, R.L.: Dynamic Server Selection in the Internet. In: Proceedings of the Third IEEE Workshop on the Architecture and Implementation of High Performance Communication Subsystems (HPCS 1995), pp. 352–360 (1995)
9. Colajanni, M., Yu, P.S., Cardellini, V.: Dynamic Load Balancing in Geographically Distributed Heterogeneous Web Servers. In: ICDCS, pp. 295–302 (1998)
10. Katz, E.D., Butler, M., McGrath, R.: A Scalable HTTP Server: The NCSA Prototype. Computer Networks and ISDN Systems 27(2), 155–164 (1994)
11. Bryhni, H., Klovning, E., Kure, O.: A Comparison of Load Balancing Techniques for Scalable Web Servers. IEEE Network, 58–64 (2000)

Research on the Principle and Application of Multiversion Data in SQL Server 2008

Aiwu Li[1] and Hongying Liu[2]

[1] Dept. of Computer Science
Guangdong Vocational College of Posts and Telecom
Guangzhou, China
[2] Dept. of Computer Science and Engineering, Guangzhou Vocational & Technical
Institute of Industry & Commerce
Guangzhou, China
law_mail@126.com, 327147616@qq.com

Abstract. In this paper, to solve the problem of read/write waiting in SQL Server, designed two additional database option parameters: read-committed-snapshot, allow-snapshot-isolation and introduced multiversion data technology, while performing modification operations, the old version data will be stored in tempdb database. Read operation can use the old version data in tempdb database, eliminate the need to use shared lock. Set a new snapshot isolation level, read operations no longer need to use shared lock. The experiment results show it can solve the read/write waiting problem in serializable isolation level.

Keywords: Multiversion data, read and write wait, transaction isolation level.

1 Introduction

In SQL Server 2000 and earlier releases, the read operation will use shared locks, the update will use exclusive locks, the two locks are not compatible with each other. Read waiting to write and vice versa will occur [1-2]. At read committed isolation level, the read operation will wait for modifications until the transaction commits. At serializable isolation level, modify operation will wait for the read operation until the transaction is complete. Since the occurrence of read/write waiting, SQL Server's operating efficiency is greatly reduced [3-4].

In order to solve the problem of read/write waiting, from 2005 release, SQL Server added two additional database option parameters: read-committed-snapshot, allow-snapshot-isolation and introduced multiversion data technology. While performing modification operations, the old version data will be stored in tempdb database [4-5].

While open read-committed-snapshot parameter in read committed isolation level, if the transaction in which modification was conducted does not finish, the read operation will use the old version data in tempdb database, eliminating the need to use shared lock [6-7].

M. Zhao and J. Sha (Eds.): ICCIP 2012, Part II, CCIS 289, pp. 707–717, 2012.

While open allow-snapshot-isolation parameter, the update will also produce multiversion data, and a new snapshot isolation level can be set, which achieved the same effect, with serializable isolation level, but read operations no longer need to use shared lock. If the data read are being modified by other connection, the read operation will read the old version data before the transaction bigan. By this way, can solve the read/write waiting problem in serializable isolation level [8-9].

2   Transaction Processing and Transaction Isolation Level in SQL Server 2008

2.1   Transaction Processing in Database System

Transaction processing is designed to maintain a computer system in a known, consistent state, by ensuring that any operations carried out on the system that are interdependent are either all completed successfully or all canceled successfully.

Databases which treat the integrity of data as paramount often include the ability to handle transactions to maintain the integrity of data.

A single transaction consists of one or more independent units of work, each reading and/or writing information to a database or other data store. When this happens it is often important to ensure that all such processing leaves the database or data store in a consistent state.

A database transaction, by definition, must be atomic, consistent, isolated and durable.

Transactions in a database environment have two main purposes:

1. To provide reliable units of work that allow correct recovery from failures and keep a database consistent even in cases of system failure, when execution stops (completely or partially) and many operations upon a database remain uncompleted, with unclear status.
2. To provide isolation between programs accessing a database concurrently. If this isolation is not provided the programs outcome are possibly erroneous.

Transaction processing allows multiple individual operations to be linked together automatically as a single, indivisible transaction. The transaction-processing system ensures that either all operations in a transaction are completed without error, or none of them are. If some of the operations are completed but errors occur when the others are attempted, the transaction-processing system "rolls back" all of the operations of the transaction (including the successful ones), thereby erasing all traces of the transaction and restoring the system to the consistent, known state that it was in before processing of the transaction began. If all operations of a transaction are completed successfully, the transaction is committed by the system, and all changes to the database are made permanent; the transaction cannot be rolled back once this is done.

Transaction processing guards against hardware and software errors that might leave a transaction partially completed, with the system left in an unknown, inconsistent state. If the computer system crashes in the middle of a transaction, the transaction processing system guarantees that all operations in any uncommitted (i.e., not completely processed) transactions are cancelled.

Most of the time, transactions are issued concurrently. If they overlap (i.e. need to touch the same portion of the database), this can create conflicts. forcing transactions to be processed sequentially (i.e. without overlapping in time) is inefficient. Therefore, under concurrency, transaction processing usually guarantees that the end result reflects a conflict-free outcome that can be reached as if executing the transactions sequentially in any order.

2.2   Transaction Isolation Level

In database systems, isolation is a property that defines how/when the changes made by one operation become visible to other concurrent operations. Isolation is one of the ACID (Atomicity, Consistency, Isolation, Durability) properties.

Of the four ACID properties in a DBMS (Database Management System), the isolation property is the one most often relaxed. When attempting to maintain the highest level of isolation, a DBMS usually acquires locks on data or implements multiversion concurrency control, which may result in a loss of concurrency. This requires adding additional logic for the application to function correctly.

Most DBMS's offer a number of transaction isolation levels, which control the degree of locking that occurs when selecting data. For many database applications, the majority of database transactions can be constructed to avoid requiring high isolation levels (e.g. SERIALIZABLE level), thus reducing the locking overhead for the system. The programmer must carefully analyze database access code to ensure that any relaxation of isolation does not cause software bugs that are difficult to find. Conversely, if higher isolation levels are used, the possibility of deadlock is increased, which also requires careful analysis and programming techniques to avoid.

The isolation levels defined by the ANSI/ISO SQL standard are listed as follows.

SERIALIZABLE:This is the highest isolation level.

With a lock-based concurrency control DBMS implementation, serializability requires read and write locks (acquired on selected data) to be released at the end of the transaction. Also range-locks must be acquired when a SELECT query uses a ranged WHERE clause, especially to avoid the phantom reads phenomenon (see below).

When using non-lock based concurrency control, no locks are acquired; however, if the system detects a write collision among several concurrent transactions, only one of them is allowed to commit. See snapshot isolation for more details on this topic.

REPEATABLE READ:In this isolation level, a lock-based concurrency control DBMS implementation keeps read and write locks (acquired on selected data) until the end of the transaction. However, range-locks are not managed, so the phantom reads phenomenon can occur

READ COMMITTED:In this isolation level, a lock-based concurrency control DBMS implementation keeps write locks (acquired on selected data) until the end of the transaction, but read locks are released as soon as the SELECT operation is performed (so the non-repeatable reads phenomenon can occur in this isolation level, as discussed below). As in the previous level, range-locks are not managed.

READ UNCOMMITTED:This is the lowest isolation level. In this level, dirty reads are allowed (see below), so one transaction may see not-yet-committed changes made by other transactions.

Above four isolation levels are defined in the ANSI SQL-92 standard.

2.3   ACID Implementations

There are two popular families of techniques to implement ACID properties: write ahead logging and shadow paging. In both cases, locks must be acquired on all information that is updated, and depending on the level of isolation, possibly on all data that is read as well. In write ahead logging, atomicity is guaranteed by copying the original (unchanged) data to a log before changing the database. That allows the database to return to a consistent state in the event of a crash.

In shadowing, updates are applied to a partial copy of the database, and the new copy is activated when the transaction commits.

Many databases rely upon locking to provide ACID capabilities. Locking means that the transaction marks the data that it accesses so that the DBMS knows not to allow other transactions to modify it until the first transaction succeeds or fails. The lock must always be acquired before processing data, including data that are read but not modified. Non-trivial transactions typically require a large number of locks, resulting in substantial overhead as well as blocking other transactions. For example, if user A is running a transaction that has to read a row of data that user B wants to modify, user B must wait until user A's transaction completes. Two phase locking is often applied to guarantee full isolation.

An alternative to locking is multiversion concurrency control, in which the database provides each reading transaction the prior, unmodified version of data that is being modified by another active transaction. This allows readers to operate without acquiring locks. I.e., writing transactions do not block reading transactions, and readers do not block writers. Going back to the example, when user A's transaction requests data that user B is modifying, the database provides A with the version of that data that existed when user B started his transaction. User A gets a consistent view of the database even if other users are changing data. One implementation relaxes the isolation property, namely snapshot isolation.

2.4   Snapshot Isolation Level

In databases, and transaction processing (transaction management), snapshot isolation is a guarantee that all reads made in a transaction will see a consistent snapshot of the database (in practice it reads the last committed values that existed at the time it started), and the transaction itself will successfully commit only if no updates it has made conflict with any concurrent updates made since that snapshot.

Snapshot isolation arose from work on multiversion concurrency control databases, where multiple versions of the database are maintained concurrently to allow readers to execute without colliding with writers. Such a system allows a natural definition and implementation of such an isolation level.

Unfortunately, the ANSI SQL-92 standard was written with a lock-based database in mind, and hence is rather vague when applied to MVCC systems. Berenson et al. wrote a paper in 1995 [10] critiquing the SQL standard, and cited snapshot isolation as an example of an isolation level that did not exhibit the standard anomalies described in the ANSI SQL-92 standard, yet still had anomalous behaviour when compared with serializable transactions.

Snapshot isolation has been adopted by several major database management systems, such as SQL Anywhere, InterBase, Firebird, Oracle, PostgreSQL. The main reason for its adoption is that it allows better performance than serializability, yet still avoids most of the concurrency anomalies that serializability avoids (but not always all). In practice snapshot isolation is implemented within multiversion concurrency control (MVCC), where generational values of each data item (versions) are maintained: MVCC is a common way to increase concurrency and performance by generating a new version of a database object each time the object is written, and allowing transactions' read operations of several last relevant versions (of each object).

2.5   Transaction Isolation Levels Surported in Sql Server

In SQL Server 2000 and earlier releases, the above four isolation levels were supported, and were implemented using locks. Different locks needed in different isolation levels are shown in table 1 as following.

Table 1. Lock needed in different isolation levels

Isolation level	write lock	read lock	range lock
Read uncommitted		-	-
Read committed	V	-	-
Repeatable read	V	V	-
Serializable	V	V	V

Using locks means one operation may block another operation. Besides block occuring. there can be three different read phenomena as showing in table 2.

Table 2. Lock needed in different isolation levels

Isolation level	write lock	read lock	range lock
Read uncommitted	may occur	may occur	may occur
Read committed	-	may occur	may occur
Repeatable read	-	-	may occur
Serializable	-	-	-

In SQL Server 2008 ACID properties is implemented by multiversion concurrency control, namely, multiversion data. By using multiversion data, it does not need to use lock to acquire data consistency in read committed isolation level. And snapshot isolation level was added in SQL Server 2008. The effect of snapshot isolation level is same as serializable, but there is no need to use lock.

3   Multiversion Data Generated after Opening Read-Committed-Snapshot

3.1   Multiversion Data Generated by Insert Operation

Execute following commands to create a test table and insert one record before and after opening read-committed-snapshot parameter respectively.

```
use db
create table t(a int identity, b char(5) default 'xxxxx')
insert into t default values
alter database db set read-committed-snapshot on
insert into t default values
go
```

Following is the original hex data of above two records, the 1st record is shown as follows:

```
10000d00
01000000
78787878
78020000
```

The 2nd record is shown as follows:

```
50000d00
02000000
78787878
78020000
00000000
00000000
51010000
0000
```

The row header data of 1st record is 0x10, which indicates that this row is a common heap record including null bitmap data. The row header data of 2nd record is 0x50, which indicates that this row is a common heap record including null bitmap data and version data.

The additional 14 bytes data is used to store version information. Its first 8 bytes is the RowID of the old version data in tempdb database. Its latter 6 bytes is the ID number of the transaction in which the modification is running. Because there is no old version data generated, the first 8 bytes' values are all 0.

3.2   Multiversion Data Generated by Update Operation

To get old version data, execute following command to update above first record:

```
begin tran
update t set b='aaaaa' where a=1
go
```

Check its original data, can find there are newly added version data. Following is the new hex data, the bold part in the end of the record is the version data:

50000d00
01000000
61616161
61020000
c0000000
01000000
87010000
00

Its first 8 bytes of version data indicates the address or RowID of old version data in tempdb database, which is (1:192:0), the latter 6 bytes is the ID number of the transaction in which modification is running. The meaning of every part in version data can be explained by Figure.1.

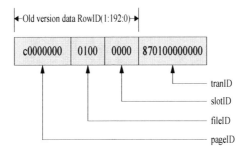

Fig. 1. Meaning of version dat

We can find the old version data as following by dumping out the #192 data page of tempdb database:

10000d
00010000
00787878
78780200
00

The above process of data change can be indicated by Figure.2.

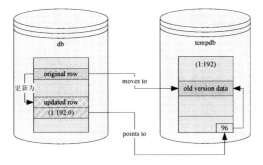

Fig. 2. Process of data change

3.3   Multiversion Data Generated by Delete Operation

As for delete operation, if the transaction in which it is running has not finished, the deleted records will be removed to tempdb database, the original data will only reserve 14 bytes version data to store its address in tempdb database and the transaction ID number.

After setting on read-committed-snapshot option parameters, in order to get old version data generated by delete operation, execute following commands to recreate table t in database db, and insert two rows as testing data.

```
drop table t
create table t(a int identity, b char(5) default 'xxxxx')
go
insert into t default values
go 2
Dump out two rows' original hex data, the first row is:
50000d00
 01000000
78787878
78020000
00000000
00000000
4c010000
0000
the second row is:
50000d00
02000000
78787878
78020000
00000000
00000000
4d010000
0000
```

The dumped hex data indicates that the version data has been generated, but the version data, the last 14 bytes, is null.

```
Start a transaction, and delete the second row.
begin tran
delete from t where a=2
go
```

Dump the hex data again, can find that the version data is inserted into the free part of the data page at the page tail, and there is no row data in the version data, the original row is deleted.

```
The dumped hex data is as following.
4eb80000 00010000 007d0100 000000
```

It indicates the rowID,(1:184:0),of the old version data, which is moved into tempdb database. Dump the old version data in tempdb database as following.

```
50000d
00020000
00787878
78780200
00000000
00000000
004d0100
000000
```

It is the very data of the deleted row, if rollback the above transaction, the deleted row will be added to the original data page again. If commit the transaction, the offset value of second row will be set to 0, indicating it is deleted.

4 Multiversion Data Generated after Opening Allow-Snapshot-Isolation

From SQL Server 2005 release on, a new transaction isolation level, snapshot was added, at the same time, a new database option parameter, allow-snapshot-isolation was added. To use snapshot isolation level in a connection, the allow-snapshot-isolation parameter must be set to on first.

After snapshot isolation level being set in a connection, it only reads the data committed before its transaction begins. The effect of this aspect is same as serializable isolation level. But in snapshot isolation level, the read operation does not need shared lock, so it allows other connection to modify the data being read, the multiversion data plays the key role to get this effect, that is, there are multiple versions corresponding to one record being read. In serializable isolation level, there is no old version data generated, the data being read is not allowed to modify until the transaction in which the read operation is running completes

Supposed the database has set on its allow-snapshot-isolation option parameter, and 3 sessions, A,B,C, have connected to the database, by using update operation as sample, we can explain the generating process of   multiversion data as following.

1. Set section A to snapshot isolation level;
2. In section A, begin a transaction, execute query_A, get a row row_A which is stored in page_A;
3. In section B, update row_A, the updated result of row_B is stored in page_A, the original data is stored in tempdb database as old version data. The address of row_A in tempdb database is stored in row_B as its version data;
4. Section B committed its transaction before section A committed its transaction. To guarantee the data read by section A does not change, the old version data row_A in tempdb database would be retained if the transaction of section A does not complete. Corresponding to the record read section A,

there are two versions' data, the one is row_A which stored in tempd database, and the other is row_B   which stored in page_A of original database;

5. If start another section C, and set its isolation level as snapshot, the data read by query_A will always be row_B untill the transaction completes;
6. Section C updated row_B and commits the transaction, the result row_C is stored in page_A, and row_B is stored in tempdb database, the address of row_B in tempdb database is stored in row_C as version data.

If start other connections to continue above processes, more versions' data of row_A can be generated.

There are three versions' data corresponding to the record read by section A, the newst version, row_C, which is stored in original database's page_A, another 2 old versions are stored in tempdb database, the newer version data store the address of its previous older version data. The different version data will be read by same query query_A in different transactions beginning at different time.The storing format of version data is same as openning the read-committed-snapshot parameter, so we do not repeat it here.

The relation of above multiversion data can be indicated by Figure.3.

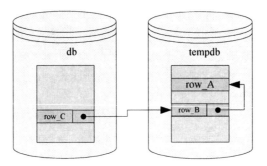

Fig. 3. Relation of multiversion data

5   Conclusion

Designed two additional database option parameters: read-committed-snapshot, allow-snapshot-isolation and introduced multiversion data technology, While performing modification operations, the old version data will be stored in tempdb database. If the transaction in which modification was conducted does not finish, read operation can use the old version data in tempdb database, eliminate the need to use shared lock. Set a new snapshot isolation level, read operations no longer need to use shared lock, can achieve the same effect. The experiment results show it can solve the read/write waiting problem in serializable isolation level.

Oracle has been using multiversion data technology for many years, By using multiversion data technology, SQL Server solves the problem of read/write waiting, which perplexing for many years, and its running efficiency was greatly raised, reducing the technology gap between Oracle and SQL Server. However, this technology in SQL Server is not perfect, its function is not available by default setting, needing to open read-committed-snapshot or allow-snapshot-isolation option parameters, which affects read committed and snapshot isolation level respectively. We look forward to using this feature by default database setting in future versions, not requring manual setting like current SQL Server release.

References

1. Bernstein, P.A., Cseri, I., Dani, N., Ellis, N., Kalhan, A., Kakivaya, G., Lomet, D.B., Manne, R., Novik, L., Talius, T.: Adapting Microsoft SQL server for cloud computing. In: 2011 IEEE 27th International Conference on Data Engineering (ICDE), pp. 1255–1263 (2011)
2. Fang, Y., Friedman, M., Nair, G., Rys, M., Schmid, A.-E.: Spatial indexing in microsoft SQL server 2008. In: Proceedings of the 2008 ACM SIGMOD International Conference on Management of Data, pp. 1207–1216 (2008)
3. Daudjee, K., Salem, K.: Lazy database replication with snapshot isolation. In: Proceedings of the 32nd International Conference on Very Large Data Bases, pp. 715–726 (2006)
4. Bernabé-Gisbert, J.M., Salinas-Monteagudo, R., Irún-Briz, L., Muñoz-Escoí, F.D.: Managing Multiple Isolation Levels in Middleware Database Replication Protocols. In: Guo, M., Yang, L.T., Di Martino, B., Zima, H.P., Dongarra, J., Tang, F. (eds.) ISPA 2006. LNCS, vol. 4330, pp. 511–523. Springer, Heidelberg (2006)
5. Cahill, M.J., Röhm, U., Fekete, A.D.: Serializable isolation for snapshot databases. ACM Transactions on Database Systems 34(4) (2009)
6. Jain, S., Shafique, F., Djeric, V., Goel, A.: Application-level isolation and recovery with solitude. In: Proceedings of the 3rd ACM SIGOPS/EuroSys European Conference on Computer Systems 2008, vol. 42(4) (2008)
7. Haustein, M., Härder, T.: Optimizing lock protocols for native XML processing. Knowledge Engineering 65(1), 147–173 (2008)
8. Wrembel, R., Bębel, B.: Metadata Management in a Multiversion Data Warehouse. In: Spaccapietra, S., Atzeni, P., Fages, F., Hacid, M.-S., Kifer, M., Mylopoulos, J., Pernici, B., Shvaiko, P., Trujillo, J., Zaihrayeu, I. (eds.) Journal on Data Semantics VIII. LNCS, vol. 4380, pp. 118–157. Springer, Heidelberg (2007)
9. Arigon, A.-M., Miquel, M., Tchounikine, A.: Multimedia data warehouses: a multiversion model and a medical application. Multimedia Tools and Applications 35(1), 91–108 (2007)
10. Berenson, H., Bernstein, P., Gray, J., Melton, J., O'Neil, E., O'Neil, P.: A Critique of ANSI SQL Isolation Levels. In: Proceedings of the 1995 ACM SIGMOD International Conference on Management of Data, pp. 1–10 (1995)
11. Oracle Database Concepts 10g Release 1 (10.1) Chapter 13 : Data Concurrency and Consistency — Oracle Isolation Levels
12. PostgreSQL 9.0 Documentation: 13.2.2.1. Serializable Isolation versus True Serializability
13. Cahill, M.J., Röhm, U., Fekete, A.D.: Serializable isolation for snapshot databases. In: Proceedings of the 2008 ACM SIGMOD International Conference on Management of Data, pp. 729–738 (2008)
14. Fekete, A., Liarokapis, D., O'Neil, E., O'Neil, P., Shasha, D.: Making Snapshot Isolation Serializable. ACM Transactions on Database Systems 30(2), 492–528 (2005)
15. Weikum, G., Vossen, G.: Transactional information systems: theory, algorithms, and the practice of concurrency control and recovery. Morgan Kaufmann (2002)

The Personal Information Privacy Protection Strategy in Social Security Information System

Xuefang Wang[1] and Hongrong Xue[2]

[1] ShijiaZhuang Railway University,
ShijiaZhuang, 050043, China
[2] The 54th Research Institute of CETC,
ShijiaZhuang, 050020, China
{wangxuefang80,xuehongrong2010}@163.com

Abstract. Social security information system bears all the social security business, playing an increasingly important role in the cause of labor and social security, but it also have a great deal of personal information of citizens. How to protect private information becomes the most public concerns. In the analysis of the privacy protection of personal information in the social security information system, this paper presents the strategies to protect the privacy by converting the original data, which provides some research ideas for the implementation of privacy protection.

Keywords: Privacy, Social Security, Personal Information.

1   Introduction

Social security has developed rapidly in recent years. Social security departments have a great deal of personal information of citizens in the performance of public administration and social service functions. Therefore the information privacy issues should be taken seriously enough. Development of network technology and network applications in depth makes vast amounts of personal information data to be more convenient to store and query. Worrying is that in the actual use, a great deal of information has been used indiscriminately without restrictions and disclosure of confidential information has seriously impacted on people's daily lives and even social stability. Social security provide convenient and efficient information services for citizens, but also need to face the resulting information security problems. Therefore, how to protect privacy information in social security information system has become an extremely urgent problem in the study of social security information.

2   Privacy and Protection of Privacy

The concept of privacy includes a wide range of content. Usually we will be understood aspart of their narrow individual information and data. And to protect the rights of such information and data is known as privacy. Privacy of the emergence

M. Zhao and J. Sha (Eds.): ICCIP 2012, Part II, CCIS 289, pp. 718–724, 2012.

and development is closely linked to the process of human civilization. The richer people's emotions, sense of shame and awareness of their rights more strongly, the more sensitive to privacy. In modern society, many countries and international organizations attach great importance to the protection of privacy and have at different periods of the relevant regulations and documents [1]. In the seventies, U.S. Department of Health Education and Welfaredepartments passed the "Privacy Protection", which made for personal data collection, record, modify and publish principles. New Zealand, Canada and China's Hong Konghave also passed for the protection of privacy laws and regulations. ROC, in the privacyprotection issues still in its infancy. Early on, no specific laws and regulations provide effective protection of privacy. To solve this problem, China adopted the draft Civil Code in the near future to highlight the protection ofmoral rights, in particular, the inclusion of moral rights to privacy, which fully reflects that the 21st century will be more respect for human dignity and human values. Recently, the first"Personal Information Protection Act" has entered the legislative stages, which are reflected China's growing concern about privacy issues.

Regulations and system of continuous improvement is on behalf of the government and the social concerns on protection of the privacy. However, with network and database technology, privacy is facing increasing challenges, the concept and scopehas become more complex. The research on Data privacy is essential in modern society.

3   Privacy Problems in Social Security System

Social security information system is an important part of the national social security, which is connected insured persons, agencies, and management. It bears all the social security business, playing an increasingly important role in the cause of labor and social security, but it also has a great deal of personal information of citizens. The information privacy issues are also increasingly prominent. Overall, the privacy of information security issues in the social security system focus on confidentiality and availabilitybalance.

3.1   How to Protect Information Security

Extensive application of modern information technology make communication faster and more subtle. Therefore, there is more difficult to protect private information. Network information technologies make people's ability to deal with growing mass of information, all kinds of information dissemination faster and faster, increasing precision search technology, so that people can easily find all kinds of information they need. Social security provide convenient and efficient information services for citizens, but also need to face the resulting information security problems. For example, some local agencies when conducting online publicity, often publish the name and identity of all 18 numbers. Some lawless elements, often through the use of networkprobes and other tools to easily collect a large number of citizen's name and identification number for credit card fraud and other illegal activities.

3.2   How to Define Private Information

Different definitions for private information are often different. What is the"personal information" is needed to protect the privacy of information, often require personal information to determine the carrier, which has brought to the difficulty of protecting private information. However, the collection of personal information department should take a conservative principle, to open the collection to the minimum personal information of citizens. Currently, many business areas are established within the industry of personal information collection and privacy management practices, but the government departments in this area is lagging behind. Therefore, how to properly handle the protection of personal privacy information in the social security system is an important task in the construction of social security information.

4   Privacy Policies of Social Security Systems

Analysis of the protection of private information, which of the two roots of the problem is: the improper collection of personal information and inappropriate use. Improper collection is over-collection of unnecessary information.For the social security departments, the purpose of collecting personal information of citizens is to record basic information of citizens, or the approved base pay and benefits and maintain appropriate links with citizens. In practice, we need to note that the information collected whether there is sufficient need, whether that is necessary for the completion of business operations. No reason to over-collect citizen information, particularly those relating to work-related items of information collected on the one hand lead to work overload, distortion of information increases; on the other hand, the maintenance and safety management on collected information has also increased the organization's workload. Improper use is the deviation from the target of using information, including improper disclosure, improper passing, etc. More specifically, in the process,the work should reduce the use of personal information, only use the most necessary personal information to complete business, without using of work-related personal information. For example, the health insurance sector in the charge of business operations audit process, audit staff focused on the hospital's treatment and medication for post-audit, auditors need to focus only in the course of their work projects and prescriptions to treatment, but not necessary to understand the patient's name and location of the unit and other personal information, so that information systems should withheld the doctor's name or ID number and other irrelevant information to protect the personal privacy of medical treatment records. In the business aspects of information disclosure within the field of social security, there are many details need to focus on privacy. On the one hand, the lack of effective means of protection should be avoided under the premise of personal information transmitted to other unrelated individuals. For example, some places use the Internet for public services, there is no information on the privacy of publicity filtration treatment, when asked to enter the Internet to check the parameter is too small, the lack of appropriate technical protection measures, so that the insured person's basic personal information can be easily queried by other persons. On the other hand, in the absence of the necessary security conditions, the subject of mastering personal information should avoid transmiting the personal information which it has to the third parties. Commissioned by the developer for data cleaning and data processing and other business, such institutions not only in legal proceedings ensure the information protection obligations of service units and service personnel, also need to take the necessary technical management means in the restrictions on workplace and working equipment, thereby reducing the possibility of leakage of the personal information in the transmission process.

4.1   Privacy Protected Program

Based on the above analysis, the study found that there are many problems in existing privacy protection. First, the study about how to determine the privacy object in the raw data is relatively rare.Thesis that privacy between the data object is associated, if not get the association, even if the data users can be inferred with high confidence level of a part of the data values, he can not make these two types of data effectively linking data to gain a better understanding of the individual characteristics of useful information. As the user the amount of deposits and depositors can not be linked to the name, identity can not be linked to illness and disease, as only informed of the data will not have a part of the privacy threat.

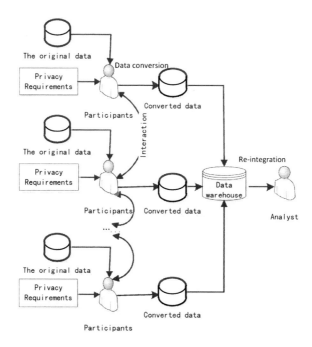

Fig. 1. Privacy protection program

Furthermore, the protection of privacy data analysis process will inevitably cause some impact on the results. How to take into account the degree of protection of data privacy and the accuracy of data analysis and how to retain data availability are also worth considering. Privacy object is no longer just a combination of several attributes, but by the specific data associated with the composition. The correlation between data collection can not be obtained directly from the data, so the object of that type of privacy protection should deal with specific attribute values from the start.To this end, the paper presents a protection strategy: converting private information. Figure 1 shows the overall process to achieve privacy protection structures and processes.

In the implementation process, assuming that all of the data sources are homogeneous, and each participant has a different privacy requirements. So each participant will independently generate a transformation matrix to transform their data. And this transformation matrix represents participants' different privacy requirements of the different attribute variables. Then participants will send the converted data to the data warehouse. Finally, the analyst will integrate these data. Through matrix transformation, all the data attributes associated will be converted to retain the data required in the case of the statistical properties. As all values' conversion in the raw data matrix has been carried out, there can be no access to the associated privacy.

4.2   Privacy Algorithm

The specific elements of the matrix having been addressed, is associated with the importance of each attribute to achieve the purpose of custom privacy needs.As the re-arrangement of the orthogonal matrix of rows or columns does not affect the orthogonality, we can rearrange a random orthogonal matrix of row vectors and column vectors, making it the diagonal elements arranged in a certain order, customized to meet privacy protection needs. Assuming the data owners want to protect all data attributes according to their degree of descending sort, they can generate a random orthogonal matrix H according to the literature [2] algorithm, and generate a custom privacy transformation matrix by Algorithm 1.

In algorithm 1, the data owner first randomly select from the matrix H or the pre-specified melements, and make each row and each column have one and only one element be selected. The algorithm assumes that the selected matrix elements have made up the vector S. Then the data owner makes the elements in S arranged in a specific order, such as in the algorithm in an ascending order. This order also represents each property different emphasis by the data owner. For example, if all elements in S are in an ascending order, then the importance of each attribute (that is, the owner concerned about the extent of the property) will meet in a descending order. Then in accordance with each element si in S, the data owners rearrange the position of each row vector in H. Similarly, column vectors in H are arranged in accordance with this method, resulting in the matrix G. The vectors consisted of the diagonal matrix elements in G are the sorted vector S. Assuming that the data provided by participants are made up of m attributes, then the time complexity of Algorithm 1 is O (m log m).Accordance with the above algorithm, if the m attributes are just by descending order of importance, the diagonal elements of the orthogonal transformation matrix in the algorithm will be arranged from small to big. Similarly, the order of property importance arranged by the data provider may be changing, but a similar approach can be used to customize privacy orthogonal transformation matrix.

```
Algorithm 1   Algorithm for privacy custom
Input:data matrix D,m×m orthogonal matrix H
Output:orthogonal matrix G with customized privacy
begin
     S:=?;
     G:=H;
     while H=NULL do
       begin
         choose an element hij from H;
         delete the ith row and jth column in H;
         S:=S∪hij;
       end
     sort the elements of S in ascending order;
     for i:=1 to m do
       begin
         find sk∈S which is also from the ith row of G;
        if i=k then
           begin
             swap the ith and the kth rows of G;
           end
       end
     for i:=1 to m do
       begin
         find sk∈S which is also from the ith column of
G;
         if i=k then
           begin
             swap the ith and the kth columns of G;
           end
       end
     output matrix G;
   end
```

In practice, the data owner will usually have different levels of interest in different properties. In general, they can follow their own experience, according to the field of the magnitude of the actual business impact, and sort the importance of attributes. For example, the personnel records in the social security system may include age, address, contact details, occupation, work unit, and so on. System administrators can reveal the risks because of disclosing the value of each property, and then sort descending based on risk. With this level of importance of attributes, we can introduce it to the data conversion process, which allows data owners in accordance with the privacy of their own to customize conversion process, which allows different attributes have different levels of protection of privacy.

5   Conclusion

Protecting the privacy of citizens from infringement for government departments is a basic requirement. By the impact of operational characteristics, the social security departments should not only attach importance to the protection of private information of citizens and strengthen the construction of related systems, but also design and implement a reasonable technical protection for the classified information in terms of technology. The paper presents the personal information privacy strategy, which not only provides a feasible way to protect privacy for the social security system and improves the grasp of the details of information security, but also effectively guarantee the work necessary to support the normal conduct of business and the leakage of personal information of citizens minimize the risk.

Acknowledgment. This work was supported by Hebei Province,2011 issue of Human Resources and Social Security Fund, Issue number: JRS-2011-6052.

References

1. Nan, D.: Data Mining Privacy: Legal and technical. Theory and Exploration 31(7), 772–775 (2007)
2. Stewart, G.W.: The Efficient Generation of Random Orthogonal Matrices with an Application to Condition Estimators. SIAM Journal on Numerical Analysis 17(3), 403–409 (1980)
3. Amiri, A.: Dare to share:Protecting sensitive knowledge with data sanitization. Decision Support Systems 43(1), 181–191 (2007)
4. Dougherty, D.J., Fisler, K., Krishnamurthi, S.: Specifying and Reasoning About Dynamic Access-Control Policies. In: Furbach, U., Shankar, N. (eds.) IJCAR 2006. LNCS (LNAI), vol. 4130, pp. 632–646. Springer, Heidelberg (2006)
5. Aggarwal, C.C., Yu, P.S.: A survey of randomization methods for privacy-preserving data mining. In: Privacy-Preserving Data Mining. Advances in Database Systems, vol. 34, pp. 137–156. Springer US (2008)
6. Agrawal, R., Strikant, R.: Privacy-preserving data mining. In: Proceedings of the 2000 ACM SIGMOD International Conference on Management of Data, Dallas,Texas, pp. 439–450 (May 2000)
7. Amiri, A.: Dare to share: Protecting sensitive knowledge with data sanitization. Decision Support Systems 43(1), 181–191 (2007)
8. Bayardo, R.J., Agrawal, R.: Data privacy through optimal k-anonymization. In: Proc.of the 21th International Conference on Data Engineering, pp. 217–228 (2005)
9. Bethencourt, J., Song, D., Waters, B.: New constructions and practical applications for private stream searching. In: Proc. of the 2006 IEEE Symposium on Security and Privacy, pp. 132–139 (2006)

Topic Diffusion Behavior Tracking in Online Social Network

Zheng Liang, Yan Jia, Bin Zhou, and Baida Zhang

Institute of Software, Department of Computer, National University of Defense Technology,
Changsha 410073, China
zliang@nudt.edu.cn, yanjiajy@vip.sina.com,
{bin.zhou.cn,zhangbaida}@gmail.com

Abstract. Information Diffusion in social network is of much importance in tracking public opinion, launching new products, and other applications. In this paper, we formally define the problem of Topic Diffusion Behavior Tracking and propose a novel model by investigating users' topic interest. Our algorithm is developed based on the combination of personal interest and friend influence. First, probability topic model is defined to model topic content efficiently by historical behavior. Second, to integrate topic content and friend influence, we develop a topic behavior tracking model based on random walk. Finally, we propose a novel measure called Topic-Interest-Rank (TIR), which ranks users according to how important they are in sociological phenomena, to predict the topic behavior in future. Comprehensive experimental studies on two different real world data sets show that our approach outperforms existing ones and well matches the practice.

Keywords: Topic diffusion behavior, personal affinity, topic influence, random walk, online social network.

1 Introduction

In the Web 2.0 age, the popularity of online social networks (Twitter[1], Digg[2] and Sina Weibo[3]) successfully facilitates the information creation and diffusion among the users [1]. Recent research on pair relationship has demonstrated that homophily [2] can be exploited to improve the predictive accuracy of information diffusion. For example, researchers have found that user's topic diffusion behavior is influenced by topological features such as influence from friends [3, 4]. Also, some approaches based on content analysis exploit personal interest to improve the accuracy of the predictor [5].

However, according to the behavior theory, human's actions happen by both internal and external cause [6]. Most of existing work focus on either friend influence

---

[1] http://twiiter.com/
[2] http://digg.com/
[3] http://weibo.com/

M. Zhao and J. Sha (Eds.): ICCIP 2012, Part II, CCIS 289, pp. 725–733, 2012.
© Springer-Verlag Berlin Heidelberg 2012

or content semantics, but do not simultaneously consider combining both features to predict topic diffusion behavior in text data. As a result, it is desirable to capture the interplay between textual content and topological information. To solve the problems, propose a novel model by investigating users' topic interest. First, probability topic model is defined to model topic content efficiently by historical behavior. Second, to integrate topic content and friend influence, we develop a Topic Diffusion Behavior Tracking model (TDBT) based on random walk. Finally, we demonstrate the proposed model on the micro-blog corpus. The experimental results indicate that our analysis is useful and interesting, and our methods are effective and efficient.

The rest of the paper is organized as follows. Section 2 provides an overview on existing probabilistic topic diffusion modeling and prediction methods based on topological information. Section 3 introduces a topic behavior tracking model based on random walk in detail. Section 4 describes the experiments conducted on real world data set to validate the effectiveness of the proposed methods. Section 5 concludes the paper and discusses future work.

2   Related Work

In this section, we review the existing work for topic diffusion behavior tracking.

Individuals in networks usually influence each other directly or indirectly, which indicates that behavior of one's adoption of innovation or information can "spread" through the network [7]. To model and predict topic diffusion, several kinds of approaches are based on the idea that two nodes x and y are more likely to form a link in the future if their sets of neighbors have large overlap. Adamic-Adar Coefficient [8] considers a similar measure, which refines the simply counting of common features by weighting rarer features more heavily.

One of the most well-known approaches for content analysis is Probabilistic Latent Semantic Analysis (PLSA) [9]. These models are statistical generative models which treat each topic as a probability distribution over words, viewing a document as a probability distribution over words. Recently, Author-Topic (AT) model [10] is proposed based on LDA, to recognize which part of the document is contributed by which co-author. To be appropriate for social network analysis, McCallum et al. further extend the AT model to the Author-Recipient-Topic (ART) model [11] to capture the distribution over topics of author-recipient relationship without taking the temporal nature of blog into consideration.

3   Topic Diffusion Behavior Tracking Model

3.1   Terminology

Definition 1 Document: Let $D = \{d_1, d_2, ..., d_M\}$ be the documents collections in social network, where Document $d \in D$ is the text document(s) published by user u_i.

Definition 2 Reply: Let R_{ij} be the Reply-Document set of user u_i replied by u_j, such as the comment of Twitter and reply of Digg. Besides, we use S_i to denote the Self-Reply.

Definition 3 Topic-Interest: For a given Topic E, user u has a certain level of interest to join Topic-Community at time window t_k. Topic-Interest $h_{i,k}^E \in H_k^E$ reflects the probability of user u_j join topic discussion at time window t_k, which is measured as a floating value.

3.2   Personal Affinity Model

To model Personal Affinity of topic E, we need to exploit the frequency of self-documents $C_{1,...,k-1}$ which users have ever post and content similarity between $C_{1,...,k-1}$ and topic feature vector θ^E.

   To model the content similarity between users' self-documents and topic feature vector θ^E, let us first regard how to model the documents as a feature vector efficiently and effectively. Usually, the documents can be represented with words vector. However, the problem using words vector is high data dimensionality. As demonstrated in [11], when the data dimensionality is too high, the performance of cosine similarity will become worse. To solve this problem, we perform Probabilistic Latent Semantic Analysis (PLSA) to reduce data dimensionality and to generate a latent topic space for representing content feature vector.

   PLSA model is a probabilistic generative model which regards documents as probabilistic mixtures θ^d of latent topics z, and each latent topic $z \in \theta^d$ is a probability distribution over words. Given the number of latent topic T, a document d can be represented by latent topic vectors $\theta^d = \{z_1, z_2, ..., z_T\}$ with the probability $P(z \mid d)$.

   After representing each document as a feature vector, cosine similarity can be used to calculate the dissimilarity. Subsequently, the personal affinity sh_i^E to topic E of user u_i is then calculated as in Eq. (1).

$$sh_i^E = \sum_{d \in C} Co \sin e(\theta^d, \theta^E)$$
(1)

Where $Co \sin e(\theta^d, \theta^E)$ is the cosine distance based on PLSA model, which can be represented as Eq. (2). In Eq. (2), $z \in \theta^E$ is the latent themes generated for topic E with and $z \in \theta^d$ is the feature vector for users' documents correspondingly.

$$Co \sin e(\theta^d, \theta^E) = \frac{\sum z^E z^d}{\sqrt{[(z^E)^2][(z^d)^2]}} \qquad (2)$$

Finally, the normalized vector of Personal Affinity values $Q^E = \{q_1, q_2, ..., q_M\}$ is given by Eq. (3)

$$q_i^E = \frac{sh_i^E}{\sum_{i=1}^{M} sh_i^E} \qquad (3)$$

Personal Affinity vector Q^E show how likely topic content "attract" users to join topic discussion.

3.3   Topic Influence Diffusion Model

Now we consider topic influence which shows how likely users influence each other in adoptions of a topic. According to the historical behavior of reply relationship, we first construct the affinity Matrix $w_{ij} \in W_k (i, j \in [1, M])$ associated to the influential network G, where w_{ij} represent the influence strength from u_i to u_j.

$$W = \begin{bmatrix} 0 & \cdots & w_{1M} \\ \vdots & \ddots & \vdots \\ w_{M1} & \cdots & w_{MM} \end{bmatrix}$$

Given a special topic E, we define topic influence like personal interest as Eq. (4).

$$w_{ij}^E \propto \sum_{d \in R_{ij}} Co \sin e(d, E) \qquad (4)$$

Furthermore, the frequency that user u_j replies user u_i is directly proportional to the strong strength the user u_i influence u_j. To integrate these two important factors, the influence value w_{ij}^E associated to topic E is defined as Eq. (5).

$$w_{ij}^E = Num(R_{ij}) * Co \sin e(\theta^d, \theta^E) \qquad (5)$$

3.4   Topic Interest Ranking Model

Given Personal Affinity Vector Q_k^E and Topic Influence Matrix W_k^E at time window t_k, we address this problem as ranking problem and propose a novel Topic Interest Rank Algorithm (TIR Algorithm) based on random walk.

Topic-Interest-Rank (TIRank) which combines Topic Influence and Intrinsic Interest can be defined as the following Eq. (6).

$$TIR_k^E = \beta w_{ij}^E \sum_{j \in Nb(i)} TIR_j^E + (1-\beta)q_i^E \tag{6}$$

The part $\beta w_{ij}^E \sum_{j \in Nb(i)} TIR_j^E$ represents the Topic Influence generated from the Neighbors $Nb(i)$ of u_i, while the other part $(1-\beta)q_i^E$ represents Intrinsic Interest of u_i generated by its own. One can imagine there is a hidden node which links all the vertexes to contribute Intrinsic Interest to the network. The interest source balance parameter β is used to control the balance of topic influence and Intrinsic Interest.

TIRank is analogous to personalized PageRank [12] and corresponds to a problem of Random Walks with Restarts [13] which consists of nodes, hidden nodes, and the links among them. So Topic Influence Network can be modeled as an ergodic Markov chain with primitive transition probability matrix to guarantee the convergence of the power of the matrix. To achieve this ergodic Markov chain, the revised transition probability matrix $\overline{W}_k^E$ determining the random walk on G is defined as Eq. (7).

$$\overline{w_k^E} = \begin{cases} \dfrac{w_{ij}^E}{\sum_{j=1}^{M} w_{ij}^E} & if \sum_{j=1}^{M} w_{ij}^E \neq 0 \\ \dfrac{1}{M} & if \sum_{j=1}^{M} w_{ij}^E = 0 \end{cases} \tag{7}$$

Moreover, due to the presence of dangling nodes which do not have any out-links and cyclic paths in the network, we apply the remedy of "random jumps" as what PageRank does. The normalized Topic Influence matrix W after the adjustment can be written as Eq. (8), where α is the probability that the random walk follows a link.

$$C_k^E = \alpha \overline{W}_k^E + (1-\alpha)ee^T / M \tag{8}$$

When a Markov chain is ergodic, the stationary distribution of its Markov matrix is guaranteed to exist, so we obtain the close form as Eq. (9).

$$TIR_k^E = (1-\beta)(1-\beta(C_k^E)^T)^{-1}Q_k^E \tag{9}$$

Now, the prediction of topic diffusion behavior is ranked by the topic interest rank TIR_k^E at future time window.

4   Experiment

In this section we present our experimental results comprising a description of dataset, Evaluation Metrics, Parameter Settings and comparative study of our method.

4.1   Datasets

We perform our experiment on two different genres of dataset: Digg and Sina Weibo. Digg is a news aggregator website, where user can submit various categories of stories. In total, this dataset comprises 21,919 users, 187,277 stories, 687,616 comments and 477,320 replies of 51 popular "Newsroom" in this time range. Sina Weibo is a free social networking and the most popular micro-blog service of China. The data set consists of the full text of Chinese articles for 6 months (from June to December, 2010) which contains 1.5 million records and 3.3 million comments.

4.2   Experiment Setup

To measure the performance of our model, we evaluate the accuracy of predicting topic community joining behavior of special group in future time window. The two dataset are partitioned into 12 continuous time window and each time window is two week long. We assign one with 8 time windows into training for model turning and other with the left 4 time windows into test set for model validation.

We employ the Precision at Top-K as evaluation metrics, i.e., how many of top K users estimated by our algorithm actually comment or cite the new post. This measure is particularly appropriate in the context of topic diffusion where we generate a rank list of users to examine whether the users appear at the next time window.

4.3   Compared Predictive Methods

We compare the following methods for Predicting topic diffusion behavior in future time window t_{k+1} .

Method 1 Historical Information (HI): Method 1 is a basic form of probability based on user historical post number. The calculate method is show as Eq. (10).

$$P(i \mid E, t_k) = \frac{Num(D_{i,1,...,k})}{\sum_{j=1}^{M} Num(D_{j,1,...,k})} \tag{10}$$

In Eq. (10), $Num(D_{i,1,...,k})$ represents the document number of user u of the group while $\sum_{j=1}^{M} Num(D_{j,1,...,k})$ is total number of all the members.

Method 2 Adamic-Adar Coefficient (AAC): According to the analysis on approaches which are based on topological Feature, Adamic-Adar Coefficient is the most effective ways [8]. This method conducts the result only by Network Topological Feature.

Method 3 Content Analysis (CA): This method only considers users' content feature with personal affinity sh_i^E . So the probability of user u_i to joining topic community TC_k^E is estimated by Eq. (3).

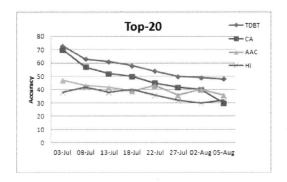

Fig. 1. Accuracy of Top-20 Metric over Time

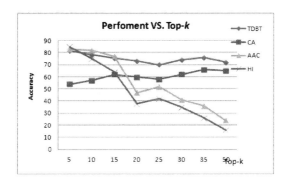

Fig. 2. Performance VS. Top-K

4.4   Prediction Performance Result

Here we address the problem of whether it is possible to infer who will possibly send a comment by communication records and the content of post-comment behavior.

In Fig. 1, we illustrate the prediction performance by comparing the HI, AAC, CA and the proposed TDBT model. The result shows that the TDBT model beats CA by 10% on accuracy. Moreover, the CA is better than AAC because that the importance of topic-interest is more significant than friend-interest. Furthermore the HI method is worst. Moreover, we obtain strong evidence of this hypothesis by observing that the performance of these models monotonically decays because that personal contacts evolve over time, which induces the models built at a specific time have decreasing predicting capability over time. This also implies our models well match the practice.

Fig.2 shows average precision curves for different K values highlighting the goodness of our approaches. Note that $\text{Pr}_{avg}(K)$ may not monotonically decrease with increasing k, which is result from the number of candidates in the denominator depends on K. Another Interesting thing is that the performance of HI and AAC methods is better than CA and TDBT models when the K is small, but sharp drops appear with the increase of K, which indicates that HI and AAC methods are only helpful for choosing the limit close friends. Comparing with the other methods, TDBT model performs best in most of K values, since the model not only exploits the content of link but also mining the most important factor which affect human topic diffusion behavior successfully.

To sum up, by comprehensively considering historic, textual and structured information into a unified model, TDBT generates more accurate trends in social network.

5   Conclusions

In this paper, we propose a new way to automatic track topic diffusion behavior. Our algorithm is developed based on the intuition that a user's inclination to join topic discussion is motivated by personal interest in topic content and topic influence from his friends. We develop a topic behavior tracking model based on random walk to combine topic content and friend influence. Moreover, a novel measure called Topic-Interest-Rank (TIR) is   propose to rank users according to how important they are in sociological phenomena. The experimental results indicate that our analysis is useful and interesting, and our methods are effective and efficient.

Acknowledgment. The research in this paper was supported in part by the National High-tech R&D Program of China (GrantNo.2010AA012505) and Chinese National Science Foundation (Grant No.60933005, No.60873204 and No.2011A010).

References

1. Eason, G., Noble, B., Sneddon, I.N.: On certain integrals of Lipschitz-Hankel type involving products of Bessel functions. Phil. Trans. Roy. Soc. London A247, 529–551 (1955)
2. Dretske, F.: Explaining behavior: Reasons in a world of causes. MIT Press (1991)
3. Liben-Nowell, D., Kleinberg, J.: The link-prediction problem for social networks. Journal of the American Society for Information Science and Technology 58(7), 1019–1031 (2007)
4. Kahanda, I., Neville, J.: Using transactional information to predict link strength in online social networks. In: Proceedings of the Third International Conference on Weblogs and Social Media, ICWSM (2009)
5. Wohlfarth, T., Ichise, R.: Semantic and event-based approach for link prediction. Practical Aspects of Knowledge Management, 50–61 (2008)

6. Liu, L., Tang, J., Han, J., Jiang, M., Yang, S.: Mining topic-level influence in heterogeneous networks. In: Proceedings of the 19th ACM International Conference on Information and Knowledge Management, pp. 199–208. ACM (2010)
7. Song, X., Lin, C., Tseng, B., Sun, M.: Modeling and predicting personal information dissemination behavior. In: Proceedings of the Eleventh ACM SIGKDD International Conference on Knowledge Discovery in Data Mining, pp. 479–488. ACM (2005)
8. Adamic, L., Adar, E.: Friends and neighbors on the web. Social Networks 25(3), 211–230 (2003)
9. Hofmann, T.: Probabilistic latent semantic analysis. In: Proc. of Uncertainty in Artificial Intelligence, UAI 1999, p. 21. Citeseer (1999)
10. Rosen-Zvi, M., Griffiths, T., Steyvers, M., Smyth, P.: The authortopic model for authors and documents. In: Proceedings of the 20th Conference on Uncertainty in Artificial Intelligence, pp. 487–494. AUAI Press (2004)
11. Steyvers, M., Griffiths, T.: Probabilistic topic models. In: Handbook of Latent Semantic Analysis, vol. 427 (2007)
12. Langville, A., Meyer, C.: Deeper inside pagerank. Internet Mathematics 1(3), 335–380 (2004)
13. Lovasz, L.: Random walks on graphs: A survey. Combinatorics, Paul Erdos is Eighty 2(1), 1–46 (1993)

Ant Colony Algorithms and Logistics Distribution Solutions

Jianhua Zhang[1] and Zhe Zhang[2]

[1] General Education Center
Beijing Normal University Zhuhai Campus, P.R. China
zhuhaijianhua@yahoo.com.cn
[2] Technical Logistics, University Duisburg-Essen,
Duisburg, Germany
engel_2002@msn.com

Abstract. First, the article briefly introduces the ant colony algorithm, and then focuses on the use it to solve the VRP (vehicle routing problem) and its application. Next, we analyzed the data structure and the characteristics of the actual logistics program. Finally, this article details the multi-parameter multi-objective algorithm and program design. The algorithm for the modern logistics management, this also has practical significance.

Keywords: Ant Colony Algorithms, TSP, VRP, Logistics management.

1   Introduction

Let's start with talking about the following: TSP, VRP, ACO.

1.1   Traveling Salesman Problem

Traveling Salesman Problem (TSP), the first description is to study the knight tour problem in 1759 for Euler (Swiss mathematician and physicist).

The easiest method for solving the TSP problem is the enumeration method. Its solution is a multi-dimensional, multi-local extreme tend to the infinity space of the complex solution. We can visualize the space as an infinite hilly area, the height of the peaks or valleys, that is, the extreme values of the problem. To solve the TSP, that is to climb to reach the top of the hill or the bottom of the process. Such problems are belong NP-Complete problem, the traveling salesman problem are mostly concentrated in the heuristic solution. Bodin (1983) divided them into three categories, the commonly used are: Nearest Neighbor Procedure, Clark and Wright Saving, Insertion procedures.

1.2   Vehicle Routing Problem

Vehicle routing problem (VRP) was first proposed by Dantzig and Ramser in 1959, it refers to a certain number of customers, each with a different number of goods

M. Zhao and J. Sha (Eds.): ICCIP 2012, Part II, CCIS 289, pp. 734–740, 2012.

demand, distribution centers to provide customers with the goods, by a team responsible for distribution of goods, organization of appropriate traffic routes, the goal is to make the customer's needs are met, and under certain constraints, to achieve the shortest distance, minimum cost, least time-consuming and so on purpose.

The TSP is a special case of VRP, due to Gaery has proved the TSP problem is NP-hard, therefore, the VRP is one of NP. Since 1959, the vehicle routing problem be proposed, it has been one of the most fundamental problems in the network optimization problem, due to its wide application and significant economic value, it has been subject to extensive attention from scholars.

About TSP and VRP, the two issues seem to have similarities, but after careful analysis, we will find is very different between the two. The latter is be solved, but must be have subject to many conditions, the algorithm of which belongs to solve the problem of multiple parameters, that is a much more complex problem.

In reality, transportation logistics companies plan a programs of the actual logistics and distribution, will be affected by a variety of constraints, such as: certain goods in transit are not allowed to mix load, there are transit time limits for certain goods, LTL cargo to used transit mode, the optimal path selection, the design of multi-start node and multi-objective node and so on. With the expansion of scale of operations, the algorithm will be more complex, the program design will be had more difficulty. The reality of Transportation and distribution programs is belong of the multi-parameters multi-objective algorithm to solve VRP.

1.3   Ant Colony Optimization

Ant colony optimization (ACO), M.Dorigo in 1991 first proposed the ant colony algorithm. Its main features are, by positive feedback, distributed collaboration to find the optimal path. This is a based of population optimization heuristic search algorithm.

The colony algorithm for TSP applications, as early as ten years ago, there are a considerable number of scholars have carried out fruitful research and has been applied in many engineering. The use of ant colony algorithm to solve the VRP, is only in recent years having proposed research topic. The difficulty does not lie in the difficulty of ant colony algorithm, but in logistics management, the transport and distribution plan are face the more conditions and requirements is too complicated. In fact, using different search options, there will be some differences in the results obtained. Also, the algorithm optimization and efficiency is very different too.

Based of our recent research work on this, we propose, this solution can be called the ACALDS (Ant Colony Algorithms and Logistics Distribution Solutions).

Below, we first talking are with VRP research about the status quo, and then we will briefly introduce the colony algorithm to solve the VRP and its Evolution, last, through data analysis, focusing on the transport and distribution plan of modern logistics management, introduced for the program design.

2   The Reality of the VRP Research

The academic literature of the vehicle routing problem have more, a considerable number is solution strategies and methods, Bodin and Golden (1981), grouped them into the following seven: Exact Procedure; Interactive Optimization; Cluster First–Route Second; Route First–Cluster Second; Saving or Insertion; Improvement or Exchanges; Mathematical programming.

Based of the basic vehicle routing problem (VRP), the vehicle routing problem have many different extension and change already in academic research and practical application. Including the vehicle routing problems with time windows(VRPTW); the fleet size and mix vehicle routing problems(FSVRP); the vehicle routing problems with multiple use of vehicle(VRPM); the vehicle routing problems with backhauls(VRPB); the vehicle routing problem with stochastic demand(VRPSD); and so on.

Solving methods are constantly evolving, can be divided into the exact algorithms and the heuristics algorithms.

In this paper to Involved the research for ACALDS (Ant Colony Algorithms and Logistics Distribution Solutions) belong to the latter. According to the investigation, very few relevant data, detailed information is rare. Hope this can play a valuable role, with the majority of researchers in this study, space has opened broader field.

3   Basic Ant Colony Algorithm and Mathematical Model

Ant colony algorithm model is based on the set of discrete points formed the plane, its solution space is used from an important mathematical tool - graph to describe. The simple description of TSP is: given N cities, there is a traveling salesman starting from a certain city, visiting each city once and only once, then back to the original city, asked to find a shortest path. Mathematical description of the TSP is: $C = \{C_1, C_2, ..., C_n\}$ is a set of cities, $L = \{L_{ij} \mid C_i, C_j \in C\}$ is a collection of C elements (City) between two connected collection; D_{ij} (i, j =1, 2, ...,n) is L_{ij} of Euclidean distance, namely:

$$d_{ij} = \sqrt{(x_i - x_j)^2 + (y_i - y_j)^2} \tag{1}$$

$G = (C, L)$ is a directed graph, TSP is to search getting the length of the shortest Hamiltion Circlehe of a directed graph G, and every node is to be access one time and only once time. The two cities in the same round-trip distance is called the symmetric TSP; otherwise known as an asymmetric TSP.

The $b_i(t)$: Is expressed the total number of ants at time t for the i element. $\tau(t)$: is expressed the amount of information to be existed on the distance from i to j, n be pressed the scale for TSP; m is the amount of ants. Then,

$$m = \sum_{i=1}^{n} b_i(t) \quad \text{And} \quad \Gamma = \{\tau_{ij}(t) \mid c_i, c_j \subset C\} \tag{2}$$

Γis the residue information between two C elements on the connection of them, at Initial time, the amount of information on each path are equal.

And set $\tau_{ij}(0) = $ const, the ant colony algorithm to find the optimal solution is through a directed graph $g = (C, L, \Gamma)$ be achieved.

Ants k (k = 1, 2…, m in the course of the campaign, is according to the amount of information on each path to determine its transfer direction. The Tabu List is used to record the all of information when the ant traversing the city. This data in the list are dynamic data to be adjusted in processing on time. In the search process, the ant is according to the amount of information and the inspired information of the path to calculate the state transition probability. $p^k_{ij}(t)$, It is the state transition probability of one ant from the city i to other city j in t time.

$$\text{If } j \in allowed_k, \quad p^k_{ij}(t) = \frac{[\tau_{ij}(t)]^{\alpha} \cdot [\eta_{ik}(t)]^{\beta}}{\sum_{s \subset allowed_k}[\tau_{is}(t)]^{\alpha} \cdot [\eta_{is}(t)]^{\beta}} \tag{3}$$

$$\text{Otherwise:} \quad p^k_{ij}(t) = 0 \tag{4}$$

Where, $allowed_k = \{c - tabu_k\}$ is to be selected the next node for an ant. a It's the factor of inspired information reflected in the ant movement, and the greater the more to be likely chosen to go that path. Inspired factor β is expected to reflect the degree of attention for the choose path with the heuristic information, the greater, and its state transition probability closer to the greedy rule: $\eta_{ij}(t)$ for the heuristic function, the formula is as follows:

$$\eta_{ij}(t) = \frac{1}{d_{ij}} \tag{5}$$

Here d_{ij} is the distance between the two cities.

In order to avoid causing too much residual pheromone information flooded heuristic information, when the ant have been completed or completed each step through all the city, you must update the residual information, as the human brain's memory of information law: new information continuously into the brain, at the same time, the old information in the brain, over time will be gradually fade and forgotten. Therefore, always in the path (i to j), the amount of information can be adjusted in accordance with the following rules in time (t + n):

$$\tau_{ij}(t+n) = (1-\rho) \cdot \tau_{ij}(t) + \Delta\tau_{ij}(t) \tag{6}$$

$$\Delta\tau_{ij}(t) = \sum_{k=1}^{m} \Delta\tau^k_{ij}(t) \tag{7}$$

Where P coefficient is to be volatile of pheromone; that is 1-P that is the information residual factor, in order to prevent unlimited accumulation of information, the P is range [0, 1) between them. $\Delta\tau_{ij}(t)$: is the pheromone increment on this cycle path (i to j); initial time $\Delta\tau_{ij}$ (0) = 0, $\Delta\tau^k_{ij}(t)$ is the amount of information stay in the loop in the path (i to j) for the k-ant.

4   Evolution of the Ant Colony Algorithm in the VRP

4.1   Evolution for the Current State Transition Probability

In the VRP, for get the optimal solution, there are two conditions: Necessary to consider the shortest distance in one transport, but also consider the minimum transportation costs. The basic unit of transport costs: the transport mileage multiplied by the load. For other conditions, we can simplify it in the algorithm, Such as, the special requirements of an order, we should be given priority. To this end, in the algorithm, we should be given priority. To this end, in the algorithm, we can increase the value of task priority factor, in order to achieve as much as possible simplified algorithm. After simplified, affecting "the current state transition probability" that is the most basic parameters can be only two: the first is a path distance between two nodes, the second is the tonnage.

So, the formula (1) should be changed to:

$$D_{ij} = \sqrt{(x_i - x_j)^2 + (y_i - y_j)^2} \times P_{ij} \tag{8}$$

P_{ij} : That is a factor involved in the second parameter.

The heuristic function should change accordingly. The formula (5) should be changed to:

$$\eta_{ij}(t) = \frac{1}{D_{ij}} \tag{9}$$

4.2   The Handling of the Initial State Transition Probability

According to the original basic ant colony algorithm assumptions and processing,, at first, we should be to set an arbitrary value, that is the initial state transition probability, next step will be comparative analysis between the initial state transition probability and obtained by calculating from the real-time status of individual ants, to determine the ant's expected initial target and to the next node. This hypothesis and processing, greatly increase the complexity of the algorithm, and not meet the true state of VRP. In fact, we can directly set the value is zero, then comparative analysis the process, select the state transition probability biggest node that is forward to next target node.

$$\tau_{ij}(0) = 0 \tag{10}$$

4.3   Residual of Information Processing

Ant colony algorithm to solve VRP is completely different from the ant colony algorithm. To solve TSP, must need to consider the impact of the previous step, but must need to prevent the residual pheromone is too much, flooded the heuristic information. After the step of searching, you need update the residual information. VRP do not need consider such problem. For VRP in the search process, the search to local optimal solution, before next step, the node must be deleted in the Current Transport Tasks List, then continue the remaining tasks. Step by step solution, until all tasks are completed.

4.4   Set the Search Method

From a global point of view, the purpose of each step of the search is to find the local optimal solution, but in the local search, to try to take into account the local scale as large as possible. For example, every step forward before, in order to obtain the expected target, taking into account the status of all not identified the target node, as much as possible.

4.5   The Last Step Can Avoid for the Search

For the last node, it is the only one currently established target, no need for complex calculations.

5   Transport Distribution of the Basic Plan and Program

The vehicle routing problem had been divided the following three types by Scholars Ballou (1992), the first type is the "single starting point and a single end point", second type is the "a single start point and mult-end points", third type is the "mult-start points and mult-end points".

We think that this classification is only considering the transport surface phenomena too rough. In order to facilitate depth to study algorithm and program design, by means of the related concepts of mathematics, we divided them as the following three types: "Single-parameter single-target algorithm"; "Multi-parameter single-objective algorithm"; "Multi-parameter multi-objective algorithm".

5.1   Single-Parameter Single-Target Algorithm and Program Design

As mentioned earlier, for the transport of bulk goods, the first constrain condition is the limited of fully loaded cargo. Therefore, in general, in the distribution program, the first plan is fully loaded cargo, and according the of truck fully loaded cargo size, arrangement the transport order, this is the descending order. Working until all cargo be sending to target node.

It is the simplest distribute solution.

5.2   Multi-parameter Single-objective Algorithm and Program Design

Multi-parameter single-objective, that is in a batch of orders, there is only one "the starting node" in a transport task, the goods will be send to other nodes.

In practice, as the "fully loaded vehicle can get the high transport efficiency", so, at first we must arrange transport vehicle according of the fully loaded to plan for all of node. The remaining LTL tasks, according of the "loading merge" method, it will be merged and can be combined into some of other transport tasks. Of course, the principle of the method is as much as possible so that the vehicle fully loaded or similarly to fully loaded. However, the weight of the LTL goods is different. Also, the path length is different between two nodes. So, according of formula (8), the algorithm will produce a variety of programs. Therefore, the "loading merge" method will increase the complexity of the algorithm.

With "as much as possible so that the vehicle fully loaded or similarly to fully loaded" is as the first condition of carpool way. Then we consider the transport cost, That is "Ton-kilometer", as small as possible, all meet the above two conditions are taken into the programs, and according to the aforementioned "evolution of the colony algorithm and using in the VRP", searching the path of the largest "state transition probability", this is the best current target node, forward step by step searching until all the target nodes has been send their goods. The plan completed.

After delivery of goods, all transportation vehicles should return the starting point, which is the starting node.

This is the "multi-parameter single-objective" of the algorithm and program design emphasis.

5.3   Multi-parameter Multi-objective Algorithm and Program Design

In fact, the true situation of an plan working in logistics company : an order involve various transport point, all of the each of point may be a "starting point", to send a cargo to other node, but also it may be the target node, to be received the goods from another node.

"Multi-parameter multi-objective" algorithm and the aforementioned "multi-parameter single-target" algorithm and program design process is very different.

6   Conclusions

Transport distribution programs are based on the "multi-parameter multi-objective" of the algorithm and program design, but the two are very different, the latter algorithm and program design complexity and difficulty greatly increased.

In addition, in the search process, all of the data are interrelated, and, the data is always changing. Through programming, we control all of task and processing, ultimately we get the satisfaction results. Of course, the program design is essential; it is a very important aspect.

References

1. Haibin, D.: Ant Colony Algorithm and its Applications. Sciences Press, China (December 2005); ISBN: 978-7-03-016204-5
2. Cao, C., Wang, N.: Intelligent Computing. Tsinghua University Press, China (September 2004); ISBN: 7-302-09412-8/TP.6570
3. Yun, G.S., Ling, Q.W.: Discrete Mathematics. Higher Education Press, China (2004)
4. Yuan, P., Xu, B.: In: 2011 6th IEEE Joint International Information Technology and Artificial Intelligence Conference, vol. 2, pp. 424–426 (2011)

Mobile Internet-Based Compression-Aware Scalable Video Coding - Rate Control for Enhancement Layers

Yu Cai, Lin Mei[*], Dazhou Wu, Rui Zhao, Lili Jia, and Weifei Wang

R&D Center of Cyber-Physical Systems,
The Third Research Institute of the Ministry of Public Security Shanghai, China
cai309569029@163.com

Abstract. The scalable video codec extension to the H.264 standard (H.264 SVC) is designed deliver the benefits described in the preceding ideal scenario. That is, it can yield decoded video at different frame rates, resolutions, or quality levels. In view of adaptive reference image of FGS (Adaptive Reference FGS, Mt-FOS) algorithm of H.264-SVC, we put forward a new algorithm called adaptive leakage predictors FGS (ALF.FGS) in this paper. ALF.FGS can not only well adapted to fluctuations in network bandwidth, but also provides greater flexibility to the macro block encoded video frame based on motion characteristics and texture characteristics of adaptive selecting a different reference macro block. Experimental results show that the ALF.FGS algorithm can effectively eliminate error at low bit rate and improve the FGS coding efficiency.

Keywords: Scalable video, FGS, H.264-SVC.

1 Introduction

With the development of society and the progress of science, video is used in increasingly diverse applications with a correspondingly diverse set of client devices—from computers viewing Internet video to portable digital assistants (PDAs) and even the humble cell phone. The video streams for these devices are necessarily different. To be made more compatible with a specific viewing device and channel bandwidth, the video stream must be encoded many times with different settings. Each combination of settings must yield a stream that targets the bandwidth of the channel carrying the stream to the consumer as well as the decode capability of the viewing device. If the original uncompressed stream is unavailable, the encoded stream must first be decoded and then re-encoded with the new settings. This quickly becomes prohibitively expensive.

The SVC extension introduces a notion not present in the original H.264 AVC co-dec−that of layers within the encoded stream. A base layer encodes the lowest temporal, spatial, and quality representation of the video stream. Enhancement layers encode additional information that, using the base layer as a starting point, can be used

---

[*] Corresponding author.

M. Zhao and J. Sha (Eds.): ICCIP 2012, Part II, CCIS 289, pp. 741–746, 2012.

to reconstruct higher quality, resolution, or temporal versions of the video during the decode process. By decoding the base layer and only the subsequent enhancement layers required, a decoder can produce a video stream with certain desired characteristics. Figure 1 shows the layered structure of an H.264 SVC stream. During the encode process, care is taken to encode a particular layer using reference only to lower level layers. In this way, the encoded stream can be truncated at any arbitrary point and still remain a valid, decodable stream.

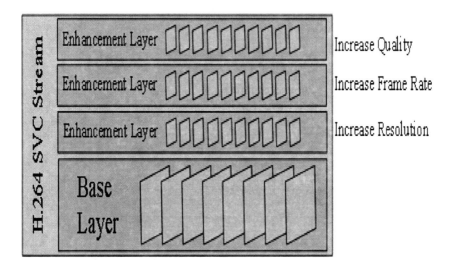

Fig. 1. The layered structure about H.264 SVC stream

2   The Key Technology about Traditional FGS

2.1   FGS in MPEG-4

The MPEG-4 fine granularity scalability (FGS) video coding standard offers flexible adaptation to varying network bandwidths and different application needs. This paper presents a MPEG-4 FGS video CODEC based watermarking scheme to embed watermark during encoding. Watermark is embedded into base layer, and can be extracted from both base layer and enhanced video through eliminating the influence of enhancement layer on watermark. This scheme eliminates error propagation caused by watermark for normal video, and utilizes error propagation caused by watermark adjustment to protect the video content. This scheme provides dual protection for intellectual property rights (IPR): watermark and video content protection utilizing error propagation in temporal motion compensation prediction.

2.2   FGS Video Coding Based on H.264

In H.264 video coding standard, the combination encoding frame was adopted. It introduces some new algorithms, and modifies several aspects of the encoding scheme. So the encoding scheme improves the encoding efficiency obviously. But the H.264 standard is not supporting FGS encoding. So a H.264 based self-adaptive FGS (Fine Granular Scalable) (H.264-FGS) encoding scheme is proposed in this paper. In this encoding scheme, the base layer of encoder is keeping H.264 encoder architecture, which consists of the motion estimation, motion compensation, intra predictive, integer transformation, loop filtering, content based arithmetic encoding, and etc. In the base layer generated block we obtain base code flux of FGS. Subtracting the original image from the reconstruction image of the base layer, we get the residual error. Then after the DCT transform and the variable length encoding compresses, we obtain the enhanced code flux of FGS. Compared with the original MPEG-4 FGS encoding scheme, the proposed FGS encoding scheme has the feature of increasing encoding efficiency by 1~3 dB and keep the all properties that MPEG-4 FGS encoding technology provided.

2.3   The Flow Chart on FGS and the Problem in Traditional FGS

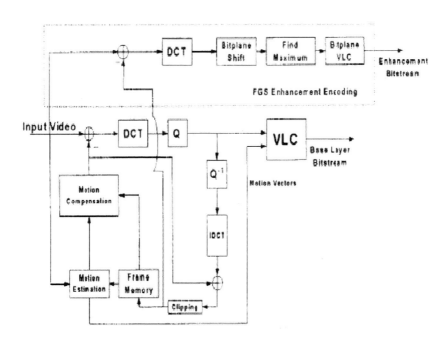

Fig. 2. The flow chart of FGS

The coding method of FGS enhancement layer is the original image and the basic layer encoded image reconstruction of the residual DCT transform, search out a maximum value in these coefficients, and then to 8 x 8 block units based on bit-plane coding using VLC. FGS is essentially the enhancement layer coding method, what is put for the basic layer of variable length codes into place plane coding method, not using the coefficient of relatedness between to eliminate redundant or other methods to achieve higher coding efficiency.

3   ALF.FGS Algorithm

In order to further improve the efficiency of coding, we must be able to adaptive select leakage predictors about α and β values .The features about video coding include two parts: the motion features and texture features. Motion feature is the movement of the video sequence. The movement smaller, the motion estimation and accuracy of compensating higher.

Supposed that the number of the current code block closed to available number of blocks is N, and difference of motion vector d_{MV}, calculated as follows:

$$d_{MV} = \frac{1}{N}\sum_{i=0}^{N}\{(mv_x^i - mv_x^c)^2 + (mv_y^i - mv_y^c)^2\}$$

(mv_x^c, mv_y^c) is the motion vector of current block. (mv_x^i, mv_y^i) is the motion vector of around the block.

We did a lot of experiments, and set α and β values as follows:

Sheet 1. α adaptive parameter

Type of MB	$d_{MV} \leq 16$	$d_{MV} > 16$
P_L0_16*16	$\Delta\alpha = 1/32$	$\Delta\alpha = 0$
P_L0_L0_16*8	$\Delta\alpha = -1/32$	$\Delta\alpha = -2/32$
P_L0_L0_8*16	$\Delta\alpha = -1/32$	$\Delta\alpha = -2/32$
P_8*8,P_8*8ref0,P_L0_8*8	$\Delta\alpha = -3/32$	$\Delta\alpha = -4/32$
P_8*8,P_8*8ref0,P_L0_8*4,P_L0_4*8	$\Delta\alpha = -5/32$	$\Delta\alpha = -6/32$
P_8*8,P_8*8ref0,P_L0_4*4	$\Delta\alpha = -6/32$	$\Delta\alpha = -7/32$

Supposed the initial value about α is α_{eff}, so the end value about α: $\alpha = \max(\min(\alpha_{eff} + \Delta\alpha, 1), 0)$.

Sheet 2. β adaptive parameter

Type of MB	$d_{MV} \leq 16$	$d_{MV} > 16$
P_L0_16*16	$\Delta\beta = 1/32$	$\Delta\beta = 0$
P_L0_L0_16*8	$\Delta\beta = -1/32$	$\Delta\beta = -2/32$
P_L0_L0_8*16	$\Delta\beta = -1/32$	$\Delta\beta = -2/32$
P_8*8,P_8*8ref0,P_L0_8*8	$\Delta\beta = -2/32$	$\Delta\beta = -3/32$
P_8*8,P_8*8ref0,P_L0_8*4,P_L0_4*8	$\Delta\beta = -3/32$	$\Delta\beta = -4/32$
P_8*8,P_8*8ref0,P_L0_4*4	$\Delta\beta = -4/32$	$\Delta\beta = -5/32$

Supposed the initial value about β is β_{eff}, so the end value about β is : $\beta = \max\left(\min\left(\beta_{eff} + \Delta\beta, 1\right), 0\right)$.

4   Simulation Setup

To examine the encoding performance, we do experiment used JSVM and the test sequence used FOREMAN and MOBILE, CIF, the frame rate is 15Hz. The experiment show that the difference between AR-FGS and ALF.FGS about the performance of coding.

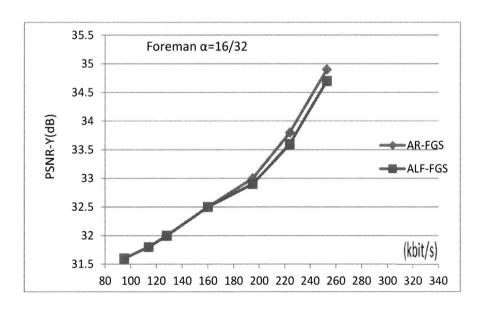

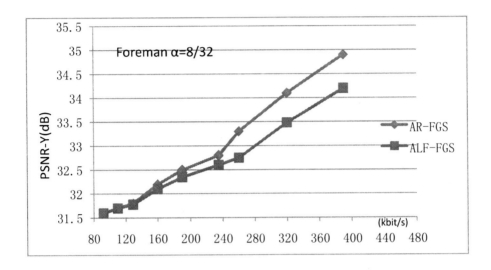

5   Conclusion

In H.264 AVC (for Baseline Profile where only unidirectional predicted frames are used), all the frames would need to be decoded irrespective of the desired display rate. To transit to a low bandwidth network, the entire stream would need to be decoded, the unwanted frames discarded, and then re-encoded. In this paper, Experimental results show that the ALF.FGS algorithm can effectively eliminate error at low bit rate and improve the FGS coding efficiency.

Acknowledgment. This work was supported by the Science and Technology Commission of Shanghai Municipality (Grants No. 10511500700).

References

1. Wiegand, T., Sullivan, G., Reichel, J., Schwarz, H., Wien, M.: Joint Draft 11: Scalable Video Coding. Doc.JVT-X201, Geneva, Switzerland (July 2007)
2. Li, H., Li, Z.G., Wen, C.: Fast Mode Decision Algorithm for Inter-Frame Coding in Fully Scalable Video Coding. IEEE Trans. Circuits Syst. Video Technol. 16(7), 889–895 (2006)
3. H.264/AVC Reference Softwares, http://iphome.hhi.de/suehring/tml
4. Zhao, T., Wang, H., Kwong, S., Kuo, C.-C.J.: Fast Mode Decision Based on Mode Adaptation. IEEE Trans. Circuits Syst. Video Technol. 20(5), 697–795 (2010)
5. Li, W.: Overview of fine granularity scalability in MPEG-4 video standard. IEEE Trans. Circuits Syst. Video Technology 11(3), 301–317 (2001)
6. Li, W., Ling, F., Chen, X.: Fine Granularity Scalability in MPEG-4 for Streaming Video. In: Proc. IEEE Int. Symp. Circuits Syst., Geneva, Switzerland (May 2000)
7. Li, W.: Frequency weighting for FGS. ISO/IEC JTCI/SC29/WG11, MPEG99/M5589 (December 1999)

Real-Time Hand Gesture Detection and Recognition by Random Forest

Xian Zhao[1,2], Zhan Song[2,3,*], Jian Guo[1], Yanguo Zhao[2], and Feng Zheng[2]

[1] Faculty of Materials, Optoelectronics and Physics, Xiangtan University,
411105 Xiangtan, China
[2] Shenzhen Institutes of Advanced Technology, Chinese Academy of Sciences,
518055 Shenzhen, China
[3] The Chinese University of Hong Kong,
00852 Hong Kong, China
{xian.zhao,zhan.song,yg.zhao,feng.zheng}@siat.ac.cn,
guojian@xtu.edu.cn

Abstract. Detection and recognition of an unconstrained hand in a natural video sequence has gained wide applications in HCI (human computer interaction). This paper presents an unsupervised approach for the training of an efficient and robust hand gesture detector. Different with traditional hand feature descriptors, the proposed approach use pair-patch comparison features to describe the samples. And the random forest is introduced to establish a machine learning model. The pair-patch comparison features could rapidly describe a sample and the distributions of them have some similarity between the same classes. In the training procedure, a database which consists of a large number of hand images with corresponding labels and background images are established. Experimental results show that the proposed approach can achieve a detection and accuracy rate of 92.23% on the dataset.

Keywords: Hand detection, decision trees, random forest.

1   Introduction

Hand detection and hand gestures recognition has been an important research topic in computer vision domain with the development of HCI techniques [1]. However, such techniques are still lack of robustness and accuracy especially to the complicate scenarios. Previous hand detection and recognition methods usually use specific markers such as colored digital gloves to make the hand more distinct compare with its backgrounds.

To make hand gesture recognitions work with naked hands, more and more visual information have been considered such as color, shape, or depth information etc. A number of different techniques have been suggested to deal with this case [2-6]. In [3], a hand detection algorithm that can detect five different gestures is proposed. The

---

[*] Corresponding author.

M. Zhao and J. Sha (Eds.): ICCIP 2012, Part II, CCIS 289, pp. 747–755, 2012.

algorithm is based on the use of active learning and boosted classifiers, which allows obtaining a much better performance than similar boosting-based systems. The system could be implemented in real video sequences, but the accuracy is unsatisfied. In [4], a novel real-time hands detection method is presented. The multi-resolution Histogram of oriented gradient (HOG) operator is employed for the hands detection as a basic feature representation. A coarse-to-fine partition strategy is introduced to increase approximation precision, and the linear or quasi-linear classifiers are used for the recognition.

In this article, an accurate and robust hand gesture detection and recognition algorithm is investigated. The method is based on random forest algorithm, which is a classifier first proposed in [7] and has been widely applied in computer vision domain [8-10]. The main contribution of this work is the use of pair-patch comparison features to describe samples. And the random forest algorithm is used to establish a machine learning model. The pair-patch comparison features could rapidly describe a sample and the distributions of them have some similarity between the same classes. In order to improve efficiency and accuracy, an effective skin detection process has been used before the implementation of random forest classifier [11, 12].

The paper is organized as follows. The proposed feature description and the random forest classifier are presented in Section 2. Experimental results on real video sequences are given in Section 3. Conclusion and future work are offered in Section 4.

2   Learning via Random Forest

The main modules of the proposed hand detection and gesture recognition system are as shown in Figure1. The system contains two stages: the offline training phase and the online detection phase.

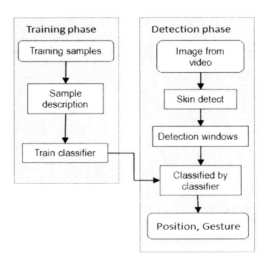

Fig. 1. Work flow of the proposed hand gesture detection and recognition system

In the training phase, we get a classifier by training a mass of samples, whose class labels are known in advance. The training set contains a mass of negative and positive samples. In the detection phase, the skin-like areas are detected firstly so as to improve the efficiency and accuracy. And then, a random forest classifier obtained via the training procedure is used to determine the potential hand regions.

2.1   Building the Training Set

Three different hand gestures are selected in this paper as shown in Figure 2. For each gesture, we collected 3,000 samples from dozens of people with different background. And there are 6,000 negative samples, which contain none hand features which used to train the classifier. By analysis of the samples, we could find that main difference between the same class samples is the different background of each target, but the pixels of gestures distribute generally consistently. So we have to collect enough samples with different background for each gesture, according to the diversity of surroundings. Another important training set issue is the negative sample set. The negative sample set should consider almost all of the possible background, and they are got from the images which contain no gestures or contain some part of gesture. For the complexity and uncertainty of the background, we set the number of negative samples twice than positive samples.

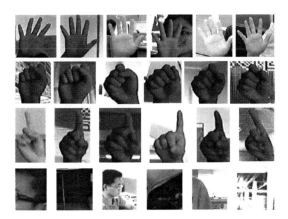

Fig. 2. A part of the three different hand gesture sample sets and the negative sample set

2.2   Description of the Samples

Sample description is as important as the classification. In this paper, we proposed pair-compare features to express samples. Firstly, all of the samples from the training set are preprocessed to remove some variations within the classes attributable to perspective distortion and noise. The accepted view is using a filter to smooth the samples. We implement a mean shift filter to these samples from the training set. This preprocess could largely reduce the diversity between the samples from the same class.

Illumination change is a serious problem in computer vision system. Based on normal features, the detection rate will be seriously affected, whether the environment is too bright or dark. In order to avoid the influence from global illumination, we choose pair-compare features to describe the sample. This type of features for classification relies on the difference of pixel values between different image pixels and thus is more robust to illumination change.

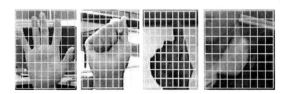

Fig. 3. Point sampling in an image

As shown in Figure 3, we evenly choose 10×10 points from a sample, and then calculate the difference between two pixels from these N points.

$$x(p1, p2) = \begin{cases} 1, & if \, |f(p1) - f(p2)| \geq \tau \\ 0, & if \, |f(p1) - f(p2)| < \tau \end{cases} \tag{1}$$

where f(p) is the intensity of the sample at p(x,y). The parameter τ is a threshold to decide in which range two intensities should be considered as similar. In this paper, we set the value of τ to 20. In order to make the pair-compare features more robust, we adopt a 3×3 mean filter before compare the difference:

$$f(x, y) = \frac{1}{9} \sum_{i,j=-1}^{1} f(x+i, y+j) \tag{2}$$

Thus, for each two pixels in the N points, we get K values of pair-compare features by Equation 1. Each sample could be described by a feature vector X:

$$X = \{x_1, x_2 ... x_K, b\} \,, \; K = C_N^2 \tag{3}$$

The value of x_i is the i-th pair-compare feature, and x_i=1 or 0. The last value of the feature vector b is the label of the sample which defined as:

$$b = \begin{cases} 1, & palm \\ 2, & finger \\ 3, & fist \\ 0, & background \end{cases} \tag{4}$$

2.3   Classifier Learning Using Random Forest

A decision tree classifier [1] is trained at the same time with the features selection. As shown in Figure 4, at each node of a tree, we choose one pair-compare feature x_i from the feature vector X randomly. The next step will turn to the left node if the value is 1. Else if the current node value is 0, next step will go to the right node.

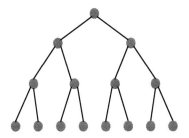

Fig. 4. Binary decision tree structure

Each sample from the training set is input from the root of a decision tree, and it will arrive at a leaf node at the bottom of the tree. After all of the training samples are classified by a tree, three will be a distribution, which contains different numbers of different classes, at each leaf node. According to the distribution, we could set a class label b which is defined in the last function for each leaf node. When an unknown sample arrives at a leaf, we could judge its class via the leaf label obtained in the training phase.

Decision tree could not train the best classifier, even is easy to explain the results and performs simply. In order to get more accurate and robust classifier result, the so-called forest refers to multi trees which are generated independently based on the features vectors are usually used.

Fig. 5. Random forest model

According to the theory of random forest, a set of random trees T is created. For the *i-th* tree, its feature vector is randomly got from X in Section 2.2. The feature vector for each tree in the forest is independent with other trees. Once the random forest is built, the trees T_1, ..., T_N can estimate a testing sample. We get N labels from the random forest $L_i (1 \leq i \leq N)$. Thus, the prediction of the forest for this unknown sample could be got by this formulation:

$$L = \arg\max\{L_i\}, \quad 1 \le i \le N \qquad (5)$$

To make the random forest classifier work well, every tree should be independent and the features which are adopted at each node should be different. If there were two trees with similar structures, their classification results are similar also. To avoid this similarity, to establish each tree, we randomly choose the features from the feature set X to be the criterion of splitting the node, and these features for each tree are different. Thus, the trees are all different in the forest.

2.4   Hand Detection

According to the above description, we know that an unknown sample could get its possible label by extracting its features $X=\{x_1, x_2, \ldots, x_K\}$ and using a random forest classifier to predict. However, in our system, the purpose of detection is finding the target from an image and judge the class of the target.

We propose a multi-scale detection method in this paper, by using a multi-scale window sliding in the image, and then predict every window by our classifier. In order to improve the detection efficiency, we implement a skin segmentation process before the multi-scale detection. As shown in the middle image in Figure 6, after the skin segmentation, the region of non-skin has effectively removed. This could largely reduce the number of the windows to predict using the classifier.

Fig. 6. Detection of the hand target

After using a skin detect process, the multi-scale windows are sliding in the region whose skin area ration is 50% to 80%. Then we predict the label of these windows by random forest classifier. The yellow rectangles in Figure 6 are the window got from skin detection, and the red rectangles are the target detected by random forest classifier.

3   Experiments and Analysis

As mentioned in Section 2, we established the feature matrix by extracting the pair-patch comparison features from the training set which contained 3000 palm samples, 3000 fist samples, 3000 finger samples and 6000 negative samples. The experiments are running on a PC with Pentium Dual-Core 3.2G CPU and 2G RAM under VS2008 platform. A low-cost web camera is used to get images with the resolution of 320×240 pixels.

3.1   Detection Accuracy

By analyzing the structure of the random forest, we found that two main factors which affect the performance of the classifier are the depth of a tree and the number of the trees in the forest. In this paper, we define this two parameters of the forest by *(D,N)*, in which *D* is the depth of a tree and   *N*   is the number of trees.

At the training phase, the depth *D* of the tree is bigger, the trees in the forest split the more layers, and class of samples in the leaf nodes will be purer and the classifier will perform better. With the increase of number *N* of trees in the forest, the classifier could have the more votes. Therefore, the result of the forest classifier will be more robust. As shown by the curves in Figure 7, we observe information about the structure of the obtained classifiers.

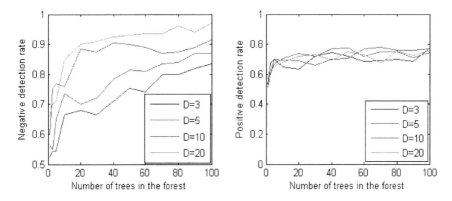

Fig. 7. Accuracy evaluation of different (D, N)

From the result, we can see that the correct rate of negative is increasing with the growth of the number of trees and the increasing of the layers of the trees. However, this change performance would not very obvious relatively after the value of *(D,N)* arrived at *(10,30)*. We also see that the correct rate of positive is affected slightly by the change of *(D,N)*, and its value is always about 70%-80%.

From the curves shown in Figure 7, when we choose *(10,30)* as the value of *(D,N)*, we can get a satisfied result in the application as shown in Figure 8.

Fig. 8. The detection results with (D, N) set to (10, 30)

3.2   Efficiency Evaluation

Our method is designed to use in a real-time video system, so the processing speed of the detection is also an important performance to analyze. In the above context, we have proposed a process of skin detection before using the random forest classifier to detect the gestures, and it save a lot of time. However, efficiency of the random forest classifier is crucial for the efficiency of the whole system. It is obvious that the less number of the trees and the less depth, the system will cost less time.   We have tested many times at different *(D, N)*, and the result is shown in Table 1.

Table 1. Average processing time of the different values of (D, N)

Parameters (D,N)	Accuracy	Time
(10,30)	92.23%	0.08s
(10,50)	92.82%	0.13s
(10,100)	93.53%	0.17s
(20,30)	92.48%	0.15s
(20,50)	92.87%	0.16s

Here, the accuracy refers to the accuracy of detection and recognition in a full of image, and the accuracy in Figure 7 is different, which means the accuracy of classification of the testing samples. From the above table we choose *(10,30)* as the parameter of the random forest, for the good efficiency and acceptable accuracy.

4   Conclusion and Future Work

In this paper, a real-time hand gesture detection and recognition method is proposed. The main contribution of this work is the use of pair-patch comparison features to describe samples, and the random forest algorithm is used to establish a machine learning model. The pair-patch comparison features could rapidly describe a sample and the distributions of them have some similarity between the same classes. In order to improve efficiency and accuracy, an effective skin detection process has been used before the implementation of random forest classifier. Real experimental results show that, the system performs with a reasonable high performance in different environments. We can get a 92.23% correct detection rate in the experiment on a video. And the speed of it is about 12 fps.

The main problem is that the speed of detection would slow down when the area of skin in the image is increasing. Future work can address how to better express the features and how to improve the structure of the random forest to boast it performance further.

Acknowledgments. The work described in this article was supported partially by the grants from the Introduced Innovative R&D Team of Guangdong Province "Robot and Intelligent Information Technology", Shenzhen Key Laboratory of Precision Engineering (project no. CXB201005250018A), National Natural Science Foundation of China (NSFC, grant no. 61002040, 60903115), and NSFC-GuangDong (grant no. 10171782619-2000007).

References

1. Nielsen, M., Störring, M., Moeslund, T.B., Granum, E.: A Procedure for Developing Intuitive and Ergonomic Gesture Interfaces for HCI. In: Camurri, A., Volpe, G. (eds.) GW 2003. LNCS (LNAI), vol. 2915, pp. 409–420. Springer, Heidelberg (2004)
2. Kolsch, M., Turk, M.: Robust Hand Detection. In: 6th IEEE International Conference on Automatic Face and Gesture Recognition, pp. 614–619. IEEE Press, Seoul (2004)
3. Francke, H., Ruiz-del-Solar, J., Verschae, R.: Real-Time Hand Gesture Detection and Recognition Using Boosted Classifiers and Active Learning. In: Mery, D., Rueda, L. (eds.) PSIVT 2007. LNCS, vol. 4872, pp. 533–547. Springer, Heidelberg (2007)
4. Zhao, Y., Song, Z., Zheng, F., Yang, H.: A Novel Multi-Resolution HOG Based Algorithm for Real-Time Hands Detection. In: 3rd IEEE International Conference on Signal Processing Systems. IEEE Press, Yantai (2011)
5. Stenger, B., Thayananthan, A., Cipolla, R.: Hand Pose Estimation Using Hierarchical Detection. In: N.Sebe et al. (eds.) HCI/ECCV2004. LNCS, vol. 3058, pp.105–116. Springer, Berlin Heidelberg (2004)
6. Liu, N., Lovell, B.C.: Gesture Classification Using Hidden Markov Models and Viterbi Path Counting. In: 7th Biennial Australian Pattern Recognition Society Conference, pp. 273–282. CSIRO Press, Sydney (2003)
7. Breiman, L.: Random Forests. Machine Learning 45(1), 5–32 (2001)
8. Gall, J.L.: Random Trees and Applications. Probability Surveys 2, 245–311 (2005)
9. Lepetit, V., Lagger, P., Fua, P.: Randomized Trees for Real-Time Keypoint Recognition. Computer Vision and Pattern Recognition 2, 775–881 (2005)
10. Marée, R., Geurts, P., Wehenkel, L.: Content-Based Image Retrieval by Indexing Random Subwindows with Randomized Trees. In: Yagi, Y., Kang, S.B., Kweon, I.S., Zha, H. (eds.) ACCV 2007, Part II. LNCS, vol. 4844, pp. 611–620. Springer, Heidelberg (2007)
11. Aznaveh, M.M., Mirzae, H., Roshan, E., Saraee, M.: A New Color Based Method for Skin Detection Using RGB Vector Space. In: IEEE Conference on Human System Interactions, Krakow, pp. 932–935 (2008)
12. Zhu, Q., Cheng, K., Wu, C., Wu, Y.: Adaptive Learning of an Accurate Skin-Color Model. In: 6th IEEE International Conference on Automatic Face and Gesture Recognition, Washington, pp. 37–42 (2004)

Web-Based Material Science Data Sharing Platform for Highway Engineering

Ting Peng[1] and Xiaoling Wang[2]

[1] MOE Special Region Highway Engineering Lab
Chang'an University, Xi'an,710049 China
t.peng@ieee.org
[2] Xi'an Branch of the People's Bank of China
Xi'an, 710004, China

Abstract. Construction materials account for significant part of highway construction cost. Performance and cost of the materials should be considered comprehensively. However, most performance data of the materials are kept in literatures, research reports, standards and specifications. It is hard to collect these data of different forms from corresponding orgranizations. So, in practice, these data are not used in material selection of highway engineering at all.

In order to apply the valuable data into practice, in this work, performance data of the materials are gathered from various sources. All the data are processed to a standard form provided by the system. Thus, the users of related areas can access the data easily. In order to make the system more friendly to the end users, full-text search engine is integrated in the system.

In this work, metadata of each material performance data record is kept in the database managment system. When each record is added in the system, lucene is employed to create full-text index of the data. Thus, both metadata search and full-text search of materials data are available.

The system has been used in practice for ten months. According to the practical application results, the users can easily share their data and access them. The data are also presented intuitively and vividly.

1 Introduction

Most performance data of the materials are kept in literatures, research reports, standards and specifications. They are owned by various organizations and in hardcopy or electronic forms. Currently, performance data of materials are not available in practice. In order to apply the valuable data into practice, in this work, performance data of materials are gathered from various sources. All the data are processed to a standard form provided by the system. Thus, the users of related area can access the data easily. In order to make the system more friendly to the end users, full-text search engine is integrated in the system.

In this work, metadata of each record of data is kept in the database managment system. When each record is added in the system, full-text index engine is

M. Zhao and J. Sha (Eds.): ICCIP 2012, Part II, CCIS 289, pp. 756–765, 2012.

employed to create full-text index of the data. Thus, both meta data search and full-text search of materials data are available.

With the system, users can search the material performance data within metadata or full-text of the material performance data. The GUI component of the system is developed with Java Script and Flex. It is provided as web pages. With support of current popular browsers and Adobe Flash plugin, the authorized users easily search for the desired data and view the full-text version of the data via browsers.

The rest of the paper is structed as follows. we discuss the challenges confronted in the next section. Then, the structure of the proposed material performance data sharing system is given in Section 3. The implementation and main functions of the system is described in section 4. At the end, this paper is concluded in Section 5.

2 Challenges

Traditionally, all the data are stored as tables in database. In this way, users can easily query them by columns via SQL. However, for material performance data have existed in various forms for years. Tables, charts, unit and description with complex characters are essential for the users. If these data are stored as traditional tables, some useful information for the users could not be properly stored.

So, in this system, metadata of the records are stored as tables, the other information is stored as full-text field, such as binary object, which is used in Rational Database Managment System.

2.1 Data Format

In the system, data are formated as documents with metadata. As shown in Tab.1, metadata of each data record is stored as a table. In the table, id, chinese name, english name, person in charge, data provider, upload date, record type, content and source of the data record. Each field of the recordd is define as corresponding data type in order to store the data properly.

In this way, metadata content and document content are both stored in the database. Thus, flexible query methods are possible.

2.2 Storage Requirements

If data are prepared as two-dimension table, it may be stored as a table in database. When large objects are involved, such as graphs and tables embded documents, data file can be stored as binary oject in Database Management System(DBMS). It can also be stored as file in the file system.

In the system we implemented here, the format of the data is relatively complex. Complex tables, charts and extraordinary characters and layout style are involved. If these data are stored as traditional tables in DBMS, it is very hard to store, retrieve and restore the infomation to original stated.

Table 1. Format of Material Data Record

Field Name	Data Type	Description
id	int(8)	Identification of each record
Chinese Name	varchar(255)	Name of the material data record, in Chinese.
English Name	varchar(255)	Name of the material data record, in English.
PersonInCharge	varchar(255)	The name of the person who is in charge of the data record.
Provider	varchar(255)	Provider of the data record.
UploadDate	data	Upload date of the record.
RecordType	int(4)	The number of data types.
Content	Blob	The content of the data record.
Source	varchar(255)	Where the data record come from.

In order to avoid these trouble, in this sytem, data are stored as their orginal document file format. In this way, data files are located on the file system, they can be easily retrieved and restored their orginal state.

3   User Requirements and System Structure

In the system, data can be shared among the users. All user can browse and search the data of the system. Registered user with certain authorization can download full-text data of the corresponding categroy.

The users in the research intitutions and construction material vendors with authorization can upload their material performance data and share them with others through the system.

All the privileged users should register at the system, then, the administrator of the system can authorize the users and grant them corresponding privileges. Thus all the users can access their athorized data. If spcecified privileges are ganted to the users, they can also have upload, modify and delete permission of some categories.

3.1   Data Integration

As shown in Fig.1, data in the system are collected from specifications, literatures, research reports, mannuals, et al. At first, they are processed into standard form defined by the data sharing system. Then, data are rechecked, if the data are corrected, they are transfered to the next move. Otherwise, the corresponding responsible persons will adapt the data and put them to the data recheck stage.

If the data are evaluated as correct at the recheck stage, they entered the data quality evaluation process. During the process, data quality is determined according to its accuracy, reliability, integraty, reachability.

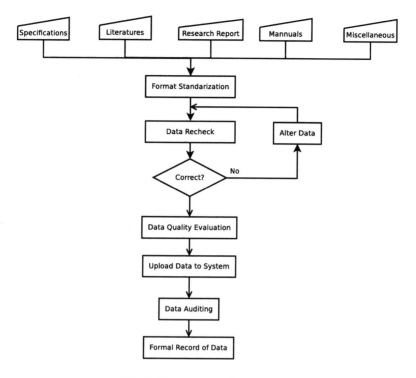

Fig. 1. Data Integration Process

Then, the data are uploaded to the system by the user with data sharing privilege. Data administrators audit the corresponding data, the qualified data are flaged as formal record data in the system. If the data is not qualified, they are rejected by the data administrators.

Search Manner. In highway engineering practice, there are two widely used information query methods. One is query the material data by their specified performance. The other is query the data by their text content. In order to make this system useful in practice, key word and full-text search methods are both provided in the system.

As discussed above, the users can query the data by their corresponding key words for meta data are stored in the database. They can also query the data by full-text content of the records.

In the system, Lucene is employed to provide full-text search function. At first lucence analyzes the data, then indexs of the data are generated. Then, the system provides full-text search service based on these index.

Present Method. Traditionally, data in database are formated as tables. In these tables, each column stands for a specified performance index of the materials. Each row of the table stands for the detail performance test result of a specified material. Thus, the records of material performance can be query by each index of its performance. However, the data may contain charts, tables, formulas. They are not easily to be stored in the table. Even if they are stored in the tables, retrieve and restore of them may be a complex process.

In our implementation, we use content database to avoid these troubles. In this system, the data files are prepared as document files such as word files. When these files are upload into the system, they are transfer into pdf files automatically.

In order to present these information perfectly, web page based pdf view function should be provided. In this system, Adobe Flex is employed to full fill this requirement.

3.2   Function Design

In this system, function of the system is categrized as: data search, material data type management, system privileges assignment, data file management, data file auditing, system logging, user management.

Through data search function, users can query the data by key word, meta data, et al. In addition, the data can also be query via words. Apache Lucene is popularily used as full-text search engine[1,3]. It is widely used as full-text search engine for web contents[4]. With the help of Apache Lucene, full-text index of the data records are generated when the data are uploaded to the system. Then, these data can also be queried by the words in the data records.

In the data type management, data administrators can define the material categories and parent category for each material type. In this way, all the data in the system are organized in a tree.

Permission management system is an essential part of this system. Permission of the users are granted according to the material types. Each user is granted with specified categories of material types. Then, the permissions are divided as read, write, delete and modify. All the users can only operate their authorized category with the granted permission. In this way, incorrect manipuation and unauthorized operation of the system is avoided. Security of the system is ensured.

3.3   Components

As shown in Fig.2, the system comprises three layers. They are called database, applications and user interface.

Documnets, metadata and user permission are all stored in database layer. Metadata and user permission are stored as table in the DBMS. Documents are stored as blob field in the databse. Thus, metadata based and full-text based indexing are made possible.

In applications layer, data audit system, lucene indexing, system log and data record management are implemented. In order to prevent unauthorized operation of the data, access control componet are also implemented in the layer. If a specified request of the system is not granted according to the user permission system, the request will be denied. The function of the corresponding component will not be invoked.

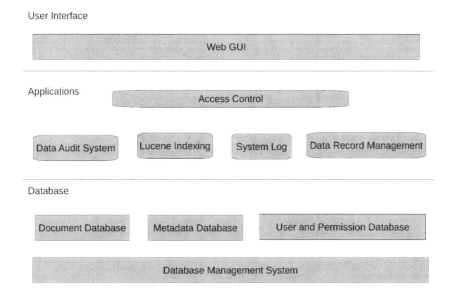

Fig. 2. System Structure

In the user interface layer, graphical user interface is implemented as browser conte. Thus, all the functions are provided as web services, the users of various platform can use them in the same manner. Platform independent is guaranteed.

3.4 Data Structure

The data in the system are categorized as five classes. they are user, user permission, material data type, material data, system log.

As shown in Fig.3, they exist in the data bases system as five tables. Key of the tables and reference relations between the tables are also given in the figure.

In this way, all the data are organized properly according to their content and relations between them. The system is made clear and effective.

4 Implementation and Typical Functions

The system is designed to use in material science data sharing among the researchers, engineers, educators and learners. All the protential users must be able to use the shared data without limitation of their information termial type, location and accessing time.

According to the requirements, JavaEE platform is employed and deployed on a high performance server in a professional data center.

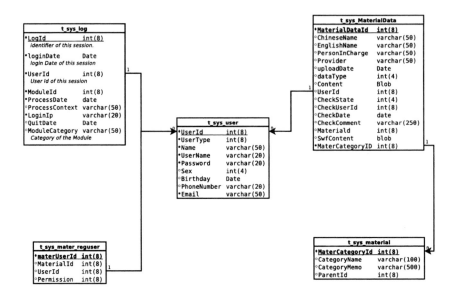

Fig. 3. Database Design

4.1   System Configuration

Currently, JavaEE is a proven nice content management system[5,2]. The system is also implemented according to JavaEE framework. It is developed as a javaEE service.

In order to make the system reliable and effective, high performance and extensive verified software components are employed. In the system, Ubuntu Linux is selected as operation system. MySQL is used as database management system. Tomcat is used as application server. OpenJDK is selected as runtime enviroment.

In order to provied document converting and present service, openoffice and swftools are both used. Apache Lucene is also integrated to provied full-text indexing for material data search purpose.

4.2   Typical Functions

In the system, material types and their belonging relationship can be defined easily. Each material type node can be edited in the intuitive interface. As shown in the left part of the figure, the nodes are defined as childs of the root node or the predefined node, the material types are organized as a tree. In this way, the categories of materials are uniformly with practice.

With the system, users can search the material performance data by metadata or full-text of the material performance data. The GUI component of the system is developed with Java Script and Flex. It runs as a web page. With support of current mainstream browser and Adobe Flash plugin, users can easily search for desired data and view the full-text version of the data in the browsers.

In the system, text based search function is provied as the recommended search method. In this way, the data can be found by specified key words. As shown in Fig.4, the system is indexing the material database by the key words. If a spcefied word is typed in the input area, with the surpport of the full-text search engine, the matched items will be returned and displayed. Thus, the users can view their detail information or download them if the users have corresponding privileges.

Fig. 4. Results of Text Search

In the system, material performance data of highway engineering contain com-plex tables and special characters. Charts and formulas may also be included. In order to conserve these data properly and retored them to the original state, they are stored as binary objects in the system. In order to present them at the users end in their origional pattern, flex is used to read the data and displayed in the browser with the help of Adobe Flash plugin. The effect of this function is shown in Fig.5. In this way, the data are presented in the conventional man-ner, the users can easily accept the system. The system also presents the data intuitively and vividly.

Fig. 5. Browser Embedded Content View

5   Conclusions and Future Work

Currently, Most of the required functions of related users are implemented in the system. Performance data of the materials are deposited in the system. Meta data of each record is also provided. Furthermore, mata data based and full-text based search engine for the data are provided.

With the system, users from research and industrial domains can easily search, view the data. Authorized users can also easily upload and share the data with other users.

However, some nice functions may be interesting to the users such as materials performance index based search is not provided in the current system. This can be provided in the future.

Acknowledgment. The project was supported by the Special Fund for Basic Scientific Research of Central Colleges, Chang'an University under Grant No. CHD2011JC097, the R&D Infrastructure and Facility Development Program under Grant No. 2005DKA32800.

References

1. Ding, Y., Yi, K., Xiang, R.: Design of paper duplicate detection system based on lucene. In: 2010 Asia-Pacific Conference on Wearable Computing Systems (APWCS), pp. 36–39 (April 2010)
2. Kwok, K.H.S., Chiu, D.K.W.: A web services implementation framework for financial enterprise content management. In: Proceedings of the 37th Annual Hawaii International Conference on System Sciences, p. 10 (January 2004)
3. Li, S., Lv, X., Ling, F., Shi, S.: Study on efficiency of full-text retrieval based on lucene. In: International Conference on Information Engineering and Computer Science, ICIECS 2009, p. 1 (December 2009)
4. Liu, C., Guo, Q.: Analysis and research of web chinese retrieval system based lunece. In: First International Workshop on Education Technology and Computer Science, ETCS 2009, vol. 1, pp. 1051–1055 (March 2009)
5. Zi-jing, J.: The analysis and design of the content management system based on j2ee. In: 2009 International Conference on Signal Processing Systems, pp. 829–833 (May 2009)

Author Index